Intermediate Algebra for College Students

Sixth Edition

Bernard Kolman
emeritus, Drexel University

Arnold Shapiro
emeritus, Temple University

BVT
PUBLISHING

Project Development Manager: Brae Buhnerkemper

Project Development Assistant: Brandi Cornwell

Managing Editor: Joyce Bianchini

Photo Researcher: Michelle Hipkins

Design and Illustrations: Rachel Weathersbee

Typesetter: Della Brackett

Text and Cover Printing: BR Printers

Sales Manager: Robert Rappeport

Marketing Manager: Richard Schofield

Permissions Coordinator: Suzanne Schmidt

Art Director: Esther Scannell

All rights reserved. Printed in the United States of America. No part of this book may be used or reproduced in any manner whatsoever without written permission, except in the case of brief quotations embodied in critical articles and reviews. For information address BVT Publishing, LLC, P.O. Box 492831, Redding, CA 96049–2831

Some ancillaries, including electronic and print components, may not be available to customers outside the United States.

ISBN: 978-1-93274-155-1

Copyright © 2011 by BVT Publishing, LLC

BVT
PUBLISHING
The publisher of affordable textbooks

To the memory of my mother, Eva.

— B K

To the memory of my parents.

— A S

Contents

Chapter 3 ▪ Mathematical Models and Word Problems   87

Chapter 4 ▪ Polynomials   113

Chapter 7 ■ The Straight Line   237

Chapter 8 ■ Exponents, Radicals, and Complex Numbers   273

Chapter 9 ■ Second-Degree Equations and Inequalities 317

Chapter 10 ■ Roots of Polynomials   355

Chapter 11 ■ Exponential and Logarithmic Functions   387

Chapter 12 ■ Analytic Geometry: The Conic Sections   441

Chapter 15 ▪ Topics in Algebra   561

To the Instructor

The authors are indebted to the faculty at those institutions that have adopted and have steadfastly continued to use the earlier editions of this text. Your letters and comments are genuinely appreciated and will always receive a prompt response.

Objectives of This Text

This sixth edition of *Intermediate Algebra for College Students* maintains our objective of providing a textbook designed for *use by the student*. We have adopted an informal, supportive style to encourage the student to read the book and to develop confidence under its guidance. We introduce concepts first by example with accompanying diagrams and illustrations that bolster the "reasonableness" of the resulting rules. We immediately reinforce every new mathematical technique or result with fully worked-out examples and captions clarifying their purpose. After each example, the student is presented with the opportunity to tackle a parallel problem, called a Progress Check, with the answer following it in the text.

This edition emphasizes applied problems. Numerous practical applications accompany the methods for solving linear equations and inequalities (see Chapter 2). In addition, Chapter 3 is devoted exclusively to the solution of word problems through the creation of a "model." The student is invited to participate in the process of translating words to algebraic expressions via a model or chart that greatly simplifies the process.

New in This Edition

Although the structure of earlier editions has been retained, we have made significant additions and improvements in this edition.

- Completely new chapter openers with motivational applications and references to many websites of mathematical interest

- Brand new chapter projects at the end of each chapter

- Many new exercises, most of which emphasize the use of graphing calculators

- New explanatory material for graphing calculator use

- Extensive copy-editing and proofing to ensure the accuracy of this text

Pedagogic Devices

We have continued to employ those pedagogic devices that instructors have found useful in the earlier editions.

Split Screens

Many algebraic procedures are described with the aid of a "split screen" that displays simultaneously both the steps of an algorithm and a worked-out example.

✔ Progress Checks

A problem (with answers) accompanies every numbered example in the text to enable the student to test his or her understanding of the material just described.

Warnings

To help eliminate misconceptions and prevent bad mathematics habits, we have inserted numerous **Warnings** that point out the incorrect practices most commonly found in homework and exam papers.

Vignettes

In each chapter we have inserted one or more vignettes, elements that are independent of the text yet are often related to the mathematical concepts. The vignettes are intended to catch the attention of the student and heighten interest in the material. (We hope they will provide interesting reading for the instructor as well.)

Exercises

Abundant, carefully graded exercises provide practice in the mechanical and conceptual aspects of algebra. Exercises requiring the use of a calculator or graphing calculator are indicated by the calculator icons shown to the left. Exercises of a more challenging nature are indicated by an *. Answers to odd-numbered exercises, review exercises, and progress tests appear in an appendix at the back of the book. Answers to even-numbered exercises appear in the Instructor's Manual. The Instructor's Manual, which includes an extensive Test Bank, is available to the instructor upon request.

End-of-Chapter Material

Every chapter contains a summary that includes the following:

Terms and Symbols   with appropriate page references

Key Ideas for Review to stress the concepts

Review Exercises to provide additional practice

Progress Tests to provide self-evaluation and reinforcement

Chapter Projects

This edition has added chapter openers and related projects at the end of each chapter. These emphasize additional applications and demonstrate the widening relevance of algebra in many areas. Some feature a "look ahead" to topics of future courses, such as polynomial curve fitting or calculus applications. Students may be excited by the career possibilities suggested by some of these sections. Instructors may wish to review the projects first; they provide one possible means of selecting which material and which exercises to emphasize. Some of the projects include essay components; the increasing importance of communication skills in scientific careers and upper-level courses seems to make this new emphasis advisable. Projects could be modified or expanded to involve students working in groups. Significant opportunities for Internet research and graphing calculator exploration are also offered.

Answers

The answers to all Review Exercises and Progress Tests appear in the back of the book.

Solutions

Worked-out solutions to selected Review Exercises appear in a separate section at the back of the book. The solved problems provide one more level of reassurance to the student using the Review Exercises in preparation for the Progress Tests. In addition, a *Student Solution Manual* containing fully worked-out solutions to selected exercises will be made available to the bookstore.

A Note on the Use of Calculators

Some of the new exercises in this edition call for the use of a graphing calculator. It is recommended that all students have one and read its manual in order to become proficient in its use. Many instructors view graphing calculators as essential tools for students of algebra, and their use becomes even more pronounced in more advanced courses. The aid these calculators provide in visualization, rapid evaluation of functions, use of graphs to discover unsuspected relationships between concepts, and offering new approaches and a greater variety of problem-solving methods, more than balances the additional challenge in becoming skilled and comfortable with them.

Many models of graphing calculators are now available, and most offer the additional benefit of links which can be used to share programs and applications between students, from instructor to student, or from the Internet.

Supplementary Material

Instructor's Solutions Manual by Jorge Cossio

Instructor's Manual with Tests by Gail Edinger

Acknowledgments

We thank the following for their review of the manuscript and for their helpful comments in this edition: Ken Klopfenstein, Colorado State University; C. Donald Smith, Louisiana State University at Shreveport; Kim Luna, Eastern New Mexico University; David Rearick, University of Colorado at Denver. We would like to acknowledge the following reviewers of the previous edition: David Lunsford, Grossmont College; Donald W. Bellairs, Grossmont College; Neil S. Dickson, Weber State College; Wayne Bishop, California State University, Los Angeles; and Patricia Martin, University of Illinois.

The staff at BVT Publishing has provided us with extensive and unflagging support. We also wish to express our appreciation to Connie Massey, Project Editor, and Brae Buhnerkemper, Project Coordinator.

New to This Edition!

BVT*Lab*

For Students

BVT*Lab* the most affordable, comprehensive online lab for college math students, provides the practice questions, learning aids, and communication tools that students need for success.

Practice Questions

Students can work through an expansive set of practice questions online. Questions are all multiple choice or true/false and are graded instantly for immediate feedback.

www.BVTLab.com

Worked Solutions

BVT*Lab* includes fully worked solutions for many of the odd-numbered questions from the textbook. An extended set of worked solutions is available with the purchase of the Student Solutions package, available at www.BVTLab.com.

Tutorials

Online video clips, audio files, or animated tutorials—all playable in any web browser—reinforce challenging concepts.

Additional Help

Helpful hints accompany selected questions, and the instructors may provide additional tips specific to their students. An "Ask the Instructor" button is also available on homework assignments and practice questions.

Discussion Forum

An online discussion forum allows students to interact with each other and the instructor to explore challenging concepts and share other resources, while providing an online community for distance learning.

Review

Students can view their grades for all completed work and also review prior homework and quizzes to identify areas that require additional study.

New to This Edition!

For Instructors

BVT*Lab*—a simple, robust, online lab for college math instructors and their students—provides essential teaching, assessment, and communication tools. It is an affordable option for students, with student lab fees costing only $19.99 for a full-semester course.

Course Set-up

BVT*Lab* has an easy-to-use, intuitive interface that allows instructors to quickly set up their courses and grade books, and replicate them from section to section and semester to semester. Multiple choice and true/false questions can be delivered online as practice questions, homework assignments, quizzes, and tests, each of which draws from a separate bank of questions.

Homework, quizzes, and tests have assigned start and end times; and tests can be proctored in the computer lab, or self-proctored for distance learners. Homework and quizzes offer optional hints and instructor tips. In addition, practice questions can be linked to fully worked solutions and multimedia tutorials.

Instructors can preview and manually select questions assigned to students, or they can use the "quick-pick" feature in **BVT***Lab* to generate sets of questions.

Grade Book

Using an assigned passcode, students register themselves into the grade book. All homework, quizzes, and tests are automatically graded and recorded in the grade book. In addition, instructors can manually enter or modify scores, with provisions for extra credit, attendance, and participation grades.

Grade books can be replicated from section to section, semester to semester, and can be easily edited or modified if required.

Communications Tools

Instructors can post discussion threads to a class forum and then monitor and moderate student replies. Important notifications can also be sent directly to each student via email.

www.BVTLab.com

To the Student

This book was written for you. It gives you every possible chance to succeed—if you use it properly.

We would like to have you think of mathematics as a challenging game—but not as a spectator sport. This wish leads to our primary rule: *Read this textbook with pencil and paper handy.* We illustrate every new idea or technique with fully worked-out examples. As you read the text, carefully follow the examples and then do the **Progress Checks**. The key to success in a math course is working problems, and the **Progress Checks** are there to provide immediate practice with the material you have just learned.

Your instructor will assign homework from the extensive selection of exercises that follows each section in the book. *Do the assignments regularly, thoroughly, and independently.* By doing many problems, you will develop the necessary skills in algebra, and your confidence will grow. Since algebraic techniques and concepts build on previous results, you can't afford to skip any of the work.

To help prevent or eliminate improper habits and to help you avoid the errors that we see each semester as we grade papers, we have interspersed **Warnings** throughout the book. The **Warnings** point out common errors and emphasize the proper method. They are summarized at the end of the chapter under the heading **Common Errors**.

We provide important review material at the end of each chapter. The **Terms and Symbols** should all be familiar by the time you reach them. If your understanding of a term or symbol is hazy, use the page reference to find the place in the text where it is introduced. Go back and read the definition.

It is possible to become so involved with the details of techniques that you lose track of the broader concepts. The list of **Key Ideas for Review** at the end of each chapter will help you focus on the principal ideas.

The **Review Exercises** at the end of each chapter can be used as part of your preparation for examinations. The section covering each exercise is indicated so that, if needed, you can go back to restudy the material. If you get stuck on a problem, see if the problem that is giving you difficulty or a similar problem is numbered in bold, indicating that a worked-out solution appears in the back of the book in the Solutions appendix. You are then ready to try **Progress Test A**. You will soon pinpoint your weak spots and can go back for further review and more exercises in those areas. Only then should you proceed to **Progress Test B**.

We believe that the eventual "payoff" in studying mathematics is an improved ability to tackle practical problems in your field of interest. To that end, this book places special emphasis on word problems, which recent surveys show often trouble students. Since algebra is the basic language of the mathematical techniques used in virtually all fields, the mastery of algebra is well worth your effort.

1 The Real Number System

> *"God made integers, all else is the work of man."*
> —Leopold Kronecker

Meteorologists are scientists who study weather phenomena, like hurricanes, hoping to be better able to predict their occurrences and effects. Like all scientists, they use numbers to measure, compare, and classify their information. For example, the Saffir-Simpson Hurricane Scale uses small **natural numbers** (1, 2, 3, 4, and 5) to classify hurricanes according to the amount of damage they are likely to cause. The recent Hurricane Katrina reached category 5 status. Scales like this often employ natural numbers because (as their name suggests) these are the types of numbers with which most people are comfortable. **Inequalities** may be used to express the range of wind speeds in miles per hour; for a category 5 storm, the speeds are > 155 mph (greater than 155 mph). For a category 1 hurricane, the speeds are between 74 and 95 mph, which can be written as $74 \leq$ wind speed ≤ 95.

http://www.noaa.gov/

Scientists require other types of numbers too—for instance, **rational numbers** like 28.92 inches (the smallest central pressure for a category 1 hurricane). Many more examples for the uses of numbers and inequalities to describe hurricanes and other meteorological phenomena can be found at http://www.noaa.gov/.

What other uses do meteorologists and other specialists make of the real number system, number lines, inequalities, and operations with real numbers? The chapter project will suggest some ideas.

■ ■ ■

Arithmetic teaches us that the rule "two plus two equals four" is truly independent of the kind of objects to which the rule applies; it doesn't matter whether the objects are apples or ants, countries or cars. Observations such as this one led to the study of the properties of numbers in an abstract sense, that is, the study of those properties that apply to *all* numbers, regardless of what the numbers represent.

Since we be dealing in much of our work with the *real numbers*, our studies will begin with a review of the *real number system*. We then introduce symbols to denote arbitrary numbers, a practice characteristic of algebra. The remainder of the chapter is devoted to explaining some of the fundamental properties of the real number system.

1.1   The Real Number System

Although this text does not stress the set approach to algebra, the concept and notation of sets is useful at times.

Sets

A **set** is a collection of objects or numbers, which are called the **elements** or **members** of the set. The elements of a set are written within braces, so that

$$A = \{4, 5, 6\}$$

tells us that the set A consists of the numbers 4, 5, and 6. The set

$$B = \{\text{Squibb, Ford, Honeywell}\}$$

consists of the names of these three corporations. We also write $4 \in A$, which we read as "4 is a member of the set A" or "4 belongs to the set A." Similarly, Ford $\in B$ is read as "Ford is a member of the set B," and I.B.M. $\notin B$ is read as "I.B.M. is not a member of the set B."

If every element of a set A is also a member of a set B, then A is a **subset** of B. For example, the set of all robins is a subset of the set of all birds.

EXAMPLE 1   WORKING WITH SETS

The set C consists of the names of all coins whose denomination is less than 50 cents.

(a) Write C in set notation.   (b) Is dime $\in C$?

(c) Is half-dollar $\in C$?   (d) Is $H = \{\text{nickel, dime}\}$ a subset of C?

SOLUTIONS

(a) We have $C = \{\text{penny, nickel, dime, quarter}\}$

(b) yes   (c) no   (d) yes

✔ **Progress Check 1**

The set V consists of the vowels in the English alphabet.

(a) Write V in set notation.
(b) Is the letter k a member of V?
(c) Is the letter u a member of V?
(d) List the subsets of V having four elements.

Answers

(a) $V = \{a, e, i, o, u\}$ (b) no   (c) yes
(d) $\{a, e, i, o\}, \{e, i, o, u\}, \{a, i, o, u\}, \{a, e, o, u\}, \{a, e, i, u\}$

The Real Number System

Much of our work in algebra deals with the set of real numbers. Let's review the composition of this number system.

The numbers $1, 2, 3, \ldots$, used for counting, form the set of **natural numbers**. If we had only these numbers to use to show the profit earned by a company, we would have no way to indicate that the company had no profit or had a loss. To indicate no profit we introduce 0, and for losses we need to introduce negative numbers. The numbers

$$\ldots, -2, -1, 0, 1, 2, \ldots$$

form the set of **integers**. Thus, every natural number is an integer. However, not every integer is a natural number.

When we try to divide two apples equally among four people, we find no number in the set of integers that will express how many apples each person should get. We need to introduce the **rational numbers**, which are numbers that can be written as a ratio of two integers,

$$\frac{p}{q} \quad \text{with } q \text{ not equal to zero}$$

Examples of rational numbers are

$$0 \quad \frac{2}{3} \quad -4 \quad \frac{7}{5} \quad \frac{-3}{4}$$

Thus, when we divide two apples equally among four people, each person gets half, or $\frac{1}{2}$ an apple. Since every integer n can be written as $\frac{n}{1}$, we see that every integer is a rational number. The number 1.3 is also a rational number, since $1.3 = \frac{13}{10}$.

We have now seen three fundamental number systems: the natural number system, the system of integers, and the rational number system. Each system we have introduced includes the previous system or systems, and each is more complicated than the one before. However, the rational number system is still inadequate for sophisticated uses of mathematics since there exist numbers that are not rational, that is, numbers that cannot be written as the ratio of two integers. These are called **irrational numbers.** It can be shown that the number a that satisfies $a \cdot a = 2$ is such a number. The number π, which is the ratio of the circumference of a circle to its diameter, is also such a number.

The decimal form of a rational number will either terminate, as

$$\frac{3}{4} = 0.75 \qquad -\frac{4}{5} = -0.8$$

or will form a repeating pattern, as

$$\frac{2}{3} = 0.\underset{\sim}{6}66\ldots \qquad \frac{1}{11} = 0.\underset{\sim}{09}0909\ldots \qquad \frac{1}{7} = 0.\underset{\sim}{1428571}\ldots.$$

Remarkably, the decimal form of an irrational number *never* forms a repeating pattern. Although we sometimes write $\pi = 3.14$, this is only an approximation, as is

$$\pi = 3.1415926536\ldots$$

Similarly, the decimal form of $\sqrt{2}$ can be approximated by $1.4142136\ldots$, which goes on forever and never forms a repeating pattern.

The rational and irrational numbers together form the **real number system** (Figure 1).

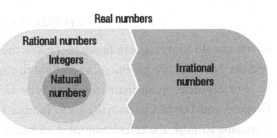

Figure 1   **The Real Number System**

The Real Number Line

To obtain a simple and useful geometric description of the set of real numbers we can draw a horizontal straight line, which we will call the **real number line;** pick a point, label it with the number 0, call it the **origin,** and denote it by O; and then we choose the **positive direction** to the right of the origin and the **negative direction** to the left of the origin. An arrow indicates the positive direction.

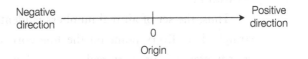

Now we select a unit of length for measuring distance. With each positive real number r, we associate the point that is r units to the right of the origin; and with each negative number $-s$, we associate the point that is s units to the left of the origin. We can now show some points on the real number line.

Mnemonic Math

> How I want a drink
> Alcoholic of course
> After the heavy lectures
> Involving quantum mechanics!

This "poem" appeared in the *Science Times* on July 5, 1988. The same article contained yet another creative gem:

> How I wish I could
> Enumerate pi easily,
> Since all these (censored) mnemonics
> Prevent recalling any of pi's sequence
> More simply

This second poem gives you a hint as to the "meaning" of these words. If you list the number of letters in each word, you have the sequence

3-1-4-1-5-9-2-6-5-3-5-8-9-7-9-3-2-3-8-4-5

Now, stick a decimal point after the first digit and you have

3.14159265358979323845

which should look vaguely familiar. This is the value of π accurate to 20 decimal places, and the "poems" are mnemonics recalling the value of this famous irrational number.

For centuries mathematicians have been fascinated by the challenge of calculating π. Gregory and David Chudnovsky of Columbia University recently became the first mathematicians to push the calculation of π to better than one billion places. And, should your interest run to poetry, π mnemonics exist in French, German, Greek, and Spanish.

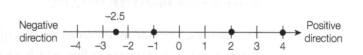

Conversely, let P be a point on the real number line. If P is to the right of the origin and r units from the origin, we associate the real number r with P. If P is to the left of the origin and s units from the origin, we associate the real number $-s$ with P.

Thus, the set of all real numbers is identified with the set of all points on a straight line. Every point on the line corresponds to a real number, called its **coordinate**; and for every real number there is a point on the line. We often say that the set of real numbers and the set of points on the real number line are in **one-to-one correspondence**. The numbers to the right of the origin are called **positive**. The numbers to the left of the origin are called **negative**. The positive numbers and zero together are called the **nonnegative** numbers, whereas the negative numbers and zero together are called the **nonpositive** numbers.

EXAMPLE 2   POINTS ON A REAL NUMBER LINE

Draw a real number line and plot the following points: $-\dfrac{3}{2}$, 2, $\dfrac{13}{4}$.

SOLUTION

✔ **Progress Check 2**

Determine the real numbers denoted on the real number line as A, B, C, and D.

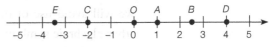

Answers

A: $\dfrac{7}{2}$ B: $-\dfrac{3}{2}$ C: 5 D: $-\dfrac{13}{4}$

Exercise Set 1.1

In Exercises 1–12 choose the correct answer(s) from the following: (a) rational number, (b) natural number, (c) real number, (d) integer, (e) irrational number.

1. The number 2 is
2. The number -3 is
3. The number $-\frac{2}{3}$ is
4. The number 0.8 is
5. The number 3 is
6. The numbers -1, -2, and -3 are
7. The numbers 0, 1, and 2 are
8. The numbers 0, $\frac{1}{2}$, 1, $\frac{2}{3}$, and $-\frac{4}{5}$ are
9. The numbers $\sqrt{2}$ and π are
10. The numbers 0.5 and 0.8 are
11. The numbers $\frac{\pi}{3}$ and 2π are
12. The numbers 0, $\frac{1}{2}$, $\sqrt{2}$, π, 4, and -4 are

In Exercises 13–21 determine whether the given statement is true (T) or false (F).

13. -14 is a natural number.
14. $-\frac{4}{5}$ is a rational number.
15. $\frac{\pi}{3}$ is a rational number.
16. 2.5 is an integer.
17. $\frac{1.75}{18.6}$ is an irrational number.
18. 0.75 is an irrational number.
19. $\frac{4}{5}$ is a real number.
20. 3 is a rational number.
21. $\sqrt{2}$ is a real number.
22. Draw a real number line and plot the following points.

    (a) 4   (b) -2 (c) $\dfrac{5}{2}$ (d) -3.5 (e) 0

23. Draw a real number line and plot the following points.

    (a) -5 (b) 4   (c) -3.5 (d) $\dfrac{7}{2}$ (e) $-\pi$

24. Estimate the real number associated with the points A, B, C, D, O, and E on the accompanying real number line.

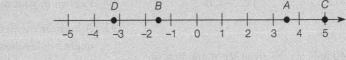

25. Represent each of the following by a positive or negative integer.

    (a) a profit of $10

    (b) a loss of $20

    (c) a temperature of 20° above zero

    (d) a temperature of 5° below zero

In Exercises 26–31 indicate which of the two given numbers appears first, viewed from left to right, on the real number line.

26. 4, 6

27. 2, 0

28. −2, 3

29. 0, −4

30. −5, −2

31. 4, −5

In Exercises 32–37 indicate which of the two given numbers appears second, viewed from left to right, on the real number line.

32. 9, 8

33. 0, 3

34. −4, 2

35. −4, 0

36. −3, −4

37. −2, 5

In Exercises 38–40 indicate the given set of numbers on the real number line.

38. The natural numbers less than 8

39. The natural numbers greater than 4 and less than 10

40. The integers that are greater than 2 and less than 7

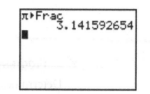 41. Your graphing calculator can convert a decimal number to a fraction. However, when we input π, we get a decimal back:

Explain in your own words why this is the case.

42. A hurricane with a central pressure of 27.25 inches might be classified as a category 4 storm. What subset of the real numbers does this number belong to? Can you verify this using your graphing calculator (see Exercise 41)?

1.2   Arithmetic Operations: Fractions

The vocabulary of arithmetic carries over to our study of algebra. In multiplying two real numbers, each of the numbers is called a **factor** and the result is called the **product**.

$$6 \cdot 5 = 30$$

factors   product

Terminology and Order of Operations

In this text we will indicate multiplication by a dot, as in the example just given, or by parentheses.

$$(6)(5) = 30$$

We will avoid use of the multiplication sign ×, since it may be confused with other algebraic symbols.

Let's look at the terminology of division.

$$30 \div 6 = 5$$

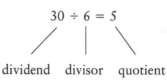

dividend   divisor   quotient

Most of the time we write division this way:

$$\frac{30}{6} = 5$$

Numbers to be multiplied have the same name (factors), whereas in division the numbers have different names (dividend, divisor). This suggests that we can interchange the factors in multiplication without altering the product, but that interchanging the dividend and divisor in division will alter the quotient. In general:

> Addition can be performed in any order.
> Multiplication can be performed in any order.
> Subtraction must be performed in the given order.
> Division must be performed in the given order.

What happens when more than one operation appears in a problem? To avoid ambiguity, we adopt the following simple rule:

> Always do multiplication and division before addition and subtraction.

EXAMPLE 1 ORDER OF ARITHMETIC OPERATIONS

Perform the indicated operations.

(a) $2 + (3)(4) - 5 = 2 + 12 - 5 = 9$

(b) $\frac{10}{5} + 7 + 3 \cdot 6 = 2 + 7 + 18 = 27$

✔ Progress Check 1

Perform the indicated operations.

(a) $2 \cdot 4 - 6 + 3$ (b) $(3)(4) - 2 + \frac{9}{3}$

Answers

(a) 5   (b) 13

We will provide complete rules for the order of operations in the next section.

Fractions

It is important to master the *arithmetic* of fractions since this serves as background for the *algebra* of fractions. We prefer to write $10 \div 5$ in the form $\frac{10}{5}$, which we call a **fraction**. The number above the line is called the **numerator**; that below the line is called the **denominator**.

$$\text{numerator} \longrightarrow \frac{10}{5} \longleftarrow \text{denominator}$$

Multiplication of fractions is straightforward.

Multiplication of Fractions

> **Step 1.** Multiply the numerators of the given fractions to find the numerator of the product.
>
> **Step 2.** Multiply the denominators of the given fractions to find the denominator of the product.

EXAMPLE 2   MULTIPLICATION OF FRACTIONS

Multiply.

(a) $\dfrac{3}{5} \cdot \dfrac{7}{2}$ (b) $\dfrac{2}{9} \cdot \dfrac{5}{3} \cdot 4$

SOLUTIONS

(a) $\dfrac{3}{5} \cdot \dfrac{7}{2} = \dfrac{3 \cdot 7}{5 \cdot 2} = \dfrac{21}{10}$

(b) $\dfrac{2}{9} \cdot \dfrac{5}{3} \cdot 4 = \dfrac{2}{9} \cdot \dfrac{5}{3} \cdot \dfrac{4}{1} = \dfrac{2 \cdot 5 \cdot 4}{9 \cdot 3 \cdot 1} = \dfrac{40}{27}$

> ✔ **Progress Check 2**
>
> Multiply.
>
> (a) $\dfrac{4}{3} \cdot \dfrac{7}{3}$ (b) $\dfrac{5}{12} \cdot \dfrac{7}{3} \cdot \dfrac{1}{2}$
>
> **Answers**
>
> (a) $\dfrac{28}{9}$ (b) $\dfrac{35}{72}$

Reciprocal

The **reciprocal** of $\frac{3}{4}$ is found by inverting $\frac{3}{4}$ to obtain $\frac{4}{3}$. Thus, $\frac{4}{3}$ is the reciprocal of $\frac{3}{4}$. Similarly, $\frac{1}{5}$ is the reciprocal of 5, and $\frac{1}{\pi}$ is the reciprocal of π. Note that the product of a real number and its reciprocal is always equal to 1. The number 0 does not have a reciprocal since the product of 0 and any number is 0.

> • Every real number, except 0, has a reciprocal such that the product of the number and its reciprocal is equal to 1.
>
> • The number 0 does not have a reciprocal, and *division by 0 is not permitted.*

Division of fractions can always be converted into a multiplication problem by forming the reciprocal.

Division of Fractions

Step 1. Invert the divisor.

Step 2. Multiply the resulting fractions.

Since 0 has no reciprocal, division by 0 is not defined.

EXAMPLE 3   DIVISION OF FRACTIONS

Divide.

(a) $\dfrac{4}{9} \div \dfrac{3}{5}$ (b) $\dfrac{\frac{2}{3}}{\frac{5}{7}}$

SOLUTIONS

(a) $\dfrac{4}{9} \div \dfrac{3}{5} = \dfrac{4}{9} \cdot \dfrac{5}{3} = \dfrac{4 \cdot 5}{9 \cdot 3} = \dfrac{20}{27}$ (b) $\dfrac{\frac{2}{3}}{\frac{5}{7}} = \dfrac{2}{3} \div \dfrac{5}{7} = \dfrac{2}{3} \cdot \dfrac{7}{5} = \dfrac{14}{15}$

✔ **Progress Check 3**

Divide.

(a) $\dfrac{8}{7} \div \dfrac{3}{2}$ (b) $\dfrac{\frac{1}{2}}{3}$ (c) $\dfrac{2}{11} \div \dfrac{5}{3}$

Answers

(a) $\dfrac{16}{21}$ (b) $\dfrac{1}{6}$ (c) $\dfrac{6}{55}$

The same fractional value can be written in many ways. Thus,

$$\frac{3}{2} = \frac{6}{4} = \frac{18}{12} = \frac{72}{48}$$

are four forms of the same fractional value.

Equivalent Fractions

The value of a fraction is not changed by multiplying or dividing *both* the numerator and denominator by the same number (other than 0). The result is called an **equivalent fraction**.

If we multiply a fraction, say $\frac{5}{2}$ by $\frac{3}{3}$, we are really multiplying by a "disguised" equivalent form of 1, since $\frac{3}{3} = 1$. Thus,

$$\frac{5}{2} = \frac{5}{2} \cdot \frac{3}{3} = \frac{15}{6}$$

EXAMPLE 4   FINDING AN EQUIVALENT FRACTION

Find the equivalent fraction.

$$\frac{7}{3} = \frac{?}{12}$$

SOLUTION

Since $12 = 3 \cdot 4$, we multiply the original denominator by 4 to obtain the new denominator. Then we must also multiply the numerator by 4.

$$\frac{7}{3} \cdot \frac{4}{4} = \frac{7 \cdot 4}{3 \cdot 4} = \frac{28}{12}$$

✔ Progress Check 4

Find the equivalent fraction.

(a) $\dfrac{5}{4} = \dfrac{?}{20}$ (b) $6 = \dfrac{?}{4}$ (c) $\dfrac{2}{3} = \dfrac{8}{?}$

Answers

(a) $\dfrac{25}{20}$ (b) $\dfrac{24}{4}$ (c) $\dfrac{8}{12}$

Now let's reverse the process. We saw that $\frac{7}{3}$ can be written as

$$\frac{7}{3} \cdot \frac{4}{4} = \frac{28}{12}$$

which is equivalent to $\frac{7}{3}$. Beginning with $\frac{28}{12}$, we can write the numerator and denominator as a product of factors:

$$\frac{28}{12} = \frac{7 \cdot 4}{3 \cdot 4} = \frac{7}{3} \cdot \frac{4}{4} = \frac{7}{3} \cdot 1 = \frac{7}{3}$$

We say that $\frac{7}{3}$ is the **reduced form** of $\frac{28}{12}$. This illustrates the **cancellation principle**.

Cancellation Principle

Common factors appearing in both the numerator and denominator of a fraction can be canceled without changing the value of the fraction. When a fraction has no common factors in its numerator and denominator, it is said to be in reduced form.

EXAMPLE 5   OBTAINING REDUCED FORM

Write $\frac{15}{27}$ in reduced form.

SOLUTION

$$\frac{15}{27} = \frac{5 \cdot 3}{9 \cdot 3} = \frac{5}{9} \cdot \frac{3}{3} = \frac{5}{9} \cdot 1 = \frac{5}{9}$$

Finding all the Primes up to *N*: The Sieve of Eratosthenes

Prime Integers Less Than or Equal to 100

2 3 ~~4~~ 5 ~~6~~ 7 ~~8~~
~~9~~ ~~10~~ 11 ~~12~~ 13 ~~14~~ ~~15~~
~~16~~ 17 ~~18~~ 19 ~~20~~ ~~21~~ ~~22~~
23 ~~24~~ ~~25~~ ~~26~~ ~~27~~ ~~28~~ 29
~~30~~ 31 ~~32~~ ~~33~~ ~~34~~ ~~35~~ ~~36~~
37 ~~38~~ ~~39~~ ~~40~~ 41 ~~42~~ 43
~~44~~ ~~45~~ ~~46~~ 47 ~~48~~ ~~49~~ ~~50~~
~~51~~ ~~52~~ 53 ~~54~~ ~~55~~ ~~56~~ 57
~~58~~ 59 ~~60~~ 61 ~~62~~ ~~63~~ ~~64~~
~~65~~ ~~66~~ 67 ~~68~~ ~~69~~ ~~70~~ 71
~~72~~ 73 ~~74~~ ~~75~~ ~~76~~ ~~77~~ ~~78~~
79 ~~80~~ ~~81~~ ~~82~~ 83 ~~84~~ ~~85~~
~~86~~ 87 ~~88~~ 89 ~~90~~ ~~91~~ ~~92~~
~~93~~ ~~94~~ ~~95~~ ~~96~~ 97 ~~98~~ ~~99~~
~~100~~

An integer $p > 1$ is called a **prime** if the only positive integers that divide p are p and 1. For example, 3, 5, 11, and 2 are primes. The number 2 is the only even prime, since every even integer greater than 2 is divisible by 2. A positive integer that is not a prime is said to be a **composite**. For example, 4, 10, and 15 are composite integers.

A method for listing all the primes up to a given integer N was developed by the Greek scientist and mathematician Eratosthenes (275–194 B.C.), who was a friend of Archimedes. We will describe this method, called the **Sieve of Eratosthenes**, and apply it to the accompanying table, which lists the positive integers less than or equal to 100.

Step 1. Make a list of all integers from 2 to N.

Step 2. Since 2 is the first prime, cross out all multiples of 2. The next integer in the list that has not been crossed out is 3, which is a prime. Now cross out all multiples of 3. The next integer in the list that has not been crossed out is 5, which is a prime. Next, cross out all multiples of 5. Repeat the process until the list is exhausted.

Step 3. The numbers that have not been crossed out are the primes less than N.

You probably noticed that no additional cross-outs occurred after you crossed out the multiples of 7. In general, you can stop when you reach a number K such that K times K is at least N.

The number of computations required for executing the "sieve" rises dramatically as N increases. For this reason, the "sieve" has become a favorite benchmark program for comparing computer hardware and software.

✔ Progress Check 5

Write in reduced form.

(a) $\dfrac{22}{60}$ (b) $\dfrac{90}{15}$ (c) $\dfrac{32}{12}$

Answers

(a) $\dfrac{11}{30}$ (b) 6   (c) $\dfrac{8}{3}$

WARNING

Only multiplicative factors common to both the *entire* numerator and the *entire* denominator can be canceled. *Don't* write

$$\frac{6+5}{3} = \frac{\overset{2}{\cancel{6}}+5}{\underset{1}{\cancel{3}}} = \frac{7}{1} = 7$$

Since 3 is not a multiplicative factor common to the entire numerator, we may not cancel.

The addition and subtraction of fractions can sometimes be more complicated than their multiplication. We begin by stating the key idea for adding and subtracting fractions.

Addition and Subtraction Principle

> We can add or subtract fractions directly only if they have the same denominator.

When fractions do have the same denominator, the process is easy: Add or subtract the numerators and keep the common denominator. Thus,

$$\frac{3}{4} + \frac{15}{4} = \frac{3+15}{4} = \frac{18}{4} = \frac{9}{2}$$

Least Common Denominator

If the fractions we wish to add or subtract do not have the same denominator, we must rewrite them as equivalent fractions that do have the same denominator. There are easy ways to find the **least common denominator (LCD)** of two or more fractions, that is, the smallest number that is divisible by each of the given denominators.

To find the LCD of two or more fractions, say, $\frac{1}{2}$, $\frac{5}{6}$, and $\frac{4}{9}$, we first write each denominator as a product of prime numbers. Recall that a **prime number** is a natural number greater than 1 whose only factors are itself and 1. For example, 5 is a prime number, since it is divisible only by 5 and 1. Other examples of numbers written as a product of primes are:

$$2 = 2$$
$$6 = 2 \cdot 3$$
$$9 = 3 \cdot 3$$

We then form a product in which each distinct prime factor appears the greatest number of times that it occurs in any single denominator. This product is the LCD. In our example, the prime factor 2 appears, at most, once in any denominator, while the prime factor 3 appears twice in a denominator. Thus, the LCD is $2 \cdot 3 \cdot 3 = 18$.

The LCD is the tool we need to add or subtract fractions with different denominators. Here is an example of the process.

EXAMPLE 6   USING THE LCD IN THE ADDITION OF FRACTIONS

Find the following sum:

$$\frac{2}{5} + \frac{3}{4} - \frac{2}{3}$$

SOLUTION

Addition and Subtraction of Fractions

Step 1. Find the LCD of the fractions.

$$LCD = 5 \cdot 2 \cdot 2 \cdot 3 = 60$$

Step 2. Convert each fraction to an equivalent fraction with the LCD as its denominator.

$$\frac{2}{5} = \frac{2}{5} \cdot \frac{12}{12} = \frac{24}{60}$$

$$\frac{3}{4} = \frac{3}{4} \cdot \frac{15}{15} = \frac{45}{60}$$

$$\frac{2}{3} = \frac{2}{3} \cdot \frac{20}{20} = \frac{40}{60}$$

Step 3. The fractions now have the same denominator. Add and subtract the numerators as indicated.

$$\frac{2}{5} + \frac{3}{4} - \frac{2}{3} = \frac{24}{60} + \frac{45}{60} - \frac{40}{60}$$

$$= \frac{24 + 45 - 40}{60}$$

$$= \frac{29}{60}$$

Step 4. Write the answer in reduced form.

Answer: $\dfrac{29}{60}$

✔ Progress Check 6

Find the sum $\dfrac{2}{3} + \dfrac{4}{7}$.

Answer

$\dfrac{26}{21}$

EXAMPLE 7   ADDING AND SUBTRACTING FRACTIONS

Perform the indicated operations and simplify.

(a) $\dfrac{1}{2} - \dfrac{1}{6} + \dfrac{1}{3}$ (b) $\dfrac{\dfrac{4}{3} - \dfrac{1}{2}}{\dfrac{1}{3} + \dfrac{3}{4}}$

SOLUTIONS

(a) We see that the LCD is 6 and

$$\frac{1}{2} = \frac{1}{2} \cdot \frac{3}{3} = \frac{3}{6}$$

$$\frac{1}{6} = \frac{1}{6} \cdot \frac{1}{1} = \frac{1}{6}$$

$$\frac{1}{3} = \frac{1}{3} \cdot \frac{2}{2} = \frac{2}{6}$$

Thus,

$$\frac{1}{2} - \frac{1}{6} + \frac{1}{3} = \frac{3}{6} - \frac{1}{6} + \frac{2}{6} = \frac{3 - 1 + 2}{6} = \frac{4}{6} = \frac{2}{3}$$

(b) The LCD of the fractions in the numerator is 6, and hence the numerator is

$$\frac{4}{3} - \frac{1}{2} = \frac{4}{3} \cdot \frac{2}{2} - \frac{1}{2} \cdot \frac{3}{3} = \frac{8}{6} - \frac{3}{6} = \frac{5}{6}$$

The LCD of the fractions in the denominator is 12, and hence the denominator is

$$\frac{1}{3} + \frac{3}{4} = \frac{1}{3} \cdot \frac{4}{4} + \frac{3}{4} \cdot \frac{3}{3} = \frac{4}{12} + \frac{9}{12} = \frac{13}{12}$$

Then the given fraction is

$$\frac{\dfrac{5}{6}}{\dfrac{13}{12}} = \frac{5}{\cancel{6}^{1}} \cdot \frac{\cancel{12}^{2}}{13} = \frac{10}{13}$$

✔ Progress Check 7

Perform the indicated operations and simplify.

(a) $\dfrac{3}{2} + \dfrac{5}{9} - \dfrac{1}{3}$

(b) $\dfrac{\dfrac{2}{3} + \dfrac{5}{6}}{\dfrac{1}{2} + \dfrac{2}{3}}$

Answers

(a) $\dfrac{31}{18}$

(b) $\dfrac{9}{7}$

Percent

Percent is a way of writing a fraction whose denominator is 100. The percent sign, %, following a number means "place the number over 100." Thus, 7% means $\frac{7}{100}$.

A fraction whose denominator is 100 is converted to decimal form by moving the decimal point in the numerator two places to the left and eliminating the denominator.

$$\frac{65}{100} = 0.65$$

Since a percent is understood to mean a fraction whose denominator is 100, we see that

$$7\% = 0.07$$

Similarly, we change a decimal to a percent by moving the decimal point two places to the right and adding the percent sign.

$$0.065 = 6.5\%$$

To write a fraction as a percent, we multiply the fraction by 100 and divide the new fraction by its denominator. For example, to write $\frac{1}{20}$ as a percent, we form

$$\frac{100}{20} = 5$$

so $\frac{1}{20} = 5\%$. Similarly, to write $\frac{1}{7}$ as a percent, we form

$$\frac{100}{7} = 14.28$$

so $\frac{1}{7} = 14.28\%$.

EXAMPLE 8 CONVERTING PERCENTS, DECIMALS, AND FRACTIONS

Write each percent as a decimal and as a fraction, and each decimal or fraction as a percent.

(a) 25% (b) 142% (c) 0.06 (d) 2.1 (e) $\frac{3}{4}$ (f) $\frac{21}{5}$ (g) $\frac{1}{6}$

SOLUTIONS

(a) $25\% = 0.25$; $25\% = \frac{25}{100} = \frac{1}{4}$ (b) $142\% = 1.42$; $142\% = \frac{142}{100} = \frac{71}{50}$

(c) $0.06 = 6\%$ (d) $2.1 = 210\%$

(e) $\frac{3}{4} = \frac{75}{100} = 75\%$ (f) $\frac{21}{5} = \frac{420}{100} = 420\%$

(g) $\frac{1}{6} = 0.167$ (rounded) $= 16.7\%$

✔ Progress Check 8

Write each percent as a decimal and as a fraction, and each decimal or fraction as a percent.

(a) 62.5%   (b) $\frac{1}{2}$%   (c) 0.26   (d) 3.475

(e) $\frac{1}{8}$ (f) $\frac{5}{2}$ (g) $\frac{1}{9}$

Answers

(a) 0.625, $\frac{5}{8}$ (b) 0.005, $\frac{1}{200}$ (c) 26%   (d) 347.5%

(e) 12.5%   (f) 250%   (g) 11.1%

It is common practice to state business problems in terms of percent. You have heard and read statements such as:

> Ms. Smith was promised an 8% salary increase.
> The Best Savers Bank pays 5.75% interest per year.
> Automobile prices will increase 4.62% on July 1.
> During the sale period, all merchandise is reduced by 20%.

To find the **percent of a number**, we must convert the percent to a decimal or fraction and then *multiply* by the number.

EXAMPLE 9   FINDING THE PERCENT OF A NUMBER

(a) What is 30% of 15?

(b) What is 5% of 400?

(c) A bank pays 6.75% interest per year. What will the annual interest be on a deposit of $500?

(d) The price of a refrigerator selling at $600 is to be reduced by 20%. What is the sale price?

SOLUTIONS

(a) 30% = 0.3 and (0.3)(15) = 4.5

(b) 5% = 0.05 and (0.05)(400) = 20

(c) 6.75% = 0.0675 and (0.0675)($500) = $33.75

(d) 20% = 0.2 and (0.2)($600) = $120 = amount of discount

Sale price = original price − discount

= $600 − $120

= $480

✔ **Progress Check 9**

(a) What is 40% of 60?

(b) What is 2% of 1200?

(c) How much interest will be earned during one year on a deposit of $2500 at 7.5% per year?

(d) The price of an automobile selling at $6800 will be increased by 4%. What is the new price?

Answers

(a) 24   (b) 24   (c) $187.50   (d) $7072

Exercise Set 1.2

In Exercises 1–14 perform the indicated operations.

1. $\dfrac{2(6+2)}{4}$

2. $\dfrac{(4+5)6}{18}$

3. $\dfrac{6(3+1)}{2} + 3 \cdot 5$

4. $\dfrac{8(6-1)}{4} - 3 \cdot 2$

5. $\dfrac{(4+5)(2+3)}{3} - 3 \cdot 5$

6. $\dfrac{(7-2)(8-2)}{3} + 7 \cdot 4$

7. $\dfrac{2}{11} \cdot \dfrac{10}{3} \cdot \dfrac{2}{5}$

8. $\dfrac{7}{5} \cdot \dfrac{4}{3} \cdot 2$

9. $\dfrac{\frac{2}{3}}{\frac{1}{5}}$

10. $\dfrac{\frac{3}{4}}{\frac{4}{3}}$

11. $\dfrac{\frac{2}{5}}{\frac{3}{10}}$

12. $\dfrac{\frac{1}{2}}{\frac{5}{6}}$

13. $\dfrac{2}{3} \div \dfrac{4}{9}$

14. $\dfrac{3}{5} \div \dfrac{9}{25}$

In Exercises 15–20 find the number that makes the fractions equivalent.

15. $\dfrac{4}{3} = \dfrac{?}{9}$

16. $\dfrac{3}{4} = \dfrac{15}{?}$

17. $1 = \dfrac{7}{?}$

18. $2 = \dfrac{?}{14}$

19. $\dfrac{5}{4} = \dfrac{?}{20}$

20. $\dfrac{4}{7} = \dfrac{12}{?}$

In Exercises 21–24 find the least common denominator of the given fractions.

21. $\dfrac{1}{4}, \dfrac{1}{2}, \dfrac{2}{15}$

22. $\dfrac{1}{3}, \dfrac{1}{9}, \dfrac{1}{5}$

23. $\dfrac{1}{20}, \dfrac{1}{30}, \dfrac{1}{45}$

24. $2, \dfrac{1}{4}, \dfrac{5}{36}$

In Exercises 25–32 perform the indicated operations and simplify.

25. $\dfrac{3}{4} + \dfrac{2}{3}$

26. $\dfrac{2}{3} + \dfrac{5}{6}$

27. $\dfrac{1}{4} + \dfrac{2}{3} - \dfrac{1}{2}$

28. $\dfrac{1}{5} - \dfrac{1}{2} + \dfrac{1}{3}$

29. $\dfrac{\frac{1}{6}+\frac{1}{2}}{\frac{5}{4}+\frac{2}{3}}$

30. $\dfrac{\frac{3}{2}-\frac{3}{8}}{\frac{1}{3}+\frac{1}{4}}$

31. $\dfrac{2-\frac{1}{3}}{3+\frac{1}{4}}$

32. $\dfrac{\frac{3}{5}-\frac{1}{10}}{1+\frac{1}{2}}$

In Exercises 33–42 change the given percent to both fractional and decimal forms.

33. 20%
34. 60%
35. 65.5%
36. 32.5%
37. 4.8%
38. 5.5%
39. 120%
40. 160%
41. $\dfrac{1}{5}\%$
42. $\dfrac{1}{10}\%$

In Exercises 43–54 convert each number to a percent.

43. 0.05
44. 0.03
45. 0.425
46. 0.345
47. 6.28
48. 7.341
49. $\dfrac{3}{5}$
50. $\dfrac{5}{6}$

51. $\dfrac{9}{4}$ 52. $\dfrac{6}{5}$

53. $\dfrac{2}{7}$ 54. $\dfrac{4}{3}$

55. What is 35% of 60?   56. What is 60% of 80?

57. What is 140% of 30?   58. What is 160% of 50?

59. What is $\frac{1}{2}$% of 40?   60. What is $\frac{2}{3}$% of 20?

In Exercises 61–64 use a calculator to convert each number to decimal form and then determine the smallest number.

61. $\dfrac{5}{32}, \dfrac{11}{64}, \dfrac{8}{50}$ 62. $\dfrac{20}{27}, \dfrac{28}{39}, \dfrac{78}{103}$

63. $\dfrac{150}{171}, \dfrac{78}{88}, \dfrac{125}{144}$ 64. $\dfrac{814}{653}, \dfrac{910}{731}, \dfrac{3875}{3107}$

In Exercises 65–68 use a calculator to convert each number to a percent and determine the largest number.

65. $\dfrac{32}{55}, \dfrac{15}{27}, \dfrac{52}{89}$ 66. $\dfrac{75}{61}, \dfrac{941}{765}, \dfrac{66}{54}$

67. $\dfrac{137}{49}, \dfrac{850}{304}, \dfrac{267}{96}$ 68. $\dfrac{999}{1077}, \dfrac{67}{73}, \dfrac{297}{321}$

69. A bank pays 7.25% interest per year. If a depositor has $800 in a savings account, how much interest will the bank pay him at the end of one year?

70. Suppose that you buy a $5000 General Motors bond that pays 9.3% interest per year. What will be the amount of the dividend when mailed to you by G.M. at the end of the year?

71. A savings bank pays 8% interest per year. If a depositor has $6000 in a savings account, what will be the amount in the account at the end of one year, assuming that no withdrawals are made?

72. A student has borrowed $3000 at a rate of 7% per year. How much interest is owed to the bank at the end of one year?

73. A record store embarks on an advertising campaign to raise its profits by 20%. If this year's profits were $96,000, what will next year's profits be if the campaign succeeds?

*74. An $800 stereo system will be sold at a 25% reduction. What will be the new price?

*75. In order to cope with rising costs, an oil producer plans to raise prices by 15%. If a barrel of oil now sells for $28.00, what will be the new price?

*76. A boat that originally sold for $600 is now on sale for $540. What is the percentage of discount?

*77. The holder of an $8000 savings certificate gets a $640 check at the end of the year. What is the annual rate of simple interest?

*78. A department store runs the following sale on a brand of stereo equipment. During the first week of the sale, the merchandise is discounted by 10%. If the merchandise is not sold by the second week, it is discounted by 20% of the sale price that was in effect during the first week. (This is called **chain discount**.) What is the price during the second week of a receiver that originally sold for $400?

*79. On September 1, an automobile manufacturer introduces the new model of a car and increases by 6% the price that was in effect for the car on August 31. Since demand for the new model exceeds supply, on October 1 the manufacturer raises the price by 2% of the price in effect on September 30. What is the new price of a car that on August 31 sold for $8000? (This is known as **chain percent increase.**)

80. Use your graphing calculator to convert each number to a fraction in lowest terms (see your manual for instructions): 0.12, 0.1278, $0.\overline{63}$ (this is 0.636363 . . .) how many repetitions must you enter before your calculator will interpret this as a repeating decimal?

81. According to the Bipartisan Task Force on Funding Disaster Relief (1995), hurricanes accounted for 39.9% of insurance payouts for the period 1984–1993. For every million dollars paid out in this period, how many dollars were paid out for hurricanes?

82. Agricultural damages accounted for 1.52 billion dollars out of a total of 30 billion dollars of damages related to hurricane Andrew, which struck Florida in August 1992. What percentage of the total damages were agricultural?

Source for data in Exercises 81–82: Pielke Jr., Roger A., and Roger A. Pielke Sr. *Hurricanes: Their Nature and Impacts on Society.* Chichester: John Wiley & Sons, 1997.

1.3 Algebraic Expressions

A rational number is one that can be written as p/q where p and q are integers (and q is not zero). These symbols can take on more than one distinct value. For example, when $p = 5$ and $q = 7$, we have the rational number $\frac{5}{7}$; when $p = -3$ and $q = 2$, we have the rational number $\frac{-3}{2}$. The symbols p and q are called **variables**, since various values can be assigned to them.

If we invest P dollars at an interest rate of 6% per year, we will have $P + 0.06P$ dollars at the end of the year. We call $P + 0.06P$ an **algebraic expression**. Note that an algebraic expression involves **variables** (in our case, P), **constants** (such as 0.06), and **algebraic operations** (such as $+, -, \cdot, \div$). Virtually everything we do in algebra involves algebraic expressions, sometimes as simple as our example and sometimes very complicated.

When we assign a value to each variable in an algebraic expression and carry out the indicated operations, we are "evaluating" the expression.

EXAMPLE 1   EVALUATING AN ALGEBRAIC EXPRESSION

Evaluate.

(a) $2x + 5$ when $x = 3$ (b) $\dfrac{3m + 4n}{m + n}$ when $m = 3, n = 2$

SOLUTIONS

(a) Substituting 3 for x, we have
$$2(3) + 5 = 6 + 5 = 11$$

(b) Substituting, we have
$$\frac{3(3) + 4(2)}{3 + 2} = \frac{9 + 8}{3 + 2} = \frac{17}{5}$$

✔ **Progress Check 1**

Evaluate.

(a) $\dfrac{r + 2s}{s - r}$ when $r = 1, s = 3$

(b) $4x + 2y - z$ when $x = 1, y = 4, z = 2$

Answers

(a) $\dfrac{7}{2}$ (b) 10

Order of Operations

If we want to evaluate

$$3 + \frac{5y}{2} \quad \text{when } y = 4$$

in what order should we perform the operations? The interpretation

$$\frac{3 + 5y}{2}$$

doesn't produce the same result as the interpretation

$$3 + \frac{5y}{2}$$

Fortunately, most calculators and computer languages use the same convention for determining the order of operations. This order or **hierarchy of operations** is shown below.

Hierarchy of Operations

1. Perform all operations within parentheses.
2. Compute any squares or powers (see Section 1.4).
3. Perform multiplication and division, working from left to right.
4. Perform addition and subtraction, working from left to right.

To evaluate an expression, substitute the given values for the variables and then apply the rules for the hierarchy of operations.

EXAMPLE 2   EVALUATING AN ALGEBRAIC EXPRESSION

Evaluate the expression

$$\frac{3(x - 1)}{y + 2} + (x - y)(x + y) \quad \text{when } x = 5, y = 2$$

SOLUTION

Substituting, we have

$$\frac{3(5 - 1)}{(2 + 2)} + (5 - 2)(5 + 2) = \frac{3(4)}{4} + (3)(7) \quad \text{Operations in parentheses}$$

$$= 3 + 21 \qquad \text{Multiplication and division}$$

$$= 24 \qquad \text{Addition}$$

✔ **Progress Check 2**

Evaluate.

(a) $\dfrac{2(x-1)}{(x+1)+(x+3)}$ when $x = 2$

(b) $1 + (2-x) + \dfrac{y}{y-1}$ when $x = 1, y = 2$

Answers

(a) $\dfrac{1}{4}$ (b) 4

Exercise Set 1.3

In Exercises 1–4 determine whether the given statement is true (T) or false (F).

1. $3x + 2 = 8$ when $x = 2$

2. $5x - 1 = 11$ when $x = 2$

3. $2xy = 12$ when $x = 2, y = 3$

4. $\dfrac{2x + y}{7} = 7$ when $x = 3, y = 1$

In Exercises 5–12 evaluate the given expression when $x = 4$.

5. $2x + 3$

6. $3x - 2$

7. $\dfrac{1}{2}x$

8. $3(x - 1)$

9. $(2x)(2x)$

10. $(2x + 1)x$

11. $\dfrac{1}{2x + 3}$

12. $\dfrac{x}{2x - 4}$

In Exercises 13–20 evaluate the given expression when $a = 3, b = 4$.

13. $2a + b$

14. $3a - b$

15. $2b - a$

16. ab

17. $3(a + 2b)$

18. $\dfrac{1}{3a + b}$

19. $\dfrac{2a - b}{b}$

20. $\dfrac{a + b}{b - a}$

In Exercises 21–28 evaluate the given expression when $r = 2, s = 3, t = 4$.

21. $r + 2s + t$

22. rst

23. $\dfrac{rst}{r + s + t}$

24. $(r + s)t$

25. $\dfrac{r + s}{t}$

26. $\dfrac{r + s + t}{t}$

27. $\dfrac{t - r}{rs}$

28. $\dfrac{3(r + s + t)}{s}$

29. Evaluate $2\pi r$ when $r = 3$. (Recall that π is approximately 3.14.)

30. Evaluate $\dfrac{9}{5}C + 32$ when $C = 37$.

31. Evaluate $0.02r + 0.314st + 2.25t$ when $r = 2.5$, $s = 3.4$, and $t = 2.81$.

32. Evaluate $10.421x + 0.821y + 2.34xyz$ when $x = 3.21, y = 2.42$, and $z = 1.23$.

In Exercises 33–36 evaluate the given expression when $x = -3.25$ and $y = 0.75$.

33. $3 + x \div 6 \cdot x - 1$

34. $3 \div (x + y) - y$

35. $2 \cdot y + 1 \div (x + 1)$

36. $-1 + (2x - y) \div 2 + y \div (1 - x)$

*37. If P dollars are invested for t years at a simple interest rate of r percent per year, the amount on hand at the end of t years is $P + Prt$. Suppose $2000 is invested at 8% per year ($r = 0.08$). How much money is on hand after

(a) one year   (b) three years
(c) half a year   (d) eight months

(*Hint:* Express eight months as a fraction of a year.)

*38. The perimeter of a rectangle is given by the formula $P = 2(L + W)$, where L is the length and W is the width of the rectangle. Find the perimeter if

(a) $L = 2$ feet, $W = 3$ feet.

(b) $L = \frac{1}{2}$ meter, $W = \frac{1}{4}$ meter.

(c) $L = 13$ inches, $W = 15$ inches.

39. Al purchases 3 boxes of cereal at $1.25 per box, 2 bottles of soda at $1.10 per bottle, and $1\frac{1}{2}$ pounds of salad at $2.29 per pound. Write an expression for the total cost.

40. If apples cost a cents per pound, pears cost p cents per pound, and cucumbers cost c cents each, write an expression for the total bill when Joan purchases 2 pounds of apples, $3\frac{1}{2}$ pounds of pears, and 6 cucumbers.

41. The campus cafeteria sells hamburgers for $1.35, hot dogs for 85¢, and french fries for 80¢ per order. Write an expression for the total cost when Jim purchases d hot dogs, h hamburgers, and f orders of french fries.

42. Hi-Fi House is offering a 10% discount on all record and cassette purchases. Write an expression for the total cost when a student purchases N cassettes at $5.99 each, M cassettes at $6.99 each, and K records at $6 each.

43. Use your calculator to evaluate the expression

$$\frac{140x - 319y}{500y}$$

for $x = 200$, $y = 200$. First, store the values under variable names. Then, enter the expression using those variable names. Now you can store new values and retrieve the expression you entered (it should not be necessary to enter it again). Evaluate the same expression for $x = 210$ and $y = 199$.

```
200→X
            200
200→Y
            200
(140X-319Y)/(500
Y)
```

1.4   Operating with Signed Numbers; Exponents

Let's review the rules for operating with signed numbers before using them in more complicated problems.

We say that $-a$ is the **opposite** of a if a and $-a$ are equidistant from the origin and lie on opposite sides of the origin.

Since $-a$ is opposite in direction to a, then $-(-a)$ must have the same direction as a. We see that

$$-(-a) = a$$

We also refer to $-a$ as the **negative** of a. Of course, the negative of a number need not be negative: $-(-5) = 5$.

Here are the rules for addition with signed numbers:

Addition with Like Signs

> Ignoring the signs, add the numbers. The sign of the answer is the same as the common sign of the original numbers.
>
> $$5 + 2 = 7$$
> $$(-5) + (-2) = -7$$

Addition with Unlike Signs

> Ignoring the signs, find the difference of the numbers. The sign of the answer is the sign of the number that is larger in absolute value.
>
> $$6 + (-4) = 2 \qquad 3 + (-5) = -2$$
> $$(-7) + 3 = -4 \qquad (-5) + 8 = 3$$

EXAMPLE 1 ADDING SIGNED NUMBERS

(a) $2 + 4 = 6$ (b) $2 + (-4) = -2$ (c) $(-2) + (-4) = -6$

(d) $(-2) + 4 = 2$ (e) $3 + [(-5) + (-2)] = 3 + (-7) = -4$

(f) $[(-4) + (-7)] + 3 = -11 + 3 = -8$ (g) $8 + 0 = 8$

✔ Progress Check 1

Add.

(a) $(-3) + (-7)$ (b) $(-5) + 1$ (c) $2 + (-6)$

(d) $-2 + [5 + (-4)]$ (e) $0 + (-8)$ (f) $[3 + (-6)] + (-1)$

Answers

(a) -10 (b) -4 (c) -4

(d) -1 (e) -8 (f) -4

Subtraction problems can be converted into addition of signed numbers.

Subtraction

> Change $a - b$ to $a + (-b)$ and follow the rules for addition of signed numbers.
>
> $$5 - 2 = 5 + (-2) = 3$$
> $$-3 - 4 = -3 + (-4) = -7$$
> $$2 - (-6) = 2 + (+6) = 8$$
> $$-6 - (-5) = -6 + (+5) = -1$$

EXAMPLE 2 SUBTRACTING SIGNED NUMBERS

(a) $7 - 4 = 7 + (-4) = 3$

(b) $10 - (-6) = 10 + (+6) = 16$

(c) $-8 - 2 = -8 + (-2) = -10$

(d) $-5 - (-4) = -5 + (+4) = -1$

(e) $-7 - (-7) = -7 + (+7) = 0$

(f) $(-2 - 5) + 6 = [-2 + (-5)] + 6 = -1$

✔ Progress Check 2

Perform the operations.

(a) $3 - 8$ (b) $-6 - 7$ (c) $-9 - (-5)$ (d) $16 - (-9)$

(e) $(14 - 5) - 4$ (f) $(-11 + 2) - 4$ (g) $(-6 - 4) - 2$

Answers

(a) -5 (b) -13 (c) -4 (d) 25

(e) 5 (f) -13 (g) -12

The rules for determining the sign in multiplication and division are straightforward.

If both numbers have the same sign, the result is positive. If the numbers have opposite signs, the result is negative.

$$3 \cdot 4 = 12 \qquad\qquad \frac{6}{3} = 2$$

$$(-2)(-5) = 10 \qquad\qquad \frac{-8}{-4} = 2$$

$$(-4)(6) = -24 \qquad\qquad \frac{-10}{2} = -5$$

Multiplication and Division

$$(7)(-3) = -21 \qquad\qquad \frac{12}{-3} = -4$$

EXAMPLE 3   MULTIPLYING AND DIVIDING SIGNED NUMBERS

(a) $4 \cdot \left(-\dfrac{1}{5}\right) = -\dfrac{4}{5}$ (b) $\left(-\dfrac{2}{3}\right)(-3) = 2$ (c) $\dfrac{-4}{8} = -\dfrac{1}{2}$

(d) $\dfrac{-16}{-24} = \dfrac{2}{3}$ (e) $(-5) \cdot \dfrac{1}{4} = -\dfrac{5}{4}$ (f) $\dfrac{18}{-2} = -9$

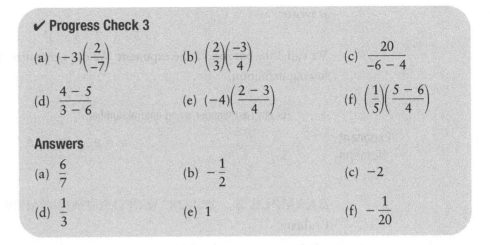

✔ **Progress Check 3**

(a) $(-3)\left(\dfrac{2}{-7}\right)$ (b) $\left(\dfrac{2}{3}\right)\left(\dfrac{-3}{4}\right)$ (c) $\dfrac{20}{-6-4}$

(d) $\dfrac{4-5}{3-6}$ (e) $(-4)\left(\dfrac{2-3}{4}\right)$ (f) $\left(\dfrac{1}{5}\right)\left(\dfrac{5-6}{4}\right)$

Answers

(a) $\dfrac{6}{7}$ (b) $-\dfrac{1}{2}$ (c) -2

(d) $\dfrac{1}{3}$ (e) 1 (f) $-\dfrac{1}{20}$

Let's apply the rules for operating with signed numbers to the evaluation of algebraic expressions.

EXAMPLE 4 EVALUATING AN ALGEBRAIC EXPRESSION

Evaluate the given expression when $x = -1$, $y = -1$.

(a) $2x + \dfrac{x-1}{y+2}$ (b) $-3(2x - y) + (-4)(2y - x)$

SOLUTIONS

(a) Substituting, we have

$$2(-1) + \frac{(-1-1)}{-1+2} = -2 + \frac{-2}{1} = -2 + (-2) = -4$$

(b) Substituting, we have

$$-3[2(-1) - (-1)] + (-4)[2(-1) - (-1)]$$
$$= -3(-2+1) + (-4)(-2+1)$$
$$= -3(-1) + (-4)(-1) = 3 + 4 = 7$$

✔ **Progress Check 4**

Evaluate the given expression when $x = 2$, $y = -1$.

(a) $-(-y)$ (b) $2 - 3x + y$ (c) $\dfrac{2-2x}{2-2y}$ (d) $\dfrac{x+y}{x-y}$

Answers

(a) -1 (b) -5 (c) $-\dfrac{1}{2}$ (d) $\dfrac{1}{3}$

Mathematicians use a special notation to indicate a product of repeated factors. For example, the product

$$3 \cdot 3 \cdot 3 \cdot 3 \cdot 3$$

is written as

$$3 \cdot 3 \cdot 3 \cdot 3 \cdot 3 = 3^5$$

We call 3 the **base** and 5 the **exponent.** We can generalize this notation by the following definition.

Exponent Notation

For any real number a and natural number n,

$$a^n = a \cdot a \cdot a \cdots a$$

EXAMPLE 5   WORKING WITH EXPONENT NOTATION
Evaluate.

(a) 2^6 (b) 0.1^3 (c) $(-2)^4$ (d) $(-5)^3$

SOLUTIONS

(a) $2^6 = 2 \cdot 2 \cdot 2 \cdot 2 \cdot 2 \cdot 2 = 64$ (b) $0.1^3 = (0.1)(0.1)(0.1) = 0.001$

(c) $(-2)^4 = (-2)(-2)(-2)(-2) = 16$ (d) $(-5)^3 = (-5)(-5)(-5) = -125$

✔ **Progress Check 5**
Evaluate.

(a) 10^3 (b) $(-4)^4$ (c) $(-2)^5$ (d) 3^4 (e) $\left(\dfrac{2}{3}\right)^3$

Answers

(a) 1000 (b) 256 (c) -32 (d) 81 (e) $\dfrac{8}{27}$

Exercise Set 1.4

In Exercises 1–54 simplify the given expression by carrying out the indicated operations.

1. $3 + 5$

2. $-2 + (-3)$

3. $(-3) + (-4)$

4. $2 + (-3)$

5. $4 + (-2)$

6. $-4 + 6$

7. $-4 + 2$

8. $0 + (-2)$

9. $3 + 0$

10. $3 + (-3)$

11. $5 - 3$

12. $5 - 8$

13. $5 - (-3)$

14. $4 - (-4)$

15. $-8 - (-3)$

16. $-6 - (-7)$

17. $5 - (-6)(-3)$

18. $4 - (-1)(2)$

19. $[-3 - (-2)] - 1$

20. $[-8 - (-4)] - 5$

21. $(-4 - 2) - (-3)$

22. $2\left(\dfrac{3}{4}\right)$

23. $(-2)(-5)$

24. $(-3)\left(-\dfrac{8}{6}\right)$

25. $\left(-\dfrac{5}{6}\right)\left(\dfrac{9}{15}\right)$

26. $\left(\dfrac{3}{5}\right)\left(-\dfrac{10}{4}\right)$

27. $\dfrac{8}{2}$

28. $\dfrac{-10}{-2}$

29. $\dfrac{-15}{5}$

30. $\dfrac{20}{-4}$

31. $\dfrac{-15}{25}$

32. $\dfrac{15}{-\frac{3}{4}}$

33. $\dfrac{-12}{-\frac{2}{3}}$

34. $(-4)\left(-\dfrac{5}{2}\right)$

35. $\dfrac{3}{5}\left(-\dfrac{15}{2}\right)$

36. $\left(-\dfrac{3}{4}\right)0$

37. $\left(-\dfrac{4}{5}\right)\left(-\dfrac{15}{2}\right)$

38. $-(-2)$

39. $\dfrac{4-4}{2}$

40. $\dfrac{14+1}{-5-(-2)}$

41. $\dfrac{5+(-5)}{3}$

42. $\dfrac{-18}{-3-6}$

43. $\dfrac{15}{2-7}$

44. $\dfrac{24}{2-8}$

45. $\dfrac{-8-4}{3}$

46. $-5(2-4)$

47. $-4(4-1)$

48. $\dfrac{3(-5+1)}{-4(2-6)}$

49. $-(-2x+3y)$

50. $(-x)(-y)$

51. $\dfrac{-x}{-y}$

52. $\dfrac{-x}{\frac{1}{2}}$

53. $\dfrac{2}{\frac{x}{-2}}$

54. $\dfrac{-a}{(-b)(-c)}$

In Exercises 55–57 evaluate the given expression when $x = -2$.

55. $x - 5$

56. $-2x$

57. $\dfrac{x}{x-1}$

In Exercises 58–60 evaluate the given expression when $x = -3, y = -2$.

58. $x + 2y$

59. $x - 2y$

60. $\dfrac{4x - y}{y}$

In Exercises 61–68 evaluate a^n for the given values of a and n.

61. $a = -1, n = 5$

62. $a = 4, n = 2$

63. $a = 6, n = 3$

64. $a = -2, n = 4$

65. $a = \dfrac{2}{5}, n = 3$

66. $a = 0.2, n = 3$

67. $a = \dfrac{5}{3}, n = 4$

68. $a = -1, n = 100$

69. Subtract 3 from -5.

70. Subtract -3 from -4.

71. Subtract -5 from -2. 72. Subtract -2 from 8.

73. At 2 P.M. the temperature is 10°C above zero, and at 11 P.M. it is 2°C below zero. How many degrees has the temperature dropped?

74. Repeat the previous exercise if the temperature at 2 P.M. is 8°C and it is -4°C at 11 P.M.

75. A stationery store had a loss of $400 during its first year of operation and a loss of $800 during its second year. How much money did the store lose during the first two years of its existence?

76. A bicycle repair shop had a profit of $150 for the month of July and a loss of $200 for the month of August. How much money did the shop gain or lose over the two-month period?

*77. E. & E. Fabrics had a loss of x dollars during its first business year and a profit of y dollars its second year. Write an expression for the net profit or loss after two years.

*78. S. & S. Hardware had a profit of x dollars, followed by a loss that exceeded twice the profit by $200. Write an expression for the net loss.

*79. The Student Stereo Shoppe had a loss of $200 during its first year of business, a profit of $800 during its second year, and a profit of $900 during its third year. What was the average profit (or loss) over the three-year period?

80. Use your calculator to evaluate the expression

$$3200x - 2900y$$

for $x = -2900, y = 3200$. First, store the values under variable names. Then, enter the expression using those variable names. Now you can store new values and retrieve the expression you entered (it should not be necessary to enter it again). Evaluate the same expression for $x = -3200$ and $y = -2900$.

1.5   Properties of Real Numbers

The real numbers obey laws that enable us to manipulate algebraic expressions with ease. We'll use the letters a, b, and c to denote real numbers.

To begin, note that the sum of two real numbers is a real number and the product of two real numbers is a real number. These are known as the **closure properties**.

Closure Properties

> **Property 1.** The sum of a and b, denoted by $a + b$, is a real number.
>
> **Property 2.** The product of a and b, denoted by $a \cdot b$ or ab, is a real number.

We say that the set of real numbers is **closed** with respect to the operations of addition and multiplication, since the sum and product of two real numbers are also real numbers.

We know that

$$3 + 4 = 7 \qquad \text{and} \qquad 3 \cdot 4 = 12$$
$$4 + 3 = 7 \qquad\qquad 4 \cdot 3 = 12$$

That is, we may *add or multiply real numbers in any order*. Writing this in algebraic symbols, we have the following:

Commutative Properties

> **Property 3.** $a + b = b + a$ Commutative property of addition
>
> **Property 4.** $ab = ba$ Commutative property of multiplication

EXAMPLE 1   USING THE COMMUTATIVE PROPERTIES

(a) $5 + 7 = 7 + 5; 5 \cdot 7 = 7 \cdot 5$

(b) $3 + (-6) = -6 + 3; 3 \cdot (-6) = (-6) \cdot 3$

(c) $3x + 4y = 4y + 3x; (3x)(4y) = (4y)(3x)$

✔ Progress Check 1

Use the commutative properties to write each expression in another form.

(a) $(-3) + 6$ (b) $(-4) \cdot 5$ (c) $-2x + 6y$ (d) $\left(\dfrac{3}{2}x\right)\left(\dfrac{1}{2}y\right)$

Answers

(a) $6 + (-3)$ (b) $5 \cdot (-4)$ (c) $6y + (-2x)$ (d) $\left(\dfrac{1}{2}y\right)\left(\dfrac{3}{2}x\right)$

When we add $2 + 3 + 4$, does it matter in what order we group the numbers? No. We see that

$$(2 + 3) + 4 = 5 + 4 = 9$$

and

$$2 + (3 + 4) = 2 + 7 = 9$$

Similarly, for multiplication of $2 \cdot 3 \cdot 4$ we have

$$(2 \cdot 3) \cdot 4 = 6 \cdot 4 = 24$$

and

$$2 \cdot (3 \cdot 4) = 2 \cdot 12 = 24$$

Clearly, *when adding or multiplying real numbers, we may group them in any order.* Translating into algebraic symbols, we have the following:

Associative Properties

> **Property 5.** $(a + b) + c = a + (b + c)$ Associative property of addition
>
> **Property 6.** $(ab)c = a(bc)$ Associative property of multiplication

EXAMPLE 2 USING THE ASSOCIATIVE PROPERTIES

(a) $5 + (2 + 3) = (5 + 2) + 3 = 10$ (b) $5 \cdot (2 \cdot 3) = (5 \cdot 2) \cdot 3 = 30$

(c) $(3x + 2y) + 4z = 3x + (2y + 4z)$ (d) $3(4y) = (3 \cdot 4)y = 12y$

(e) $(-2)[(-5)(-x)] = [(-2)(-5)](-x) = 10(-x) = -10x$

✔ Progress Check 2

Use the associative properties to simplify.

(a) $3 + (2 + x)$ (b) $6 \cdot 2xy$

Answers

(a) $5 + x$ (b) $12xy$

We can combine the commutative and associative properties to simplify algebraic expressions.

EXAMPLE 3 SIMPLIFYING AN EXPRESSION

Use the commutative and associative properties to simplify.

(a) $(3 + x) + 5$ (b) $\left(\frac{2}{3}y\right)\left(\frac{3}{4}\right)$ (c) $(2x - 4) + 7$

SOLUTIONS

(a) $(3 + x) + 5 = (x + 3) + 5$ Commutative property of addition

$\qquad\qquad\quad = x + (3 + 5)$ Associative property of addition

$\qquad\qquad\quad = x + 8$

(b) $\left(\frac{2}{3}y\right)\left(\frac{3}{4}\right) = \frac{3}{4} \cdot \left(\frac{2}{3}y\right)$ Commutative property of multiplication

$\qquad\qquad\quad = \left(\frac{3}{4} \cdot \frac{2}{3}\right)y$ Associative property of multiplication

$\qquad\qquad\quad = \frac{1}{2}y$

(c) $(2x - 4) + 7 = [2x + (-4)] + 7$
$$= 2x + (-4) + 7 \qquad \text{Associative property of addition}$$
$$= 2x + 3$$

✔ Progress Check 3

Use the commutative and associative properties to simplify.

(a) $4 + (2x + 2)$ (b) $\left(\dfrac{4}{5}x\right)\left(\dfrac{10}{2}\right)$ (c) $(5 - 3x) + 6$

Answers

(a) $6 + 2x$ (b) $4x$ (c) $11 - 3x$

The **distributive properties** deal with both addition and multiplication. For instance,

$$2(3 + 4) = 2(7) = 14 \quad \text{and} \quad (1 + 2)5 = (3)5 = 15$$

We may notice that

$$2(3) + 2(4) = 6 + 8 = 14$$

and

$$1(5) + 2(5) = 5 + 10 = 15$$

produce the same results as the first two equations. The distributive properties tell us that this is not an accident; rather, it is a rule that we may always use.

Distributive Properties

> **Property 7.** $a(b + c) = ab + bc$
>
> **Property 8.** $(a + b)c = ac + bc$

The distributive properties can be extended to factors that are a sum of more than two terms. Thus,

$$3(5x + 2y - 4z) = 3(5x) + 3(2y) + 3(-4z)$$
$$= 15x + 6y - 12z$$

EXAMPLE 4   USING THE DISTRIBUTIVE PROPERTIES

(a) $4(2x + 3) = 4(2x) + 4(3) = 8x + 12$

(b) $(4x + 2)6 = (4x)(6) + (2)(6) = 24x + 12$

(c) $2(x + 5y - 2z) = 2x + 2(5y) + 2(-2z)$
$$= 2x + 10y - 4z$$

(d) $-(2y - x) = (-1)(2y - x) = (-1)(2y) + (-1)(-x) = -2y + x$

Note that a negative sign in front of parentheses is treated as multiplication by -1.

> **✔ Progress Check 4**
> Simplify, using the distributive properties.
>
> (a) $5(3x + 4)$ (b) $(x + 3)7$ (c) $-2(3a - b + c)$
>
> **Answers**
> (a) $15x + 20$ (b) $7x + 21$ (c) $-6a + 2b - 2c$

It is easy to show that the commutative and associative properties *do not* hold for subtraction and division. For example,

$$2 - 5 = -3 \quad \text{but} \quad 5 - 2 = 3$$

and, in general,

$$a - b = -(b - a) \neq b - a$$

Similarly, $12 \div 3 \neq 3 \div 12$ shows that the commutative property does not hold for division.

The student is encouraged to provide counterexamples to show that the associative property does not hold for subtraction and division (see Exercise 19 in Exercise Set 1.5.)

Table 1 summarizes some of the important properties of real numbers.

TABLE 1 Properties of Real Numbers

For all real numbers *a*, *b*, and *c*:

Closure properties

$a + b$ is a real number.
ab is a real number.

Commutative properties

$a + b = b + a$
$ab = ba$

Associative properties

$(a + b) + c = a + (b + c)$
$(ab)c = a(bc)$

Distributive properties

$a(b + c) = ab + ac$
$(a + b)c = ac + bc$

Identity properties

There is a unique real number 0 called the ***additive identity*** such that

$$a + 0 = a \quad \text{and} \quad 0 + a = a$$

There is a unique real number 1 called the ***multiplicative identify*** such that

$$a \cdot 1 = a \quad \text{and} \quad 1 \cdot a = a$$

Inverse properties

For every real number a there is a unique number $-a$ called the ***additive inverse*** or ***opposite*** of a such that

$$a + (-a) = 0$$

For every real number a (other than 0) there is a unique real number $\frac{1}{a}$ called the ***multiplicative inverse*** or ***reciprocal*** such that

$$a \cdot \frac{1}{a} = 1$$

Exercise Set 1.5

In Exercises 1–18 justify the given equation by using one or more properties of real numbers.

1. $2 + 5 = 5 + 2$

2. $(3 \cdot 2)(-4) = 3[(2)(-4)]$

3. $-2 \cdot 5 = 5(-2)$

4. $2(4 + 5) = 2 \cdot 4 + 2 \cdot 5$

5. $(4 + 3)2 = 4 \cdot 2 + 3 \cdot 2$

6. $3(2 - 4) = 3 \cdot 2 - 3 \cdot 4$

7. $-2(4 - 5) = (-2)(4) - 2(-5)$

8. $(3 + 2) + 4 = 3 + (2 + 4)$

9. $-3 + (2 + 5) = (-3 + 2) + 5$

10. $(2 - 5) + 8 = 2 + (-5 + 8)$

11. $3 + a = a + 3$ 12. $2(x + 2) = 2x + 4$

13. $2(ab) = (2a)b$ 14. $5(a + b) = 5(b + a)$

15. $2(xy) = x(2y)$ 16. $4(a + b) = 4b + 4a$

17. $5 + (a + 2) = 2 + (5 + a)$ 18. $(5x)y = 5(yx)$

19. Give examples showing that the commutative and associative properties do not hold for the operation of subtraction.

In Exercises 20–25 find and correct the mistake.

20. $a + 2a = 2a^2$ 21. $2(a + 2) = 2a + 2$

22. $3(x - 2) = x - 6$ 23. $(a - b)2 = 2a - b$

24. $3(ab) = (3a)(3b)$

25. $(2a + 3) + a = 3(a + 2)$

In Exercises 26–54 simplify the given expression.

26. $(2 + x) + 4$ 27. $(2 - x) + 2$

28. $(x - 3) - 4$ 29. $(x - 5) - 2x$

30. $(2x)(-5)$ 31. $(-3x)(-4)$

32. $2(-3x)$ 33. $a(2b)(3c)$

34. $4\left(\dfrac{3}{2}a\right)$ 35. $\dfrac{2}{3}(9 + 12a - 6b)$

36. $\dfrac{4x}{-2}$ 37. $\dfrac{-2}{4x}$

38. $\dfrac{-8x}{-4}$ 39. $(3x)\left(-\dfrac{4}{9}y\right)$

40. $\dfrac{1}{4}(4a)$ 41. $\dfrac{1}{5}(10ab)$

42. $\dfrac{4(b + 2)}{3}$ 43. $\dfrac{3(5x - y)}{12}$

44. $6x + \dfrac{(y - 1)4}{2}$ 45. $3a + \dfrac{(b - 3c)}{2}(-5)$

46. $3(a - 2) - 2(b + 4)$ 47. $4(x + y) - 2(z - 2w)$

48. $3\left(\dfrac{2u + v}{6}\right) + \dfrac{1}{2}(4w)$

49. $2\left(\dfrac{x}{2} + y - 2\right) - (-2u + 4)$

50. $4\left(\dfrac{a - 2b + 4}{2}\right) + \dfrac{1}{3}(6c + 9)$

51. $-3.65\left(\dfrac{0.47 - 2.79}{6.44}\right)$

52. $\dfrac{6.92}{4.7}\left(\dfrac{2.01}{1.64 - 3.53}\right)$

53. $0.40\left(\dfrac{17.52 - 6.48 + 2.97}{3.60}\right) - 0.25(-4.75 + 2.92)$

54. $16.33\left(\dfrac{14.94}{3.87} - \dfrac{2.22 + 7.46}{2.96}\right)$

In Exercises 55–58 find a counterexample for each given statement; that is, find real values for the variables that make the statement false.

*55. $a(b + c) = ab + c$

*56. $\dfrac{a}{b} = \dfrac{b}{a}$

*57. $(b - c)a = b - ca$

*58. $(a + b)(c + d) = ac + bd$

1.6 Absolute Value and Inequalities

When we introduced the real number line, we pointed out that positive numbers lie to the right of the origin and negative numbers lie to the left of the origin.

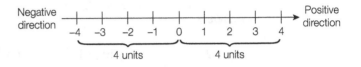

Suppose we are interested in the *distance* between the origin and the points labeled 4 and −4. Each of these points is four units from the origin, that is, the *distance is independent of the direction.*

When we are interested in the size of a number *a* and don't care about the direction or sign, we use the notation of **absolute value**, which we write as $|a|$. Thus,

$$|4| = 4$$
$$|-4| = 4$$

EXAMPLE 1 WORKING WITH ABSOLUTE VALUE

(a) $|-6| = 6$ (b) $|17.4| = 17.4$ (c) $|0| = 0$

(d) $|4 - 9| = |-5| = 5$ (e) $\left|\dfrac{2}{5} - \dfrac{6}{5}\right| = \left|-\dfrac{4}{5}\right| = \dfrac{4}{5}$

✔ Progress Check 1

Find the values.

(a) $|22|$ (b) $\left|-\dfrac{2}{7}\right|$ (c) $|4 - 4|$ (d) $|6 - 8|$ (e) $\left|\dfrac{1}{7} - \dfrac{3}{7}\right|$

Answers

(a) 22 (b) $\dfrac{2}{7}$ (c) 0 (d) 2 (e) $\dfrac{2}{7}$

The absolute value bars act as grouping symbols. We must work inside these grouping symbols before we can remove them.

EXAMPLE 2 ORDER OF OPERATIONS WITH ABSOLUTE VALUE

(a) $|-3| + |-6| = 3 + 6 = 9$

(b) $|3 - 5| - |8 - 6| = |-2| - |2| = 2 - 2 = 0$

(c) $\dfrac{|4 - 7|}{|-6|} = \dfrac{|-3|}{|-6|} = \dfrac{3}{6} = \dfrac{1}{2}$

(d) $\left|\dfrac{2 - 8}{3}\right| = \left|\dfrac{-6}{3}\right| = |-2| = 2$

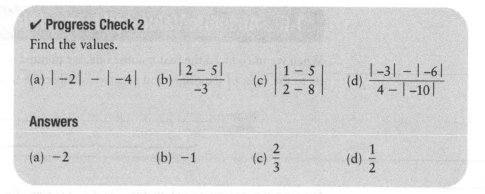

✔ **Progress Check 2**

Find the values.

(a) $|-2| - |-4|$ (b) $\dfrac{|2 - 5|}{-3}$ (c) $\left|\dfrac{1 - 5}{2 - 8}\right|$ (d) $\dfrac{|-3| - |-6|}{4 - |-10|}$

Answers

(a) -2 (b) -1 (c) $\dfrac{2}{3}$ (d) $\dfrac{1}{2}$

The absolute value of a number is, then, always nonnegative. What can we do with the absolute value of a variable, say, $|x|$? We don't know whether x is positive or negative, so we can't write $|x| = x$. For instance, when $x = -4$, we have

$$|x| = |-4| = 4 \neq x$$

and when $x = 4$, we have

$$|x| = |4| = 4 = x$$

We must define absolute value so that it works for both positive and negative values of a variable.

Absolute Value

$$|a| = \begin{cases} a & \text{when } a \text{ is 0 or positive} \\ -a & \text{when } a \text{ is negative} \end{cases}$$

When a is positive, say, $a = 4$, the absolute value is the number itself; when a is negative, say, $a = -4$, the absolute value is the negative of a, or $+4$. Thus, the absolute value is always nonnegative.

The following properties of absolute value follow from the definition.

Properties of Absolute Value

For all real numbers a and b,

1. $|a|$ is nonnegative
2. $|a| = |-a|$
3. $|a - b| = |b - a|$

We began by showing how absolute value can be used to denote distance from the origin without regard to direction. We will conclude by demonstrating the use of absolute value to denote the distance between any two points a and b on the real number line. In Figure 2, the distance between the points labeled 2 and 5 is 3 units and can be obtained by evaluating either $|5 - 2|$ or $|2 - 5|$. Similarly, the distance between the points labeled -1 and 4 is given

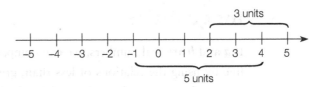

Figure 2   Distance Expressed by Absolute Value

by either $|4 - (-1)| = 5$ or $|-1 - 4| = 5$. Using the notation to denote the distance between the points A and B, we provide the following definition.

Distance on the Real Number Line

> The distance $\overline{AB}$ between points A and B on the real number line, whose coordinates are a and b, respectively, is given by
> $$\overline{AB} = |b - a|$$

Property 3 then tells us that $\overline{AB} = |b - a| = |a - b|$. Viewed another way, Property 3 states that the distance between any two points on the real number line is independent of the direction.

EXAMPLE 3   ABSOLUTE VALUE AND DISTANCE

Let points A, B, and C have coordinates -4, -1, and 3, respectively, on the real number line, and let the origin, with coordinate 0, be denoted by O. Find the following distances.

(a) $\overline{AB}$ (b) $\overline{CB}$ (c) $\overline{OB}$

SOLUTIONS

Using the definition, we have

(a) $\overline{AB} = |-1 - (-4)| = |-1 + 4| = |3| = 3$

(b) $\overline{CB} = |-1 - 3| = |-4| = 4$

(c) $\overline{OB} = |-1 - 0| = |-1| = 1$

✔ Progress Check 3

The points P, Q, and R on the real number line have coordinates -6, 4, and 6, respectively. Find the following distances.

(a) $\overline{PR}$ (b) $\overline{QP}$ (c) $\overline{PQ}$ (d) $\overline{PO}$

Answers

(a) 12   (b) 10   (c) 10   (d) 6

Inequalities

If a and b are real numbers, we can compare their positions on the real number line by using the relations of **less than**, **greater than**, **less than or equal to**, and **greater than or equal to**, denoted by the **inequality symbols** $<$, $>$, $\leq$, and $\geq$, respectively. Table 2 describes both algebraic and geometric interpretations of the inequality symbols.

Here is a helpful way to remember the meaning of the symbols $>$ and $<$. We can think of the symbols $>$ and $<$ as pointers that always point to the lesser of the two numbers.

EXAMPLE 4   USING THE INEQUALITY SYMBOLS
(a) $2 < 5$ (b) $-1 < 3$ (c) $6 > 4$

✔ Progress Check 4

Make a true statement by replacing the square with the symbol $<$ or $>$.

(a) $7 \ \square \ 10$ (b) $16 \ \square \ 8$ (c) $4 \ \square \ -2$

Answers

(a) $<$ (b) $>$ (c) $>$

We can use the real number line to illustrate the relations $<$ and $>$. For example, in Figure 3 we show that the inequality $x < 3$ is satisfied by *all* points to the left of 3.

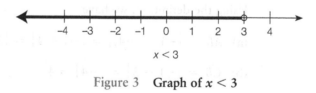

$x < 3$

Figure 3   **Graph of $x < 3$**

Similarly, in Figure 4 we show that the inequality $x \geq -1$ is satisfied by *all* points to the right of (and including) -1.

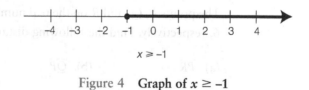

$x \geq -1$

Figure 4   **Graph of $x \geq -1$**

For $x < 3$, the point labeled 3 does not satisfy the inequality; we indicate this by an open circle.

TABLE 2 Inequalities and the Real Number Line

Algebraic Statement	Equivalent Statement	Location on the Number Line
$a > b$	a is greater than b. or b is less than a.	a lies to the right of b.
$a > 0$	a is greater than zero. or a is positive.	a lies to the right of the origin.
$a < b$	a is less than b. or b is greater than a.	a lies to the left of b.
$a < 0$	a is less than zero. or a is negative.	a lies to the left of the origin.
$a \geq b$	a is greater than or equal to b. or b is less than or equal to a.	a coincides with b or lies to the right of b.
$a \geq 0$	a is greater than or equal to zero. or a is nonnegative.	a coincides with or lies to the right of the origin.
$a \leq b$	a is less than or equal to b. or b is greater than or equal to a.	a coincides with b or lies to the left of b.
$a \leq 0$	a is less than or equal to zero. or a is nonpositive.	a coincides with or lies to the left of the origin.

For $x \geq -1$, the point labeled -1 does satisfy the inequality; we indicate this by a solid circle.

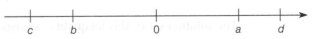

In Figures 3 and 4, the shading indicates the "set" of all points whose coordinates satisfy the given inequality. The set of all such coordinates is called the **solution set** of the inequality, and we are said to have **graphed** the solution set of the inequality or to have graphed the inequality.

EXAMPLE 5 INEQUALITIES AND THE REAL NUMBER LINE

In the following figure,

(a) $a > b$, since a is to the right of b. (b) $c < a$, since c is to the left of a.
(c) $b < 0$, since b is to the left of 0. (d) $d > a$, since d is to the right of a.

✔ **Progress Check 5**

For the figure in Example 5, make a true statement by replacing each square with the symbol < or >.

(a) $b \,\square\, d$ (b) $a \,\square\, c$ (c) $d \,\square\, 0$ (d) $b \,\square\, a$

Answers

(a) <   (b) >   (c) >   (d) <

EXAMPLE 6   GRAPHING AN INEQUALITY

Graph the solution set of the inequality on the real number line.

(a) $x \geq 2$ (b) $x < 2$

SOLUTIONS

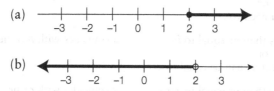

✔ **Progress Check 6**

Graph the inequality on the real number line.

(a) $x < 0$ (b) $x \geq -1$ (c) $x < -2$

Answers

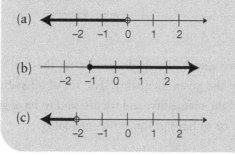

We also write compound inequalities, such as

$$-1 \leq x < 2$$

The solution set to this inequality consists of all real numbers that satisfy

$$-1 \leq x \quad \text{and} \quad x < 2$$

that is, all numbers between -1 and 2 and including -1 itself. We can easily graph the solution set on a real number line.

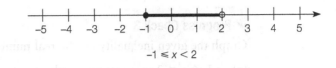

$$-1 \leq x < 2$$

EXAMPLE 7 GRAPHING A COMPOUND INEQUALITY

Graph $-3 < x < -1$, x a real number.

SOLUTION

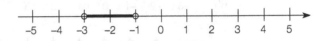

> ✔ **Progress Check 7**
>
> Graph $-2 \leq x \leq 3$, x a real number.
>
> **Answer**
>
>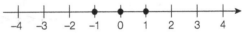

We can also graph the solution set to the inequality

$$-1 \leq x < 2, \ x \text{ an integer}$$

that is, the set of integers greater than or equal to -1 and less than 2. The solution set is $\{-1, 0, 1\}$.

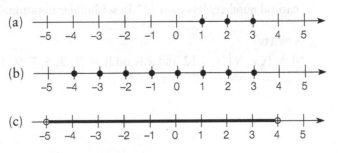

EXAMPLE 8 GRAPHING A COMPOUND INEQUALITY

Graph the given inequality on the real number line.

(a) $-5 < x < 4$, x a natural number

(b) $-5 < x < 4$, x an integer

(c) $-5 < x < 4$, x a real number

SOLUTIONS

(a)

(b)

(c)

✔ **Progress Check 8**

Graph the given inequality on the real number line.

(a) $-3 \leq x \leq 2$, x a natural number

(b) $-3 \leq x < 3$, x an integer

(c) $-4 \leq x \leq 0$, x a real number

Answers

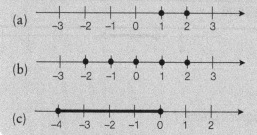

(a)

(b)

(c)

It is sometimes convenient to use **set-builder notation** as a way of writing statements such as "A is the set of integers between -3 and 2." If we let I represent the set of integers, we write

$$A = \{x \in I \mid -3 < x < 2\}$$

Each part of this symbolic expression has an explicit meaning.

$\{\ \ \}$	*read*	the set of all
$x \in I$	*read*	integers x
$\mid$	*read*	such that
$-3 < x < 2$	*read*	x is between -3 and 2

EXAMPLE 9   WORKING WITH SET-BUILDER NOTATION

If N is the set of natural numbers, write the statement "the set A of all natural numbers less than 10" in set-builder notation. List the elements of A.

SOLUTION

$A = \{x \in N \mid x < 10\} = \{1, 2, 3, 4, 5, 6, 7, 8, 9\}$

✔ **Progress Check 9**

If N is the set of natural numbers, write the statement "A is the set of all odd natural numbers less than 12" in set-builder notation. List the elements of A.

Answer

$A = \{x \in N \mid x < 12 \text{ and } x \text{ is odd}\} = \{1, 3, 5, 7, 9, 11\}$

Exercise Set 1.6

In Exercises 1–24, find the value of the given expression.

1. $|2|$

2. $\left|-\dfrac{2}{3}\right|$

3. $|1.5|$

4. $|-0.8|$

5. $-|2|$

6. $-\left|-\dfrac{2}{5}\right|$

7. $|2 - 3|$

8. $|2 - 2|$

9. $|2 - (-2)|$

10. $|2| + |-3|$

11. $\dfrac{|14 - 8|}{|-3|}$

12. $\dfrac{|2 - 12|}{|1 - 6|}$

13. $\dfrac{|3| - |2|}{|3| + |2|}$

14. $\dfrac{|4 - 2| |4| |-3|}{|4 - 3|}$

15. $|x| - |y|$ when $x = -1, y = -2$

16. $|x| - |x \cdot y|$ when $x = -3, y = 4$

17. $|x + y| + |x - y|$ when $x = -3, y = 2$

18. $\dfrac{|a - 2b|}{2a}$ when $a = 1, b = 2$

19. $\dfrac{|x| + |y|}{|x| - |y|}$ when $x = -3, y = 4$

20. $\dfrac{|-|2a + b||}{|a - b|}$ when $a = -3, b = 2$

21. $\dfrac{|-|3a - 2b| + c|}{|a - b|}$ when $a = 1, b = 3, c = 1$

22. $\dfrac{|a - b| - 2|c - a|}{|a - b + c|}$ when $a = -2, b = 3, c = -5$

23. $\dfrac{|2a - b| - |c + a|}{a|a + b - 2c|}$ when $a = 1.69, b = -7.43,$ $c = 2.98$

24. $\dfrac{|-b| c - a||}{c |b - a|}$ when $a = 12.44, b = 4.74,$ $c = -5.83$

In Exercises 25–30 the coordinates of points A and B are given. Find $\overline{AB}$.

25. $2, 5$

26. $-3, 6$

27. $-3, -1$

28. $-4, \dfrac{11}{2}$

29. $-\dfrac{4}{5}, \dfrac{4}{5}$

30. $2, 2$

In Exercises 31–36, write each given statement using the symbols $<, >, \leqslant, \geqslant$.

31. 4 is greater than 1.

32. -2 is less than -1.

33. 2 is not greater than 3.

34. 3 is not less than 1.

35. 3 is nonnegative.

36. -2 is nonpositive.

In Exercises 37–51 make a true statement by replacing the square with the symbol $<$ or $>$.

37. $3 \,\square\, 5$

38. $8 \,\square\, 2$

39. $4 \,\square\, -3$

40. $4 \,\square\, -6$

41. $-3 \,\square\, -2$

42. $-5 \,\square\, -4$

43. $-\dfrac{1}{2} \,\square\, \dfrac{1}{3}$

44. $\dfrac{1}{2} \,\square\, -\dfrac{1}{4}$

45. $-\dfrac{1}{5} \,\square\, -\dfrac{1}{3}$

46. $|-3| \,\square\, |5|$

47. $-|3| \,\square\, |4|$

48. $|-4| \,\square\, |-3|$

49. $|-2| \,\square\, 1$

50. $|4| \,\square\, 0$

51. $-|4| \,\square\, 0$

In Exercises 52–57 replace the square with the symbol $<$ or $>$ to make a true statement, referring to the number line below.

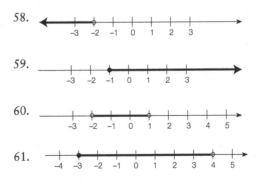

52. $a \,\square\, 0$

53. $b \,\square\, a$

54. $e \,\square\, f$

55. $d \,\square\, c$

56. $0 \,\square\, e$

57. $d \,\square\, a$

In Exercises 58–61 state the inequality represented on the given number line.

58.

59.

60.

61.

In Exercises 62–73 graph the inequality.

62. $x \leq -2$

63. $x \geq -3$

64. $x < 4$

65. $x > 1$

66. $-3 \leq x \leq 2$

67. $-4 < x < -2$

68. $-2 < x < 0$

69. $1 < x < 3$

70. $-2 < x \leq 3$, x an integer

71. $1 < x < 5$, x a natural number

72. $-3 \leq x \leq -1$, x an integer

73. $-3 \leq x < 2$, x a natural number

In Exercises 74–77 I is the set of integers, N is the set of natural numbers, and R is the set of real numbers. Write each statement in set-builder notation.

74. The set of natural numbers between -3 and 4, including -3

75. The set of integers between 2 and 4, including 4

76. The set of negative integers

77. The set of even natural numbers less than 6

In Exercises 78–83 list the elements of the given set. I is the set of integers, and N is the set of natural numbers.

78. $\{x \in I \mid -5 < x \leq -1\}$

79. $\{x \in I \mid -4 \leq x < 0\}$

80. $\{x \in N \mid -2 \leq x < 4\}$

81. $\{x \in N \mid 0 \leq x \leq 6\}$

82. $\{x \in I \mid -4 \leq x \leq 10 \text{ and } x \text{ is even}\}$

83. $\{x \in N \mid 1 < x \leq 6 \text{ and } x \text{ is odd}\}$

*84. Using the indicated values for a and b, verify the following properties of absolute value.

(a) $|a| \geq 0$ $a = 2; a = -4$

(b) $|a| = |-a|$ $a = -5; a = 3; a = 0$

(c) $|a - b| = |b - a|$ $a = 3, b = 1;$
$a = -2, b = -1$

(d) $|ab| = |a||b|$ $a = -2, b = -4$

(e) $\left|\dfrac{a}{b}\right| = \dfrac{|a|}{|b|}$ $a = 3, b = -5$

*85. Let a and b be the coordinates of two distinct points on the real number line. What does property (c) in the previous exercise say about measuring the distance between the two points?

*86. Verify that
$$|a + b| \leq |a| + |b|$$
using the following values of a and b:
$$a = 3, b = 2; a = -3, b = 2;$$
$$a = 3, b = -2; a = -3, b = -2$$

▪ ▪ ▪

Chapter Summary

Terms and Symbols

$<, >, \leq, \geq$	38	equivalent fraction	11	percent, %	17
$\in, \notin$	3	exponent	28	prime number	14
absolute value, | |	35	factor	8	product	8
algebraic expression	21	fraction	9	quotient	8
associative properties	31	graph of an inequality	39	rational number	4
base	28	hierarchy of operations	22	real number line	5
cancellation principle	12	identity properties	33	real number system	5
closure properties	30	inequality symbols	38	reciprocal	10
common factor	12	integer	4	reduced form	12
commutative properties	30	inverse properties	33	set	13
constant	21	irrational number	5	set-builder notation	42
denominator	9	LCD	14	set notation	3
distributive properties	32	member	3	solution set	39
dividend	8	natural number	4	subset	3
divisor	8	numerator	9	variable	21
element	3	origin	5		

Key Ideas for Review

Topic	Page	Key Idea
Fractions	8	
multiplication	10	Find the product of the numerators and then divide by the product of the denominators.
division	11	Multiply the numerator by the reciprocal of the denominator.
addition and subtraction	14	If the denominators are the same, add or subtract the numerators and keep the common denominator.
		If the denominators are different, find the LCD and convert each fraction to an equivalent with the LCD as the denominator.
Percent	17	Percent is a fraction whose denominator is 100.
Conversions	17	Fractions, decimals, and percents are different ways of writing the same thing; you can always convert any form to any other form.
Rational number	4	A rational number is a quotient of two integers, p/q, with $q \neq 0$. The decimal form of a rational number either terminates or forms a repeating pattern.
Irrational number	5	An irrational number cannot be written as a quotient of two integers; the decimal equivalent never forms a repeating pattern.
Real number system	3	The real number system consists of the rational numbers and the irrational numbers.

continues

Topic	Page	Key Idea
Hierarchy of operations	22	Operations within parentheses are done *before* multiplication and division; addition and subtraction are done last.
Properties of the real numbers	33	See Table 2.
Absolute value	35	Absolute value is defined by $$|a| = \begin{cases} a & \text{when} & a \geq 0 \\ -a & \text{when} & a < 0 \end{cases}$$
Distance from origin	35	Absolute value represents distance and is always nonnegative. The distance from the origin to a point whose coordinate is a on the real number line is $|a|$.
Distance between points	37	The distance between points A and B, whose coordinates on the real number line are a and b, respectively, is $$\overline{AB} = |b - a| = |a - b|$$

Common Errors

1. $2x - y \neq 2(x - y)$. *Don't* assume grouping where it isn't indicated.

2. $3(a - b) = 3a - 3b$. *Don't* write $3(a - b) = 3a - b$.

3. $(-2)(-3)(-4) = -24$, not $+24$. When the number of negative factors is odd, the product is negative.

4. To evaluate an expression such as
$$\frac{3x + 2y}{x + 3y} \quad \text{when } x = 2 \text{ and } y = 1$$
work independently on the numerator and denominator before dividing.
$$\frac{3(2) + 2(1)}{2 + 3(1)} = \frac{6 + 2}{2 + 3} = \frac{8}{5}$$

Don't write
$$\frac{3(\cancel{2}) + \cancel{2}(1)}{\cancel{2} + 3(1)} = \frac{3 + 1}{1 + 3} = \frac{4}{4} = 1$$

5. The absolute value bars act as grouping symbols. We must work *inside* these grouping symbols before we can remove them.

6. The number π is irrational; therefore, we cannot say $\pi = \frac{22}{7}$ or $\pi = 3.14$. These are approximations for computational use only. We write $\pi \approx 3.14$ where the symbol $\approx$ is read as "is approximately equal to."

Review Exercises

Solutions to exercises whose numbers are in bold are in the Solutions section in the back of the book.

1.1 In Exercises 1–3 write each set by listing its elements within braces.

1. The set of natural numbers between -5 and 4, inclusive.

2. The set of integers between -3 and -1, inclusive.

3. The subset of $x \in S$, $S = \{0.5, 1, 1.5, 2\}$, such that x is an even integer.

In Exercises 4–7 determine whether the statement is true (T) or false (F).

4. $\sqrt{7}$ is a real number.

5. -35 is a natural number.

6. -14 is not an integer.

7. 0 is an irrational number.

8. Draw a real number line and plot the following points.

  (a) 3 (b) -5 (c) $\dfrac{1}{2}$ (d) -1.5

In Exercises 9–11 determine which of the two numbers appears second when viewed from left to right on the real number line.

  9. $3, 2$ 10. $-4, -5$ 11. $0, -2$

1.2 In Exercises 12–17 perform the indicated operations.

12. $\dfrac{(2+3)4}{10} + 4 \cdot 3$ 13. $\dfrac{(3-5)(4-16)}{(3+1)(-2)} + \dfrac{1}{2}$

14. $\dfrac{2}{3} \cdot \dfrac{4}{5} \cdot \dfrac{6}{7}$ 15. $\dfrac{3}{4} \div \dfrac{5}{8}$

16. $\dfrac{1 + \dfrac{1}{2}}{\dfrac{3}{4} + \dfrac{1}{2}}$ 17. $\dfrac{\dfrac{2}{3} + \dfrac{1}{6}}{\dfrac{2}{9} - \dfrac{3}{2}}$

In Exercises 18 and 19 change the given percent to both fractional and decimal forms.

18. 7% 19. 2.25%

In Exercises 20 and 21 convert the given number to percent.

20. 4.52 21. 0.021

22. Suppose that your school tax bill reads: "$800 in taxes due Nov 1, reduced to $784 if paid by Oct 15." What is the percent of the discount?

1.3 In Exercises 23–26 determine whether the given statement is true (T) or false (F).

23. $2x + 4 = 10$ when $x = 3$

24. $3x - 2 = 6$ when $x = 3$

25. $3x - 4y = 6$ when $x = 1, y = 2$

26. $2x + 5y = 11$ when $x = -2, y = 3$

27. A salesperson receives $3.25x + 0.15y$ dollars, where x is the number of hours worked and y is the number of miles of automobile usage.

Find the amount due the salesperson if $x = 12$ hours and $y = 80$ miles.

1.4 In Exercises 28–33 simplify.

28. $3 + (-5)$ 29. $6 - 8$

30. $(-5) + (-3)$ 31. $(-3) - (-2)$

32. $(-2)\left(-\dfrac{1}{2}\right)$ 33. $\dfrac{-16}{-2}$

34. Evaluate $x - 3y$ when $x = 2, y = -3$.

35. A stereo shop had the following financial history during its first three years of operation. It lost x dollars during the first year and made a profit of y dollars during the second year. Its profit during the third year was $1000. Write an expression for the net profit or loss after three years.

1.5 In Exercises 36–39 identify the property (or properties) that justifies the given statement.

36. $(3 + 4)x = 3x + 4x$

37. $a + (b + c) = c + (a + b)$

38. $c(a + b) = bc + ac$

39. $3(ab) = b(3a)$

In Exercises 40–43 find and correct the mistake.

40. $2(a + 3) = 2a + 3$

41. $\dfrac{4 + a}{2} = 2 + a$

42. $-2(a - 3) = -2a - 6$

43. $2(ab) = (2b)(2a)$

1.6 In Exercises 44–45 find the value of the expression.

44. $\dfrac{|3| - |4|}{|2| + |-5|}$

45. $\dfrac{|2 - 2b| + |a - b|}{|ab|}$ when $a = -2, b = 3$

46. Provide a counterexample for the following statement:

  If a and b are real numbers such that $|a| = |b|$, then $a = b$.

In Exercises 47–48 the coordinates of points A and B are given. Find $\overline{AB}$.

47. $-3, 2$

48. $-4, -8$

In Exercises 49–50 state the inequality represented on the given number line.

49.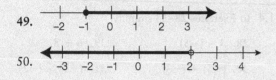

50.

In Exercises 51–52 graph the inequality on the real number line.

51. $x > -2$

52. $-2 \leqslant x < 5$

Progress Test 1A

1. The numbers $3, -\frac{2}{3}$, and 0.72 are all
   (a) natural numbers   (b) rational numbers
   (c) irrational numbers   (d) none of these

2. The numbers $-\frac{\pi}{2}, \sqrt{3}$, and $-\frac{4}{5}$ are all
   (a) irrational numbers   (b) rational numbers
   (c) real numbers   (d) none of these

3. On a real number line, indicate the integers that are greater than -3 and less than 4.

4. Evaluate $\dfrac{3a - 4b}{2a - b}$ when $a = 3, b = 2$.

5. Evaluate $\dfrac{2x - 6y}{x - y}$ when $x = -1, y = 1$.

6. Evaluate $\dfrac{3[(a + 2b) - (2b - a)]}{c}$ when $a = -2$, $b = -1, c = -6$.

7. Simplify $5(x - y) - 3(2x - y)$.

8. Simplify $2\left(\dfrac{a + b}{4}\right) + \left(\dfrac{b - a}{2}\right)$.

9. Evaluate $\dfrac{|2 - 8|}{|2| + |-8|}$.

10. Evaluate $3|x| - 2|2y|$ when $x = -2, y = -3$.

11. Evaluate $\left|\dfrac{-2|3x| + 3|-y|}{|x + y|}\right|$ when $x = -2$, $y = 1$.

12. Evaluate $|x| \cdot |y| - 2|x \cdot y|$ when $x = -1$, $y = 2$.

13. Graph the inequality $-1 \leqslant x < 3$.

14. Graph the inequality $-4 \leqslant x \leqslant 1$, x an integer.

15. Give the inequality represented on the following number line.

Progress Test 1B

1. The numbers $-2, 0.45$, and $\frac{7}{9}$ are all
   (a) integers   (b) irrational numbers
   (c) rational numbers   (d) none of these

2. The numbers $-\sqrt{7}, 2\pi$, and -0.49 are all
   (a) natural numbers   (b) irrational numbers
   (c) real numbers   (d) none of these

3. On a real number line, indicate the integers that are greater than -5 and less than -1.

4. Evaluate $\dfrac{2m - 5n}{3m - n}$ when $m = 2, n = 4$.

5. Evaluate $\dfrac{x + 2y}{2x - y}$ when $x = 3, y = -5$.

6. Evaluate $\dfrac{-2[(p - 2q) - 2r - p]}{p \cdot q}$ when $p = 2$, $q = -3$, $r = \frac{1}{2}$.

7. Simplify $7(x + 2y) - 2(3x - y)$.

8. Simplify $3\left(\dfrac{a - 2b}{6}\right) - \left(\dfrac{b - 2a}{2}\right)$.

9. Evaluate $\dfrac{|-3| - |4 - 7|}{|-4| + |-2|}$.

10. Evaluate $\dfrac{|x|}{2} - 3|3y|$ when $x = -4, y = -5$.

11. Evaluate $\dfrac{3\,|\,2y\,|\,-\,3\,|\,x\,|}{-\,|\,x-2y\,|}$ when $x = -2,\ y = 1$.

12. Evaluate $\left|\,\dfrac{x}{3}\cdot\dfrac{y}{2}\,\right| - 3\,|\,2x \cdot y\,|$ when $x = -6$, $y = 4$.

13. Graph the inequality $-2 < x \le 5$.

14. Graph the inequality $-5 \le x \le -1$, x an integer.

15. Give the inequality represented on the following number line.

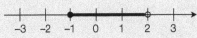

Chapter 1 Project

To study the nature and impact of hurricanes, from a scientific as well as a human standpoint, it is necessary to use and understand real numbers. In the chapter opener, you read about the Saffir-Simpson Hurricane Scale. What subset of the real numbers does this scale use?

Look at Exercise 42 in Section 1.1, and Exercises 81 and 82 in Section 1.2. Now do some additional research on hurricanes. Use percents, inequalities, and number lines to make a report on the data you discover. For example, what percentage of deaths due to weather were caused by hurricanes in your area last year? What range of wind speeds are associated with a category 3 hurricane?

■ ■ ■

11. Evaluate $\dfrac{3|2x| - 2|3y|}{2x + 3y}$ when $x = -2, y = 1$.

12. Evaluate $\left| \dfrac{x}{3} \right| - \left| \dfrac{y}{2} \right|$; $2x$; π; when $y = 6$.

13. Graph the inequality $-2 < x < 5$.

14. Graph the inequality $-5 \le x < 1$, x an integer.

15. Give the inequality represented on the following number line.

$\longleftarrow \;\;|\!\!-\!\!-\!\!-\!\!|\!\!-\!\!-\!\!-\!\!|\!\!-\!\!-\!\!-\!\!|\!\!-\!\!-\!\!-\!\!|\!\!-\!\!-\!\!-\!\!|\!\!-\!\!-\!\!-\!\!|\!\!-\!\!-\!\!-\!\!|\longrightarrow$
$\;\; -3 \; -2 \; -1 \;\; 0 \;\; 1 \;\; 2 \;\; 3 \;\; 4$

Chapter 1 Project

To understand the nature and impact of hurricanes, from a scientific as well as a human standpoint, it is necessary to use and understand a lot of numbers. In the chapter opener, you read about the Saffir–Simpson Hurricane Scale. What subset of the real numbers does the scale use?

Look at Exercise 42 in Section 1.1, and Exercises 81 and 82 in Section 1.2. Now do some additional research on hurricanes. Use percents, inequalities, and number lines to make a report on the data you discover. For example, what percentage of deaths due to weather were caused by hurricanes in your area last year. What range of wind speeds are associated with a category 3 hurricane?

2 Linear Equations and Inequalities

> **"**Neglect of mathematics works injury to all knowledge since he who is ignorant of it cannot know the other sciences or the things of this world.**"**
>
> —Roger Bacon

Nutritionists and dietitians use algebra to determine an appropriate balance of amounts and types of food in a healthy diet. To any mathematician, the word "balance" immediately suggests equations! Metaphorically, the operations we perform to solve an equation are a "balancing act." For example, we must never add more to one side of an equation than we do to the other.

How does a dietitian determine the correct number of calories for a person who wants to maintain a certain weight? Actually, this determination should be made on an individual basis and must include details about the individual other than just the desired weight. However, in this chapter's project we will look at a simplified version of answering this question using a linear equation.

http://www.bls.gov

(By the way, the U.S. Department of Labor's Bureau of Labor Statistics suggests that courses in mathematics are a healthy part of a balanced dietitian's background. See how many careers require algebra at www.bls.gov.)

■ ■ ■

Finding solutions to equations has long been a major concern of algebra. Recent work in inequalities, much of it since World War II, has elevated the importance of solving inequalities as well. Oil refining and steel producing are among the major industries using computers daily to solve problems involving thousands of inequalities. The solutions enable these companies to optimize their "product mix" and their profitability.

In this chapter we learn to solve the most basic forms of equations and inequalities. Even this rudimentary capability proves adequate to allow us to tackle a wide range of applications in both this and the following chapter.

2.1 Linear Equations in One Variable

Here are some examples of equations in the variable x.

$$x - 2 = 0 \qquad\qquad x(x - 3) = 10$$
$$3(2x - 5) = 3 \qquad\qquad 2x + 5 = x - 7$$
$$\frac{1}{2x + 3} = 5 \qquad\qquad \frac{x + 2}{x - 3} = -1$$

An **equation** states that two algebraic expressions are equal. The expression to the left of the equal sign is called the **left-hand side** of the equation, and the expression to the right of the equal sign is called the **right-hand side.**

Our task is to find values of the variable for which the equation holds true. These values are called **solutions** or **roots** of the equation, and the set of all solutions is called the **solution set.** For example, the equation

$$x - 5 = 3$$

is a true statement only when $x = 8$. Then 8 is a solution of the equation, and $S = \{8\}$ is the solution set.

Solving an Equation

When we say that we want to "solve an equation," we mean that we want to find all the solutions, or roots. If we can replace an equation by another, simpler, equation that has the same roots, we will have an approach to solving equations. Equations having the same roots are called **equivalent equations.** There are two important rules that allow us to replace an equation by an equivalent equation.

Simplifying Equations

> The solutions of a given equation are not affected by the following operations:
>
> • Addition or subtraction of a number or expression on both sides of the equation
>
> • Multiplication or division of both sides of the equation by a number other than 0

Let's solve the equation

$$2x + 5 = 13$$

By the rules for the order of equations, we see that x has first been multiplied by 2 and then 5 has been added to the result. To return to the original value of x, we need to subtract 5 and then divide by 2. Since these operations are permitted by the rules for simplifying equations, we begin by *subtracting +5 from both sides of the equation.*

$$2x + 5 - 5 = 13 - 5$$
$$2x + 0 = 8$$
$$2x = 8$$

Now, *dividing both sides of the last equation by 2* yields

$$\frac{2x}{2} = \frac{8}{2}$$
$$x = 4$$

We have arrived at the solution $x = 4$. It is a good idea to check that 4 does indeed satisfy the original equation.

$$2x + 5 = 13$$
$$2(4) + 5 \stackrel{?}{=} 13$$
$$13 \stackrel{\checkmark}{=} 13$$

Then 4 is a root, or solution, of the equation $2x + 5 = 13$.

In simplifying equations, we often reach a point at which the equation looks like this:

$$5x + 4x = -18$$

Here, simplification of the left-hand side relies on the distributive property of the real numbers:

$$5x + 4x = (5 + 4)x$$
$$= 9x$$

We say that $5x$ and $4x$ are **like terms** and we see that the distributive property allows us to combine like terms. You may think of this as "adding apples and apples." For example, the expression

$$3x + 2y - x + 6y$$

becomes

$$3x - x + 2y + 6y \qquad \text{Commutative property}$$
$$= 2x + 8y \qquad \text{Distributive property}$$

Why can't we simplify further? Because we cannot add "apples and oranges"!

EXAMPLE 1   SOLVING AN EQUATION

Solve the equation $3x - 1 = x + 9$.

SOLUTION

We gather the terms involving x on one side of the equation and the constant terms on the other. Here are the steps.

$$3x - 1 = x + 9$$
$$3x - 1 + 1 = x + 9 + 1 \qquad \text{Add 1 to both sides.}$$
$$3x = x + 10 \qquad \text{Simplify.}$$
$$3x - x = x + 10 - x \qquad \text{Subtract } x \text{ from both sides.}$$
$$2x = 10 \qquad \text{Combine like terms.}$$

Now it is easy to solve for x.

$$\frac{2x}{2} = \frac{10}{2} \qquad \text{Divide both sides by 2.}$$
$$x = 5$$

Check:

$$3(5) - 1 \overset{?}{=} 5 + 9$$
$$15 - 1 \overset{?}{=} 5 + 9$$
$$14 \overset{\checkmark}{=} 14$$

✔ **Progress Check 1**

Solve and check.

(a) $4x + 7 = 3$ (b) $x - 6 = 5x - 26$

Answers

(a) -1 (b) 5

When the equation we seek to solve involves fractions, we can eliminate the fractions to ease the solution process.

EXAMPLE 2   SOLVING AN EQUATION WITH FRACTIONS

Solve $\dfrac{5}{6}x - \dfrac{4}{3} = \dfrac{3}{5}$.

SOLUTION

The LCD of all fractions appearing in the equation is 30. We multiply both sides of the equation by the LCD to clear the equation of fractions.

$$30\left(\frac{5}{6}x - \frac{4}{3}\right) = 30\left(\frac{3}{5}\right)$$

$$30\left(\frac{5}{6}x\right) + 30\left(-\frac{4}{3}\right) = 30\left(\frac{3}{5}\right) \qquad \text{Distributive property}$$

$$25x - 40 = 18$$

$$25x = 58 \qquad \text{Add 40 to both sides.}$$

$$x = \frac{58}{25} \qquad \text{Divide both sides by 25.}$$

Verify that $\dfrac{58}{25}$ is a solution of the original equation!

✔ Progress Check 2

Solve and check.

(a) $-\dfrac{2}{3}(x - 5) = \dfrac{3}{2}(x + 1)$ (b) $\dfrac{1}{3}x + 2 - 3\left(\dfrac{x}{2} + 4\right) = \left(\dfrac{x}{4} - 1\right)$

Answers

(a) $\dfrac{11}{13}$ (b) $-\dfrac{108}{17}$

Solving a Linear Equation

The equations we have solved are all of the first degree and involve only one unknown. Such equations are called **first-degree equations in one unknown** or, more simply, **linear equations**. By rearranging and collecting like terms, any such equation can be put into the general form

$$ax + b = 0$$

where a and b are any real numbers and $a \neq 0$. Let's see how we would solve this equation.

$$ax + b = 0$$

$$ax + b - b = 0 - b \qquad \text{Subtract } b \text{ from both sides.}$$

$$ax = -b$$

$$\frac{ax}{a} = \frac{-b}{a} \qquad \text{Divide both sides by } a.$$

$$x = -\frac{b}{a}$$

Substituting in Equation (1) shows that $-\frac{b}{a}$ is indeed a solution and leads to the following:

Roots of a Linear Equation

> The linear equation $ax + b = 0$, $a \neq 0$, has exactly one solution: $-\frac{b}{a}$.

Identities and Conditional Equations

Does every equation have a solution? Can an equation have multiple solutions? No solutions? We explore these questions in depth throughout this text as we develop more sophisticated tools for tackling these problems.

We can, however, begin our exploration with some simple observations. Some equations, such as

$$3x = 2x + x$$

are true for all values of x and are called **identities**. (It's not always possible to establish that an equation is an identity by just looking at it.) Those equations that are true for only certain values of the unknown (namely, the solutions) are called **conditional equations**. Every linear equation

$$ax + b = 0, a \neq 0$$

is a conditional equation since it has precisely one solution.

Finally, we point out that some equations have no solutions. For example, consider the equation

$$3x = 3x + 1$$

Adding $-3x$ to both sides we have

$$3x - 3x = 3x + 1 - 3x$$
$$0 = 1$$

Since this last equation is a contradiction, we conclude that the given equation has no solution. (Write the given equation in the form $ax + b = 0$ and carefully note the value of a.)

EXAMPLE 3   IDENTITIES AND CONDITIONAL EQUATIONS

Determine whether each of the following is a conditional equation, an identity, or has no solution.

(a) $4(x - 1) = 3x - 1$

(b) $5(x + 2) + x = 6x + 10$

(c) $4(x - 3) = 4x - 3$

SOLUTIONS

We'll let the student supply a reason for each step.

(a)

$$4(x - 1) = 3x - 1$$
$$4x - 4 = 3x - 1$$
$$4x - 4 + 4 = 3x - 1 + 4$$
$$4x = 3x + 3$$
$$4x - 3x = 3x + 3 - 3x$$
$$x = 3$$

Since the original equation is true only for $x = 3$, it is a conditional equation.

(b)

$$5(x + 2) + x = 6x + 10$$
$$5x + 10 + x = 6x + 10$$
$$6x + 10 = 6x + 10$$

Since the left- and right-hand sides of the last equation are identical, substituting any real value for x will make the equation true. We conclude: the equation is an identity.

(c)

$$4(x - 3) = 4x - 3$$
$$4x - 12 = 4x - 3$$
$$4x - 12 - 4x = 4x - 3 - 4x$$
$$-12 = -3$$

Since this is a contradiction, the original equation has no solution.

✔ **Progress Check 3**

Determine whether each of the following is a conditional equation (C), an identity (I), or has no solution (N).

(a) $-2(x - 5) + 2 = -2(x - 6)$ (b) $3(2x + 1) = -4(x + 1) + 10x$

(c) $-5(x - 2) = 2x + 17$

Answers

(a) I   (b) N   (c) C

Exercise Set 2.1

In Exercises 1–8 determine whether the given statement is true (T) or false (F).

1. $x = 2$ is a solution to $3x = 6$.

2. $x = -2$ is a solution to $4x = -6$.

3. $x = 3$ is a solution to $3x - 1 = 10$.

4. $x = -5$ is a solution to $2x + 3 = -7$.

5. $x = \dfrac{3}{2}$ is a solution to $2x + 1 = 4$.

6. $x = \dfrac{5}{2}$ is a solution to $3x - 4 = \dfrac{5}{2}$.

7. $x = 6/(4 - k)$ is a solution to $kx + 6 = 4x$.

8. $x = \dfrac{7}{3}k$ is a solution to $2kx + 7 = 5x$.

In Exercises 9–42 solve the given linear equation and check your answer.

9. $2x = 8$

10. $3x = -6$

11. $2x = -\dfrac{5}{2}$

12. $2x + 3 = 7$

13. $3x + 5 = -1$

14. $5r + 10 = 0$

15. $3s - 1 = 2$

16. $4 - x = 2$

17. $2 - 3a = 6$

18. $2 = 3x + 4$

19. $3 = 2x - 1$

20. $\dfrac{1}{2}s + 2 = 4$

21. $\dfrac{3}{2}t - 2 = 7$

22. $-\dfrac{2}{3}x + 3 = 2$

23. $-1 = -\dfrac{2}{3}x + 1$

24. $0 = -\dfrac{1}{2}a - \dfrac{2}{3}$

25. $2x + 2 = x + 6$

26. $4r + 3 = 3r - 2$

27. $-5x + 8 = 3x - 4$

28. $2x - 1 = 3x + 2$

29. $-2x + 6 = -5x - 4$

30. $6x + 4 = -3x - 5$

31. $2(3b + 1) = 3b - 4$

32. $-3(2x + 1) = -8x + 1$

33. $4(2x - 1) = 5x + 5$

34. $-3(3x - 1) = -4x - 2$

35. $4(x - 1) = 2(x + 3)$

36. $-3(x - 2) = 2(x + 4)$

37. $2(x + 4) - 1 = 0$

38. $3a + 2 - 2(a - 1) = 3(2a + 3)$

39. $-2(x - 1) + 3(x - 1) = 4(x + 5)$

40. $2(y - 1) + 3(y + 2) = 8$

41. $-4(2x + 1) - (x - 2) = -11$

42. $3(a + 2) - 2(a - 3) = 0$

In Exercises 43–46 solve for x.

43. $kx + 8 = 5x$

44. $8 - 2kx = -3x$

45. $2 - k + 5(x - 1) = 3$

46. $3(2 + 3k) + 4(x - 2) = 5$

In Exercises 47–52 determine whether the equation is an identity (I), a conditional equation (C), or has no solution (N).

47. $3x + 5 = 2(x - 4)$

48. $3x - 4 = 4(x - 3) - x$

49. $-5(x + 2) = -2(x + 5) - 3x$

50. $\dfrac{2}{3}x + 1 = x - \dfrac{x - 1}{3} + \dfrac{2}{3}$

51. $\dfrac{1}{2}x - 1 = \dfrac{3}{4}x - 2$

52. $\dfrac{x + 1}{2} = \dfrac{x - 1}{2}$

*53. If $x = 2$ is a solution to the equation $2a + 3x = 14$, find a.

*54. If $x = -3$ is a solution to the equation $5a - 2x = 3a - 10$, find a.

*55. If $y = 4$ is a solution to the equation $40 - 4y = 2b - 6y + 8$, find b.

*56. If $z = -\frac{1}{2}$ is a solution to the equation $-4b + 2z = -4$, find b.

*57. After many hours of work, an analyst for the Safety Lock Company finds that the equation

$$0.5(2x - 5) = -x + 18$$

can be used to determine (in thousands of units) the manufacturing capacity x of a plant. Find the manufacturing capacity.

*58. A business consultant tells the board of directors of the Super Computer Corporation that the profit or loss (in thousands of dollars) for the current year can be found by solving the equation

$$2x - 23 = 2(5 - 0.5x)$$

(a) Solve the equation for x.

(b) Will the board of directors announce a profit or a loss for the year?

59. You can use a graphing calculator to determine whether an equation is an identity. When a mathematical statement like an equation is entered, using symbols like "=," "<," or ">," the calculator will return a "1" if the statement is true, and "0" if it is false. (Look under TEST for the equality and inequality symbols, or check your manual.) An identity must be true for any value of the variable, so you should store one value, test the equation, then try again with a different value.

    Use this method to verify your answers to Exercises 47–52.

60. A simple rule of thumb for determining a healthy body weight W for a man of a given height h in inches is given by the equation

$$W = 6(h - 60) + 106$$

    According to this formula, how tall should a man who weighs 148 pounds be? (Note that in the real world other factors like body type and muscle mass affect healthy weights.)

61. Another rule of thumb relates desired weight to number of calories consumed each day. For a person with a moderately active lifestyle, this formula suggests that the daily intake of calories should be fifteen times the desired weight in pounds. To lose one pound in one week, a person who weighs 170 pounds would need to consume x calories each day, according to the equation

$$7(170(15) - x) = 3500$$

    Solve for x. (The 3500 on the right-hand side of this equation suggests that cutting 3500 calories out of one's diet results in a loss of one pound. Do some research to determine how accurate this simplified model is.)

    Now explain in your own words what each number and symbol in this equation refers to, and why the equation "works."

2.2 Problem Solving: From Words to Algebra

The larger of two numbers is 1 more than the smaller. Five times the larger exceeds four times the smaller by 12. Find the numbers.

How do you go about solving a word problem? The words are your clues, but you must translate these clues into algebraic expressions and then form an equation or inequality that you can solve. In this section, we're going to show you how to attack a word problem and how to recognize the "code words" that appear time and again in applications.

These are the typical steps used in solving word problems.

Step 1. Read the problem until you understand what is required.

Step 2. Isolate what is known and what is to be found.

Step 3. In many problems, the unknown quantity is the answer to a question such as "how much" or "how many." Let an algebraic symbol, say, x, represent the unknown.

Step 4. Represent other quantities in the problem in terms of x.

Step 5. Find the relationship in the problem that lets you write an equation (or an inequality).

Step 6. Solve. Check your answer to see that it

    (a) satisfies the original question, and

    (b) satisfies the equation (or inequality).

Words and Phrases

Some students have trouble with word problems because they are unfamiliar with the mathematical interpretation of certain words and phrases. Practice, of course, will help; we also suggest that you read the problem very carefully. Table 1 may be helpful; it has a list of words and phrases you will come across, with examples of how they are used.

Let's apply our steps to the problem that we stated at the outset of this section.

EXAMPLE 1   SOLVING A WORD PROBLEM

The larger of two numbers is 1 more than the smaller. Five times the larger exceeds four times the smaller by 12. Find the numbers.

SOLUTION

After reading the problem, it is clear that the unknown may represent either the larger or smaller number. If we let

$$n = \text{the smaller number} \qquad \text{Step 3}$$

then

$$n + 1 = \text{the larger number} \qquad \text{Step 4}$$

TABLE 1   Translating Words and Phrases to Algebra

Word or phrase	Algebraic Symbol	Example	Algebraic Expression
Sum	+	Sum of two numbers	$a + b$
Difference	−	Difference of two numbers	$a - b$
		Difference of a number and 3	$x - 3$
Product	× or ·	Product of two numbers	$a \cdot b$
Quotient	÷ or /	Quotient of two numbers	$\frac{a}{b}$ or a/b
Exceeds		a exceeds b by 3.	$a = b + 3$
More than		a is 3 more than b.	or
More of		There are 3 more of a than of b.	$a - 3 = b$
Twice		Twice a number	$2x$
		Twice the difference of x and 3	$2(x - 3)$
		3 more than twice a number	$2x + 3$
		3 less than twice a number	$2x - 3$
Is or equals	=	The sum of a number and 3 is 15.	$x + 3 = 15$
Percent of	%	30% of a number	$0.3x$

The relationship between these numbers specified in the problem is

$$5 \times \text{larger} = (4 \times \text{smaller}) + 12$$ Step 5

or, in terms of our unknowns,

$$5(n + 1) = 4n + 12$$ Step 5a

Solving,

$$5n + 5 = 4n + 12$$ Step 6

$$n = 7 = \text{the smaller number}$$

$$n + 1 = 8 = \text{the larger number}$$

You can verify that the solution (a) answers the original question and (b) satisfies the equation of Step 5a.

> ✔ **Progress Check 1**
> Write the number 30 as the sum of two numbers such that twice the larger is 3 less than 7 times the smaller.
>
> **Answer**
> 7 + 23

EXAMPLE 2   A WORD PROBLEM IN GEOMETRY

The length of a rectangle is 2 feet more than twice its width. If the perimeter is 22 feet, find the dimensions of the rectangle.

SOLUTION

Drawing a figure is a necessity when dealing with geometric applications. In Figure 1, we let

$$w = \text{the width of the rectangle}$$

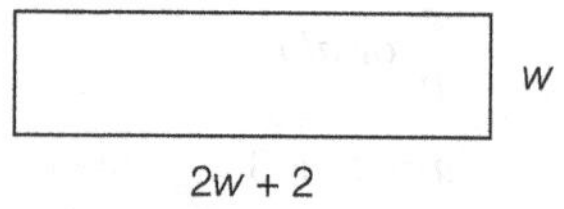

since the length is expressed in terms of the width. The problem states that

$$\text{length} = 2(\text{width}) + 2$$

$$= 2w + 2$$

From Figure 1, we see that

$$\text{perimeter} = 2(\text{length} + \text{width})$$

2w + 2

Figure 1   Diagram for Example 2

or, in terms of our problem,

$$22 = 2[(2w + 2) + w]$$
$$22 = 2(3w + 2)$$
$$22 = 6w + 4$$
$$18 = 6w$$
$$w = 3$$

We conclude: The width w is 3 feet and the length is $2w + 2$ or 8 feet. The rectangle has dimensions 3 feet by 8 feet.

> ### ✔ Progress Check 2
> One side of a triangle is 3 cm longer than the shortest side; the third side is 1 cm more than twice the shortest side. If the perimeter of the triangle is 20 cm, find the dimensions of the three sides.
>
> ### Answer
> 4, 7, and 9 cm

EXAMPLE 3   A WORD PROBLEM IN BUSINESS

A department store advertises that all appliances are on sale at a 20% discount. If the sale price of a microwave oven is $160, what was its original price?

SOLUTION

It's clear that

> sale price = original price − discount

where *discount* is the reduction in dollars and not in percent. If we let

$$p = \text{original price}$$

then the discount is 20% of the original price or

$$\text{discount} = 0.2p$$

Substituting in the equation above,

$$160 = p - 0.2p$$
$$160 = 0.8p$$
$$200 = p$$

The oven was originally priced at $200.

> ✔ **Progress Check 3**
> If you pay \$63 for a car radio after receiving a 30% discount, what was the price of the radio before the discount?
>
> **Answer**
> \$90

EXAMPLE 4   A WORD PROBLEM IN INTEGERS
Find three consecutive integers whose sum is 54.

SOLUTION
Let's have the unknown represent the first of the three consecutive integers. Then

$$n = \text{the first integer}$$
$$n + 1 = \text{the second integer}$$

and

$$n + 2 = \text{the third integer}$$

However, the sum of these three integers is to be 54, that is,

> first integer + second integer + third integer = 54

or, in terms of the unknown n,

$$n + (n + 1) + (n + 2) = 54$$
$$3n + 3 = 54$$
$$3n = 51$$
$$n = 17$$

Then 17, 18, and 19 are the three consecutive integers we seek.

> ✔ **Progress Check 4**
> Find three consecutive integers whose sum is 78.
>
> **Answer**
> 25, 26, 27

WARNING

Don't be fooled into thinking that every problem has a solution. For example, try to find three consecutive integers whose sum is 23. You will have a very frustrating experience—there simply are no such numbers.

EXAMPLE 5   A WORD PROBLEM USING AVERAGE

John has taken two quizzes in algebra and has received scores of 90 and 96. What score must he receive on his third quiz to achieve an average of 92?

SOLUTION

We let the unknown represent the third quiz score:

$$x = \text{score on the third quiz}$$

Since

$$\text{average} = \frac{\text{sum of scores}}{\text{number of scores}}$$

we must have

$$92 = \frac{90 + 96 + x}{3}$$

We then multiply both sides of the equation by 3, the denominator of the fraction. This will clear the equation of fractions.

$$(92)(3) = 90 + 96 + x$$
$$276 = 186 + x$$
$$90 = x$$

John must achieve a grade of 90 on his third quiz.

✔ Progress Check 5

A golf pro has an average of 71 in the last four tournaments. If the scores were 68, 70, and 72 in three of the events, what was the score in the fourth tournament?

Answer

74

EXAMPLE 6   A WORD PROBLEM IN GEOMETRY

A right triangle whose area is 12 square feet has a base that measures 3 feet. What is the altitude?

SOLUTION

It is a good idea to draw a figure for problems of this type (see Figure 2). We have labeled the figure to indicate that the base measures 3 feet and the altitude is our unknown h. Since

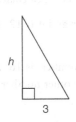

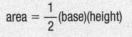
$$\text{area} = \frac{1}{2}(\text{base})(\text{height})$$

Figure 2 **Diagram for Example 6**

$$12 = \frac{1}{2}(3)(h)$$

$$12(2) = 3h$$

$$\frac{24}{3} = h$$

$$8 = h$$

We have found that the altitude is 8 feet.

✔ Progress Check 6

A carpenter is instructed to build a rectangular room with a perimeter of 18 meters. If one side of the room measures 5 meters, what are the dimensions of the room?

Answer

4 meters by 5 meters

Exercise Set 2.2

1. A vacation club charters an airplane to carry its 200 members to Rome. If the airline charges the club $50,000 for the round trip, how much will each member pay for the trip?

2. Suppose that a camp director needs to provide each camper with a small portable radio that sells for $4. The director has been given $900 for the purchase of the radios. How many campers will receive a radio?

3. How many $7 transistor radios can a dealer buy with $350?

4. Suppose that 12.5 gallons of special fuel are required to fill the tank of a tractor. If it costs $7.50 to fill the tank, what is the price per gallon?

5. If a dozen rolls cost $1.02, what is the price per roll?

6. A school district tries to give each of 110 typewriters a routine maintenance check, which costs $12 per typewriter once a year. This year the school has $960 on hand for the typewriter maintenance program. Will all typewriters be checked? If not, how many will not be checked?

7. 78 is 30% of what number?

8. 24 is 60% of what number?

9. 96 is 120% of what number?

10. 2 is $\frac{1}{2}$% of what number?

11. A car dealer advertises a $5400 sedan at a "30% discount" for $4000. Is the dealer telling the truth?

12. The local discount store sells a camera for $180, which is a 25% discount from the suggested retail price. What is the suggested retail price?

13. A stationery store sells a dozen ballpoint pens for $3.84, which represents a 20% discount from the price charged when a dozen pens are bought individually. How much does it cost to buy three pens?

14. A copying service advertises as follows: "   cents per copy for 4 or fewer copies per page; 12 cents per copy, a 20% reduction, for 5 or more copies per page." Since the typesetter forgot to set the original prediscount price per copy, calculate it.

15. The sum of a certain number and 4 is 12. Find the number.

16. The difference between two numbers is 16. If one of the numbers is 16, find the other number or numbers.

17. The difference between two numbers is 24. If one of the numbers is 14, find the other number or numbers.

18. Find a number that when subtracted from 4 times itself yields 36.

19. Find a number that when added to 3 times itself gives 24.

20. Find three consecutive integers whose sum is 21.

21. A certain number is 3 more than another number. If their sum is 21, find the numbers.

22. A certain number is 5 less than another number. If their sum is 11, find the numbers.

23. A certain number is 2 more than 3 times another number. If their sum is 14, find the numbers.

24. A certain number is 5 less than twice another number. If their sum is 19, find the numbers.

25. A young man is 3 years older than his brother. Thirty years from now the sum of their ages will be 111. Find the current ages of the brothers.

26. An elderly man is 22 years older than his daughter. Fifty years ago, the sum of their ages was 34. Find the current age of the man.

27. Joan is 3 times as old as Anne. Fifteen years from now Joan will be twice as old as Anne will be then. How old is each now?

28. The sum of the ages of a woman and her son is 36 years. Six years from now the woman will be twice as old as her son. How old is each now?

29. John is presently 12 years older than Joseph. Four years ago John was twice as old as Joseph. How old is each now?

30. At the present time Albert is 20 years old and Steven is 16 years old. How many years ago was Albert $1\frac{1}{2}$ times as old as Steven?

31. At the present time Lisa is 24 years old and Erica is 16 years old. How many years ago was Lisa twice as old as Erica?

32. A certain number is 3 more than twice another. If their sum is increased by 8, the result is 41. Find the numbers.

33. The larger of two numbers is 3 more than twice the smaller. If the sum is 18, find the numbers.

34. Separate 36 into two parts so that 4 times the smaller minus 3 times the larger is 11.

35. A resort guarantees that the average temperature over the period Friday, Saturday, and Sunday will be exactly 80°F, or else each guest pays only half price for the facilities. If the temperatures on Friday and Saturday were 90°F and 82°F respectively, what must the temperature be on Sunday so that the resort does not lose half of its revenue?

36. A patient's temperature was taken at 6 A.M., 12 noon, 3 P.M., and 8 P.M. The first, third, and fourth readings were 102.5°, 101.5°, and 102°F, respectively. The nurse forgot to write down the second reading but remembered that the average of the four readings was 101.5°F. What was the second temperature reading?

37. Suppose that an investor buys 100 shares of stock on each of four successive days at $10 per share on the first day, $10.50 per share on the second day, and $12 per share on the fourth day. If the average price of the stock is $11.20 per share, what was the price per share on the third day?

38. In an election for president of a local volunteer organization, there were 84 votes cast. If candidate A received 24 votes more than candidate B, how many votes did each candidate receive?

39. A 12-meter-long steel beam is to be cut into two pieces so that one piece will be 4 meters longer than the other. How long will each piece be?

40. A rectangular grazing field whose length is 10 meters longer than its width is to be enclosed with 100 meters of fencing material. What are the dimensions of the field?

41. The perimeter of a rectangle is 36 meters. If the width is 3 times the length, find the dimensions.

42. The length of a rectangle is 4 meters more than 3 times its width. If the perimeter is 24 meters, find the dimensions.

43. A triangle whose area is 36 square centimeters has an altitude that measures 8 centimeters. What is the length of the base?

44. The perimeter of an isosceles triangle is 32 centimeters. The two equal sides are each 2 centimeters shorter than the base. Find the dimensions of the triangle.

45. In an isosceles triangle, the two equal angles are each 15° more than the third angle. Find the measure of each angle. (Recall that the sum of the angles of a triangle is 180°.)

46. An investor invested $4000 at 5% per year. How much additional money should be invested at 8% per year so that the total invested will pay 6% per year?

47. The length of a rectangle is 5 feet more than twice its width. If the perimeter is 40 feet, find the dimensions of the rectangle.

48. The length of a rectangle is 3 cm less than four times its width. If the perimeter is 34 cm, find the dimensions of the rectangle.

49. A farmer plans to enclose a rectangular field, whose length is 16 meters more than its width,

with 140 meters of chain-link fencing. What are the dimensions of the field?

50. Suppose that one angle of a triangle is 20° larger than the smallest angle, while the third angle is 10° larger than the smallest angle. Find the number of degrees in each angle.

51. One side of a triangle is 1 meter more than twice the shortest side, while the third side is 3 meters more than the shortest side. If the perimeter is 24 meters, what is the length of each side?

2.3 Formulas

We can think of a **formula** (sometimes called a **literal equation**) as a rule that expresses a relationship between two or more variables. For example, the familiar formula from geometry

$$A = \frac{1}{2}bh$$

allows us to calculate the area A of a right triangle if we know the length of both the base b and the altitude h. In the next example we'll use a formula to convert between different temperature scales.

EXAMPLE 1   USING A FORMULA FOR TEMPERATURE CONVERSION

The formula

$$C = \frac{5}{9}(F - 32)$$

tells us how to obtain the temperature C in Celsius if we know the temperature F in Fahrenheit. If the thermostat in a room reads 68° Fahrenheit, what is the equivalent Celsius temperature?

SOLUTION

Substituting $F = 68$ in the formula, we have

$$C = \frac{5}{9}(F - 32) = \frac{5}{9}(68 - 32) = \frac{5}{9}(36) = 20$$

and we see that the corresponding Celsius temperature is 20°.

✔ **Progress Check 1**

The formula for simple interest I is $I = Prt$, where P is the amount invested, r is the rate of interest, and t is the time (in years). Find the interest earned if $1500 is invested at 8% for 3 years.

Answer

$360

The formula of Example 1 is adequate for converting from the Fahrenheit scale to the Celsius scale. But what if we know the Celsius temperature C and want to find the corresponding Fahrenheit temperature F? It would appear worthwhile to *turn the formula around*, that is, to solve for F in terms of C. We can do this by using the familiar steps of algebraic manipulation. Thus,

$$C = \frac{5}{9}(F - 32)$$

$$\frac{9}{5}C = F - 32 \qquad \text{Multiply by } \frac{9}{5}$$

$$\frac{9}{5}C + 32 = F \qquad \text{Add } +32$$

Now, given a value of C we can determine the value of F, that is, we can convert from temperature on the Celsius scale to temperature on the Fahrenheit scale.

EXAMPLE 2   SOLVING A FORMULA IN FINANCE

If an amount P is invested at the simple annual interest rate r, then the amount A available at the end of t years is

$$A = P + Prt$$

Solve for P.

SOLUTION

$$A = P + Prt$$

$$A = P(1 + rt) \qquad \text{Distributive property}$$

$$\frac{A}{1 + rt} = \frac{P(1 + rt)}{1 + rt} \qquad \text{Divide both sides by } 1 + rt.$$

$$\frac{A}{1 + rt} = P$$

✔ Progress Check 2

Solve for t.

$$d = v + 0.5at$$

Answer

$$t = \frac{2d - 2v}{a}$$

The steps in solving a formula for another variable are the same as those you would use in obtaining a numerical solution. We always seek to consolidate the variable we are solving for on one side of the equals sign and then isolate this variable.

EXAMPLE 3   SOLVING A FORMULA WITH FRACTIONS

Solve for a:

$$c = \frac{1}{a} + \frac{1}{b}$$

SOLUTION

We first multiply by the LCD, ab, obtaining

$$cab = b + a$$

Putting all the terms that contain the unknown a on one side, we have

$$cab - a = b$$

Applying the distributive property to the left-hand side,

$$(cb - 1)a = b$$

then

$$a = \frac{b}{cb - 1}$$

✔ **Progress Check 3**

Solve for a:

$$\frac{1}{a} + \frac{1}{y} = \frac{1}{c}$$

Answer

$$a = \frac{cy}{y - c}$$

Sometimes we need to know a specific formula in order to solve a problem. Chapter 3 presents a range of problems of this type; an example follows.

EXAMPLE 4   APPLYING A FORMULA IN FINANCE

A student wins $500 in a state lottery and decides to invest this sum in a bank that pays 8% simple interest. How long will it take for the original investment to double?

SOLUTION

The formula needed to handle this problem was presented in Example 2. The sum A available when P dollars is invested at a simple interest rate r for a period of t years is

$$A = P + Prt$$

We are told that $P = 500$ dollars and that $r = 8\%$. Since the investment P is to double, we must have $A = 1000$ dollars. We then substitute in the formula above

$$1000 = 500 + 500(0.08)t$$

being careful to use the decimal value 0.08 for the rate $r = 8\%$. Solving for t,

$$500 = 500(0.08)t \qquad \text{Subtract 500.}$$
$$500 = 40t \qquad \text{Simplify.}$$
$$12.5 = t \qquad \text{Divide by 40.}$$

Conclusion: It takes 12.5 years for an investment to double in value at an 8% simple interest rate.

✔ **Progress Check 4**

How long does it take for an investment to double at a simple interest rate of 10%?

Answer

10 years

Exercise Set 2.3

In Exercises 1–20 solve the formula for the specified variable.

1. $C = 2\pi r$ for r (geometry: circumference of a circle)

2. $I = Prt$ for t (finance: simple interest)

3. $S = 2\pi rh$ for h (geometry: lateral surface area of a right circular cylinder)

4. $E = IR$ for I (physics: electricity, Ohm's law)

5. $A = \dfrac{1}{2}h(b + b')$ for b (geometry: area of a trapezoid)

6. $P = 2L + 2W$ for W (geometry: perimeter of a rectangle)

7. $A = P + Prt$ for t (finance: simple interest)

8. $y - y_1 = m(x - x_1)$ for x_1 (analytic geometry: point-slope form)

9. $a_n = a_1 + (n - 1)d$ for n (nth term of an arithmetic sequence)

10. $S = \dfrac{n}{2}(a_1 + a_n)$ for a_1 (sum of an arithmetic series)

11. $S = \dfrac{a_1}{1 - r}$ for r (sum of an infinite geometric series)

12. $\dfrac{1}{f} = \dfrac{1}{a} + \dfrac{1}{b}$ for f (physics: optics, focal length)

13. $A = 2\pi r(r + h)$ for h (geometry: surface area of a right circular cylinder)

14. $d = v + 0.5at$ for a (physics: motion of a falling body)

15. $V = \dfrac{1}{3}\pi r^2 h$ for h (geometry: volume of a cone)

16. $E = mc^2$ for m (physics: energy in terms of mass and the speed of light)

17. $s = \dfrac{1}{2}gt^2$ for g (physics: distance of a falling body)

18. $A = \dfrac{1}{3}h(y_0 + 4y_1 + y_2)$ for h (mathematics: Simpson's Rule)

19. $S = P(1 + r)^t$ for P (finance: compound interest)

20. $x^2 = 4py$ for y (geometry: equation of a parabola)

21. Solve the equation $A = bt + c$ for t.

22. Solve the equation $S = 3abt + 2ab$ for b.

23. Solve the equation $5Av + 3bvt + 2kt = 0$ for v.

24. Solve $F = \dfrac{9}{5}C + 32$ for C.

25. For the linear equation $A = P + Prt$

   (a) solve for r.

   (b) solve for t.

*26. Solve the equation for a:

$$\frac{1}{a-1} + \frac{1}{b} = c$$

*27. Solve the equation for b:

$$A = \frac{b-a}{b+a}$$

*28. Solve the equation for s:

$$R = \frac{gs}{g+s}$$

*29. Solve the equation for r:

$$S = \frac{rt-a}{r-t}$$

2.4   Linear Inequalities

To solve an inequality such as

$$2x + 5 > x - 3$$

means to find its solution set, that is, to find *all* values of x that make it true. We need to know what operations we can perform on inequalities to simplify the expressions and allow us to isolate the variable.

Let's see if we can deduce the rules for inequalities. If we begin with

$$8 > 3$$

and add a positive number, say, $+12$, to both sides, we have

$$8 + 12 \overset{?}{>} 3 + 12$$
$$20 > 15$$

Similarly, if we add a negative number, say, -4, to both sides, we have

$$8 + (-4) \overset{?}{>} 3 + (-4)$$
$$4 > -1$$

We can say that

> Any number can be added to or subtracted from both sides of an inequality without affecting the inequality.

Now let's see what happens when we multiply both sides of the inequality

$$8 > 3$$

by a positive number, say, $+6$. We see that

$$8 \cdot 6 \overset{?}{>} 3 \cdot 6$$
$$48 > 18$$

If we multiply both sides by a negative number, say, -4, we have

$$(8)(-4) \overset{?}{>} (3)(-4)$$
$$-32 < -12$$

Look at what happened! Multiplication by a negative number changed the direction of the inequality sign. We can summarize the rules for handling inequalities in this way:

Rules for Inequalities

> The same operations can be performed with inequalities as with equations, except that multiplication or division by a *negative* number reverses the inequality sign.

EXAMPLE 1   SOLVING AN INEQUALITY

Solve the inequality $2x + 5 \geq x - 3$ and graph the solution set.

SOLUTION

We will perform addition and subtraction to collect terms in x just as we did for equations.

$$2x + 5 \geq x - 3$$
$$2x + 5 - 5 \geq x - 3 - 5$$
$$2x \geq x - 8$$
$$2x - x \geq x - 8 - x$$
$$x \geq -8$$

The graph of the solution set consists of -8 and all points to the right of -8.

The circle at -8 has been filled in to indicate that -8 belongs to the solution set. The arrow indicates that the solution set includes all points to the right of -8.

> ✔ **Progress Check 1**
>
> Solve the inequality $3x - 2 \geq 2x + 4$ and graph the solution set.
>
> **Answer**
>
> $x \geq 6$
>
>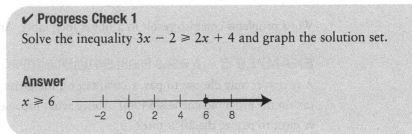

EXAMPLE 2   SOLVING AN INEQUALITY

Solve the inequality $5x < 2(x - 1)$ and graph the solution set.

SOLUTION

We proceed just as if we were dealing with an equation.

$$5x < 2(x - 1)$$
$$5x < 2x - 2$$
$$3x < -2$$

To solve for x we must divide by $+3$. Our rules say we may divide by a positive number without affecting the direction of the inequality sign.

$$\frac{3x}{3} < \frac{-2}{3}$$
$$x < -\frac{2}{3}$$

The graph of the solution set looks like this:

The circle at $-\frac{2}{3}$ has been left open to indicate that $-\frac{2}{3}$ does not belong to the solution set. The arrow indicates that the solution set consists of all points to the left of $-\frac{2}{3}$.

✔ **Progress Check 2**

Solve the inequality $8x + 2 \leq 3(x - 1)$ and graph the solution set.

Answer

$x \leq -1$

Applications

Word problems can also result in a linear inequality. An example follows.

EXAMPLE 3   A WORD PROBLEM USING INEQUALITIES

A taxpayer may choose to pay a 20% tax on the gross income or to pay a 25% tax on the gross income less $4000. Above what income level should the taxpayer elect to pay at the 20% rate?

SOLUTION

If we let x = gross income, then the choice available to the taxpayer is

(a) pay at the 20% rate on the gross income, that is, pay $0.20x$, or

(b) pay at the 25% rate on the gross income less $4000, that is, pay $0.25(x - 4000)$.

To determine when (a) produces a lower tax than (b), we must solve

$$0.20x < 0.25(x - 4000)$$
$$0.20x < 0.25x - 1000$$
$$-0.05x < -1000$$

This time we must divide by -0.05. Our rule says that division by a negative number will change the direction of the inequality, so that $<$ becomes $>$. Thus,

$$\frac{-0.05x}{-0.05} > \frac{-1000}{-0.05}$$
$$x > 20{,}000$$

The taxpayer should choose to pay at the 20% rate if the income exceeds $20,000.

✔ Progress Check 3

A customer is offered the following choice of telephone services:

(a) unlimited local calls at a $20 monthly charge, or

(b) a base rate of $8 per month plus 6 cents per message unit.

When does it cost less to choose the unlimited service?

Answer

It costs less when the anticipated use exceeds 200 units.

Compound Inequalities

We can solve compound inequalities such as

$$1 < 3x - 2 \leq 7$$

by operating on all three parts at the same time.

$$3 < 3x \leq 9 \qquad \text{Add } +2 \text{ to all three parts.}$$
$$1 < x \leq 3 \qquad \text{Divide each part by 3.}$$

EXAMPLE 4   SOLVING A COMPOUND INEQUALITY

Solve the inequality

$$-3 \leq 1 - 2x < 6$$

SOLUTION

Operating on both inequalities, we have

$$-4 \leq -2x < 5 \qquad \text{Add } -1 \text{ to all three parts.}$$
$$2 \geq x > -\frac{5}{2} \qquad \text{Divide each part by } -2.$$

✔ **Progress Check 4**

Solve the inequality $-5 < 2 - 3x < -1$.

Answer

$$\frac{7}{3} > x > 1$$

Exercise Set 2.4

In Exercises– 1–4 select the values of x that satisfy the given inequality.

1. $x < 3$
   (a) 4   (b) 5   (c) −2   (d) 0   (e) 1.2

2. $x > 4$
   (a) 8   (b) 4   (c) 6   (d) −3   (e) 9.1

3. $x \leq 5$
   (a) 3   (b) 7   (c) 5   (d) 4.3   (e) −5

4. $x \geq -1$
   (a) 0   (b) −4   (c) 1   (d) −2   (e) −1

In Exercises 5–44 solve the given inequality and graph the solution set.

5. $x + 4 < 8$

6. $x + 5 < 4$

7. $x + 3 < -3$

8. $x - 2 \leq 5$

9. $x - 3 \geq 2$

10. $x + 5 \geq -1$

11. $2 < a + 3$

12. $-5 > b - 3$

13. $2y < -1$

14. $3x < 6$

15. $2x \geq 0$

16. $-\frac{1}{2}y \geq 4$

17. $2r + 5 < 9$

18. $3x - 2 > 4$

19. $3x - 1 \geq 2$

20. $4x + 3 \leq 11$

21. $\frac{1}{2}y - 2 \leq 2$

*22. $\frac{3}{2}x + 1 \geq 4$

23. $3 \leq 2x + 1$

24. $4 \geq 3b - 2$

25. $-3x - 2 \leq 4$

26. $-5x + 2 > -8$

27. $4(2x + 1) < 16$

28. $3(3r - 4) \geq 15$

29. $2(x - 3) < 3(x + 2)$

30. $4(x - 3) \geq 3(x - 2)$

31. $3(2a - 1) < 4(2a - 3)$

32. $2(3x - 1) + 4 < 3(x + 2) - 8$

33. $3(x + 1) + 6 \geq 2(2x - 1) + 4$

34. $4(3x + 2) - 1 \leq -2(x - 3) + 15$

35. $-2 < 4x \leq 5$

36. $3 \leq 6x < 12$

37. $4 < -3x < 10$

38. $-5 < -2x < 9$

39. $-4 \leq 2x + 2 \leq -2$

40. $5 \leq 3x - 1 \leq 11$

41. $3 \leq 1 - 2x < 7$

42. $5 < 2 - 3x \leq 11$

43. $-8 < 2 - 5x \leq 7$

44. $-10 < 5 - 2x < -5$

45. You can rent a compact car from firm A for $160 per week with no charge for mileage, or from firm B for $100 per week plus 20 cents for each mile driven. Above what mileage does it cost less to rent from firm A?

46. An appliance salesperson is paid $30 per day plus $25 for each appliance sold. How many appliances must be sold for the salesperson's income to exceed $130 per day?

47. A pension trust invests $6000 in a bond that pays 5% interest per year. It also wishes to invest additional funds in a more speculative bond paying 9% interest per year so that the return on the total investment will be at least 6%. What is the minimum amount that must be invested in the more speculative bond?

48. A book publisher spends $25,000 on editorial expenses and $6 per book for manufacturing and other expenses in the course of publishing a psychology textbook. If the book sells for $25.00, how many copies must be sold to show a profit?

*49. Suppose that the base of a right triangle is 10 inches. If the area is to be at least 20 square inches and is not to exceed 80 square inches, what values may be assigned to the altitude h?

*50. A total of 70 meters of fencing material is available with which to enclose a rectangular area whose width is 15 meters. If the area must be at least 180 square meters, what values can be assigned to the length L?

2.5   Absolute Value in Equations and Inequalities

Let's review the definition of absolute value given in Chapter 1.

$$|x| = \begin{cases} x & \text{when } x \geq 0 \\ -x & \text{when } x < 0 \end{cases}$$

For example,

$$|5| = 5 \qquad |-5| = 5 \qquad |0| = 0$$

Equations

We can apply the definition of absolute value to solving the equation

$$|x - 3| = 5 \tag{1}$$

From the definition of absolute value, we then have

$$x - 3 = 5 \quad \text{or} \quad -(x - 3) = 5$$

which can be rewritten as

$$x - 3 = 5 \quad \text{or} \quad x - 3 = -5$$

This last pair of equations says that the *quantity* $x - 3$ in Equation (1) can have the values 5 or -5, which is exactly what we mean by absolute value. Solving, we have

$$x = 8 \quad \text{or} \quad x = -2$$

It's a good idea to check the answers by substituting.

$$|8 - 3| \overset{?}{=} 5 \qquad |-2 - 3| \overset{?}{=} 5$$
$$|5| \overset{?}{=} 5 \qquad |-5| \overset{?}{=} 5$$
$$5 \overset{\checkmark}{=} 5 \qquad 5 \overset{\checkmark}{=} 5$$

EXAMPLE 1   ABSOLUTE VALUE IN AN EQUATION

Solve the equation $|2x - 7| = 11$.

SOLUTION

We have to solve two equations.

$$2x - 7 = 11 \quad \text{or} \quad -(2x - 7) = 11$$
$$2x = 18 \qquad\qquad -2x + 7 = 11$$
$$x = 9 \qquad\qquad\qquad x = -2$$

> **✔ Progress Check 1**
>
> Solve and check.
>
> (a) $|x + 8| = 9$ (b) $|3x - 4| = 7$
>
> **Answers**
>
> (a) $1, -17$ (b) $\dfrac{11}{3}, -1$

By focusing on the definition of absolute value as the distance of a point on the real number line from the origin, we can provide a slightly different way to solve equations involving absolute value.

EXAMPLE 2   ABSOLUTE VALUE AS DISTANCE

Solve the equation $|2 - x| = 6$.

SOLUTION

The *point* on the real number line whose coordinate is $2 - x$ must lie precisely 6 units from the origin, that is,

$$2 - x = 6 \quad \text{or} \quad 2 - x = -6$$
$$-x = 4 \qquad\qquad -x = -8$$
$$x = -4 \qquad\qquad x = 8$$

> **✔ Progress Check 2**
>
> Solve as in Example 2 and check: $\left|\dfrac{x}{2} - 4\right| = 5$
>
> **Answer**
>
> $18, -2$

Here's a trick question: Does the equation

$$|x + 2| = -3$$

have a solution? The answer is an emphatic "No!" since the absolute value of a quantity is always greater than or equal to 0.

Inequalities

To solve inequalities involving absolute value, we again recall that $|x|$ is the distance between the origin and x on the real number line. We can then easily graph the solution set for each of the inequalities $|x| < a$ and $|x| > a$.

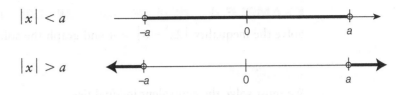

$|x| < a$

$|x| > a$

We can summarize the result this way:

> For a given positive number a,
>
> $|x| < a$ is equivalent to $-a < x < a$
>
> $|x| > a$ is equivalent to $x > a$ or $x < -a$

EXAMPLE 3 ABSOLUTE VALUE IN AN INEQUALITY

Solve the inequality $|2x - 5| \leq 7$ and graph the solution set.

SOLUTION

We must solve the equivalent compound inequality.

$$-7 \leq 2x - 5 \leq 7$$
$$-2 \leq 2x \leq 12 \qquad \text{Add } +5 \text{ to each part.}$$
$$-1 \leq x \leq 6 \qquad \text{Divide each part by 2.}$$

The graph of the solution set is then

✔ **Progress Check 3**

Solve, and graph the solution set.

(a) $|x| < 3$　　(b) $|3x - 1| \leq 8$　(c) $|x| < -2$　　(d) $|x| > -5$

Answers

(a) $-3 < x < 3$

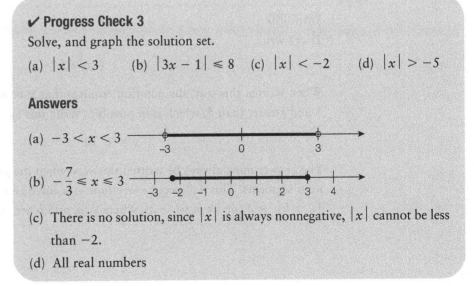

(b) $-\dfrac{7}{3} \leq x \leq 3$

(c) There is no solution, since $|x|$ is always nonnegative, $|x|$ cannot be less than -2.

(d) All real numbers

EXAMPLE 4   ABSOLUTE VALUE IN AN INEQUALITY

Solve the inequality $|2x - 6| > 4$ and graph the solution set.

SOLUTION

We must solve the equivalent inequalities.

$$2x - 6 > 4 \qquad \text{or } 2x - 6 < -4$$
$$2x > 10 \qquad\qquad 2x < 2$$
$$x > 5 \qquad\qquad x < 1$$

The graph of the solution set is then

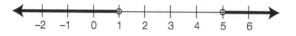

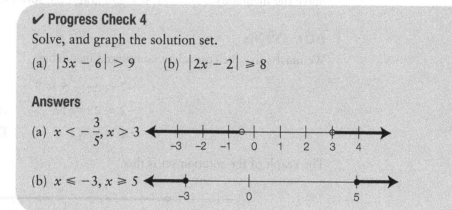

✔ **Progress Check 4**

Solve, and graph the solution set.

(a) $|5x - 6| > 9$ (b) $|2x - 2| \geq 8$

Answers

(a) $x < -\dfrac{3}{5}, x > 3$

(b) $x \leq -3, x \geq 5$

WARNING

Don't write

$$1 > x > 5$$

When written this way, the notation requires that x be *simultaneously* less than 1 and greater than 5, which is impossible. Write this as

$$x < 1 \quad \text{or} \quad x > 5$$

The answer must always be written this way when the graph consists of disjoint segments. This will occur every time you solve an inequality of the form $|x \pm b| \geq a$ (or $|x \pm b| > a$), where x, a, and b are real numbers.

Exercise Set 2.5

1. Which of the following are solutions to $|x - 3| = 5$?
   (a) -8 (b) 8 (c) 2 (d) -2
   (e) none of these

2. Which of the following are solutions to $|2x + 5| = 6$?
   (a) $\dfrac{1}{2}$ (b) $-\dfrac{1}{2}$ (c) $-\dfrac{11}{2}$ (d) $\dfrac{11}{2}$
   (e) none of these

3. Which of the following are solutions to $|3a + 5| < 20$?
   (a) 5 (b) 4 (c) -10 (d) -8
   (e) none of these

4. Which of the following are solutions to $|2b - 3| \le 6$?
   (a) -1 (b) 0 (c) 5 (d) 4 (e) -2

5. Which of the following are solutions to $|-3x + 2| > 11$?
   (a) -3 (b) -4 (c) 5 (d) 2 (e) 4

6. Which of the following are solutions to $|3x - 5| \ge 7$?
   (a) $-\dfrac{1}{2}$ (b) 4 (c) 1 (d) 6 (e) -1

7. Which of the following are solutions to $|x - 3| < -5$?
   (a) -2 (b) 1 (c) 8 (d) 0
   (e) none of these

8. Which of the following are solutions to $|3x + 1| > -2$?
   (a) $\dfrac{1}{3}$ (b) -1 (c) 0 (d) 1
   (e) all of these

In Exercises 9–20 solve and check.

9. $|x + 2| = 3$ 10. $|x - 3| = 5$

11. $|r - 5| = \dfrac{1}{2}$ 12. $|2r - 4| = 2$

13. $|2x + 1| = 3$ 14. $|3x - 1| = 5$

15. $|3y - 2| = 4$ 16. $|5y + 1| = 11$

17. $|-3x + 1| = 5$ 18. $|-4x - 3| = 9$

19. $|2t + 2| = 3$ 20. $|2t + 2| = 0$

In Exercises 21–46 solve and graph.

21. $|x| < 5$ 22. $|x| \le 3$

23. $|x| > 4$ 24. $|x| \ge 8$

25. $|x| > -3$ 26. $|x| > 0$

27. $|x + 3| < 5$ 28. $|x - 2| \le 4$

29. $|x + 1| > 3$ 30. $|x + 2| > -3$

31. $|x - 3| \ge 4$ 32. $|2x + 1| < 5$

33. $|3x + 6| \le 12$ 34. $|4x - 1| > 3$

35. $|3x + 2| \ge -1$ 36. $|2x + 3| \ge 7$

37. $|1 - 2x| \le 3$ 38. $\left|\dfrac{1}{3} - x\right| < \dfrac{2}{3}$

39. $|1 - 3x| > 4$ 40. $|1 + 2x| < 0$

41. $\left|\dfrac{1}{2} + x\right| > \dfrac{1}{2}$ 42. $|1 - 2x| < 0$

43. $\left|\dfrac{x - 1}{2}\right| < 3$ 44. $\dfrac{|2x + 1|}{3} < 0$

45. $\dfrac{|2x - 1|}{4} < 2$ 46. $\dfrac{|3x + 2|}{2} < 4$

47. A machine that packages 100 vitamin pills per bottle can make an error of 2 pills per bottle. If x is the number of pills in a bottle, write an inequality using absolute value that indicates a maximum error of 2 pills per bottle. Solve the inequality.

48. The weekly income of a worker in a manufacturing plant differs from \$300 by no more than \$50. If x is the weekly income, write an inequality using absolute value that expresses this relationship. Solve the inequality.

*49. If $x = 2$ is a solution to $|a + x| = 5$, find all possible values of a.

*50. If $x = -3$ is a solution to $|2a - 3x| = 2$, find all possible values of a.

*51. If $x = 3$ is a solution to the inequality $|2a - x| < 3$, find all possible values of a.

*52. If $x = 4$ is a solution to the inequality $|3a + x| \le 5$, find all possible values of a.

*53. If $x = -2$ is a solution to the inequality $|2a + 5x| > 4$, find all possible values of a.

*54. If $x = 4$ is a solution to the inequality $|3a - 2x| \ge 3$, find all possible values of a.

■ ■ ■

Chapter Summary

Terms and Symbols

absolute value	77	formula	68	literal equation	68
compound inequality	75	identity	57	right-hand side	53
conditional equations	57	left-hand side	53	root	53
equation	53	like terms	54	solution	53
equivalent equation	53	linear equation	56	solution set	53
first-degree equation	56	linear inequality	72		

Key Ideas for Review

Topic	Page	Key Idea
Solving an equation	53	
equivalent equations	53	Solutions of an equation are found by changing the equation into a succession of simpler equivalent equations that have the same roots.
linear equation	56	The linear equation $ax + b = 0$, $a \neq 0$, has exactly one solution.
formula	68	A formula is an equation giving the relationship between two or more variables. You can "solve" a formula for any variable using the usual steps of algebra.
Solving an inequality	72	
caution on multiplication	73	Linear inequalities are solved in a manner very similar to that of linear equations, except that multiplication or division by a negative number reverses the direction of the inequality sign.
solution set	80	Assuming $a > 0$, the solution set to the inequality $\|x\| < a$ is the interval $-a < x < a$, whereas the solution set to the inequality $\|x\| > a$ consists of two disjoint intervals: $x < -a$ or $x > a$.
Absolute value	77	
equations and inequalities	77	Linear equations and inequalities involving absolute value can be solved using the definition of absolute value.

Common Errors

1. When multiplying an equation or inequality by a constant, remember to multiply both sides by the constant. This requires that each term of each side be multiplied by the constant, and the constant must never be zero.

2. When multiplying or dividing an inequality by a negative number, remember to change the direction of the inequality sign. Write

$$-3x \leq 6$$
$$x \geq -2$$

Don't write

$$-3x \leq 6 \qquad -3x \leq 6$$
$$x \geq 2 \quad \text{or} \quad x \leq -2$$

Both of these are wrong!

3. Inequalities of the form

$$\|x - 4\| \geq 9$$

will result in the two disjoint segments $x \leq -5$ or $x \geq 13$. This result must be written as shown; *don't* write $-5 \geq x \geq 13$, since this notation makes no sense.

Review Exercises

Solutions to exercises whose numbers are in bold are in the Solutions section in the back of the book.

2.1 In Exercises 1–6 solve the given linear equation and check your answer.

1. $3x = 5$
2. $5x = 15$
3. $2x + 3 = 15$
4. $5a + 2 = 12$
5. $2(x - 1) = 4x - 3$
6. $3(2b - 1) = 4b - 2$

2.2 7. The XYZ company consists of two divisions: the foreign division and the domestic division. A stockbroker tells her mathematically minded client that the domestic division's annual profit (in millions of dollars) was 4 more than twice the profit of the foreign division, and that the total annual profit of the XYZ company was $19 million. Find the annual profit of each division.

8. In a certain sociology course there are two textbooks. If one book costs $6 less than the other book, and the total book expense for the course is $44, what is the cost of each book?

9. A photographer working in the darkroom makes four test prints before deciding on the proper exposure time for the final print. If the first three test prints have been exposed for 5, 12, and 15 seconds, and the average of the four exposure times is 13 seconds, determine the exposure time of the fourth test print.

10. The perimeter of a parallelogram is 46 inches. If the shorter sides are one inch shorter than the longer sides, find the dimensions.

2.3 11. Solve the equation $r = 2s + 4tu$ for u.

12. Solve the equation $3A - 2B = C + D$ for A.

13. Solve the equation $3A - 2B + C = D$ for B.

14. Solve the equation $2a + 3cd = ef - g$ for c.

2.4 In Exercises 15–22 solve the given inequality.

15. $x + 3 < 6$
16. $x - 2 \leqslant 4$
17. $2x + 3 > 5$
18. $3x - 2 \geqslant 3$
19. $2(x + 2) < 3(x - 1)$

20. $3(2x - 3) \geqslant 2(3x - 4)$
21. $3 < 2x < 6$
22. $-3 < 3x + 2 \leqslant 4$

In Exercises 23–30 solve the given inequality and graph the solution set.

23. $x - 2 < 1$
24. $2x - 1 \leqslant 3$
25. $3x - 2 > -5$
26. $2x + 4 \geqslant 0$
27. $2x < 3(x - 1)$
28. $3(x - 1) < 2(x - 3)$
29. $-1 < 2x + 1 < 4$
30. $0 \leqslant 2x + 2 \leqslant 2$

31. An hour of exercising on machine A burns up 400 calories, while an hour on machine B burns up 300 calories. If a woman exercises one hour on machine B, how many hours should she also exercise on machine A so that a total of 1500 calories will be burned up?

32. Sportsview Rental provides a projection screen TV for a charge of $8.00 for the first day and $5.00 for each additional day. Actionview Rental provides the same equipment for $6.50 per day. If you are planning to rent a projection screen TV for t days, for what values of t would you prefer to rent from Sportsview Rental?

33. A telephone salesperson is paid a salary of $120 per week, plus $1.50 for each person who places an order. How many persons must place orders so that the salesperson's weekly income will exceed $180?

34. The author of a mathematics textbook determines that it takes 30 minutes to read a certain section and 4 minutes to solve each exercise. How many exercises should an instructor assign in addition to the reading so that the student will spend at least 70 minutes on the assignment?

2.5 In Exercises 35–40 solve and check.

35. $|3x - 4| = 5$
36. $|2x + 3| = 1$
37. $|-y + 3| = 2$
38. $|-3s - 2| = 4$

39. $\left| 3r + 3 \right| = 0$ 40. $\left| 4t - 2 \right| = 0$

In Exercises 41–50 solve and graph.

41. $\left| 3x \right| < 3$ 42. $\left| 3x \right| > 6$

43. $\left| 2x + 3 \right| \leq 2$ 44. $\left| 3x - 2 \right| \geq 1$

45. $\left| 2x + 1 \right| = 2$ 46. $\left| -3x + 6 \right| = 0$

47. $\left| 2 + 2x \right| < 0$ 48. $\left| 2 - 2x \right| \geq 0$

49. $\dfrac{\left| 3x + 1 \right|}{2} < 2$ 50. $\dfrac{\left| 4x - 2 \right|}{3} \geq 4$

Progress Test 2A

1. Solve and check: $4x - 6 = 9$.

2. Solve and check: $2(x - 2) = 3(2x + 4)$.

3. True or false: -1 is a root of $2x - 1 = 3x + 1$.

4. Solve for h: $V = \pi r^2 h$.

5. Solve for x: $-2x + 3 = 4 + kx$.

6. 28 is 40% of what number?

7. 8 is $\frac{1}{4}$% of what number?

8. The length of a rectangle is 3 meters longer than its width. If the perimeter is 36 meters, find the dimensions of the rectangle.

9. Find three consecutive even integers whose sum is 48.

10. Part of a $5000 trust fund is invested in a mutual fund yielding 6% per year in dividends, and the balance in a corporate bond yielding 7% interest per year. If the total annual interest is $320, how much is invested in each?

11. Solve and graph: $3(2 - x) < 12$.

12. Solve and graph: $5(3x - 2) \geq 2(4 - 5x) + 7$.

13. Solve: $\left| 2x - 2 \right| = 5$.

14. Solve and graph: $\left| 2 - x \right| \leq 12$.

15. Solve and graph: $\left| 2x + 5 \right| > 7$.

Progress Test 2B

1. Solve and check: $5x + 4 = -6$.

2. Solve and check: $-(x + 3) = 4(x - 7)$.

3. True or false: -2 is a root of $-3x - 5 = 2x - 3$.

4. Solve for b: $A = \frac{1}{2}h(b + c)$.

5. Solve for x: $2(3 - kx) = (5 - 2x)$.

6. 44 is 110% of what number?

7. 56 is 70% of what number?

8. The width of a rectangle is 1 centimeter less than twice its length. If the perimeter is 22 centimeters, find the dimensions of the rectangle.

9. A certain number is 4 less than another number. If their sum is 46, find the numbers.

10. An $8000 pension fund is invested in two parts yielding 5% and 8% interest per year, respectively. If the total annual interest is $520, how much is invested in each part?

11. Solve and graph: $5(4 - 2x) > 45$.

12. Solve and graph: $4(x + 2) \leq 3(2 - 3x) - 11$.

13. Solve: $\left| 3x - 4 \right| = 5$.

14. Solve and graph: $\left| 3 - 2x \right| \geq 12$.

15. Solve and graph: $\left| 3x - 1 \right| < 2$.

Chapter 2 Project

How do dietitians design healthy diets for people of different shapes and sizes? Factors like muscle mass, height, age, and gender play a role. Algebra is an important tool for solving problems that involve numerical data like these.

Do Exercises 60 and 61 in Section 2.1. Now do some research into how age, height, body shape, and other factors like these affect determinations about healthy weights and caloric intake. Remember that the formulas given here are simple examples intended to show how dietitians may use algebra; they are not proven laws. If you can, interview a real dietitian or nutritionist and ask him or her how mathematics is utilized in human health science.

Adapt the equation given in Exercise 61 for a man who wishes to lose 1.5 pounds in one week, with a starting weight of 200 pounds. If the man's goal weight is 180 pounds, how tall does the formula in Exercise 60 suggest he might be?

■ ■ ■

3 Mathematical Models and Word Problems

"A great discovery solves a great problem but there is a grain of discovery in the solution of any problem. Your problem may be modest; but if it challenges your curiosity and brings into play your inventive faculties, and if you solve it by your own means, you may experience the tension and enjoy the triumph of discovery."
—George Pólya

Scientists and mathematicians work together to learn about, and hopefully to solve, serious problems facing all of us. One of these problems is global warming. The Earth's surface is about one degree Fahrenheit warmer than it was just 100 years ago. The presence in our atmosphere of increasing amounts of so-called greenhouse gases like methane and carbon dioxide is largely responsible.

If human activities like burning fossil fuels add methane to our air, how do scientists determine what proportion of the atmosphere is methane? One figure indicates that the concentration of methane has increased by 150% in the last 250 years. What does this figure mean? Problems dealing with the concentrations of substances in combination are called

http://www.epa.gov

mixture problems, and they are one of the several types of word problems that this chapter addresses. The chapter project will look at some more examples related to global warming, and you can learn more at this informative government website, www.epa.gov.

■ ■ ■

When engineers want to test a new idea, they build a model upon which to experiment. A properly constructed model is expected to behave in the same manner as the final product. In the same way, a physicist may build a model that facilitates exploration of the behavior of a natural phenomenon. Similarly, a biologist may build a model to explain the interaction between body mechanisms.

Mathematicians also build models, but they do so on paper. A **mathematical model** consists of mathematical expressions and equations that are an abstract representation of the problem. The steps in the process consist of

    (a) determining the variables,

    (b) creating the model,

    (c) using the model to find a solution or solutions,

    (d) verifying that the solution satisfies the original problem.

The steps in the process of mathematical modeling should sound familiar. They are precisely the steps we used in Chapter 2 when we introduced you to the intriguing world of word problems. You have seen that the challenge in solving word problems lies in translating from words into mathematical equivalents, that is, in building the mathematical model.

We are now going to explore a variety of word problems in which we will show you how to build a model in an organized manner that will lead to the appropriate algebraic expressions and equations. In short, *we are going to demonstrate a method for solving word problems that is virtually foolproof.*

We pointed out in Section 2.2 that sometimes you must use a formula in order to solve a problem. This need not frighten you. For example, you already know one of the formulas we will use:

$$\text{distance} = \text{rate} \times \text{time}$$

Often, these formulas express a relationship that you use all of the time but have never written down. For example, if you have a pocketful of change and want to know how wealthy you are, you would determine the number of coins of each type (the technical term is *denomination*) and multiply each by the number of cents in that type. The formula

$$\text{value in cents} = \text{number of coins} \times \text{number of cents in each coin}$$

explicitly states the relationship that you intuitively used.

Having successfully translated from words into algebra, you must now solve the equation that you have formulated. That's the easy part: straightforward algebraic steps will lead you to a numerical solution. The final step: always check to ensure that the answer "makes sense" in the context of the problem.

3.1 Coin Problems

In building a model for coin problems, you must distinguish between the *number* of coins and the *value* of the coins. For example,

n nickels have a value of $5n$ cents

n dimes have a value of $10n$ cents

n quarters have a value of $25n$ cents

If you have 8 quarters, what is their value? You find the answer by using this relationship.

> For any denomination of coins,
>
> number of coins × number of cents in each coin = value in cents

Since each quarter has a value of 25 cents, the total value of the quarters is

$$8 \times 25 = 200 \text{ cents}$$

EXAMPLE 1   A COIN PROBLEM

A purse contains $3.20 in quarters and dimes. If there are 3 more quarters than dimes, how many coins of each type are there?

SOLUTION

In our model, we may let the unknown represent the number of quarters or the number of dimes. We make a choice. Let

$$n = \text{number of quarters}$$

then

$$n - 3 = \text{number of dimes}$$

since "there are 3 more quarters than dimes."

We can begin to build our model by gathering the data in the form of a chart, using the relationship

> value in cents = number of coins × number of cents in each coin

to guide us.

In our problem, we are told that

$$\text{total value} = (\text{value of quarters}) + (\text{value of dimes})$$

	Number of coins	× Number of cents in each coin	=	Value in cents
Quarters	n	25		$25n$
Dimes	$n - 3$	10		$10(n - 3)$
Total				320

Substituting from the chart and solving,

$$320 = 25n + 10(n - 3)$$
$$320 = 25n + 10n - 30$$
$$350 = 35n$$
$$10 = n$$

Then

$$n = \text{number of quarters} = 10$$
$$n - 3 = \text{number of dimes} = 7$$

Now verify that the value is $3.20.

✔ **Progress Check 1**

(a) Solve Example 1, letting the unknown n represent the number of dimes.

(b) A class collected $3.90 in nickels and dimes. If there were 6 more nickels than dimes, how many coins were there of each type?

Answers

(a) 10 quarters, 7 dimes   (b) 24 dimes, 30 nickels

EXAMPLE 2   A COIN PROBLEM

A jar contains 25 coins worth $3.05. If the jar contains only nickels and quarters, how many coins are there of each type?

SOLUTION

We'll choose a variable to represent the number of nickels:

$$n = \text{number of nickels}$$

Can our model represent the number of quarters in terms of n? Since there is a total of 25 coins, we must have

$$25 - n = \text{number of quarters}$$

The model can then be built in the form of a chart.

	Number of coins	× Number of cents in each coin	=	Value in cents
Nickels	n	5		$5n$
Quarters	$25 - n$	25		$25(25 - n)$
Total				305

We know that

$$\text{total value} = (\text{value of nickels}) + (\text{value of quarters})$$
$$305 = 5n + 25(25 - n)$$
$$305 = 5n + 625 - 25n$$
$$-320 = -20n$$
$$n = 16 = \text{number of nickels}$$
$$25 - n = \ \ 9 = \text{number of quarters}$$

Verify that the coins have a total value of $3.05.

✔ **Progress Check 2**

A pile of coins worth $10 consisting of quarters and half-dollars is lying on a desk. If there are twice as many quarters as half-dollars, how many half-dollars are there?

Answer

10

EXAMPLE 3   A DISGUISED COIN PROBLEM

A man purchased 10-cent, 15-cent, and 20-cent stamps with a total value of $8.40. If the number of 15-cent stamps is 8 more than the number of 10-cent stamps and there are 10 more of the 20-cent stamps than of the 15-cent stamps, how many of each did he receive?

SOLUTION

This problem points out two things: (a) it is possible to phrase coin problems in terms of stamps or other objects, and (b) a "wordy" problem can be attacked by the same type of analysis.

	Number of stamps ×	Denomination of each stamp	=	Value in cents
10-cent	$n - 8$	10		$10(n - 8)$
15-cent	n	15		$15n$
20-cent	$n + 10$	20		$20(n + 10)$
Total				840

We let n be the number of 15-cent stamps (since the 10-cent and 20-cent stamps are specified in terms of the 15-cent stamps). Since

$$\text{total value} = \begin{pmatrix} \text{value of} \\ \text{10-cent stamps} \end{pmatrix} + \begin{pmatrix} \text{value of} \\ \text{15-cent stamps} \end{pmatrix} + \begin{pmatrix} \text{value of} \\ \text{20-cent stamps} \end{pmatrix}$$

we have

$$840 = 10(n - 8) + 15n + 20(n + 10)$$
$$840 = 10n - 80 + 15n + 20n + 200$$
$$840 = 45n + 120$$
$$720 = 45n$$
$$16 = n$$

Thus,

$$n = \text{number of 15-cent stamps} = 16$$
$$n - 8 = \text{number of 10-cent stamps} = 8$$
$$n + 10 = \text{number of 20-cent stamps} = 26$$

Verify that the total value is $8.40.

✔ Progress Check 3

The pretzel vendor finds that her coin-changer contains $8.75 in nickels, dimes, and quarters. If there are twice as many dimes as nickels and 10 fewer quarters than dimes, how many of each kind of coin are there?

Answer

15 nickels, 30 dimes, and 20 quarters

Exercise Set 3.1

1. A soda machine contains $3.00 in nickels and dimes. If the number of dimes is 5 times more than twice the number of nickels, how many coins of each type are there?

2. A donation box has $8.50 in nickels, dimes, and quarters. If there are twice as many dimes as nickels, and 4 more quarters than dimes, how many coins of each type are there?

3. A wallet has $460 in $5, $10, and $20 bills. The number of $5 bills exceeds twice the number of $10 bills by 4, while the number of $20 bills is 6 fewer than the number of $10 bills. How many bills of each type are there?

4. A traveler buys $990 in traveler's checks, in $10, $20, and $50 denominations. The number of $20 checks is 3 less than twice the number of $10 checks, while the number of $50 checks is 5 less than the number of $10 checks. How many traveler's checks were bought in each denomination?

5. A movie theater charges $5 admission for an adult and $3 for a child. If 700 tickets were sold and the total revenue received was $2900, how many tickets of each type were sold?

6. At a gambling casino a red chip is worth $5, a green one $2, and a blue one $1. A gambler buys $27 worth of chips. The number of green chips is 2 more than 3 times the number of red ones, while the number of blue chips is 3 less than twice the number of red ones. How many chips of each type did the gambler get?

7. A student buys 5-cent, 10-cent, and 15-cent stamps, with a total value of $6.70. If the number of 5-cent stamps is 2 more than the number of 10-cent stamps, while the number of 15-cent stamps is 5 more than one half the number of 10-cent stamps, how many stamps of each denomination did the student obtain?

8. A railroad car, designed to carry containerized cargo, handles crates that weigh 1, $\frac{1}{2}$, and $\frac{1}{4}$ ton. On a certain day, the railroad car carries 17 tons of

cargo. If the number of $\frac{1}{2}$-ton containers is twice the number of 1-ton containers, while the number of $\frac{1}{4}$-ton containers is 8 more than 4 times the number of 1-ton containers, how many containers of each type are in the car?

9. An amateur theater group is converting a large classroom into an auditorium for a forthcoming play. The group will sell $3, $5, and $6 tickets. They want to receive exactly $503 from the sale of the tickets. If the number of $5 tickets to be sold is twice the number of $6 tickets, and the number of $3 tickets is 1 more than 3 times the number of $6 tickets, how many tickets of each type are there?

10. An amusement park sells 25-cent, 50-cent, and $1 tickets and a teacher purchases $32.50 worth of tickets. A student remarks that there are twice as many 50-cent tickets as there are $1 tickets and

that the number of 25-cent tickets is 30 more than the number of 50-cent tickets. How many tickets of each type are there?

11. During its annual picnic, a company supplies lemonade for all employees and their families. The picnic committee has purchased twice as many pint jugs as quart jugs and 8 fewer gallon jugs than quart jugs. How many jugs of each type are there if 22 gallons of lemonade were purchased? (*Hint*: There are 2 pints to a quart and 4 quarts to a gallon.)

12. A gym offers a variety of weights for use by its members. If there are 6 more 50-pound weights than 100-pound weights and three times as many 20-pound weights as 50-pound weights, for a total of 3180 pounds, how many of each weight are there?

3.2   Investment Problems

The class of investment problems that we are going to solve involves simple interest. As an example, assume that you invest $500 (called the **principal**) at an annual interest rate of 6%. Then the interest I available at year's end is

$$I = (0.06)(500) = 30$$

In this example, you have earned $30 in interest. We can generalize and develop a formula that will form the basis for our modeling of these investment problems.

> simple annual interest = principal · annual rate
>
> or
>
> $$I = P \cdot r$$

This formula will be used in all investment problems.

EXAMPLE 1   INVESTING AT SIMPLE INTEREST

A part of $7000 is invested at 6% annual interest and the remainder at 8%. If the total amount of annual interest is $460, how much was invested at each rate?

SOLUTION
Let

$$n = \text{amount invested at 6\%}$$

then

$$7000 - n = \text{amount invested at 8\%}$$

since the total amount is $7000. The model can then be built in the form of a chart.

	Principal	×	Rate	=	Interest
6% portion	n		0.06		$0.06n$
8% portion	$7000 - n$		0.08		$0.08(7000 - n)$
Total					460

Since the total interest is the sum of the interest from the two parts,

$$460 = 0.06n + 0.08(7000 - n)$$
$$460 = 0.06n + 560 - 0.08n$$
$$0.02n = 100$$
$$n = \$5000 = \text{portion invested at 6\%}$$
$$7000 - n = \$2000 = \text{portion invested at 8\%}$$

✔ **Progress Check 1**

A club decides to invest a part of $4600 in stocks earning 4.5% annual dividends, and the remainder in bonds paying 7.5%. How much must the club invest in each to obtain a net return of 5.4%?

Answer
$3220 in stocks, $1380 in bonds

EXAMPLE 2   INVESTING AT SIMPLE INTEREST

A part of $12,000 is invested at 5% annual interest, and the remainder at 9%. The annual income on the 9% investment is $100 more than the annual income on the 5% investment. How much is invested at each rate?

SOLUTION

Let

$$n = \text{amount invested at 5\%}$$

then

$$12,000 - n = \text{amount invested at 9\%}$$

We can then model the information in the form of a chart.

	Principal	×	Rate	=	Interest
5% investment	n		0.05		$0.05n$
9% investment	$12,000 - n$		0.09		$0.09(12,000 - n)$

Since the interest on the 9% investment is $100 more than the interest on the 5% investment,

$$0.09(12{,}000 - n) = 0.05n + 100$$
$$1080 - 0.09n = 0.05n + 100$$
$$980 = 0.14n$$
$$n = 7000$$

Thus, $7000 is invested at 5% and $5000 at 9%.

✔ Progress Check 2

$7500 is invested in two parts yielding 5% and 15% annual interest. If the interest earned on the 15% investment is twice that earned on the 5% investment, how much is invested in each?

Answer
$4500 at 5%, $3000 at 15%

EXAMPLE 3   AN INVENTORY INVESTMENT PROBLEM

A shoe store owner had $6000 invested in inventory. The profit on women's shoes was 35%, while the profit on men's shoes was 25%. If the profit on the entire stock was 28%, how much was invested in each type of shoe?

SOLUTION

Let

$$n = \text{amount invested in women's shoes}$$

then

$$6000 - n = \text{amount invested in men's shoes}$$

In chart form, the model now looks like this:

	Principal	×	Rate	=	Interest
Women's shoes	n		0.35		$0.35n$
Men's shoes	$6000 - n$		0.25		$0.25(6000 - n)$
Total stock	6000		0.28		$0.28(6000)$

The profit on the entire stock was equal to the sum of the profits on each portion:

$$0.28(6000) = 0.35n + 0.25(6000 - n)$$
$$1680 = 0.35n + 1500 - 0.25n$$
$$180 = 0.1n$$
$$n = 1800$$

The store owner had invested $1800 in women's shoes and $4200 in men's shoes.

✔ **Progress Check 3**

An automobile dealer has $55,000 invested in compacts and midsize cars. The profit on sales of the compacts is 10%, and the profit on sales of midsize cars is 16%. How much did the dealer invest in compact cars if the overall profit on the total investment is 12%?

Answer

$36,666.67

Exercise Set 3.2

1. A part of $8000 was invested at 7% annual interest and the remainder at 8%. If the total annual interest is $590, how much was invested at each rate?

2. A $20,000 scholarship endowment fund is to be invested in two ways: part in a stock paying 5.5% annual interest in dividends and the remainder in a bond paying 7.5%. How much should be invested in each to obtain a net yield of 6.8%?

3. To help pay for his child's college education, a father invests $10,000 in two separate investments: part in a certificate of deposit paying 8.5% annual interest, the rest in a mutual fund paying 7%. The annual income on the certificate of deposit is $200 more than the annual income on the mutual fund. How much is invested in each type of investment?

4. A bicycle store selling 3-speed and 10-speed models has $16,000 in inventory. The profit on a 3-speed is 11%, while the profit on a 10-speed model is 22%. If the profit on the entire stock is 19%, how much was invested in each type of bicycle?

5. A film shop carrying black-and-white film and color film has $4000 in inventory. The profit on black-and-white film is 12%, and the profit on color film is 21%. If the annual profit on color film is $150 less than the annual profit on black-and-white film, how much was invested in each type of film?

6. A widow invested one third of her assets in a certificate of deposit paying 6% annual interest, one sixth of her assets in a mutual fund paying 8%, and the remainder in a stock paying 8.5%. If her total annual income from these investments is $910, what was the total amount invested by the widow?

7. A trust fund has invested $8000 at 6% annual interest. How much additional money should be invested at 8.5% to obtain a return of 8% on the total amount invested?

8. A businessman invested a total of $12,000 in two ventures. In one he made a profit of 8% and in the other he lost 4%. If his net profit for the year was $120, how much did he invest in each venture?

9. A retiree invested a certain amount of money at 6% annual interest; a second amount, which is $300 more than the first amount, at 8%; and a third amount, which is 4 times as much as the first amount, at 10%. If the total annual income from these investments is $1860, how much was invested at each rate?

10. A finance company lends a certain amount of money to Firm A at 7% annual interest; an amount $100 less than that lent to Firm A is lent to Firm B at 8%; and an amount $200 more than that lent to Firm A is lent to Firm C at 8.5%. If the total annual income is $126.50, how much was lent to each firm?

11. A prospective bridegroom wants to buy an engagement ring. Two jewelry stores each show him a ring at a cost of $2400. One jeweler requires a 20% down payment with the balance to be paid at the end of one year at 11% simple interest. The other jeweler requires a 25% down payment with the balance to be paid at the end of one year at 12% simple interest. What is the difference in total cost?

12. Because payment is one month overdue, a customer receives a department store bill for $332.92 that includes a 1.5% interest charge for late payment. What was the original amount of the bill?

13. An art dealer is ready to sell a Goya drawing and a Monet watercolor for which he paid a total of $45,000. If the Goya appreciated 83% and the Monet appreciated 72%, how much profit will he realize on each if he is offered $80,700 for both?

14. A small firm borrows $1000 from a stockholder at a simple interest rate of 7.5%. The company secretary lends the firm an additional sum at a simple interest rate of 8.25%. At the end of one year, the firm repays a total of $3997.75. How much did the secretary lend the firm and what is the simple interest rate on the total loan?

15. Use your graphing calculator to investigate what happens if you calculate interest more often than once per year (this is called *compound interest*).

Suppose $1000 is invested at an interest rate of 1.5% and the interest is computed after 6 months; then this interest is added to the principal so that it may earn interest for the next 6 months. (See the following.)

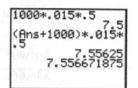

The total interest for the year is $7.50 plus $7.56, or $15.06, rather than the $15.00 we would expect from simple interest.

Repeat the procedure above for quarterly (four times per year) and monthly compounding. Put your findings in a table.

3.3   Distance (Uniform Motion) Problems

Here is the basic formula for solving distance problems:

$$\text{distance} = \text{rate} \times \text{time}$$
$$\text{or}$$
$$d = r \cdot t$$

For instance, an automobile traveling at an average speed of 50 miles per hour for 3 hours will travel a distance of

$$d = r \cdot t$$
$$= 50 \cdot 3 = 150 \text{ miles}$$

The relationships that permit you to write an equation are sometimes obscured by the words. Here are some questions to ask as you set up a distance problem:

(a) Are there two distances that are equal? Will two objects have traveled the same distance? Is the distance on a return trip the same as the distance going?

(b) Is the sum (or difference) of two distances equal to a constant? When two objects are traveling toward each other, they meet when the sum of the distances traveled by each equals the original distance between them.

EXAMPLE 1   A DISTANCE PROBLEM

Two trains leave New York for Chicago. The first train travels at an average speed of 60 miles per hour while the second train, which departs an hour later, travels at an average speed of 80 miles per hour. How long will it take the second train to overtake the first train?

SOLUTION

Since we are interested in the time the second train travels, we choose to let

$$t = \text{number of hours second train travels}$$

and then

$$t + 1 = \text{number of hours first train travels}$$

since the first train departs one hour earlier. In chart form, the model now looks like this:

	Rate	×	Time	=	Distance
First train	60		$t + 1$		$60(t + 1)$
Second train	80		t		$80t$

At the moment the second train overtakes the first, they must both have traveled the *same* distance.

$$60(t + 1) = 80t$$
$$60t + 60 = 80t$$
$$60 = 20t$$
$$3 = t$$

It will take the second train 3 hours to catch up with the first train.

✔ Progress Check 1

A light plane leaves the airport at 9 a.m. traveling at an average speed of 200 miles per hour. At 11 a.m. a jet plane departs and follows the same route. If the jet travels at an average speed of 600 miles per hour, at what time will the jet overtake the light plane?

Answer

12 noon

WARNING

The units of measurement of rate, time, and distance must be consistent. If a car travels at an average speed of 40 miles per hour for 15 minutes, then the distance covered is

$$d = r \cdot t$$

$$d = 40 \cdot \frac{1}{4} = 10 \text{ miles}$$

since 15 minutes = $\frac{1}{4}$ hour.

EXAMPLE 2   A DISTANCE PROBLEM

A jogger running at the rate of 4 miles per hour takes 45 minutes more than a car traveling at 40 miles per hour to cover a certain course. How long does it take the jogger to complete the course, and what is the length of the course?

SOLUTION

Notice that time is expressed in both minutes and hours. Let's choose hours as the unit of time and let

$$t = \text{time for the jogger to complete the course}$$

and then

$$t - \frac{3}{4} = \text{time for the car to complete the course}$$

since the car takes 45 minutes ($= \frac{3}{4}$ hour) less time. We can then model the information in the form of a chart.

	Rate	×	Time	=	Distance
Jogger	4		t		$4t$
Car	40		$t - \dfrac{3}{4}$		$40\left(t - \dfrac{3}{4}\right)$

Since the jogger and car travel the same distance,

$$4t = 40\left(t - \frac{3}{4}\right) = 40t - 30$$
$$30 = 36t$$
$$\frac{5}{6} = t$$

The jogger takes $\frac{5}{6}$ hour or 50 minutes. The distance traveled is

$$4t = 4 \cdot \frac{5}{6} = \frac{20}{6} = 3\frac{1}{3} \text{ miles}$$

✔ **Progress Check 2**

The winning horse finished the race in 3 minutes; a losing horse took 4 minutes. If the average rate of the winning horse was 5 feet per second more than the average rate of the slower horse, find the average rates of both horses.

Answer

Winner: 20 feet per second; loser: 15 feet per second

EXAMPLE 3   A DISTANCE PROBLEM

At 2 P.M. a plane leaves Boston for San Francisco, traveling at an average speed of 500 miles per hour. Two hours later a plane departs from San Francisco to Boston traveling at an average speed of 600 miles per hour. If the cities are 3200 miles apart, at what time do the planes pass each other?

SOLUTION

Let

t = the number of hours after 2 P.M. at which the planes meet

Let's piece together the information that we have. The model can then be built in the form of a chart.

	Rate	×	Time	=	Distance
From Boston	500		t		$500t$
From San Francisco	600		$t - 2$		$600(t - 2)$

At the moment that the planes pass each other, the sum of the distances traveled by both planes must be 3200 miles.

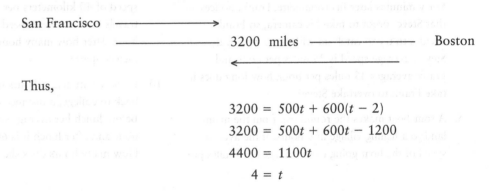

Thus,

$$3200 = 500t + 600(t - 2)$$
$$3200 = 500t + 600t - 1200$$
$$4400 = 1100t$$
$$4 = t$$

The planes meet 4 hours after the departure of the plane from Boston.

✔ Progress Check 3

Two cyclists start at the same time from the same place and travel in the same direction. If one cyclist averages 16 miles per hour and the second averages 20 miles per hour, how long will it take for them to be 12 miles apart?

Answer

3 hours

Exercise Set 3.3

1. Two trucks leave Philadelphia for Miami. The first truck to leave travels at an average speed of 50 kilometers per hour. The second truck, which leaves 2 hours later, travels at an average speed of 55 kilometers per hour. How long will it take the second truck to overtake the first truck?

2. Jackie either drives or bicycles from home to school. Her average speed when driving is 36 miles per hour, and her average speed when bicycling is 12 miles per hour. If it takes her $\frac{1}{2}$ hour less to drive to school than to bicycle, how long does it take to drive to school, how long does it take to bicycle to school, and how far is the school from her home?

3. Professors Roberts and Jones, who live 676 miles apart, are exchanging houses and jobs for four months. They start out for their new locations at exactly the same time, and they meet after 6.5 hours of driving. If their average speeds differ by 4 miles per hour, what is each professor's average speed?

4. Steve leaves school by moped for spring vacation. Forty minutes later his roommate, Frank, notices that Steve forgot to take his camera, so Frank decides to try to catch up with Steve by car. If Steve's average speed is 25 miles per hour and Frank averages 45 miles per hour, how long does it take Frank to overtake Steve?

5. A tour boat makes the round trip from the mainland to a fishing village in 6 hours. If the average speed of the boat going to the village is 15 miles per hour and the average speed returning is 12 miles per hour, how far from the mainland is the island?

6. Two cars start out from the same point at the same time and travel in opposite directions. If their average speeds are 36 and 44 miles per hour, respectively, after how many hours will they be 360 miles apart?

7. An express train and a local train start out from the same point at the same time and travel in opposite directions. The express train travels twice as fast as the local train. If after 4 hours they are 480 kilometers apart, what is the average speed of each train?

8. Two planes start out from the same place at the same time and travel in the same direction. One plane has an average speed of 400 miles per hour and the other plane has an average speed of 480 miles per hour. After how many hours will they be 340 miles apart?

9. Two cyclists start out at the same time from points that are 395 kilometers apart and travel toward each other. The first cyclist travels at an average speed of 40 kilometers per hour, and the second travels at an average speed of 50 kilometers per hour. After how many hours will they be 35 kilometers apart?

10. It takes a student 8 hours to drive from her home back to college, a distance of 580 kilometers. Before lunch her average speed is 80 kilometers per hour and after lunch it is 60 kilometers per hour. How many hours does she travel at each rate?

3.4   Mixture Problems

One type of mixture problem involves mixing commodities, say, two or more types of nuts, to obtain a mixture with a desired value. To form a suitable model, we will need to use a number of "common sense" relationships. If the commodities are measured in pounds, these are

> number of pounds × price per pound = value of commodity
>
> pounds in mixture = sum of pounds of each commodity
>
> value of mixture = sum of values of individual commodities

EXAMPLE 1   A COFFEE MIXTURE

How many pounds of Brazilian coffee worth $5 per pound must be mixed with 20 pounds of Colombian coffee worth $4 per pound to produce a mixture worth $4.20 per pound?

SOLUTION

Let

$$n = \text{number of pounds of Brazilian coffee}$$

The model can then be built in the form of a chart.

Type of coffee	Number of pounds	$\times$	Price per pound	$=$	Value in cents
Brazilian	n		500		$500n$
Colombian	20		400		8000
Mixture	$n + 20$		420		$420(n + 20)$

(Note that the weight of the mixture equals the sum of the weights of the Brazilian and Colombian coffees going into the mixture.) Since the value of the mixture is the sum of the values of the two types of coffee, we have

$$420(n + 20) = 500n + 8000$$
$$420n + 8400 = 500n + 8000$$
$$400 = 80n$$
$$5 = n$$

We must add 5 pounds of Brazilian coffee.

✔ **Progress Check 1**

How many pounds of macadamia nuts worth $4 per pound must be mixed with 4 pounds of cashews worth $2.50 per pound and 6 pounds of pecans worth $3 per pound to produce a mixture that is worth $3.20 per pound?

Answer

5 pounds

EXAMPLE 2   A MIXTURE OF CHOCOLATES

Caramels worth $1.75 per pound are to be mixed with cream chocolates worth $2 per pound to make a 5-pound mixture that will be sold at $1.90 per pound. How many pounds of each are needed?

SOLUTION

Let n = number of pounds of caramels. Displaying all of the information, we have

Type of candy	Number of pounds	×	Price per pound	=	Value in cents
Caramels	n		175		$175n$
Cream chocolates	$5 - n$		200		$200(5 - n)$
Mixture	5		190		950

(Note that the number of pounds of cream chocolates is the weight of the mixture less the weight of the caramels.) Since the value of the mixture is the sum of the values of the two components, we have

$$950 = 175n + 200(5 - n)$$
$$950 = 175n + 1000 - 200n$$
$$25n = 50$$
$$n = 2$$

We must have 2 pounds of caramels and 3 pounds of cream chocolates.

✔ **Progress Check 2**

How many gallons of oil worth 55¢ per gallon and how many gallons of oil worth 75¢ per gallon must be mixed to obtain 40 gallons of oil worth 60¢ per gallon?

Answer
30 gallons of the 55-cent oil and 10 gallons of the 75-cent oil

---

Liquid Mixtures

A second type of mixture problem involves solutions containing different concentrations of materials. For instance, a 40-gallon drum of a solution that is 75% acid contains $(40)(0.75) = 30$ gallons of acid. If the solutions are measured in gallons, the relationship we need is

number of gallons of solution	×	% of component A	=	number of gallons of component A

The other relationships we need are really the same as in our first type of mixture problem.

number of gallons in mixture	=	sum of the number of gallons in each solution
number of gallons of component A in mixture	=	sum of the number of gallons of component A in each solution

EXAMPLE 3   A LIQUID MIXTURE

A 40% acid solution is to be mixed with a 75% acid solution to produce 140 gallons of a solution that is 50% acid. How many gallons of each solution must be used?

SOLUTION

For our model, we let

$$n = \text{number of gallons of the 40\% acid solution}$$

Then

$$140 - n = \text{number of gallons of the 75\% acid solution}$$

since the number of gallons in the mixture is the sum of the number of gallons in each contributing solution. We can then model the information in the form of a chart.

	Number of gallons	×	% acid	=	Number of gallons of acid
40% solution	n		40		$0.40n$
75% solution	$140 - n$		75		$0.75(140 - n)$
Mixture	140		50		70

Since the number of gallons of acid in the mixture is the sum of the number of gallons of acid in each solution (see Figure 1), we have

$$70 = 0.40n + 0.75(140 - n)$$
$$70 = 0.40n + 105 - 0.75n$$
$$-35 = -0.35n$$
$$n = 100 \text{ gallons}$$
$$140 - n = 40 \text{ gallons}$$

Thus, we mix 100 gallons of the 40% solution with 40 gallons of the 75% solution to produce 140 gallons of the 50% solution.

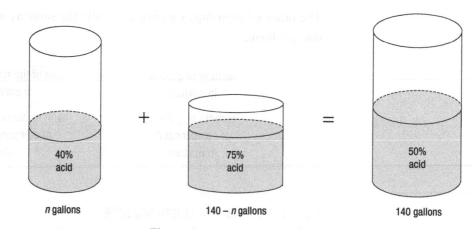

Figure 1   **Concentration of Acid**

✔ Progress Check 3

How many gallons of milk that is 22% butterfat must be mixed with how many gallons of cream that is 60% butterfat to produce 19 gallons of a mixture that is 40% butterfat?

Answer

10 gallons of milk and 9 gallons of cream

EXAMPLE 4   A MIXTURE OF ALLOYS

How many ounces of an alloy that is 30% tin must be mixed with 15 ounces of an alloy that is 12% tin to produce an alloy that is 24% tin?

SOLUTION

Let n = number of ounces of the 30% tin alloy. The alloy may be treated as a solution, and we can display the information for our model.

	Number of ounces	×	% tin	=	Number of ounces of tin
30% alloy	n		30		$0.30n$
12% alloy	15		12		1.8
Mixture	$n + 15$		24		$0.24(n + 15)$

(Note that the number of ounces in the mixture is the sum of the number of ounces in the alloys going into the mixture.) Since the number of ounces of *tin* in the mixture is the sum of the number of ounces of tin in each alloy, we have

$$0.24(n + 15) = 0.30n + 1.8$$
$$0.24n + 3.6 = 0.30n + 1.8$$
$$1.8 = 0.06n$$
$$n = 30$$

Thus, we need to add 30 ounces of the 30% alloy to 15 ounces of the 12% alloy.

> **✔ Progress Check 4**
> How many pounds of a 25% copper alloy must be added to 50 pounds of a 55% copper alloy to produce an alloy that is 45% copper?
>
> **Answer**
> We need to add 25 pounds of 25% copper alloy.

EXAMPLE 5   REDUCING A MIXTURE

A tank contains 40 gallons of water and 10 gallons of alcohol. How many gallons of water must be removed if the remaining solution is to be 30% alcohol?

SOLUTION

Let n = number of gallons of water to be removed. This problem is different since we are removing water. We can model the information in the form of a chart.

	Number of gallons	×	% alcohol	=	Gallons of alcohol
Original solution	50		20		10
Water removed	n		0		0
New solution	$50 - n$		30		$0.3(50 - n)$

(Note that the water removed has 0% alcohol!) The number of gallons of alcohol in the new solution is the same amount as in the original solution since only water has been removed.

$$0.3(50 - n) = 10$$
$$15 - 0.3n = 10$$
$$5 = 0.3n$$
$$n = 16\frac{2}{3}$$

Thus, we must remove $16\frac{2}{3}$ gallons of water.

✔ **Progress Check 5**

A tank contains 90 quarts of an antifreeze solution that is 50% antifreeze. How much water should be removed to raise the antifreeze level to 60% in the new solution?

Answer

15 quarts of water should be removed.

Exercise Set 3.4

1. How many pounds of raisins worth $1.50 per pound must be mixed with 10 pounds of peanuts worth $1.20 per pound to produce a raisin-peanut mixture worth $1.40 per pound?

2. How many ounces of Ceylon tea worth $1.50 per ounce and how many ounces of Formosa tea worth $2.00 per ounce must be mixed to obtain a mixture of 8 ounces that is worth $1.85 per ounce?

3. A copper alloy that is 40% copper is to be combined with a copper alloy that is 80% copper to produce 120 kilograms of an alloy that is 70% copper. How many kilograms of each alloy must be used?

4. How many liters of an ammonia solution that is 20% ammonia must be mixed with 20 liters of an ammonia solution that is 48% ammonia to produce a solution that is 36% ammonia?

5. A vat contains 60 gallons of a 15% saline solution. How many gallons of water must be evaporated so that the resulting solution will be 20% saline?

6. How many grams of pure silver must be added to 30 grams of an alloy that is 50% silver to obtain an alloy that is 60% silver?

7. How much water must be added to dilute 10 quarts of a solution that is 18% iodine so that the resulting solution will be 12% iodine?

8. A vat contains 27 gallons of water and 9 gallons of acetic acid. How many gallons of water must be evaporated if the remaining solution is to be 40% acetic acid?

9. How many pounds of a fertilizer worth $3 per pound must be combined with 12 pounds of a weed killer worth $6 per pound and 18 pounds of phosphate worth $6 per pound to produce a mixture worth $4.80 per pound?

10. A producer of packaged frozen vegetables wants to market the product at $1.20 per kilogram. How many kilograms of green beans worth $1 per kilogram must be mixed with 100 kilograms of corn worth $1.30 per kilogram and 90 kilograms of peas worth $1.40 per kilogram to produce the required mixture?

■ ■ ■

Chapter Summary

Key Ideas for Review

Topic	Page	Key Idea
Mathematical model	89	When you convert a word problem into mathematical expressions, equations, and inequalities, you create a mathematical model for the problem.
Formulas associated with word problems		
coin problems	90	number of coins $\times$ number of cents in each coin $=$ value in cents
investment problems	94	principal $\times$ rate $=$ interest
distance (uniform motion) problems	98	rate $\times$ time $=$ distance
mixture problems	102	number of pounds $\times$ price per pound $=$ value amount of solution $\times$ % of component A $=$ amount of component A

Review Exercises

Solutions to exercises whose numbers are in bold are in the Solutions section in the back of the book.

3.1 1. A church collection box contains $5.35 in dimes, quarters, and half-dollars. If the number of dimes is twice the number of quarters and the number of half-dollars is one less than three times the number of quarters, how many coins of each denomination are there?

2. A certain electronic device consists of 16-transistor, 48-transistor, and 64-transistor components. The number of 48-transistor components is two less than the number of 16-transistor components, and the number of 64-transistor components is three less than twice the number of 16-transistor components. If the device contains a total of 480 transistors, how many components of each type are required?

3. A freighter carries a load of 2-ton, 5-ton, and 8-ton slabs of steel. The number of 5-ton slabs is 20 fewer than the number of 2-ton slabs and the number of 8-ton slabs is one more than twice the number of 2-ton slabs. If the load being carried weighs 575 tons, how many slabs of each type are being carried?

4. Suppose that you receive a package with a total postage of $5.60 that is made up of 20-cent, 40-cent, and 1-dollar stamps. If the number of 40-cent stamps is three more than the number of 20-cent stamps and the number of 1-dollar stamps is two fewer than the number of 20-cent stamps, how many stamps of each denomination are there on the package?

3.2 5. Part of a lump-sum death payment of $40,000 was invested at 10% annual interest, and the rest was invested at 8% annual interest. If the total annual interest is $3500, how much was invested at each rate?

6. A record shop selling classical and popular music has $12,000 worth of music in inventory. The profit on classical music is 15%, while the profit on popular music is 20%. If the annual profit on classical music is $1000 less

than the annual profit on popular music, how much inventory does the shop carry in each type of music? (Assume that the entire inventory is sold.)

7. An investment club invested a total of $7000 in two real estate limited partnerships. In one partnership they make a profit of 10% for the year and in the other they have a loss of 5% for the year. If the net annual profit is $325, how much was invested in each limited partnership?

8. A finance company lent a certain amount of money to the AB company at 8% annual interest. An amount $500 more than that lent to the AB company was lent to the CD company at 10% annual interest, and an amount $400 less than the amount lent to the AB company was lent to the EF company at 12% annual interest. If the total annual interest received by the finance company is $1502, how much was lent to each borrower?

3.3 9. Two aircraft start from the same point at the same time flying in opposite directions. The faster aircraft travels twice as fast as the other one. After 5 hours of travel they are 1500 miles apart. Find the average speed of each aircraft.

10. Two joggers start to run toward each other at the same time from points that are 12 miles apart, at average speeds of 10 miles per hour and 9 miles per hour, respectively. After how many hours will they be 0.6 mile apart?

11. Two buses, traveling at average speeds of 50 and 55 miles per hour, respectively, leave Los Angeles for Chicago at the same time. After how many hours are they 60 miles apart?

12. Two airplanes leave at the same time from points 3150 miles apart, traveling toward each other, and they pass each other after 3.5 hours of flying. If their average speeds differ by 100 miles per hour, what is the average speed of each airplane?

3.4 13. How many pounds of cashews worth $4.00 per pound must be mixed with 6 pounds of

walnuts worth $2.00 per pound to yield a mixture worth $2.50 per pound?

14. A vat contains 100 gallons of a 20% potassium solution. How many gallons of water must be evaporated to get a 25% solution?

15. How many pounds of ground beef that is 25% fat must be blended with 10 pounds of ground veal that is 10% fat to produce a mixture that is 15% fat?

16. How many pounds of Colombian coffee worth $4.00 per pound must be mixed with how many pounds of Jamaican coffee worth $5.00 per pound to produce 25 pounds of a mixture that will be sold at $4.80 per pound?

17. Atmospheric concentrations are usually measured in parts per billion, by volume (ppbv). So, a concentration of carbon dioxide equal to 13 ppbv means that, for every billion volume units (say, milliliters) of the atmosphere, there are 13 units of carbon dioxide.

   Convert an atmospheric concentration of carbon dioxide of 13 ppbv to a percent. (That is, what percent of this atmosphere would be carbon dioxide?)

18. In 2002 the atmospheric concentration of the greenhouse gas methane was about 1751 parts per billion by volume (ppbv). This means that in a one-billion liter volume of the atmosphere, we should find about 1751 liters of methane gas.

   Suppose we had a 100 L sample of gas with this concentration of methane. How much methane, in mL, would have to be added to increase the concentration to 150% of its current level? (Hint: We want to increase the concentration to 1.5×1751, or 2626.5 ppbv.)

19. Store the following values in your graphing calculator as A and B: $A = 0.1$, $B = 0.3$ (see the calculator screen on top of next page). Then, enter the expression

$$\frac{112A + (172 - 112)B}{172}$$

   Suppose the 112 in the above expression represents liters of CO_2, and the values of A and B represent 10% and 30%, respectively.

a. What might the 172 represent? What about the 0.17?

b. Experiment with changing the values of A and B. How can this expression help you solve certain mixture problems?

Progress Test 3A

1. Translate into algebra: "The number of chairs is 3 less than 4 times the number of tables."

2. Steve is presently 6 years younger than Lisa. If the sum of their ages is 40, how old is each?

3. The width of a rectangle is 4 cm less than twice its length. If the perimeter is 12 cm, find the dimensions of the rectangle.

4. A donation box contains 30 coins consisting of nickels, dimes, and quarters. The number of dimes is 4 more than twice the number of quarters. If the total value of the coins is $2.60, how many coins of each type are there?

5. A fruit grower ships crates of oranges that weigh 30, 50, and 60 pounds each. A certain shipment weighs 1140 pounds. If the number of 30-pound crates is 3 more than one half the number of 50-pound crates, and the number of 60-pound crates is 1 less than twice the number of 50-pound crates, how many crates of each type are there?

6. A college fund has invested $12,000 at 7% annual interest. How much additional money must be invested at 9% to obtain a return of 7.8% on the total amount invested?

7. A businessperson invested a certain amount of money at 6.5% annual interest; a second amount, which is $200 more than the first amount, at 7.5%; and a third amount, which is $300 more than twice the first amount, at 9%. If the total annual income from these investments is $1962, how much was invested at each rate?

8. A moped and a car leave from the same point at the same time and travel in opposite directions. The car travels 3 times as fast as the moped. If after 5 hours they are 300 miles apart, what is the average speed of each vehicle?

9. A bush pilot in Australia picks up mail at a remote village and returns to home base in 4 hours. If the average speed going is 150 miles per hour and the average speed returning is 100 miles per hour, how far from the home base is the village?

10. An alloy that is 60% silver is to be combined with an alloy that is 80% silver to produce 120 ounces of an alloy that is 75% silver. How many ounces of each alloy must be used?

11. A beaker contains 150 cubic centimeters of a solution that is 30% acid. How much water must be evaporated so that the resulting solution will be 40% acid?

Progress Test 3B

1. Translate into algebra: "The number of Democrats is 4 more than one third the number of Republicans."

2. Separate 48 into two parts so that the larger part plus 3 times the smaller is 80.

3. One side of a triangle is 2 cm shorter than the third side, while the second side is 3 cm longer than one half the third side. If the perimeter is 15 cm, find the length of each side.

4. An envelope contains 20 discount coupons in $1, $5, and $10 denominations. The number of $5 coupons is twice the number of $10 coupons. If the total value of the coupons is $54, how many coupons of each type are there?

5. A cheese sampler with a total weight of 25 ounces of cheese contains 1-ounce, 2-ounce, and 3-ounce samples. If the number of 1-ounce samples is 3

more than the number of 3-ounce samples and the number of 2-ounce samples is 1 less than twice the number of 3-ounce samples, how many samples of each weight are there?

6. Part of an $18,000 trust fund is to be invested in a stock paying 6% in dividends, and the remainder in a bond paying 7.2% annual interest. How much should be invested in each to obtain a net yield of 7%?

7. A woman invested a certain amount of money at 8% annual interest and a second amount of money, $2000 greater than the first amount, at 6%. If the annual incomes on the two investments are equal, how much was invested at each rate?

8. Two trains start out at 10 A.M. from stations that are 1120 kilometers apart and travel toward each

other at average speeds of 80 and 60 kilometers per hour, respectively. At what time will they pass each other?

9. Two charter buses leave New York for Los Angeles. The first one travels at an average speed of 40 miles per hour. The second one leaves 3 hours later and travels at an average speed of 50 miles per hour. How long will it take the second bus to overtake the first one?

10. How many pounds of lawn seed worth $4.00 per pound must be mixed with 15 pounds of fertilizer worth $3.00 per pound to produce a mixture worth $3.20 per pound?

11. A vat contains 12 gallons of acid and 48 gallons of water. How much acid must be added to make a solution that is 40% acid?

Chapter 3 Project

GREENHOUSE GAS CONCENTRATIONS AND GLOBAL WARMING

The atmosphere of the Earth is a mixture of gases. The relative proportions of the major components of the atmosphere (nitrogen and oxygen) don't change very much over time, but there are small amounts of other gases that can have a big effect on the planet's climate and on its inhabitants (us!).

Greenhouse gases like carbon dioxide and methane trap heat that would otherwise be radiated out into space. A little of this is a good and necessary thing, but some human activities (like the burning of fossil fuels) release these gases and increase the concentration of greenhouse gases. This has the world's scientists concerned that we may have too much of a good thing!

In this chapter project, you will learn about how concentrations of these gases are measured, and how to use percents to get an idea of what proportion of our atmosphere is composed of greenhouse gases. You will try to determine how much this proportion can change with the addition of greater quantities of these atmospheric components. Start by reading more at www.epa.gov; and then do Exercises 17, 18, and 19 in Section 3.4.

Create a table showing how much the composition of the atmosphere changes with the addition of different amounts of CO_2 and methane. (You might want to use scientific notation to express small percents more compactly.) Explain how you can use your calculator to make these computations more quickly. (Hint: See Exercise 19 in Section 3.4.)

Using the information at the website listed above, or other sources, make a graph of the changes in quantities of methane in our atmosphere over the past 200 years.

■ ■ ■

4 Polynomials

"Algebra is generous: she often gives more than is asked of her.**"**
—Jean le Rond D'Alembert

Mathematics is required in unexpected places. The United States Postal Service considers a package to have a combined length and girth of up to 84 inches. (The girth is the perimeter around the widest part of the package.) A "large package" may have a combined length and girth of up to 130 inches. Suppose I created a package by cutting squares out of the corners of a rectangle of cardboard, then folding up the sides. How can we write an algebraic expression that gives the volume of such a package? We would call this expression a polynomial—in this case, a cubic polynomial.

The facts about package volume discussed above suggest how useful mathematics is in many careers, including packaging. The chapter project will explore these ideas more fully.

Are you fascinated by numbers, patterns, and statistics? Learn more about them (and some careers in mathematics) at http://www.amstat.org/.

■ ■ ■

Much of the work that is carried out in algebra involves expressions of a special form that are called polynomials. Since you will be dealing with polynomials throughout this book, we will devote this chapter to making sure that you can handle basic operations with polynomials.

4.1   Polynomials

Exponents

Let's review the notation of exponents that we introduced in Chapter 1. We write

$$a^1 = a$$
$$a^2 = a \cdot a$$
$$a^3 = a \cdot a \cdot a$$
$$\vdots \qquad \vdots$$
$$a^n = \underbrace{a \cdot a \cdot \,\cdots\, \cdot a}_{n \text{ factors}}$$

where n is a natural number and a is a real number. The notation a^n means "a is used as a **factor** n times" and is read as "a to the nth **power**" or simply as "a to the n." We call a the **base** and n the **exponent**. When $n = 1$, we simply write a rather than a^1. When $n = 2$, a^2 is referred to as "a squared." And when $n = 3$, a^3 is referred to as "a cubed."

Definition of a^n

> If n is a natural number, then
> $$a^n = a \cdot a \cdot \,\ldots\, \cdot a$$
> for every real number a.

EXAMPLE 1   EXPONENT NOTATION

Expand (write without exponents).

(a) $\left(\dfrac{1}{2}\right)^3$ (b) x^4 (c) $2x^3$ (d) $-3x^2y^3$ (e) $(3x)^2$

SOLUTIONS

(a) $\left(\dfrac{1}{2}\right)^3 = \dfrac{1}{2} \cdot \dfrac{1}{2} \cdot \dfrac{1}{2} = \dfrac{1}{8}$ Base is $\dfrac{1}{2}$; exponent is 3

(b) $x^4 = x \cdot x \cdot x \cdot x$ Base is x; exponent is 4

(c) $2x^3 = 2 \cdot x \cdot x \cdot x$

(d) $-3x^2y^3 = -3 \cdot x \cdot x \cdot y \cdot y \cdot y$

(e) $(3x)^2 = 3x \cdot 3x$

Note that, as demonstrated in (c) and (d) of Example 1, the exponent applies only to the factor *immediately* preceding it.

✔ **Progress Check 1**

Write without using exponents.

(a) 2^4 (b) $\left(\dfrac{1}{3}\right)^2$ (c) x^3y (d) $\dfrac{1}{2}xy^3$

Answers

(a) $2 \cdot 2 \cdot 2 \cdot 2$ (b) $\dfrac{1}{3} \cdot \dfrac{1}{3}$ (c) $x \cdot x \cdot x \cdot y$ (d) $\dfrac{1}{2} \cdot x \cdot y \cdot y \cdot y$

⚠ **WARNING**

Note the difference between

$$(-3)^2 = (-3)(-3) = 9$$

and

$$-3^2 = -(3 \cdot 3) = -9$$

There is a rule of exponents that we will need later in this chapter. We see that

$$a^2 \cdot a^3 = \underbrace{(a \cdot a)}_{2 \text{ factors}} \cdot \underbrace{(a \cdot a \cdot a)}_{3 \text{ factors}}$$

$$= \underbrace{(a \cdot a \cdot a \cdot a \cdot a)}_{2 + 3 = 5 \text{ factors}} = a^5$$

We can generalize this rule as follows:

Product Rule for Exponents

If m and n are natural numbers and a is a real number, then

$$a^m \cdot a^n = a^{m+n}$$

EXAMPLE 2   THE PRODUCT RULE FOR EXPONENTS

Multiply.

(a) $x^2 \cdot x^3$ (b) $(3x)(4x^4)$

SOLUTIONS

(a) $x^2 \cdot x^3 = x^{2+3} = x^5$

(b) $(3x)(4x^4) = 3 \cdot 4 \cdot x \cdot x^4 = 12x^{1+4} = 12x^5$

✔ **Progress Check 2**

Multiply.

(a) $x^5 \cdot x^2$ (b) $(2x^6)(-2x^4)$

Answers

(a) x^7 (b) $-4x^{10}$

Polynomials

When we combine exponent forms in one or more variables, as in

$$2x^2 + 3xy - x + 4$$

each part connected by addition is called a **term** and the entire expression is called a **polynomial**. The constants 2, 3, -1, and 4 are also given a special name: **coefficients**. Thus,

$2x^2$	$+$	$3xy$	$- \quad x$	$+ \quad 4$	Polynomial
$2x^2,$		$3xy,$	$-x$	4	Terms
$2,$		$3,$	-1	4	Coefficients

We'll state these observations in a formal manner.

Definition of a Polynomial

> A **polynomial** is a sum of terms in which
>
> **(a)** the exponent of each variable must be a nonnegative integer, and
>
> **(b)** no variables appear in the denominator.

EXAMPLE 3   THE TERMS AND COEFFICIENTS OF A POLYNOMIAL

Find the terms and coefficients.

(a) $x^2y - y^2 + 3xy$ (b) $\dfrac{1}{2}x^3 - \dfrac{2}{3}y^3$

SOLUTIONS

(a)

Term	x^2y	$-y^2$	$3xy$
Coefficient	1	-1	3

(b)

Term	$\dfrac{1}{2}x^3$	$-\dfrac{2}{3}y^3$
Coefficient	$\dfrac{1}{2}$	$-\dfrac{2}{3}$

✔ **Progress Check 3**

Find the terms and coefficients.

(a) $\dfrac{1}{4}x^7$ (b) $2x^2y^2 + 4xy - y^2$

Answers

(a) Term: $\dfrac{1}{4}x^7$; coefficient: $\dfrac{1}{4}$ (b) Terms: $2x^2y^2$, $4xy$, $-y^2$; coefficients: 2, 4, -1

Here are some examples of polynomials:

$$2x, \qquad \frac{1}{2}x^3, \qquad xy^2, \qquad 3x - 2, \qquad x^3 + 6x^2,$$
$$4x^2 - 2x + 1, \qquad 3x^2 + 4x^2y - xy^2 - 5y^3$$

We will later see that the product of two polynomials, such as

$$(2x + 1)(x^2 - 2x + 1)$$

is also a polynomial. Be careful, however, when dealing with the quotient of polynomials.

The quotient of two polynomials, such as

$$\frac{2x + 1}{x^2 - 2x + 1}$$

is not always a polynomial.

EXAMPLE 4   RECOGNIZING POLYNOMIALS

Which of the following are not polynomials?

(a) $3x^{1/2} + xy^2 + 2y$ (b) $2x^2y - 5$ (c) $x^5 - x^{-1} + 2$ (d) $-2x^3 + \dfrac{1}{x}$

SOLUTION

Every exponent of a variable in a polynomial must be a nonnegative integer. Thus, (a) is not a polynomial since x appears with the fractional exponent $\frac{1}{2}$; (c) is not a polynomial since x appears with the negative exponent -1. Further, no variable may appear in the denominator of a polynomial, which rules out (d).

✔ **Progress Check 4**

Which of the following are not polynomials?

(a) $-2xy + 3x - 3y$ (b) $xy^{2/5} - 2x^2$ (c) $-3xy + 3x^{-3}y$

Answer

(b) and (c)

Degree of a Polynomial

The **degree of a term** of a polynomial is found by adding the exponents of all the variables in that term. (The degree of a constant term is zero.) For instance, the terms of

$$2x^3 - 3xy^2 + 5x^2y^2 + xy - 7$$

have the following degrees:

$2x^3$	is of degree 3.
$-3xy^2 = -3x^1y^2$	is of degree $1 + 2 = 3$.
$5x^2y^2$	is of degree $2 + 2 = 4$.
$xy = x^1y^1$	is of degree $1 + 1 = 2$.
-7	is of degree 0 and is often called the constant term.

The **degree of a polynomial** is the degree of the term with a nonzero coefficient that has the highest degree in the polynomial. The polynomial

$$2x^3 - 3xy^2 + 5x^2y^2 + xy - 7$$

is of degree 4 since the term of highest degree, $5x^2y^2$, is of degree 4.

EXAMPLE 5   DEGREE OF A POLYNOMIAL AND ITS TERMS

Find the degree of each term and of the polynomial.

$$4x^5 - 2x^3y + x^2y^2 - 3$$

SOLUTION

$4x^5$	degree 5
$-2x^3y$	degree 4 (since $3 + 1 = 4$)
x^2y^2	degree 4 (since $2 + 2 = 4$)
-3	degree 0

Degree of the polynomial = 5 (degree of highest-degree term)

✔ Progress Check 5

Find the degree of each term and of the polynomial $2x^6y - x^3y^2 + 7xy^2 - 12$.

Answers

Degree of each term, in sequence: 7, 5, 3, 0; degree of the polynomial: 7

Applications of Polynomials

Many problems lead to algebraic expressions that are polynomials. We will now look at several simple examples; many others will occur later throughout the book.

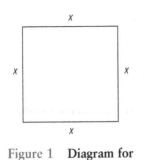

Figure 1   **Diagram for Example 6**

EXAMPLE 6 POLYNOMIALS FOR AREA AND PERIMETER

Find polynomials giving the perimeter of the square and the area of the square shown in Figure 1.

SOLUTION

Each side is of length x. The polynomial $4x$ gives the perimeter of the square. The polynomial x^2 gives the area of the square.

✔ **Progress Check 6**

Consider the rectangle in Figure 2, whose sides are x and y.

(a) Write the polynomial representing the perimeter of the rectangle.

(b) Write the polynomial representing the area of the rectangle.

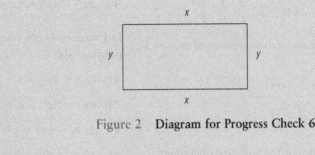

Figure 2   **Diagram for Progress Check 6**

Answers

(a) $2x + 2y$ (b) xy

EXAMPLE 7 A POLYNOMIAL EXPRESSION FOR TOTAL COST

A grocery bag contains x apples, each costing 12 cents, and y pears, each costing 10 cents. What does the polynomial $12x + 10y$ represent?

SOLUTION

The term $12x$ gives the total cost (in cents) of the apples in the bag, and the term $10y$ gives the total cost (in cents) of the pears in the bag. Thus, the polynomial $12x + 10y$ represents the total cost (in cents) of the contents of the grocery bag.

✔ **Progress Check 7**

If a car travels at the rate of r miles per hour for t hours, what does the polynomial rt represent?

Answer

the distance traveled in t hours

Exercise Set 4.1

In Exercises 1–8 identify the base(s) and exponent(s) in each expression.

1. 2^5

2. $(-2)^4$

3. t^4

4. w^6

5. $3y^5$

6. $-2t^3$

7. $3x^2y^3$

8. $-4u^3v^4$

In Exercises 9–14 write the given expression using exponents.

9. $3 \cdot 3 \cdot 3$

10. $(-5)(-5)(-5)(-5)$

11. $\left(\frac{1}{3}\right)\left(\frac{1}{3}\right)\left(\frac{1}{3}\right)\left(\frac{1}{3}\right)$

12. $x \cdot x \cdot x \cdot x \cdot x \cdot x$

13. $3 \cdot y \cdot y \cdot y \cdot y$

14. $-2 \cdot \frac{1}{p} \cdot \frac{1}{p} \cdot \frac{1}{p}$

In Exercises 15–16 evaluate each expression when $x = 3$ and $y = -2$.

15. (a) $(-xy)^2$ (b) $-(xy)^2$

16. (a) $-\left(\frac{x}{y}\right)^2$ (b) $\left(-\frac{x}{y}\right)^2$

In Exercises 17–26 carry out the indicated operations.

17. $b^5 \cdot b^2$

18. $x^3 \cdot x^5$

19. $(3x^2)(2x^4)$

20. $(6x^3)(5x)$

21. $(4y^3)(-5y^6)$

22. $(-6x^4)(-4x^7)$

23. $\left(\frac{4}{3}v^3\right)\left(\frac{5}{7}v^5\right)$

24. $\left(\frac{4}{3}w^2\right)\left(\frac{5}{2}w^4\right)$

25. $\left(\frac{3}{2}x^3\right)(-2x)$

26. $\left(-\frac{5}{3}x^6\right)\left(-\frac{3}{10}x^3\right)$

27. Which of the following expressions are not polynomials?

(a) $-3x^2 + 2x + 5$ (b) $-3x^2y$

(c) $-3x^{2/3} + 2xy + 5$ (d) $-2x^{-4} + 2xy^3 + 5$

28. Which of the following expressions are not polynomials?

(a) $4x^5 - x^{1/2} + 6$ (b) $\frac{2}{5}x^3 + \frac{4}{3}x - 2$

(c) $4x^5y$ (d) $x^{4/3}y + 2x - 3$

In Exercises 29–34 give the terms and coefficients for each given polynomial.

29. $4x^4 - 2x^2 + x - 3$

30. $\frac{1}{3}x^2 + 2x - 5$

31. $\frac{2}{3}x^3y + \frac{1}{2}xy - y + 2$

32. $2.5x^3y - 3xy^2 + 4x^2 + 8$

33. $\frac{1}{3}x^3 + \frac{1}{2}x^2y - 2x + y + 7$

34. $-4x^4 + 3x^3y - y^3 + 12$

In Exercises 35–40 find the degree of each term in the given polynomial.

35. $3x^3 - 2x^2 + 3$

36. $4x^2 + 2x - y + 3$

37. $4x^4 - 5x^3 + 2x^2 - 5x + 1$

38. $5x^5 + 2x^2y^2 + xy^3 + 3y$

39. $\frac{3}{2}x^4 + 2xy^2 + y^3 - y + 2$

40. $3x^8 - 3y^5 + 4x + 2$

In Exercises 41–46 find the degree of each of the given polynomials.

41. $2x^3 + 3x^2 - 5$

42. $4x^5 - 8x^3 + x + 5$

43. $3x^2y + 2x^2 - y^2 + 2$

44. $4xy^3 + xy^2 + 4y^2 - y$

45. $\frac{3}{5}x^4 + 2x^2 - x^2y + 4$

46. $4x^5y^2 + x^3y - 2xy^2 + 7$

47. The degree of the polynomial $\frac{3}{5}x^4 + 2x^2 + 3x - 2$ is

(a) $\frac{3}{5}$ (b) 4   (c) 1   (d) none of these

48. The degree of the polynomial $-2x^3y + y^3 + x^2 + 3$ is

(a) -2 (b) 3   (c) 4   (d) none of these

49. Find the value of the polynomial $2x^2 - 2x + 1$ when $x = 3$.

50. Find the value of the polynomial $2x^3 + x^2 - x + 4$ when $x = -2$.

51. Find the value of the polynomial $3x^2y^2 + 2xy - x + 2y + 7$ when $x = 2, y = -1$.

52. Find the value of the polynomial $0.02x^2 + 0.3x - 0.5$ when $x = 0.3$.

53. Find the value of the polynomial $2.1x^3 + 3.3x^2 - 4.1x - 7.2$ when $x = 4.1$.

54. Find the value of the polynomial $0.3x^2y^2 - 0.5xy + 0.4x - 0.6y + 0.8$ when $x = 0.4, y = 0.25$.

*55. Write a polynomial giving the area of a circle of radius r.

*56. Write a polynomial giving the area of a triangle of base b and height h.

*57. Figure 3 shows a field consisting of a rectangle and a square. What does each of the following polynomials represent?

  (a) $x^2 + xy$ (b) $2x + 2y$
  (c) $4x$ (d) $4x + 2y$

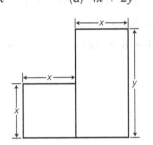

Figure 3   Diagram for Exercise 57

*58. An investor buys x shares of GE stock at $55 per share, y shares of Exxon stock at $45 per share, and z shares of AT&T stock at $20 per share. What does the polynomial $55x + 45y + 20z$ represent?

*59. Show that

$$-(ab)^2 = -\left|\, ab \,\right|^2 \text{ and } (-ab)^2 = \left|\, ab \,\right|^2$$

60. Store the value -3 as x in your graphing calculator. Do you think the value of the polynomial $x^5 + 3x^4 + x^3 + 2x^2 + 3$ will be positive, negative, or zero when $x = -3$? Enter the polynomial and see if you were correct.

```
-3→X
                        -3
X^5+3X^4+X^3+2X²
+X+3█
```

4.2   Addition and Subtraction of Polynomials

Those terms of a polynomial that differ only in their coefficients are called **like terms**. Following are some examples of like terms:

$$4x^2 \qquad \text{and} \qquad -3x^2$$
$$-5xy^3 \qquad \text{and} \qquad 17xy^3$$
$$2x^2y^2 \qquad \text{and} \qquad -2x^2y^2$$

Once again, the distributive property makes it easy to add like terms. For example,

$$-5xy^3 + 17xy^3 = (-5 + 17)xy^3 = 12xy^3$$

This leads to a simple rule for the addition of polynomials.

> To add polynomials, combine like terms by adding their coefficients.

It is often helpful to regroup the terms before adding. For example,

x^2 terms x terms   constant terms

$$(3x^2 - 2x + 5) + (x^2 + 4x - 9)$$
$$= 3x^2 + x^2 - 2x + 4x + 5 - 9$$
$$= 4x^2 + 2x - 4$$

EXAMPLE 1   ADDITION OF POLYNOMIALS

Add.

(a) $4x^2 - 3xy + 2y^2$ and $2x^2 - xy - y^2$

(b) $x^3 - 2x^2 + 6x$, $x^2 - 4$, and $2x^3 - x + 6$

SOLUTIONS

(a) Grouping like terms and then adding, we see that

$$4x^2 + 2x^2 - 3xy - xy + 2y^2 - y^2 = 6x^2 - 4xy + y^2$$

(b) Grouping like terms and then adding, we have

$$x^3 + 2x^3 - 2x^2 + x^2 + 6x - x - 4 + 6 = 3x^3 - x^2 + 5x + 2$$

✔ Progress Check 1

Simplify by combining like terms.

(a) $2x^2 + x - 3 + 4x^2 - 5x - 8$

(b) $-2x^3 + 2x^2y^2 - 4y^2 + 4x^3 + 2y^2 + xy - 7$

Answers

(a) $6x^2 - 4x - 11$ (b) $2x^3 + 2x^2y^2 - 2y^2 + xy - 7$

Sometimes we must remove parentheses before we can combine terms. Again, the key is the distributive property. For example,

$$2(x - 3y) - 3(2x + 4y)$$
$$= 2x - 6y - 6x - 12y \qquad \text{Distributive property}$$
$$= -4x - 18y \qquad \text{Combine like terms}$$

The same idea permits us to subtract polynomials. For example, to subtract $x^2 - 3x + 1$ from $3x^2 - x - 5$, we have

$$(3x^2 - x - 5) - (x^2 - 3x + 1)$$
$$= 3x^2 - x - 5 - x^2 + 3x - 1$$
$$= 2x^2 + 2x - 6$$

WARNING

Don't write

$$(x + 5) - (x + 2) = x + 5 - x + 2 = 7$$

The coefficient -1 in front of $(x + 2)$ is understood (but not written) and must be multiplied by each term in the parentheses:

$$(x + 5) - (x + 2) = x + 5 - x - 2 = 3$$

EXAMPLE 2   SIMPLIFYING EXPRESSIONS WITH POLYNOMIALS

Simplify.

(a) $3(x^2 - 2xy + \frac{1}{3}y^2) - 2(2y^2 + x^2 - \frac{1}{2}xy)$ (b) $2x(x - 5) + 4(x - 3)$

SOLUTIONS

(a) $3(x^2 - 2xy + \frac{1}{3}y^2) - 2(2y^2 + x^2 - \frac{1}{2}xy)$

$= 3x^2 - 6xy + y^2 - 4y^2 - 2x^2 + xy$

$= 3x^2 - 2x^2 - 6xy + xy + y^2 - 4y^2$

$= x^2 - 5xy - 3y^2$

(b) $2x(x - 5) + 4(x - 3)$

$= 2x^2 - 10x + 4x - 12$

$= 2x^2 - 6x - 12$

✔ **Progress Check 2**

Simplify.

(a) $6(r^2 + 2rs - 1) - 4(-rs - 2 + 2r^2)$

(b) $4\left(\frac{1}{2}x^2 + \frac{1}{4}x + 1\right) + 5\left(2x^2 - \frac{2}{5}x - 1\right)$

Answers

(a) $-2r^2 + 16rs + 2$ (b) $12x^2 - x - 1$

Exercise Set 4.2

In Exercises 1–11 add the given polynomials.

1. $5x; 2x$
2. $5y; -3y$
3. $3x^3; -6x^2$
4. $-3x^2; -5x^2$
5. $x^2 - 3x + 1; 3x^2 + 2x + 3$
6. $2x^2 + \frac{5}{2}x + 2; -3x^2 - \frac{5}{3}x + 7$
7. $2x^3 + 2x^2 - x + 1; -2x^3 + 5x^2 + x + 2$
8. $3xy; 4xy$
9. $2rs; -5rs$
10. $2x^2y^2 - xy + 2x + 3y + 3; x^2y^2 + 3xy + 2x + 7$
11. $\frac{2}{5}rs^3 + 4r^2s^2 + 2r^2 + 2; \frac{4}{5}rs^3 - 6r^2s^2 - r^2s + 5$

In Exercises 12–15 find the mistake(s) in each statement. Obtain the correct answer.

12. $(x + 3) - (x + 5) = 8$
13. $(x^2 + 2x + 4) - 2(x^2 + 3x - 5) = -x^2 + 5x - 1$
14. $(x^2y^2 + 2x^2 + y) - (3x^2y^2 + x^2 - y + 2) =$
    $-x^2y^2 + x^2 - 2$

15. $(y^2 + xy + y) - 2(x^2 + xy - 3y)$
    $= y^2 - 2x^2 - xy - 2y$

In Exercises 16–25 subtract the second polynomial from the first.

16. $8x; 3x$
17. $18y; -6y$
18. $3x^2; 4x^2$
19. $3x^2 + 2x - 5; -3x^2 + 2x - 2$
20. $\frac{3}{2}x^3 + 2x^2 + 5; \frac{5}{2}x^3 - x^2 - \frac{1}{2}x + 3$
21. $3x^2y^2 + 2xy - y; 2x^2y^2 - xy + x + 2y + 3$
22. $4x^2 + 2x - 5; 3x^2 - 3x + 5$
23. $\frac{5}{2}x^3 - 2x^2 + x - 2; \frac{3}{5}x^3 + x^2 - 4$
24. $2xy^2 + xy + x - 3; 2x^2y - xy^2 + y + x - 2$
25. $3rs^3 - 2rs^2 + rs + 3; -2rs^2 + 3rs - r + s$

In Exercises 26–35 simplify by combining like terms.

26. $(4x^2 + 3x + 2) + (3x^2 - 2x - 5)$

27. $5x^2 + 2x + 7 - 3x^2 - 8x + 2$

28. $(2x^2 + 3x + 8) - (5 - 2x + 2x^2)$

29. $3xy + 2x + 3y + 2 + (1 - y - 2x + xy)$

30. $4xy^2 + 2xy + 2x + 3 - (-2xy^2 + xy - y + 2)$

31. $(3r^2s^2 + rs^2 - rs + r) + (2r^2s^2 - r^2s + s + 1)$

32. $3a^2b - ba^2 + 2a - b + 2a^2b - 3ba^2 + b + 1$

33. $(2s^2t^3 - st^2 + st - s + t) - (3s^2t^2 - 2s^2t - 4st^2 - t + 3)$

34. $3xy^2z - 4x^2yz + xy + 3 - (2xy^2z + x^2yz - yz + x - 2)$

35. $a^2bc + ab^2c + 2ab^3 - 3a^2bc - 4ab^3 + 3$

36. On Monday morning an investor buys x shares of Honeywell stock at \$60 per share and y shares of Sears stock at \$50 per share. On Monday afternoon the same investor buys x shares of GE stock at \$55 per share and y shares of Bethlehem Steel stock at \$20 per share. Write polynomials to answer the following questions:

    (a) How much money was invested during the morning transactions?

    (b) How much money was invested during the afternoon transactions?

    (c) How much money was invested by the end of Monday?

37. At Thursday's opening of the stock market, an investor buys x shares of IBM stock at \$110 per share. Later in the day, he sells y shares of Kindercare stock at \$13 per share and z shares of Lotus stock at \$17 per share. Write a polynomial that expresses the net of his transactions for the day.

38. To obtain a mat for a painting, an artist takes a rectangular piece of cardboard with sides x and y and cuts out a square of side $x/2$ (see Figure 4). Write a polynomial giving the area of the mat; that is, what is the area of the remaining figure?

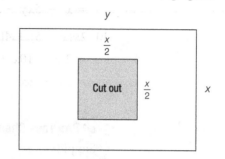

Figure 4   **Diagram for Exercise 38**

*39. The polynomial, all of whose coefficients are zero, is called the **zero polynomial** and is denoted by O. By use of an example, show that if P is a polynomial of degree n, then

$$P + O = O + P = P$$

*40. Let P be a polynomial and let $-P$ be the polynomial obtained from P by negating the sign of the coefficient of each term in P. By use of an example, show that

$$P + (-P) = O$$

where O is the zero polynomial (see Exercise 39).

4.3   Multiplication of Polynomials

We have already dealt with multiplication of some simple polynomial forms such as

$$3x^2 \cdot x^4 = 3x^6$$

and

$$2x(x + 4) = 2x^2 + 8x$$

By using the rule for exponents

$$a^m \cdot a^n = a^{m+n}$$

and the distributive properties

$$a(b + c) = ab + ac$$
$$(a + b)c = ac + bc$$

we can handle the product of any two polynomials.

EXAMPLE 1   MULTIPLYING POLYNOMIALS

Multiply.

(a) $3x^3(2x^3 - 6x^2 + 5)$ (b) $-x^2y(x^3 - 4xy^2 + 6y^3)$

SOLUTIONS

(a) $3x^3(2x^3 - 6x^2 + 5)$

$= (3x^3)(2x^3) + (3x^3)(-6x^2) + (3x^3)(5)$

$= (3 \cdot 2)x^{3+3} + 3(-6)x^{3+2} + 3 \cdot 5x^3$

$= 6x^6 - 18x^5 + 15x^3$

(b) $-x^2y(x^3 - 4xy^2 + 6y^3)$

$= (-x^2y)(x^3) + (-x^2y)(-4xy^2) + (-x^2y)(6y^3)$

$= -x^5y + 4x^3y^3 - 6x^2y^4$

✔ **Progress Check 1**

Multiply.

(a) $2x^2\left(\dfrac{1}{2}x^2 - 3x - 4\right)$ (b) $-xy(x^2 - 2x^2y - 3xy^2)$

Answers

(a) $x^4 - 6x^3 - 8x^2$ (b) $-x^3y + 2x^3y^2 + 3x^2y^3$

Let's try to find the product.

$$(x + 2)(3x^2 - x + 5)$$

The key here is to "rename" terms and groups of terms to fit into the alternate form of the distributive property $(a + b)c = ac + bc$. Here is how we can do it.

$$(x + 2)\underbrace{(3x^2 - x + 5)}_{} = x\underbrace{(3x^2 - x + 5)}_{} + 2\underbrace{(3x^2 - x + 5)}_{}$$

$$\underset{(a+b)}{} \quad \underset{c}{} \qquad = \qquad \underset{ac}{} \quad + \quad \underset{bc}{}$$

$$= 3x^3 - x^2 + 5x + 6x^2 - 2x + 10$$

$$= 3x^3 + 5x^2 + 3x + 10$$

In general, we can multiply two polynomials by multiplying one polynomial by each term of the other polynomial and adding the resulting products.

EXAMPLE 2   MULTIPLYING POLYNOMIALS

Multiply.

(a) $(3x - 2)(x + 4)$ (b) $(2x - 3)(-4x^2 + x + 5)$

SOLUTIONS

(a) $(3x - 2)(x + 4)$
$$= 3x(x + 4) - 2(x + 4)$$
$$= 3x^2 + 12x - 2x - 8$$
$$= 3x^2 + 10x - 8$$

(b) $(2x - 3)(-4x^2 + x + 5)$
$$= 2x(-4x^2 + x + 5) - 3(-4x^2 + x + 5)$$
$$= -8x^3 + 2x^2 + 10x + 12x^2 - 3x - 15$$
$$= -8x^3 + 2x^2 + 12x^2 + 10x - 3x - 15$$
$$= -8x^3 + 14x^2 + 7x - 15$$

✔ **Progress Check 2**
Multiply.

(a) $(3x - 1)(x - 3)$ (b) $(x^2 + 2)(x^2 - 3x + 1)$

Answers

(a) $3x^2 - 10x + 3$ (b) $x^4 - 3x^3 + 3x^2 - 6x + 2$

Long Form

The work done in multiplying polynomials can be arranged in a "long multiplication" format. Here is an example.

EXAMPLE 3   "LONG MULTIPLICATION" FORM
Find the product of $2x - 3$ and $-4x^2 + x + 5$.

SOLUTION
We arrange the work as follows:

$$
\begin{array}{r}
-4x^2 + x + 5 \\
2x - 3 \\
\hline
-8x^3 + 2x^2 + 10x \quad = 2x(-4x^2 + x + 5) \\
12x^2 - 3x - 15 \quad = -3(-4x^2 + x + 5) \\
\hline
-8x^3 + 14x^2 + 7x - 15
\end{array}
$$

✔ **Progress Check 3**
Repeat Progress Check 2(b) using long multiplication.

Mental Multiplication

Products of the form $(2x + 3)(5x - 2)$ are so important that we must learn to handle them mentally. Let's work through the following problem:

$$\begin{aligned}
(2x + 3)(5x - 2) &= 2x(5x - 2) + 3(5x - 2) \\
&= (2x)(5x) + 2x(-2) + 3(5x) + 3(-2) \\
&= 10x^2 - 4x + 15\text{x} - 6
\end{aligned}$$

We have stopped just short of the last step because we want to show the relationships between the factors and the products. If we take the product of the first terms of each expression

$$(2x + 3)(5x - 2)$$
$$10x^2$$

we have the term containing x^2. Similarly, taking the product of the last terms of each expression

$$(2x + 3)(5x - 2)$$
$$-6$$

we have the constant term. The term containing x can be found by adding the product of the "inners" and the product of the "outers."

$$(2x + 3)(5x - 2)$$

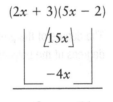

$$15x$$
$$-4x$$
$$\text{Sum} = 11x$$

Thus, $(2x + 3)(5x - 2) = 10x^2 + 11x - 6$.

EXAMPLE 4   MENTAL MULTIPLICATION

Multiply.

(a) $(x - 1)(2x + 3)$ (b) $(2x + 2)(2x - 2)$

SOLUTIONS

(a) We diagram the process so that you can learn to do these mentally.

$$\begin{array}{ccc}
(x - 1)(2x + 3) & (x - 1)(2x + 3) & (x - 1)(2x + 3) \\
2x^2 & -2x & -3 \\
& 3x & \\
& \text{Sum} = +x &
\end{array}$$

Thus, $(x - 1)(2x + 3) = 2x^2 + x - 3$.

(b) Once more, we have

$$(2x + 2)(2x - 2) \quad\quad (2x + 2)(2x - 2) \quad\quad (2x + 2)(2x - 2)$$

$$4x^2 \quad\quad\quad\quad\quad 4x \quad\quad\quad\quad\quad -4$$

$$-4x$$

$$\text{Sum} = + 0x$$

Thus, $(2x + 2)(2x - 2) = 4x^2 - 4$.

✔ **Progress Check 4**

Multiply mentally.

(a) $(x + 2)(x + 1)$ (b) $(t - 2)(2t + 3)$

(c) $(2x - 3)(3x - 2)$ (d) $(3x + 2)(3x - 2)$

Answers

(a) $x^2 + 3x + 2$ (b) $2t^2 - t - 6$ (c) $6x^2 - 13x + 6$ (d) $9x^2 - 4$

In Examples 2 and 3, the product of polynomials of degrees one and two is seen to be a polynomial of degree three. From the multiplication process, it is easy to derive the following useful rule:

Degree of a Product

> The degree of the product of two nonzero polynomials is the sum of the degrees of the polynomials.

Special Forms

Here are three forms that occur frequently and are worthy of special attention.

$$(x + y)^2 = (x + y)(x + y) = x^2 + 2xy + y^2$$
$$(x - y)^2 = (x - y)(x - y) = x^2 - 2xy + y^2$$
$$(x + y)(x - y) = x^2 - y^2$$

EXAMPLE 5   MULTIPLYING WITH SPECIAL FORMS

Multiply mentally.

(a) $(x + 2)^2$ (b) $(x - 3)^2$ (c) $(x + 4)(x - 4)$

SOLUTIONS

(a) $(x + 2)^2 = (x + 2)(x + 2) = x^2 + 4x + 4$

(b) $(x - 3)^2 = (x - 3)(x - 3) = x^2 - 6x + 9$

(c) $(x + 4)(x - 4) = x^2 - 16$

✔ **Progress Check 5**

Multiply mentally.

(a) $(x - 4)^2$ (b) $(x + 1)^2$

(c) $(2x - 3)^2$ (d) $(2x + 3)(2x - 3)$

Answers

(a) $x^2 - 8x + 16$ (b) $x^2 + 2x + 1$

(c) $4x^2 - 12x + 9$ (d) $4x^2 - 9$

Exercise Set 4.3

In Exercises 1–16 perform the indicated multiplication.

1. $(2x^3)(3x^2)$ 2. $(6x^2)(-5x^4)$

3. $(3ab^2)(2ab)$ 4. $(-3s^2t)(4s)$

5. $2x(x^2 + 3x - 5)$ 6. $6x^2(2x^3 - 2x^2 + 5)$

7. $-2s^3(2st^2 - 2st + 6)$ 8. $a^3(-3a^2 - a + 2)$

9. $4a^2b^2(2a^2 + ab - b^2)$ 10. $4y(2y^3 - 3y + 3)$

11. $(x + 2)(x - 3)$ 12. $(x - 1)(x + 4)$

13. $(y + 5)(y + 2)$ 14. $(a - 3)(a - 4)$

15. $(x + 3)^2$ 16. $(y - 2)(y - 2)$

In Exercises 17–30 perform the indicated multiplication mentally.

17. $(s + 3)(s - 3)$ 18. $(t + 6)(t - 6)$

19. $(3x + 2)(x - 1)$ 20. $(2x - 3)(x + 1)$

21. $(a - 2)(2a + 5)$ 22. $(a + 3)(3a - 2)$

23. $(2y + 3)(3y + 2)$ 24. $(3x - 2)(2x + 3)$

25. $(2a + 3)(2a + 3)$ 26. $(3x + 2)(3x + 2)$

27. $(2y + 5)(2y - 5)$ 28. $(4t + 3)(4t - 3)$

29. $(3x - 4)(3x + 4)$ 30. $(5b - 2)(5b + 2)$

In Exercises 31–54 perform the indicated multiplication. Use long multiplication where convenient.

31. $(x^2 + 2)(x^2 + 2)$ 32. $(y^2 - 3)(y^2 - 3)$

33. $(x^2 - 2)(x^2 + 2)$ 34. $(2x^2 - 5)(2x^2 + 5)$

35. $(x + 1)(x^2 + 2x - 3)$ 36. $(x - 2)(2x^3 + x - 2)$

37. $(2s - 3)(s^3 - s + 2)$

38. $(-3s + 2)(-2s^2 - s + 3)$

39. $(a + 2)(3a^2 - a + 5)$

40. $(b + 3)(-3b^2 + 2b + 4)$

41. $(x^2 + 3)(2x^2 - x + 2)$

42. $(2y^2 + y)(-2y^3 + y - 3)$

43. $(x^2 + 2x - 1)(2x^2 - 3x + 2)$

44. $(a^2 - 4a + 3)(4a^3 + 2a + 5)$

45. $(3x^2 - 2x + 2)(2x^3 - 4x + 2)$

46. $(-3y^3 + 3y - 4)(2y^2 - 2y + 3)$

47. $(2a^2 + ab + b^2)(3a - b^2 + 1)$

48. $(-3a + ab + b^2)(3b^2 + 2b + 2)$

49. $5(2x - 3)^2$ 50. $2(3x - 2)(2x + 3)$

51. $x(2x - 1)(x + 2)$ 52. $3x(2x + 1)^2$

53. $(x - 1)(x + 2)(x + 3)$

54. $(3x + 1)(2x - 4)(3x + 2)$

55. In the product $(x - 1)(x^2 - 2x + 3)$ give the coefficient of

   (a) x^2 (b) x

56. In the product $(3x - 2)(2x^2 + 3x - 4)$ give the coefficient of

   (a) x^2 (b) x

57. In the product $(x^2 - 2x + 1)^2$ give the coefficient of

   (a) x^4 (b) x^2

58. In the product $(x^2 - 2x + 3)(x^2 - 3x - 5)$ give the coefficient of

   (a) x^3 (b) x^2

In Exercises 59–66 simplify the expression.

59. $3x(yx^2 + xy) + xy(x^2 - x)$

60. $(x - y)(x + y) - x(x + y)$

61. $(x - 1)(x + 3) - x^2$

62. $(2x - 1)(3x + 2) - (x - 2)(x + 3)$

63. $2x(x - 3) - 4(x^2 - 4)$

64. $x(-x - 3) + (-x + 4)^2$

65. $(x + 4)(x - 4) - (x - 2)^2$

66. $(x - 2)^2 - x(x - 1)$

67. When a polynomial of degree 3 is multiplied by a polynomial of degree 4, the degree of the product is

    (a) 12   (b) 1   (c) 7   (d) $\dfrac{4}{3}$

68. When a polynomial of degree 6 is multiplied by a polynomial of degree 3, the degree of the product is

    (a) 18   (b) 3   (c) 2   (d) 9
    (e) none of these

In Exercises 69–74 simplify the expression.

69. $(1.25x - 3.67)^2$ 70. $(-3.74 + 7.39y)^2$

71. $(5.74y^2 - 2.82)(3.96y^2 + 1.15)$

72. $2.62x(4.78x - 16.42)(3.76x + 4.91)$

73. $(x - 0.04)(3.25x - 2.00)(6.67x + 3.48)$

74. $(6.94 - 10.01x^2)(4.72 + 9.97x^2)$

*75. If P and Q are nonzero polynomials, can their product be the zero polynomial?

In Exercises 76–78 give a counterexample that disproves each statement.

*76. $(a + b)^2 = a^2 + b^2$

*77. $(a + b)(a^2 + b^2) = a^3 + b^3$

*78. $(a + b)(a^2 + b^2) = (a + b)^3$

79. Construct a polynomial expression to model the situation described in the chapter opener. A square piece of cardboard measuring 60 inches on each side is made into a rectangular box by cutting identical squares from the four corners, then folding up the flaps. Let x represent the length of the side of each discarded square. Write an expression for the length, width, and height of the open-top box. Now multiply these binomials together to get a cubic polynomial in standard form. This polynomial represents the volume of the box.

80. Evaluate the polynomial you found in Exercise 79, using your graphing calculator, by selecting various values of x and storing them, as you did in Exercise 60 in section 4.1. For what value of x does the volume seem to be largest? Would a package designed this way satisfy the postal requirements discussed in the chapter opener?

4.4   Factoring

Now that we can find the product of two polynomials, let's consider the reverse problem: Given a polynomial, can we find factors whose product will yield the given polynomial? This process is known as **factoring**. We will approach factoring by learning to recognize the situations in which factoring is possible.

Common Factors

Look at the polynomial

$$x^2 + x$$

Is there some factor common to *both* terms? Yes—each term contains the variable x. If we remove x and write

$$x^2 + x = x(\quad + \quad)$$

we can see that we must have

$$x^2 + x = x(x + 1)$$

EXAMPLE 1   REMOVING COMMON FACTORS

Factor.

(a) $15x^3 - 10x^2$ 　　　　(b) $4x^2y - 8xy^2 + 6xy$

SOLUTIONS

(a) Both 5 and x^2 are common to *both* terms.

$$15x^3 - 10x^2 = 5x^2(3x - 2)$$

(b) Here, we see that 2, x, and y are common to all three terms.

$$4x^2y - 8xy^2 + 6xy = 2xy(2x - 4y + 3)$$

✔ **Progress Check 1**

Factor.

(a) $4x^2 - x$ 　　　　(b) $3x^4 - 9x^2$

Answers

(a) $x(4x - 1)$ 　　　　(b) $3x^2(x^2 - 3)$

EXAMPLE 2   REMOVING COMMON FACTORS

Factor.

(a) $2ab - 8bc$ 　　　　(b) $2x(x + y) - 5y(x + y)$

SOLUTIONS

(a) We see that both 2 and b are found in each term. Don't be misled by the position of b to the right of the first term and to the left in the second term. Remember, multiplication is commutative!

$$2ab - 8bc = 2b(a - 4c)$$

(b) Here, $(x + y)$ is found in both terms. Factoring, we have

$$2x\underbrace{(x + y)} - 5y\underbrace{(x + y)} = (x + y)(2x - 5y)$$

common factor

✔ **Progress Check 2**

Factor.

(a) $3r^2t - 15t^2u + 6st^3$ 　　　　(b) $3m(2x - 3y) - n(2x - 3y)$

Answers

(a) $3t(r^2 - 5tu + 2st^2)$ 　　　　(b) $(2x - 3y)(3m - n)$

Factoring by Grouping

It is sometimes possible to discover common factors by first grouping terms. The best way to learn the method is by studying some examples.

EXAMPLE 3   FACTORING BY GROUPING

Factor.

(a) $2ab + b + 2ac + c$ (b) $2x - 4x^2y - 3y + 6xy^2$

SOLUTIONS

(a) Begin by grouping those terms containing b and those terms containing c.

$$2ab + b + 2ac + c = (2ab + b) + (2ac + c) \quad \text{Grouping}$$
$$= b(2a + 1) + c(2a + 1) \quad \text{Factoring out } b \text{ and } c$$
$$= (2a + 1)(b + c) \quad \text{Factoring out } 2a + 1$$

(b) $2x - 4x^2y - 3y + 6xy^2$
$$= (2x - 4x^2y) + (-3y + 6xy^2) \quad \text{Grouping}$$
$$= 2x(1 - 2xy) + (-3y)(1 - 2xy) \quad \text{Factoring out } 2x \text{ and } -3y$$
$$= (1 - 2xy)(2x - 3y) \quad \text{Factoring out } 1 - 2xy$$

✔ Progress Check 3

Factor.

(a) $2m^3n + m^2 + 2mn^2 + n$ (b) $2a^2 - 4ab^2 - ab + 2b^3$

Answers

(a) $(2mn + 1)(m^2 + n)$ (b) $(a - 2b^2)(2a - b)$

Factoring Second-Degree Polynomials

Another type of factoring involves second-degree polynomials. We now know that

$$(x + 2)(x + 3) = x^2 + 5x + 6$$

and can do the multiplication mentally. We will need these mental gymnastics to allow us to reverse the process.

Let's look at

$$x^2 + 5x + 6$$

and think of this in the form

$$x^2 + 5x + 6 = (\quad)(\quad)$$

If we restrict ourselves to positive integer coefficients, then the term x^2 can only have come from $x \cdot x$, so we can write

$$x^2 + 5x + 6 = (x \quad)(x \quad)$$

The constant 6 can be the product of either two positive numbers or two negative numbers. (If we choose one positive factor and one negative factor, we can't produce a positive product.) However the middle term is positive and results from adding two terms. Then the signs must both be positive.

$$x^2 + 5x + 6 = (x + \quad)(x + \quad)$$

Finally, the number 6 can be written as the product of two positive integers in just two ways:

$$1 \cdot 6 \quad \text{or} \quad 2 \cdot 3$$

The factors of 6 whose sum is 5 are 2 and 3, so that

$$x^2 + 5x + 6 = (x + 2)(x + 3)$$

EXAMPLE 4   FACTORING A SECOND-DEGREE POLYNOMIAL

Factor.

(a) $x^2 - 7x + 10$ (b) $x^2 - 3x - 4$

SOLUTIONS

(a) Since the constant term is positive and the middle term is negative, we must have

$$x^2 - 7x + 10 = (x - \quad)(x - \quad)$$

The possible positive integer factors of 10 are

$$1 \cdot 10 \quad \text{and} \quad 2 \cdot 5$$

The factors of 10 whose sum is 7 are 2 and 5, so that

$$x^2 - 7x + 10 = (x - 2)(x - 5)$$

(b) Since the constant term is negative, we must have

$$x^2 - 3x - 4 = (x + \quad)(x - \quad)$$

The positive integer factors of 4 are

$$1 \cdot 4 \quad \text{and} \quad 2 \cdot 2$$

The factors of 4 whose difference is 3 are 1 and 4. Associating 4 with the negative sign, we have

$$x^2 - 3x - 4 = (x + 1)(x - 4)$$

✔ Progress Check 4

Factor.

(a) $x^2 - 11x + 24$ (b) $x^2 + 6x + 9$ (c) $x^2 - 2x - 8$

Answers

(a) $(x - 3)(x - 8)$ (b) $(x + 3)(x + 3)$ (c) $(x + 2)(x - 4)$

Irreducible Polynomial

Before you get the impression that every second-degree polynomial with integer coefficients can be factored as a product of polynomials of lower degree with integer coefficients, try your hand at factoring

$$x^2 + x + 1$$

There are no polynomials with integer coefficients that allow us to factor $x^2 + x + 1$. Such polynomials are said to be **irreducible** over the integers.

Leading Coefficient Other Than One

Now we will try something a bit more difficult, for example,

$$2x^2 - x - 6$$

When the coefficient of x^2 is a number other than 1, we can use the same approach but the number of possible combinations increases.

First, we see that $2x^2$ can only result from the factors $2x$ and x if we restrict ourselves to positive integer coefficients. Thus, we write

$$2x^2 - x - 6 = (2x \quad)(x \quad)$$

Since the constant term is negative, we must have

$$2x^2 - x - 6 = (2x + \quad)(x - \quad)$$

or

$$2x^2 - x - 6 = (2x - \quad)(x + \quad)$$

The possible positive integer factors of 6 are

$$1 \cdot 6 \quad \text{and} \quad 2 \cdot 3$$

We need factors of 6 such that the difference between one factor and two times the other factor is -1. We thus find that the correct factorization is

$$2x^2 - x - 6 = (2x + 3)(x - 2)$$

EXAMPLE 5   FACTORING A SECOND-DEGREE POLYNOMIAL

Factor.

(a) $3x^2 + 7x + 4$ (b) $6x^2 + 5x - 4$

SOLUTIONS

(a) We start with

$$3x^2 + 7x + 4 = (3x + \quad)(x + \quad) \quad \text{(Why?)}$$

The possible positive integer factors of 4 are

$$1 \cdot 4, \quad 4 \cdot 1, \quad 2 \cdot 2$$

We need factors of 4 such that one factor plus three times the other is 7. Thus,

$$3x^2 + 7x + 4 = (3x + 4)(x + 1)$$

(b) The coefficient of x^2 is 6, and the only positive integer factors of 6 are

$$1 \cdot 6 \quad \text{and} \quad 2 \cdot 3$$

The factorization (if it exists) must look like one of the following:

$$6x^2 + 5x - 4 = (x - \quad)(6x + \quad)$$
$$6x^2 + 5x - 4 = (x + \quad)(6x - \quad)$$
$$6x^2 + 5x - 4 = (2x - \quad)(3x + \quad)$$
$$6x^2 + 5x - 4 = (2x + \quad)(3x - \quad)$$

We next turn to the positive integer factors of 4. The possible factors are

$$1 \cdot 4 \quad \text{and} \quad 2 \cdot 2$$

By trial and error, we see that the choice that produces $+5$ for the middle term is

$$6x^2 + 5x - 4 = (2x - 1)(3x + 4)$$

✔ Progress Check 5

Factor.

(a) $3x^2 - 16x + 21$ (b) $2x^2 + 3x - 9$ (c) $4x^2 + 12x + 5$

Answers

(a) $(3x - 7)(x - 3)$ (b) $(2x - 3)(x + 3)$ (c) $(2x + 1)(2x + 5)$

No-Fuss Factoring

If you found the trial and error approach used in Example 5 to be a bit tedious, we can offer you an alternative factoring method to use when the coefficient of x^2 is a number other than 1. The steps are outlined as follows:

Factoring $ax^2 + bx + c$	Example: $6x^2 + 5x - 6$
Step 1. Find two integers whose product is $a \cdot c$ and whose sum is b.	*Step 1.* $a \cdot c = (6)(-6) = -36$. Two integers whose product is -36 and sum is 5 are 9 and -4.
Step 2. Write the middle term bx in terms of these integers.	*Step 2.* $5x = 9x - 4x$ and $6x^2 + 5x - 6 = 6x^2 + (9x - 4x) - 6$
Step 3. Group.	*Step 3.* $\qquad = (6x^2 + 9x) - (4x + 6)$
Step 4. Remove the common factors in each group.	*Step 4.* $\qquad = 3x(2x + 3) - 2(2x + 3)$
Step 5. Factor out the common linear term.	*Step 5.* $\qquad = (2x + 3)(3x - 2)$

EXAMPLE 6   FACTORING BY THE NO-FUSS METHOD

Factor $4x^2 + 11x + 6$ by the No-Fuss Method.

SOLUTION

The product of the coefficients of the first and last terms is

$$(4)(6) = 24$$

Two integers whose product is 24 and whose sum is 11 (the coefficient of the first-degree term) are 3 and 8, that is,

$$11x = 3x + 8x$$

Then

$$4x^2 + 11x + 6 = 4x^2 + 3x + 8x + 6$$
$$= (4x^2 + 3x) + (8x + 6)$$
$$= x(4x + 3) + 2(4x + 3)$$
$$= (4x + 3)(x + 2)$$

✔ Progress Check 6

Factor $6x^2 + x - 2$ by the No-Fuss Method.

Answer

$(2x - 1)(3x + 2)$

Combining Methods

We conclude with problems that combine the various methods of factoring that we have studied. Here is a good rule to follow:

> Always remove common factors before attempting any other factoring techniques.

EXAMPLE 7   COMBINING METHODS OF FACTORING

Factor.

(a) $x^3 - 6x^2 + 8x$

(b) $2x^3 + 4x^2 - 30x$

(c) $3y(y + 3) + 2(y + 3)(y^2 - 1)$

SOLUTIONS

(a) Following our rule, we first remove the common factor x.

$$x^3 - 6x^2 + 8x = x(x^2 - 6x + 8)$$
$$= x(x - 2)(x - 4)$$

(b) Removing $2x$ as a common factor, we have

$$2x^3 + 4x^2 - 30x = 2x(x^2 + 2x - 15)$$
$$= 2x(x - 3)(x + 5)$$

(c) Removing the common factor $y + 3$, we have

$$3y(y + 3) + 2(y + 3)(y^2 - 1) = (y + 3)[3y + 2(y^2 - 1)]$$
$$= (y + 3)(3y + 2y^2 - 2)$$
$$= (y + 3)(2y^2 + 3y - 2)$$
$$= (y + 3)(2y - 1)(y + 2)$$

common factor

✔ **Progress Check 7**

Factor.

(a) $x^3 + 5x^2 - 6x$ (b) $2x^3 - 2x^2y - 4xy^2$

(c) $-3x(x + 1) + (x + 1)(2x^2 + 1)$

Answers

(a) $x(x + 6)(x - 1)$ (b) $2x(x + y)(x - 2y)$

(c) $(x + 1)(2x - 1)(x - 1)$

Exercise Set 4.4

In Exercises 1–20 factor by removing common factors.

1. $2x + 6$
2. $5x - 15$
3. $3x - 9y$
4. $\frac{1}{2}x + \frac{1}{4}y$
5. $-2x - 8y$
6. $3x + 6y + 15$
7. $4x^2 + 8y - 6$
8. $3a + 4ab$
9. $5bc + 25b$
10. $2x^2 - x$
11. $y - 3y^3$
12. $2x^4 + x^2$
13. $-3y^2 - 4y^5$
14. $-\frac{1}{2}y^2 + \frac{1}{8}y^3$
15. $3abc + 12bc$
16. $3x^2 + 6x^2y - 9x^2z$
17. $5r^3s^4 - 40r^4s^3t$
18. $9a^3b^3 + 12a^2b - 15ab^2$
19. $8a^3b^5 - 12a^5b^2 + 16$
20. $7x^2y^3z^4 - 21x^4yz^5 + 49x^5y^2z^3$

In Exercises 21–58 factor each second degree polynomial.

21. $x^2 + 4x + 3$
22. $x^2 + 2x - 8$
23. $y^2 - 8y + 15$
24. $y^2 + 7y - 8$
25. $a^2 - 7ab + 12b^2$
26. $x^2 - 14x + 49$
27. $y^2 + 6y + 9$
28. $a^2 - 7a + 10$
29. $25 - 10x + x^2$
30. $4b^2 - a^2$
31. $x^2 - 5x - 14$
32. $x^2 - \frac{1}{9}$
33. $4 - y^2$
34. $a^2 + ab - 6b^2$
35. $x^2 - 6x + 9$
36. $a^2 - 4ab + 4b^2$
37. $x^2 - 12x + 20$
38. $x^2 - 8x - 20$
39. $x^2 + 11x + 24$
40. $y^2 + 4y + 3$
41. $2x^2 - 3x - 2$
42. $2x^2 + 7x + 6$
43. $3a^2 - 11a + 6$
44. $4x^2 - 9x + 2$

45. $6x^2 + 13x + 6$

46. $4y^2 + 4y - 3$

47. $8m^2 - 6m - 9$

48. $9x^2 + 24x + 16$

49. $10x^2 - 13x - 3$

50. $6a^2 + ab - 2b^2$

51. $6a^2 - 5ab - 6b^2$

52. $4x^2 + 20x + 25$

53. $10r^2s^2 + 9rst + 2t^2$

54. $16 - 24xy + 9x^2y^2$

55. $6 + 5x - 4x^2$

56. $8n^2 - 18n - 5$

57. $25r^2 + 4s^2$

58. $15 + 4x - 4x^2$

In Exercises 59–86 factor by using a combination of methods.

59. $2x^2 - 2x - 12$

60. $3y^2 + 6y - 45$

61. $30x^2 + 28x - 16$

62. $30x^2 - 35x + 10$

63. $12x^2b^2 + 2xb^2 - 24b^2$

64. $x^4y^4 + x^2$

65. $18x^2m + 33xm + 9m$

66. $8x^3 + 14x^2 - 15x$

67. $25m^2n^3 - 5m^2n$

68. $12x^2 - 22x^3 - 20x^4$

69. $xy + \frac{1}{4}x^3y^3$

70. $10r^2 - 5rs - 15s^2$

71. $x^4 + 2x^2y^2 + y^4$

72. $a^4 - 8a^2 + 16$

73. $b^4 + 2b^2 - 8$

74. $4b^4 + 20b^2 + 25$

75. $6b^4 + 7b^2 - 3$

76. $4(x + 1)(y + 2) - 8(y + 2)$

77. $2(x + 1)(x - 1) + 5(x - 1)$

78. $3(x + 2)^2(x - 1) - 4(x + 2)^2(2x + 7)$

79. $3xy - 6x + 3y - 6$

80. $2ac - bc + 2a - b$

81. $2x^3y - 3x^2 - 2xy^2 + 3y$

82. $4a^2 - 4b^2 - 3a^3b + 3ab^3$

83. $4(2x - 1)^2(x + 2)^3(x + 1) - 3(2x - 1)^5(x + 2)^2$ $(x + 3)$

84. $5(x - 1)^2(y - 1)^3(x + 2) - (3x - 1)(x - 1)^3(y - 1)$

85. $(7 - 2x)^3(2)(5x)(5) + (5x)^2(3)(7 - 2x)^2(-2)$

86. $3(4x)^2(4)(7x - 2)^2 + (4x)^3(2)(7x - 2)(6)$

*87. Show that the polynomial $x^2 + 1$ cannot be written as the product $(x + r)(x + s)$, where r and s are integers.

*88. Show that the polynomial $x^2 + x + 1$ cannot be written as the product $(x + r)(x + s)$, where r and s are integers.

In Exercises 89–92 factor the given polynomial by the "no-fuss" factoring method.

*89. $2x^2 + 5x - 12$

*90. $4x^2 - 2x - 2$

*91. $6x^2 - 7x - 3$

*92. $6x^2 + 5x - 6$

93. Using your graphing calculator, you can check whether a polynomial has been factored correctly. Consider the following possible factorings:

(a) $x^5 + x^4 + 5x^3 - x^2 + 2x - 8 =$ $(x^2 + x - 2)(x^3 + 3x + 4)$

(b) $x^5 + x^4 + 5x^3 - x^2 + 2x - 8 =$ $(x^2 + x + 2)(x^3 + 3x - 4)$

Both equations are valid for $x = 1$. What about $x = 7.523$? Try several values of x and determine which of the two is correct.

4.5 Special Factors

There is a special case of the second-degree polynomial that occurs frequently and factors easily. Given the polynomial $x^2 - 9$, we see that each term is a perfect square. You may easily verify that

$$x^2 - 9 = (x + 3)(x - 3)$$

In general, the following rule is one that works whenever we are dealing with a difference of two squares.

Difference of Two Squares

$$a^2 - b^2 = (a + b)(a - b)$$

EXAMPLE 1   FACTORING A DIFFERENCE OF TWO SQUARES

Factor.

(a) $x^2 - 16$ (b) $4x^2 - 25$ (c) $9x^2 - 16y^2$

SOLUTIONS

(a) $x^2 - 16 = (x + 4)(x - 4)$

(b) With $a = 2x$ and $b = 5$,
$$4x^2 - 25 = (2x + 5)(2x - 5)$$

(c) With $a = 3x$ and $b = 4y$,
$$9x^2 - 16y^2 = (3x + 4y)(3x - 4y)$$

✔ Progress Check 1

Factor.

(a) $x^2 - 49$ (b) $16x^2 - 9$ (c) $25x^2 - y^2$

Answers

(a) $(x + 7)(x - 7)$ (b) $(4x + 3)(4x - 3)$ (c) $(5x + y)(5x - y)$

 WARNING

Don't confuse a *difference* of two squares, such as $4x^2 - 9$, and a *sum* of two squares, such as $x^2 + 25$. In the case of a difference of two squares,

$$4x^2 - 9 = (2x + 3)(2x - 3)$$

However, a sum of two squares such as $x^2 + 25$ cannot be factored.

The formulas for a sum of two cubes and a difference of two cubes can be verified by multiplying the factors on the right-hand sides of the following equations.

Sum and Difference of Two Cubes

$$a^3 + b^3 = (a + b)(a^2 - ab + b^2)$$

$$a^3 - b^3 = (a - b)(a^2 + ab + b^2)$$

These formulas provide a direct means for factoring a sum and a difference of two cubes and are used in the same way as the formula for a difference of two squares. Be careful as to the placement of plus and minus signs when using these formulas.

Greek Algebra

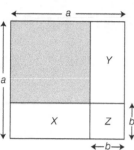

The Greek mathematicians of antiquity viewed algebra from a geometric perspective. They had no need for negative numbers since measurements of distance are positive values. From earliest times they recognized the need for (positive) rational numbers and believed that this number system was adequate for all their needs. When they discovered that the hypotenuse of a right triangle whose sides are 1 unit in length is *not* a rational number, they were forced to extend their concept of numbers to the (positive) real numbers. Modern mathematicians have introduced more sophisticated number systems for similar reasons: the need to represent solutions to problems.

An example of "Greek algebra" is illustrated in the accompanying figure. The Greeks used a geometric argument to establish the identity

$$(a - b)^2 = a^2 - 2ab + b^2 \tag{1}$$

The shaded area is a square whose side is of length $a - b$ and whose area is $(a - b)^2$. The area of the entire region is obviously a^2, the area of the regions labeled X and Y are both ab, and the area of the small square Z is b^2. From the figure,

area of shaded region = (area of entire region) − (area of region X)
− (area of region Y) − (area of region Z)

On substitution, we obtain the identity in (1) above.

EXAMPLE 2   FACTORING A SUM OR DIFFERENCE OF TWO CUBES

Factor each of the following.

(a) $x^3 + 1$ (b) $27m^3 - 64n^3$

SOLUTIONS

(a) When $a = x$ and $b = 1$, the formula for a sum of two cubes yields

$$x^3 + 1 = (x + 1)(x^2 - x + 1)$$

(b) Note that $27m^3 - 64n^3 = (3m)^3 - (4n)^3$. We then use the formula for a difference of two cubes with $a = 3m$ and $b = 4n$.

$$27m^3 - 64n^3 = (3m - 4n)(9m^2 + 12mn + 16n^2)$$

> ✔ **Progress Check 2**
> Factor.
>
> (a) $8x^3 + y^3$ (b) $8s^3 - 27t^3$
>
> **Answers**
>
> (a) $(2x + y)(4x^2 - 2xy + y^2)$ (b) $(2s - 3t)(4s^2 + 6st + 9t^2)$

EXAMPLE 3   RECOGNIZING SPECIAL FACTORS

Factor each of the following.

(a) $\dfrac{1}{27}u^3 - 8v^3$ (b) $125x^6 + 8y^3$

SOLUTIONS

(a) Since

$$\frac{1}{27}u^3 - 8v^3 = \left(\frac{u}{3}\right)^3 - (2v)^3$$

we may use the formula for a difference of two cubes with $a = \dfrac{u}{3}$ and $b = 2v$.

$$\frac{1}{27}u^3 - 8v^3 = \left(\frac{u}{3} - 2v\right)\left(\frac{u^2}{9} + \frac{2}{3}uv + 4v^2\right)$$

(b) Rewrite the polynomial as $(5x^2)^3 + (2y)^3$. With $a = 5x^2$ and $b = 2y$, the formula for a sum of two cubes tells us that

$$125x^6 + 8y^3 = (5x^2 + 2y)(25x^4 - 10x^2y + 4y^2)$$

✔ Progress Check 3

Factor each of the following.

(a) $125r^3 + \dfrac{1}{125}s^3$ (b) $27a^6 - 64b^6$

Answers

(a) $\left(5r + \dfrac{s}{5}\right)\left(25r^2 - rs + \dfrac{s^2}{25}\right)$ (b) $(3a^2 - 4b^2)(9a^4 + 12a^2b^2 + 16b^4)$

Exercise Set 4.5

In Exercises 1–10 use the formulas for the sum of two cubes and the difference of two cubes to find the given product.

1. $(2x + y)(4x^2 - 2xy + y^2)$

2. $(x + 3y)(x^2 - 3xy + 9y^2)$

3. $(x - 2y)(x^2 + 2xy + 4y^2)$

4. $(4x - y)(16x^2 + 4xy + y^2)$

5. $(3r + 2s)(9r^2 - 6rs + 4s^2)$

6. $(2a - 3b)(4a^2 + 6ab + 9b^2)$

7. $(2m - 5n)(4m^2 + 10mn + 25n^2)$

8. $(4a + 3b)(16a^2 - 12ab + 9b^2)$

9. $\left(\dfrac{x}{2} - 2y\right)\left(\dfrac{1}{4}x^2 + xy + 4y^2\right)$

10. $\left(3x - \dfrac{y}{3}\right)\left(9x^2 + xy + \dfrac{1}{9}y^2\right)$

In Exercises 11–30 factor the expression.

11. $x^2 - 49$

12. $9 - x^2$

13. $y^2 - \dfrac{1}{9}$

14. $\dfrac{1}{16} - y^2$

15. $4b^2 - a^2$

16. $16r^2 - 25s^2$

17. $x^2y^2 - 9$

18. $a^4 - 16$

19. $x^3 + 27y^3$

20. $8x^3 + 125y^3$

21. $27x^3 - y^3$

22. $64x^3 - 27y^3$

23. $a^3 + 8$

24. $8r^3 - 27$

25. $\frac{1}{8}m^3 - 8n^3$

26. $8a^3 - \frac{1}{64}b^3$

27. $(x + y)^3 - 8$

28. $27 + (x + y)^3$

29. $8x^6 - 125y^6$

30. $a^6 + 27b^6$

In Exercises 31 and 32 factor the expression as a difference of squares and as a difference of cubes. Compare answers.

31. $x^6 - y^6$

32. $64a^6 - \frac{1}{64}b^{12}$

33. Determine whether the following factoring is valid by storing any value of x, then entering the entire equation (refer to your calculator manual to find the equals sign). If the calculator returns a value of "0", the equation is not an identity and the factoring is not valid. If it returns a "1", then the equation is valid for the value of x you chose. Does this mean the factoring is correct? (Refer back to Exercise 93 in Section 4.4!)

$$x^{100} - 81 = (x^{50} + 9)(x^{50} - 9)$$

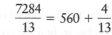

34. Use the method of Exercise 33 to check your answers to other exercises in this section.

4.6   Division of Polynomials

There is a procedure for polynomial division that parallels the long division process of arithmetic. In arithmetic, if we divide an integer p by an integer $d \neq 0$, we obtain a quotient q and a remainder r, so we can write

$$\frac{p}{d} = q + \frac{r}{d} \tag{1}$$

where

$$0 \leqslant r < d \tag{2}$$

This result can also be written in the form

$$p = qd + r, \qquad 0 \leqslant r < d \tag{3}$$

For example,

$$\frac{7284}{13} = 560 + \frac{4}{13}$$

or

$$7284 = (560)(13) + 4$$

In the long division process for polynomials, we divide the dividend $P(x)$ by the divisor $D(x) \neq 0$ to obtain a quotient $Q(x)$ and a remainder $R(x)$. We have

$$\frac{P(x)}{D(x)} = Q(x) + \frac{R(x)}{D(x)} \tag{4}$$

where $R(x) = 0$ or where

$$\text{degree of } R(x) < \text{degree of } D(x) \tag{5}$$

This result can also be written as

$$P(x) = Q(x)D(x) + R(x) \tag{6}$$

Note that Equations (1) and (4) have the same form and that Equation (6) has the same form as Equation (3). Equation (2) requires that the remainder be less than the divisor, and the parallel requirement for polynomials in Equation (5) is that the *degree* of the remainder be less than that of the divisor.

EXAMPLE 1   DIVIDING POLYNOMIALS

Divide $3x^3 - 7x^2 + 1$ by $x - 2$.

SOLUTION

Polynomial Division

Step 1. Arrange the terms of both polynomials by descending powers of x. If a power is missing, write the term with a zero coefficient.

$$x - 2 \overline{)3x^3 - 7x^2 + 0x + 1}$$

Step 2. Divide the first term of the dividend by the first term of the divisor. The answer is written above the first term of the dividend.

$$\begin{array}{r} 3x^2 \\ x - 2 \overline{)3x^3 - 7x^2 + 0x + 1} \end{array}$$

Step 3. Multiply the divisor by the quotient obtained in Step 2, and then subtract the product.

$$\begin{array}{r} 3x^2 \\ x - 2 \overline{)3x^3 - 7x^2 + 0x + 1} \\ \underline{3x^3 - 6x^2 } \\ -\ x^2 + 0x + 1 \end{array}$$

Step 4. Repeat Steps 2 and 3 until the remainder is zero or the degree of the remainder is less than the degree of the divisor.

$$\begin{array}{r} 3x^2 -\ x\ -\ 2 \qquad = Q(x) \\ x - 2 \overline{)3x^3 - 7x^2 + 0x + 1} \\ \underline{3x^3 - 6x^2 } \\ -\ x^2 + 0x + 1 \\ \underline{-\ x^2 + 2x } \\ -\ 2x + 1 \\ \underline{-\ 2x + 4} \\ -3 \qquad = R(x) \end{array}$$

Step 5. Write the answer in the form of Equation (4) or Equation (6).

$$\begin{aligned} P(x) &= 3x^3 - 7x^2 + 1 \\ &= \underbrace{(3x^2 - x - 2)}_{Q(x)} \underbrace{(x - 2)}_{\ \cdot\ \ D(x)} \underbrace{-3}_{+\ R(x)} \end{aligned}$$

✔ Progress Check 1

Divide $\dfrac{3x^3 - 4x - 5}{x - 2}$.

Answer

$3x^2 + 6x + 8 + \dfrac{11}{x - 2}$

EXAMPLE 2   DIVIDING POLYNOMIALS

Divide $x^3 + 1$ by $x + 1$.

SOLUTION

Note that there are terms missing in the dividend. We fill in these terms with zero coefficients and proceed as before.

$$
\begin{array}{r}
x^2 - x + 1 \\
x + 1 \overline{) x^3 + 0x^2 + 0x + 1} \\
\underline{x^3 + x^2} \\
-x^2 + 0x + 1 \\
\underline{-x^2 - x} \\
x + 1 \\
\underline{x + 1} \\
0
\end{array}
$$

$$\frac{x^3 + 1}{x + 1} = x^2 - x + 1$$

We see that it is possible for the remainder to be 0. We then say that $x + 1$ is a factor of $x^3 + 1$.

✔ Progress Check 2

Divide $x^5 - 5x^3 + 3x^2 + 6x - 6$ by $x^2 - 2$.

Answer

$x^3 - 3x + 3$

Exercise Set 4.6

In Exercises 1–38 perform the indicated division. Be sure to write your answers in the form of Equation (4).

1. $\dfrac{10x + 25}{5}$

2. $\dfrac{8x - 4}{-2}$

3. $\dfrac{4 - 12x}{-3}$

4. $\dfrac{14 - 7x}{7}$

5. $\dfrac{12x^2 - 6x + 3}{3}$

6. $\dfrac{15x^3 + 20x^2 - 5}{5}$

7. $\dfrac{12x^2 - 8x}{2x}$

8. $\dfrac{6x - 15x^3}{3x}$

9. $\dfrac{10a^2 - 12a^4}{4a^2}$

10. $\dfrac{27a^4 - 18a^3}{9a^2}$

11. $\dfrac{4x^3 - 12x^2 + 16x}{4x}$

12. $\dfrac{-12y^4 - 18y^3 + 6y^2}{6y^2}$

13. $\dfrac{x^2 - 16}{x + 4}$

14. $\dfrac{y^2 + 2y - 3}{y + 2}$

15. $\dfrac{a^2 - 2a - 8}{a - 2}$

16. $\dfrac{x^2 + 7x + 10}{x + 2}$

17. $\dfrac{x^2 - 7x + 12}{x - 5}$

18. $\dfrac{b^2 - b - 6}{b + 4}$

19. $\dfrac{2x^2 + 5x + 3}{2x + 1}$

20. $\dfrac{6x^2 - x - 2}{2x - 3}$

21. $\dfrac{6a^2 + a - 1}{2a - 1}$

22. $\dfrac{9x^2 + 6x - 8}{3x - 2}$

23. $\dfrac{10x^2 + x - 3}{5x + 1}$

24. $\dfrac{6x^2 + 2x}{3x - 1}$

25. $\dfrac{4s^2 - 9}{2s + 3}$

26. $\dfrac{-6y^2 - 4y + 2}{4 - 2y}$

27. $\dfrac{4s^2 + 9}{2s + 3}$

28. $\dfrac{2x^3 + x^2 - 4x - 1}{x - 2}$

29. $\dfrac{3y^3 + 6y^2 - y - 2}{y + 2}$

30. $\dfrac{x^3 + x^2}{x - 1}$

31. $\dfrac{x^3 - 8}{x + 2}$

32. $\dfrac{x^3 + 8}{x + 2}$

33. $\dfrac{x^3 - x^2 - x + 1}{x + 1}$

34. $\dfrac{y^3 - 4y^2 + y + 6}{y + 3}$

35. $\dfrac{a^3 + 3a^2 - 4a + 2}{4 - a^2}$

36. $\dfrac{a^3 + 3a^2 - 10a - 24}{a^2 - a - b}$

37. $\dfrac{1.27x^3 - 22.42x + 3.05}{x^2 - 2}$

38. $\dfrac{6.49x^3 + 9.47x^2 - 7.84}{x^2 + x - 1}$

39. If a polynomial of degree 6 is divided by a polynomial of degree 2, the degree of the quotient is

(a) 3   (b) 8   (c) 4   (d) 12

(e) none of these

40. If a polynomial of degree 18 is divided by a polynomial of degree 6, the degree of the quotient is

(a) 3   (b) 108   (c) 24   (d) 12

(e) none of these

■ ■ ■

Chapter Summary

Terms and Symbols

base	114	degree of a term	118	like terms	121
coefficient	116	exponent	114	polynomial	116
constant term	118	factoring	130	power	114
degree of a polynomial	118	irreducible polynomial	134	term	116

Key Ideas for Review

Topic	Page	Key Idea
Product rule for exponents	115	$a^m \cdot a^n = a^{m+n}$
Degree of a term	118	The degree of a term is the sum of the exponents of all the variables within the term.
Polynomial	116	A polynomial is a sum of terms of the form $3x^2$, $-5x^2y$, and so on, where the exponent of each variable must be a nonnegative integer.
degree	118	The degree of a polynomial is the degree of the term of highest degree.
addition	121	To add two polynomials, add like terms. To subtract two polynomials, subtract like terms.
multiplication	124	To multiply two polynomials, multiply one polynomial by each term of the other and add the products. $$(a + b)^2 = a^2 + 2ab + b^2$$ $$(a - b)^2 = a^2 - 2ab + b^2$$ $$(a + b)(a - b) = a^2 - b^2$$

continues

Topic	Page	Key Idea
Factoring	130	A polynomial is said to be factored when it is written as a product of two or more polynomials of lower degree.
methods	130	Factoring methods include the removal of common factors and grouping. To find the factors of a second-degree polynomial, you may use trial-and-error and the no-fuss factoring methods.
difference of squares	139	$a^2 - b^2 = (a + b)(a - b)$
sum and difference of cubes	139	$a^3 + b^3 = (a + b)(a^2 - ab + b^2)$ $a^3 - b^3 = (a - b)(a^2 + ab + b^2)$

Common Errors

1. *Don't* write

$$(2x + 3) - (x + 3) = 2x + 3 - x \oplus 3 = x + 6$$

This is probably the most common and persistent error made by algebra students! You must use the distributive law to give

$$(2x + 3) - (x + 3) = 2x + 3 - x \ominus 3 = x$$

2. The notation $a \div b$ is read "a divided by b" and is equivalent to $\frac{a}{b}$, *not* $\frac{b}{a}$.

Review Exercises

Solutions to exercises whose numbers are in bold are in the Solutions section in the back of the book.

4.1 In Exercises 1–4 determine whether the given expression is a polynomial.

1. $-2xy^2 + x^2y$ 2. $3b^2 + 2b - 6$

3. $x^{-1/2} + 5x^2 - x$ 4. $7.5x^2 + 3x - \frac{1}{2}x^0$

In Exercises 5–8 write the terms and the coefficients of the terms.

5. $3x^3 - 4x + 2$ 6. $4x^4 - x^2 + 2x - 3$

7. $-4x^2y^2 + 3x^2y - xy^2 + xy - 1$

8. $2xy^2 - 3xy + x + 3$

In Exercises 9–12 indicate the degree of the polynomial.

9. $-0.5x^7 + 6x^3 - 5$ 10. $2x^2 + 3x^4 - 7x^5$

11. $3x^2 - 2x + 2$ 12. $\frac{1}{2}x^4 - 2x + 3$

In Exercises 13–16 find the value of the given polynomial for the indicated value(s) of x (and y).

13. $3x^4 - 2x^2 + 2x - 1$, $x = -2$

14. $2x^2y^2 - 2xy^2 + x - 2y$, $x = 2, y = -1$

15. $-3x^3y + xy^2 - 2xy + 3$, $x = 1, y = -2$

16. $3x^3 - 2x^2 + x - 3$, $x = 3$

4.2/ In Exercises 17–28 perform the indicated
4.3   operations.

17. $(2x^3 - 3x + 1) + (3x^3 + 2x^2 - 3)$

18. $(3a^2b^3 - 2a^2b + ab - a) - (-2a^3b^3 + ab^2 - 2ab + b)$

19. $(x^2y - xy^2 + x - 1) + (3xy^2 - 2x + y + 3)$

20. $(4x^4 - 2x^3 + x - 3) - (3x^3 - x^2 + 2x - 5)$

21. $(2x + 1)(3x - 2)$ 22. $x(2x - 1)^2$

23. $(3y - 1)(2y + 2)$ 24. $(3y - 1)(2y^2 + 2)$

25. $ab(a - 1)(a + 2)^2$

26. $(a^2 + 2a + 3)(a^2 - a - 1)$

27. $(x - 2)(x + 2)(x^2 - 2x + 3)$

28. $(b + 1)^2(2b - 1)^2$

29. In the product $(x^2 - 1)(x^2 + 3x - 4)$, find the coefficient of x^3.

30. In the product $(x^2 - 2x + 3)(x^3 + 2x^2 - 3x - 1)$, find the coefficient of x^4.

31. In the product $x^2(2x - 3)^2$, find the coefficient of x^3.

32. In the product $(x^2y + x - y)(x^2y - x + y)$, find the coefficient of x^3y.

4.4 In Exercises 33–46 factor completely.

33. $x^3 + x^2 - 2x$

34. $y^4 - y^3 - 6y^2$

35. $x^3 + 2x^2 - 3x$

36. $2x^2 - 5x - 3$

37. $6x^2 - 7x + 2$

38. $16x^2 - y^2$

39. $18x^2 - 24x + 6$

40. $2rs + s - 2r - 1$

41. $9a^4 + 6a^2 + 1$

42. $2x^2 + xy - 2y^2$

43. $y^2 - \dfrac{1}{4}x^2$

44. $3a^2 + 2ab - 2b - 3a$

45. $2ab + ac - 2b - c$ 46. $a^4 - 2a^2 + 1$

4.5 In Exercises 47–52 factor completely.

47. $a^2 - \dfrac{1}{4}b^2$ 48. $x^2y^2 - 9$

49. $8a^3 + 27b^3$ 50. $8x^3 + 125y^3$

51. $8a^3 - 27b^3$ 52. $8x^3 - 125y^3$

4.6 In Exercises 53–60 perform the indicated division. Be sure to write the answer in the form of Equation (4).

53. $\dfrac{16x - 8}{4}$ 54. $\dfrac{6x - 18x^3}{3x}$

55. $\dfrac{4y^5 - 6y^4 + 2y^3}{2y^2}$ 56. $\dfrac{4y^2 - 25}{y + 5}$

57. $\dfrac{x^3 + 27}{x + 3}$ 58. $\dfrac{x^3 - 27}{x + 3}$

59. $\dfrac{y^3 - 3y + 2}{y - 2}$ 60. $\dfrac{a^3 - 3a^2 - 2a + 6}{a^2 + 2}$

Progress Test 4A

1. In $\left(-\dfrac{1}{5}\right)^4$, what is the base? What is the exponent?

2. Find the degree of the polynomial.
$$-3x^5 + 2x^3 + xy^2 - 2$$

3. Find the value of the polynomial
$$3x^2y + 2xy - 3x + 1$$
when $x = -2$, $y = 3$.

4. Find a polynomial giving the volume of a cube of side s.

5. Add the polynomials.
$$2x^3 + 3x^2 + 1 \quad \text{and} \quad -5x^3 + x - 3$$

6. Simplify.
$$x - 3x^2y + 2y + 1 + 3y - 2x + 5x^2y + y - 3$$

7. Find $(2x^3 + x^2 - 2x + 1) - (3x^3 + 4x - 2)$.

8. Subtract $2xy^2 + x^2 - y + 2$ from $3x^2y + 5xy^2 + 3y$.

9. Multiply mentally $(2x - 5y)^2$.

10. Multiply $(x^2 + 2)(3x^2 - 2x + 5)$.

11. Factor $x^2 + 4x - 12$.

12. Factor completely $2x^2y - 8xy + 6y$.

13. Factor $4a^2 - 49$.

14. Factor $3x^2 - 13xy - 10y^2$.

15. Factor $\dfrac{x^3}{125} - 125y^3$.

16. Divide $\dfrac{x^3 + 2x^2 - 2x + 1}{x - 2}$.

17. Divide $2a^4 - 3a^3 - 2a^2 - 3a - 4$ by $a^2 + 1$.

18. If a polynomial of degree 12 is divided by a polynomial of degree 5, what is the degree of the quotient?

Progress Test 4B

1. State the base and exponent in $\left(-\dfrac{2}{3}\right)^5$.

2. Find the degree of the polynomial.
$$2x^4 - x^3y^2 + 4y^3 + 7$$

3. Evaluate the polynomial
$$-x^3 + 2x^2y - y + 1$$
when $x = -2$, $y = -1$.

4. Find a polynomial giving the area of a square of side s, less the area of an isosceles right triangle of side s.

5. Add the polynomials.
$$6x^5 - x^3 + x^2 \quad \text{and} \quad 4x^4 + 3x^3 - 2x^2 + 1$$

6. Simplify.
$$2x^2 - 3x^2y + y^2 - 7 + 4x^2y - 4y^2 + 4x^2 - 3$$

7. Find $(-3x^3 - 2x^2 + x - 3) - (2x^3 - 4x^2 - 2x + 5)$.

8. Subtract $2x^2y^2 - 3xy^2 - 2$ from $6x^2y^2 - 4xy^2 + xy$.

9. Multiply mentally $(3x - 4)^2$.

10. Multiply $(x + y)(2x - 3y - 2)$.

11. Factor $r^2 + 9r + 14$.

12. Factor completely $3x^2 + 6x + 3$.

13. Factor $16y^2 - 64x^2$.

14. Factor $3x^2 - 17x + 10$.

15. Factor $8a^3 + \dfrac{b^3}{8}$.

16. Divide $\dfrac{4x^3 - 2x^2 + 6x - 5}{x - 3}$.

17. Divide $r^4 - 3r^3 + 4r - 2$ by $r^2 - 1$.

18. If a polynomial of degree 17 is divided by a polynomial of degree 7, what is the degree of the quotient?

Chapter 4 Project

As discussed in the chapter opener, packages must often be designed to meet certain requirements. As you saw in Exercises 79 and 80 in Section 4.3, cubic polynomials can be used to express the volume of packages whose dimensions must meet certain requirements.

For this project, we will design a fourth degree (quartic) polynomial with two variables, x and y, to represent the cost of mailing a package. Suppose the variable y represents the cost per cubic inch of mailing a package. Suppose we have a package with a width 3 inches greater than the length and a height $2\frac{1}{2}$ inches greater than the width. If the length is x inches, write a polynomial expression that represents the cost of mailing this package. Multiply it out. Is it a fourth degree polynomial?

Suppose $x = 5\frac{1}{2}$ inches, and $y = 1\frac{1}{2}$ cents. How much would it cost to mail this package? Can it be mailed more cheaply?

■ ■ ■

5 Rational Expressions

> *From the intrinsic evidence of his creation, the Great Architect of the Universe now begins to appear as a pure mathematician.*
> —Sir James Hopwood Jeans

Game theory is an exciting and ever-growing branch of mathematics. Game theorists (like John Nash, the subject of the book and film *A Beautiful Mind*) study the mathematical properties of simple conflict situations to determine which strategies should be used to maximize gains and minimize losses. The lessons mathematicians learn from simple games with dice or coins can be of great use when applied to more complicated "games" like international finance or competitions between animal species.

Suppose you are playing a game with two possible actions each turn. Perhaps the actions are "move" or "stand still." You might decide to move 3/5 of the time and stand still 2/5 of the time. In this case, the **ratio** of "move" turns to "stand still" turns would be

http://www.awm-

3:2 ("three to two"). If you wanted a *move* to *stand still* ratio of $x{:}y$ then you would move $\frac{x}{x+y}$ of the time. What **rational expression,** like $\frac{x}{x+y}$, would represent how often you "stand still"?

In this chapter's project, you will see how rational expressions like the one above can be used to describe some basic aspects of simple games, like strategies, oddments, and payoffs.

Linda Goldway Keen is a mathematician who has worked with dynamical systems, which can be used to study the complex "game" played by predators and prey in the wild, where the payoff is survival. Learn about her and other women in mathematics at www.awm-math.org.

▪   ▪   ▪

In algebra we are often faced with complex fractions such as

$$\frac{1-\dfrac{1}{x}}{\dfrac{1}{x^2}+\dfrac{1}{x}}$$

that must be simplified. We also, at times, need to find the sum of expressions such as

$$\frac{x}{x-2}+\frac{2x^2}{x-3}$$

Our objective is to learn to handle such problems. We will study the rules for basic operations with fractions (addition, subtraction, multiplication, and division) and will see that a simple idea forms the cornerstone for much of our work: *multiplying a number or expression by a fraction equivalent to 1 does not change its value.*

We will also solve equations, involving algebraic fractions, and word problems leading to such equations.

5.1   Simplifying Rational Expressions

At the start of this book we defined a **rational number** as the quotient $\frac{p}{q}$ where p and q are integers and q is not zero. In an analogous manner, we define a **rational expression** as the quotient of two polynomials. Following are some examples of rational expressions (which are also called **algebraic fractions**):

$$\frac{2x}{5} \qquad \frac{x+2}{x-2} \qquad \frac{-2x^2+3x+4}{x^2-4} \qquad \frac{a^3-b^3}{a^2+2ab+b^2}$$

A rational expression is not defined when the denominator is zero. In subsequent chapters we will be very careful to avoid assigning values to variables that can create a zero denominator. For now, we will let you concentrate on the operations involved and will assume that all denominators represent nonzero real numbers.

We begin our study by examining the rule that enables us to simplify rational expressions.

Cancellation Principle

$$\frac{ab}{ac}=\frac{b}{c} \quad \text{if } a \neq 0$$

This is not anything new; we have used cancellation in arithmetic before.

$$\frac{2}{3}\cdot\frac{3}{5}=\frac{2}{5}$$

Why does this work? Why are we allowed to "cancel" the number 3? Because $\frac{3}{3}=1$. In fact, for any nonzero number a, $\frac{a}{a}=1$, so that if $a\neq 0$ is a factor of both the numerator *and* denominator of the product of two fractions, we can cancel the number a.

The same principle applies to rational expressions. Cancellation of a factor that is common to the numerator and denominator does not change the value of a rational expression. Thus,

$$\frac{x^2(x-1)}{2x(x-2)} = \frac{x \cdot x \cdot (x-1)}{2 \cdot x \cdot (x-2)} = \frac{x(x-1)}{2(x-2)}$$

EXAMPLE 1   SIMPLIFYING A RATIONAL EXPRESSION
Simplify.

(a) $\dfrac{-4x^2y}{8xy^2}$ (b) $\dfrac{-6(a-1)(b+1)^2}{-21a(b+1)}$

SOLUTIONS

(a) $\dfrac{-4x^2y}{8xy^2} = \dfrac{-\cancel{4} \cdot x \cdot x \cdot \cancel{y}}{2 \cdot \cancel{4} \cdot x \cdot \cancel{y} \cdot y} = \dfrac{-x}{2y} = -\dfrac{x}{2y}$

(b) $\dfrac{-6(a-1)(b+1)^2}{-21a(b+1)} = \dfrac{-2 \cdot \cancel{3} \cdot (a-1)(b+1)\cancel{(b+1)}}{-\cancel{3} \cdot 7 \cdot a\cancel{(b+1)}} = \dfrac{2(a-1)(b+1)}{7a}$

✔ Progress Check 1
Simplify.

(a) $\dfrac{14ab^3}{-63a^2b}$ (b) $\dfrac{9(x-1)^2(y^2+1)}{3(y^2+1)(x-1)}$

Answers

(a) $-\dfrac{2b^2}{9a}$ (b) $3(x-1)$

Note in Example 1b that we wrote the integers 6 and 21 as a product of their prime factors. This technique makes it easy to discover common integer factors that can be canceled.

WARNING
Although the numbers

$$-\frac{1}{2} \qquad \frac{-1}{2} \qquad \frac{1}{-2}$$

are all equivalent, mathematicians prefer the format $-\frac{1}{2}$. Get in the habit of writing your answers so that the negative sign precedes the rational expression rather than appearing in either the numerator or the denominator.

We summarize a systematic procedure for the simplification of rational expressions.

Simplifying Rational Expressions

Step 1. Factor the numerator completely.

Step 2. Factor the denominator completely.

Step 3. Cancel factors that are common to both the numerator and denominator.

EXAMPLE 2   SIMPLIFYING A RATIONAL EXPRESSION

Simplify $\dfrac{x^2 - 4}{x^2 + 5x + 6}$.

SOLUTION

Simplifying	Example
Step 1. Factor the numerator completely.	$x^2 - 4 = (x + 2)(x - 2)$
Step 2. Factor the denominator completely.	$x^2 + 5x + 6 = (x + 3)(x + 2)$
Step 3. Cancel factors that are common to both the numerator and the denominator.	$\dfrac{x^2 - 4}{x^2 + 5x + 6} = \dfrac{\cancel{(x + 2)}(x - 2)}{(x + 3)\cancel{(x + 2)}} = \dfrac{x - 2}{x + 3}$

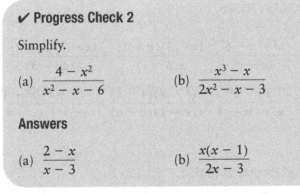

✔ Progress Check 2

Simplify.

(a) $\dfrac{4 - x^2}{x^2 - x - 6}$ (b) $\dfrac{x^3 - x}{2x^2 - x - 3}$

Answers

(a) $\dfrac{2 - x}{x - 3}$ (b) $\dfrac{x(x - 1)}{2x - 3}$

WARNING

(a) Only multiplicative factors of the entire numerator and denominator can be canceled. Don't write

$$\frac{2x - y}{x} = 2 - y$$

Since x is not a multiplicative factor of the *whole* numerator, we may not cancel it.

(b) *Don't write*

$$\frac{y^2 - x^2}{y - x} = y - x$$

To simplify correctly, write

$$\frac{y^2 - x^2}{y - x} = \frac{(y + x)\cancel{(y - x)}}{\cancel{y - x}} = y + x$$

We finish our discussion of cancellation with a somewhat subtle technique. Can you do anything with the following expression?

$$\frac{x - 5}{5 - x}$$

At first glance you might say, "No, there are no common factors." However, if you recognize that $5 - x = -(x - 5)$, then you can see that

$$\frac{x - 5}{5 - x} = \frac{x - 5}{-(x - 5)} = \frac{1\cancel{(x - 5)}}{-1\cancel{(x - 5)}} = \frac{1}{-1} = -1$$

EXAMPLE 3   SIMPLIFYING RATIONAL EXPRESSIONS

Simplify.

(a) $\dfrac{x^2 - x - 6}{3x - x^2}$ (b) $\dfrac{16 - x^2}{x^2 - 3x - 4}$

SOLUTIONS

(a) $\dfrac{x^2 - x - 6}{3x - x^2} = \dfrac{(x - 3)(x + 2)}{x(3 - x)} = \dfrac{\cancel{(x - 3)}(x + 2)}{-x\cancel{(x - 3)}} = \dfrac{x + 2}{-x} = -\dfrac{x + 2}{x}$

(b) $\dfrac{16 - x^2}{x^2 - 3x - 4} = \dfrac{(4 + x)(4 - x)}{(x + 1)(x - 4)} = \dfrac{-(4 + x)\cancel{(x - 4)}}{(x + 1)\cancel{(x - 4)}} = -\dfrac{x + 4}{x + 1}$

✔ Progress Check 3

Simplify.

(a) $\dfrac{x^2 + 7x - 8}{x - x^2}$ (b) $\dfrac{9y^2 - x^2}{x - 3y}$ (c) $\dfrac{8 - 2x}{x^2 - 16}$

Answers

(a) $-\dfrac{x + 8}{x}$ (b) $-(3y + x)$ (c) $-\dfrac{2}{x + 4}$

Exercise Set 5.1

In Exercises 1–50 simplify the rational number or rational expression.

1. $\dfrac{3}{24}$

2. $\dfrac{-5}{15}$

3. $\dfrac{63}{-9}$

4. $\dfrac{17}{68}$

5. $-\dfrac{6}{21}$

6. $-\dfrac{18}{8}$

7. $\dfrac{12}{52}$

8. $\dfrac{72}{-30}$

9. $\dfrac{-75}{25}$

10. $\dfrac{19}{21}$

11. $\dfrac{9ab^3}{3ab}$

12. $\dfrac{-7xy^2}{49y^3}$

13. $\dfrac{-16x(z + 3)^2}{24x^2(z + 3)}$

14. $\dfrac{14(m^2 + 1)^2(n - 2)}{-42(n - 2)^2(m^2 + 1)}$

15. $\dfrac{-16(r + 4)^3 s}{6(s - 1)(r + 4)^2}$

16. $\dfrac{8a^2b(c + 1)}{18ab^2(c + 1)^2}$

17. $\dfrac{3(y^2 + z^2)^2}{-12(y^2 + z^2)}$

18. $\dfrac{63(a - 1)(b - 1)(c - 1)}{-9(b - 1)(a - 1)^2}$

19. $\dfrac{4(z^2 + z + 1)^2}{34(z^2 + z + 1)}$

20. $\dfrac{63(r - 3)^3 s^3(t + 2)}{9s^4(t + 2)^2(r - 3)^2}$

21. $\dfrac{3x^2 - 6x}{-9x + 18}$

22. $\dfrac{9xy^2 - 9x}{-21xy}$

23. $\dfrac{2x^4 + x^2}{6x^2 + 3}$

24. $\dfrac{x^2 + 2x + 4}{xy + 2y}$

25. $\dfrac{2x^3 + 2x^2}{x + 1}$

26. $\dfrac{24m^2n^2 + 48m^2n}{10mn + 20}$

27. $\dfrac{3abc + 12bc}{15ac + 60c}$

28. $\dfrac{2t^2 + 4t - 16}{t^2 - 4t + 4}$

29. $\dfrac{x^3 + 5x^2 - 6x}{2x^2 + 12x}$

30. $\dfrac{3xy - 6x + 3y - 6}{x^2 + 2x + 1}$

31. $\dfrac{t^3 + 1}{t^2 + t}$

32. $\dfrac{27x^3 - y^3}{9x^2 - 3xy}$

33. $\dfrac{4a^2 - 9}{2a^2 - 3a - 9}$

34. $\dfrac{9s^2t - 4t}{3st^2 + 2t^2}$

35. $\dfrac{4(xy + 2x + y + 2) - 8(x + 1)}{(x + 1)y}$

36. $\dfrac{16r^2 - 25t^2}{16r^2 - 40t + 25t^2}$

37. $\dfrac{3t^4 - 27t^2}{2t^2 - 6t}$

38. $\dfrac{8r^3 - 27}{4r^2 - 9}$

39. $\dfrac{9a^2b^3 - a^2b}{3ab^2 - ab}$

40. $\dfrac{4x^2 + 6x - 4}{3x^2 + 12x + 4}$

41. $\dfrac{2x^2 + 9x + 9}{9 - x^2}$

42. $\dfrac{3x^2 - 2x^3}{2x^2 - 3x}$

43. $\dfrac{a^3 - 5a^2 + 6a}{2a - a^2}$

44. $\dfrac{16 - n^2}{2n^2 - 7n - 4}$

45. $\dfrac{12r^2b^2 - 4rb}{rb - 3r^2b^2}$

46. $\dfrac{9x^2 - 36y^2}{36y - 18x}$

47. $\dfrac{6t - 4t^2}{6t^3 - 7t^2 - 3t}$

48. $\dfrac{9r^3s - 16rs}{4s^2 - 3rs}$

49. $\dfrac{-2x^2 - 5x + 3}{x - 2x^2}$

50. $\dfrac{2a^2 - a + 2ab - b}{ab - 2a^2b}$

51. Check the following simplification with your graphing calculator, by first storing values for x and y. (See the figure below.)

$$\frac{x^2 - 3xy + 2y^2}{x - 2y} = x - y$$

```
3→X
                     3
5→Y
                     5
(X²-3XY+2Y²)/(X-
2Y)
                    -2
```

Use the same method to verify your answer to Exercise 50.

5.2   Multiplication and Division of Rational Expressions

If we think of a rational expression as a fraction, then we see that the rule for multiplication is already familiar to us from arithmetic.

Multiplication of Fractions

$$\frac{a}{b} \cdot \frac{c}{d} = \frac{ac}{bd}, \quad b \neq 0, d \neq 0$$

That is, when multiplying two given fractions, we obtain a new fraction whose numerator is the product of the numerators of the given fractions and whose denominator is the product of the denominators of the given fractions. The same rule holds for both rational numbers and rational expressions.

EXAMPLE 1   MULTIPLICATION OF RATIONAL NUMBERS AND RATIONAL EXPRESSIONS

Multiply.

(a) $\dfrac{5}{2} \cdot \dfrac{3}{4}$ 　(b) $\dfrac{3}{4} \cdot \dfrac{x-1}{2}$ 　(c) $\dfrac{x-1}{2} \cdot \dfrac{x+1}{x}$ 　(d) $\dfrac{3}{4x} \cdot \dfrac{x-3}{2y} \cdot \dfrac{x+3}{y-1}$

SOLUTIONS

(a) $\dfrac{5}{2} \cdot \dfrac{3}{4} = \dfrac{5 \cdot 3}{2 \cdot 4} = \dfrac{15}{8}$

(b) $\dfrac{3}{4} \cdot \dfrac{x-1}{2} = \dfrac{3(x-1)}{4 \cdot 2} = \dfrac{3(x-1)}{8}$

(c) $\dfrac{x-1}{2} \cdot \dfrac{x+1}{x} = \dfrac{(x-1)(x+1)}{2 \cdot x} = \dfrac{x^2-1}{2x}$

(d) $\dfrac{3}{4x} \cdot \dfrac{x-3}{2y} \cdot \dfrac{x+3}{y-1} = \dfrac{3(x-3)(x+3)}{4x \cdot 2y(y-1)} = \dfrac{3(x^2-9)}{8xy(y-1)}$

✔ **Progress Check 1**

Multiply.

(a) $\dfrac{2x}{y} \cdot \dfrac{y+1}{y^2+1}$ 　(b) $\dfrac{3}{a} \cdot \dfrac{b^2}{2a} \cdot \dfrac{c}{d-3}$

Answers

(a) $\dfrac{2x(y+1)}{y(y^2+1)}$ 　(b) $\dfrac{3b^2c}{2a^2(d-3)}$

To divide two fractions, we multiply the numerator by the reciprocal of the divisor.

Division of Fractions

$$\frac{\dfrac{a}{b}}{\dfrac{c}{d}} = \frac{a}{b} \cdot \frac{d}{c} = \frac{ad}{bc}, \qquad b, c, d \neq 0$$

This rule "works" because we are really multiplying by a cleverly disguised form of 1, namely

$$\frac{\dfrac{d}{c}}{\dfrac{d}{c}} = 1$$

Observe that

$$\frac{\dfrac{a}{b}}{\dfrac{c}{d}} \cdot \frac{\dfrac{d}{c}}{\dfrac{d}{c}} = \frac{\dfrac{ad}{bc}}{\dfrac{cd}{cd}} = \frac{\dfrac{ad}{bc}}{1} = \frac{ad}{bc}$$

EXAMPLE 2 DIVISION OF RATIONAL NUMBERS AND RATIONAL EXPRESSIONS

Divide.

(a) $\dfrac{\dfrac{2}{5}}{\dfrac{3}{4}}$ (b) $\dfrac{\dfrac{2x}{x-1}}{\dfrac{x-2}{x}}$ (c) $\dfrac{\dfrac{3a^3b^2}{2cd}}{\dfrac{c-1}{2a^2b}}$ (d) $\dfrac{2x}{y} \div \dfrac{3y^3}{x-3}$ (e) $\dfrac{\dfrac{x}{2x+1}}{x-2}$

SOLUTIONS

(a) $\dfrac{\dfrac{2}{5}}{\dfrac{3}{4}} = \dfrac{2}{5} \cdot \dfrac{4}{3} = \dfrac{2 \cdot 4}{5 \cdot 3} = \dfrac{8}{15}$

(b) $\dfrac{\dfrac{2x}{x-1}}{\dfrac{x-2}{x}} = \dfrac{2x}{x-1} \cdot \dfrac{x}{x-2} = \dfrac{2x^2}{(x-1)(x-2)}$

(c) $\dfrac{\dfrac{3a^3b^2}{2cd}}{\dfrac{c-1}{2a^2b}} = \dfrac{3a^3b^2}{2cd} \cdot \dfrac{2a^2b}{c-1} = \dfrac{6a^5b^3}{2c(c-1)d}$

(d) $\dfrac{2x}{y} \div \dfrac{3y^3}{x-3}$

To solve this problem, we write the expression as a fraction and simplify.

$$\dfrac{\dfrac{2x}{y}}{\dfrac{3y^3}{x-3}} = \dfrac{2x}{y} \cdot \dfrac{x-3}{3y^3} = \dfrac{2x(x-3)}{3y^4}$$

(e) $\dfrac{\dfrac{x}{2x+1}}{x-2} = \dfrac{\dfrac{x}{2x+1}}{\dfrac{x-2}{1}} = \dfrac{x}{2x+1} \cdot \dfrac{1}{x-2} = \dfrac{x}{(2x+1)(x-2)}$

✔ **Progress Check 2**

Divide.

(a) $\dfrac{\dfrac{5(y-1)^2}{x}}{\dfrac{2(x-1)^2}{y}}$

(b) $\dfrac{3a^2b}{a+1} \div \dfrac{2(b-1)}{a-1}$

Answers

(a) $\dfrac{5y(y-1)^2}{2x(x-1)^2}$

(b) $\dfrac{3a^2(a-1)b}{2(a+1)(b-1)}$

EXAMPLE 3   OPERATIONS ON AND SIMPLIFICATION OF RATIONAL EXPRESSIONS

Perform the indicated operations and simplify.

(a) $\dfrac{3x^2-27}{12-6x} \cdot \dfrac{2x^2-4x}{x+3}$

(b) $\dfrac{2x^3+3x^2}{10-20x} \div \dfrac{2x^2+3x}{10x-5}$

SOLUTIONS

(a) $\dfrac{3x^2-27}{12-6x} \cdot \dfrac{2x^2-4x}{x+3} = \dfrac{3(x^2-9)}{6(2-x)} \cdot \dfrac{2x(x-2)}{x+3}$ Remove common factors.

$$= \dfrac{3(x+3)(x-3)2x(x-2)}{6(2-x)(x+3)}$$ Complete factoring and multiply.

$$= -x(x-3)$$ Cancel common factors.

(b) $\dfrac{2x^3 + 3x^2}{10 - 20x} \div \dfrac{2x^2 + 3x}{10x - 5} = \dfrac{x^2(2x + 3)}{10(1 - 2x)} \cdot \dfrac{5(2x - 1)}{x(2x + 3)}$ Invert denominator and factor.

$= -\dfrac{x}{2}$ Cancel common factors.

✔ Progress Check 3

Perform the indicated operations and simplify.

(a) $\dfrac{-2}{3x^2 + 4x + 1} \cdot \dfrac{6x^2 - 4x - 2}{x^2 - 1}$ (b) $\dfrac{10x - 2x^2}{-x^2 + 5x - 6} \div \dfrac{x^2 - 25}{-x^2 + 2x}$

Answers

(a) $\dfrac{-4}{(x + 1)^2}$ (b) $-\dfrac{2x^2}{(x - 3)(x + 5)}$

Exercise Set 5.2

In Exercises 1–8 determine whether each statement is true (T) or false (F).

1. $\dfrac{3}{8} \cdot \dfrac{x + 5}{4} = \dfrac{3(x + 5)}{32}$ 2. $\dfrac{2}{3} \cdot \dfrac{x + 4}{7} = \dfrac{2x + 4}{21}$

3. $\dfrac{5}{2} \cdot \dfrac{4x + 7}{15} = \dfrac{2x + 7}{3}$

4. $\dfrac{2x}{5y} \cdot \dfrac{5x + 15}{4} = \dfrac{x(x + 5)}{2y}$

5. $\dfrac{\dfrac{1}{3}}{\dfrac{2x}{x - 1}} = \dfrac{x - 1}{6x}$ 6. $\dfrac{\dfrac{x}{2x + 1}}{\dfrac{2}{x}} = \dfrac{2}{2x + 1}$

7. $\dfrac{\dfrac{2}{3}}{\dfrac{4x}{3x + 6}} = \dfrac{x + 6}{2x}$ 8. $\dfrac{\dfrac{x^2 - y^2}{xy}}{\dfrac{x + y}{x^2}} = \dfrac{x(x - y)}{y}$

In Exercises 9–22 simplify, if possible.

9. $\dfrac{6x + 3}{3}$ 10. $\dfrac{8x - 4}{2}$

11. $\dfrac{3x + 2}{3}$ 12. $\dfrac{6x - 3}{5}$

13. $\dfrac{5}{10x^2 - 15}$ 14. $\dfrac{3}{6x - 12y^2}$

15. $\dfrac{5a^4}{25a^2}$ 16. $\dfrac{18}{27} \cdot \dfrac{a^2 b^4}{a^3 b^2}$

17. $\dfrac{x + 4}{x^2 - 16}$ 18. $\dfrac{y^2 - 25}{y + 5}$

19. $\dfrac{x^2 - 8x + 16}{x - 4}$ 20. $\dfrac{5x^2 - 45}{2x - 6}$

21. $\dfrac{6x^2 - x - 1}{2x^2 + 3x - 2}$ 22. $\dfrac{2x^3 + x^2 - 3x}{3x^2 + x + 2}$

In Exercises 23–56 compute and simplify your answer.

23. $\dfrac{x + 1}{3} \cdot \dfrac{2x + 3}{4}$ 24. $\dfrac{3x - 1}{2y} \cdot \dfrac{2x + 3}{3x + 1}$

25. $\dfrac{a - 4}{3} \cdot \dfrac{9(a + 4)}{b}$ 26. $\dfrac{x + 1}{3x + 6} \cdot \dfrac{6}{x + 1}$

27. $\dfrac{a^2}{4} \div \dfrac{a}{2}$ 28. $\dfrac{2a^2 b^4}{3c^3} \div \dfrac{a^3 b^2}{6c^5}$

29. $\dfrac{2}{3x - 6} \div \dfrac{3}{2x - 4}$ 30. $\dfrac{5x + 15}{8} \div \dfrac{3x + 9}{4}$

31. $\dfrac{3x^2 + x}{2x + 4} \cdot \dfrac{4}{x^2 + 2x}$ 32. $\dfrac{a^2 - a}{b + 1} \cdot \dfrac{2b}{a^3 - a^2}$

33. $\dfrac{25 - a^2}{b + 3} \cdot \dfrac{2b^2 + 6b}{a - 5}$ 34. $\dfrac{2xy^2}{x + y} \cdot \dfrac{x + y}{4xy}$

35. $\dfrac{2x}{x - 3} \div \dfrac{6x^2}{x + 3}$ 36. $\dfrac{a - a^2}{b - 1} \div \dfrac{a^2 - a}{b}$

37. $\dfrac{4y^2 - 9}{x^2 - 1} \cdot \dfrac{x^2 - x}{3 - 2y}$

38. $\dfrac{9 - 25b^2}{a^3 + a^2} \div \dfrac{5b - 3}{a + 1}$

39. $\dfrac{x^2 - 4}{x + 1} \div \dfrac{2x + 3}{2x - 4}$

40. $\dfrac{9}{a^2 - 16} \div \dfrac{3}{a + 4}$

41. $\dfrac{x + 2}{3y} \div \dfrac{x^2 - 2x - 8}{15y^2}$

42. $\dfrac{3x}{x + 2} \div \dfrac{6x^2}{x^2 - x - 6}$

43. $\dfrac{6x^2 - x - 2}{2x^2 - 5x + 3} \cdot \dfrac{2x^2 - 7x + 6}{3x^2 + x - 2}$

44. $\dfrac{3x^2 - 5x - 2}{4x^2 - 3x - 1} \cdot \dfrac{5x^2 - 3x - 2}{3x^2 + 7x + 2}$

45. $\dfrac{x^2 + 3x - 10}{x^2 + 4x + 3} \div \dfrac{x^2 + 2x - 15}{x^2 - x - 2}$

46. $\dfrac{25 - 15x}{x^2 - 4} \div \dfrac{3x^2 - 8x + 5}{x + 2}$

47. $(x^2 - 4) \cdot \dfrac{2x + 3}{x^2 + 2x - 8}$

48. $(a^2 - 2a) \cdot \dfrac{a + 1}{6 - a - a^2}$

49. $\dfrac{b^2 - 1}{3 - 2b - b^2} \cdot (-b^2 - 3b)$

50. $\dfrac{25 - x^2}{10 - 3x - x^2} \div \dfrac{x}{2 - x}$

51. $(x^2 - 2x - 15) \div \dfrac{x^2 - 7x + 10}{x^2 + 1}$

52. $\dfrac{2y^2 - 5y - 3}{y - 4} \div (y^2 + y - 12)$

*53. $\dfrac{x^2 - 4}{x^2 + 2x - 3} \cdot \dfrac{x^2 + 3x - 4}{x^2 - 7x + 10} \cdot \dfrac{x + 3}{x^2 + 3x + 2}$

*54. $\dfrac{x^2 - 9}{6x^2 + x - 1} \cdot \dfrac{2x^2 + 5x + 2}{x^2 + 4x + 3} \cdot \dfrac{x^2 - x - 2}{x^2 - 3x}$

*55. $\left(\dfrac{x + 4}{x + 1} \cdot \dfrac{x - 3}{x - 2}\right) \div \dfrac{x + 4}{x^3 - x^2 - 2x}$

*56. $\dfrac{x - 2}{2x^2 + 5x - 3} \div \left(\dfrac{2x - 1}{x - 2} \cdot \dfrac{x + 4}{x + 3}\right)$

5.3 Addition and Subtraction of Rational Expressions

Following is a basic principle of addition and subtraction that must be remembered:

Addition and Subtraction Principle

> We can add or subtract fractions directly only if they have the same denominator.

The process is already familiar to you.

Addition and Subtraction Rule

$$\frac{a}{c} + \frac{b}{c} = \frac{a + b}{c}$$

$$\frac{a}{c} - \frac{b}{c} = \frac{a - b}{c}$$

Here c is the common denominator. We add the numerators ($a + b$) to find the numerator of the sum and retain the common denominator. Similarly, we subtract b from a to find the numerator of the difference and retain the common denominator. For example,

$$\frac{2}{x} - \frac{4}{x} + \frac{5}{x} = \frac{2 - 4 + 5}{x} = \frac{3}{x}$$

How do we handle the addition of fractions if the denominators are not the same? We must rewrite each fraction as an equivalent fraction so that they all have the same denominator. Although any common denominator will do, we will concentrate on finding the least common denominator, or LCD. Here is the procedure:

Least Common Denominator	Example

$$\frac{1}{x^3 - x^2} \qquad \frac{-2}{x^3 - x} \qquad \frac{3x}{x^2 + 2x + 1}$$

Step 1. Factor the denominator of each fraction completely.

$$\frac{1}{x^2(x - 1)} \qquad \frac{-2}{x(x - 1)(x + 1)} \qquad \frac{3x}{(x + 1)^2}$$

Step 2. Determine the different factors in the denominators of the fractions, and the highest power to which each factor occurs in any denominator.

Factor	Highest power	Final factor
x	2	x^2
$x - 1$	1	$x - 1$
$x + 1$	2	$(x + 1)^2$

Step 3. The product of the factors to their highest power, as determined in Step 2, is the LCD.

The LCD is

$$x^2(x - 1)(x + 1)^2$$

EXAMPLE 1   FINDING THE LEAST COMMON DENOMINATOR

Find the LCD of the fractions.

$$\frac{y + 2}{2x^2 - 18} \qquad \frac{4y}{3x^3 + 9x^2} \qquad \frac{y + 1}{(x - 3)^2(y - 1)^2}$$

SOLUTION

Factoring each denominator completely, we have

$$\frac{y + 2}{2(x + 3)(x - 3)} \qquad \frac{4y}{3x^2(x + 3)} \qquad \frac{y + 1}{(x - 3)^2(y - 1)^2}$$

The different factors and the highest power of each factor in any denominator are

Factor	Highest Power	Final Factor
2	1	2
3	1	3
x	2	x^2
$x + 3$	1	$x + 3$
$x - 3$	2	$(x - 3)^2$
$y - 1$	2	$(y - 1)^2$

The LCD is then the product

$$6x^2(x + 3)(x - 3)^2(y - 1)^2$$

✔ Progress Check 1

Find the LCD of the fractions.

$$\frac{2a}{(3a^2 + 12a + 12)b} \qquad \frac{-7b}{a(4b^2 - 8b + 4)} \qquad \frac{3}{ab^3 + 2b^3}$$

Answer

$$12ab^3(a + 2)^2(b - 1)^2$$

Having determined the LCD, we must convert each fraction to an equivalent fraction with the LCD as its denominator. We have already seen that multiplying a fraction by 1 yields an equivalent fraction. We can accomplish this conversion by multiplying the fraction by the appropriate equivalent of 1. Here is the process.

Addition of Fractions	**Example**
	$\dfrac{4}{3x(x + 3)} + \dfrac{x - 1}{x^2(x - 2)}$
Step 1. Find the LCD.	LCD is $3x^2(x + 3)(x - 2)$.
Step 2. Examine the first fraction. Multiply it by a fraction whose numerator and denominator are the same and consist of all factors of the LCD that are missing in the denominator of the first fraction.	$\left[\dfrac{4}{3x(x + 3)}\right] \cdot \dfrac{x(x - 2)}{x(x - 2)}$ first fraction · factors of LCD missing in denominator $3x(x + 3)$
	$= \dfrac{4x(x - 2)}{3x^2(x + 3)(x - 2)}$
	$= \dfrac{4x^2 - 8x}{3x^2(x + 3)(x - 2)}$

continues

Addition of Fractions	Example

Step 3. Repeat Step 2 for each fraction.

$$\overset{\text{second}}{\underset{\text{fraction}}{\left[\dfrac{x-1}{x^2(x-2)}\right]}} \cdot \dfrac{3(x+3)}{3(x+3)}$$

factors of LCD missing
in denominator $x^2(x-2)$

$$= \dfrac{3(x-1)(x+3)}{3x^2(x-2)(x+3)}$$

$$= \dfrac{3(x^2+2x-3)}{3x^2(x+3)(x-2)}$$

$$= \dfrac{3x^2+6x-9}{3x^2(x+3)(x-2)}$$

Step 4. The fractions now all have the same denominator. Apply the addition principle. (Do not multiply out the denominators; it may be possible to perform cancellation.)

$$\dfrac{4}{3x(x+3)} + \dfrac{x-1}{x^2(x-2)} \quad \text{Original example}$$

$$= \dfrac{4x^2-8x}{3x^2(x+3)(x-2)} + \dfrac{3x^2+6x-9}{3x^2(x+3)(x-2)}$$

$$= \dfrac{4x^2-8x+3x^2+6x-9}{3x^2(x+3)(x-2)}$$

$$= \dfrac{7x^2-2x-9}{3x^2(x+3)(x-2)}$$

EXAMPLE 2   FINDING THE SUM OF RATIONAL EXPRESSIONS

Find the sum:

(a) $\dfrac{3}{2xy} - \dfrac{4}{x^2} + \dfrac{2}{y^2}$ (b) $\dfrac{2x}{x^2-4} + \dfrac{1}{x(x+2)} - \dfrac{1}{x-2}$

SOLUTIONS

(a) The LCD is $2x^2y^2$. (Verify.) Then

$$\dfrac{3}{2xy} \cdot \dfrac{xy}{xy} - \dfrac{4}{x^2} \cdot \dfrac{2y^2}{2y^2} + \dfrac{2}{y^2} \cdot \dfrac{2x^2}{2x^2} = \dfrac{3xy}{2x^2y^2} - \dfrac{8y^2}{2x^2y^2} + \dfrac{4x^2}{2x^2y^2}$$

$$= \dfrac{3xy - 8y^2 + 4x^2}{2x^2y^2}$$

(b) Since $x^2 - 4 = (x + 2)(x - 2)$, the LCD is $x(x + 2)(x - 2)$. Then

$$\frac{2x}{(x + 2)(x - 2)} \cdot \frac{x}{x} + \frac{1}{x(x + 2)} \cdot \frac{x - 2}{x - 2} - \frac{1}{x - 2} \cdot \frac{x(x + 2)}{x(x + 2)}$$

$$= \frac{2x^2}{x(x + 2)(x - 2)} + \frac{x - 2}{x(x + 2)(x - 2)} - \frac{x(x + 2)}{x(x + 2)(x - 2)}$$

$$= \frac{2x^2 + x - 2 - (x^2 + 2x)}{x(x + 2)(x - 2)} = \frac{2x^2 + x - 2 - x^2 - 2x}{x(x + 2)(x - 2)}$$

$$= \frac{x^2 - x - 2}{x(x + 2)(x - 2)} = \frac{(x - 2)(x + 1)}{x(x + 2)(x - 2)} = \frac{x + 1}{x(x + 2)}$$

✔ Progress Check 2

Find the sum.

(a) $\dfrac{4r - 3}{9r^3} - \dfrac{2r + 1}{4r^2} + \dfrac{2}{3r}$ (b) $\dfrac{2}{n} + \dfrac{3}{n + 1} - \dfrac{5}{n + 2}$

Answers

(a) $\dfrac{6r^2 + 7r - 12}{36r^3}$ (b) $\dfrac{7n + 4}{n(n + 1)(n + 2)}$

Exercise Set 5.3

In Exercises 1–10 find the LCD.

1. $\dfrac{4}{x}, \dfrac{x - 2}{y}$

2. $\dfrac{x}{x - 1}, \dfrac{x + 4}{x + 2}$

3. $\dfrac{5 - a}{a}, \dfrac{7}{2a}$

4. $\dfrac{x + 2}{x}, \dfrac{x - 2}{x^2}$

5. $\dfrac{2b}{b - 1}, \dfrac{3}{(b - 1)^2}$

6. $\dfrac{2 + x}{x^2 - 4}, \dfrac{3}{x - 2}$

7. $\dfrac{4x}{x - 2}, \dfrac{5}{x^2 + x - 6}$

8. $\dfrac{3}{y^2 - 3y - 4}, \dfrac{2y}{y + 1}$

9. $\dfrac{3}{x + 1}, \dfrac{2}{x}, \dfrac{x}{x - 1}$

10. $\dfrac{4}{x}, \dfrac{3}{x - 1}, \dfrac{x}{x^2 - 2x + 1}$

In Exercises 11–58 perform the indicated operations and simplify.

11. $\dfrac{2}{x} + \dfrac{5}{x}$

12. $\dfrac{12}{b + 1} + \dfrac{3}{b + 1}$

13. $\dfrac{x}{y} + \dfrac{2x}{y}$

14. $\dfrac{x^2 + 5}{x + 1} - \dfrac{x^2 + 3}{x + 1}$

15. $\dfrac{2a - 3}{a - 2} + \dfrac{1 - a}{a - 2}$

16. $\dfrac{x + 2}{x - 1} - \dfrac{2x - 3}{x - 1}$

17. $\dfrac{x^2 + 4x}{x + 3} - \dfrac{9 + 4x}{x + 3}$

18. $\dfrac{x^2 + x}{x + 2} + \dfrac{2x + 2}{x + 2}$

19. $\dfrac{2y - 16}{y^2 - 16} + \dfrac{2 - y}{y^2 - 16}$

20. $\dfrac{3x - 5}{x - 4} - \dfrac{x + 3}{x - 4}$

21. $\dfrac{8}{a - 2} + \dfrac{4}{2 - a}$

22. $\dfrac{x}{x^2 - 4} + \dfrac{2}{4 - x^2}$

23. $\dfrac{3y}{2 - y} - \dfrac{5y}{3y - 6}$

24. $\dfrac{a - 1}{a - 3} - \dfrac{a}{12 - 4a}$

25. $\dfrac{3}{x - 1} - \dfrac{x}{x - 1} + \dfrac{3x - 5}{x - 1}$

26. $\dfrac{y^2}{y^2 - 9} + \dfrac{9}{y^2 - 9} - \dfrac{6y}{y^2 - 9}$

27. $\dfrac{2}{x} + \dfrac{1}{5}$

28. $\dfrac{x}{4} - \dfrac{y}{3}$

29. $5 - \dfrac{2}{x}$

30. $\dfrac{x-1}{3} + 2$

31. $\dfrac{1}{x-1} + \dfrac{2}{x-2}$

32. $\dfrac{1}{a+2} + \dfrac{3}{a-2}$

33. $\dfrac{a}{8b} - \dfrac{b}{12a}$

34. $\dfrac{4}{3x} - \dfrac{5}{xy}$

35. $\dfrac{4x-1}{6x^3} + \dfrac{2}{3x^2}$

36. $\dfrac{5}{2x+6} - \dfrac{x}{x+3}$

37. $\dfrac{2x}{x-3} + \dfrac{4x-2}{9-3x}$

38. $\dfrac{3}{a^2-16} - \dfrac{2}{a-4}$

39. $\dfrac{x}{x-y} - \dfrac{y}{x+y}$

40. $\dfrac{5x}{2x^2-18} + \dfrac{4}{3x-9}$

41. $\dfrac{x}{x-y} + \dfrac{y}{x+y}$

42. $\dfrac{2x}{x^2-9} + \dfrac{5}{3x+9}$

43. $\dfrac{4}{r} - \dfrac{3}{r+2}$

44. $2 + \dfrac{4}{a^2-4}$

45. $\dfrac{1}{x-1} + \dfrac{2x-1}{(x-2)(x+1)}$

46. $\dfrac{2x}{2x+1} - \dfrac{x-1}{(2x+1)(x-2)}$

47. $\dfrac{a+2}{a^2-a} - \dfrac{2a}{a+1}$

48. $\dfrac{2x}{x^2+x-2} + \dfrac{3}{x+2}$

49. $\dfrac{2}{x-2} + \dfrac{x}{x^2-x-6}$

50. $\dfrac{2x-1}{x^2+5x+6} - \dfrac{x-2}{x^2+4x+3}$

51. $\dfrac{2x-1}{x^3-4x} - \dfrac{x}{x^2+x-2}$

52. $\dfrac{2x}{x^2-1} + \dfrac{x+1}{x^2+3x-4}$

53. $\dfrac{2}{x+2} + \dfrac{3}{x-2} - \dfrac{5}{x+3}$

54. $\dfrac{2x}{x+2} + \dfrac{x}{x-2} - \dfrac{1}{x^2-4}$

55. $\dfrac{2}{y^2-y} - \dfrac{y}{y+1} + \dfrac{y+1}{y}$

56. $\dfrac{3}{x^2+5x+6} - \dfrac{2}{x^2+4x+3} + \dfrac{4}{x^2+x-2}$

*57. $\left(\dfrac{2}{x-1} + \dfrac{3}{x-2}\right) \cdot \left(\dfrac{x^2+x-6}{5x-7}\right)$

*58. $\left[\dfrac{3}{y+3} - \dfrac{2y}{(y+3)(y-1)}\right] \div \left(\dfrac{y^2-y-6}{y^2+2y-3}\right)$

59. Look at the chapter opener. Suppose you are playing a game in which there are two possible actions you may perform each turn. Let's say you decide to perform these actions in a ratio of $x : y$ This would mean that you perform the first action $\frac{x}{x+y}$ of the time and the second action $\frac{y}{x+y}$ of the time. (Here's an example. Your opponent flips a coin, and you call out heads or tails. If you performed these actions in a ratio of 3:2, then you would call out heads 3/5 of the time and tails 2/5 of the time.)

Add the two expressions.

$$\frac{x}{x+y} + \frac{y}{x+y}$$

Why does the value of the sum make sense in the given context?

60. A *strategy* for a player with two possible "moves" or choices each time a game is played can be expressed as the ratio $x : y$ described in Exercise 59. Suppose a player receives $5 each time she makes the first choice and $3 each time she makes the second choice. Then the average amount earned per turn would be given by the expression

$$V = \frac{5x + 3y}{x+y}$$

If a player uses the strategy 3:2, what would be the average amount earned per turn?

5.4   Complex Fractions

At the beginning of this chapter, we said that we would like to simplify fractions such as

$$\frac{1 - \dfrac{1}{x}}{\dfrac{1}{x^2} + \dfrac{1}{x}}$$

This is an example of a **complex fraction**, which is an algebraic expression with a fraction or fractions in the numerator or denominator, or both.

    There are two methods commonly used to simplify complex fractions. Fortunately, we already have all the tools needed and will apply both methods to the problem.

EXAMPLE 1   SIMPLIFYING A COMPLEX FRACTION

Simplify.

$$\frac{1 - \dfrac{1}{x}}{\dfrac{1}{x^2} + \dfrac{1}{x}}$$

SOLUTION

| Method 1 |

Step 1. Find the LCD of all fractions appearing in the numerator and denominator.

The LCD of $\dfrac{1}{1}, \dfrac{1}{x},$ and $\dfrac{1}{x^2}$ is x^2

Step 2. Multiply the numerator and denominator by the LCD. Since this is multiplication by 1, the result is an equivalent fraction. Then simplify.

$$\frac{x^2 \left(1 - \dfrac{1}{x}\right)}{x^2 \left(\dfrac{1}{x^2} + \dfrac{1}{x}\right)} = \frac{x^2 - x}{1 + x} = \frac{x(x - 1)}{x + 1}$$

| Method 2 |

Step 1. Combine the terms in the numerator into a single fraction.

$$1 - \frac{1}{x} = \frac{x}{x} - \frac{1}{x} = \frac{x - 1}{x} \quad \text{(numerator)}$$

Step 2. Combine the terms in the denominator into a single fraction.

$$\frac{1}{x^2} + \frac{1}{x} = \frac{1}{x^2} + \frac{x}{x^2} = \frac{1 + x}{x^2} \quad \text{(denominator)}$$

Step 3. Apply the rule for division of fractions, that is, multiply the numerator by the reciprocal of the denominator.

$$\frac{\dfrac{x - 1}{x}}{\dfrac{1 + x}{x^2}} = \frac{x - 1}{1\,x} \cdot \frac{x\,x^2}{1 + x} = \frac{x(x - 1)}{x + 1}$$

✔ **Progress Check 1**

Simplify.

(a) $\dfrac{2+\dfrac{1}{x}}{1-\dfrac{2}{x}}$ (b) $\dfrac{a-1}{1-\dfrac{1}{a}}$

Answers

(a) $\dfrac{2x+1}{x-2}$ (b) a

EXAMPLE 2 SIMPLIFYING A COMPLEX FRACTION

Simplify.

$$\dfrac{\dfrac{a}{b}+\dfrac{b}{a}}{\dfrac{1}{a}-\dfrac{1}{b}}$$

SOLUTION

The LCD of all the fractions is ab. Then, using Method 1, we have

$$\dfrac{\dfrac{a}{b}+\dfrac{b}{a}}{\dfrac{1}{a}-\dfrac{1}{b}}=\dfrac{ab\left(\dfrac{a}{b}+\dfrac{b}{a}\right)}{ab\left(\dfrac{1}{a}-\dfrac{1}{b}\right)}=\dfrac{\dfrac{a^2b}{b}+\dfrac{ab^2}{a}}{\dfrac{ab}{a}-\dfrac{ab}{b}}$$

$$=\dfrac{a^2+b^2}{b-a}=-\dfrac{a^2+b^2}{a-b}$$

Using Method 2, we first compute the numerator. Since the LCD is ab, we have

$$\dfrac{a}{b}+\dfrac{b}{a}=\dfrac{a}{b}\cdot\dfrac{a}{a}+\dfrac{b}{a}\cdot\dfrac{b}{b}=\dfrac{a^2+b^2}{ab}$$

We next compute the denominator. Again, since the LCD is ab, we have

$$\dfrac{1}{a}-\dfrac{1}{b}=\dfrac{1}{a}\cdot\dfrac{b}{b}-\dfrac{1}{b}\cdot\dfrac{a}{a}=\dfrac{b-a}{ab}$$

Then

$$\dfrac{\dfrac{a}{b}+\dfrac{b}{a}}{\dfrac{1}{a}-\dfrac{1}{b}}=\dfrac{\dfrac{a^2+b^2}{ab}}{\dfrac{b-a}{ab}}=\dfrac{a^2+b^2}{ab}\cdot\dfrac{ab}{b-a}=\dfrac{a^2+b^2}{b-a}$$

which is equivalent to the answer obtained by Method 1.

✔ Progress Check 2
Simplify.

(a) $\dfrac{\dfrac{y}{x}+\dfrac{1}{y}}{\dfrac{x}{y}-\dfrac{1}{x}}$ (b) $\dfrac{\dfrac{1}{x}-y}{\dfrac{1}{y}-x}$

Answers

(a) $\dfrac{x+y^2}{x^2-y}$ (b) $\dfrac{y}{x}$

EXAMPLE 3   WORKING WITH COMPLEX FRACTIONS
Write as a simple fraction.

$$1+\dfrac{1+\dfrac{1}{x}}{\dfrac{2}{x}-\dfrac{1}{x-1}}$$

SOLUTION
We first work on the complex fraction to simplify it. The LCD of all the fractions is $x(x-1)$. We multiply numerator and denominator by the LCD.

$$\dfrac{x(x-1)\left(1+\dfrac{1}{x}\right)}{x(x-1)\left(\dfrac{2}{x}-\dfrac{1}{x-1}\right)}=\dfrac{(x^2-x)+(x-1)}{2(x-1)-x}=\dfrac{x^2-1}{x-2}$$

We now substitute this equivalent fraction in the original problem and carry out the addition.

$$1+\dfrac{1+\dfrac{1}{x}}{\dfrac{2}{x}-\dfrac{1}{x-1}}=1+\dfrac{x^2-1}{x-2}=\dfrac{x-2}{x-2}+\dfrac{x^2-1}{x-2}=\dfrac{x^2+x-3}{x-2}$$

✔ Progress Check 3
Write as a simple fraction.

(a) $\dfrac{1}{\dfrac{1}{x}+1}-1$ (b) $2+\dfrac{x}{1-\dfrac{1}{x}}$

Answers

(a) $-\dfrac{1}{x+1}$ (b) $\dfrac{x^2+2x-2}{x-1}$

Exercise Set 5.4

In Exercises 1–24 simplify.

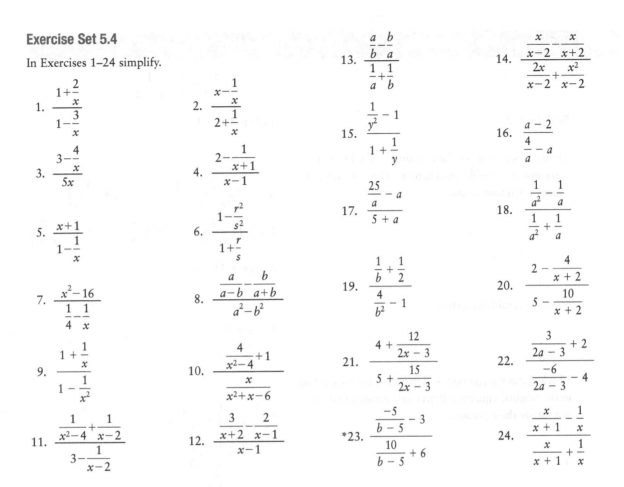

1. $\dfrac{1 + \dfrac{2}{x}}{1 - \dfrac{3}{x}}$

2. $\dfrac{x - \dfrac{1}{x}}{2 + \dfrac{1}{x}}$

3. $\dfrac{3 - \dfrac{4}{x}}{5x}$

4. $\dfrac{2 - \dfrac{1}{x+1}}{x-1}$

5. $\dfrac{x+1}{1 - \dfrac{1}{x}}$

6. $\dfrac{1 - \dfrac{r^2}{s^2}}{1 + \dfrac{r}{s}}$

7. $\dfrac{x^2 - 16}{\dfrac{1}{4} - \dfrac{1}{x}}$

8. $\dfrac{\dfrac{a}{a-b} - \dfrac{b}{a+b}}{a^2 - b^2}$

9. $\dfrac{1 + \dfrac{1}{x}}{1 - \dfrac{1}{x^2}}$

10. $\dfrac{\dfrac{4}{x^2-4} + 1}{\dfrac{x}{x^2+x-6}}$

11. $\dfrac{\dfrac{1}{x^2-4} + \dfrac{1}{x-2}}{3 - \dfrac{1}{x-2}}$

12. $\dfrac{\dfrac{3}{x+2} - \dfrac{2}{x-1}}{x-1}$

13. $\dfrac{\dfrac{a}{b} - \dfrac{b}{a}}{\dfrac{1}{a} + \dfrac{1}{b}}$

14. $\dfrac{\dfrac{x}{x-2} - \dfrac{x}{x+2}}{\dfrac{2x}{x-2} + \dfrac{x^2}{x-2}}$

15. $\dfrac{\dfrac{1}{y^2} - 1}{1 + \dfrac{1}{y}}$

16. $\dfrac{a - 2}{\dfrac{4}{a} - a}$

17. $\dfrac{\dfrac{25}{a} - a}{5 + a}$

18. $\dfrac{\dfrac{1}{a^2} - \dfrac{1}{a}}{\dfrac{1}{a^2} + \dfrac{1}{a}}$

19. $\dfrac{\dfrac{1}{b} + \dfrac{1}{2}}{\dfrac{4}{b^2} - 1}$

20. $\dfrac{2 - \dfrac{4}{x+2}}{5 - \dfrac{10}{x+2}}$

21. $\dfrac{4 + \dfrac{12}{2x-3}}{5 + \dfrac{15}{2x-3}}$

22. $\dfrac{\dfrac{3}{2a-3} + 2}{\dfrac{-6}{2a-3} - 4}$

*23. $\dfrac{\dfrac{-5}{b-5} - 3}{\dfrac{10}{b-5} + 6}$

24. $\dfrac{\dfrac{x}{x+1} - \dfrac{1}{x}}{\dfrac{x}{x+1} + \dfrac{1}{x}}$

5.5 Equations and Inequalities with Fractions

Suppose we are interested in solving the equation

$$\frac{2}{x-1} + \frac{1}{3} = \frac{1}{x-1}$$

for x. We must first try to clear the equation of all fractions. Once again, the least common denominator (LCD) is exactly what we need. We will explain the method and illustrate it with this equation.

Solving Equations with Fractions   Example

$$\frac{2}{x-1} + \frac{1}{3} = \frac{1}{x-1}$$

Step 1. Find the LCD.

LCD is $3(x-1)$.

Step 2. Multiply both sides of the equation by the LCD. Then carry out all possible cancellations. This will leave an equation without fractions.

$$3(x-1)\left(\frac{2}{x-1} + \frac{1}{3}\right) = 3(x-1)\left(\frac{1}{x-1}\right)$$

$$3\cancel{(x-1)}\,\frac{2}{\cancel{x-1}} + 3(x-1)\frac{1}{\cancel{3}} = 3\cancel{(x-1)} \cdot \frac{1}{\cancel{x-1}}$$

$$6 + (x-1) = 3$$

Step 3. Solve the resulting equation.

$$5 + x = 3$$

$$x = -2$$

Step 4. Check the answer(s) obtained in Step 3 by substituting in the original equation. Reject any answers that do not satisfy the equation.

$$\frac{2}{-2-1} + \frac{1}{3} \overset{?}{=} \frac{1}{-2-1}$$

$$-\frac{2}{3} + \frac{1}{3} \overset{?}{=} -\frac{1}{3}$$

$$-\frac{1}{3} \overset{\checkmark}{=} -\frac{1}{3}$$

⚠ WARNING

When we multiply an expression by a factor, we must multiply each term in the expression by that factor.

If you are multiplying an expression by the factor 2x, don't write

$$2x\left(\frac{1}{2x} + 5x\right) = 1 + 5x$$

The correct procedure is

$$2x\left(\frac{1}{2x} + 5x\right) = 1 + 10x^2$$

Note that it is not enough to clear the given equation of all fractions and proceed to find an answer. *The answer may not be a solution of the original equation.* Substituting the answer in the original equation may produce a denominator of 0, and division by 0 is not permitted. Thus, when dealing with equations that involve fractions, *you must always check that the answer is a solution* by substituting in the original equation The following example illustrates this point.

EXAMPLE 1   SOLVING AN EQUATION

Solve and check.

$$\frac{8x + 1}{x - 2} + 4 = \frac{7x + 3}{x - 2}$$

SOLUTION

Step 1. The LCD is $x - 2$.

Step 2.

$$(x - 2)\left(\frac{8x + 1}{x - 2} + 4\right) = (x - 2)\left(\frac{7x + 3}{x - 2}\right)$$

$$(x - 2)\frac{8x + 1}{x - 2} + (x - 2) \cdot 4 = (x - 2)\frac{7x + 3}{x - 2}$$

$$8x + 1 + 4x - 8 = 7x + 3$$

Step 3.

$$5x = 10$$

$$x = 2.$$

Step 4. Check: 2 is not a solution since substituting 2 in the original equation yields a denominator of 0, and we cannot divide by 0. Thus, the given equation has no solution.

✔ **Progress Check 1**

Solve and check.

(a) $\dfrac{3}{x} - 1 = \dfrac{1}{2} - \dfrac{6}{x}$ (b) $-\dfrac{2x}{x + 1} = 1 + \dfrac{2}{x + 1}$

Answers

(a) $x = 6$ (b) no solution

Solving Inequalities with Fractions

In this chapter we will limit ourselves to inequalities with fractions that only have constants in the denominators. When the LCD is a positive number, we may proceed to clear fractions in exactly the same manner as with equations.

EXAMPLE 2   SOLVING AN INEQUALITY

Solve for x.

$$\frac{x}{2} - 9 < \frac{1 - 2x}{3}$$

SOLUTION

Step 1. The LCD is $2 \cdot 3 = 6$.

Step 2. Multiply both sides by the LCD.

$$6\left(\frac{x}{2} - 9\right) < 6\left(\frac{1 - 2x}{3}\right)$$

$$\frac{6x}{2} - 54 < \frac{{}^{2}\cancel{6}(1 - 2x)}{\cancel{3}}$$

$$3x - 54 < 2(1 - 2x) = 2 - 4x$$

Step 3.

$$3x - 54 < 2 - 4x$$

$$3x + 4x < 2 + 54$$

$$7x < 56$$

$$x < 8$$

✔ Progress Check 2

Solve.

(a) $\dfrac{3x - 1}{4} + 1 > 2 + \dfrac{x}{3}$ (b) $\dfrac{2 + 3x}{5} - 1 \leqslant \dfrac{x + 1}{3}$

Answers

(a) $x > 3$ (b) $x \leqslant \dfrac{7}{2}$

In Chapter 2 we provided examples of equations that have no solutions. The same situation applies for inequalities. Here is an example.

EXAMPLE 3   SOLVING AN INEQUALITY

Solve.

$$\frac{2(x + 1)}{3} < \frac{2x}{3} - \frac{1}{6}$$

SOLUTION

The LCD is 6. Then

$$6\left[\frac{2(x + 1)}{3}\right] < 6\left(\frac{2x}{3} - \frac{1}{6}\right) \qquad \text{Multiply both sides by 6.}$$

$$4(x + 1) < 6\left(\frac{2x}{3}\right) - 6 \cdot \frac{1}{6}$$

$$4x + 4 < 4x - 1$$

$$4 < -1$$

Our procedure has led to a contradiction, indicating that there is no solution to the inequality.

✔ **Progress Check 3**
Solve.

$$\frac{2x-3}{2} \geqslant x + \frac{2}{5}$$

Answer
no solution

Exercise Set 5.5

In Exercises 1–30 solve and check.

1. $\dfrac{x}{2} = \dfrac{5}{3}$

2. $\dfrac{3x}{4} - 5 = \dfrac{1}{4}$

3. $\dfrac{2}{x} + 1 = \dfrac{3}{x}$

4. $\dfrac{5}{a} - \dfrac{3}{2} = \dfrac{1}{4}$

5. $\dfrac{x}{x+3} = \dfrac{3}{5}$

6. $\dfrac{a}{a-2} = \dfrac{3}{5}$

7. $\dfrac{2y-3}{y+3} = \dfrac{5}{7}$

8. $\dfrac{1-4x}{1-2x} = \dfrac{9}{8}$

9. $\dfrac{1}{x-2} + \dfrac{1}{2} = \dfrac{2}{x-2}$

10. $\dfrac{4}{x-4} - 2 = \dfrac{1}{x-4}$

11. $\dfrac{3r+1}{r+3} + 2 = \dfrac{5r-2}{r+3}$

12. $\dfrac{2x-1}{x-5} + 3 = \dfrac{3x-2}{5-x}$

13. $\dfrac{2x-3}{2x+1} + 3 = \dfrac{2}{2x+1}$

14. $\dfrac{4t+3}{2t-1} - 2 = \dfrac{5}{2t-1}$

15. $\dfrac{2}{x-2} + \dfrac{2}{x^2-4} = \dfrac{3}{x+2}$

16. $\dfrac{3}{x-1} + \dfrac{2}{x+1} = \dfrac{5}{x^2-1}$

17. $\dfrac{4-3x}{3x-1} = \dfrac{3}{2} - \dfrac{2x+3}{1-3x}$

18. $\dfrac{3a+2}{a-3} + 1 = \dfrac{a+8}{a-3}$

19. $\dfrac{x}{x-1} - 1 = \dfrac{3}{x+1}$

20. $\dfrac{2}{x-2} + 1 = \dfrac{x+2}{x-2}$

21. $\dfrac{4}{b} - \dfrac{1}{b+3} = \dfrac{3b+2}{b^2+2b-3}$

22. $\dfrac{3}{x^2-2x} + \dfrac{2x-1}{x^2+2x-8} = \dfrac{2}{x+4}$

23. $\dfrac{x}{2} - 3 < \dfrac{1}{2}$

24. $\dfrac{a}{3} - 2 > \dfrac{2}{3}$

25. $\dfrac{x}{2} - 2 \geqslant x - \dfrac{3}{2}$

26. $\dfrac{t}{3} - 1 \leqslant t + \dfrac{2}{3}$

27. $\dfrac{4-x}{3} \geqslant 2 - x$

28. $\dfrac{x}{3} - 5 < \dfrac{2-3x}{4}$

29. $\dfrac{3x-2}{3} \geqslant x + \dfrac{1}{2}$

30. $\dfrac{2x-1}{3} \geqslant x + 2$

*31. Solve for y:

$$a + \frac{4}{y-1} = \frac{2}{3}$$

*32. Solve for t:

$$b + \frac{2}{t-1} = \frac{3}{1-t}$$

*33. Solve the inequality for r.

$$\frac{r-1}{2} \leqslant \frac{r+1}{a}; \qquad a > 2$$

*34. Solve the inequality for s.

$$\frac{3s}{a} \leqslant \frac{a+1}{a^2}; \qquad a > 0$$

35. Refer to Section 5.3, Exercise 60. In Game Theory the word "oddment" is sometimes used to express the value of one part of a ratio. Thus, 3 and 2 would be the oddments of the ratio 3:2.

Using the rational expression

$$V = \frac{5x+3y}{x+y}$$

what value of the x oddment would result in a game with value $V = 4.5$, if the y oddment is equal to 1?

5.6 Applications; Work Problems

Many applications involve equations or inequalities with rational expressions. To handle these, you will have to use everything you have learned about "setting up" word problems and then follow the techniques given in the prior section to solve the equation or inequality.

EXAMPLE 1   SOLVING A WORD PROBLEM

A certain number is 3 times another number. If the sum of their reciprocals is $\frac{20}{3}$, find the numbers.

SOLUTION

Let

$$x = \text{the smaller number}$$

Then

$$3x = \text{the larger number}$$

The reciprocals of these numbers are $\dfrac{1}{x}$ and $\dfrac{1}{3x}$, so that

$$\frac{1}{x} + \frac{1}{3x} = \frac{20}{3}$$

We multiply both sides by the LCD, which is $3x$.

$$3x\left(\frac{1}{x} + \frac{1}{3x}\right) = 3x\left(\frac{20}{3}\right)$$

$$3 + 1 = 20x$$

$$4 = 20x$$

$$x = \frac{4}{20} = \frac{1}{5}$$

The numbers are then $\frac{1}{5}$ and $\frac{3}{5}$.

Check: We add the reciprocals.

$$\frac{5}{1} + \frac{5}{3} = \frac{15}{3} + \frac{5}{3} = \frac{20}{3}$$

and verify that $\frac{1}{5}$ and $\frac{3}{5}$ constitute a solution.

✔ Progress Check 1

One number is twice another. If the difference of their reciprocals is $\frac{8}{3}$, find the numbers.

Answers

$\dfrac{3}{8}$ and $\dfrac{3}{16}$; $-\dfrac{3}{8}$ and $-\dfrac{3}{16}$

EXAMPLE 2   SOLVING A WORD PROBLEM

The denominator of a fraction is 2 more than its numerator. If $\frac{5}{2}$ is added to the fraction, the result is $\frac{17}{6}$. Find the fraction.

SOLUTION

Let

$$x = \text{the numerator of the fraction}$$

Then

$$x + 2 = \text{the denominator of the fraction}$$

The fraction is then $\dfrac{x}{x + 2}$, and we have

$$\frac{x}{x + 2} + \frac{5}{2} = \frac{17}{6}$$

We multiply both sides by the LCD, which is $6(x + 2)$.

$$6(x + 2)\left(\frac{x}{x + 2} + \frac{5}{2}\right) = 6(x + 2)\left(\frac{17}{6}\right)$$

$$6x + 15(x + 2) = 17(x + 2)$$

$$21x + 30 = 17x + 34$$

$$4x = 4$$

$$x = 1$$

Then

$$\frac{x}{x + 2} = \frac{1}{3}$$

is the fraction. (Verify that the fraction $\frac{1}{3}$ does satisfy the given conditions.)

✔ Progress Check 2

The numerator of a fraction is 3 more than its denominator. If the fraction is subtracted from $\frac{11}{4}$, the result is 1. Find the fraction.

Answer

$\dfrac{7}{4}$

EXAMPLE 3   SOLVING A DISTANCE PROBLEM

An airplane flying against the wind travels 150 miles in the same time that it can travel 180 miles with the wind. If the wind speed is 10 miles per hour, what is the speed of the airplane in still air?

SOLUTION

Let r = the rate (or speed) of the airplane in still air. Let's display the information that we have.

	Rate	×	Time	=	Distance
With wind	$r + 10$		t		180
Against wind	$r - 10$		t		150

From the equation rate × time = distance, we know

$$\text{time} = \frac{\text{distance}}{\text{rate}}$$

Since we are told that the time of travel with the wind is the same as that against the wind, we have

$$\text{time with wind} = \text{time against wind}$$

$$\frac{180}{r + 10} = \frac{150}{r - 10}$$

Multiplying both sides of the equation by the LCD, which is $(r + 10)(r - 10)$, we have

$$(r + 10)(r - 10)\left(\frac{180}{r + 10}\right) = (r + 10)(r - 10)\left(\frac{150}{r - 10}\right)$$

$$180(r - 10) = 150(r + 10)$$

$$180r - 1800 = 150r + 1500$$

$$30r = 3300$$

$$r = 110$$

The rate of the plane in still air is 110 miles per hour.

✔ Progress Check 3

An express train travels 200 miles in the same time that a local train travels 150 miles. If the express train travels 20 miles per hour faster than the local train, find the rate of each train.

Answer

local: 60 miles per hour; express: 80 miles per hour

Work Problems

There is a class of problems called **work problems** that lead to equations with fractions. Work problems typically involve two or more people or machines working on the same task. The key to these problems is to express the rate of work per unit of time, whether an hour, a day, a week, or some other unit. For example, if a machine can do a job in 5 days, then

$$\text{rate of machine} = \frac{1}{5} \text{ job per day}$$

If this machine were used for two days, it would perform $\frac{2}{5}$ of the job. In summary:

> If a machine (or person) can complete a job in n days, then
>
> $$\text{rate of machine (or person)} = \frac{1}{n} \text{job per day}$$
>
> $$\text{work done} = \text{rate} \times \text{time}$$

The assumption made in these problems is that the people or machines involved work at the same rate at all times, whether working alone or together.

EXAMPLE 4 SOLVING A WORK PROBLEM

A firm with two factories receives an order for the manufacture of circuit boards. Factory A can complete the order in 20 days, and factory B can complete the order in 30 days. How long will it take to complete the order if both factories are assigned to the task?

SOLUTION

Let x = number of days for completing the job when both factories are assigned. We can display the information in a table.

	Time alone	Rate	× Time	= Work done
Factory A	20	$\frac{1}{20}$	x	$\frac{x}{20}$
Factory B	30	$\frac{1}{30}$	x	$\frac{x}{30}$

Since

$$\text{work done by factory A} + \text{work done by factory B} = 1 \text{ whole job}$$

we have

$$\frac{x}{20} + \frac{x}{30} = 1$$

Multiplying both sides by the LCD, which is 60, we have

$$60\left(\frac{x}{20} + \frac{x}{30}\right) = 60 \cdot 1$$

$$3x + 2x = 60$$

$$5x = 60$$

$$x = 12$$

Thus, it takes 12 days to complete the job if both factories are assigned to the task.

✔ **Progress Check 4**

An electrician can complete a job in 6 hours; his assistant requires 12 hours to do the same job. How long would it take the electrician and assistant, working together, to do the job?

Answer

4 hours

EXAMPLE 5   SOLVING A WORK PROBLEM

Using a small mower, a student begins to mow a lawn at 12 noon, a job that would take him 9 hours. At 1 P.M. another student, using a tractor, joins him; and they complete the job together at 3 P.M. How many hours would it take to do the job by tractor only?

SOLUTION

Let x = number of hours to do the job by tractor alone. The small mower worked from 12 noon to 3 P.M., or 3 hours; the tractor was used from 1 P.M. to 3 p.m., or 2 hours. All of the information can be displayed in a table.

	Time alone	Rate	× Time	= Work done
Small mower	9	$\frac{1}{9}$	3	$\frac{3}{9}$
Tractor	x	$\frac{1}{x}$	2	$\frac{2}{x}$

since

$$\text{work done by small mower} + \text{work done by tractor} = 1 \text{ whole job}$$

we have

$$\frac{3}{9} + \frac{2}{x} = 1$$

To solve, multiply both sides by the LCD, which is $9x$.

$$9x\left(\frac{3}{9} + \frac{2}{x}\right) = 9x \cdot 1$$

$$3x + 18 = 9x$$

$$18 = 6x$$

$$x = 3$$

Thus, by tractor alone, the job can be done in 3 hours.

✔ Progress Check 5

A printing press can print the morning newspaper in 6 hours. After the press has been in operation for 2 hours, a second press joins in printing the paper; both presses finish the job in 2 more hours. How long would it take the second press to print the morning newspaper if it had to do the entire job alone?

Answer

6 hours

Exercise Set 5.6

1. If two thirds of a certain number is added to one half of the number, the result is 21. Find the number.

2. If one fourth of a certain number is added to one third of the number, the result is 14. Find the number.

3. A certain number is twice another. If the sum of their reciprocals is 4, find the numbers.

4. A certain number is 3 times another. If the difference of their reciprocals is 8, find the numbers. (There are two solutions.)

5. The denominator of a fraction is one more than its numerator. If $\frac{1}{2}$ is added to the fraction, the result is $\frac{5}{4}$. Find the fraction.

6. The numerator of a certain fraction is 3 less than its denominator. If $\frac{1}{10}$ is added to the fraction, the result is $\frac{1}{2}$. Find the fraction.

7. If $\frac{3}{2}$ is added to twice the reciprocal of a certain number, the result is 2. Find the number.

8. If $\frac{1}{3}$ is subtracted from 3 times the reciprocal of a certain number, the result is $\frac{25}{6}$. Find the number.

9. John can mow a lawn in 2 hours, and Peter can mow the same lawn in 3 hours. How long would it take to mow the lawn if they worked together?

10. Computer A can carry out an engineering analysis in 4 hours, and computer B can do the same job in 6 hours. How long would it take to complete the job if both computers worked together?

11. Jackie can paint a certain room in 3 hours, Lisa in 4 hours, and Susan in 2 hours. How long will it take to paint the room if they all work together?

12. A mechanic and assistant, working together, can repair an engine in 3 hours. Working alone, the mechanic can complete the job in 5 hours. How long would it take the assistant to do the job alone?

13. Copying machine A and B, working together, can prepare enough copies of the annual report for the board of directors meeting in 2 hours. Machine A, working alone, requires 3 hours to do the job. How long would it take machine B to do the job by itself?

14. A 5-horsepower snowblower together with an 8-horsepower snowblower can clear a parking lot in 1 hour. The 5-horsepower blower, working alone, can do the job in 3 hours. How long would it take the 8-horsepower blower to do the job by itself?

15. Hoses A and B together can fill a swimming pool in 5 hours. If hose A alone takes 12 hours to fill the pool, how long would it take hose B to fill the pool?

16. A senior copy editor together with a junior copy editor can edit a book in 3 days. The junior editor, working alone, would take twice as long to complete the job as the senior editor would require if working alone. How long would it take each editor to complete the job by herself?

17. Hose A can fill a certain vat in 3 hours. After 2 hours of pumping, hose A is turned off. Hose B is then turned on and completes filling the vat in 3 hours. How long would it take hose B alone to fill the vat?

18. A shovel dozer together with a large backhoe can complete a certain excavation project in 4 hours. The shovel dozer is half as fast as the large backhoe. How long would it take each piece of equipment to complete the job by itself?

19. A printing shop starts a job at 10 A.M. using press A. Using this press alone, it would take 8 hours to complete the job. At 2 P.M. press B is also turned on, and both presses together finish the job at 4 P.M. How long would it take press B to do the job by itself?

20. A moped covers 40 miles in the same time that a bicycle covers 24 miles. If the rate of the moped is 8 miles per hour faster than the bicycle, find the rate of each vehicle.

21. A boat travels 20 kilometers upstream in the same time that it would take the same boat to travel 30 kilometers downstream. If the rate of the stream is 5 kilometers per hour, find the speed of the boat in still water.

22. An airplane flying against the wind travels 300 miles in the same time that it would take the same plane to travel 400 miles with the wind. If the wind speed is 20 miles per hour, find the speed of the airplane in still air.

23. Car A can travel 20 kilometers per hour faster than car B. If car A covers 240 kilometers in the same time that car B covers 200 kilometers, what is the speed of each car?

24. A sedan is 20 miles per hour slower than a sports car. If the sedan can travel 160 miles in the same time that the sports car travels 240 miles, find the speed of each car.

5.7   Ratio and Proportion

Suppose that in looking about your mathematics classroom you find there are 10 male and 14 female students. If we understand **ratio** to be the quotient of two quantities, we see that the ratio of male students to female students is $\frac{10}{14}$ or $\frac{5}{7}$, which we can also write as 10:14 (read "10 to 14").

Ratio

EXAMPLE 1   SIMPLE RATIOS

The entire stock of a small photography store consists of 75 Kodak and 60 Polaroid cameras.

(a) What is the ratio of Kodak to Polaroid cameras?

(b) What is the ratio of Polaroid cameras to the entire stock?

SOLUTIONS

(a) $\dfrac{\text{Kodak}}{\text{Polaroid}} = \dfrac{75}{60} = \dfrac{5}{4}$ (or Kodak:Polaroid = 5:4)

(b) $\dfrac{\text{Polaroid}}{\text{entire stock}} = \dfrac{60}{135} = \dfrac{4}{9}$ (or Polaroid:entire stock = 4:9)

✔ **Progress Check 1**

The American alligator is an endangered species. On an American alligator reserve, there are 600 females and 900 males. Find the ratio of the following:

(a) males to females

(b) females to males

(c) females to total number of alligators

Answers

(a) 9:6 or $\dfrac{3}{2}$ (b) 6:9 or $\dfrac{2}{3}$ (c) 6:15 or $\dfrac{2}{5}$

Ratios can often be used to solve word problems. They enable us to set up equations that can then be solved.

EXAMPLE 2   USING RATIOS IN A WORD PROBLEM

The length and width of a rectangular room are in the ratio 3:4. If the perimeter of the room is 70 feet, what are the dimensions of the room?

SOLUTION

Let $3x$ denote the length of the room. Then the width must be $4x$, since

$$\frac{\text{length}}{\text{width}} = \frac{3}{4} = \frac{3x}{4x}$$

The perimeter P of the rectangle is given by

$$P = \text{length} + \text{length} + \text{width} + \text{width}$$
$$70 = 2(\text{length} + \text{width})$$
$$70 = 2(3x + 4x)$$
$$70 = 14x$$
$$x = 5 \text{ feet}$$

Thus,

$$length = 3x = 3(5) = 15 \, feet$$
$$width = 4x = 4(5) = 20 \, feet$$

✔ **Progress Check 2**

The ratios of two angles of a triangle to the smallest angle are 1:2 and 1:3, respectively. Find the measure of each angle. (*Hint:* The sum of the angles of a triangle is 180°.)

Answer

30°, 60°, 90°

Proportion

When two ratios are set equal to each other, we have what is called a **proportion**. We shall soon see that proportions will be useful in solving many word problems. First we practice the mechanics of operating with proportions.

EXAMPLE 3   PROPORTIONS

Solve for x.

$$\frac{x}{12} = \frac{4}{9}$$

SOLUTION

Multiplying both sides of the equation by 12, we have

$$\frac{x}{12} \cdot \frac{12}{1} = \frac{4}{9} \cdot \frac{12}{1} = \frac{48}{9} = \frac{16}{3}$$

Thus,

$$x = \frac{16}{3}$$

✔ **Progress Check 3**

Solve for r.

(a) $\dfrac{3}{r-1} = \dfrac{1}{4}$ (b) $\dfrac{4}{2} = \dfrac{2r}{5}$

Answers

(a) $r = 13$ (b) $r = 5$

The Most Pleasing Rectangle

From the time of the ancient Greeks, certain ratios have played a surprising role in aesthetics and, in particular, in architecture.

Suppose that a line segment of length L is divided into two parts of lengths a and b, as in Figure 1. If

$$\frac{L}{a} = \frac{a}{b}$$

then the ratio $a{:}b$, denoted by ϕ (the Greek letter phi) is called the **golden ratio**. The great German astronomer Kepler called it the "divine proportion," and many extraordinary properties of this number have been developed since the Middle Ages. We will show in Section 9.2 that the numerical value of ϕ is approximately 1.61803.

The ancient Greek architects observed that a rectangle the lengths of whose adjacent sides are in the ratio $\phi{:}1$ appears to be the most pleasing rectangle to a majority of viewers. This rectangle, shown in Figure 2, is called the **golden rectangle**; and psychological experiments in the late 1800s backed up the findings of the early Greeks, whose architects put great faith in the golden rectangle. The proportions of the Parthenon in Athens, built in the fifth century B.C., are those of the golden rectangle.

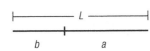

Figure 1 Golden Ratio

Figure 2 Golden Rectangle

Golden Rectangle			
L	a	b	φ
1	.618033989	.381966011	1.61803399
2	1.23606798	.763932023	1.61803399
3	1.85410197	1.14589803	1.61803399
4	2.47213596	1.52786405	1.61803399
5	3.09016994	1.90983006	1.61803399
6	3.70820393	2.29179607	1.61803399
7	4.32623792	2.67376208	1.61803399
8	4.94427191	3.05572809	1.61803399
9	5.56230590	3.43769410	1.61803399
10	6.18033989	3.81966011	1.61803399

Applications

We now turn to the use of proportions in the solution of applied problems.

EXAMPLE 4   PROPORTIONS IN A WORD PROBLEM

ABC University has determined that a student-teacher ratio of 19:2 is ideal. If there will be 855 students next fall, how large a teaching staff will be required, assuming that the ideal student-faculty ratio will be maintained?

SOLUTION

Let x denote the number of teachers. Then

$$\frac{\text{students}}{\text{teachers}} = \frac{19}{2} = \frac{855}{x}$$

Then, multiplying by $2x$ to clear fractions, we have

$$19x = 2(855) = 1710$$

$$x = \frac{1710}{19} = 90$$

Thus, 90 teachers are required.

✔ Progress Check 4

Four out of every five homes in suburban Philadelphia have two telephones. If 25,000 new homes are to be built, how many of these will have two telephones?

Answer

20,000

EXAMPLE 5   PROPORTIONS IN A WORD PROBLEM

A landscaping service advertises that the cost of sodding a 1500-square-foot area is $240. What would be the proportional cost of sodding an area of 3500 square feet?

SOLUTION

Let x be the cost of sodding the larger area. Then

$$\frac{\text{area}}{\text{cost}} = \frac{1500}{240} = \frac{3500}{x}$$

or, after clearing fractions,

$$1500x = 840,000$$

$$x = 560$$

Thus, the proportional cost is $560.

✔ Progress Check 5

The cost of an airplane flight of 600 miles is $75. What is the proportional cost of a flight of 1600 miles?

Answer

$200

Exercise Set 5.7

In Exercises 1–6 write as a ratio.

1. 5.08 centimeters to 2 inches

2. 2 inches to 5.08 centimeters

3. 8 feet to 2.5 feet

4. 1.3 inches to 12 inches

5. 12 cubic feet to 16 cubic feet

6. 2.12 quarts to 2 liters

7. One side of a triangle is 8 centimeters. The other two sides are in the ratio 5:4. If the perimeter of the triangle is 44 centimeters, find the dimension of the other two sides.

8. An artist wants to make a rectangular frame whose length and width are in the ratio 2:3. If the amount of framing material that is available is 25 inches, find the dimensions of the frame.

In Exercises 9–14 solve for the unknown in each proportion.

9. $\dfrac{x}{3} = \dfrac{6}{5}$

10. $\dfrac{y}{4} = \dfrac{2}{3}$

11. $\dfrac{5}{2} = \dfrac{3}{4r}$

12. $\dfrac{6}{5r} = \dfrac{2}{3}$

13. $\dfrac{2}{r+1} = \dfrac{1}{3}$

14. $\dfrac{5}{s-1} = \dfrac{3}{2}$

15. Two numbers whose sum is 30 are in the ratio of 3:7. Find the numbers.

16. A stockbroker charges a commission of $42 on the purchase or sale of 500 shares of stock. What would be the proportional commission on the purchase or sale of 800 shares of stock?

17. A taxpayer pays a state tax of $400 on an income of $12,000. What is the proportional tax on an income of $15,000?

18. In a certain county of Ohio, the ratio of Republicans to Democrats is 3:2.

    (a) If there are 1800 Republicans, how many Democrats are there?

    (b) If there are 1800 Democrats, how many Republicans are there?

19. A toy train manufacturer makes a $\frac{1}{2}$-foot-long locomotive model of a 40-foot-long actual locomotive. If the same scale is maintained, how long is a sleeping car whose scale model is 0.75 foot long?

20. On a certain map, 2 centimeters represents 25 kilometers. How many kilometers does 8 centimeters represent?

21. If 5 out of 6 people in Philadelphia read *The Inquirer*, how many readers of this paper are there in an area with a population of 66,000 people?

22. A car uses 12 gallons of gasoline to travel 216 miles. Assuming the same type of driving, how many gallons of gasoline will be used on a 441-mile trip?

23. If a photocopying machine can produce 740 copies in 40 minutes, how many copies can it produce in 52 minutes?

24. A chemical plant that makes 120 tons daily of a certain product discharges 500 gallons of waste products into a nearby stream. If production is increased to 200 tons daily, how many gallons of waste products will be dumped into the stream?

25. A 150-pound person is given 18 cubic centimeters of a certain drug for a metabolic disorder. How much of the drug will be required by a 200-pound person, assuming the same dose-to-weight ratio?

26. A marketing research firm has determined that two out of five suburban car owners have a station wagon. How many station wagon owners are there among 40,000 suburban car owners?

27. Solve the following proportion for r:

$$\frac{3}{r-1} = \frac{4}{a}$$

28. Solve the following proportion for s:

$$\frac{2s}{a} = \frac{s-1}{2}$$

■ ■ ■

Chapter Summary

Terms and Symbols

algebraic fraction	151	LCD	161	rational expression	153
cancellation principle	151	proportion	182	rational number	151
complex fraction	166	ratio $a:b$	180	work problems	176

Key Ideas for Review

Topic	Page	Key Idea
Cancellation principle	151	Nonzero *factors* appearing in both the numerator and denominator of a fraction may be canceled, provided they are factors of the entire numerator and the entire denominator.
Simplifying a rational expression	151	To simplify a rational expression, follow these steps: *Step 1.* Factor the numerator completely. *Step 2.* Factor the denominator completely. *Step 3.* Use the cancellation principle to cancel factors that are common to both the numerator and the denominator.
Multiplication and division of rational expressions	156	$$\frac{a}{b}\cdot\frac{c}{d}=\frac{ac}{bd} \qquad \frac{\dfrac{a}{b}}{\dfrac{c}{d}}=\frac{a}{b}\cdot\frac{d}{c}=\frac{ad}{bc}$$
Addition and subtraction of rational expressions	160	To add or subtract rational expressions with the same denominator, follow these rules: $$\frac{a}{c}+\frac{b}{c}=\frac{a+b}{c}$$ $$\frac{a}{c}-\frac{b}{c}=\frac{a-b}{c}$$
Least Common Denominator (LCD)	161	The LCD of two or more algebraic fractions is found by forming the product of all the different factors in the denominators, each factor raised to the highest power that it has in any denominator.
Complex fractions	166	Complex fractions can be simplified by two methods: *Method 1.* Multiply the numerator and denominator by the LCD of all the fractions appearing in the complex fraction. *Method 2.* Reduce the numerator and denominator, independently, into simple fractions, and then perform the division.
Equations and inequalities with fractions	169	To solve an equation involving fractions, find the LCD and multiply both sides of the equation by the LCD. This will produce an equation without fractions. If the LCD involved the unknown, then the answer *must be checked*. Inequalities with only constants in the denominator can be handled in the same manner as equations, if we choose the LCD to be a positive number.

Common Errors

1. It is essential to factor completely before attempting cancellation. This will allow you to see which factors are common to the entire numerator and the entire denominator.

2. *Don't* write
$$\frac{xy - 2y}{x} = y - 2y$$
Since x is not a factor of the entire numerator, we may not cancel.

3. *Don't* write
$$\frac{x^2 - y^2}{x - y} = x - y$$
After factoring completely, we see that
$$\frac{x^2 - y^2}{x - y} = \frac{(x + y)\cancel{(x - y)}}{\cancel{x - y}} = x + y$$

4. If an equation is multiplied by an LCD involving a variable, you must check that the answer is a solution of the original equation. The answer may result in a zero in a denominator, in which case it is not a solution.

Review Exercises

Solutions to exercises whose numbers are in bold are in the Solutions section in the back of the book.

5.1 In Exercises 1–4 simplify the given expression, if possible.

1. $\dfrac{5x + 10}{5}$
2. $\dfrac{2x - 3}{2}$

3. $\dfrac{x^2 - 2x - 8}{x + 2}$
4. $\dfrac{4x^3 - 2x^2 + 6x}{2x}$

5.2 In Exercises 5–10 compute and simplify.

5. $\dfrac{x - 1}{2} \cdot \dfrac{x - 2}{3}$
6. $\dfrac{2x - 1}{3} \cdot \dfrac{2x + 1}{2}$

7. $\dfrac{4x}{x + 1} \div \dfrac{2x^2}{x - 1}$
8. $\dfrac{2x^3 - 8x}{x^2 - 3x - 4} \div \dfrac{x^2 - 2x}{x^2 - 1}$

9. $\dfrac{2x^2 + 3x - 2}{3x^2 + x - 2} \cdot \dfrac{2x^2 + 5x + 3}{2x^2 + 5x + 2}$

10. $\dfrac{x^2 + x - 6}{x^2 - 9} \div \dfrac{x^2 + 5x + 6}{x^2 - 4x + 3}$

5.3 In Exercises 11–14 find the least common denominator.

11. $\dfrac{5}{x + 2}, \dfrac{2}{x - 2}$
12. $\dfrac{3x}{x - 2}, \dfrac{5 + x}{(x - 2)^2}$

13. $\dfrac{3y}{y^2 - 4}, \dfrac{2}{y + 2}, \dfrac{4y^2}{y^2 - 2y}$

14. $\dfrac{2x}{3y}, \dfrac{x - 1}{y^2}, \dfrac{x^2 + 2x}{y - 1}$

In Exercises 15–20 perform the indicated operations and simplify.

15. $\dfrac{2 - x^2}{x} + \dfrac{4 + 2x^2}{3x}$
16. $\dfrac{2a - 1}{a - 1} + \dfrac{2a}{a + 1}$

17. $3 - \dfrac{2a}{a - 2}$

18. $\dfrac{2y}{(2x + 3)(x - 1)} - \dfrac{y - 1}{2x + 3}$

19. $\dfrac{x + 1}{2(x^2 - 9)} + \dfrac{x - 3}{3(x - 3)} - \dfrac{x}{x + 3}$

20. $2 - \dfrac{x}{x^2 - 1} + \dfrac{2x - 3}{2(x + 1)}$

5.4 In Exercises 21–26 simplify the given expression.

21. $\dfrac{2 - \dfrac{1}{x}}{1 + \dfrac{5}{x}}$
22. $\dfrac{a - \dfrac{1}{a - 1}}{3a - \dfrac{1}{a - 1}}$

23. $\dfrac{\dfrac{1}{a^2} - \dfrac{1}{a}}{\dfrac{1}{a^2} + \dfrac{1}{a}}$
24. $\dfrac{\dfrac{3}{y^2 - 9} - 3}{\dfrac{2}{y^2 - 2y - 3}}$

25. $\dfrac{\dfrac{x}{x + 1} - \dfrac{1}{x}}{\dfrac{x}{x + 1} + \dfrac{1}{x}}$
26. $\dfrac{\dfrac{x^2}{x - 3} + \dfrac{x}{x - 3}}{\dfrac{2x}{x - 3} - \dfrac{x}{x + 3}}$

5.5   In Exercises 27–32 solve and check.

27. $\dfrac{x}{2} = \dfrac{2}{7}$ 28. $\dfrac{2x - 1}{3} = \dfrac{2}{3}$

29. $\dfrac{2a}{5} + 1 = \dfrac{3}{4}$ 30. $\dfrac{y}{2y - 1} = \dfrac{2}{5}$

31. $\dfrac{2x + 1}{2x - 1} = -\dfrac{2}{3}$ 32. $\dfrac{2r - 1}{2r + 3} - 2 = \dfrac{3}{2r + 3}$

5.6 33. The denominator of a fraction is 2 less than its numerator. If $\frac{2}{3}$ is added to the fraction, the result is $\frac{7}{3}$. Find the fraction.

34. A certain number is three times another. If the difference of their reciprocals is $\frac{2}{3}$, find the number. (There are two answers.)

35. If $\frac{1}{2}$ is added to three times the reciprocal of a certain number, the result is 2. Find the number.

36. A typing service finds that employee A can type a complete manuscript in 10 days, and employee B can type it in 15 days. How long will it take to type the manuscript if both employees work on it?

37. Two photographers working together can complete a fashion assignment in 3 hours. Working alone, the senior photographer can complete the job in 5 hours. How long would it take the junior photographer to complete the job?

38. The first author of a mathematics textbook starts to work on the book on January 1, 2005, and can complete the book on December 31, 2005, if he works on it alone. On July 1, 2005, his co-author starts to work on the book, and together they complete the book on October 1, 2005. How long would it take the second author to write the book by himself? Assume that each month has 30 days.

39. John can decorate the gym for the Saturday night dance in 4 hours, Mary in 6 hours, and

Stacy in 8 hours. How long will the job take if all three work together?

40. A canoe travels 30 kilometers upstream in the same time that it would take the canoe to travel 50 kilometers downstream. If the rate of the stream is 4 kilometers per hour, what is the speed of the canoe in still water?

41. Computer A does 200 million computations in the same time that computer B does 120 million computations. If computer A is 10 million computations per second faster than computer B, how many operations per second does each computer carry out?

42. A cyclist riding against the wind travels 120 miles in the same time that she can travel 600 miles with the wind. If wind speed is 20 miles per hour, what is the speed of the cyclist in still air?

5.7   In Exercises 43–46 solve for the unknown in each proportion.

43. $\dfrac{3x}{4} = \dfrac{3}{2}$ 44. $\dfrac{2y - 1}{3} = \dfrac{5}{3}$

45. $\dfrac{2}{2r + 3} = \dfrac{1}{2}$ 46. $\dfrac{3}{r - 2} = \dfrac{2}{r + 3}$

47. If 2 out of 7 students in your English class smoke, how many smokers are there if the class has 35 students?

48. Suppose that the annual return on a $5000 investment is $12.50. What is the proportional return on a $1250 investment?

49. The cost of a 180-square-foot carpet is $600. What is the cost of a 240-square-foot carpet that is made of the same material?

50. The ratio of nuts to raisins in a health food snack is 2:3. How many ounces of raisins are there in a 2-pound (32-ounce) pack of the snack?

Progress Test 5A

1. Multiply $\dfrac{-8x^2(4 - x^2)}{2y^2} \cdot \dfrac{3y}{x - 2}$

2. Divide $\dfrac{2x^2 - x - 6}{x^2 + x - 12}$ by $\dfrac{-x^2 - 2x + 8}{3x^2 - 10x + 3}$

3. Compute $\dfrac{2x^2 - 5x + 2}{5 - x} \div \dfrac{3x}{x^2 - 6x + 5}$

4. Find the LCD of $\dfrac{2}{(x - 1)y}, \dfrac{-4}{y^2}$, and $\dfrac{x + 2}{5(x - 1)^2}$

5. Find $\dfrac{2}{x - 5} - \dfrac{11}{5 - x}$

6. Find $\dfrac{4}{y(y + 1)} - \dfrac{3y}{y + 1} + \dfrac{y - 1}{2y}$

7. Simplify $\dfrac{6x - 3}{2 - \dfrac{1}{x}}$

8. Simplify $\dfrac{1 - \dfrac{7}{x^2 - 9}}{\dfrac{x - 4}{x^2 + x - 6}}$

9. Solve $\dfrac{-5x - 2}{2x + 6} - 2 = \dfrac{x + 4}{x + 3}$

10. Solve $\dfrac{2x + 3}{2} \leqslant \dfrac{x}{6} - 4$

11. An apprentice plumber can complete a job in 6 hours. After he has been working on the assignment for 2 hours, he is joined by a master plumber, and the two complete the job in 1 more hour. How long would it take the master plumber working alone to do the entire job?

12. Solve $\dfrac{3}{n + 2} = \dfrac{1}{2}$

13. The interest on a $3000 loan is $125. What is the interest on a $7000 loan at the same interest rate for the same length of time?

Progress Test 5B

1. Multiply $\dfrac{14(y - 1)}{3(x^2 - y^2)} \cdot \dfrac{9(x + y)}{-7y^2}$

2. Divide $\dfrac{5 - x}{3x^2 + 5x - 2}$ by $\dfrac{x^2 - 4x - 5}{2x^2 + 3x - 2}$

3. Compute $\dfrac{x^4 - x^2}{x^2 - 4} \div \dfrac{x^2 - x}{-2x + 4}$

4. Find the LCD of $\dfrac{y - 1}{x^2(y + 1)}, \dfrac{x - 2}{2x(y - 1)}$, and $\dfrac{3x}{4(y + 1)^2}$

5. Find $\dfrac{x + 1}{3 - x} + \dfrac{x - 1}{x - 3}$

6. Find $\dfrac{3}{4(v - 1)} + \dfrac{v + 2}{v^2(v - 1)} - \dfrac{v + 1}{2v}$

7. Simplify $\dfrac{2x - 4}{\dfrac{2}{x} - 1}$

8. Simplify $\dfrac{\dfrac{x^2 - x - 6}{2x + 2}}{\dfrac{3}{x^2 - 1} - 1}$

9. Solve $\dfrac{1 - 4x}{2x - 2} + 6 = \dfrac{2x}{1 - x}$

10. Solve $\dfrac{3 - x}{3} + 3 \geqslant \dfrac{x}{2}$

11. A fast collator can do a job in 4 hours while a slower-model collator requires 6 hours. They are both assigned to a job, but after one hour the slower collator is reassigned. How long will it take the faster collator to finish the job?

12. Solve $\dfrac{4}{t - 1} = \dfrac{2}{3}$

13. A golfer cards a 36 for the first 8 holes. What is her proportional score for 18 holes?

Chapter 5 Project

To get more out of this chapter project, try reading a little of the classic book *The Compleat Strategyst* by J. D. Williams, © 1954. The subject of game theory is complex but rewarding. Rational expressions may be used to represent the value of a game. The value of a game is the average payoff you may expect to receive each time you play, if you play using the appropriate strategy! A payoff may be measured in points, dollars, or any countable units.

Look at Exercises 59 and 60 in Section 5.3, and Exercise 35 in Section 5.5. Now invent a simple game, perhaps using coins or dice. It should involve two players and have a set number of options for each player on each turn. Include a description of payoffs to each player; i.e., what is the reward if you win on any given turn? Look for a description of the classic finger game Morra for a good example.

What strategies (plans of action) would improve the payoffs for either player in your game? Or is it completely random?

▪ ▪ ▪

6 Functions

"The concept of function is of the greatest importance not only in pure mathematics but also in practical applications."

—Richard Courant and Herbert Robbins

Try this experiment. Listen to a cricket chirping, and count the number of times it chirps in one minute. Divide that number by 4; then add 40. Now compare that result to the temperature in degrees Fahrenheit. Is your result close? It probably is.

This is one example of a *function*. For this experiment, the outside temperature in degrees Fahrenheit is treated as a function of the number of times a cricket chirps in fifteen seconds. This rule of thumb has actually been shown to have validity. Find out how by looking up Svante Arrhenius at http://scienceworld.wolfram.com/biography/.

We will look at this function more closely in several sections of this chapter. By looking at its graph, determining the slope, finding its inverse, etc., you will see how functions help us to predict events in the world around us. (See the chapter project.)

■ ■ ■

http://scienceworld
.wolfram.com/biography/

What is the result of increased fertilization on the growth of an azalea? If the minimum wage is increased, what will be the effect on the number of unemployed workers? When a submarine dives, can we calculate the water pressure against the hull at a given depth?

Each of the questions posed above seeks a relationship between phenomena. The search for relationships, or correspondence, is a central activity in our attempts to understand the universe; it is used in mathematics, engineering, the physical and biological sciences, the social sciences, business and economics.

The concept of a **function** has been developed as a means of organizing and assisting the study of relationships. Since graphs are powerful means of exhibiting relationships, we begin with a study of the Cartesian, or rectangular, coordinate system. We then formally define a function and offer a number of ways of viewing the concept of a function. **Function notation** will be introduced to provide a convenient means of writing functions.

We will also explore some special types of functional relationships (**increasing and decreasing functions**), the effect of combining functions in various ways, and how functions can be used to describe certain processes.

6.1   Rectangular Coordinate Systems

In Chapter 1 we associated the system of real numbers with points on the real number line. That is, we saw that there is a one-to-one correspondence between the system of real numbers and points on the real number line.

We will now develop an analogous way to handle points in a plane. We begin by drawing a pair of perpendicular lines intersecting at a point O called the **origin**. One of the lines, called the **x-axis**, is usually drawn in a horizontal position. The other line, called the **y-axis**, is usually drawn vertically.

If we think of the x-axis as a real number line, we may mark off some convenient unit of length, with positive numbers to the right of the origin and negative numbers to the left of the origin. Similarly, we may think of the y-axis as a real number line. Again, we may mark off a convenient unit of length (usually the same as the unit of length on the x-axis), with the upward direction representing positive numbers and the downward direction negative numbers. The x- and y-axes are called **coordinate axes**, and together they constitute a **rectangular coordinate system**, also called a **Cartesian coordinate system** (Figure 1).

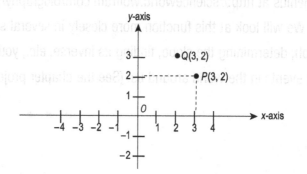

Figure 1   **Coordinates of a Point**

By using coordinate axes, we can outline a procedure for labeling a point P in the plane (see Figure 1). From P, draw a perpendicular line to the x-axis and note that it meets the x-axis at $x = 3$. Now draw a perpendicular line from P to the y-axis and note that it meets the y-axis at $y = 2$. We say that the **coordinates** of P are given by the **ordered pair** (3, 2). The term "ordered pair" means that the order is significant, that is, the ordered pair (3, 2) is different from the ordered pair (2, 3). In fact, the ordered pair (2, 3) gives the coordinates of the point Q shown in Figure 1.

The first number of the ordered pair (a, b) is sometimes called the **abscissa** of P and the second number is called the **ordinate** of P. We will use a simpler terminology. We call a the **x-coordinate** (since we measure it along the x-axis) and b the **y-coordinate** (since we measure it along the **y-axis**).

Let's recap what we have done. We now have a procedure by which each point P in the plane determines a unique ordered pair of real numbers (a, b). It is customary to write the point P as $P(a, b)$. It is also true that every ordered pair of real numbers (a, b) determines a unique point P in the plane that is a units from the y-axis and b units from the x-axis.

We can note a few additional facts, using Figure 2:

- The coordinate axes divide the plane into four **quadrants**, which we label I, II, III, and IV, as shown in Figure 2. The point $(-3, 2)$ is in Quadrant II; the point $(2, -4)$ is in Quadrant IV.

- All points on the x-axis have a **y-coordinate** of 0. For example, point A has coordinates $(-1, 0)$; point E has coordinates $(3, 0)$.

- All points on the y-axis have an x-coordinate of 0. For example, point C has coordinates $(0, 3)$ and point F has coordinates $(0, -3)$.

- The x-coordinate of a point is the distance of the point from the y-axis; the y-coordinate is the distance from the x-axis. Point $D(2, 3)$ is 2 units from the y-axis and 3 units from the x-axis.

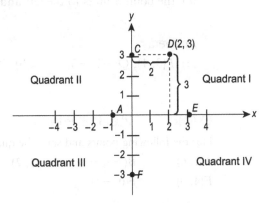

Figure 2   **The Four Quadrants**

EXAMPLE 1   FINDING THE COORDINATES OF A POINT

Find the coordinates of the points *A*, *B*, *C*, *D*, and *E* in Figure 3.

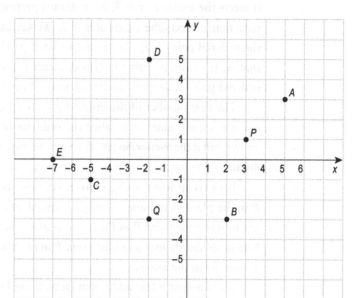

Figure 3   **Finding the Coordinates of a Point**

SOLUTIONS

$A(5, 3)$ $B(2, -3)$ $C(-5, -1)$ $D(-2, 5)$ $E(-7, 0)$

✔ **Progress Check 1**

Using Figure 3 in Example 1, find the following coordinates:

(a) *P* and *Q*

(b) the point 1 unit to the right and 2 units below *A*

(c) the point 3 units to the left and 4 units up from *C*

Answers

(a) $P(3, 1)$, $Q(-2, -3)$ (b) $(6, 1)$ (c) $(-8, 3)$

EXAMPLE 2   PLOTTING POINTS

Plot the following points and state the quadrant in which each point lies.

$A(1, 6)$ $B(-3, -3)$ $C(-3, 2)$ $D(2, -5)$

$E(4, 0)$ $F(0, -1)$

SOLUTIONS

See Figure 4.

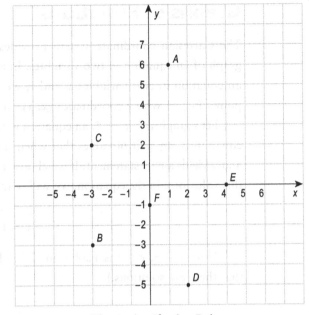

Figure 4   **Plotting Points**

A: Quadrant I   B: Quadrant III   C: Quadrant II

D: Quadrant IV   E: Not in a quadrant   F: Not in a quadrant

✔ **Progress Check 2**

Plot each of the following points and state the quadrant in which it lies.

L(−4, −2)   R(2, 5)   M(0, 3)

S(−1, 0)   T(−2, 3)   U(3, −1.5)

Answers

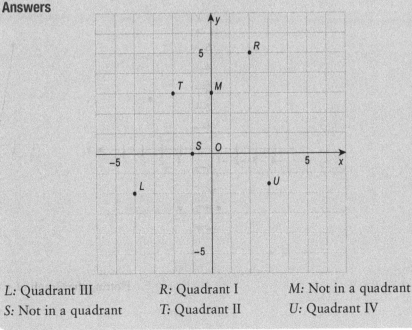

L: Quadrant III   R: Quadrant I   M: Not in a quadrant

S: Not in a quadrant   T: Quadrant II   U: Quadrant IV

Graphs of Equations

The Cartesian coordinate system provides a means of drawing a "picture" or **graph of an equation in two variables.** In general, when we refer to the graph of an equation in two variables x and y, we shall mean the set in the plane of all points $P(x, y)$ whose coordinates (x, y) satisfy the given equation.

Let's graph $y = x^2 - 4$, an equation in the variables x and y. A solution to this equation is any pair of values that when substituted in the equation in place of x and y yields a true statement. If we choose a value for x, say, $x = 3$, and substitute this value of x in the equation, we will obtain the corresponding value of y.

$$y = x^2 - 4$$
$$y = (3)^2 - 4 = 5$$

Thus, $x = 3, y = 5$ is a solution. Table 1 shows a number of solutions. (Verify that these are solutions.)

TABLE 1 Points on the Graph of $y = x^2 - 4$

x	-3	-2	-1	0	1	2	$\dfrac{5}{2}$
$y = x^2 - 4$	5	0	-3	-4	-3	0	$\dfrac{9}{4}$

We can treat the numbers in Table 1 as ordered pairs (x, y) and plot the points that they represent. Figure 5a shows the points; in Figure 5b we have joined the points to form a smooth curve, which is the graph of the equation.

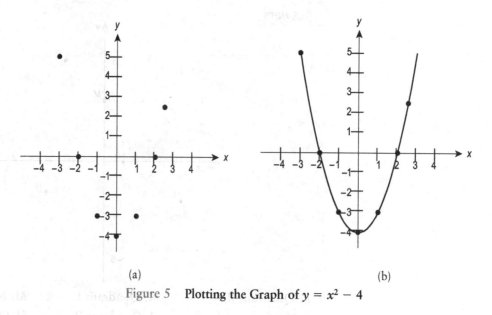

(a)   (b)

Figure 5 **Plotting the Graph of $y = x^2 - 4$**

EXAMPLE 3   ABSOLUTE VALUE IN GRAPHING

Graph the equation $y = |x + 1|$.

SOLUTION

Form a table by assigning values to x and then calculating the corresponding values of y.

x	-3	-2	-1	0	1	2	3	4
$y = |x + 1|$	2	1	0	1	2	3	4	5

(Verify that the table entries are correct. Remember—we are dealing with absolute value.) Now we plot the points and join the points in a "smooth" curve (Figure 6). The curve of $y = x + 1$ appears to be two rays intersecting at the point $(-1, 0)$. (A ray is a line segment of indefinite length starting from a fixed point.)

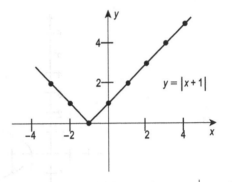

Figure 6   **Graph of the Equation $y = |x + 1|$**

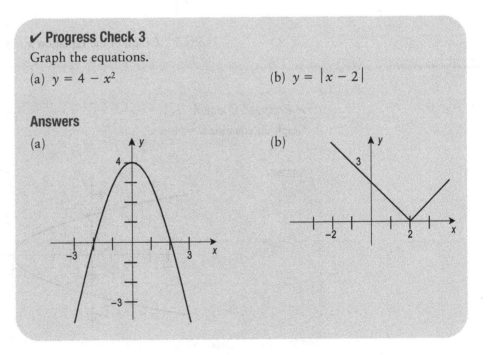

✔ Progress Check 3

Graph the equations.

(a) $y = 4 - x^2$ (b) $y = |x - 2|$

Answers

(a)

(b)

EXAMPLE 4   FINDING THE ORDERED PAIRS (X, Y)

Graph the equation $x = y^2 + 1$.

SOLUTION

We need to find ordered pairs (x, y) that will satisfy the given equation. In this case it is easiest to pick a value of y and find the corresponding value of x from the given equation. Thus, if $y = 0$, then $x = 1$; and if $y = 1$, then $x = 2$. In this manner we obtain the following table;

y	-3	-2	-1	0	1	2	3
x	10	5	2	1	2	5	10
(x, y)	$(10, -3)$	$(5, -2)$	$(2, -1)$	$(1, 0)$	$(2, 1)$	$(5, 2)$	$(10, 3)$

The graph is shown in Figure 7.

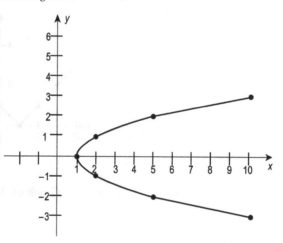

Figure 7   **Graph of the Equation $x = y^2 + 1$**

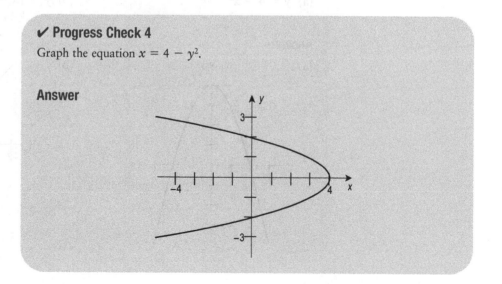

✔ **Progress Check 4**

Graph the equation $x = 4 - y^2$.

Answer

Exercise Set 6.1

In Exercises 1 and 2 find the coordinates of the points A, B, C, D, E, F, G, and H from the graphs.

1.

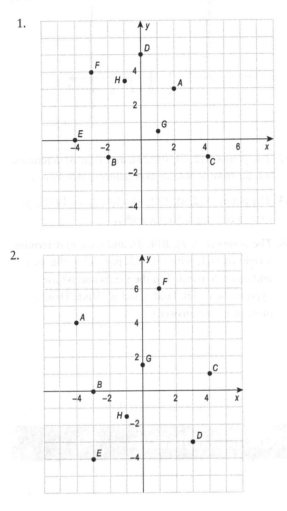

2.

In Exercises 3–8 plot the given points.

3. $(2, 3)$, $(-3, -2)$, $(-1, 0)$, $(4, -4)$, $(-1, 1)$, $(0, -2)$

4. $(-3, 4)$, $(3, 0)$, $(3, 2)$, $(3, -3)$, $(0, 4)$, $(-1, -2)$

5. $(4, -3)$, $(1, 4)$, $(-5, 2)$, $(0, 0)$, $(-4, 0)$, $(-4, -5)$

6. $(-4, -2)$, $(2, 1)$, $(-3, 1)$, $(-2, 0)$, $(0, 2)$, $(1, -3)$

7. $\left(-\frac{1}{2}, \frac{1}{2}\right)$, $(2.5, 1.5)$, $(-7.5, -2.5)$, $\left(1, -\frac{1}{2}\right)$, $\left(-\frac{1}{2}, 0\right)$, $\left(0, \frac{1}{4}\right)$

8. $\left(-\frac{5}{2}, -\frac{3}{2}\right)$, $\left(0, -\frac{1}{2}\right)$, $\left(\frac{1}{4}, 1\right)$, $\left(-1, \frac{3}{2}\right)$, $\left(0, \frac{3}{2}\right)$, $\left(\frac{1}{2}, 0\right)$

9. Using the figure in Exercise 1, find the coordinates of
   (a) the point 2 units to the left and 1 unit above B.
   (b) the point 4 units to the right and 5 units below A.

10. Using the figure in Exercise 2, find the coordinates of
    (a) the point 3 units to the right and 2 units above A.
    (b) the point 2 units to the left and 1 unit below H.

In Exercises 11–22, without plotting, name the quadrant in which the given point is located.

11. $(2, 4)$

12. $(-3, 80)$

13. $(200, -80)$

14. $(-5, 20)$

15. $(-8, -26)$

16. $(40, -20.1)$

17. $(\pi, 8)$

18. $(-2, 0.3)$

19. $(-84.7, -12.8)$

20. $(2.84, -80)$

21. $\left(\frac{17}{4}, \frac{4}{5}\right)$

22. $(-0.5, 0.3)$

23. Which of the following are solutions to $2x - 3y = 12$?
    (a) $(0, -4)$ (b) $(1, 3)$ (c) $(3, 1)$ (d) $(3, -2)$

24. Which of the following are solutions to $3x + 2y = 18$?
    (a) $(-4, 15)$ (b) $\left(0, -\frac{3}{2}\right)$ (c) $(-9, 0)$ (d) $(4, 3)$

25. Which of the following are solutions to $2x + 3y^2 = 18$?
    (a) $(3, -2)$ (b) $(2, 1)$ (c) $(9, 0)$ (d) $(15, 4)$

26. Which of the following are solutions to $3x^2 - 2y = 12$?
    (a) $(0, -6)$ (b) $(4, 30)$ (c) $(2, 0)$ (d) $(-2, 12)$

27. Consider the equation $4x + 3y = 12$. Complete the following table so that each ordered pair (x, y) is a solution of the given equation.

x	1		0		-3	
y		-2	0			2

28. Consider the equation $2x - 3y = 6$. Complete the following table so that each ordered pair (x, y) is a solution of the given equation.

x	6		0		-3	
y		-6	0			2

In Exercises 29–59 graph the given equation. (Use a calculator for Exercises 54–59.)

29. $y = 2x$

30. $y = 3x$

31. $y = 2x + 4$

32. $y = -3x + 5$

33. $3x - 2y = 6$

34. $x = 2y + 3$

35. $3x + 5y = 15$

36. $x = 2$

37. $y = -3$

38. $y = x^2 + 3$

39. $y = 3 - x^2$

40. $y = 3x - x^2$

41. $x = y^2 - 1$

42. $x = 2 - y^2$

43. $y = x^3 + 1$

44. $y = x^3 - 2$

45. $x = y^3 - 1$

46. $x = 2 - y^3$

47. $y = |x - 2|$

48. $y = |x + 3|$

49. $y = |x| + 1$

50. $y = \dfrac{1}{2x + 1}$

51. $xy = 2$

52. $2x^2 + y = 4$

53. $x^2 - y + 8 = 0$

54. $2.23y - 6.47x + 3.41 = 0$

55. $7.37y + 2.75x = 9.46$

56. $3.17x^2 - 2.02y - 3.73 = 0$

57. $6.59x^2 + 3.72y = -9.82$

58. $4.81y^2 - 3.07x + 4.21 = 0$

59. $8.07y^2 + 0.11x = 3.46$

60. Graph the set of all points whose y-coordinate is 3.

61. What is the equation whose graph is shown below?

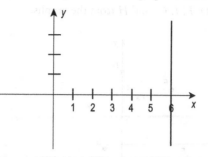

*62. The points $A(2, 7)$, $B(4, 3)$, and $C(x, 3)$ determine a right triangle whose hypotenuse is AB. Find x.

*63. The points $A(2, 6)$, $B(4, 6)$, $C(4, 8)$, and $D(x, y)$ form a rectangle. Find x and y.

*64. The points $A(2, 7)$, $B(4, 3)$, and $C(x, y)$ determine a right triangle with one side parallel to the x-axis and one side parallel to the y-axis and whose hypotenuse is AB. Find x and y. (*Hint:* There is more than one answer.)

6.2   Functions and Function Notation

Functions

The equation

$$y = 2x + 3$$

can be thought of as a rule that assigns a value to y for every value of x. If we let X denote the set of values that we can assign to x and let Y denote the set of values that the equation assigns to y, we can show the correspondence schematically (Figure 8).

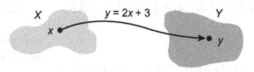

Figure 8   **Correspondence Determined by an Equation**

We are particularly interested in those rules that assign exactly one y in Y for a given x in X. This type of correspondence plays a fundamental role in many mathematical applications and is given a special name.

> A **function** is a rule that, for each x in a set X, assigns exactly one y in a set Y. The element y is called the **image** of x. The set X is called the **domain** of the function, and the set of all images is called the **range** of the function.

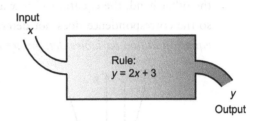

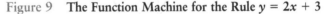

Figure 9   The Function Machine for the Rule $y = 2x + 3$

We can think of the rule defined by the equation $y = 2x + 3$ as a function machine (see Figure 9). Each time we drop a value of x into the input hopper, exactly one value of y falls out of the output hopper. If we drop in $x = 5$, the function machine follows the rule and produces $y = 13$. If the rule in the machine drops out more than one value of y for a given x, then it is not a function. Since we are free to choose those values of x that we drop into the machine, we call x the **independent variable**; the value of y that drops out depends upon the choice of x, and y is called the **dependent variable**. We say the dependent variable is a function of the independent variable; that is, *the output is a function of the input.*

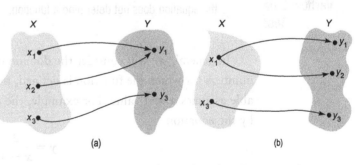

Figure 10   Function and Non-function Correspondence

Let's look at a few schematic presentations. The correspondence in Figure 10a is a function; for each x in X there is exactly one corresponding value of y in Y. True, y_1 is the **image** of both x_1 and x_2, but this does not violate the definition of a function! However, the correspondence in Figure 10b is not a function, since x_1 is assigned to both y_1 and y_2, which does violate the definition of a function.

Vertical Line Test

There is a graphic way to test if an equation determines a function. Let's graph the equations $y = x^2$ and $y^2 = x$ in which x is the independent variable. Now draw vertical lines on both graphs in Figure 11. No vertical line intersects the graph of $y = x^2$ in more than one point; however, some vertical lines intersect the graph of $y^2 = x$ in two points. This is another way of saying that the equation $y = x^2$ assigns exactly one y for each x and therefore determines y as a function of x. On the other hand, the equation $y^2 = x$ assigns two values of y to some values of x, so the correspondence does not determine y as a function of x. Thus, *not every equation in two variables determines one variable as a function of the other.*

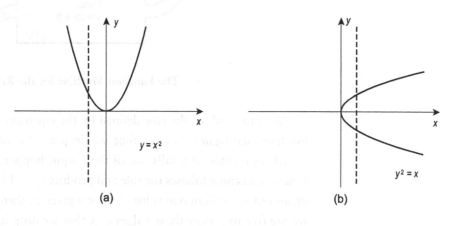

(a)   (b)

Figure 11   **The Vertical Line Test**

Vertical Line Test

If any vertical line meets the graph of an equation in more than one point, then the equation does not determine a function.

In general, we will consider the **domain** of a function to be the set of all real numbers for which the function is defined, that is, for which the dependent variable assumes a real value. For example, the domain of the function determined by the equation

$$y = \frac{2}{x - 1}$$

is the set of real numbers other than $x = 1$, since division by 0 is not defined.

The **range** of a function is, in general, not as easily determined as is the domain. The range is the set of all y values that occur in the correspondence; that is, it is the set of all outputs of the function. For our purposes it will be adequate to determine the range by examining the graph of the function.

EXAMPLE 1   GRAPHS AND FUNCTIONS

Graph the equation. If the correspondence determines a function, find the domain and range.

$$y = 4 + x, \quad 0 \le x \le 5$$

SOLUTION

See Figure 12. The graph is a line segment, and it is clear that no vertical line meets the graph in more than one point. The equation, therefore, determines a function.

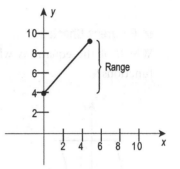

Figure 12   Graph of $y = 4 + x$, $0 \leqslant x \leqslant 5$

We are given that $0 \leqslant x \leqslant 5$, and since the function is defined for all such x, the domain is $\{x | 0 \leqslant x \leqslant 5\}$. We see from the graph that the range is $\{y | 4 \leqslant y \leqslant 9\}$.

✔ Progress Check 1

Graph the equation $y = x^2 - 4$, $-3 \leqslant x \leqslant 3$. If the correspondence determines a function, find the domain and range.

Answer

The desired graph is the portion of the curve shown in Figure 5b of Section 6.1 for the values of x between -3 and 3. The domain is $\{x | -3 \leqslant x \leqslant 3\}$; the range is $\{y | -4 \leqslant y \leqslant 5\}$.

EXAMPLE 2   GRAPHS AND FUNCTIONS

Which of the equations whose graphs are shown in Figure 13 determine functions?

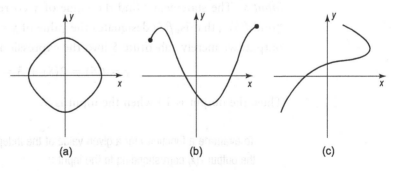

Figure 13   Which Graphs Determine a Function?

SOLUTIONS

(a) Not a function, because some vertical lines meet the graph in more than one point.

(b) A function, passes the vertical line test

(c) Not a function, fails the vertical line test

✔ **Progress Check 2**

Which of the equations whose graphs are shown in Figure 14 determine functions?

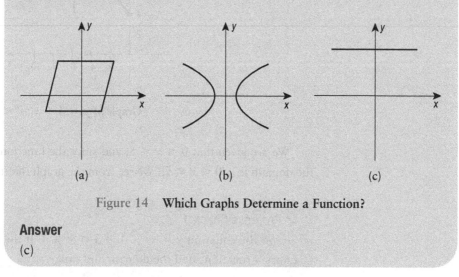

(a)   (b)   (c)

Figure 14   **Which Graphs Determine a Function?**

Answer

(c)

Function Notation

There is a special notation used for functions. We express the functional relation

$$y = 2x + 3$$

by writing

$$f(x) = 2x + 3$$

The symbol $f(x)$ is read "f of x" and denotes the *output* corresponding to the *input* x. The statement "find the value of y corresponding to $x = 5$" becomes "find $f(5)$"; that is, $f(5)$ designates the value of $y = f(x)$ when $x = 5$. To find this output, we merely substitute 5 into the expression in place of x. We then obtain

$$y = f(5) = 2(5) + 3 = 13$$

Thus, the output is 13 when the input is 5.

> To **evaluate** a function f for a given value of the independent variable x is to find the output $f(x)$ corresponding to the input x.

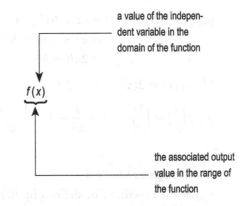

a value of the independent variable in the domain of the function

$f(x)$

the associated output value in the range of the function

A function may be denoted by a letter other than f. Thus, F, g, h, and C may all denote a function.

EXAMPLE 3   USING FUNCTION NOTATION

(a) If $f(x) = 2x^2 - 2x + 1$, find $f(-1)$.

(b) If $f(t) = 3t - 1$, find $f(a^2)$.

SOLUTIONS

(a) We substitute -1 in place of x.

$$f(-1) = 2(-1)^2 - 2(-1) + 1 = 5$$

(b) We substitute a^2 in place of t.

$$f(a^2) = 3(a^2) - 1 = 3a^2 - 1$$

✔ **Progress Check 3**

(a) If $f(u) = u^3 + 3u - 4$, find $f(-2)$.

(b) If $f(t) = t^2 + 1$, find $f(t - 1)$.

Answers

(a) -18 (b) $t^2 - 2t + 2$

EXAMPLE 4   USING FUNCTION NOTATION

Let the function f be defined by $f(x) = x^2 - 1$. Find the following:

(a) $f(-2)$ (b) $f(a + h)$ (c) $f(a + h) - f(a)$ (d) $2f(x)$ (e) $f\left(\dfrac{1}{x}\right)$

SOLUTIONS

(a) $f(-2) = (-2)^2 - 1 = 4 - 1 = 3$

(b) $f(a + h) = (a + h)^2 - 1 = a^2 + 2ah + h^2 - 1$

(c) $f(a + h) - f(a) = (a + h)^2 - 1 - (a^2 - 1)$
$$= a^2 + 2ah + h^2 - 1 - a^2 + 1$$
$$= 2ah + h^2$$

(d) $2f(x) = 2(x^2 - 1) = 2x^2 - 2$

(e) $f\left(\dfrac{1}{x}\right) = \left(\dfrac{1}{x}\right)^2 - 1 = \dfrac{1}{x^2} - 1 = \dfrac{1 - x^2}{x^2}$

✔ **Progress Check 4**

Let the function f be defined by $f(t) = t^2 + t - 1$. Find the following:

(a) $f(0)$ (b) $f(a + h)$ (c) $f(a + h) - f(a)$

Answers

(a) -1 (b) $a^2 + 2ah + h^2 + a + h - 1$ (c) $2ah + h^2 + h$

    WARNING

(a) *Don't* write

$$f(a + 3) = f(a) + f(3)$$

Function notation is not to be confused with the distributive law.

(b) *Don't* write

$$f(a + 3) = f(a) + 3$$

To evaluate $f(a + 3)$, substitute $a + 3$ for each occurrence of the independent variable.

(c) *Don't* write

$$f(x^2) = f \cdot x^2$$

The use of parentheses in function notation does not imply multiplication.

(d) *Don't* write

$$f(x^2) = [f(x)]^2$$

Squaring x is not the same as squaring $f(x)$.

(e) *Don't* write

$$f(3x) = 3f(x)$$

EXAMPLE 5   A FORMULA IN FUNCTION NOTATION

The correspondence between Fahrenheit temperature F and Celsius temperature C is given by

$$F(C) = \frac{9}{5}C + 32$$

which is often simply written as $F = \frac{9}{5}C + 32$.

(a) Find the Fahrenheit temperature corresponding to a Celsius reading of 37° (normal body temperature).

(b) Write C as a function of F.

(c) Find the Celsius temperature corresponding to a Fahrenheit reading of 212° (the boiling point of water).

SOLUTIONS

(a) We substitute $C = 37$ to find $F(37)$.

$$F(37) = \frac{9}{5}(37) + 32 = 98.6$$

Normal body temperature is 98.6° Fahrenheit.

(b) We solve the equation for C.

$$F(C) = \frac{9}{5}C + 32$$

$$F - 32 = \frac{9}{5}C$$

$$C = \frac{5}{9}(F - 32)$$

or

$$C(F) = \frac{5}{9}(F - 32)$$

(c) We substitute $F = 212$ to find $C(212)$.

$$C = \frac{5}{9}(F - 32)$$

$$C(212) = \frac{5}{9}(212 - 32) = \frac{5}{9}(180) = 100$$

Water boils at 100° Celsius.

✔ **Progress Check 5**

Suppose that an object is dropped from a fixed height. If we neglect air resistance, the distance s (in feet) that the object has fallen after t seconds is a function of t given by

$$s(t) = 16t^2$$

(Note that the function does *not* depend upon the mass of the object.) Find the distance traveled by an object when t is as follows:

(a) 2 seconds

(b) 4 seconds

(c) How long does it take an object to fall 400 feet?

Answers

(a) 64 feet   (b) 256 feet   (c) 5 seconds

Exercise Set 6.2

In Exercises 1–10 graph the given equation. If the correspondence is a function, determine the domain and range.

1. $y = 3 + x,\ 0 \leqslant x \leqslant 4$ 2. $y = 2 - x,\ -2 \leqslant x \leqslant 5$

3. $y = x^2 + 1$ 4. $y = 9 - x^2$

5. $y = x^2 - 4$ 6. $y = -4 - x^2$

7. $y = |x|,\ -2 \leqslant x \leqslant 3$

8. $y = |x + 1|,\ -3 \leqslant x \leqslant 1$

9. $y = |2x - 1|,\ -1 \leqslant x \leqslant 2$

10. $y = |x| - 1,\ -2 \leqslant x \leqslant 2$

In Exercises 11–18 determine the domain of the given function.

11. $f(x) = 2x^2 + x - 3$ 12. $g(t) = \dfrac{1}{t - 2}$

13. $f(v) = \dfrac{1}{(v - 3)(v + 1)}$ 14. $g(x) = \dfrac{x - 3}{(x + 2)(x - 4)}$

15. $f(x) = \dfrac{x - 2}{x + 1}$ 16. $h(t) = \dfrac{t}{(t - 3)(t + 5)}$

17. $f(x) = \dfrac{5}{x}$ 18. $g(s) = \dfrac{5s}{s - 2}$

In Exercises 19–30 determine whether or not the given curve is the graph of a function.

19.

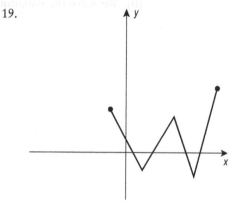

20.

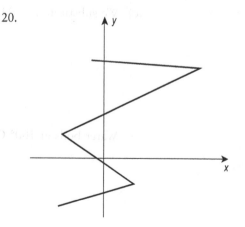

21.

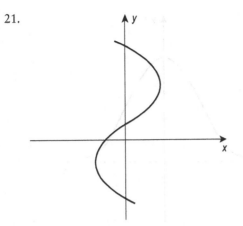

24.

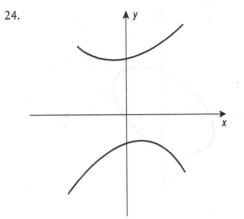

22.

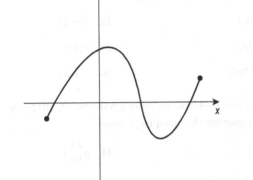

25.

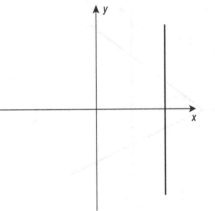

23.

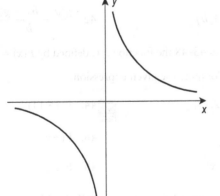

26.

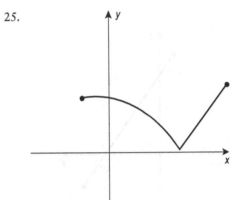

27.

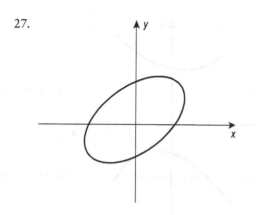

30.

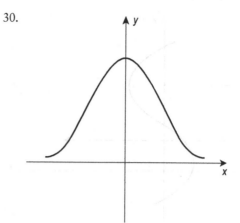

28.

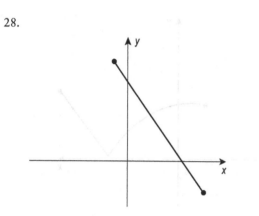

29.

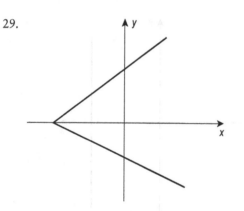

In Exercises 31–36 the function f is defined by $f(x) = 2x^2 + 5$. Compute the given expression.

31. $f(0)$ 32. $f(-2)$

33. $f(a)$ 34. $f(3x)$

35. $3f(x)$ 36. $-f(x)$

In Exercises 37–42 the function g is defined by $g(x) = x^2 + 2x$. Compute the given expression.

37. $g(-3)$ 38. $g\left(\dfrac{1}{x}\right)$

39. $\dfrac{1}{g(x)}$ 40. $g(-x)$

41. $g(a + h)$ 42. $\dfrac{g(a + h) - g(a)}{h}$

In Exercises 43–48 the function F is defined by $F(x) = \dfrac{x^2 + 1}{3x - 1}$. Compute the given expression.

43. $F(-2.73)$ 44. $F(16.11)$

45. $\dfrac{1}{F(x)}$ 46. $F(-x)$

47. $2F(2x)$ 48. $F(x^2)$

In Exercises 49–54 the function r is defined by $r(t) = \dfrac{t - 2}{t^2 + 2t - 3}$. Compute the given expression.

49. $r(-8.27)$ 50. $r(2.04)$

51. $r(2a)$ 52. $2r(a)$

53. $r(a + 1)$ 54. $r(1 + h)$

55. A tour operator who runs charter flights to Rome has established the following pricing schedule. For a group of no more than 100 people, the round trip fare per person is $300. For a group that has more than 100 but fewer than 150 people, the fare will be $250 for each person in excess of 100 people. Write the tour operator's total revenue R as a function of the number of people x in the group.

56. A firm packages and ships 1-pound jars of instant coffee. The cost C of shipping is 40 cents for the first pound and 25 cents for each additional pound.

    (a) Write C as a function of the weight w (in pounds) for $0 < w < 30$.

    (b) What is the cost of shipping a package containing 24 jars of instant coffee?

57. Suppose that x dollars are invested at 7% interest per year compounded annually. Express the amount A in the account at the end of one year as a function of x.

58. The rate of a car rental firm is $19 daily, plus 18¢ per mile that the rented car is driven.

    (a) Express the cost c of renting a car as a function of the number of miles m traveled in one day.

    (b) What is the domain of the function?

    (c) How much would it cost to rent a car for a one-day 100-mile trip?

59. In a wildlife preserve, the population P of eagles depends upon the population x of rodents, its basic food supply. Suppose that P is given by

    $$P(x) = 0.002x + 0.004x^2$$

    What is the eagle population when the rodent population is

    (a) 500?   (b) 2000?

60. A record club offers the following sale. If 3 records are bought at the regular price of $7.98 each, you may purchase up to 7 more records at half price.

    (a) Express the total cost c to a customer as a function of the number r of half-price records bought.

    (b) What is the domain of this function?

    (c) How much will it cost to buy a total of 8 records?

*61. A function f is called **even** if $f(-x) = f(x)$ for every value x in the domain of f; it is called **odd** if $f(-x) = -f(x)$ for all such values x. Determine whether the following functions are even, odd, or neither.

    (a) $f(x) = x^2 + 1$ (b) $f(x) = x^3$

    (c) $f(x) = x^2 + x$ (d) $f(x) = |x|$

*62. Express the area A of an equilateral triangle as a function of the length s of its side.

63. Express the diameter d of a circle as a function of its circumference C.

64. Express the perimeter P of a square as a function of its area A.

65. Read the chapter opening.

    (a) Express the outside temperature T in degrees Fahrenheit as a function of the number of times n that a cricket is heard to chirp in one minute.

    (b) What would the outside temperature be if a cricket was heard to chirp 130 times?

66. (a) Find $f(80)$ for the function

    $$f(t) = \frac{E}{R}\left(\frac{1}{T} - \frac{1}{t}\right)$$

    if E, R, and T are constants equal to 49,000, 8.3145, and 296, respectively. (This is a formula from chemistry that is the basis for the cricket rule-of-thumb in Exercise 65).

    (b) Use your graphing calculator to set up a LIST of values for the constant t: {71, 76, 84, 89, 90}; then reevaluate the function using the LIST.

67. MATHEMATICS IN WRITING:

    (a) Explain in your own words the phrase *domain of a function*.

    (b) Give an example of a function whose domain excludes the number 2. Explain in a complete sentence.

    (c) Give an example of a function whose domain excludes all real numbers less than 5. Explain in a complete sentence.

    (d) How can your graphing calculator help you to determine the range of a function? Give an example.

6.3   Graphs of Functions

We have used the graph of an equation to help us find out whether or not the equation determines a function. It is therefore natural that when we speak of the **graph of a function** such as

$$f(x) = -2x + 4$$

we mean the graph of the equation

$$y = -2x + 4$$

We can therefore use the method of plotting points developed in Section 6.1 to plot the graph of a function determined by an equation.

At times, functions are defined other than by equations. In many important applications, a function may be defined by a table or by several formulas. We illustrate this by several examples.

EXAMPLE 1   A FUNCTION DEFINED BY SEVERAL RULES

The commission earned by a door-to-door cosmetics salesperson is determined as shown in the following table:

Weekly Sales	Commission
Less than $300	20% of sales
$300 or more but less than $400	$60 + 35% of sales over $300
$400 or more	$95 + 60% of sales over $400

(a) Express the commission C as a function of sales s.

(b) Find the commission if the weekly sales are $425.

(c) Sketch the graph of the function.

SOLUTIONS

(a) The function C can be described by three equations:

$$C(s) = \begin{cases} 0.2s & \text{if } s < 300 \\ 60 + 0.35(s - 300) & \text{if } 300 \leq s < 400 \\ 95 + 0.60(s - 400) & \text{if } s \geq 400 \end{cases}$$

(b) When $s = 425$, we must use the third equation and substitute to determine $C(425)$.

$$C(425) = 95 + 0.6(425 - 400)$$
$$= 95 + 0.6(25)$$
$$= 110$$

The commission on sales of $425 is $110.

(c) The graph of the function C consists of three line segments (Figure 15).

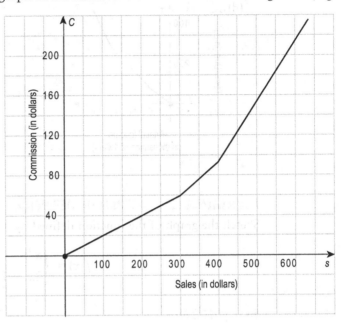

Figure 15   **Graph of a Function Defined by Several Rules**

✔ Progress Check 1

The state tax due is given in the following table:

Annual Income	Tax Due
Under $5000	1% of income
$5000 or more, but less than $15,000	$50 + 2% of income over $5000
$15,000 or more	$250 + 4% of income over $15,000

(a) Express the tax T as a function of income d.

(b) Find the tax due if the income is $7000.

(c) Find the tax due if the income is $18,000.

(d) Sketch the graph of the function T.

Answers

(a) $$T(d) = \begin{cases} 0.01d & \text{if } d < 5000 \\ 50 + 0.02(d - 5000) & \text{if } 5000 \leq d < 15{,}000 \\ 250 + 0.04(d - 15{,}000) & \text{if } d \geq 15{,}000 \end{cases}$$

(b) $T(7000) = 90$

(c) $T(18,000) = 370$

(continues)

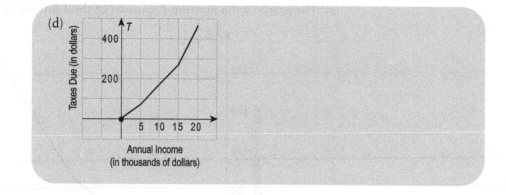

(d)

Taxes Due (in dollars)

Annual Income
(in thousands of dollars)

EXAMPLE 2   A FUNCTION DEFINED BY SEVERAL EQUATIONS

Sketch the graph of the function defined by

$$f(x) = \begin{cases} x^2 & \text{if } -2 \leq x \leq 2 \\ 2x + 1 & \text{if } 2 < x \leq 5 \end{cases}$$

SOLUTION

We form a table of points to be plotted.

x	-2	-1	0	1	2	3	4	5
$f(x)$	4	1	0	1	4	7	9	11

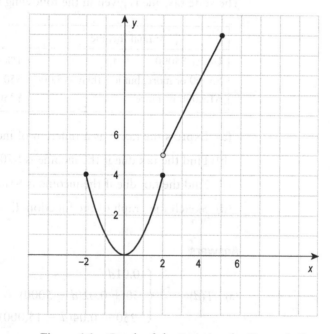

Figure 16   **Graph of the Function for Example 2**

See Figure 16. Note that the graph has a gap. Also note that the point (2, 5) has been marked with an open circle to indicate that it is not on the graph of the function. Had the point (2, 5) been included, we would have two values of y corresponding to $x = 2$, and we would not have a function.

✔ **Progress Check 2**
Sketch the graph of the function defined by

$$f(x) = \begin{cases} 2x, & -2 \leq x < 4 \\ 5, & x \geq 4 \end{cases}$$

Answer

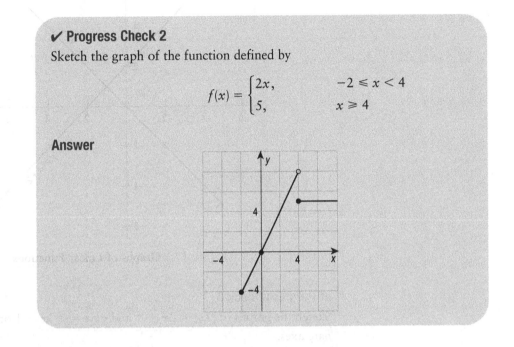

Linear Functions

The function

$$f(x) = ax + b$$

is called a **linear function**. We will study this function in detail in the next chapter and will show that its graph is a straight line. For now, we sketch the graphs of a few linear functions to "convince" ourselves that the graphs appear to be straight lines.

EXAMPLE 3   GRAPHING LINEAR FUNCTIONS
Sketch the graphs of $f(x) = x$ and $g(x) = -x + 2$ on the same coordinate axes.

SOLUTION
We need to graph $y = x$ and $y = -x + 2$. We form a table of values, plot the corresponding points, and connect these by "smooth" curves. See Figure 17.

x	$y = x$	$y = -x + 2$
-4	-4	6
-2	-2	4
0	0	2
1	1	1
3	3	-1

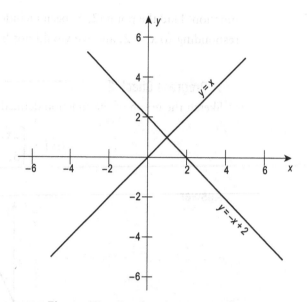

Figure 17   **Graphs of Linear Functions**

✔ **Progress Check 3**

Sketch the graphs of $f(x) = 2x + 1$ and $g(x) = -3x + 1$ on the same coordinate axes.

Answer

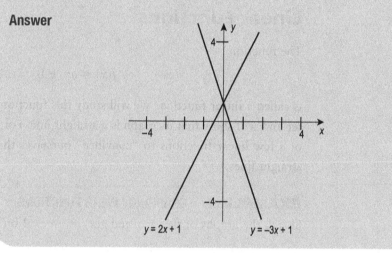

Quadratic Functions

The function

$$f(x) = ax^2 + bx + c, \quad a \neq 0$$

is called a **quadratic function**. The graph of this function is called a **parabola** and will be studied in detail in a later chapter.

EXAMPLE 4 GRAPHING A QUADRATIC FUNCTION

Sketch the graph of $f(x) = 2x^2 - 4x + 3$.

SOLUTION

We need to graph $y = 2x^2 - 4x + 3$. We form a table of values, plot the corresponding points, and connect these by a "smooth" curve. See Figure 18.

x	y
−1	9
0	3
1	1
2	3
3	9

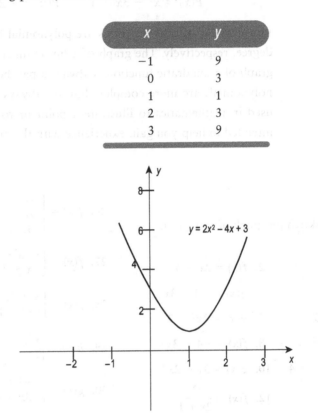

Figure 18 **Graph of a Quadratic Equation**

✔ **Progress Check 4**

Sketch the graph of $f(x) = -x^2 + 4x - 5$.

Answer

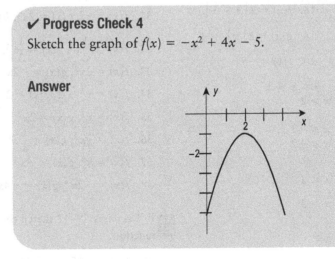

Polynomial Functions

In Chapter 2 we were introduced to polynomials and were shown how to determine the degree of a polynomial. Polynomials in one variable are of particular interest because they always determine a function. The following are some examples:

$$P(x) = x^2 - 3x + 1 \qquad P(x) = -2x^5 + \frac{1}{2}x^3 + 2x - 4$$

Linear and quadratic functions are **polynomial functions** of the first and second degree, respectively. The graph of a linear function is always a straight line; the graph of a quadratic function is always a parabola. The graphs of higher-degree polynomials are more complex, but are always "smooth curves" and are often used in mathematics to illustrate a point or to test an idea. The exercises are intended to help you gain experience with the graphs of polynomial functions.

Exercise Set 6.3

In Exercises 1–30 sketch the graph of each given function.

1. $f(x) = 3x + 4$

2. $f(x) = 2x - 3$

3. $f(x) = 3 - x$

4. $g(x) = -4 - 3x$

5. $f(x) = 2x^2 + 3$

6. $h(x) = 2x^2 - 3$

7. $g(x) = 5 - 2x^2$

8. $f(x) = -4 - 3x^2$

9. $h(x) = x^2 - 4x + 4$

10. $g(x) = 3x - 2x^2$

11. $f(x) = \dfrac{2}{x - 3}$

12. $f(x) = \dfrac{3}{2x + 1}$

13. $g(x) = \dfrac{3x - 4}{2}$

14. $h(x) = \dfrac{4 - x}{3}$

15. $h(x) = |x - 1|$

16. $f(x) = 2|1 - x|$

17. $f(x) = |x| + 1$

18. $g(x) = 2|x| - 1$

19. $f(x) = 3$

20. $f(x) = -5$

21. $f(x) = \begin{cases} -3x, & -4 \leq x \leq 2 \\ -3, & x > 2 \end{cases}$

22. $f(x) = \begin{cases} 3, & x < -2 \\ -2x, & x \geq -2 \end{cases}$

23. $g(x) = \begin{cases} \dfrac{1}{2}x + 1, & x \leq 2 \\ -2x + 6 & x > 2 \end{cases}$

24. $f(x) = \begin{cases} |x + 1|, & x < -1 \\ x, & x \geq -1 \end{cases}$

25. $f(x) = \begin{cases} 2, & x < 3 \\ 1, & x > 3 \end{cases}$

26. $f(x) = \begin{cases} 2, & x < 3 \\ 1, & x = 3 \\ -3, & x > 3 \end{cases}$

27. $f(x) = \begin{cases} -4x - 1, & x \leq -1 \\ -x + 2, & x > -1 \end{cases}$

28. $f(x) = \begin{cases} x + 1, & x < -1 \\ -x^2 + 1, & x > -1 \end{cases}$

29. $h(x) = \begin{cases} x^2, & x < 1 \\ 2, & x \geq 1 \end{cases}$

30. $g(x) = \begin{cases} -x^2 + 2, & x \leq 2 \\ -3x + 1, & x > 2 \end{cases}$

In Exercises 31–38 sketch the graphs of the given functions on the same coordinate axes.

31. $f(x) = x^2$, $g(x) = 2x^2$, $h(x) = \dfrac{1}{2}x^2$

32. $f(x) = \dfrac{1}{2}x^2$, $g(x) = \dfrac{1}{3}x^2$, $h(x) = \dfrac{1}{4}x^2$

33. $f(x) = 2x^2$, $g(x) = -2x^2$

34. $f(x) = x^2 - 2$, $g(x) = 2 - x^2$

35. $f(x) = x^3$, $g(x) = 2x^3$

36. $f(x) = \dfrac{1}{2}x^3$, $g(x) = \dfrac{1}{4}x^3$

37. $f(x) = x^3$, $g(x) = -x^3$

38. $f(x) = -2x^3$, $g(x) = -4x^3$

In Exercises 39–42 sketch the graph of each given function.

39. $f(x) = 0.65x^2 - 0.44$

40. $f(x) = 0.84x^2 + 0.17x - 0.55$

41. $f(x) = 0.15x^3 - 2.1x^2 + 4.6$

42. $f(x) = -3.4x^2 - 1.8x + 6.3$

43. Graph the shipping function of Exercise 56, Section 6.2.

44. Graph the temperature function of Example 5, Section 6.2.

*45. The telephone company charges a fee of $6.50 per month for the first 100 message units and an additional fee of 6 cents for each of the next 100 message units. A reduced rate of 5 cents is charged for each message unit after the first 200 units. Express the monthly charge C as a function of the number of message units x. Graph this function.

*46. The annual dues of a union are as shown in the table.

Employee's annual salary	Annual dues
Less than $8000	$60
$8000 or more, but less than $15,000	$60 + 1% of the salary in excess of $8000
$15,000 or more	$130 + 2% of the salary in excess of $15,000

Express the annual dues d as a function of the salary. Graph this function.

47. MATHEMATICS IN WRITING: Store the LIST {3,4,5,6} as L_1; then graph

$$y = 3x + L_1$$

Write a brief paragraph explaining your results.

48. Refer to Exercise 65 in section 6.2.

(a) Graph the function you found in part a.

(b) Find the slope of the line.

(c) What is the y-intercept of the line?

49. The Celsius temperature C is related to Fahrenheit temperature F by the formula

$$C = \frac{5}{9}(F - 32)$$

Refer to exercise 48 above.

(a) Write a linear equation expressing the outside temperature in degrees Celsius in terms of n, the number of times a cricket chirps in one minute.

(b) Graph this linear relationship.

6.4 Increasing and Decreasing Functions

We say that the straight line in Figure 19a is increasing or rising, since the values of y increase as we move from left to right. Since the graph of a function f is obtained by sketching $y = f(x)$, we can give a precise definition of **increasing** and **decreasing functions**.

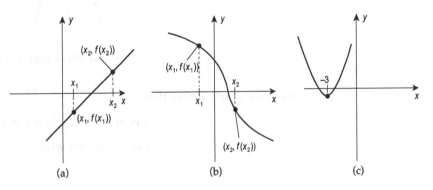

Figure 19 **Graphs of Increasing and Decreasing Functions**

Increasing and Decreasing Functions

- A function f is increasing if $f(x_2) > f(x_1)$ whenever $x_1 < x_2$.
- A function f is decreasing if $f(x_2) < f(x_1)$ whenever $x_1 < x_2$.

In other words, if a function is increasing, the dependent variable y assumes larger values as we move from left to right (Figure 19a); for a decreasing function (Figure 19b), y takes on smaller values as we move from left to right. The function pictured in Figure 19c is neither increasing, nor decreasing, according to this definition. In fact, one portion of the graph is decreasing and another is increasing. We can modify our definition of increasing and decreasing functions so as to apply to intervals in the domain. A function may then be increasing in some intervals and decreasing in others.

Returning to Figure 19c, we see that the function whose graph is shown is decreasing when $x \leq -3$ and increasing when $x \geq -3$. This is the "usual" situation for a function—there are intervals in which the function is increasing and intervals in which it is decreasing. Of course, there is another possibility. The function may have the same value over an interval, in which case we call it a **constant function** over that interval.

EXAMPLE 1   DETERMINING WHERE A FUNCTION IS INCREASING AND DECREASING

Given the function $f(x) = 1 - x^2$, determine where the function is increasing and where it is decreasing.

SOLUTION

We obtain the graph of $y = 1 - x^2$ by plotting several points. See Figure 20.

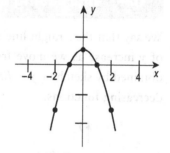

Figure 20   **Graph of $f(x) = 1 - x^2$**

From the graph we see that

$$f \text{ is increasing when } x \leq 0$$
$$f \text{ is decreasing when } x \geq 0$$

✔ **Progress Check 1**

Given $f(x) = x^2 + 2x$, determine where the function is increasing and where the function is decreasing.

Answer

increasing when $x \geq -1$; decreasing when $x \leq -1$

EXAMPLE 2   DETERMINING WHERE A FUNCTION IS INCREASING AND DECREASING

The function f is defined by

$$f(x) = \begin{cases} |x| & \text{if } x \leq 2 \\ -3 & \text{if } x > 2 \end{cases}$$

Find the values of x for which the function is increasing, decreasing, and constant.

SOLUTION

We sketch the graph of f by plotting a number of points. See Figure 21. From the graph we determine the following:

f is increasing if $0 \leq x \leq 2$

f is decreasing if $x \leq 0$

f is constant and has value -3 if $x > 2$

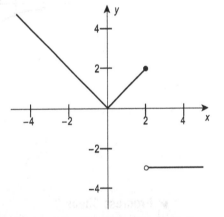

Figure 21   **Graph for Example 2**

✔ **Progress Check 2**

The function f is defined by

$$f(x) = \begin{cases} 2x + 1 & \text{if } x < -1 \\ 0 & \text{if } -1 \leq x \leq 3 \\ -2x + 1 & \text{if } x > 3 \end{cases}$$

Find the values of x for which the function is increasing, decreasing, and constant.

Answer

increasing if $x < -1$; decreasing if $x > 3$; constant if $-1 \leq x \leq 3$

EXAMPLE 3   DETERMINING WHERE A FUNCTION IS INCREASING AND DECREASING

The function f *is* defined by

$$f(x) = \frac{1}{x}$$

Find the values of x for which the function is increasing, decreasing, and constant.

SOLUTION

We obtain the graph of f by plotting several points. See Figure 22. Since the graph is made up of two parts, we must treat the question of increasing and decreasing separately for each part. From the graph we see that

$$f \text{ is decreasing if } x > 0$$

$$f \text{ is decreasing if } x < 0$$

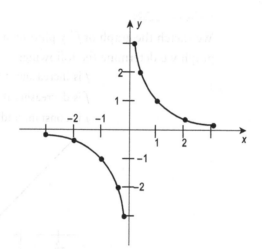

Figure 22   **Graph for Example 3**

✔ Progress Check 3

The function f is defined by

$$f(x) = \frac{1}{x + 4}$$

Find the values of x for which the function is increasing, decreasing, and constant.

Answer

decreasing if $x > -4$; decreasing if $x < -4$

Exercise Set 6.4

In Exercises 1–24 determine the values of x where the function is increasing, decreasing, and constant.

1. $f(x) = \dfrac{1}{3}x + 2$

2. $f(x) = 3 - \dfrac{1}{2}x$

3. $f(x) = x^2 + 1$

4. $f(x) = x^2 - 4$

5. $f(x) = 9 - x^2$

6. $f(x) = x^2 - 3x$

7. $f(x) = 4x - x^2$

8. $f(x) = x^2 - 2x + 4$

9. $f(x) = \dfrac{1}{2}x^2 + 3$

10. $f(x) = 4 - \dfrac{1}{2}x^2$

11. $f(x) = (x - 2)^2$

12. $f(x) = |x - 1|$

13. $f(x) = |2x + 1|$

14. $f(x) = \begin{cases} x, & x < 2 \\ 2, & x \geq \end{cases}$

15. $f(x) = \begin{cases} 2x, & x > -1 \\ -x - 1, & x \leq -1 \end{cases}$

16. $f(x) = \begin{cases} x + 1, & x > 2 \\ 1, & -1 \leq x \leq 2 \\ -x + 1, & x < -1 \end{cases}$

17. $f(x) = (x + 1)^3$

18. $f(x) = \dfrac{1}{2}(x - 1)^3$

19. $f(x) = (x - 2)^3$

20. $f(x) = x^3 + 1$

21. $f(x) = (x - 1)^4$

22. $f(x) = x^4 + 1$

*23. $f(x) = \dfrac{1}{x - 1}$

*24. $f(x) = x + \dfrac{1}{x}$

*25. A manufacturer of skis finds that the profit made from selling x pairs of skis per week is given by

$$P(x) = 80x - x^2 - 60$$

For what values of x is $P(x)$ increasing? For what values is it decreasing?

*26. A psychologist who is training chimpanzees to understand human speech finds that the number $N(t)$ of words learned after t weeks of training is given by

$$N(t) = 80t - t^2, \quad 0 \leq t \leq 80$$

For what values of t does $N(t)$ increase? For what values does it decrease?

*27. It has been found that x hours after a dosage of a standard drug has been given to a person, the change in blood pressure is given by

$$P(x) = \dfrac{x^3}{3} - \dfrac{7}{2}x^2 + 10x, \quad 0 \leq x \leq 6$$

During the 6-hour period of observation, when will the blood pressure be increasing? When will it be decreasing?

*28. Suppose that the profit made by a moped manufacturer from selling x mopeds per week is given by

$$P(x) = x^2 - 1000x + 500$$

For what values of x is $P(x)$ increasing? For what values is it decreasing?

29. MATHEMATICS IN WRITING: Explain in your own words how the slope of a line can help you to predict how the function outputs are changing with changes in the inputs. Are the graphs in Exercises 1 and 2 *rising* or *falling*? How can you tell? What is the importance of knowing whether a graph is rising or falling?

30. Graph the function $f(x) = x^3 - 12x$ in your calculator. Select an appropriate viewing window. Use the TRACE feature to determine the intervals where the function is increasing or decreasing.

6.5   Direct and Inverse Variation

Direct Variation

Two functional relationships occur so frequently that they are given distinct names. They are **direct variation** and **inverse variation**. Two quantities are said to **vary directly** if an increase in one causes a proportional increase in the other. In the table

x	1	2	3	4
y	3	6	9	12

we see that an increase in x causes a proportional increase in y. If we look at the ratios y/x, we have

$$\frac{y}{x} = \frac{3}{1} = \frac{6}{2} = \frac{9}{3} = \frac{12}{4} = 3$$

or $y = 3x$. The ratio y/x remains constant for all values of y and $x \neq 0$. This is an example of the

Principle of Direct Variation

> y varies directly as x means $y = kx$ for some constant k.

As another example, y varies directly as the square of x means $y = kx^2$ for some constant k. Direct variation, then, involves a constant k, which is called the **constant of variation**.

EXAMPLE 1   DIRECT VARIATION

Write the appropriate equation, solve for the constant of variation k, and use this k to relate the variables.

(a) d varies directly as t, and $d = 15$ when $t = 2$.

(b) y varies directly as the cube of x, and $y = 24$ when $x = -2$.

SOLUTIONS

(a) Using the principle of direct variation, the functional relationship is

$$d = kt \quad \text{for some constant } k$$

Substituting the values $d = 15$ and $t = 2$, we have

$$15 = k \cdot 2$$

$$k = \frac{15}{2}$$

Therefore,

$$d = \frac{15}{2}t$$

(b) Using the principle of direct variation, the functional relationship is

$$y = kx^3 \quad \text{for some constant } k$$

Substituting the values $y = 24$, $x = -2$, we have

$$24 = k \cdot (-2)^3 = -8k$$

$$k = -3$$

Thus,

$$y = -3x^3$$

✔ **Progress Check 1**

(a) If P varies directly as the square of V, and $P = 64$ when $V = 16$, find the constant of variation.

(b) The circumference C of a circle varies directly as the radius r. If $C = 25.13$ when $r = 4$, express C as a function of r.

Answers

(a) $\dfrac{1}{4}$ (b) $C = 6.2825r$

Inverse Variation

Two quantities are said to **vary inversely** if an increase in one causes a proportional decrease in the other. In the table

x	1	2	3	4
y	24	12	8	6

we see that an increase in x causes a proportional decrease in y. If we look at the product xy, we have

$$xy = 1 \cdot 24 = 2 \cdot 12 = 3 \cdot 8 = 4 \cdot 6 = 24$$

or $y = 24/x$. In general, we have the

Principle of Inverse Variation

y varies inversely as x means $y = \dfrac{k}{x}$ for some constant k.

Once again, k is called the constant of variation.

EXAMPLE 2   INVERSE VARIATION

Write the appropriate equation, solve for the constant of variation k, and use k to relate the variables.

(a) m varies inversely as d, and $m = 9$ when $d = -3$.

(b) y varies inversely as the square of x, and $y = 10$ when $x = 10$.

SOLUTIONS

(a) The principle of inverse variation tells us that

$$m = \frac{k}{d}$$

for some constant k. Substituting $m = 9$ and $d = -3$ yields $k = -27$. Thus,

$$m = \frac{-27}{d}$$

(b) The functional relationship is

$$y = \frac{k}{x^2} \quad \text{for some constant } k$$

Substituting $y = 10$ and $x = 10$, we have

$$10 = \frac{k}{(10)^2} = \frac{k}{100}$$

$$k = 1000$$

Thus,

$$y = \frac{1000}{x^2}$$

✔ Progress Check 2

If v varies inversely as the cube of w, and $v = 2$ when $w = -2$, find the constant of variation.

Answer

-16

Joint Variation

An equation of variation can involve more than two variables. We say that a quantity **varies jointly** as two or more other quantities if it varies directly as their product.

EXAMPLE 3   JOINT VARIATION

Express as an equation: P varies jointly as R, S, and the square of T.

SOLUTION

Since P must vary directly as $R \cdot S \cdot T^2$, we have $P = k \cdot R \cdot S \cdot T^2$ for some constant k.

✔ Progress Check 3

Express as an equation: m varies jointly as p and q, and inversely as d.

Answer

$$m = \frac{kpq}{d}$$

EXAMPLE 4   JOINT VARIATION

Find the constant of variation if x varies jointly as y and z, and $x = 30$ when $y = 2$ and $z = 3$.

SOLUTION

We have

$$x = k \cdot y \cdot z \quad \text{for some constant } k$$

and substitute for x, y, and z.

$$30 = k \cdot 2 \cdot 3$$

$$30 = 6k$$

$$k = 5$$

Thus,

$$x = 5yz$$

✔ Progress Check 4

Find the constant of variation if x varies jointly as y and the cube of z, and inversely as t, and $x = -\frac{1}{4}$ when $y = -1$, $z = -2$, and $t = 4$.

Answer

$-\dfrac{1}{8}$

Exercise Set 6.5

1. In the following table, y varies directly as x.

x	2	3	4	6	8	12		
y	8	12	16	24			80	120

   (a) Find the constant of variation.

   (b) Write an equation showing that y varies directly as x.

   (c) Complete the blanks in the table.

2. In the following table, y varies inversely as x.

x	1	2	3	6	9	12	15	18		
y	6	3	2	1	$\frac{2}{3}$	$\frac{1}{2}$			$\frac{1}{4}$	$\frac{1}{10}$

   (a) Find the constant of variation.

   (b) Write an equation showing that y varies inversely as x.

   (c) Complete the blanks in the table.

3. If y varies directly as x, and $y = -\frac{1}{4}$ when $x = 8$,

   (a) find the constant of variation.

   (b) find y when $x = 12$.

4. If C varies directly as the square of s, and $C = 12$ when $s = 6$,

   (a) find the constant of variation.

   (b) find C when $s = 9$.

5. If s varies directly as the square of t and $s = 10$ when $t = 10$,

   (a) find the constant of variation.

   (b) find s when $t = 5$.

6. If V varies directly as the cube of T, and $V = 16$ when $T = 4$,

   (a) find the constant of variation.

   (b) find V when $T = 6$.

7. If y varies inversely as x, and $y = -\frac{1}{2}$ when $x = 6$,

   (a) find the constant of variation.

   (b) find y when $x = 12$.

8. If V varies inversely as the square of p, and $V = \frac{2}{3}$ when $p = 6$,

   (a) find the constant of variation.

   (b) find V when $p = 8$.

9. If K varies inversely as the cube of r, and $K = 8$ when $r = 4$,

   (a) find the constant of variation.

   (b) find K when $r = 5$.

10. If T varies inversely as the cube of u, and $T = 2$ when $u = 2$,

    (a) find the constant of variation.

    (b) find T when $u = 5$.

11. If M varies directly as the square of r and inversely as the square of s, and if $M = 4$ when $r = 4$ and $s = 2$,

    (a) write the appropriate equation relating M, r, and s.

    (b) find M when $r = 6$ and $s = 5$.

12. If f varies jointly as u and v, and $f = 36$ when $u = 3$ and $v = 4$,

    (a) write the appropriate equation connecting f, u, and v.

    (b) find f when $u = 5$ and $v = 2$.

13. If T varies jointly as p and the cube of v and inversely as the square of u, and if $T = 24$ when $p = 3$, $v = 2$, and $u = 4$,

    (a) write the appropriate equation connecting T, p, v, and u.

    (b) find T when $p = 2$, $v = 3$, and $u = 36$.

14. If A varies jointly as the square of b and the square of c, and inversely as the cube of d, and if $A = 18$ when $b = 4$, $c = 3$, and $d = 2$,

    (a) write the appropriate equation relating A, b, c, and d.

    (b) find A when $b = 9$, $c = 4$, and $d = 3$.

15. The distance s an object falls from rest in t seconds varies directly as the square of t. If an object falls 144 feet in 3 seconds,

    (a) how far does it fall in 4 seconds?

    (b) how long does it take to fall 400 feet?

16. In a certain state the income tax paid by a person varies directly as the income. If the tax is $20 per month when the monthly income is $1600, find the tax due when the monthly income is $900.

17. The resistance R of a conductor varies inversely as the area A of its cross section. If $R = 20$ ohms when $A = 8$ square centimeters, find R when $A = 12$ square centimeters.

18. The pressure P of a certain enclosed gas varies directly as the temperature T and inversely as the volume V. Suppose that 300 cubic feet of gas exert a pressure of 20 pounds per square foot when the temperature is 500°K (absolute temperature measured in the Kelvin scale). What is the pressure of this gas when the temperature is lowered to 400°K and the volume is increased to 500 cubic feet?

19. The intensity of illumination I from a source of light varies inversely as the square of the distance d from the source. If the intensity is 200 candlepower when the source is 4 feet away,

    (a) what is the intensity when the source is 6 feet away?

    (b) how close should the source be to provide an intensity of 50 candlepower?

20. The weight of a body in space varies inversely as the square of its distance from the center of the earth. If a body weighs 400 pounds on the surface of the earth, how much does it weigh 100 miles above the surface of the earth? (Assume that the radius of the earth is 4000 miles.)

21. The equipment cost of a printing job varies jointly as the number of presses and the number of hours that the presses are run. When 4 presses are run for 6 hours, the equipment cost is $1200. If the equipment cost for 12 hours of running is $3600, how many presses are being used?

22. The current I in a wire varies directly as the electromotive force E and inversely as the resistance R. If the current of 36 amperes is obtained with a wire that has resistance of 10 ohms and the electromotive force is 120 volts, find the current produced when $E = 220$ volts and $R = 30$ ohms.

23. The illumination from a light source varies directly as the intensity of the source and inversely as the square of the distance from the source. If the illumination is 50 candlepower per square foot when 2 feet away from a light source whose intensity is 400 candlepower, what is the illumination when 4 feet away from a source whose intensity is 3840 candlepower?

24. If f varies directly as u and inversely as the square of v, what happens to f if both u and v are doubled?

▪ ▪ ▪

Chapter Summary

Terms and Symbols

abscissa	193	function notation, $f(x)$	204	origin	192
Cartesian coordinate system	192	graph of a function	212	parabola	216
constant function	220	graph of an equation in two		polynomial function	218
constant of variation	224	variables	196	quadrant	193
coordinate axes	192	image	201	quadratic functions	216
coordinates of a point	193	increasing function	219	range	201
decreasing function	219	independent variable	201	rectangular coordinate system	192
dependent variable	201	inverse variation	225	vertical line test	202
direct variation	223	joint variation	226	x-axis	192
domain	201	linear function	215	x-coordinate	193
"evaluate" a function	204	ordered pair	193	y-axis	192
function	201	ordinate	193	y-coordinate	193

Key Ideas for Review

Topic	Page	Key Idea
Rectangular coordinate system	192	In a rectangular coordinate system, every ordered pair of real numbers (a, b) corresponds to a point in the plane, and every point in the plane corresponds to an ordered pair of real numbers.
Graph of an equation	196	An equation in two variables can be graphed by plotting points that satisfy the equation and then joining the points to form a smooth curve.
Function	200	A function is a rule that assigns exactly one element y of a set Y to each element x of a set X. The domain is the set of inputs and the range is the set of outputs.
notation	204	Function notation gives both the definition of the function and the value or expression at which to evaluate the function. Thus, if f is defined by $f(x) = x^2 + 2x$, then the notation $f(3)$ denotes the result of replacing the independent variable x by 3 wherever it appears: $f(3) = 3^2 + 2(3) = 15$.
defining a function	212	An equation is not the only way to define a function. Sometimes a function is defined by a table or chart, or by several equations. Moreover, not every equation determines a function.
graph	212	To graph $f(x)$, simply graph the equation $y = f(x)$. The graph of a function can have holes or gaps, and can be defined in "pieces."
vertical line test	202	A graph represents a function $y = f(x)$ if no vertical line meets the graph in more than one point.
polynomials	218	Polynomials in one variable determine functions and have "smooth" curves as their graphs.
increasing and decreasing	219	As we move from left to right, the graph of an increasing function rises and the graph of a decreasing function falls.

continues

constant	220	The graph of a constant function neither rises nor falls; it is horizontal.
Direct and inverse variation	223	Direct and inverse variation are functional relationships. We say that y varies directly as x if $y = kx$ for some constant k. We say that y varies inversely as x if $y = k/x$ for some constant k.
Joint variation	226	We say that y varies jointly as two or more other quantities if it varies directly as their product.

Common Errors

1. Function notation is not distributive. *Don't* write

$$f(a + 3) = f(a) + f(3)$$

or

$$f(a + 3) = f(a) + 3$$

Instead, substitute $a + 3$ for the independent variable.

2. *Don't* write

$$f(x^2) = [f(x)]^2$$

or

$$f(x^2) = f \cdot x^2$$

Again, the notation $f(x^2)$ denotes the output when we replace the independent variable by x^2.

3. It is legitimate for the graph of a function to have holes or gaps. Don't force the graph of every function to be "continuous."

Review Exercises

Solutions to exercises whose numbers are in bold are in the Solutions section in the back of the book.

6.1 1. If A is the point with coordinates $(2, -3)$, find the coordinates of the point B that is 4 units to the left and 1 unit below A.

2. If A is the point with coordinates $(-3, -2)$, find the coordinates of the point B that is 3 units above A.

3. Without plotting, name the quadrant in which the point $(-3, 2)$ is located.

4. Which of the following are solutions to
$$2x^2 - 5y = -7?$$
(a) $(2, 3)$ (b) $(2, -3)$ (c) $(-2, -3)$ (d) $(-2, 3)$

5. Which of the following are solutions to
$$x - y^2 = 3?$$
(a) $(-1, 2)$ (b) $(1, 4)$ (c) $(-2, -7)$ (d) $(3, 0)$

6. Complete the following table for the equation $2x + 5y = 20$.

x	2		0		3	
y		-1		0		4

In Exercises 7–9 graph the given equation.

7. $y = -3x$

8. $x = -2y + 1$

9. $y = 3x - x^2$

10. Graph the set of all points whose x- and y-coordinates are equal.

6.2 In Exercises 11 and 12 graph the given equation. If the correspondence is a function, determine the domain and range.

11. $y = 2x - x^2$

12. $x = y^2 - 1$

In Exercises 13 and 14 determine the domain of the given function.

13. $f(x) = \dfrac{x - 3}{x + 4}$

14. $g(t) = \dfrac{3}{t^2 + t - 12}$

In Exercises 15 and 16 determine whether or not the given curve is the graph of a function.

15.

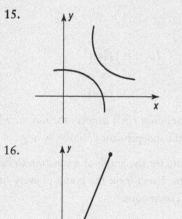

16.

17. The function f is defined by $f(x) = x^2 - x + 2$. Compute the following:

(a) $f(2)$ (b) $f(0)$ (c) $f(-3)$

18. The function g is defined by

$$g(t) = \frac{t - 3}{t + 1}$$

Compute the following:

(a) $g(-5)$ (b) $g(0)$ (c) $g(3)$

19. Suppose that an object drops from a fixed height. If we neglect air resistance, the force of the earth's gravity causes the object to hit the ground after t seconds. The relationship of t to the distance s (in feet) the object falls is given by

$$s = 16t^2$$

(Note that the function does not depend upon the mass of the body.)

(a) What is the distance traveled by an object when t is 2 seconds? What is the distance traveled in 4 seconds?

(b) How long does it take the object to fall 144 feet?

20. Express the area A of a circle as a function of its diameter d.

6.3 In Exercises 21–26 sketch the graph of the given function.

21. $f(x) = 2x - 1$

22. $g(x) = -3x + 2$

23. $h(x) = 2x + x^2$

24. $f(x) = x - x^3$

25. $g(x) = \begin{cases} x - 1, & x \le -1 \\ x^2, & -1 < x \le 2 \\ -2, & x > 2 \end{cases}$

26. $h(x) = \begin{cases} x + 2, & x < 2 \\ x^2, & x \ge 2 \end{cases}$

In Exercises 27 and 28 sketch the graphs of the given functions on the same coordinate axes.

27. $f(x) = x^2 + 1$, $g(x) = 2x^2 + 1$

28. $f(x) = x^3 + 2$, $g(x) = -x^3 + 2$

29. A photography shop sells powdered developer. The cost C of shipping an order is 15 cents for each of the first 5 pounds, and 10 cents for each additional pound.

(a) Write C as a function of the number n of pounds in an order, for $0 < n \le 20$.

(b) Sketch the graph of the function C for $0 < n \le 20$.

(c) What is the cost of shipping an order that consists of 16 pounds of developer?

30. A stereo shop runs the following advertisement: "Big sale on 90-minute tape cassettes! Pay $2.20 each for the first 10 cassettes, $2.15 each for the next 15 cassettes, and $2.05 for each cassette beyond 25."

(a) Express the cost C as a function of the number x of cassettes purchased.

(b) What is the cost of buying 32 cassettes?

6.4 In Exercises 31–38 determine the values of x where the function is increasing, decreasing, and constant.

31. $f(x) = 2 - x$

32. $f(x) = x^2 - x$

33. $f(x) = x^2 + 1$

34. $f(x) = x^2 - x - 6$

35. $f(x) = (x - 1)^2$

36. $f(x) = (x + 2)^2 - 4$

37. $f(x) = \begin{cases} x - 3, & x < 1 \\ 2, & 1 < x \le 3 \\ -x + 5, & x > 3 \end{cases}$

38. $f(x) = \begin{cases} x + 2, & x < -2 \\ x^2, & -2 \le x < 4 \\ 3, & x \ge 4 \end{cases}$

39. The cost C of manufacturing x quarts of a certain pharmaceutical is given (in dollars) by

$$C(x) = x^2 - 20x + 800$$

For what values of x is $C(x)$ increasing? For what values is it decreasing?

40. After x hours of weightlessness, it is found that a subject requires $T(x)$ minutes to solve a certain puzzle. If

$$T(x) = 20 + 4x - x^2$$

for what values of x is $T(x)$ increasing? For what values is it decreasing?

6.5 41. In the following table y varies directly as the square of t.

t	1	2	3	4	
y	$\frac{1}{2}$	2	$\frac{9}{2}$		$\frac{25}{2}$

(a) Write the appropriate equation relating y and t.

(b) Find the constant of variation.

(c) Complete the blanks in the table.

42. In the following table M varies inversely as the cube of n.

n	2	3	4	
M	$\frac{1}{12}$	$\frac{2}{81}$		$\frac{2}{375}$

(a) Write the appropriate equation relating M and n.

(b) Find the constant of variation.

(c) Complete the blanks in the table.

43. If F varies directly as the square of r, and $F = 6$ when $r = 3$,

(a) find the constant of variation.

(b) find F when $r = 6$.

44. If A varies inversely as the cube of b, and $A = \frac{3}{16}$ when $b = 2$,

(a) find the constant of variation.

(b) find A when $b = 4$.

45. If S varies jointly as t and the square of u, and $S = 18$ when $t = 4$ and $u = 9$, find S when $t = 6$ and $u = 3$.

46. If K varies jointly as b and c and inversely as the square of d, and if $K = \frac{3}{4}$ when $b = 6$, $c = 2$, and $d = 2$, find K when $b = 4$, $c = 3$, and $d = 4$.

47. In the following table z varies jointly as x and y.

x	2	3	4	2	
y	3	5	2		3
z	9	$\frac{45}{2}$	12	15	18

Complete the blanks in the table.

48. In the following table T varies directly as r and inversely as the square of s.

r	2	3	4	5	
s	3	2	5		3
T	$\frac{8}{27}$	1	$\frac{16}{75}$	$\frac{5}{3}$	$\frac{4}{9}$

Complete the blanks in the table.

49. The output of an employee on an assembly line varies directly as the number of hours on a training course. If the employee can turn out 18 items per hour after a 6-hour training course, how many items can she turn out per hour after a 10-hour course?

50. The time required by a subject to solve a certain puzzle varies jointly as the temperature of the room and the number of hours without sleep. If it takes a certain subject 10 minutes to solve the puzzle in a 60°F room after 10 hours without sleep, how long will it take the same subject to solve the puzzle in a 90° room after 20 hours without sleep?

51. A software firm finds that the revenue R received from the sale of one of its products varies directly as the amount spent on advertising and inversely as the length of the training manual. If the firm received $1,000,000 of revenue on a product with a 100-page training manual after spending $50,000 on advertising, how much revenue would it have received if the manual had been 120 pages long and $75,000 had been spent on advertising?

Progress Test 6A

1. Sketch the graph of $y = -2x^3 + 1$.

2. Find the domain of the function $f(x) = \dfrac{2x}{x + 3}$.

3. Find the domain of the function $g(y) = \dfrac{2}{y^2 - 4}$.

4. Use the vertical line test to determine if the equations
$$y = \begin{cases} |x|, & -3 \leq x \leq 3 \\ x^2, & x > 0 \end{cases}$$
define a function.

5. Is the following the graph of a function?

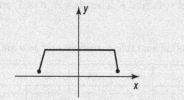

6. Evaluate $f(-\tfrac{1}{2})$ for $f(x) = x^2 - 3x + 1$.

7. Evaluate $f(2t)$ for $f(x) = \dfrac{1 - x^2}{1 + x^2}$.

8. Evaluate $\dfrac{f(a + h) - f(a)}{h}$ for $f(x) = 2x^2 + 3$.

9. Sketch the graph of the function
$$f(x) = \begin{cases} x - 1, & -5 \leq x \leq -1 \\ x^2, & -1 < x \leq 2 \\ -2, & 2 < x \leq 5 \end{cases}$$

10. Sketch the graph of $f(x) = x^2 - 4x + 2$.

11. If R varies directly as q, and $R = 20$ when $q = 5$, find R when $q = 40$.

12. If S varies inversely as the cube of t, and $S = 8$ when $t = -1$, find S when $t = -2$.

13. If P varies jointly as q and r, and inversely as the square of t, and if $P = -3$ when $q = 2$, $r = -3$, and $t = 4$, find P when $q = -1$, $r = \tfrac{1}{2}$, and $t = 4$.

14. Determine the intervals where the function $f(x) = x^2 - 2x + 1$ is increasing, decreasing, and constant.

15. Determine the intervals where the function
$$f(x) = \begin{cases} |x - 1|, & x < 3 \\ -1, & x \geq 3 \end{cases}$$
is increasing, decreasing, and constant.

Progress Test 6B

1. Sketch the graph of $y = \tfrac{1}{2}x^3 - 1$.

2. Find the domain of the function $f(t) = \dfrac{t}{2t - 1}$.

3. Find the domain of the function $g(x) = \dfrac{4x}{1 - x^2}$.

4. Use the vertical line test to determine if the equations
$$y = \begin{cases} |x - 1|, & x \leq 5 \\ 4, & x \geq 5 \end{cases}$$
define a function.

5. Is the following the graph of a function?

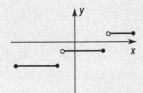

6. Evaluate $f(-1)$ for $f(x) = \dfrac{x^2 + 2}{x}$.

7. Evaluate $f\left(\dfrac{a}{2}\right)$ for $f(x) = (1 + x)^2$.

8. Evaluate $\dfrac{f(a + h) - f(a)}{h}$ for $f(x) = -x^2 + 2$.

9. Sketch the graph of the function
$$f(x) = \begin{cases} |x| + 1, & -4 \leq x < 1 \\ 2x, & 1 \leq x \leq 4 \\ 4, & x > 4 \end{cases}$$

10. Sketch the graph of $f(x) = -x^2 + 2x$.

11. If L varies directly as the cube of r, and $L = 2$ when $r = -\frac{1}{2}$, find L when $r = 4$.

12. If A varies inversely as the square of b, and $A = -2$ when $b = 4$, find A when $b = 3$.

13. If T varies jointly as a and the square of b, and inversely as the cube of c, and if $T = 64$ when $a = -1$, $b = \frac{1}{2}$, and $c = 2$, find T when $a = 2$, $b = 4$, and $c = -1$.

14. Determine the intervals where the function $f(x) = |x - 2|$ is increasing, decreasing, and constant.

15. Determine the intervals where the function
$$f(x) = \begin{cases} 5, & x < -1 \\ |x|, & -1 \leq x \leq 3 \\ -1, & x > 3 \end{cases}$$
is increasing, decreasing, and constant.

Chapter 6 Project

At the beginning of this chapter, we mentioned a function that relates the number of times a cricket chirps in one minute to the outside temperature in degrees Fahrenheit. Here is that function. (You have seen it several times!)

$$f(n) = \frac{n}{4} + 40$$

What would the temperature be if you heard 36 chirps in one minute? 52? Use your graphing calculator to set up a TABLE, pairing the inputs (number of chirps) with the outputs (temperature) for 10 values of n.

For this chapter's project, look back at Section 6.2, Exercise 65, and Section 6.3, Exercises 48 and 49. Put these results together with your table, and complete the following exercise.

MATHEMATICS IN WRITING: In your own words, explain how the concepts of *function, line,* and *slope* can be used to describe and predict phenomenon in the world around us.

Mathematics and biology go together well. The same could be said for physics, chemistry, or just about any branch of science. The concept of function is crucial to understanding how scientists model the real world with mathematics.

Explore the connections between mathematics and biology further at http://archives.math.utk.edu /mathbio/.

http://archives.math.utk.edu/mathbio/

▪ ▪ ▪

7 The Straight Line

"For as long as we can reliably reach into the past we find the development of mathematics intimately connected with the development of the whole of our civilization."

—Marc Kac

Architects throughout history have used mathematical principles to design spaces and structures of beauty and utility. From the pyramids of ancient Egypt to the subways of modern American cities, concepts of design have relied upon an understanding of the concepts of algebra.

How is algebra used to put a roof over your head? Probably, the roof you are under right now can be modeled by a straight line. Is it shallow or steep? What does a roofer mean when she says that the pitch of a roof is $\frac{5}{12}$? Expressed another way, this fraction is equal to nearly 42%. This is how the designer of a highway would express this same concept, except that he would call it a grade rather than a pitch. In this chapter's project, we will use linear equations to create a model for a roof with a pitch of $\frac{5}{12}$.

■ ■ ■

In Chapter 6 we said that functions of the form $f(x) = ax + b$ are called linear functions, and we saw that the graphs of such functions appear to be straight lines. In this chapter we will demonstrate that these conjectures are well founded: the graph of a linear function is indeed a straight line.

The concept of slope is introduced and is used to develop two important forms of the equation of the straight line: the point-slope form and the slope-intercept form. Horizontal, vertical, parallel, and perpendicular lines are also explored.

Finally, the graphs of linear inequalities are discussed, and a simple technique for sketching such graphs is developed.

7.1   Slope of the Straight Line

In Figure 1, we have drawn a straight line L that is not vertical. We have indicated the distinct points $P_1(x_1, y_1)$ and $P_2(x_2, y_2)$ on L. The increments or changes $x_2 - x_1$ and $y_2 - y_1$ in the x- and y-coordinates, respectively, from P_1 to P_2 are also indicated. Note that the increment $x_2 - x_1$ cannot be zero, since L is not vertical.

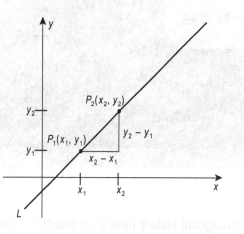

Figure 1   **Increments on the Line L**

If $P_3(x_3, y_3)$ and $P_4(x_4, y_4)$ are another pair of points on L, as shown in Figure 2, the increments $x_4 - x_3$ and $y_4 - y_3$ will, in general, be different from the increments obtained by using P_1 and P_2. Since triangles P_1AP_2 and P_3BP_4 are similar, however, the corresponding sides are in proportion; that is, the ratios

$$\frac{y_4 - y_3}{x_4 - x_3} \quad \text{and} \quad \frac{y_2 - y_1}{x_2 - x_1}$$

are the same. This ratio is called the **slope of the line** L and is denoted by m.

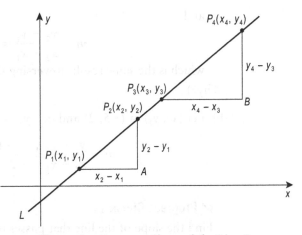

Figure 2   Constant Slope of the Line L

Slope of a Line

The slope of a line that is not vertical is given by

$$m = \frac{y_2 - y_1}{x_2 - x_1}$$

where $P_1(x_1, y_1)$ and $P_2(x_2, y_2)$ are any two distinct points on the line. For a vertical line, $x_1 = x_2$, so $x_2 - x_1 = 0$. Since we cannot divide by 0, we say that a vertical line has no slope.

For a horizontal line, $y_1 = y_2$, so $y_2 - y_1 = 0$, and the slope $m = 0$. Observe that having *no slope* is different from having *zero slope*.

EXAMPLE 1   FINDING THE SLOPE OF A LINE

Find the slope of the line that passes through the given pair of points.

(a) (4, 2) and (1, −2)   (b) (−5, 2) and (−2, −1)

SOLUTIONS

(a) We may choose either point as (x_1, y_1) and the other as (x_2, y_2). Our choice is

$$(x_1, y_1) = (4, 2)$$

$$(x_2, y_2) = (1, -2)$$

Then

$$m = \frac{y_2 - y_1}{x_2 - x_1} = \frac{-2 - 2}{1 - 4} = \frac{-4}{-3} = \frac{4}{3}$$

If we had reversed the choice we would have

$$(x_1, y_1) = (1, -2)$$

$$(x_2, y_2) = (4, 2)$$

and

$$m = \frac{y_2 - y_1}{x_2 - x_1} = \frac{2 - (-2)}{4 - 1} = \frac{4}{3}$$

which is the same result. Reversing the choice does not affect the value of m. (Why?)

(b) Let $(x_1, y_1) = (-5, 2)$ and $(x_2, y_2) = (-2, -1)$. Then

$$m = \frac{y_2 - y_1}{x_2 - x_1} = \frac{-1 - 2}{-2 - (-5)} = \frac{-3}{3} = -1$$

✔ **Progress Check 1**

Find the slope of the line that passes through the given pair of points.

(a) (2, −4) and (4, 1)   (b) (−1, −3) and (−2, −5)

Answers

(a) $\dfrac{5}{2}$ (b) 2

WARNING

Once you have chosen a point as (x_1, y_1), you must be consistent. If you have $(x_1, y_1) = (5, 2)$ and $(x_2, y_2) = (1, 6)$, *don't write*

$$m = \frac{6 - 2}{5 - 1} = \frac{4}{4} = 1$$

This answer has the wrong sign because

$$\frac{y_2 - y_1}{x_1 - x_2} \neq \frac{y_2 - y_1}{x_2 - x_1}$$

Meaning of Slope

Slope is a means of measuring the steepness of a line. That is, slope specifies the number of units we must move up or down to reach the line after moving 1 unit to the right of the line. In Figure 3, we have displayed several lines with positive and negative slopes. We can summarize this way:

Let m be the slope of a line L.

1. When $m > 0$, the line is the graph of an **increasing function**.

2. When $m < 0$, the line is the graph of a **decreasing function**.

3. When $m = 0$, the line is the graph of a **constant function**.

4. Slope does not exist for a vertical line, and a vertical line is not the graph of a function.

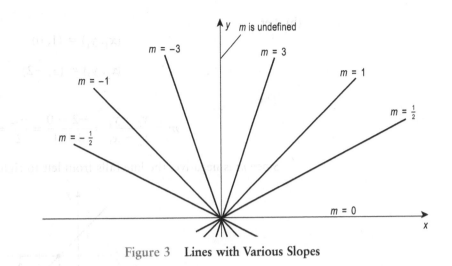

Figure 3   Lines with Various Slopes

EXAMPLE 2   FINDING THE SLOPE OF A LINE

Find the slope of the line through the given points and state whether the line is rising or falling.

(a) $(1, 2)$ and $(-2, -7)$ (b) $(1, 0)$ and $(3, -2)$

SOLUTIONS

(a) Let

$$(x_1, y_1) = (1, 2)$$

$$(x_2, y_2) = (-2, -7)$$

Then

$$m = \frac{y_2 - y_1}{x_2 - x_1} = \frac{-7 - 2}{-2 - 1} = \frac{-9}{-3} = 3$$

Since m is positive, the line rises from left to right (See Figure 4).

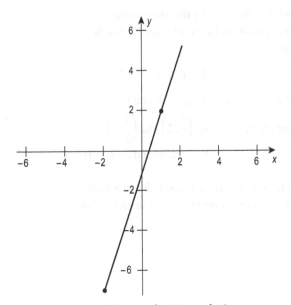

Figure 4   Diagram for Example 2a

(b) Let

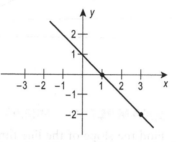

Then

$$m = \frac{y_2 - y_1}{x_2 - x_1} = \frac{-2 - 0}{3 - 1} = \frac{-2}{2} = -1$$

Since m is negative, the line falls from left to right (See Figure 5).

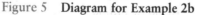

Figure 5   Diagram for Example 2b

✔ Progress Check 2

Find the slope of the line that passes through the given points and state whether the line is rising, falling, or constant.

(a) $(-1, -3)$ and $(0, 1)$ (b) $(-1, -4)$ and $(3, -4)$ (c) $(2, 0)$ and $(4, -1)$

Answers

(a) 4; rising   (b) 0; constant   (c) $-\frac{1}{2}$; falling

Exercise Set 7.1

In Exercises 1–8 find the slope of the line passing through the given points and state whether the line is rising or falling.

1. $(2, 3)$ and $(-1, -3)$ 2. $(1, 2)$ and $(-2, 5)$

3. $(1, -4)$ and $(-1, -2)$ 4. $(2, -3)$ and $(3, 2)$

5. $(-2, 3)$ and $(0, 0)$ 6. $\left(\frac{1}{2}, 2\right)$ and $\left(\frac{3}{2}, 1\right)$

7. $(2, 4)$ and $(-3, 4)$ 8. $(-2, 2)$ and $(-2, -4)$

In Exercises 9–12 refer to Figure 6 and indicate whether the slope of the given line is positive (P) or negative (N).

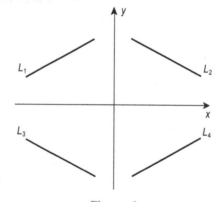

Figure 6

9. L_1 10. L_2

11. L_3 12. L_4

In Exercises 13–16 use Figure 7 to determine whether the given statement is true (T) or false (F).

13. The slope of L_1 is greater than the slope of L_2.

14. The slope of L_3 is less than the slope of L_4.

15. The slope of L_2 is greater than the slope of L_3.

16. The slope of L_4 is less than the slope of L_1.

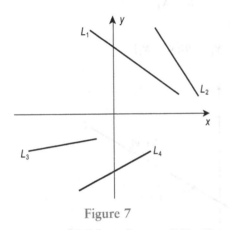

Figure 7

In Exercises 17–20 find the slope of the lines in Figure 8.

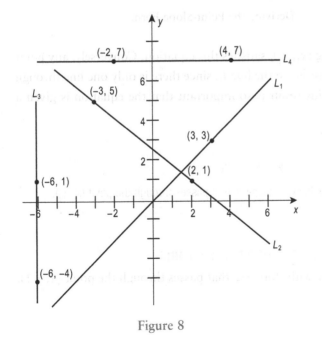

Figure 8

17. L_1 18. L_2

19. L_3 20. L_4

*21. Find a real number c so that the points $(-3, 2)$ and $(c, 4)$ lie on a straight line whose slope is 2.

*22. Find a real number c so that the points $(2, 1)$ and $(c, 2c + 1)$ lie on a straight line whose slope is 3.

23. The slope of a roof is called *pitch*, and it is usually expressed as a fraction with a denominator of 12. (See the chapter opener.) So, a roof with a slope of $\frac{1}{2}$ has a pitch of $\frac{6}{12}$. Suppose I design a roof with a triangular cross section, so that the peak of the house is 20 feet above ground level, and the eaves are 14 feet above ground level. How wide would this house be if the pitch of the roof were $\frac{3}{12}$?

24. Refer to Exercise 23. How high would the peak of a house with a triangular roof be if the house is 72 feet wide, the eaves are 40 feet above ground level, and the pitch of the roof is $\frac{2}{12}$?

25. The grade of a highway is usually expressed as a percent. So, a highway with a grade of 1% has a slope of $\frac{1}{100}$. Suppose one point on a highway is at an elevation of 300 feet above sea level, and a point 100 feet farther along the highway is at an elevation of 304 feet. What is the grade of this highway?

26. Refer to Exercise 25. Suppose the grade of a highway is 8.4%, and one point is 650 feet above sea level. What is the elevation of a point 250 feet farther up the highway?

7.2   Equations of the Straight Line

Point-Slope Form

We can apply the concept of slope to develop important forms of the equations of a straight line. In Figure 9, the point $P_1(x_1, y_1)$ lies on a line L whose slope is m. If $P(x, y)$ is any other point on L, then we may use P and P_1 to compute m, that is,

$$m = \frac{y - y_1}{x - x_1}$$

which can be written in the form

$$y - y_1 = m(x - x_1)$$

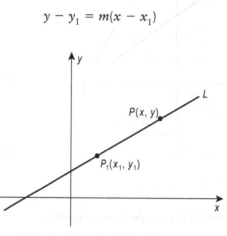

Figure 9   Deriving the Point-Slope Form

Every point on L, including (x_1, y_1), satisfies this equation. Conversely, any point satisfying this equation must lie on the line L, since there is only one line through $P_1(x_1, y_1)$ with slope m. This result is so important that the equation is given a special name.

Point-Slope Form

$$y - y_1 = m(x - x_1)$$

is an equation of the line with slope m that passes through the point (x_1, y_1).

EXAMPLE 1   APPLYING THE POINT-SLOPE FORM

Find an equation of the line with slope -2 that passes through the point $(4, -1)$. Sketch the line.

SOLUTION

We have $m = -2$ and $(x_1, y_1) = (4, -1)$. Using the point-slope form,

$$y - y_1 = m(x - x_1)$$
$$y - (-1) = -2(x - 4)$$
$$y + 1 = -2x + 8$$
$$y = -2x + 7$$

To sketch the line, we need a second point. We can substitute a value of x, such as $x = 0$, in the equation of the line to obtain another point. See Figure 10.

x	y
4	-1
0	7

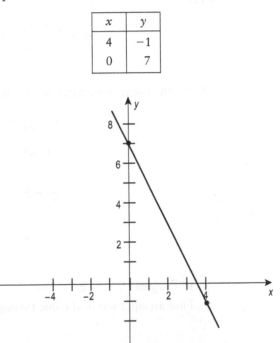

Figure 10   **Diagram for Example 1**

✔ Progress Check 1
Find an equation of the line with slope 3 that passes through the point $(-1, -5)$.

Answer
$y = 3x - 2$

It is also possible to use the point-slope form to find an equation of a line when we know two points on the line.

EXAMPLE 2   FINDING THE EQUATION OF A LINE THROUGH TWO POINTS

Find an equation of the line that passes through the points $(6, -2)$ and $(-4, 3)$.

SOLUTION

First, we find the slope. If we let

$$(x_1, y_1) = (6, -2)$$

$$(x_2, y_2) = (-4, 3)$$

Then

$$m = \frac{y_2 - y_1}{x_2 - x_1} = \frac{3 - (-2)}{-4 - 6} = \frac{5}{-10} = -\frac{1}{2}$$

Next, the point-slope form is used with $m = -\dfrac{1}{2}$ and $(x_1, y_1) = (6, -2)$.

$$y - y_1 = m(x - x_1)$$

$$y - (-2) = -\frac{1}{2}(x - 6)$$

$$y + 2 = -\frac{1}{2}x + 3$$

$$y = -\frac{1}{2}x + 1$$

✔ **Progress Check 2**

Find an equation of the line through the points $(3, 0)$ and $(-15, -6)$.

Answer

$$y = \frac{1}{3}x - 1$$

Slope-Intercept Form

There is another form of the equation of the straight line that is very useful. In Figure 11, the line L meets the y-axis at the point $(0, b)$ and is assumed to have slope m. Then we can let $(x_1, y_1) = (0, b)$ and use the point-slope form.

$$y - y_1 = m(x - x_1)$$

$$y - b = m(x - 0)$$

$$y = mx + b$$

The Pirate Treasure (Part I)

Five pirates traveling with a slave found a chest of gold coins. The pirates agreed to divide the coins among themselves the following morning.

During the night Pirate 1 awoke and, not trusting his fellow pirates, decided to remove his share of the coins. After dividing the coins into five equal lots, he found that one coin remained. The pirate took his lot and gave the remaining coin to the slave to ensure his silence.

Later that night Pirate 2 awoke and decided to remove his share of the coins. After dividing the remaining coins into five equal lots, he found one coin left over. The pirate took his lot and gave the extra coin to the slave.

That same night the process was repeated by Pirates 3, 4, and 5. Each time there remained one coin, which was given to the slave.

In the morning these five compatible pirates divided the remaining coins into five equal lots. Once again a single coin remained.

Question: What is the minimum number of coins there could have been in the chest? (For help, see Part II on page 249.)

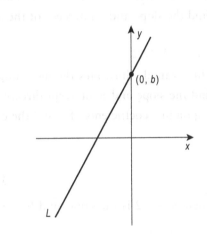

Figure 11   Deriving the Slope-Intercept Form

We call b the **y-intercept**, and we now have the following result:

Slope-Intercept Form

The graph of the equation

$$y = mx + b$$

is a straight line with slope m and y-intercept b.

The last result leads to the important conclusion mentioned in the introduction to this section. Since the graph of $y = mx + b$ is the graph of the function $f(x) = mx + b$, we have shown that the *graph of a linear function is a nonvertical straight line.*

EXAMPLE 3   APPLYING THE SLOPE-INTERCEPT FORM

Find an equation of the line with slope -1 and y-intercept 5.

SOLUTION

We substitute $m = -1$ and $b = 5$ in the equation

$$y = mx + b$$

to obtain

$$y = -x + 5$$

> **✔ Progress Check 3**
>
> Find an equation of the line with slope $\frac{1}{2}$ and y-intercept -4.
>
> **Answer**
>
> $y = \dfrac{1}{2}x - 4$

EXAMPLE 4   FINDING THE SLOPE AND Y-INTERCEPT

Find the slope and y-intercept of the line $y = -2x - 4$.

SOLUTION

This example illustrates the most important use of the slope-intercept form: to find the slope and y-intercept directly from the equation. We have to align corresponding coefficients of x and the constant terms.

$$\begin{array}{ccc} y = & -2x & - 4 \\ & | & | \\ y = & mx & + b \end{array}$$

Then $m = -2$ is the slope, and $b = -4$ is the y-intercept.

> **✔ Progress Check 4**
>
> Find the slope and y-intercept of the line $y = -\frac{1}{3}x + 14$.
>
> **Answer**
>
> slope $= m = -\dfrac{1}{3}$; y-intercept $= b = 14$

EXAMPLE 5   FINDING THE SLOPE AND Y-INTERCEPT

Find the slope and y-intercept of the line $y - 3x + 1 = 0$.

SOLUTION

The equation must be written in the form $y = mx + b$. That is, we must solve for y.

$$y = 3x - 1$$

The Pirate Treasure (Part II)

First, note that any number that is a multiple of 5 can be written in the form $5n$, where n is an integer. Since the number of coins found in the chest by Pirate 1 was one more than a multiple of 5, we can write the original number of coins C in the form $C = 5n + 1$, where n is a positive integer. Now, Pirate 1 removed his lot of n coins and gave one to the slave. The remaining coins can be calculated as

$$5n + 1 - (n + 1) = 4n$$

and since this is also one more than a multiple of 5, we can write $4n = 5p + 1$, where p is a positive integer. Repeating the process, we have the following sequence of equations.

$C = 5n + 1$	found by Pirate 1
$4n = 5p + 1$	found by Pirate 2
$4p = 5q + 1$	found by Pirate 3
$4q = 5r + 1$	found by Pirate 4
$4r = 5s + 1$	found by Pirate 5
$4s = 5t + 1$	found next morning

Solving for s in the last equation and substituting successively in the preceding equations leads to the requirement that

$$1024n - 3125t = 2101 \qquad (1)$$

where n and t are positive integers. Equations such as this that require integer solutions are called Diophantine equations, and there is an established procedure for solving them that is studied in courses in number theory.

You might want to try to solve Equation (1) using a computer program. Since

$$n = \frac{3125t + 2101}{1024}$$

you can substitute successive integer values for t until you produce an integer result for n. The BASIC program shown at the left does just that.

BASIC Program

```
10   FOR K = 1 TO 3200
20   X = (3125*K + 2101)/1024
30   I = INT(X)
40   IF X = I THEN GO TO 60
50   NEXT K
60   PRINT "MINIMUM NUMBER OF COINS = "; 5*I + 1
70   END
```

We see that $m = 3$ is the slope and that $b = -1$ is the y-intercept.

✔ **Progress Check 5**

Find the slope and y-intercept of the line $2y + x - 3 = 0$.

Answer

slope $= m = -\dfrac{1}{2}$; y-intercept $= b = \dfrac{3}{2}$

General First-Degree Equation

Throughout this chapter we have been dealing with first-degree equations in two variables. The **general first-degree equation** in x and y can always be written in the form

$$Ax + By + C = 0$$

where A, B, and C are constants and A and B are not both zero. We can rewrite this equation as

$$By = -Ax - C$$

If $B \neq 0$, the equation becomes

$$y = -\frac{A}{B}x - \frac{C}{B}$$

whose graph is a straight line with slope $-A/B$ and y-intercept $-C/B$. If $B = 0$, the equation becomes $Ax + C = 0$, whose graph is a vertical line. If $A = 0$, the equation becomes $By + C = 0$, whose graph is a horizontal line. If $C = 0$, the equation becomes $Ax + By = 0$, whose graph is a straight line passing through the origin. We have therefore proved the following:

The General First-Degree Equation

- The graph of the general first-degree equation

  $$Ax + By + C = 0 \quad (A \text{ and } B \text{ not both zero})$$

  is a straight line.

- If $B = 0$, the graph is a vertical line.

- If $A = 0$, the graph is a horizontal line.

- If $C = 0$, the line passes through the origin.

WARNING

1. Given the equation $y + 2x - 3 = 0$, *don't* write $m = 2$, $b = -3$. You must rewrite the equation by solving for y:

   $$y = -2x + 3$$

   Then obtain $m = -2$, $b = 3$.

2. Given the equation $y = 5x - 6$, *don't* write $m = 5$, $b = 6$. The sign is part of the answer, so the correct answer is $m = 5$, $b = -6$.

Exercise Set 7.2

1. Which of the following are linear equations in x and y?

   (a) $3x + 2y = 4$ (b) $xy = 2$

   (c) $2x^2 - y = 5$ (d) $2\left(x - \dfrac{3}{2}\right) + 5y = 4$

2. Which of the following are linear equations in x and y?

   (a) $2x^2 + y = 7$ (b) $3x - 2y = 7$

   (c) $\dfrac{1}{2}(2x^2 - 4) + 4y = 2$ (d) $x = 2y - 3$

In Exercises 3–10 express each equation in the form $Ax + By + C = 0$ and state the values of A, B, and C.

3. $y = 2x - 3$ 4. $y - 2 = \dfrac{3}{2}(x - 4)$

5. $y = 3$ 6. $x = \dfrac{3}{4}y - 1$

7. $3\left(x - \dfrac{1}{3}\right) - 2y = 6$ 8. $2x + 5y + 7 = 0$

9. $x = \dfrac{1}{2}$ 10. $y + 1 = -\dfrac{1}{2}(x - 2)$

11. Does the point $(-1, 3)$ lie on the straight line $2x + 3y = 7$?

12. Does the point $(4, 2)$ lie on the straight line $3x - 2y = 2$?

In Exercises 13–24 graph the equation.

13. $y = 2x + 1$ 14. $y = 3x - 2$

15. $y = -2x + 3$ 16. $y = 3x$

17. $x = 2y + 1$ 18. $x = y + 2$

19. $x = -2y + 3$ 20. $x = \dfrac{1}{2}y$

21. $y + 2x = 4$ 22. $2y - x = 0$

23. $x + 2y + 3 = 0$ 24. $x - 3y + 6 = 0$

In Exercises 25–32 find the point-slope form of the line satisfying the given conditions.

25. Its slope is 2 and it passes through the point $(-1, 3)$.

26. Its slope is $-\dfrac{1}{2}$ and it passes through the point $(1, -2)$.

27. Its slope is 3 and it passes through the point $(0, 0)$.

28. Its slope is 0 and it passes through the point $(-1, 3)$.

29. It passes through the points $(2, 4)$ and $(-3, -6)$.

30. It passes through the points $(-3, 5)$ and $(1, 7)$.

31. It passes through the points $(0, 0)$ and $(3, 2)$.

32. It passes through the points $(-2, 4)$ and $(3, 4)$.

In Exercises 33–36 find the slope-intercept form of the line satisfying the given properties.

33. Its slope is 3 and its y-intercept is 2.

34. Its slope is -3 and its y-intercept is -3.

35. Its slope is 0 and its y-intercept is 2.

36. Its slope is $-\dfrac{1}{2}$ and its y-intercept is $\dfrac{1}{2}$.

37. Does the point $(4, 2)$ lie on the line with slope -2 that passes through the point $(3, 4)$?

38. Does the point $(-1, 3)$ lie on the line passing through the points $(1, 3)$ and $(4, -3)$?

In Exercises 39–50 find the slope and y-intercept of the given line.

39. $y = 3x + 2$ 40. $y = -\dfrac{2}{3}x - 4$

41. $x = -5$ 42. $x = 3$

43. $y = 3$ 44. $y = -4$

45. $3x + 4y = 5$ 46. $2x + 3y = 6$

47. $2x - 5y + 3 = 0$ 48. $3x + 4y + 2 = 0$

49. $x = \dfrac{2}{3}y + 2$ 50. $x = -\dfrac{1}{2}y + 3$

In Exercises 51–56 determine whether the given line rises from left to right or falls from left to right.

51. $y = 2x + 3$ 52. $y = -\dfrac{3}{2}x + 5$

53. $y = -\dfrac{3}{4}x - 2$ 54. $y = \dfrac{4}{5}x - 6$

55. $x = 2y - 5$ 56. $x = 3 - 4y$

In Exercises 57–62 find the slope-intercept form of the line determined by the given points.

57. $(-1, 2)$ and $(3, 5)$ 58. $(-2, -3)$ and $(3, 4)$

59. $(32.65, -17.47)$ and $(-4.76, 19.24)$

60. $(0, 14.38)$ and $(-7.62, 3.04)$

61. $(-6.45, -12.42)$ and $(8.44, 0)$

62. $(0, 0)$ and $(-4.47, 9.31)$

In Exercises 63 and 64 find the slope-intercept form of the given line.

63.

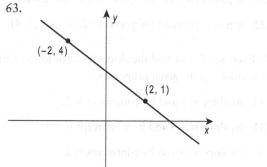

64.

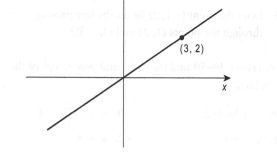

In Exercises 65–68 identify the variables and write an equation relating them.

65. A rental firm charges $8, plus $1.50 per hour, for use of a power aerator.

66. A taxi charges 60 cents, plus 35 cents per mile.

67. A brokerage firm charges $25, plus 12 cents per share.

68. A theater may be rented for $200, plus $1.25 per person.

69. The Celsius (C) and Fahrenheit (F) temperature scales are related by a linear equation. Water boils at 212°F, or 100°C; it freezes at 32°F, or 0°C.

   (a) Write a linear equation expressing F in terms of C.

   (b) What is the Fahrenheit temperature when the Celsius temperature is 20°?

70. The college bookstore sells a textbook costing $10 for $13.50 and a textbook costing $12 for $15.90. If the markup policy of the bookstore is linear, write an equation that relates sales price S and cost C. What is the cost of a textbook that sells for $22?

71. An appliance manufacturer finds that it had sales of $200,000 five years ago and sales of $600,000 this year. If the growth in sales is assumed to be linear, what will the sales be five years from now?

72. A product that sold for $250 three years ago sells for $325 this year. If price increases are assumed to be linear, how much will the product sell for six years from now?

*73. Find a real number c such that $P(-2, 2)$ is on the line $3x + cy = 4$.

*74. Find a real number c such that the line $cx - 5y + 8 = 0$ has x-intercept 4.

*75. If the points $(-2, -3)$ and $(-1, 5)$ are on the graph of a linear function f, find $f(x)$.

*76. If $f(1) = 4$ and $f(-1) = 3$ and the function f is linear, find $f(x)$.

*77. Prove that the linear function $f(x) = ax + b$ is an increasing function if $a > 0$ and is a decreasing function if $a < 0$.

*78. If x_1 and x_2 are the abscissas of two points on the graph of the function $y = f(x)$, show that the slope m of the line connecting the two points can be written as

$$m = \frac{f(x_2) - f(x_1)}{x_2 - x_1}$$

79. A manufacturing process costs $12,000 to get started, then an additional $350 to produce each unit. Set up a linear cost function and graph it with your graphing calculator. You will need to change the WINDOW to "find" the graph.

   Use your graph to determine the largest number of units that could be produced if costs must be kept under $600,000. (Hint: Graph a horizontal line $y = 600,000$ and look for the point of intersection with your original graph.)

80. Use your graphing calculator to see how changing the values of A and B affect the graph of the line $Ax + By = 0$. What do you get if A and B have the same absolute value but are opposite in sign? (Hint: Choose a SQUARE viewing window from your ZOOM menu.)

81. Investigate the concept of slope further by storing a LIST of various slopes. Let $L_1 = \{1, 2, 3, 4, 5\}$ and enter the equation seen in the graphic below:

Explain in your own words how the changing values in your list affect the lines.

82. Repeat Exercise 81 with the following list: $\{1, 0.1, 0.01\}$.

83. Suppose a roofer decided to design a roof (with a triangular cross section) by first writing the equation of a straight line. She decides to consider a point at the base of the house as the origin of a coordinate system. So, a point at the base of the roof has coordinates (0, 25), since the edge of the roof is 25 feet above ground level. If the roofer desires a pitch (slope) of $\frac{4}{12}$, what is the equation of the line she needs?

84. Refer back to exercise 83. Graph the equation you found. (You may use your graphing calculator.) Determine the heights of the peak of the roof for various possible values of x (say, 20 feet, 30 feet, and 40 feet.) Draw the house for each value of x.

7.3 Further Properties of the Straight Line

Horizontal and Vertical Lines

Horizontal and vertical lines are special cases that deserve particular attention. In Figure 12a we have a vertical line through the point (3, 2). Choose any other point on the line and answer the question: What is the x-coordinate of the point? You now see that every point on this vertical line has an x-coordinate of 3. The equation of the line is $x = 3$, since x remains constant. If we take a second point on this line, say, (3, 4), we see that the slope is

$$m = \frac{y_2 - y_1}{x_2 - x_1} = \frac{4 - 2}{3 - 3} = \frac{2}{0}$$

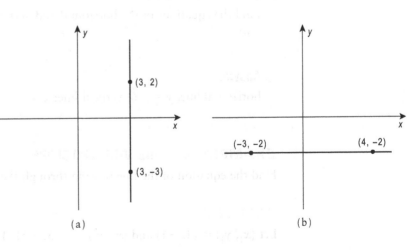

Figure 12 Deriving the Equations of Horizontal and Vertical Lines

Since we cannot divide by 0, we say that the slope is undefined.

> **The equation of the vertical line through (a, b) is**
>
> $$x = a$$
>
> A vertical line has no slope.

Vertical Lines

Looking at Figure 12b, we see that the coordinates of all points on the horizontal line through $(4, -2)$ have the form $(x, -2)$. The equation of the line is then $y = -2$, since y remains constant. If we choose a second point on the line, say $(6, -2)$, we find that the slope is

$$m = \frac{y_2 - y_1}{x_2 - x_1} = \frac{-2 - (-2)}{6 - 4} = \frac{0}{2} = 0$$

> **The equation of the horizontal line through (a, b) is**
>
> $$y = b$$
>
> The slope of a horizontal line is 0.

Horizontal Lines

EXAMPLE 1   FINDING THE EQUATIONS OF HORIZONTAL AND VERTICAL LINES

Find the equations of the horizontal and vertical lines through the point $(-4, 7)$.

SOLUTION

The horizontal line has the equation $y = 7$. The vertical line has the equation $x = -4$.

> **✔ Progress Check 1**
>
> Find the equations of the horizontal and vertical lines through the point $(5, -6)$.
>
> **Answer**
>
> horizontal line: $y = -6$; vertical line: $x = 5$

EXAMPLE 2   LINE WITH ZERO SLOPE

Find the equation of the line passing through the points $(4, -1)$ and $(-5, -1)$.

SOLUTION

Let $(x_1, y_1) = (4, -1)$ and $(x_2, y_2) = (-5, -1)$. The slope is

$$m = \frac{y_2 - y_1}{x_2 - x_1} = \frac{-1 - (-1)}{-5 - 4} = \frac{0}{-9} = 0$$

The equation then is

$$y - y_1 = m(x - x_1)$$
$$y - (-1) = 0(x - 4)$$
$$y + 1 = 0$$
$$y = -1$$

There is another way of solving this problem. Since both points have the same y-coordinate, we are dealing with a horizontal line. The equation of a horizontal line through $(a, -1)$ is $y = -1$.

✔ **Progress Check 2**

Find an equation of the line passing through $(6, -1)$ and $(6, 7)$.

Answer

$x = 6$

Parallel and Perpendicular Lines

In Figure 13 we have sketched two lines that are parallel. Clearly, the two lines have the same "steepness," or slope. In general, we can make the following statements:

Parallel Lines

> Parallel lines have the same slope.
>
> Lines that have the same slope are parallel.

Exercises 37 and 38 will guide you through a geometric proof of these results.

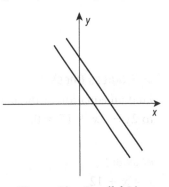

Figure 13   **Parallel Lines**

EXAMPLE 3   SLOPE AND PARALLEL LINES

Find the slope of every line parallel to the line $y = -\frac{2}{3}x + 5$.

SOLUTION

Since $y = -\frac{2}{3}x + 5$ is in the form $y = mx + b$, we see that the slope $m = -\frac{2}{3}$. Every line parallel to $y = -\frac{2}{3}x + 5$ has the same slope, so we conclude that all such lines also have slope $m = -\frac{2}{3}$.

✔ **Progress Check 3**

Find the slope of every line parallel to the line $y - 4x + 5 = 0$.

Answer

$m = 4$

EXAMPLE 4   EQUATIONS OF PARALLEL LINES

Find an equation of the line passing through the point $(2, -1)$ and parallel to $y = \frac{1}{2}x - 5$.

SOLUTION

The slope of the line $y = \frac{1}{2}x - 5$ and of every line parallel to it is $m = \frac{1}{2}$. Letting $(x_1, y_1) = (2, -1)$ we have

$$y - y_1 = m(x - x_1)$$

$$y - (-1) = \frac{1}{2}(x - 2)$$

$$y + 1 = \frac{1}{2}x - 1$$

$$y = \frac{1}{2}x - 2$$

✔ **Progress Check 4**

Find an equation of the line passing through the point $(-8, 4)$ and parallel to $2y - 2x + 17 = 0$.

Answer

$y = x + 12$

Slope can also be used to determine if two lines are perpendicular.

> If two lines with slopes m_1 and m_2 are perpendicular, then $m_2 = -1/m_1$.
>
> If the slopes m_1 and m_2 of two lines satisfy $m_2 = -1/m_1$, then the two lines are perpendicular.

Perpendicular Lines

This criterion for perpendicularity, which applies only when neither line is vertical, can be established by a geometric argument. (See Exercises 39 and 40.) The following example illustrates the use of this criterion.

EXAMPLE 5   EQUATIONS OF PERPENDICULAR LINES

Find an equation of the line passing through the point $(-3, 4)$ and perpendicular to the line $y = 3x - 2$. Sketch both lines.

SOLUTION

The line $y = 3x - 2$ has slope $m_1 = 3$. The line we seek has slope $m_2 = -1/m_1$ $= -1/3$ and passes through $(x_1, y_1) = (-3, 4)$. See Figure 14.

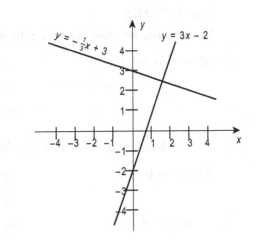

Figure 14   **Perpendicular Lines**

Thus,

$$y - y_1 = m(x - x_1)$$

$$y - 4 = -\frac{1}{3}[x - (-3)]$$

$$y - 4 = -\frac{1}{3}(x + 3) = -\frac{1}{3}x - 1$$

$$y = -\frac{1}{3}x + 3$$

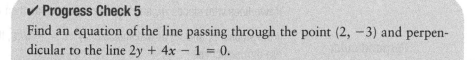

✔ **Progress Check 5**

Find an equation of the line passing through the point $(2, -3)$ and perpendicular to the line $2y + 4x - 1 = 0$.

Answer

$$y = \frac{1}{2}x - 4$$

EXAMPLE 6   DETERMINING IF LINES ARE PARALLEL OR PERPENDICULAR

State whether each pair of lines is parallel, perpendicular, or neither.

(a) $y - 3x + 11 = 0$; $2y = 6x - 4$

(b) $y = -4x + 1$; $2y = -4x + 9$

(c) $3y - x - 7 = 0$; $2y + 6x + 8 = 0$

SOLUTIONS

In each case, we must determine the slope of each of the lines.

(a) $\quad y - 3x + 11 = 0 \qquad\qquad 2y = 6x - 4$

$$y = 3x - 11 \qquad\qquad y = 3x - 2$$

$$m_1 = 3 \qquad\qquad\quad m_2 = 3$$

The lines are parallel since they have the same slope.

(b) $\quad y = -4x + 1 \qquad\qquad 2y = -4x + 9$

$$y = -2x + \frac{9}{2}$$

$$m_1 = -4 \qquad\qquad\qquad m_2 = -2$$

Since $m_1 \neq m_2$, the lines cannot be parallel. Also, since

$$-\frac{1}{m_1} = -\frac{1}{-4} = \frac{1}{4} \neq m_2$$

the lines are not perpendicular. Therefore, the lines are neither parallel nor perpendicular.

(c) $\quad 3y - x - 7 = 0 \qquad\qquad 2y + 6x + 8 = 0$

$$3y = x + 7 \qquad\qquad\quad 2y = -6x - 8$$

$$y = \frac{1}{3}x + \frac{7}{3} \qquad\qquad\quad y = -3x - 4$$

$$m_1 = \frac{1}{3} \qquad\qquad\qquad\quad m_2 = -3$$

Since

$$m_2 = -3 \quad \text{and} \quad -\frac{1}{m_1} = -3$$

we see that

$$m_2 = -\frac{1}{m_1}$$

and the lines are perpendicular.

✔ **Progress Check 6**

State whether each pair of lines is parallel, perpendicular, or neither.

(a) $4y - 6x = 11$; $3y + 2x - 7 = 0$

(b) $9y - x + 16 = 0$; $3y = 9x + 4$

(c) $5y = x - 4$; $25y - 5x + 17 = 0$

Answers

(a) perpendicular   (b) neither   (c) parallel

Exercise Set 7.3

In Exercises 1–4 write an equation of the line satisfying the given conditions.

1. It is horizontal and passes through the point $(3, 2)$.

2. It is horizontal and passes through the point $(-2, 4)$.

3. It is vertical and passes through the point $(-2, 3)$.

4. It is vertical and passes through the point $(3, -2)$.

In Exercises 5–14 write an equation of (a) the horizontal line passing through the point, and (b) the vertical line passing through the point.

5. $(-6, 3)$ 6. $(-5, -2)$

7. $(4, -5)$ 8. $(11, -14)$

9. $(0, 0)$ 10. $(0, -4)$

11. $(-7, 0)$ 12. $(-1, -1)$

13. $(0, 5)$ 14. $(5, 0)$

In Exercises 15 and 16 write an equation of the line shown in each graph.

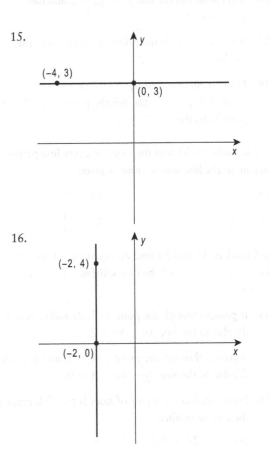

15.

16.

In Exercises 17–20 let L be the line determined by P_1 and P_2, and let L' be the line determined by P_3 and P_4. Determine whether L and L' are parallel, and sketch both L and L'.

17. $P_1(1, -1), P_2(3, 4); P_3(2, 3), P_4(-1, 8)$

18. $P_1(2, 1), P_2(4, 4); P_3(0, -2), P_4(-2, -5)$

19. $P_1(1, 3), P_2(0, 5); P_3(-4, 8), P_4(-2, 4)$

20. $P_1(4, 2), P_2(6, -1); P_3(4, 5), P_4(1, 8)$

In Exercises 21–24 find the slope of every line parallel to the given line.

21. $y = -\dfrac{2}{5}x + 4$ 22. $x - 2y + 5 = 0$

23. $3x + 2y = 6$ 24. $x = 3y - 2$

In Exercises 25–27 find the slope-intercept form of the line satisfying the given conditions.

25. It is parallel to the line $y = \frac{3}{2}x + 5$ and has y-intercept -2.

26. It is parallel to the line $y = -\frac{1}{2}x - 2$ and has y-intercept 3.

27. It passes through the point $(1, 3)$ and is parallel to the line $y = -3x + 2$.

28. Find an equation, of the form $Ax + By + C = 0$, of the line passing through the point $(-1, 2)$ and parallel to the line $3y + 2x = 6$.

In Exercises 29–32 find the slope of every line perpendicular to the line whose slope is given.

29. 2   30. -3

31. $-\dfrac{1}{2}$ 32. $-\dfrac{3}{4}$

In Exercises 33 and 34 find an equation, of the form $Ax + By + C = 0$, of the line satisfying the given conditions.

33. It passes through the point $(-3, 2)$ and is perpendicular to the line $3x + 5y = 2$.

34. It passes through the point $(-1, -3)$ and is perpendicular to the line $3y + 4x - 5 = 0$.

35. State whether each pair of lines is parallel, perpendicular, or neither.

    (a) $3x + 2y = 7; 3y - 2x = 4$

(b) $y - 3x + 1 = 0; 3y + x = 8$

(c) $y = \dfrac{2}{3}x + 3; 6y - 4x + 8 = 0$

36. State whether each pair of lines is parallel, perpendicular, or neither.

    (a) $y - 3x + 1 = 0; x = \dfrac{y}{3} + 2$

    (b) $2x + 5y = 1; x + y = 2$

    (c) $3x + 2y = 6; 12y - 8x + 7 = 0$

*37. In the accompanying figure, lines L_1 and L_2 are parallel. Points A and D are selected on lines L_1 and L_2, respectively. Lines parallel to the x-axis are constructed connecting points A and D to points B and E, respectively, on the y-axis. Supply a reason for each of the steps in the following proof.

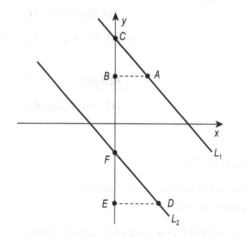

(a) Angles ABC and DEF are equal.

(b) Angles ACB and DFE are equal.

(c) Triangles ABC and DEF are similar.

(d) $\dfrac{\overline{CB}}{\overline{BA}} = \dfrac{\overline{FE}}{\overline{ED}}$

(e) $m_1 = \dfrac{\overline{CB}}{\overline{BA}}, m_2 = \dfrac{\overline{FE}}{\overline{ED}}$

(f) $m_1 = m_2$

(g) Parallel lines have the same slope.

*38. Prove that if two lines have the same slope, they are parallel.

*39. In the accompanying figure, lines L_1 and L_2, are perpendicular to each other with slopes m_1 and m_2, respectively, and intersect at a point Q. A perpendicular line from Q to the x-axis intersects the x-axis at the point C. Supply a reason for each of the steps in the following proof.

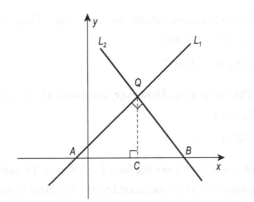

(a) Angles CAQ and BQC are equal.

(b) Triangles ACQ and BCQ are similar.

(c) $\dfrac{\overline{CQ}}{\overline{AC}} = \dfrac{\overline{CB}}{\overline{CQ}}$

(d) $m_1 = \dfrac{\overline{CQ}}{\overline{AC}}, m_2 = -\dfrac{\overline{CB}}{\overline{CQ}}$

(e) $m_2 = -\dfrac{1}{m_1}$

*40. Prove that if two lines have slopes m_1 and m_2 such that $m_2 = -1/m_1$, the lines are perpendicular.

41. Look back at Exercise 80 in the previous section. What do you now know about how the values of A and B affect the graph of the line $Ax + By = 0$? Why is a SQUARE viewing window needed to see this?

7.4   Linear Inequalities in Two Variables

When we draw the graph of a linear equation, say

$$y = 2x - 1$$

we can readily see that the graph of the line divides the set of points in the plane that are not on the line into two regions, which we call **half-planes**. (See Figure 15.) If, in the equation $y = 2x - 1$, we replace the equals sign with any of the symbols $<, >, \leq, \geq$, we have a **linear inequality in two variables**. By the **graph of a linear inequality** such as

$$y < 2x - 1$$

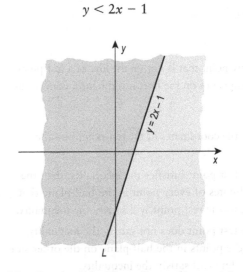

Figure 15   **Graph of the Linear Inequality:** $y < 2x - 1$

we mean the set of all points whose coordinates satisfy the inequality. Thus, the point $(4, 2)$ lies on the graph of $y < 2x - 1$, since

$$2 < (2)(4) - 1 = 7$$

shows that $x = 4$, $y = 2$ satisfies the inequality. However, the point $(1, 5)$ does not lie on the graph of $y < 2x - 1$, since

$$5 < (2)(1) - 1 = 1$$

is not true. Since the coordinates of every point on the line L in Figure 15 satisfy the *equation* $y = 2x - 1$, we readily see that the coordinates of those points in the half-plane below the line must satisfy the *inequality* $y < 2x - 1$. Similarly, the coordinates of those points in the half-plane above the line must satisfy the *inequality* $y > 2x - 1$. This leads to a straightforward method for graphing linear inequalities.

EXAMPLE 1 GRAPHING A LINEAR INEQUALITY

Sketch the graph of the inequality $x + y \geq 1$.

SOLUTION

Graphing Linear Inequalities

Step 1. Replace the inequality sign with an equals sign and plot the line.

(a) If the inequality is $\leq$ or $\geq$, plot a solid line. (Points on the line will satisfy the inequality.)

(b) If the inequality is $<$ or $>$, plot a dashed line. (Points on the line will not satisfy the inequality.)

Graph $x + y = 1$.

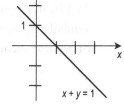

Step 2. Choose any point that is not on the line as a test point. If the origin is not on the line, it is the most convenient choice.

Choose $(0, 0)$ as a test point.

Step 3. Substitute the coordinates of the test point into the inequality.

(a) If the test point satisfies the inequality, then the coordinates of every point in the half-plane that contains the test point will satisfy the inequality.

(b) If the test point does not satisfy the inequality, then the points in the half-plane on the other side of the line will satisfy the inequality.

Substituting $(0, 0)$ in

$$x + y \geq 1$$

gives

$$0 + 0 \geq 1 \quad (?)$$
$$0 \geq 1$$

which is false.

(continues)

Graphing Linear Inequalities *(continued)*

Since (0, 0) is in the half-plane below the line and does not satisfy the inequality, all the points above the line will satisfy the inequality. Thus, the graph consists of the line together with the half-plane above the line. See Figure 16.

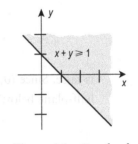

Figure 16   **Graph of** $x + y \geq 1$

✔ **Progress Check 1**

Sketch the graph of the inequality $4x + 3y \leq 12$.

Answer

See Figure 17.

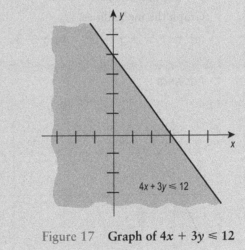

Figure 17   **Graph of** $4x + 3y \leq 12$

EXAMPLE 2   GRAPHING A LINEAR INEQUALITY

Sketch the graph of the inequality $2x - 3y > 6$.

SOLUTION

We first graph the line $2x - 3y = 6$. We draw a dashed or broken line to indicate that $2x - 3y = 6$ is not part of the graph. (See Figure 18.) Since $(0, 0)$ is not on the line, we can use it as a test point.

$$2x - 3y > 6$$
$$2(0) - 3(0) > 6 \quad (?)$$
$$0 - 0 > 6 \quad (?)$$
$$0 > 6$$

is false. Since $(0, 0)$ is in the half-plane above the line, the graph consists of the half-plane below the line.

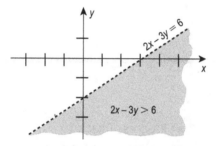

Figure 18   **Graph of $2x - 3y > 6$**

✔ **Progress Check 2**

Graph the inequalities.

(a) $y \leq 2x + 1$ (b) $y + 3x > -2$ (c) $y \geq -x + 1$

Answers

(a)   (b)   (c)

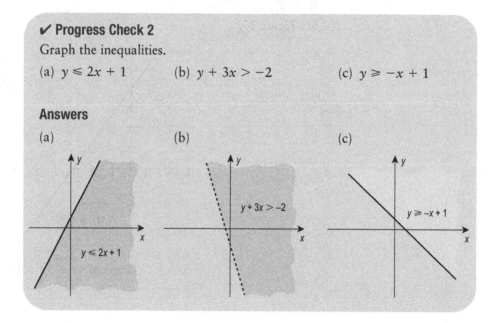

Select a test point far enough from the line for you to be certain it is above or below the line. If your graph is not accurately sketched, you might select a point that you think is above the line but is actually below it, or vice versa.

EXAMPLE 3   GRAPHS OF LINEAR INEQUALITIES

Graph the inequalities.

(a) $y < x$ (b) $2x \geqslant 5$

SOLUTIONS

(a) Since the origin lies on the line $y = x$, we choose another test point, say, (0, 1), above the line. Since (0, 1) does not satisfy the inequality, the graph of the inequality is the half-plane below the line. See Figure 19a.

(b) The graph of $2x = 5$ is a vertical line, and the graph of $2x \geqslant 5$ consists of the line together with the half-plane to the right of the line. See Figure 19b.

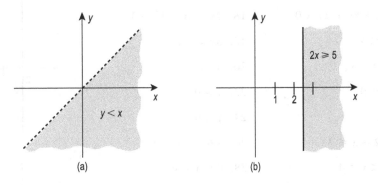

Figure 19   Diagrams for Example 3

✔ **Progress Check 3**

Graph the inequalities.

(a) $2y \geqslant 7$ (b) $x < -2$ (c) $1 \leqslant y < 3$

Answers

(a)   (b)   (c)

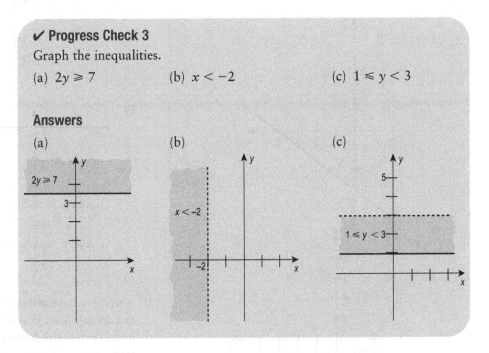

Exercise Set 7.4

In Exercises 1–28 graph the given inequality.

1. $y \le x + 2$

2. $y \ge x + 3$

3. $y > x - 4$

4. $y < x - 5$

5. $y \le 4 - x$

6. $y \ge 2 - x$

7. $y > x$

8. $y \le 2x$

9. $y \ge \frac{1}{2}x - 3$

10. $y \le 3 - \frac{2}{3}x$

11. $y < 1 - \frac{5}{2}x$

12. $y > \frac{1}{3}x + 2$

13. $3x - 5y > 15$

14. $2y - 3x < 12$

15. $3x + 8y + 24 \le 0$

16. $2x - 5y - 10 > 0$

17. $x \le 4$

18. $3x > -2$

19. $y > -3$

20. $5y \le 25$

21. $x < 0$

22. $y \ge 0$

23. $x > 0$

24. $y < 0$

25. $-2 \le x \le 3$

26. $-6 < y < -2$

27. $1 < y < 4$

28. $0 \le x \le 6$

In Exercises 29–34 give the linear inequality whose graph is shown.

29.

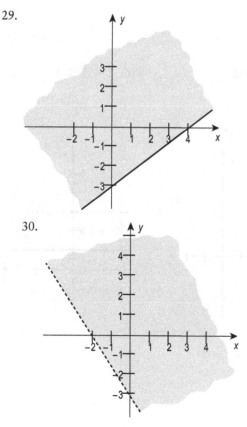

30.

31.

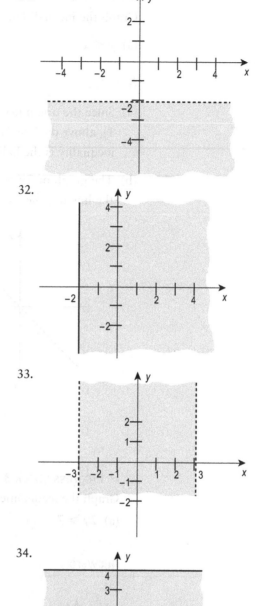

32.

33.

34.

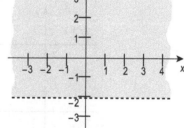

*35. A steel producer makes two types of steel: regular and special. A ton of regular steel requires 2 hours in the open-hearth furnace, and a ton of special steel requires 5 hours. Let x and y denote the numbers of tons of regular and special steel, respectively, made per day. If the open-hearth is available at most 15 hours per day, write an inequality that must be satisfied by x and y. Graph this inequality.

*36. A patient is placed on a diet that restricts caloric intake to 1500 calories per day. The patient plans to eat x ounces of cheese, y slices of bread, and z apples on the first day of the diet. If cheese contains 100 calories per ounce, bread 110 calories per slice, and apples 80 calories each, write an inequality that must be satisfied by x, y, and z.

■ ■ ■

Chapter Summary

Terms and Symbols

constant function	240	horizontal line	254	point-slope form	244
decreasing function	240	increasing function	240	slope-intercept form	246
general first-degree equation	250	linear inequality in two		slope of a line	238
graph of a linear inequality in		variables	261	vertical line	254
two variables	261	parallel lines	255	y-intercept	249
half-plane	261	perpendicular lines	257		

Key Ideas for Review

Topic	Page	Key Idea
Linear function	238	A linear function is of the form $f(x) = ax + b$.
graph	238	The graph of a linear function is a nonvertical straight line.
Slope	238	Any two distinct points $P_1(x_1, y_1)$ and $P_2(x_2, y_2)$ on a line can be used to find the slope $$m = \frac{y_2 - y_1}{x_2 - x_1}.$$
positive and negative slope	240	Positive slope indicates that a line is rising; negative slope indicates that a line is falling.
Point-slope form	244	The point-slope form of the equation of a nonvertical line is $y - y_1 = m(x - x_1)$.
Slope-intercept form	246	The slope-intercept form of the equation of a nonvertical line is $y = mx + b$.
Horizontal and vertical lines	253	The slope of a horizontal line is 0; the slope of a vertical line is undefined. The equation of a horizontal line through the point (a, b) is $y = b$. The equation of a vertical line through the point (a, b) is $x = a$.
Parallel lines	255	Parallel lines have the same slope.
Perpendicular lines	257	The slopes of perpendicular lines are negative reciprocals of each other.
General first-degree equation	250	The graph of the general first-degree equation $Ax + By + C = 0$, where A and B are not both zero, is always a straight line.
Linear inequalities	261	The graph of a linear inequality in two variables is a half-plane.

Common Errors

1. When calculating the slope

$$m = \frac{y_2 - y_1}{x_2 - x_1}$$

by using two points, you must be consistent in labeling the points. For example, if we have $(x_1, y_1) = (2, 3)$ and $(x_2, y_2) = (4, 5)$, then

$$m = \frac{5 - 3}{4 - 2} = \frac{2}{2} = 1$$

Don't write

$$m = \frac{5 - 3}{2 - 4} = \frac{2}{-2} = -1$$

2. The equation of the horizontal line through (a, b) is $y = b$. The equation of the vertical line through (a, b) is $x = a$. *Don't reverse these.*

3. The equation $y - 6x + 2 = 0$ must be rewritten in the form $y = 6x - 2$ before you can determine the slope $m = 6$ and intercept $b = -2$. Notice also that the intercept includes the sign; that is, the intercept is -2, not 2.

4. If a line L has slope $-\frac{1}{3}$, then every line perpendicular to L has slope 3, *not* -3. For instance, the line $2y = x - 1$ has slope $\frac{1}{2}$; every line perpendicular to this line has slope -2, *not* 2.

5. Do not confuse "zero slope" and "no slope." A horizontal line has zero slope, but a vertical line has no slope.

Review Exercises

Solutions to exercises whose numbers are in bold are in the Solutions section in the back of the book.

7.1 In Exercises 1 and 2 find the slope of the line passing through the given points.

  1. $(-2, 3)$ and $(2, 5)$ **2.** $(3, -1)$ and $(-3, 3)$

In Exercises 3 and 4 state whether the line whose slope is given is rising or falling.

  3. $m = 3$ **4.** $m = -2$

In Exercises 5 and 6 state whether the line passing through the given points is rising or falling.

  5. $(-3, -2)$ and $(4, -5)$ **6.** $(2, 3)$ and $(3, -2)$

Exercises 7 and 8 refer to Figure 20. Indicate if the slope of the line is positive (P) or negative (N).

  7. L_1 **8.** L_2

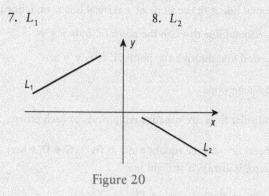

Figure 20

In Exercises 9 and 10 use Figure 21 to determine whether the given statement is true (T) or false (F).

  9. The slope of L_1 is less than the slope of L_2.

  10. The slope of L_4 is greater than the slope of L_3.

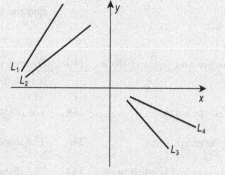

Figure 21

In Exercises 11 and 12 find the slope of the indicated line in Figure 22.

  11. L_1 **12.** L_2

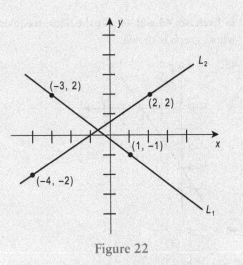

Figure 22

13. Find a real number c so that the straight line
$$3x + 2y = c$$
has y-intercept -3.

14. Find a real number c so that the point $(2, -3)$ is on the straight line
$$cx - 2y = 3$$

7.2 In Exercises 15 and 16 express the equation in the form $Ax + By = C$ and state the values of A, B, and C.

15. $3(x - 4) + 2(y + 1) = 4$

16. $x = -3y + 1$

17. Does the point $(2, -1)$ lie on the straight line $3x - 4y = 10$?

18. Show that the point $(5, -1)$ does not lie on the straight line $2x + 5y = 4$.

In Exercises 19 and 20 graph the line and label the x- and y-intercepts.

19. $3y - 2x = 12$ 20. $x = -2y + 3$

In Exercises 21 and 22 find the point-slope form of the line satisfying the given conditions.

21. Its slope is -3 and its x-intercept is 4.

22. It passes through the points $(-2, 1)$ and $(0, 3)$.

In Exercises 23 and 24 find the slope-intercept form of the line satisfying the given conditions.

23. Its slope is 4 and its y-intercept is -2.

24. It passes through the points $(0, -3)$ and $(2, 4)$.

In Exercises 25 and 26 find the slope and the y-intercept of the line.

25. $x = \dfrac{3}{2}y - 2$ 26. $2(x - 1) + y = 4$

In Exercises 27 and 28 determine whether the given line is rising or falling.

27. $2x - 3y = 6$ 28. $x = -3y + 4$

7.3 In Exercises 29 and 30 write an equation of (a) the horizontal line passing through the point, and (b) the vertical line passing through the point.

29. $(2, -3)$ 30. $(-3, 4)$

In Exercises 31 and 32 write an equation of the line shown in the graph.

31.

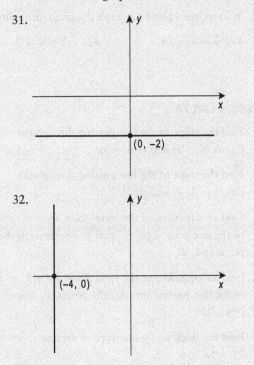

32.

In Exercises 33 and 34 let L be the line determined by P_1 and P_2, and let L' be the line determined by P_3 and P_4. Determine whether L and L' are parallel.

33. $P_1(4, 2)$, $P_2(-1, 5)$; $P_3(1, 2)$, $P_4(2, 3)$

34. $P_1(3, 2)$, $P_2(4, 3)$; $P_3(6, 2)$, $P_4(5, 1)$

In Exercises 35 and 36 find the slope-intercept form of the line satisfying the given conditions.

35. It is parallel to the line $3x - 2y = 4$ and has y-intercept 5.

36. It is parallel to the line $2x - 4y + 4 = 0$ and has x-intercept 3.

37. Find the point-slope form of the line passing through the point $(4, 1)$ and perpendicular to the line $5x - 2y = 4$.

38. Find the slope-intercept form of the line that is perpendicular to the line $3x + 4y = 6$ and whose y-intercept is 4.

In Exercises 39 and 40 state whether each pair of lines is parallel, perpendicular, or neither.

39. $2x - 3y = 4$; $2y + 3x = 6$

40. $3x - 2y = 6$; $x + 2y = 4$

7.4 In Exercises 41 and 42 graph the given inequality.

41. $y \geq 4 - 2x$ **42.** $-1 < y \leq 3$

In Exercises 43 and 44 give the linear inequality whose graph is shown.

43.

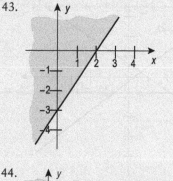

44.

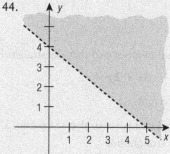

Progress Test 7A

1. Find the slope of the line passing through the points $(6, -3)$ and $(-6, -3)$.

2. Find the slope of the line passing through the points $\left(-1, \frac{3}{2}\right)$ and $\left(\frac{1}{2}, \frac{1}{2}\right)$.

3. Find an equation, of the form $Ax + By + C = 0$, of the line with slope -7 that passes through the point $(-1, 2)$.

4. Find an equation, of the form $Ax + By + C = 0$, of the line passing through the points $(6, 8)$ and $(-4, 7)$.

5. Find the slope and y-intercept of the line $2y + 5x - 6 = 0$.

6. Find the slope of the line $3y = 2x - 1$, and determine whether the line is rising or falling.

7. Find the slope of the line $2y + \frac{1}{2}x - 5 = 0$, and determine whether the line is rising or falling.

8. A telephone company charges 25 cents for the first minute and 20 cents for each additional minute.

Write an equation relating the total cost C of a phone call and the number of minutes t the parties are connected.

9. Find an equation of the vertical line passing through the point $\left(-11, \frac{3}{4}\right)$.

10. Find an equation of the horizontal line passing through the point $\left(4, -\frac{7}{3}\right)$.

11. Find the slope-intercept form of the line passing through the point $(0, 2)$ and parallel to the line $y - 3x - 2 = 0$.

12. Find the slope of every line perpendicular to the line $2y + 7x - 6 = 0$.

13. Find an equation, of the form $Ax + By + C = 0$, of the line passing through the point $(-1, -2)$ and perpendicular to the line $3y = 4x - 1$.

14. Graph the inequality $y > x - 2$.

15. Graph the inequality $x \leq -3$.

Progress Test 7B

1. Find the slope of the line passing through the points $(-4, -2)$ and $(-4, 6)$.

2. Find the slope of the line passing through the points $\left(\frac{1}{3}, -\frac{4}{3}\right)$ and $\left(-\frac{1}{2}, \frac{1}{3}\right)$.

3. Find an equation, of the form $Ax + By + C = 0$, of the line with slope 5 that passes through the point $(-6, -7)$.

4. Find an equation, of the form $Ax + By + C = 0$, of the line passing through the points $(-9, 2)$ and $(3, -6)$.

5. Find the slope and y-intercept of the line $3y - 12x + 5 = 0$.

6. Find the slope of the line $2y - 7x + 10 = 0$, and determine whether the line is rising or falling.

7. Find the slope of the line $4y + 5x - 3 = 0$, and determine whether the line is rising or falling.

8. The U.S. Postal Service charges 22 cents for the first ounce and 17 cents for every additional ounce of a first class letter. Write an equation relating the total cost C of a mailing and the number of ounces n when n is a natural number.

9. Find an equation of the horizontal line passing through the point $\left(-1, \frac{5}{4}\right)$.

10. Find an equation of the vertical line passing through the point $\left(3, -\frac{2}{3}\right)$.

11. Find an equation, of the form $Ax + By + C = 0$, of the line passing through the point $(-5, -7)$ and parallel to the line $y - 2x = 6$.

12. Find the slope of every line perpendicular to the line $-3x + 5y - 2 = 0$

13. Find the slope-intercept form of the line passing through the point $\left(\frac{1}{2}, -\frac{3}{2}\right)$ and perpendicular to the line $3y - x = 0$.

14. Graph the inequality $2y + 3x \leq 1$.

15. Graph the inequality $y > -1$.

Chapter 7 Project

To design a house, an architect must grasp some fundamental concepts of algebra, including many that we have studied in this chapter. A fundamental concept is the pitch, or slope of a roof, which is usually expressed as a fraction with a denominator of 12. So a roofer might say, if the roof has a pitch of $\frac{5}{12}$, then for every 12 feet horizontally, the roof must rise 5 feet. (Refer back to the chapter opener.)

For this chapter's project, first do Exercises 23 and 24 in Section 7.1, and Exercises 83 and 84 in Section 7.2. Write a paragraph summarizing how the algebra of straight lines can help to put a roof over your head (literally and figuratively!).

Now, repeat the Exercises listed above with different values. Use your graphing calculator to visualize your results. If the graph below represents one side of a roof, what is its pitch?

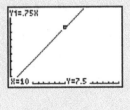

▪ ▪ ▪

8 Exponents, Radicals, and Complex Numbers

" *Mighty are numbers; joined with art, resistless.* "

—Euripides

Cosmologists, like Stephen Hawking, study the way the universe appears to us now, and use mathematics and physics to extrapolate what it may have been like billions of years ago. In particular, they look at two forces, gravitation and the electric force, which are both crucial to the way the galaxies formed after the Big Bang. However, the electric force is much stronger than the gravitational force—one trillion times one trillion times one trillion times as strong, in fact! The force of gravity is hardly a factor with small masses like molecules, so chemists can ignore it. But with huge masses like galaxies and black holes, it is so important that it helps to determine the shape of the universe.

How can we express "one trillion times one trillion times one trillion?" We need rules for expressing large numbers with exponents and multiplying them together. In this chapter's project, we will see how mathematicians, manipulating large numbers using the rules of exponents, may help to determine the final fate of the universe.

■ ■ ■

We have previously worked with exponential notation such as x^n when n is a positive integer. We now seek to expand our capability to handle any exponent, whether zero, a positive integer, a negative integer, or a rational number. We will see that the same rules apply in all these cases.

Radicals are an alternate way of writing rational exponent forms. Since the solutions of polynomial equations frequently involve radicals, we will learn to manipulate and simplify radical forms, as background to our study of polynomial equations of degree greater than 1.

We will also see that the real number system is inadequate to provide solutions to all polynomial equations. It is necessary to create a new type of number, called a complex number, which we will explore at the end of the chapter.

8.1 Positive Integer Exponents

In Chapter 4 we defined a^n by

$$a^n = \underbrace{a \cdot a \cdot \cdots \cdot a}_{n \text{ factors}}$$

where n is a natural number and a is any real number. We then saw that if m and n are natural numbers and a is any real number,

$$a^m \cdot a^n = a^{m+n}$$

We shall now develop additional rules for exponents. We see that

$$(a^2)^3 = \underbrace{a^2 \cdot a^2 \cdot a^2}_{n \text{ factors}} = a^6$$

and, in general, if m and n are any natural numbers and a is any real number, then

$$(a^m)^n = a^{mn}$$

EXAMPLE 1   SIMPLIFYING EXPRESSIONS WITH EXPONENTS
Simplify.

(a) $(2^2)^3$ (b) $(x^4)^3$ (c) $(x^2 \cdot x^3)^4$

(d) $(a^2)^n$ (e) $(r^n)^{2n}$ (f) $[(x+2)^4]^2$

SOLUTIONS

(a) $(2^2)^3 = 2^{2 \cdot 3} = 2^6$ (b) $(x^4)^3 = x^{4 \cdot 3} = x^{12}$

(c) $(x^2 \cdot x^3)^4 = (x^{2+3})^4 = (x^5)^4 = x^{5 \cdot 4} = x^{20}$ (d) $(a^2)^n = a^{2n}$

(e) $(r^n)^{2n} = r^{n \cdot 2n} = r^{2n^2}$

(f) $[(x+2)^4]^2 = (x+2)^{4 \cdot 2} = (x+2)^8$

✔ **Progress Check 1**

Simplify.

(a) $(x^3)^4$ (b) $(x^7)^7$ (c) $(x^2)^3 \cdot x^5$

(d) $(y^n)^2$ (e) $[(2a - 2)^3]^5$ (f) $x^4(x^2)^3$

Answers

(a) x^{12} (b) x^{49} (c) x^{11} (d) y^{2n} (e) $(2a - 2)^{15}$ (f) x^{10}

Now we turn to a^m/a^n. We will use our old friend, the cancellation principle, to simplify. We see that

$$\frac{a^4}{a^2} = \frac{a \cdot a \cdot a \cdot a}{a \cdot a} = \frac{a^2}{1} = a^2$$

and

$$\frac{a^2}{a^4} = \frac{a \cdot a}{a \cdot a \cdot a \cdot a} = \frac{1}{a^2}$$

We can conclude that the result depends upon which exponent is larger. If m and n are natural numbers and a is any nonzero real number, then

$$\frac{a^m}{a^n} = a^{m-n} \qquad \text{if } m > n$$

$$\frac{a^m}{a^n} = \frac{1}{a^{n-m}} \qquad \text{if } n > m$$

$$\frac{a^m}{a^n} = 1 \qquad \text{if } m = n$$

EXAMPLE 2   SIMPLIFYING EXPRESSIONS WITH EXPONENTS

Simplify.

(a) $\dfrac{5^7}{5^4}$ (b) $\dfrac{(-3)^2}{(-3)^3}$ (c) $\dfrac{-x^{17}}{x^{11}}$

(d) $\dfrac{-(2y - 1)^6}{(2y - 1)^8}$ (e) $\dfrac{x^{2n+1}}{x^n}$ (f) $\dfrac{(x^3)^4}{x^7(x^2)^5}$

SOLUTIONS

(a) $\dfrac{5^7}{5^4} = 5^{7-4} = 5^3 = 125$

(b) $\dfrac{(-3)^2}{(-3)^3} = \dfrac{1}{(-3)^{3-2}} = \dfrac{1}{-3} = -\dfrac{1}{3}$

(c) $\dfrac{-x^{17}}{x^{11}} = -x^{17-11} = -x^6$

(d) $\dfrac{-(2y-1)^6}{(2y-1)^8} = \dfrac{-1}{(2y-1)^{8-6}} = \dfrac{-1}{(2y-1)^2}$

(e) $\dfrac{x^{2n+1}}{x^n} = x^{2n+1-n} = x^{n+1}$

(f) $\dfrac{(x^3)^4}{x^7(x^2)^5} = \dfrac{x^{12}}{x^{17}} = \dfrac{1}{x^5}$

✔ Progress Check 2

Simplify, using only positive exponents.

(a) $\dfrac{6^3}{6^9}$

(b) $\dfrac{-2^4}{2^2}$

(c) $\dfrac{a^{14}}{a^8}$

(d) $\dfrac{b^{17}}{b^{25}}$

(e) $\dfrac{y^n}{y^{2n}}$

(f) $\dfrac{-2(x+1)^4}{(x+1)^{11}}$

Answers

(a) $\dfrac{1}{6^6}$
(b) -4
(c) a^6
(d) $\dfrac{1}{b^8}$
(e) $\dfrac{1}{y^n}$
(f) $\dfrac{-2}{(x+1)^7}$

Thus far, we have developed rules for multiplying and dividing exponents when there is a common base. It is also easy to develop rules for when there is a common exponent. For example,

$$(ab)^3 = (ab)(ab)(ab) = (a \cdot a \cdot a) \cdot (b \cdot b \cdot b)$$
$$= a^3 b^3$$

and, in general, if m is any natural number and a and b are any real numbers, then

$$(ab)^m = a^m b^m$$

Similarly,

$$\left(\dfrac{a}{b}\right)^3 = \left(\dfrac{a}{b}\right)\left(\dfrac{a}{b}\right)\left(\dfrac{a}{b}\right) = \dfrac{a \cdot a \cdot a}{b \cdot b \cdot b} = \dfrac{a^3}{b^3}$$

and, in general, if m is any natural number and a and b are any real numbers, $b \neq 0$, then

$$\left(\dfrac{a}{b}\right)^m = \dfrac{a^m}{b^m}$$

There is a helpful technique for keeping track of the sign. If we have $(-ab)^m$, we treat this as $[(-1)ab]^m$ and then have

$$(-ab)^m = [(-1)ab]^m = (-1)^m a^m b^m$$

The sign of the result will then depend upon whether m is even or odd. If m is even, $(-1)^m = 1$; and if m is odd, $(-1)^m = -1$. Thus, if m is even, the result is $a^m b^m$; if m is odd, the result is $-a^m b^m$. For example,

$$(-xy)^3 = -x^3 y^3 \qquad (-xy)^6 = x^6 y^6$$

EXAMPLE 3   SIMPLIFYING EXPRESSIONS WITH EXPONENTS

Simplify.

(a) $\left(\dfrac{3}{2}\right)^2$　　　　(b) $(xy)^6$　　　　(c) $-(2x)^4$　　　　(d) $(-2x)^4$

(e) $-\left(\dfrac{2}{x}\right)^3$　　　　(f) $(2x^2 y)^4$　　　　(g) $\left(\dfrac{-ab^2}{c^3}\right)^3$　　　　(h) $\dfrac{(24y)^3}{(12x)^3}$

SOLUTIONS

(a) $\left(\dfrac{3}{2}\right)^2 = \dfrac{3^2}{2^2} = \dfrac{9}{4}$　　　　　　(b) $(xy)^6 = x^6 y^6$

(c) $-(2x)^4 = -2^4 x^4 = -16x^4$　　　　(d) $(-2x)^4 = (-2)^4 x^4 = 16x^4$

(e) $-\left(\dfrac{2}{x}\right)^3 = -\dfrac{2^3}{x^3} = -\dfrac{8}{x^3}$　　　　(f) $(2x^2 y)^4 = 2^4 (x^2)^4 \cdot y^4 = 16x^8 y^4$

(g) $\left(\dfrac{-ab^2}{c^3}\right)^3 = \dfrac{(-1)^3 a^3 \cdot (b^2)^3}{(c^3)^3} = \dfrac{-a^3 b^6}{c^9}$

(h) $\dfrac{(24y)^3}{(12x)^3} = \left(\dfrac{\overset{2}{\cancel{24}}y}{\cancel{12}x}\right)^3 = \left(\dfrac{2y}{x}\right)^3 = \dfrac{2^3 y^3}{x^3} = \dfrac{8y^3}{x^3}$

✔ Progress Check 3

Simplify.

(a) $\left(\dfrac{2}{3}\right)^3$　　　　(b) $(2xy)^2$　　　　(c) $\left(\dfrac{2x^2}{y^3}\right)^4$

(d) $\left(-\dfrac{2}{5}xy^2\right)^2$　　　　(e) $(-xy)^3$　　　　(f) $\left(\dfrac{x^5 y^2}{y}\right)^3$

Answers

(a) $\dfrac{8}{27}$　　(b) $4x^2 y^2$　　(c) $\dfrac{16x^8}{y^{12}}$　　(d) $\dfrac{4}{25}x^2 y^4$　　(e) $-x^3 y^3$　　(f) $x^{15} y^3$

Exercise Set 8.1

In Exercises 1–4 evaluate the given expression. Identify the base and exponent.

1. $\left(\dfrac{1}{3}\right)^4$

2. $\left(\dfrac{2}{5}\right)^3$

3. $(-2)^5$

4. $(-0.2)^4$

In Exercises 5–8 rewrite the given expression, using exponents.

5. $(-5)(-5)(-5)(-5)$

6. $\left(\dfrac{1}{2}\right)\left(\dfrac{1}{2}\right)\left(\dfrac{1}{2}\right)\left(\dfrac{1}{3}\right)\left(\dfrac{1}{3}\right)$

7. $4 \cdot 4 \cdot x \cdot x \cdot y \cdot y \cdot y$

8. $3 \cdot x \cdot x \cdot x + 2 \cdot y \cdot y \cdot y \cdot y$

In Exercises 9–14 the right-hand side of each equation is incorrect. Correct that side.

9. $x^2 \cdot x^4 = x^8$

10. $(y^2)^5 = y^7$

11. $\dfrac{b^6}{b^2} = b^3$

12. $\dfrac{x^2}{x^6} = x^4$

13. $(2x)^4 = 2x^4$

14. $\left(\dfrac{4}{3}\right)^4 = \dfrac{4}{3^4}$

In Exercises 15–68 simplify, using the properties of exponents.

15. $\left(-\dfrac{1}{2}\right)^4\left(-\dfrac{1}{2}\right)^3$

16. $x^3 \cdot x^6$

17. $(x^m)^{3m}$

18. $(y^4)^{2n}$

19. $(x^{m+1})^m$

20. $(y^{2n})^{n-1}$

21. $\dfrac{3^6}{3^2}$

22. $\dfrac{(-4)^6}{(-4)^{10}}$

23. $-\left(\dfrac{x}{y}\right)^3$

24. $\left[\dfrac{(2x+1)^2}{(3x-2)^3}\right]^3$

25. $y^2 \cdot y^6$

26. $-3r^3r^3$

27. $(x^3)^5 \cdot x^4$

28. $[(-2)^5]^4(-2)^3$

29. $-\left(\dfrac{a}{b}\right)^5$

30. $\dfrac{x^4}{x^8}$

31. $(-2x^2)^5$

32. $-(2x^2)^5$

33. $3^{2m} \cdot 3^m$

34. $(-2)^m(-2)^n$

35. $x^{3n} \cdot x^n$

36. $y^{2m-1} \cdot y^{m+2}$

37. $(3^2)^4$

38. $(x^6)^5$

39. $\dfrac{5^{2n}}{5^{n-1}}$

40. $\dfrac{7^{3m^2-m}}{7^{2m^2+2m}}$

41. $\dfrac{x^n}{x^{n+2}}$

42. $\dfrac{x^{3+n}}{x^n}$

43. $\left(\dfrac{3x^3}{y^2}\right)^5$

44. $\left(\dfrac{2x^4y^3}{y^2}\right)^3$

45. $-(-5x^3)(-6x^5)$

46. $-(-ab)^5$

47. $(x^2)^3(y^2)^4(x^3)^7$

48. $(a^3)^4(b^2)^5(b^3)^6$

49. $\dfrac{(r^2)^4}{(r^4)^2}$

50. $\dfrac{[(x+1)^3]^2}{[(x+1)^5]^3}$

51. $[(3b+1)^5]^5$

52. $[(2x+3)^3]^7$

53. $\dfrac{(2a+b)^4}{(2a+b)^6}$

54. $\dfrac{5(3x-y)^8}{(3x-y)^2}$

55. $-(3x^3y)^3$

56. $\left(\dfrac{3}{2}x^2y^3\right)^n$

57. $\left(\dfrac{2a^n}{b^{2n}}\right)^n$

58. $\left(\dfrac{1}{3}x^{2n}y^2\right)^n$

59. $\dfrac{(3x^2)^3}{(-2x)^3}$

60. $\dfrac{(-2a^2b)^4}{(-3ab^2)^3}$

61. $(2x+1)^3(2x+1)^7$

62. $(3x-2)^6(3x-2)^5$

63. $\dfrac{y^3(y^3)^4}{(y^4)^6}$

64. $\dfrac{2[(3x-1)^3]^5[(3x-1)^2]^4}{[(3x-1)^2]^7}$

65. $(-2a^2b^3)^{2n}$

66. $\left(-\dfrac{2}{3}a^2b^3c^2\right)^3$

67. $\left(\dfrac{-2a^2b^3}{c^2}\right)^3$

68. $\left(\dfrac{8x^3y}{6xy^4}\right)^3$

In Exercises 69–76 evaluate the expression.

69. $(1.27)^2(3.65)^2$

70. $(-4.73)^3(-0.22)^3$

71. $\dfrac{-(6.14)^2(2.07)^2}{(7.93)^2}$

72. $\dfrac{(1.77)^2}{(2.85)^2(8.19)^2}$

73. $(2x-1)^3(x+1)^3$ when $x = 1.73$

74. $\dfrac{(3-x)^2}{(x+3)^2}$ when $x = 2.25$

75. $(5.46^2)^2$

76. $(3.29^2)^2$

77. Does $\dfrac{a^m}{a^n} = a^{m-n}$ for all values of a? Investigate this question by setting up a TABLE in your graphing calculator. Let $m = 6$, $n = 4$, and $y^1 = (x\char94 6)/(x\char94 4)$, $y^2 = x\char94(6 - 4)$. (NOTE: "$\char94$" refers to the exponent key on your calculator.) Then set up a TABLE. (Make sure you set it up so that you can choose your own input values. See your manual for details.) Can you find any value of x for which $y^1 = y^2$? Explain.

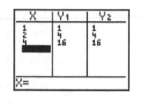

78. Perform the division: $10^{78}/(2 \times 10^9)$ using the rules of exponents.

$$\left(\text{Hint: } \frac{10^{78}}{2(10^9)} = \frac{1}{2} \times \frac{10^{78}}{10^9}\right)$$

Now perform the same operation in your calculator. Do the answers agree? Explain.

79. The ratio of the strength of the electric force (the force that holds electrons within atoms) to the gravitational force (which holds planets around the Sun) can be written as "one trillion times one trillion times one trillion." Write this number as the product of exponential expressions (base ten), and then find the product (as a larger power of ten).

8.2   Integer Exponents

Zero and Negative Exponents

We would like to expand our rules for exponents to include zero and negative exponents.

We begin with a^0, where $a \neq 0$. We will assume that the previous rules for exponents apply to a^0 and see if this leads us to a definition of a^0. For example, applying the rule $a^m a^n = a^{m+n}$ yields

$$a^m \cdot a^0 = a^{m+0} = a^m$$

Dividing both sides by a^m, we see that we must have

$$a^0 = 1$$

We *define* a^0 in this way. (We did not allow a to be zero since 0^0 has no mathematical meaning.) The student can easily verify that the other rules for exponents also hold. For example, our *definition* tells us that $(a/b)^0 = 1$, which agrees with the rule for quotients, since

$$\left(\frac{a}{b}\right)^0 = \frac{a^0}{b^0} = \frac{1}{1} = 1$$

EXAMPLE 1   USING AN EXPONENT OF ZERO
Evaluate.

(a) 3^0

(b) $(-4)^0$

(c) $\left(\dfrac{2}{5}\right)^0$

(d) $4(xy)^0$

(e) $\dfrac{-2}{(t^2 - 1)^0}$

(f) -3^0

SOLUTIONS

(a) $3^0 = 1$ (b) $(-4)^0 = 1$ (c) $\left(\dfrac{2}{5}\right)^0 = 1$

(d) $4(xy)^0 = 4(1) = 4$ (e) $\dfrac{-2}{(t^2 - 1)^0} = \dfrac{-2}{1} = -2$ (f) $-3^0 = -1$

✔ Progress Check 1

Simplify.

(a) $(-4x)^0$ (b) $-3(r^2 s)^0$ (c) $9\left(\dfrac{2}{7}\right)^0$

(d) $-4(x^2 - 5)^0$ (e) $5x^0 - 2xy^0$

Answers

(a) 1 (b) -3 (c) 9 (d) -4 (e) $5 - 2x$

The same approach will lead us to a meaning for negative exponents. For consistency, we must have, for $a \neq 0$,

$$a^m \cdot a^{-m} = a^{m-m} = a^0 = 1$$

Thus,

$$a^m \cdot a^{-m} = 1$$

If we divide both sides by a^m, we obtain

$$a^{-m} = \frac{1}{a^m}$$

Had we divided by a^{-m}, we would have obtained

$$a^m = \frac{1}{a^{-m}}$$

Thus, a^{-m} is the reciprocal of a^m, and a^m is the reciprocal of a^{-m}. Again, the student should verify that all the rules for exponents hold with this definition of a^{-m}. For example, if $a \neq 0$,

$$(a^{-m})^n = \left(\frac{1}{a^m}\right)^n = \frac{1}{a^{mn}} = a^{-mn}$$

The rules for negative exponents can be expressed in another way.

A factor moves from numerator to denominator (or from denominator to numerator) by changing the sign of the exponent.

EXAMPLE 2   WORKING WITH NEGATIVE EXPONENTS

Simplify, using positive exponents.

(a) 3^{-2}

(b) $\dfrac{1}{2^{-3}}$

(c) $(-3)^{-2}$

(d) $-x^{-7}$

(e) $\dfrac{-2}{(a-1)^{-2}}$

(f) $(2x)^{-3}$

(g) $2x^{-3}$

(h) $a + b^{-5}$

SOLUTIONS

(a) $3^{-2} = \dfrac{1}{3^2} = \dfrac{1}{9}$

(b) $\dfrac{1}{2^{-3}} = 2^3 = 8$

(c) $(-3)^{-2} = \dfrac{1}{(-3)^2} = \dfrac{1}{9}$

(d) $-x^{-7} = -(x^{-7}) = -\dfrac{1}{x^7}$

(e) $\dfrac{-2}{(a-1)^{-2}} = -2(a-1)^2$

(f) $(2x)^{-3} = \dfrac{1}{(2x)^3} = \dfrac{1}{8x^3}$

(g) $2x^{-3} = 2\left(\dfrac{1}{x^3}\right) = \dfrac{2}{x^3}$

(h) $a + b^{-5} = a + \dfrac{1}{b^5}$

✔ Progress Check 2

Simplify, using positive exponents.

(a) 4^{-2}

(b) $\dfrac{1}{3^{-2}}$

(c) $\dfrac{r^{-6}}{s^{-2}}$

(d) $x^{-2}y^{-3}$

Answers

(a) $\dfrac{1}{16}$

(b) 9

(c) $\dfrac{s^2}{r^6}$

(d) $\dfrac{1}{x^2y^3}$

EXAMPLE 3   SIMPLIFYING EXPRESSIONS WITH EXPONENTS

Simplify, using only positive exponents in the answer.

(a) $\dfrac{4a^3}{6a^{-5}}$

(b) $(x^2y^{-3})^{-5}$

(c) $a^{-3}\left(\dfrac{a^2}{b^{-2}}\right)^4$

(d) $(m^{-1} + n^{-1})^2$

SOLUTIONS

(a) $\dfrac{4a^3}{6a^{-5}} = \dfrac{2}{3}a^3a^5 = \dfrac{2}{3}a^8$

(b) $(x^2y^{-3})^{-5} = (x^2)^{-5}(y^{-3})^{-5} = x^{-10}y^{15} = \dfrac{y^{15}}{x^{10}}$

(c) $a^{-3}\left(\dfrac{a^2}{b^{-2}}\right)^4 = a^{-3}\dfrac{(a^2)^4}{(b^{-2})^4} = a^{-3}\left(\dfrac{a^8}{b^{-8}}\right) = \dfrac{a^{-3+8}}{b^{-8}} = \dfrac{a^5}{b^{-8}} = a^5b^8$

(d) $(m^{-1} + n^{-1})^2 = \left(\dfrac{1}{m} + \dfrac{1}{n}\right)^2 = \left(\dfrac{n+m}{mn}\right)^2 = \dfrac{(n+m)^2}{(mn)^2} = \dfrac{n^2 + 2nm + m^2}{m^2n^2}$

✔ **Progress Check 3**

Simplify, using only positive exponents in the answer.

(a) $\dfrac{x^7}{x^{-5}}$ (b) $(x^{-4}y^{-3})^4$ (c) $a^2\left(\dfrac{a^{-4}}{b^3}\right)^{-3}$ (d) $(3 + x)^{-1}$

Answers

(a) x^{12} (b) $\dfrac{1}{x^{16}y^{12}}$ (c) $a^{14}b^9$ (d) $\dfrac{1}{3 + x}$

⚠ **WARNING**

Don't confuse negative numbers and negative exponents.

(a) $2^{-4} = \dfrac{1}{2^4}$

 Don't write

$$2^{-4} = -2^4$$

(b) $(-2)^{-3} = \dfrac{1}{(-2)^3} = \dfrac{1}{-8} = -\dfrac{1}{8}$

 Don't write

$$(-2)^{-3} = \dfrac{1}{2^3} = \dfrac{1}{8}$$

(c) $-3^{-2} = -\dfrac{1}{3^2} = -\dfrac{1}{9}$

 Don't write

$$-3^{-2} = 3^2 = 9$$

We can now summarize the laws of exponents.

Laws of Exponents

If m and n are integers, then

$$a^m \cdot a^n = a^{m+n} \qquad\qquad \left(\dfrac{a}{b}\right)^n = \dfrac{a^n}{b^n}, \qquad b \neq 0$$

$$\dfrac{a^m}{a^n} = a^{m-n} = \dfrac{1}{a^{n-m}}, \quad a \neq 0 \qquad\qquad a^0 = 1, \qquad a \neq 0$$

$$(a^m)^n = a^{mn} \qquad\qquad\qquad a^{-n} = \dfrac{1}{a^n}, \qquad a \neq 0$$

$$(ab)^n = a^n b^n$$

Exercise Set 8.2

In Exercises 1–72 use the rules for exponents to simplify. Write the answers using only positive exponents.

1. 2^0

2. $(-1.2)^0$

3. $(xy)^0$

4. $2(a^2 - 1)^0$

5. $\dfrac{3}{(2x^2 + 1)^0}$

6. -3^0

7. $-5xy^0$

8. 2^{-4}

9. $(-3)^{-3}$

10. $\dfrac{1}{3^{-4}}$

11. $\dfrac{2}{4^{-3}}$

12. x^{-5}

13. $(-x)^3$

14. $-x^{-5}$

15. -4^{-2}

16. $-2x^{-2}$

17. $\dfrac{1}{y^{-6}}$

18. $\dfrac{1}{x^{-7}}$

19. $(2a)^{-6}$

20. $-6(3x + 2y)^{-5}$

21. $\dfrac{-4}{(5a - 3b)^{-2}}$

22. $3^4 3^{-6}$

23. $5^{-3} 5^5$

24. $x^{-4} x^2$

25. $4y^5 y^{-2}$

26. $a^4 a^{-4}$

27. $x^{-4} x^{-5} x^2$

28. $-3a^{-3} a^{-6} a^4$

29. $(3^2)^{-3}$

30. $(4^{-2})^2$

31. $[(-2)^3]^3$

32. $(x^{-2})^4$

33. $(x^{-3})^{-3}$

34. $[(x + y)^{-2}]^2$

35. $\dfrac{2^2}{2^{-3}}$

36. $\dfrac{3^{-5}}{3^2}$

37. $\dfrac{x^8}{x^{-10}}$

38. $\dfrac{3x^{-7}}{x^4}$

39. $\dfrac{4x^{-3}}{x^{-2}}$

40. $\dfrac{2x^4 y^{-2}}{x^2 y^{-3}}$

41. $2x^3 x^{-3}$

42. $(x^4 y^{-2})^{-1}$

43. $(2a^2 b^{-3})^{-3}$

44. $(ab^{-1})^{-1}$

45. $(a^{-1} b^{-1})^{-1}$

46. $\left(\dfrac{6}{9} x^{-3} y^2\right)^2$

47. $(3a^{-2} b^{-3})^{-2}$

48. $\dfrac{1}{(2xy)^{-2}}$

49. $\left(\dfrac{a^{-3} b^3}{c^{-2}}\right)^{-3}$

50. $\left(-\dfrac{1}{2} x^3 y^{-4}\right)^{-3}$

51. $\dfrac{a^2 b^4}{c}$

52. $\dfrac{(x^{-2})^2}{(3y^{-2})^3}$

53. $\dfrac{3a^5 b^{-2}}{9a^{-4} b^2}$

54. $\dfrac{8x^{-3} y^{-4}}{2x^{-4} y^{-3}}$

55. $\left(\dfrac{x^2}{x^3}\right)^{-1}$

56. $\left(\dfrac{x^3}{x^{-2}}\right)^2$

57. $\left(\dfrac{2a^2 b^{-4}}{a^{-3} c^{-3}}\right)^2$

58. $\left(\dfrac{3xy^{-1}}{2x^{-1} y^2}\right)^{-2}$

59. $\dfrac{2x^{-3} y^2}{x^{-3} y^{-3}}$

60. $(a^{-2} b^2)^{-1}$

61. $\left(\dfrac{y^{-2}}{y^{-3}}\right)^{-1}$

62. $\left(\dfrac{8x^{-3} y}{6xy^{-4}}\right)^{-3}$

63. $\left(\dfrac{-2a^{-2} b^3}{c^{-2}}\right)^{-2}$

64. $\left(-\dfrac{3}{2} a^2 b^{-2} c^{-2}\right)^{-3}$

65. $\left(\dfrac{x^3 y^{-1}}{z^{-3}}\right)^3$

66. $\left(\dfrac{x^{-3} yz^{-4}}{x^2 z}\right)^{-3}$

67. $\left(\dfrac{2a^{-2} b^3}{c^{-3}}\right)^2$

68. $\left(\dfrac{x^2 y^{-3}}{2xz^{-2}}\right)^{-2}$

69. $\dfrac{(a + b)^{-1}}{(a - b)^{-2}}$

70. $(a^{-1} + b^{-1})^{-1}$

71. $\dfrac{(x + y)^{-1}}{x^{-1} + y^{-1}}$

72. $\dfrac{(a^{-1} + b)^{-1}}{(a + b^{-1})^{-1}}$

In Exercises 73–80 evaluate the expression.

73. $(1.20^2)^{-1}$

74. $(-3.67^2)^{-1}$

75. $\left(\dfrac{7.65^{-1}}{7.65^2}\right)^2$

76. $\left(\dfrac{4.46^2}{4.46^{-1}}\right)^{-1}$

77. $\dfrac{(1.7)^{-2} (2.1)^2}{(1.7)(2.1)^{-1}}$

78. $\dfrac{(3.42 + 2.01)^{-1}}{(3.42 - 2.01)^{-2}}$

79. $\dfrac{(2x + 1)^{-1}}{(x - 1)^{-2}}$ when $x = 8.65$

80. $\dfrac{(3x - 1)(x + 2)^2}{(4 - x)^{-2}}$ when $x = 4.03$

81. The force of electrical repulsion (in Newtons) between two protons at a distance of one meter apart is given by $(8.9876 \times 10^9)(1.602 \times 10^{-19})$. Simplify this product. How strong is the gravitational force between two protons at a distance of one meter? (You must divide the product you just found by the ratio you found in Exercise 79.) (The ratio we used is rounded off, so this value is not exact. A better value is 1.876×10^{-64}).

8.3   Rational Exponents and Radicals

Suppose a square whose sides are of length a has an area of 25 square inches (Figure 1). We can write the equation

$$a^2 = 25$$

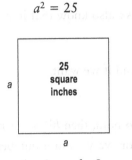

Figure 1   **Area of a Square**

and seek a number a whose square is 25. We say that a is a **square root of b** if $a^2 = b$. Similarly, we say that a is a **cube root of b** if $a^3 = b$; and in general, if n is a natural number, we say that

> a is an **nth root of b** if $a^n = b$.

Thus, 5 is a square root of 25, since $5^2 = 25$, and -2 is a cube root of -8, since $(-2)^3 = -8$.

Since $(-5)^2 = 25$, we conclude that -5 is also a square root of 25. More generally, if $b > 0$ and a is a square root of b, then $-a$ is also a square root of b. If $b < 0$, there is no real number a such that $a^2 = b$ since the square of a real number is always nonnegative. (We'll see in Section 8.5 that mathematicians have created an extended number system in which there is a root when $b < 0$ and n is even.)

Table 1 summarizes the different cases for the nth root of b. Note that when n is odd, the nth roots of b have the same sign as b.

TABLE 1   The nth Root of a Real Number b

b	n	Number of nth roots of b such that $a^n = b$	Form of nth roots	b	Examples
Positive	Even	2	$a, -a$	4	Square roots are 2, -2
Negative	Even	None	None	-1	No square roots
Positive	Odd	1	$a > 0$	8	Cube root is 2
Negative	Odd	1	$a < 0$	-8	Cube root is -2
0	All	1	0	0	Square root is 0

We would like to define rational exponents in a manner that will be consistent with the rules for integer exponents. If the rule $(a^m)^n = a^{mn}$ is to hold, then we must have

$$(b^{1/n})^n = b^{n/n} = b$$

We also know that if $a^n = b$, then a is an nth root of b. If

$$a^n = b$$

and if we want

$$(b^{1/n})^n = b$$

to hold, then $b^{1/n}$ must be the same as a; so $b^{1/n}$ must be an nth root of b. Then for every natural number n, we say that

$b^{1/n}$ is an nth root of b.

Of course, when n is even, we must also have $b \geqslant 0$.

Principal nth Root

If n is even and b is positive, Table 1 indicates that there are two numbers, a and $-a$, that are nth roots of b. For example,

$$4^2 = 16 \quad \text{and} \quad (-4)^2 = 16$$

There are then two candidates for $16^{1/2}$, namely, 4 and -4. To avoid ambiguity we say that $16^{1/2} = 4$. That is, if n is even and b is positive, we always *choose* the positive number a such that $a^n = b$ to be the nth root and call a the **principal nth root** of b. Thus, $b^{1/n}$ denotes the principal nth root of b.

EXAMPLE 1 FINDING THE PRINCIPAL nTH ROOT
Evaluate.

(a) $144^{1/2}$ (b) $(-8)^{1/3}$ (c) $(-25)^{1/2}$ (d) $-\left(\dfrac{1}{16}\right)^{1/4}$

SOLUTIONS

(a) $144^{1/2} = 12$ (b) $(-8)^{1/3} = -2$

(c) $(-25)^{1/2}$ is not a real number   (d) $-\left(\dfrac{1}{16}\right)^{1/4} = -\dfrac{1}{2}$

✔ **Progress Check 1**

Evaluate.

(a) $(27)^{1/3}$ (b) $(-27)^{1/3}$ (c) $36^{1/2}$ (d) $(-36)^{1/2}$

(e) $-36^{1/2}$ (f) $-36^{-1/2}$ (g) $\left(\dfrac{1}{8}\right)^{1/3}$

Answers

(a) 3 (b) -3 (c) 6   (d) not a real number

(e) -6 (f) $-\dfrac{1}{6}$ (g) $\dfrac{1}{2}$

WARNING

1. Note that

$$-36^{1/2} = -(36)^{1/2} = -6$$

   but $(-36)^{1/2}$ is undefined.

2. *Don't* write $16^{1/2} = -4$. The definition of an *n*th root requires that you write $16^{1/2} = 4$ (the principal *n*th root).

Rational Exponents

Now we are prepared to define $b^{m/n}$, where m is an integer (positive, negative, or zero), n is a natural number, and $b > 0$ when n is even. We want the rules for exponents to hold for rational exponents as well. That is, we want to have

$$4^{3/2} = 4^{(1/2)(3)} = (4^{1/2})^3 = 2^3 = 8$$

and

$$4^{3/2} = 4^{(3)(1/2)} = (4^3)^{1/2} = (64)^{1/2} = 8$$

To achieve this consistency, we define $b^{m/n}$, for an integer m, a natural number n, and a real number b, by

$$b^{m/n} = (b^{1/n})^m = (b^m)^{1/n}$$

where b must be positive when n is even. With this definition, all the rules of exponents continue to hold when the exponents are rational numbers.

EXAMPLE 2 WORKING WITH RATIONAL EXPONENTS

Simplify.

(a) $(-8)^{4/3}$ (b) $x^{1/2} \cdot x^{3/4}$ (c) $(x^{3/4})^2$ (d) $(3x^{2/3}y^{-5/3})^3$

SOLUTIONS

(a) $(-8)^{4/3} = [(-8)^{1/3}]^4 = (-2)^4 = 16$ (b) $x^{1/2} \cdot x^{3/4} = x^{1/2 + 3/4} = x^{5/4}$

(c) $(x^{3/4})^2 = x^{(3/4)(2)} = x^{3/2}$

(d) $(3x^{2/3}y^{-5/3})^3 = 3^3 \cdot x^{(2/3)(3)}y^{(-5/3)(3)} = 27x^2 y^{-5} = \dfrac{27x^2}{y^5}, y \neq 0$

✔ Progress Check 2

Simplify. Assume all variables are positive real numbers.

(a) $27^{4/3}$ (b) $(a^{1/2}b^{-2})^{-2}$ (c) $\left(\dfrac{x^{1/3}y^{2/3}}{z^{5/6}}\right)^{12}$

Answers

(a) 81 (b) $\dfrac{b^4}{a}$ (c) $\dfrac{x^4 y^8}{z^{10}}$

Radicals

The symbol $\sqrt{b}$ is an alternative way of writing $b^{1/2}$; that is, $\sqrt{b}$ denotes the non-negative square root of b. The symbol $\sqrt{}$ is called a **radical sign**, and $\sqrt{b}$ is called the **principal square root of b**. Thus,

$$\sqrt{25} = 5 \qquad \sqrt{0} = 0 \qquad \sqrt{-25} \text{ is undefined.}$$

In general, the symbol $\sqrt[n]{b}$ is an alternative way of writing $b^{1/n}$, the principal nth root of b. Of course, we must apply the ame restrictions to $\sqrt[n]{b}$ that we established for $b^{1/n}$. In summary,

$$\sqrt[n]{b} = b^{1/n} = a, \quad \text{where } a^n = b$$

with these restrictions:

- If n is even and $b < 0$, $\sqrt[n]{b}$ is not a real number.
- If n is even and $b \geqslant 0$, $\sqrt[n]{b}$ is the *nonnegative* number a satisfying $a^n = b$.

WARNING

Many students are accustomed to writing $\sqrt{4} = \pm 2$. This is incorrect since the symbol $\sqrt{}$ indicates the *principal* square root, which is nonnegative. Get in the habit of writing $\sqrt{4} = 2$. If you want to indicate *all* the square roots of 4, write $\pm\sqrt{4} = \pm 2$.

When Is a Proof Not a Proof?

Books of mathematical puzzles love to include "proofs" that lead to false or contradictory results. Of course, there is always an incorrect step hidden somewhere in the proof. The error may be subtle, but a good grounding in the fundamentals of mathematics will enable you to catch it.

Examine the following "proof."

$$1 = 1^{1/2} \tag{1}$$
$$= [(-1)^2]^{1/2} \tag{2}$$
$$= (-1)^{2/2} \tag{3}$$
$$= (-1)^1 \tag{4}$$
$$= -1 \tag{5}$$

The result is obviously contradictory: we can't have $1 = -1$. Yet each step seems to be legitimate. Did you spot the flaw? The rule

$$(b^m)^{1/n} = b^{m/n}$$

used in going from (2) to (3) doesn't apply when n is even and b is negative. Any time the rules of algebra are abused the results are unpredictable!

In short, $\sqrt[n]{b}$ is the **radical form** of $b^{1/n}$. The quantity b is called the **radicand**, and the integer n is called the **index**. We can switch back and forth from one form to the other.

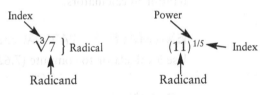

For instance,

$$\sqrt[3]{7} = 7^{1/3} \qquad (11)^{1/5} = \sqrt[5]{11}$$

Finally, we treat the radical form of $b^{m/n}$, where m is an integer and n is a natural number, as follows. We have already defined $b^{m/n}$ as $(b^m)^{1/n}$, so

$$b^{m/n} = (b^m)^{1/n} = \sqrt[n]{b^m}$$

Also, $b^{m/n}$ has been defined as $(b^{1/n})^m$, so

$$b^{m/n} = (b^{1/n})^m = \left(\sqrt[n]{b}\right)^m$$

Of course, the radicand must be such that its radical form will be defined. Thus,

$$7^{2/3} = (7^2)^{1/3} = \sqrt[3]{7^2}$$
$$7^{2/3} = (7^{1/3})^2 = (\sqrt[3]{7})^2$$

EXAMPLE 3 RADICAL FORM AND RATIONAL EXPONENT FORM

Change from radical form to rational exponent form, or vice versa. Simplify your answer and use only positive exponents. Assume all variables are nonzero.

(a) $(2x)^{-3/2}$, $x > 0$ (b) $\dfrac{1}{\sqrt[7]{y^4}}$ (c) $(-3a)^{3/7}$ (d) $\sqrt{x^2 + y^2}$

SOLUTIONS

(a) $(2x)^{-3/2} = \dfrac{1}{(2x)^{3/2}} = \dfrac{1}{\sqrt{8x^3}}$

(b) $\dfrac{1}{\sqrt[7]{y^4}} = \dfrac{1}{y^{4/7}}$

(c) $(-3a)^{3/7} = \sqrt[7]{-27a^3}$

(d) $\sqrt{x^2 + y^2} = (x^2 + y^2)^{1/2}$

✔ Progress Check 3

Change from radical form to rational exponent form, or vice versa. Simplify your answer and use only positive exponents. Assume all variables are positive real numbers.

(a) $\sqrt[4]{2rs^3}$ (b) $(x + y)^{5/2}$ (c) $y^{-5/4}$ (d) $\dfrac{1}{\sqrt[4]{m^5}}$

Answers

(a) $(2r)^{1/4}s^{3/4}$ or $(2rs^3)^{1/4}$ (b) $\sqrt{(x + y)^5}$ (c) $\dfrac{1}{\sqrt[4]{y^5}}$ (d) $\dfrac{1}{m^{5/4}}$

Calculators with a "y^x" key can be used to evaluate expressions such as $(7.62)^{3/4}$. The following example illustrates the necessary keystrokes on most hand-held calculators.

EXAMPLE 4 RATIONAL EXPONENTS AND CALCULATORS

Use a calculator to compute $(7.62)^{3/4}$.

SOLUTION

The required keystrokes are as follows:

7.62 $\boxed{y^x}$ .75 $\boxed{=}$

The displayed answer is

4.5863398

✔ Progress Check 4

Use a calculator to compute $(18.10)^{2/5}$.

Answer

3.1847213

Exercise Set 8.3

In Exercises 1–32 simplify, and write the answer using only positive exponents.

1. $16^{3/4}$

2. $4^{5/2}$

3. $(-125)^{-1/3}$

4. $(-64)^{-2/3}$

5. $\left(\dfrac{-8}{125}\right)^{2/3}$

6. $\left(\dfrac{-8}{27}\right)^{5/3}$

7. $c^{1/4}c^{-2/3}$

8. $x^{-1/2}x^{1/3}$

9. $\dfrac{2x^{1/3}}{x^{-3/4}}$

10. $\dfrac{y^{-2/3}}{y^{1/5}}$

11. $\left(\dfrac{x^{7/2}}{x^{2/3}}\right)^{-6}$

12. $\left(\dfrac{x^{3/2}}{x^{2/3}}\right)^{1/6}$

13. $\dfrac{125^{4/3}}{125^{2/3}}$

14. $\dfrac{32^{-1/5}}{32^{3/5}}$

15. $(x^2y^3)^{1/3}$

16. $(x^{1/3}y^2)^6$

17. $(16a^4b^2)^{3/2}$

18. $(x^6y^4)^{-1/2}$

19. $(a^{-3}b^2)^{-3/2}$

20. $(4a^{-4}b^{-5})^{-1/2}$

21. $(-64x^{6n})^{1/3}$

22. $(16^{8n}y^2)^{-1/4}$

23. $\left(\dfrac{x^{15}}{y^{10}}\right)^{3/5}$

24. $\left(\dfrac{x^8}{y^{12}}\right)^{3/4}$

25. $\left(\dfrac{x^{18}}{y^{-6}}\right)^{2/3}$

26. $\left(\dfrac{a^{-3/2}}{b^{-1/2}}\right)^{-5/2}$

27. $\left(\dfrac{x^3}{y^{-6}}\right)^{-4/3}$

28. $\left(\dfrac{x^9}{y^{-3/2}}\right)^{-2/3}$

29. $\left(\dfrac{-8x^9}{27y^{-3/2}}\right)^{5/3}$

30. $\left(\dfrac{-125x^{12}}{-y^{-3/2}}\right)^{-2/3}$

31. $\left(\dfrac{64x^6}{y^{12}}\right)^{1/4}$

32. $\left(-\dfrac{8}{27}\cdot\dfrac{x^6}{y^{-4}}\right)^{-2/3}$

In Exercises 33–40 write the expression in radical form.

33. $\left(\dfrac{1}{4}\right)^{2/5}$

34. $(-6)^{2/3}$

35. $x^{2/3}$

36. $(12y)^{-4/3}$

37. $(-8x^2)^{2/5}$

38. $(x^3y^3)^{1/6}$

39. $(x^2-1)^{2/3}$

40. $(3x^6+y^6)^{-3/4}$

In Exercises 41–48 write the expression in exponent form, using only positive exponents.

41. $\sqrt[4]{8^3}$

42. $\sqrt[4]{\left(\dfrac{1}{8}\right)^3}$

43. $\dfrac{1}{\sqrt[5]{(-8)^2}}$

44. $\dfrac{1}{\sqrt[3]{x^7}}$

45. $\dfrac{1}{\sqrt[4]{\dfrac{4}{9}a^3}}$

46. $\sqrt[6]{(3a^4b^6)^5}$

47. $\sqrt{(2x^{-4}y^3)^7}$

48. $\dfrac{1}{\sqrt[5]{(2a^2+3b^3)^3}}$

In Exercises 49–52 select the correct answer.

49. $\sqrt{121}=$

(a) 12 (b) 10 (c) 11

(d) ± 11 (e) not a real number

50. $\sqrt[3]{-27}=$

(a) 3 (b) $\dfrac{1}{3}$ (c) $-\dfrac{1}{3}$

(d) -3 (e) not a real number

51. $-\sqrt[3]{-\dfrac{1}{8}}=$

(a) -2 (b) 2 (c) $\dfrac{1}{2}$

(d) $-\dfrac{1}{2}$ (e) not a real number

52. $\sqrt[4]{16}=$

(a) 2 (b) -2 (c) $\dfrac{1}{2}$

(d) $-\dfrac{1}{2}$ (e) not a real number

In Exercises 53–64 evaluate the expression.

53. $\sqrt{\dfrac{4}{9}}$

54. $\sqrt{\dfrac{25}{4}}$

55. $\sqrt{-36}$

56. $\sqrt[4]{-81}$

57. $\sqrt[3]{\dfrac{1}{27}}$

58. $\sqrt[3]{-\dfrac{1}{125}}$

59. $\sqrt{(-5)^2}$

60. $\sqrt{\left(-\dfrac{1}{3}\right)^2}$

61. $\sqrt{\left(\dfrac{1}{2}\right)^2}$

62. $\sqrt{\left(\dfrac{5}{4}\right)^2}$

63. $\sqrt{\left(-\dfrac{7}{2}\right)^2}$

64. $\sqrt{(-7)^2}$

In Exercises 65–72 use a calculator to evaluate the expression.

65. $(14.43)^{3/2}$

66. $-(2.46)^{3/2}$

67. $(10.46)^{2/3}$

68. $(8.97)^{4/3}$

69. $\dfrac{(6.47)^{1/3}}{(6.47)^{4/3}}$

70. $\dfrac{(3.75)^{3/2}}{(3.75)^{1/2}}$

71. $\sqrt{3x^2 + 4y^3}$ when $x = 1.6$, $y = 5.7$

72. $\sqrt{(a^2 + b^4)^3}$ when $a = 2.5$, $b = 6.7$

8.4   Evaluating and Simplifying Radicals

Since radicals are just another way of writing exponents, the properties of radicals can be derived from the properties of exponents. By switching from radical to exponent form and back again, we can develop these properties of radicals.

Properties of Radicals

If n is a natural number, a and b are real numbers, and all radicals denote real numbers, then

1. $\sqrt[n]{b^m} = (b^m)^{1/n} = (b^{1/n})^m = (\sqrt[n]{b})^m$ $\sqrt[3]{8^2} = (\sqrt[3]{8})^2$

2. $\sqrt[n]{a} \cdot \sqrt[n]{b} = a^{1/n} \cdot b^{1/n} = (ab)^{1/n} = \sqrt[n]{ab}$ $\sqrt{4}\sqrt{9} = \sqrt{36}$

3. $\dfrac{\sqrt[n]{a}}{\sqrt[n]{b}} = \dfrac{a^{1/n}}{b^{1/n}} = \left(\dfrac{a}{b}\right)^{1/n} = \sqrt[n]{\dfrac{a}{b}}, \quad b \neq 0$ $\dfrac{\sqrt[3]{8}}{\sqrt[3]{27}} = \sqrt[3]{\dfrac{8}{27}}$

4. $\sqrt[n]{a^n} = \begin{cases} a & \text{if } n \text{ is odd} \\ |a| & \text{if } n \text{ is even.} \end{cases}$ $\sqrt{(-4)^2} = |-4| = 4$

Property 4 results from observing that

$$\sqrt[n]{a^n} = (a^n)^{1/n} = a^{n/n} = a$$

will result in a negative answer if $a < 0$ and n is even. Since we must choose the *principal* root, we must choose $|a|$, as shown in Property 4.

These properties can be used to evaluate and simplify radical forms. The key to the process is to think in terms of perfect squares when dealing with square roots, to think in terms of perfect cubes when dealing with cube roots, and so on. Here are some examples.

EXAMPLE 1   SIMPLIFYING RADICAL FORMS

Simplify.

(a) $\sqrt{72}$ (b) $\sqrt[3]{-54}$ (c) $2\sqrt[3]{8x^3y}$ (d) $\sqrt{\dfrac{16x}{9y^2}}$

SOLUTIONS

(a) $\sqrt{72} = \sqrt{36 \cdot 2} = \sqrt{36}\sqrt{2} = 6\sqrt{2}$

(b) $\sqrt[3]{-54} = \sqrt[3]{(-27)(2)} = \sqrt[3]{-27}\sqrt[3]{2} = -3\sqrt[3]{2}$

(c) $2\sqrt[3]{8x^3y} = 2\sqrt[3]{8}\sqrt[3]{x^3}\sqrt[3]{y} = 2(2)(x)\sqrt[3]{y} = 4x\sqrt[3]{y}$

(d) $\sqrt{\dfrac{16x}{9y^2}} = \dfrac{\sqrt{16x}}{\sqrt{9y^2}} = \dfrac{\sqrt{16}\sqrt{x}}{\sqrt{9}\sqrt{y^2}} = \dfrac{4\sqrt{x}}{3|y|}$

✔ Progress Check 1

Simplify.

(a) $\sqrt{45}$ (b) $\sqrt[3]{-81}$ (c) $-3\sqrt[4]{x^3y^4}$

Answers

(a) $3\sqrt{5}$ (b) $-3\sqrt[3]{3}$ (c) $-3|y|\sqrt[4]{x^3}$

WARNING

The properties of radicals state that

$$\sqrt{x^2} = |x|$$

It is a common error to write $\sqrt{x^2} = x$, but this leads to the conclusion that $\sqrt{(-6)^2} = -6$. Since the symbol $\sqrt{}$ represents the principal or nonnegative square root of a number, the result cannot be negative. It is therefore essential to write $\sqrt{x^2} = |x|$ (and, in fact, $\sqrt[n]{x^n} = |x|$ whenever n is even) unless we know that $x \geq 0$, in which case we can write $\sqrt{x^2} = x$.

Simplifying Radical Forms

There are other techniques we can use to simplify radical forms. If we have $\sqrt[3]{x^4}$, we can write it as

$$\sqrt[3]{x^4} = \sqrt[3]{x^3 \cdot x} = \sqrt[3]{x^3}\sqrt[3]{x} = x\sqrt[3]{x}$$

In general,

> $\sqrt[n]{x^m}$ can always be simplified so that the exponent within the radical is less than the index n, and x is prime (the only divisors of x are itself and 1).

Another possibility is illustrated by $\sqrt[4]{x^{10}}$, which can be written as

$$\sqrt[4]{x^{10}} = x^{10/4} = x^{5/2} = \sqrt{x^5}$$

In general,

> $\sqrt[n]{x^m}$ can always be simplified so that m and n have no common factors.

EXAMPLE 2   SIMPLIFYING RADICAL FORMS

Simplify. All variables represent positive real numbers.

(a) $\sqrt{x^3y^3}$ (b) $\sqrt{12x^5}$ (c) $\sqrt[3]{x^7y^6}$

SOLUTIONS

(a) $\sqrt{x^3y^3} = \sqrt{(x^2 \cdot x)(y^2 \cdot y)} = \sqrt{x^2y^2}\sqrt{xy} = xy\sqrt{xy}$

(b) $\sqrt{12x^5} = \sqrt{(4 \cdot 3)(x^4 \cdot x)} = \sqrt{4x^4}\sqrt{3x} = 2x^2\sqrt{3x}$

(c) $\sqrt[3]{x^7y^6} = \sqrt[3]{x^6 \cdot x}\sqrt[3]{y^6} = \sqrt[3]{x^6}\sqrt[3]{y^6}\sqrt[3]{x} = x^2y^2\sqrt[3]{x}$

✔ Progress Check 2

Simplify. All variables represent positive real numbers.

(a) $\sqrt{4xy^5}$ (b) $\sqrt[3]{16x^4y^6}$ (c) $\sqrt[4]{16x^8y^5}$

Answers

(a) $2y^2\sqrt{xy}$ (b) $2xy^2\sqrt[3]{2x}$ (c) $2x^2y\sqrt[4]{y}$

It is always possible to rewrite a fraction so that the denominator is free of radicals, a process called **rationalizing the denominator**. The key to this process is to change the fraction so that the denominator is of the form $\sqrt[n]{a^n}$, which reduces to a if n is odd and to $|a|$ if n is even.

$$\frac{5}{\sqrt{7}} = \frac{5}{\sqrt{7}} \cdot \frac{\sqrt{7}}{\sqrt{7}}$$

$$= \frac{5\sqrt{7}}{\sqrt{7^2}} = \frac{5\sqrt{7}}{7}$$

Multiply numerator and denominator by $\sqrt{7}$ to form a perfect square under the radical sign in the denominator.

If we are given

$$\frac{1}{\sqrt[3]{2x^2}}$$

we seek a factor that will change the expression under the radical sign in the denominator into the perfect cube $\sqrt[3]{2^3x^3}$. The factor is $\sqrt[3]{2^2x}$ since $\sqrt[3]{2x^2} \cdot \sqrt[3]{2^2x} = \sqrt[3]{2^3x^3}$. Thus,

$$\frac{1}{\sqrt[3]{2x^2}} = \frac{1}{\sqrt[3]{2x^2}} \cdot \frac{\sqrt[3]{2^2x}}{\sqrt[3]{2^2x}} = \frac{\sqrt[3]{4x}}{\sqrt[3]{2^3x^3}} = \frac{\sqrt[3]{4x}}{2x}$$

EXAMPLE 3   RATIONALIZING THE DENOMINATOR

Rationalize the denominator. Every variable represents a positive real number.

(a) $\dfrac{1}{\sqrt{3}}$ (b) $\dfrac{6xy^2}{5\sqrt{2x}}$ (c) $\dfrac{-3x^5y^6}{\sqrt[4]{x^3y}}$

SOLUTIONS

(a) $\dfrac{1}{\sqrt{3}} = \dfrac{1}{\sqrt{3}} \cdot \dfrac{\sqrt{3}}{\sqrt{3}} = \dfrac{\sqrt{3}}{3}$

(b) $\dfrac{6xy^2}{5\sqrt{2x}} = \dfrac{6xy^2}{5\sqrt{2x}} \cdot \dfrac{\sqrt{2x}}{\sqrt{2x}} = \dfrac{6xy^2\sqrt{2x}}{5 \cdot 2x} = \dfrac{3}{5}y^2\sqrt{2x}$

(c) $\dfrac{-3x^5y^6}{\sqrt[4]{x^3y}} = \dfrac{-3x^5y^6}{\sqrt[4]{x^3y}} \cdot \dfrac{\sqrt[4]{xy^3}}{\sqrt[4]{xy^3}}$ The multiplier $\sqrt[4]{xy^3}$ will produce $\sqrt[4]{x^4y^4}$ in the denominator.

$$= \dfrac{-3x^5y^6\sqrt[4]{xy^3}}{\sqrt[4]{x^4y^4}}$$

$$= \dfrac{-3x^5y^6\sqrt[4]{xy^3}}{xy}$$

$$= -3x^4y^5\sqrt[4]{xy^3}$$

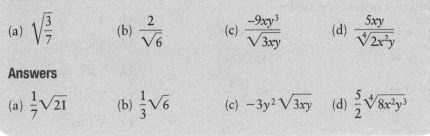

✔ **Progress Check 3**

Rationalize the denominator. Every variable represents a positive real number.

(a) $\sqrt{\dfrac{3}{7}}$ (b) $\dfrac{2}{\sqrt{6}}$ (c) $\dfrac{-9xy^3}{\sqrt{3xy}}$ (d) $\dfrac{5xy}{\sqrt[4]{2x^2y}}$

Answers

(a) $\dfrac{1}{7}\sqrt{21}$ (b) $\dfrac{1}{3}\sqrt{6}$ (c) $-3y^2\sqrt{3xy}$ (d) $\dfrac{5}{2}\sqrt[4]{8x^2y^3}$

A radical expression is said to be **simplified** when

(a) $\sqrt[n]{x^m}$ has $m < n$. (x is prime.)

(b) $\sqrt[n]{x^m}$ has no common factors between m and n.

(c) The denominator is rationalized.

EXAMPLE 4   RADICALS IN SIMPLIFIED FORM

Write in simplified form. Every variable represents a positive real number.

(a) $\sqrt[4]{x^2y^5}$ (b) $\sqrt{\dfrac{8x^3}{y}}$ (c) $\sqrt[6]{\dfrac{x^3}{y^2}}$

SOLUTIONS

(a) $\sqrt[4]{x^2y^5} = \sqrt[4]{x^2}\,\sqrt[4]{y^4 \cdot y} = \sqrt{x}\,\sqrt[4]{y^4}\,\sqrt[4]{y} = y\sqrt{x}\,\sqrt[4]{y}$

(b) $\sqrt{\dfrac{8x^3}{y}} = \dfrac{\sqrt{(4x^2)(2x)}}{\sqrt{y}} = \dfrac{\sqrt{4x^2}\sqrt{2x}}{\sqrt{y}} = \dfrac{2x\sqrt{2x}}{\sqrt{y}}$

$\qquad = \dfrac{2x\sqrt{2x}}{\sqrt{y}} \cdot \dfrac{\sqrt{y}}{\sqrt{y}} = \dfrac{2x\sqrt{2xy}}{y}$

(c) $\sqrt[6]{\dfrac{x^3}{y^3}} = \dfrac{\sqrt[6]{x^3}}{\sqrt[6]{y^2}} = \dfrac{\sqrt{x}}{\sqrt[3]{y}} = \dfrac{\sqrt{x}}{\sqrt[3]{y}} \cdot \dfrac{\sqrt[3]{y^2}}{\sqrt[3]{y^2}} = \dfrac{\sqrt{x}\,\sqrt[3]{y^2}}{y}$

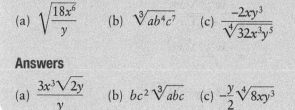

✔ **Progress Check 4**

Write in simplified form. Every variable represents a positive real number.

(a) $\sqrt{\dfrac{18x^6}{y}}$ (b) $\sqrt[3]{ab^4c^7}$ (c) $\dfrac{-2xy^3}{\sqrt[4]{32x^3y^5}}$

Answers

(a) $\dfrac{3x^3\sqrt{2y}}{y}$ (b) $bc^2\sqrt[3]{abc}$ (c) $-\dfrac{y}{2}\sqrt[4]{8xy^3}$

Exercise Set 8.4

In Exercises 1–69 simplify the expression. Every variable represents a positive real number.

1. $\sqrt{48}$

2. $\sqrt{100}$

3. $\sqrt[3]{54}$

4. $\sqrt{80}$

5. $\sqrt[3]{40}$

6. $\sqrt{\dfrac{8}{27}}$

7. $\sqrt[3]{\dfrac{8}{27}}$

8. $\sqrt[4]{16}$

9. $\sqrt[3]{\dfrac{8}{125}}$

10. $\sqrt{x^3}$

11. $\sqrt{x^8}$

12. $\sqrt[3]{y^7}$

13. $\sqrt[3]{a^{11}}$

14. $\sqrt[4]{b^{14}}$

15. $\sqrt{x^6}$

16. $\sqrt{48x^9}$

17. $\sqrt{98b^{10}}$

18. $\sqrt[3]{24x^8}$

19. $\sqrt[3]{108y^{16}}$

20. $\sqrt[4]{96x^{10}}$

21. $\sqrt{20x^4}$

22. $\sqrt{x^5y^4}$

23. $\sqrt{a^{10}b^7}$

24. $\sqrt{x^5y^3}$

25. $\sqrt[3]{x^6y^8}$

26. $\sqrt[3]{x^{14}y^{17}}$

27. $\sqrt[4]{a^5b^{10}}$

28. $\sqrt{9x^8y^5}$

29. $\sqrt{72x^7y^{11}}$

30. $\sqrt[3]{48x^6y^9}$

31. $\sqrt[3]{24b^{10}c^{14}}$

32. $\sqrt[4]{16x^8y^5}$

33. $\sqrt[4]{48b^{10}c^{12}}$

34. $\sqrt{20x^5y^7z^4}$

35. $\sqrt[3]{40a^8b^4c^5}$

36. $\sqrt[3]{72x^6y^9z^8}$

37. $\sqrt{\dfrac{1}{5}}$

38. $\dfrac{2}{\sqrt{5}}$

39. $\dfrac{4}{3\sqrt{11}}$

40. $\dfrac{3}{\sqrt{6}}$

41. $\dfrac{2}{\sqrt{12}}$

42. $\dfrac{1}{\sqrt{x}}$

43. $\dfrac{1}{\sqrt{3y}}$

44. $\sqrt{\dfrac{2}{y}}$

45. $\dfrac{4x^2}{\sqrt{2x}}$

46. $\sqrt{\dfrac{2}{x^2}}$

47. $\dfrac{6xy}{\sqrt{2x}}$

48. $\dfrac{8a^2b^2}{2\sqrt{2b}}$

49. $\dfrac{-5x^4y^5}{\sqrt[3]{x^2y^2}}$

50. $\dfrac{-4a^8b^6}{\sqrt[4]{a^3b^2}}$

51. $\dfrac{5ab}{\sqrt[3]{2ab^2}}$

52. $\sqrt{\dfrac{12x^4}{y}}$

53. $\sqrt{\dfrac{20x^5}{y^3}}$

54. $\dfrac{\sqrt{8a^5}}{\sqrt{3b}}$

55. $\sqrt[3]{\dfrac{x^5}{y^2}}$

56. $\sqrt[3]{\dfrac{2a^2}{3b}}$

57. $\sqrt[4]{\dfrac{8x^2}{3y}}$

58. $\sqrt{a^3b^5}$

59. $\sqrt{x^7y^5}$

60. $\sqrt[3]{x^2y^7}$

61. $\sqrt[4]{32x^8y^6}$

62. $\sqrt{9x^7y^5}$

63. $\sqrt[4]{48x^8y^6z^2}$

64. $\dfrac{xy}{\sqrt[3]{54x^2y^4}}$

65. $\dfrac{7xy^2}{\sqrt[4]{48x^7y^3}}$

66. $\dfrac{3a^3b^3}{\sqrt[3]{2a^2y^5}}$

67. $\dfrac{x}{\sqrt[4]{96x^6y^9}}$

68. $\dfrac{xy}{\sqrt[3]{32x^6y^4}}$

69. $\dfrac{4a^4b^2}{\sqrt[3]{125a^9b^4}}$

*70. Prove that $|ab| = |a||b|$. (*Hint:* Begin with $|ab| = \sqrt{(ab)^2}$.)

*71. Find the step in the following "proof" that is incorrect. Explain.

$$1 = \sqrt{1} = \sqrt{(-1)(-1)} = \sqrt{-1}\sqrt{-1} = -1$$

72. Enter the program below in your graphing calculator.

```
PROGRAM:RATIONAL
:Disp "X/A√(Y)"
:Input "X? ",X
:Input "A? ",A
:Input "Y? ",Y
:Disp X/(A*Y)▶Fr
ac," ROOT ",Y
```

Run the program. Use it to do Exercises 38–41 above.

8.5 Operations with Radicals

We can add or subtract expressions involving radical forms that are exactly the same. For example,

$$2\sqrt{2} + 3\sqrt{2} = (2 + 3)\sqrt{2} = 5\sqrt{2}$$
$$3\sqrt[3]{x^2y} - 7\sqrt[3]{x^2y} = (3 - 7)\sqrt[3]{x^2y} = -4\sqrt[3]{x^2y}$$

(Note that in each example we displayed an intermediate step to show that the distributive law is really the key to the addition process.)

EXAMPLE 1   ADDITION AND SUBTRACTION WITH RADICAL FORMS

Simplify and combine terms.

(a) $\sqrt{27} - \sqrt{12} = \sqrt{9 \cdot 3} - \sqrt{4 \cdot 3} = 3\sqrt{3} - 2\sqrt{3} = \sqrt{3}$

(b) $7\sqrt{5} + 4\sqrt{3} - 9\sqrt{5} = (7 - 9)\sqrt{5} + 4\sqrt{3} = -2\sqrt{5} + 4\sqrt{3}$

(c) $\sqrt[3]{x^2y} - \dfrac{1}{2}\sqrt{xy} - 3\sqrt[3]{x^2y} + 4\sqrt{xy}$

$$= (1 - 3)\sqrt[3]{x^2y} + \left(-\dfrac{1}{2} + 4\right)\sqrt{xy} = -2\sqrt[3]{x^2y} + \dfrac{7}{2}\sqrt{xy}$$

✔ Progress Check 1

Simplify and combine terms.

(a) $\sqrt{125} - \sqrt{80}$

(b) $\sqrt[3]{24} - \sqrt{8} - \sqrt[3]{81} + \sqrt{32}$

(c) $2\sqrt[5]{xy^3} - 4\sqrt[5]{x^3y} - 5\sqrt[5]{xy^3} - 2\sqrt[5]{x^3y}$

Answers

(a) $\sqrt{5}$ (b) $-\sqrt[3]{3} + 2\sqrt{2}$ (c) $-3\sqrt[5]{xy^3} - 6\sqrt[5]{x^3y}$

WARNING

Don't write

$$\sqrt{9} + \sqrt{16} = \sqrt{25}$$

You can perform addition only with identical radical forms. This is one of the most common mistakes made by students in algebra! You can easily verify that

$$\sqrt{9} + \sqrt{16} = 3 + 4 = 7$$

It is easy to simplify the product of $\sqrt[n]{a}$ and $\sqrt[m]{b}$ when $m = n$. Thus,

$$\sqrt[5]{x^2y} \cdot \sqrt[5]{xy} = \sqrt[5]{x^3y^2}$$

but $\sqrt[3]{x^2y} \cdot \sqrt[5]{xy}$ cannot be simplified in this manner.

Products of the form

$$(\sqrt{2x} - 5)(\sqrt{2x} + 3)$$

can be handled by forming all four products and then simplifying.

$$(\sqrt{2x} - 5)(\sqrt{2x} + 3) = \sqrt{2x} \cdot \sqrt{2x} + 3\sqrt{2x} - 5\sqrt{2x} - 15$$
$$= 2x - 2\sqrt{2x} - 15$$

EXAMPLE 2 MULTIPLICATION WITH RADICAL FORMS

Multiply and simplify.

(a) $2\sqrt[3]{xy^2} \cdot \sqrt[3]{x^2y^2}$ (b) $(\sqrt{3} + 2)(\sqrt{3} - 2)$

(c) $(\sqrt{2} - \sqrt{5})(\sqrt{2} + \sqrt{5})$ (d) $(2\sqrt{x} + 3\sqrt{y})^2$

SOLUTIONS

(a) $2\sqrt[3]{xy^2} \cdot \sqrt[3]{x^2y^2} = 2\sqrt[3]{x^3y^4} = 2xy\sqrt[3]{y}$

(b) $(\sqrt{3} + 2)(\sqrt{3} - 2) = \sqrt{3} \cdot \sqrt{3} - 2\sqrt{3} + 2\sqrt{3} - 4 = 3 - 4 = -1$

(c) $(\sqrt{2} - \sqrt{5})(\sqrt{2} + \sqrt{5}) = \sqrt{2} \cdot \sqrt{2} + \sqrt{2} \cdot \sqrt{5} - \sqrt{5} \cdot \sqrt{2} - \sqrt{5} \cdot \sqrt{5}$
$$= 2 - 5 = -3$$

(d) $(2\sqrt{x} + 3\sqrt{y})^2 = (2\sqrt{x})^2 + 2 \cdot 2\sqrt{x} \cdot 3\sqrt{y} + (3\sqrt{y})^2$
$$= 4x + 12\sqrt{xy} + 9y$$

✔ **Progress Check 2**

Multiply and simplify.

(a) $\sqrt[7]{a^3b^4} \cdot \sqrt[7]{3ab^3}$ (b) $\sqrt{3}(\sqrt{2} - 4)$ (c) $(\sqrt{2} - 5)(\sqrt{2} + 1)$

(d) $(\sqrt[3]{3x} - 4)(\sqrt[3]{3x} + 2)$ (e) $(\sqrt{x} - \sqrt{2y})^2$

Answers

(a) $b\sqrt[7]{3a^4}$ (b) $\sqrt{6} - 4\sqrt{3}$ (c) $-3 - 4\sqrt{2}$

(d) $\sqrt[3]{(3x)^2} - 2\sqrt[3]{3x} - 8$ (e) $x + 2y - 2\sqrt{2xy}$

Note that

$$(\sqrt{m} + \sqrt{n})(\sqrt{m} - \sqrt{n}) = m - n$$

That is, products of this form are free of radicals. This idea is used to rationalize denominators as in this example.

$$\frac{7}{\sqrt{2} + \sqrt{3}} = \frac{7}{\sqrt{2} + \sqrt{3}} \cdot \frac{\sqrt{2} - \sqrt{3}}{\sqrt{2} - \sqrt{3}} = \frac{7(\sqrt{2} - \sqrt{3})}{2 - 3}$$

$$= \frac{7(\sqrt{2} - \sqrt{3})}{-1} = -7(\sqrt{2} - \sqrt{3})$$

EXAMPLE 3 RATIONALIZING THE DENOMINATOR

Rationalize the denominator. Every variable represents a positive real number.

(a) $\dfrac{4}{\sqrt{5} - \sqrt{2}}$ (b) $\dfrac{5}{\sqrt{x} + 2}$ (c) $\dfrac{-1}{2 - \sqrt{3y}}$

SOLUTIONS

(a) $\dfrac{4}{\sqrt{5} - \sqrt{2}} = \dfrac{4}{\sqrt{5} - \sqrt{2}} \cdot \dfrac{\sqrt{5} + \sqrt{2}}{\sqrt{5} + \sqrt{2}}$ Multiply numerator and denominator by $\sqrt{5} + \sqrt{2}$.

$= \dfrac{4(\sqrt{5} + \sqrt{2})}{5 - 2} = \dfrac{4}{3}(\sqrt{5} + \sqrt{2})$

(b) $\dfrac{5}{\sqrt{x} + 2} = \dfrac{5}{\sqrt{x} + 2} \cdot \dfrac{\sqrt{x} - 2}{\sqrt{x} - 2}$ Multiply numerator and denominator by $\sqrt{x} - 2$.

$= \dfrac{5(\sqrt{x} - 2)}{x - 4}$

(c) $\dfrac{-1}{2 - \sqrt{3y}} = \dfrac{-1}{2 - \sqrt{3y}} \cdot \dfrac{2 + \sqrt{3y}}{2 + \sqrt{3y}} = \dfrac{-2 - \sqrt{3y}}{4 - 3y}$

✔ Progress Check 3

Rationalize the denominator. Every variable represents a positive real number.

(a) $\dfrac{-6}{\sqrt{2} + \sqrt{6}}$ (b) $\dfrac{2}{\sqrt{3x} - 1}$

(c) $\dfrac{-4}{\sqrt{x} + \sqrt{5y}}$ (d) $\dfrac{4}{\sqrt{x} - \sqrt{y}}$

Answers

(a) $\dfrac{3}{2}(\sqrt{2} - \sqrt{6})$ (b) $\dfrac{2(\sqrt{3x} + 1)}{3x - 1}$

(c) $\dfrac{-4(\sqrt{x} - \sqrt{5y})}{x - 5y}$ (d) $\dfrac{4(\sqrt{x} + \sqrt{y})}{x - y}$

Exercise Set 8.5

In Exercises 1–28 simplify and combine terms. Every variable represents a positive real number.

1. $2\sqrt{3} + 5\sqrt{3}$

2. $3\sqrt{5} - 5\sqrt{5}$

3. $4\sqrt[3]{11} - 6\sqrt[3]{11}$

4. $\frac{1}{2}\sqrt[3]{7} - 2\sqrt[3]{7}$

5. $3\sqrt{x} + 4\sqrt{x}$

6. $3\sqrt[3]{a} - \frac{2}{5}\sqrt[3]{a}$

7. $3\sqrt{2} + 5\sqrt{2} - 2\sqrt{2}$

8. $\sqrt[3]{4} - 3\sqrt[3]{4} + \sqrt{6} - 2\sqrt{6}$

9. $3\sqrt{y} + 2\sqrt{y} - \frac{1}{2}\sqrt{y}$

10. $\frac{1}{2}\sqrt[3]{x} - 2\sqrt[4]{x} + \frac{1}{3}\sqrt[3]{x} - \frac{1}{2}\sqrt[4]{x}$

11. $\sqrt{24} + \sqrt{54}$

12. $\sqrt{75} - \sqrt{150}$

13. $2\sqrt{27} + \sqrt{12} - \sqrt{48}$

14. $\sqrt{20} - 4\sqrt{45} + \sqrt{80}$

15. $\sqrt[3]{40} + \sqrt{45} - \sqrt[3]{135} + 2\sqrt{80}$

16. $3\sqrt[3]{128} + \sqrt{128} - 2\sqrt{72} - \sqrt[3]{54}$

17. $3\sqrt[3]{xy^2} + 2\sqrt[3]{xy^2} - 4\sqrt[3]{x^2y}$

18. $\sqrt[4]{x^2y^2} + 2\sqrt[4]{x^2y^2} - \frac{2}{3}\sqrt{x^2y^2}$

19. $2\sqrt[3]{a^4b} + \frac{1}{2}\sqrt{ab} - \frac{1}{2}\sqrt[3]{a^4b} + 2\sqrt{ab}$

20. $\sqrt{\dfrac{xy}{3}} + \sqrt{6xy}$

21. $\sqrt[5]{2x^3y^2} - 3\sqrt[5]{2x^3y^2} + 4\sqrt[5]{2x^3y^2}$

22. $\sqrt{2abc} - 3\sqrt{8abc} + \sqrt{\dfrac{abc}{2}}$

23. $-\sqrt[3]{xy^4} - 2y\sqrt[3]{xy} - \frac{1}{2}\sqrt{xy^4}$

24. $\sqrt{xy} + xy - 3\sqrt{xy} - 2\sqrt{x^2y^2}$

25. $2\sqrt{5} - (3\sqrt{5} + 4\sqrt{5})$

26. $2\sqrt{18} - (3\sqrt{12} - 2\sqrt{75})$

27. $x\sqrt[3]{x^4y} - (\sqrt[3]{x^5y} - 2x\sqrt{x^4y})$

28. $2(\sqrt{x^3y^7} - xy\sqrt[3]{y}) - 3\sqrt[3]{x^3y^7}$

In Exercises 29–50 multiply and simplify.

29. $\sqrt{3}(\sqrt{3} + 4)$

30. $\sqrt{5}(2 - \sqrt{5})$

31. $\sqrt{6}(\sqrt{2} + 2\sqrt{3})$

32. $\sqrt{8}(\sqrt{2} - \sqrt{3})$

33. $3\sqrt[3]{x^2y} \cdot \sqrt[3]{x \cdot y^2}$

34. $2\sqrt[4]{a^2b^3} \cdot \sqrt[4]{a^3b^2}$

35. $-4\sqrt[5]{x^2y^3} \cdot \sqrt[5]{x^4y^2}$

36. $\sqrt[3]{3a^2b} \cdot \sqrt[3]{9a^3b^4}$

37. $(\sqrt{2} + 3)(\sqrt{2} - 2)$

38. $(\sqrt{7} + 5)(\sqrt{7} - 3)$

39. $(2\sqrt{3} - 3)(3\sqrt{2} + 2)$

40. $(\sqrt{5} - 1)\sqrt{5} + 2)$

41. $(\sqrt{2} - \sqrt{3})^2$

42. $(\sqrt{3} + \sqrt{5})^2$

43. $(\sqrt{8} - 2\sqrt{2})(\sqrt{2} + 2\sqrt{8})$

44. $(\sqrt{x} + 2\sqrt{y})(\sqrt{x} - 3\sqrt{y})$

45. $(\sqrt{3x} + \sqrt{2y})(\sqrt{3x} - 2\sqrt{2y})$

46. $(\sqrt{2a} + 3)(\sqrt[3]{2x} - 3)$

47. $(\sqrt[3]{2x} + 3)(\sqrt[3]{2x} - 3)$

48. $(\sqrt[3]{xy^2} - 3)(\sqrt[3]{x^2y} + 2)$

49. $(\sqrt[3]{a^4} + \sqrt[3]{b^2})(\sqrt[3]{a^2} - 2\sqrt[3]{b^4})$

50. $(\sqrt[4]{x^2y^3} + 2\sqrt[4]{x^5y})(\sqrt[4]{x^2} - \sqrt[4]{y^3})$

In Exercises 51–72 rationalize the denominator.

51. $\dfrac{3}{\sqrt{2} + 3}$

52. $\dfrac{2}{\sqrt{5} - 2}$

53. $\dfrac{-3}{\sqrt{7} - 9}$

54. $\dfrac{2}{\sqrt{3} - 4}$

55. $\dfrac{2}{\sqrt{x} + 3}$

56. $\dfrac{3}{\sqrt{x} - 5}$

57. $\dfrac{-3}{3\sqrt{a} + 1}$

58. $\dfrac{-4}{2\sqrt{x} - 2}$

59. $\dfrac{4}{2 - \sqrt{2y}}$

60. $\dfrac{-3}{5 + \sqrt{5y}}$

61. $\dfrac{\sqrt{8}}{\sqrt{2} + 2}$

62. $\dfrac{\sqrt{3}}{\sqrt{3} - 5}$

63. $\dfrac{\sqrt{2} + 1}{\sqrt{2} - 1}$

64. $\dfrac{\sqrt{5} - 1}{\sqrt{5} + 1}$

65. $\dfrac{\sqrt{5} + \sqrt{3}}{\sqrt{5} - \sqrt{3}}$

66. $\dfrac{\sqrt{6} + \sqrt{2}}{\sqrt{3} - \sqrt{2}}$

67. $\dfrac{\sqrt{x}}{\sqrt{x} + \sqrt{y}}$

68. $\dfrac{2\sqrt{a}}{\sqrt{2x} + \sqrt{y}}$

69. $\dfrac{\sqrt{a} + 1}{2\sqrt{a} - \sqrt{b}}$

70. $\dfrac{4\sqrt{x} - \sqrt{y}}{\sqrt{x} + \sqrt{y}}$

71. $\dfrac{2\sqrt{x} + \sqrt{y}}{\sqrt{2x} - \sqrt{y}}$

72. $\dfrac{3\sqrt{a} - \sqrt{3b}}{\sqrt{2a} + \sqrt{b}}$

In Exercises 73 and 74 demonstrate the result by providing real values for x and y and a positive integer value for n.

*73. $\sqrt{x} + \sqrt{y} \neq \sqrt{x + y}$

*74. $\sqrt[n]{x^n + y^n} \neq x + y$

8.6   Complex Numbers

One of the central problems in algebra is to find solutions to a given polynomial equation. A key difficulty is that even a simple polynomial equation such as

$$x^2 = -4$$

has no solution since the square of a real number is always nonnegative.

To resolve this problem, mathematicians created a new number system built upon an "imaginary unit" i, defined by $i = \sqrt{-1}$. If we square both sides of the equation $i = \sqrt{-1}$, we have $i^2 = -1$, a result that cannot be obtained with real numbers. By definition,

$$i = \sqrt{-1}$$
$$i^2 = -1$$

We also assume that i behaves according to all the algebraic laws we have already developed (with the exception of the rules for inequalities for real numbers). This allows us to simplify higher powers of i by expressing the power as 1, -1, or $-i$.

$$i^3 = i^2 \cdot i = (-1)i = -i$$
$$i^4 = i^2 \cdot i^2 = (-1)(-1) = 1$$

Now it's easy to simplify i^n when n is any natural number. Since $i^4 = 1$, we simply seek the highest multiple of 4 that is less than or equal to n. For example,

$$i^5 = i^4 \cdot i = (1) \cdot i = i$$
$$i^{27} = i^{24} \cdot i^3 = (i^4)^6 \cdot i^3 = (1)^6 \cdot i^3 = i^3 = -1$$

EXAMPLE 1   WORKING WITH THE IMAGINARY UNIT i

Simplify.

(a) i^{101} (b) $-i^{74}$ (c) i^{36} (d) i^{51}

SOLUTIONS

(a) $i^{101} = i^{100} \cdot i = (i^4)^{25} \cdot i = i$

(b) $-i^{74} = -i^{72} \cdot i^2 = -(i^4)^{18} \cdot i^2 = -(1)^{18} \cdot i^2 = (-1)(-1) = 1$

(c) $i^{36} = (i^4)^9 = (1)^9 = 1$

(d) $i^{51} = i^{48} \cdot i^3 = (i^4)^{12} \cdot i^3 = (1)^{12} \cdot i^3 = i^3 = -i$

✔ Progress Check 1

Simplify.

(a) i^{22} (b) i^{15} (c) i^{29} (d) i^{200}

Answers

(a) -1 (b) $-i$ (c) i (d) 1

It is also easy to write square roots of negative numbers in terms of i. For example,

$$\sqrt{-25} = i\sqrt{25} = 5i$$

because $(5i)^2 = 5^2 i^2 = (25)(-1) = -25$, and, in general, we define

$$\sqrt{-a} = i\sqrt{a} \quad for\ a > 0$$

Any number in the form bi, where b is a real number, is called an **imaginary number**.

WARNING

$$\sqrt{-4}\sqrt{-9} \neq \sqrt{36}$$

The rule $\sqrt{a} \cdot \sqrt{b} = \sqrt{ab}$ holds only when $a \geq 0$ and $b \geq 0$. Instead, write

$$\sqrt{-4}\sqrt{-9} = 2i \cdot 3i = 6i^2 = -6$$

Having created imaginary numbers, we next combine real and imaginary numbers. We say that $a + bi$, where a and b are real numbers, is a **complex number**. The number a is called the **real part** of $a + bi$, and b is called the **imaginary part**. The following are examples of complex numbers:

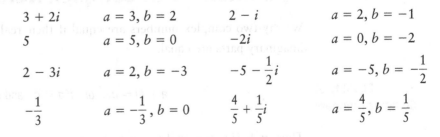

$3 + 2i$ $a = 3, b = 2$ $2 - i$ $a = 2, b = -1$

5 $a = 5, b = 0$ $-2i$ $a = 0, b = -2$

$2 - 3i$ $a = 2, b = -3$ $-5 - \frac{1}{2}i$ $a = -5, b = -\frac{1}{2}$

$-\frac{1}{3}$ $a = -\frac{1}{3}, b = 0$ $\frac{4}{5} + \frac{1}{5}i$ $a = \frac{4}{5}, b = \frac{1}{5}$

Note that every real number a can be written as a complex number by choosing $b = 0$. Thus,

$$a = a + 0i$$

We see that the real number system is a subset of the complex number system. The desire to find solutions to every quadratic equation has led mathematicians to create a more comprehensive number system, which incorporates all previous number systems.

Will you have to learn still more number systems? The answer, fortunately, is a resounding "No!" We will show in a later chapter that complex numbers are all that we need to provide solutions to any polynomial equation.

EXAMPLE 2   RADICALS AND COMPLEX NUMBERS

Write as a complex number.

(a) $-\dfrac{1}{2}$ (b) $\sqrt{-9}$ (c) $-1 - \sqrt{-4}$

SOLUTION

(a) $-\dfrac{1}{2} = -\dfrac{1}{2} + 0i$

(b) $\sqrt{-9} = i\sqrt{9} = 3i = 0 + 3i$

(c) $-1 - \sqrt{-4} = -1 - i\sqrt{4} = -1 - 2i$

✔ **Progress Check 2**

Write as a complex number.

(a) 0.2   (b) $-\sqrt{-3}$ (c) $3 - \sqrt{-9}$

Answers

(a) $0.2 + 0i$ (b) $0 - i\sqrt{3}$ (c) $3 - 3i$

Operations with Complex Numbers

We say two complex numbers are equal if their real parts are equal and their imaginary parts are equal.

Equality of Complex Numbers

$$a + bi = c + di \quad \text{if } a = c \ \text{ and } b = d$$

Thus, $x + 3i = 6 - yi$ if $x = 6$ and $y = -3$.

We add and subtract the complex numbers $3 + 4i$ and $2 - i$ by combining like terms; that is, we combine the real parts and we combine the imaginary parts.

$$(3 + 4i) + (2 - i) = (3 + 2) + (4 - 1)i = 5 + 3i$$
$$(3 + 4i) - (2 - i) = (3 - 2) + (4 + 1)i = 1 + 5i$$

Addition and Subtraction of Complex Numbers

$$(a + bi) + (c + di) = (a + c) + (b + d)i$$
$$(a + bi) - (c + di) = (a - c) + (b - d)i$$

Note that the sum or difference of two complex numbers is again a complex number.

EXAMPLE 3 ADDITION AND SUBTRACTION OF COMPLEX NUMBERS
Perform the indicated operations.

(a) $(7 - 2i) + (4 - 3i)$ (b) $3i + (-7 + 5i)$

(c) $(-11 + 5i) - (9 + i)$ (d) $14 - (3 - 8i)$

SOLUTIONS

(a) $(7 - 2i) + (4 - 3i) = (7 + 4) + (-2 - 3)i = 11 - 5i$

(b) $3i + (-7 + 5i) = (0 - 7) + (3 + 5)i = -7 + 8i$

(c) $(-11 + 5i) - (9 + i) = (-11 - 9) + (5 - 1)i = -20 + 4i$

(d) $14 - (3 - 8i) = (14 - 3) + (0 + 8)i = 11 + 8i$

✔ Progress Check 3
Perform the indicated operations.

(a) $(-9 + 3i) + (6 - 2i)$ (b) $(-17 + i) + 15$
(c) $(2 - 3i) - (9 - 4i)$ (d) $7i - (-3 + 9i)$

Answers
(a) $-3 + i$ (b) $-2 + i$ (c) $-7 + i$ (d) $3 - 2i$

Multiplication of complex numbers is analogous to multiplication of polynomials. The distributive law is used to form all the products, and the substitution $i^2 = -1$ is used to simplify. For example,

$$5i(2 - 3i) = 5i(2) - (5i)(3i) = 10i - 15i^2$$
$$= 10i - 15(-1) = 15 + 10i$$
$$(2 + 3i)(3 - 5i) = 2(3 - 5i) + 3i(3 - 5i)$$
$$= 6 - 10i + 9i - 15i^2$$
$$= 6 - i - 15(-1)$$
$$= 21 - i$$

In general,

$$(a + bi)(c + di) = a(c + di) + bi(c + di)$$
$$= ac + adi + bci + bdi^2$$
$$= ac + (ad + bc)i + bd(-1)$$
$$= (ac - bd) + (ad + bc)i$$

Thus,

Multiplication of Complex Numbers

$$(a + bi)(c + di) = (ac - bd) + (ad + bc)i$$

This result is significant because it demonstrates that the product of two complex numbers is again a complex number. It need not be memorized; simply use the distributive law to form all the products and the substitution $i^2 = -1$ to simplify.

EXAMPLE 4   MULTIPLICATION OF COMPLEX NUMBERS

Find the product of $(2 - 3i)$ and $(7 + 5i)$.

SOLUTION

$$(2 - 3i)(7 + 5i) = 2(7 + 5i) - 3i(7 + 5i)$$
$$= 14 + 10i - 21i - 15i^2$$
$$= 14 - 11i - 15(-1)$$
$$= 29 - 11i$$

✔ Progress Check 4

Find the product.

(a) $(-3 - i)(4 - 2i)$ (b) $(-4 - 2i)(2 - 3i)$

Answers

(a) $-14 + 2i$ (b) $-14 + 8i$

Complex Conjugate

The complex number $a - bi$ is called the conjugate of the complex number $a + bi$. We see that

$$(a + bi)(a - bi) = a(a - bi) + bi(a - bi)$$
$$= a^2 - abi + abi - b^2 i^2$$
$$= a^2 - b^2(-1)$$
$$= a^2 + b^2$$

which is a real number. The following result will be helpful in the division of complex numbers.

> The product of a complex number and its conjugate is a real number.
> $$(a + bi)(a - bi) = a^2 + b^2$$

EXAMPLE 5   WORKING WITH THE COMPLEX CONJUGATE

Multiply by the conjugate of the given complex number.

(a) $6 - i$ (b) $-3i$ (c) 4

SOLUTIONS

(a) The conjugate of $6 - i$ is $6 + i$, and we have

$$(6 - i)(6 + i) = 36 - i^2 = 36 + 1 = 37$$

(b) The conjugate of $0 - 3i$ is $0 + 3i$. Thus,

$$(-3i)(3i) = -9i^2 = 9$$

(c) Since $4 = 4 + 0i$, the conjugate of $4 + 0i$ is $4 - 0i = 4$. Thus, the complex conjugate of a real number is the real number itself. Hence

$$(4)(4) = 16$$

> ✔ **Progress Check 5**
>
> Multiply by the conjugate of the given complex number.
>
> (a) $3 + 2i$ (b) $-\sqrt{2} - 3i$ (c) $4i$ (d) -7
>
> **Answers**
> (a) 13   (b) 11   (c) 16   (d) 49

We can now demonstrate that the quotient of two complex numbers is also a complex number. The quotient

$$\frac{q + ri}{s + ti}, \quad s + ti \neq 0$$

can be written in the form $a + bi$ by multiplying both numerator and denominator by $s - ti$, the conjugate of the denominator. We then have

$$\frac{q + ri}{s + ti} = \frac{q + ri}{s + ti} \cdot \frac{s - ti}{s - ti} = \frac{(qs + rt) + (rs - qt)i}{s^2 + t^2}$$

$$= \frac{(qs + rt)}{s^2 + t^2} + \frac{(rs - qt)}{s^2 + t^2}i$$

which is a complex number of the form $a + bi$. Thus, we have the following result:

Early Mathematicians' Views of Complex Numbers

When mathematicians in the middle of the sixteenth century tried to solve certain quadratic equations by completing the square, they found themselves, much to their distress, having to deal with the square root of a negative quantity. For example, in 1545 Girolamo Cardano (see also Section 10.3) solved the problem of dividing the number 10 into two parts whose product is 40. If one of the parts is x, then the other part is $10 - x$, and we must solve the equation $x(10 - x) = 40$. Using methods we will describe in Chapter 9, Cardano obtained the roots

$$5 + \sqrt{-15} \quad \text{and} \quad 5 - \sqrt{-15}$$

This frustrated him terribly since he had obtained an answer that was "nonsense." He wrote, "So progresses arithmetic subtlety the end of which, as is said, is as refined as it is useless." (See Morris Klein, *Mathematical Thought from Ancient to Modern Times*, Oxford Press, New York, 1972.)

Other famous mathematicians at that time also rejected complex numbers as worthless and fictitious objects; and, in fact, it was the philosopher and scientist René Descartes who called them "imaginary." It was not until the 1700s that these numbers began to be understood and used. Those earlier mathematicians would be very surprised to learn that complex numbers have been used in thousands of applications ranging from problems in aerodynamics to explanations of the inner workings of the atom.

Division of Complex Numbers

$$\frac{q + ri}{s + ti} = \frac{qs + rt}{s^2 + t^2} + \frac{(rs - qt)}{s^2 + t^2}i, \quad s + ti \neq 0$$

EXAMPLE 6   DIVISION OF COMPLEX NUMBERS

Write in the form $a + bi$.

(a) $\dfrac{-2 + 3i}{3 - i}$ (b) $\dfrac{2i}{2 + 5i}$ (c) $\dfrac{1 - i}{2i}$

SOLUTIONS

(a) $\dfrac{-2 + 3i}{3 - i} = \dfrac{-2 + 3i}{3 - i} \cdot \dfrac{3 + i}{3 + i}$ Multiplying numerator and denominator by the conjugate $3 + i$ of the denominator

$= \dfrac{-6 - 2i + 9i + 3i^2}{9 + 3i - 3i - i^2} = \dfrac{-6 + 7i + 3(-1)}{9 - (-1)}$

$= \dfrac{-9 + 7i}{10} = -\dfrac{9}{10} + \dfrac{7}{10}i$

(b) $\dfrac{2i}{2 + 5i} = \dfrac{2i}{2 + 5i} \cdot \dfrac{2 - 5i}{2 - 5i}$ Multiplying numerator and denominator by the conjugate $2 - 5i$ of the denominator

$$= \dfrac{4i - 10i^2}{4 - 10i + 10i - 25i^2} = \dfrac{4i - 10(-1)}{4 - 25(-1)}$$

$$= \dfrac{10 + 4i}{29} = \dfrac{10}{29} + \dfrac{4}{29}i$$

(c) $\dfrac{1 - i}{2i} = \dfrac{1 - i}{2i} \cdot \dfrac{-2i}{-2i}$ Multiplying numerator and denominator by the conjugate $-2i$ of the denominator

$$= \dfrac{-2i + 2(-1)}{-4i^2} = \dfrac{-2i - 2}{4}$$

$$= -\dfrac{1}{2} - \dfrac{1}{2}i$$

✔ **Progress Check 6**

Write in the form $a + bi$.

(a) $\dfrac{4 - 2i}{5 + 2i}$ (b) $\dfrac{3}{2 - 3i}$ (c) $\dfrac{-3i}{3 + 5i}$

Answers

(a) $\dfrac{16}{29} - \dfrac{18}{29}i$ (b) $\dfrac{6}{13} + \dfrac{9}{13}i$ (c) $-\dfrac{15}{34} - \dfrac{9}{34}i$

The reciprocal of a nonzero complex number $s + ti$ can also be written in the form $a + bi$ by multiplying numerator and denominator by $s - ti$, the conjugate of the denominator. We will let the student verify that we obtain the following result:

The Reciprocal of a Complex Number

$$\dfrac{1}{s + ti} = \dfrac{s}{s^2 + t^2} - \dfrac{t}{s^2 + t^2}i, \quad s + ti \neq 0$$

EXAMPLE 7 FINDING THE RECIPROCAL OF A COMPLEX NUMBER

Write the reciprocal in the form $a + bi$.

(a) $2 - 2i$ (b) $3i$

SOLUTIONS

(a) The reciprocal is

$$\dfrac{1}{2 - 2i}$$

Multiplying both numerator and denominator by the conjugate $2 + 2i$ of the denominator, we have

$$\frac{1}{2-2i} \cdot \frac{2+2i}{2+2i} = \frac{2+2i}{4-4i^2} = \frac{2+2i}{4+4}$$

$$= \frac{2+2i}{8} = \frac{1}{4} + \frac{1}{4}i$$

Verify that the product of the original complex number and its reciprocal equals 1, that is, $(2 - 2i)(\frac{1}{4} + \frac{1}{4}i) = 1 + 0i = 1$.

(b) The reciprocal is $\dfrac{1}{3i}$ and

$$\frac{1}{3i} = \frac{1}{3i} \cdot \frac{-3i}{-3i} = \frac{-3i}{-9i^2} = \frac{-3i}{9} = -\frac{1}{3}i$$

It is easy to see that $(3i)\left(-\dfrac{1}{3}i\right) = -i^2 = 1$.

✔ **Progress Check 7**

Write the reciprocal in the form $a + bi$.

(a) $3 - i$ (b) $1 + 3i$ (c) $-2i$

Answers

(a) $\dfrac{3}{10} + \dfrac{1}{10}i$ (b) $\dfrac{1}{10} - \dfrac{3}{10}i$ (c) $\dfrac{1}{2}i$

Why have mathematicians created complex numbers? In the next chapter we will show that complex numbers are indispensable in solving second-degree equations. Beyond that, advanced mathematics in science and engineering has many uses for complex numbers. The real number system simply isn't adequate.

Exercise Set 8.6

In Exercises 1–14 simplify.

1. i^{60}

3. i^{27}

5. $-i^{48}$

7. $-i^{33}$

9. i^{-15}

11. $-i^{-26}$

13. $-i^{-25}$

2. i^{58}

4. i^{83}

6. $-i^{54}$

8. $-i^{95}$

10. i^{-84}

12. $-i^{39}$

14. $i^{8/3}$ [*Hint:* $(i^8)^{1/3}$]

In Exercises 15–30 write each complex number in the form $a + bi$.

15. 2

17. $-\dfrac{1}{2}$

19. $\sqrt{-16}$

21. $-\sqrt{-5}$

23. $-\sqrt{-36}$

25. $2 + \sqrt{-16}$

16. -4

18. -0.3

20. $\sqrt{-25}$

22. $\sqrt{-8}$

24. $-\sqrt{-18}$

26. $3 - \sqrt{-49}$

27. $-\dfrac{3}{2} - \sqrt{-72}$

28. $-2 + \sqrt{-128}$

29. $0.3 - \sqrt{-98}$

30. $-0.5 + \sqrt{-32}$

In Exercises 31–60 perform the indicated operations and write the answer in the form $a + bi$.

31. $2i + (3 - i)$

32. $-3i + (2 - 5i)$

33. $2 + (6 - i)$

34. $3 - (2 - 3i)$

35. $2 + 3i + (3 - 2i)$

36. $(3 - 2i) - \left(2 + \dfrac{1}{2}i\right)$

37. $-3 - 5i - (2 - i)$

38. $\left(\dfrac{1}{2} - i\right) + \left(1 - \dfrac{2}{3}i\right)$

39. $(2i)(4i)$

40. $(-3i)(6i)$

41. $-2i(3 + i)$

42. $3i(2 - i)$

43. $i\left(-\dfrac{1}{2} + i\right)$

44. $\dfrac{i}{2}\left(\dfrac{4 - i}{2}\right)$

45. $(2 + 3i)(2 + 3i)$

46. $(1 + i)(-3 + 2i)$

47. $(2 - i)(2 + i)$

48. $(5 + i)(2 - 3i)$

49. $(-2 - 2i)(-4 - 3i)$

50. $(2 + 5i)(1 - 3i)$

51. $(3 - 2i)(2 - i)$

52. $(4 - 3i)(2 + 3i)$

53. $(3 + 2i)^2$

54. $(2 - 5i)^2$

55. $(3 - i)^2$

56. $(5 + 3i)^2$

57. $2i^2$

58. $(2i)^2$

59. $-4i^2$

60. $(-4i)^2$

In Exercises 61–66 multiply by the conjugate and simplify.

61. $2 - i$

62. $3 + i$

63. $3 + 4i$

64. $2 - 3i$

65. $-4 - 2i$

66. $5 + 2i$

In Exercises 67–76 perform the indicated division and write the answer in the form $a + bi$.

67. $\dfrac{2 + 5i}{1 - 3i}$

68. $\dfrac{1 + 3i}{2 - 5i}$

69. $\dfrac{3 - 4i}{3 + 4i}$

70. $\dfrac{4 - 3i}{4 + 3i}$

71. $\dfrac{3 - 2i}{2 - i}$

72. $\dfrac{2 - 3i}{3 - i}$

73. $\dfrac{2 + 5i}{3i}$

74. $\dfrac{5 - 2i}{-3i}$

75. $\dfrac{4i}{2 + i}$

76. $\dfrac{-2i}{3 - i}$

In Exercises 77–84 find the reciprocal and write it in the form $a + bi$.

77. $3 + 2i$

78. $4 + 3i$

79. $\dfrac{1}{2} - i$

80. $1 - \dfrac{1}{3}i$

81. $-7i$

82. $-5i$

83. $\sqrt{2} - i$

84. $2 - \sqrt{3}i$

*85. Show that the reciprocal of $s + ti$ is

$$\dfrac{s}{s^2 + t^2} - \dfrac{t}{s^2 + t^2}i$$

*86. Show that the commutative law of addition holds for the set of complex numbers.

*87. Show that the commutative law of multiplication holds for the set of complex numbers.

*88. Show that $0 + 0i$ is the additive identity and $1 + 0i$ is the multiplicative identity for the set of complex numbers.

*89. Show that $-a - bi$ is the additive inverse of the complex number $a + bi$.

*90. Demonstrate the distributive property for the set of complex numbers.

*91. For what values of x is $\sqrt{x - 3}$ a real number?

*92. For what values of y is $\sqrt{2y - 10}$ a real number?

93. Your graphing calculator probably has an "i" key. Use it to find the following product (see the graphic below for an example).

```
(501+25i)(-254-3
60i)
   -118254-186710i
```

94. Use your graphing calculator to find the quotient:

$$\dfrac{10^6 - 14^{-2}i}{10^9 - 13^{-2}i}$$

95. Use your graphing calculator to find the quotient:

$$\dfrac{1000 + 1000i}{1001 - 1001i}$$

Chapter Summary

Terms and Symbols

complex number, $a + bi$	303	index	289	rationalizing the denominator	294
conjugate of a complex number	306	nth root, $\sqrt[n]{a}$	285	real part	303
cube root, $\sqrt[3]{a}$	285	principal nth root	286	reciprocal of a complex number	309
imaginary number	303	principal square root	288		
imaginary part	303	radical form	289	simplified radical	294
imaginary unit, i	302	radical sign, $\sqrt{\ }$	288	square root, $\sqrt{a}$	285
		radicand	289		

Key Ideas for Review

Topic	Page	Key Idea
Exponents	280	The laws of exponents hold for all rational exponents.
zero exponent	280	Zero as an exponent produces a result of 1. Thus, $a^0 = 1$, for $a \neq 0$.
negative exponents	280	Since $a^{-m} = \dfrac{1}{a^m}$ and $a^m = \dfrac{1}{a^{-m}}$, $\quad a \neq 0$ we can change the sign of the exponent by moving the factor from numerator to denominator or from denominator to numerator.
Radicals	288	Radicals are an alternate means of writing rational exponent forms. Thus, $$a^{m/n} = \sqrt[n]{a^m} = \left(\sqrt[n]{a}\right)^m, \quad \text{if } a \geq 0$$
identities	292	The identities $$\left(\sqrt[n]{a}\right)^n = \sqrt[n]{a^n} = \begin{cases} a & \text{if } n \text{ is odd} \\ |a| & \text{if } n \text{ is even} \end{cases}$$ $$\sqrt[n]{ab} = \sqrt[n]{a}\sqrt[n]{b}$$ $$\sqrt[n]{\dfrac{a}{b}} = \dfrac{\sqrt[n]{a}}{\sqrt[n]{b}}, \quad b \neq 0$$ are useful in simplifying expressions with radicals when all radicals denote real numbers.

simplified form	293	A radical expression is in simplified form if
		   (a) $\sqrt[n]{x^m}$ has $m < n$, x prime,
		   (b) $\sqrt[n]{x^m}$ has no common factors between m and n, and
		   (c) the denominator does not contain a radical.

addition and subtraction	298	Addition and subtraction of radical expressions can be performed only if exactly the same radical form is involved.
product	299	The product $\left(\sqrt[m]{a}\right)\left(\sqrt[n]{b}\right)$ can be easily simplified if $m = n$.
Imaginary unit i	302	The identities $i = \sqrt{-1}$ and $i^2 = -1$ can be used to simplify an expression of the form i^n and to rewrite $\sqrt{-a}$ as $i\sqrt{a}$, $a > 0$.
Complex numbers	303	Every complex number can be written in the form $a + bi$, where a and b are real numbers.
operations	304	The sum, difference, product, and quotient of two complex numbers can always be expressed in the form $c + di$. (Of course, we cannot divide by zero.)
subsets	304	The real number system is a subset of the complex number system since any real number a can be written as $a + 0i$.

Common Errors

1. *Don't* perform intermediate steps on any polynomial, no matter how complicated, that is raised to the zero power since 1 is the answer.

$$(y^2 + x^2 - 2y + 4)^0 = 1$$

2. Don't confuse negative *numbers* and negative *exponents*. *Don't* write

$$(-2)^{-3} = \frac{1}{2^3} = \frac{1}{8}$$

When the factor is moved to the denominator, only the sign of the exponent changes.

$$(-2)^{-3} = \frac{1}{(-2)^3} = \frac{1}{-8} = -\frac{1}{8}$$

$$-2^{-3} = -\frac{1}{2^3} = -\frac{1}{8}$$

3. *Don't* write

$$\sqrt{4} + \sqrt{60} = \sqrt{64}$$

You can add only if the radical forms are identical:

$$\sqrt{2x} + 5\sqrt{2x} = 6\sqrt{2x}$$

4. *Don't* write

$$\sqrt{-2} \cdot \sqrt{-8} = \sqrt{16} = 4$$

When dealing with negative numbers under the radical sign, first write the expressions in terms of the imaginary unit i such that

$$\sqrt{-2} \cdot \sqrt{-8} = (i\sqrt{2})(i\sqrt{8})$$
$$= i^2\sqrt{16} = (-1)(4) = -4$$

5. *Don't* write

$$\sqrt{25} = \pm 5$$

The number indicated by $\sqrt{25}$ is the *positive* square root of 25. Thus,

$$\sqrt{25} = 5 \quad \text{and} \quad -\sqrt{25} = -5$$

6. Remember that

$$\sqrt{x^2} = |x|$$

Don't write

$$\sqrt{x^2} = x$$

unless you know that $x \geq 0$.

Review Exercises

Solutions to exercises whose numbers are in bold are in the Solutions section in the back of the book.

8.1 In Exercises 1–8 simplify, using the properties of exponents.

1. $(x^2)^{3n}$

2. $y^4 y^5$

3. $\left(-\dfrac{a}{b}\right)^5$

4. $(x^3)^4(x^2)^5$

5. $\dfrac{(b^2)^3(b^3)^2}{(b^4)^2}$

6. $[(2a - 1)^2]^5$

7. $(2x + y)^2(2x + y)^3$

8. $\dfrac{(3a^3b^2)^3}{(-2a^4b^3)^4}$

8.2 In Exercises 9–16 use the rules for exponents to simplify. Write the answers using only positive exponents.

9. $(-2)^{-5}$

10. $\dfrac{3}{x^{-3}}$

11. $2y^2 y^{-4}$

12. $a^{-4} a^4 a^2$

13. $(-3x^3 y^{-2})^0$

14. $\dfrac{12a^{-4}b^{-2}}{3a^{-2}b^{-5}}$

15. $\left(\dfrac{2xy^{-2}}{3x^{-2}y^{-3}}\right)^{-4}$

16. $\left(\dfrac{-3x^{-2}y^{-3}}{2x^{-3}y^{-4}}\right)^{-3}$

8.3 In Exercises 17–24 simplify, and write the answer using only positive exponents. Every variable represents a positive real number.

17. $32^{2/5}$

18. $(x^2)^{1/6}$

19. $a^{1/4} a^{2/3}$

20. $\dfrac{81^{1/4}}{81^{5/4}}$

21. $(x^3 y^4)^{1/6}$

22. $(x^4 y^{2/5})^{-1/2}$

23. $\left(\dfrac{x^{2/3}}{x^{4/3}}\right)^{1/4}$

24. $\left(\dfrac{x^2}{y^{-2/5}}\right)^{-3/2}$

8.4 In Exercises 25–30 write the expression in simplified form. Every variable represents a positive real number.

25. $\sqrt{60}$

26. $\sqrt[3]{\dfrac{125}{27}x^8}$

27. $\dfrac{2}{\sqrt{4x}}$

28. $\dfrac{4ab}{\sqrt[3]{3a^2b}}$

29. $\dfrac{6a^7}{\sqrt{3b}}$

30. $\sqrt[4]{\dfrac{16x^8}{5y^2}}$

8.5 In Exercises 31–34 simplify, and combine terms. Every variable represents a positive real number.

31. $5\sqrt{5} - 2\sqrt{5}$

32. $\sqrt[4]{x^2y^2} + 2\sqrt[4]{x^2y^2}$

33. $\sqrt[3]{3xy^2} + \sqrt[3]{5xy^2}$

34. $\sqrt{\dfrac{xy}{2}} + 2\sqrt{xy}$

In Exercises 35–38 rationalize the denominator.

35. $\dfrac{-3}{3 - \sqrt{x}}$

36. $\dfrac{\sqrt{3x} - 1}{\sqrt{3x} + 1}$

37. $\dfrac{2}{\sqrt{x - y}}$

38. $\dfrac{\sqrt{2ab}}{\sqrt{a} - \sqrt{b}}$

8.6 In Exercises 39–50 perform the indicated operations and write the answer in the form $a + bi$.

39. i^{68}

40. $-i^{29}$

41. $\sqrt{-20}$

42. $2 + \sqrt[3]{-54}$

43. $3i - (4 - 5i)$

44. $(3 + 4i)(3 - 4i)$

45. $(5i)(3 - 2i)$

46. $(4 - 3i)^2$

47. $\dfrac{1}{\sqrt{3} + 2i}$

48. $\dfrac{2 - 3i}{1 + i}$

49. $\dfrac{1}{i}$

50. $\dfrac{i}{1 - i}$

Progress Test 8A

In Problems 1–7 simplify, and write the answer using only positive exponents.

1. $\dfrac{(x + 1)^{2n-1}}{(x + 1)^{n+1}}$

2. $\left(\dfrac{1}{2}x^3y^2\right)^4$

3. $\left(\dfrac{-2xy^3}{5x^2y}\right)^3$

4. $\dfrac{5(a^2 - 2a + 1)^0}{(x^{-2})^3}$

5. $(2x^{2/5} \cdot 4x^{2/5})^{-2}$

6. $\dfrac{x^{-2/3}y^{1/2}}{x^{-2}y^{-3/2}}$

7. $\left(\dfrac{27x^{-6}z^0}{125y^{-3/2}}\right)^{-2/3}$

8. Write $(2y - 1)^{5/2}$ in radical form.

9. Write $\sqrt[3]{6y^5}$ in rational exponent form.

10. Simplify $-\sqrt{32x^4y^9}$.

11. Simplify $\sqrt{\dfrac{x}{5}}$.

12. Simplify $\dfrac{-4a^2b\sqrt[3]{a^7b^6}}{\sqrt[3]{a}}$.

13. Simplify $\sqrt[3]{24} - 3\sqrt[3]{81}$.

14. Simplify $2\sqrt{xy^2} - 6\sqrt{x^2y} + 3\sqrt{xy^2} - 2\sqrt{x^2y}$.

15. Multiply and simplify $3(2\sqrt{x} - 3\sqrt{y})(2\sqrt{x} + 3\sqrt{y})$.

16. Write in the form $a + bi$: $4 - \sqrt{-4}$.

17. Compute $2 + \sqrt{-27} - 3\sqrt{-3}$.

18. Simplify $-i^{47}$.

19. Write in the form $a + bi$: $(-4 - 2i) \div (3 - 4i)$.

20. Write the reciprocal of $4 + 3i$ in the form $a + bi$.

Progress Test 8B

In Problems 1–7 simplify, and write the answer using only positive exponents.

1. $(x^{3n-1})^2$

2. $\left(-\dfrac{1}{3}a^2b\right)^3$

3. $\left(\dfrac{-3y^{-2}}{x^{-3}}\right)^{-3}$

4. $\dfrac{4(x+1)^5(2x+1)^0}{(x+1)^6}$

5. $(-2y^{1/3} \cdot 3y^{1/6})^{-3}$

6. $\dfrac{x^{1/2}y^{-1/5}}{x^{-2}y^{3/5}}$

7. $\left(\dfrac{27x^{-3/2}y^{4/5}}{x^{5/2}y^{1/5}}\right)^{-2/5}$

8. Write $(3x+1)^{2/3}$ in radical form.

9. Write $\sqrt[5]{4x^3}$ in rational exponent form.

10. Simplify $-3\sqrt[4]{16x^6z^2}$.

11. Simplify $\sqrt{\dfrac{2x^3}{y}}$.

12. Simplify $\dfrac{-2x^3y^2\sqrt{x^5y^6}}{\sqrt{xy}}$.

13. Simplify $2\sqrt[3]{54} - 4\sqrt[3]{16}$.

14. Simplify $-\sqrt{(a-1)b^2} + 2\sqrt{(a-1)^3b} - 2\sqrt{(a-1)b^2} - 3\sqrt{(a-1)^3b}$

15. Multiply and simplify $-2(3\sqrt{a} - \sqrt{b})(2\sqrt{a} - 3\sqrt{b})$.

16. Write in the form $a + bi$: $2 + \sqrt{-8}$.

17. Compute $-3 - 3\sqrt{-8} + 2\sqrt{-18}$.

18. Simplify $-3i^{25}$.

19. Write in the form $a + bi$: $(2 - i) \div (2 - 3i)$.

20. Write the reciprocal of $3 - 5i$ in the form $a + bi$.

Chapter 8 Project

Physicists are accustomed to dealing with very large numbers. Without exponents, they would have no convenient way to express or deal with these quantities. For instance, there are about 10^{78} atoms in the observable universe. If all of these atoms contained one proton each (and most of them do) and if there are about 2×10^9 times as many photons in the universe as protons, how many photons are there? You must use the laws of exponents to answer this question.

Look at Exercises 78 and 79 in Section 8.1, and Exercise 81 in Section 8.2.

What will the final fate of the universe be? Some scientists think it will probably keep expanding forever—the galaxies getting farther and farther away from each other. Some, however, think that there may be a "Big Crunch," a sort of reverse Big Bang in which gravitational forces will cause the galaxies to stop moving outward and collapse toward each other again.

Do some research on cosmology, and determine how many atoms of "dark matter" there may be in the universe. What is the ratio of dark matter to bright matter, and how do the laws of exponents help to calculate it? How does this ratio help cosmologists to think about the possibility of a "Big Crunch?"

■ ■ ■

9 Second-Degree Equations and Inequalities

> "All the effects of nature are only the mathematical consequences of a small number of immutable laws."
> —Pierre-Simon de Laplace

Number theory is a classic area of mathematical investigation. Number theorists hunt for formulas that reveal interesting properties of positive integers. Sometimes, these formulas are arrived at after lengthy study; at other times, they may appear in a flash of insight. Such flashes often happened to the brilliant mathematical prodigy Srinivasa Ramanujan (1887–1920), who is famous for providing remarkably complicated mathematical formulas. No one else has ever been able to derive some of these formulas!

Second-degree equations like the ones we will study in this chapter often play a role in number-theoretic formulas. For instance, how do you find the product of two numbers without multiplying them directly? One way is with the "quarter squares rule," which we will look at in this chapter's project.

■ ■ ■

The function

$$f(x) = ax^2 + bx + c, \quad a \neq 0$$

is called a **quadratic function**. We are interested in finding the **zeros** of the function, that is, the values of x for which $f(x) = 0$. This is equivalent to finding the roots of the equation

$$ax^2 + bx + c = 0, \quad a \neq 0$$

which we call a **quadratic equation** or **second-degree equation in one variable**. We will look at techniques for solving quadratic equations and at applications that lead to this algebraic form. We will also study methods of attacking second-degree inequalities in one variable.

9.1   Solving Quadratic Equations

The Form $ax^2 + c = 0$

When the quadratic equation $ax^2 + bx + c = 0$ has the coefficient $b = 0$, we have an equation of the form

$$2x^2 - 10 = 0$$

which is easily solved. We begin by isolating x^2.

$$2x^2 - 10 = 0$$
$$2x^2 = 10$$
$$x^2 = 5$$

At this point we ask: Is there a number whose square is 5? There are actually two such numbers: $\sqrt{5}$ and $-\sqrt{5}$.

$$x^2 = 5$$
$$x = \pm\sqrt{5}$$

(Note that we have used the shorthand notation, $\pm\sqrt{5}$, as a way of indicating $\sqrt{5}$ and $-\sqrt{5}$. We will see that a quadratic equation always has two solutions.)

EXAMPLE 1   SOLVING "SIMPLE" QUADRATIC EQUATIONS

Solve the equation.

(a) $3x^2 - 8 = 0$ (b) $4x^2 + 11 = 0$ (c) $(x - 5)^2 + 9 = 0$

SOLUTIONS

(a) We isolate and solve for x.

$$3x^2 - 8 = 0$$

$$3x^2 = 8$$

$$x^2 = \frac{8}{3}$$

$$x = \pm\sqrt{\frac{8}{3}} = \pm\frac{2\sqrt{2}}{\sqrt{3}}$$

To attain simplest radical form, we must rationalize the denominator.

$$x = \pm\frac{2\sqrt{2}}{\sqrt{3}} \cdot \frac{\sqrt{3}}{\sqrt{3}} = \pm\frac{2\sqrt{6}}{3} \text{ or } \pm\frac{2}{3}\sqrt{6}$$

(b) We isolate and solve for x.

$$4x^2 + 11 = 0$$

$$4x^2 = -11$$

$$x^2 = -\frac{11}{4}$$

$$x = \pm\sqrt{\frac{-11}{4}} = \pm\frac{i\sqrt{11}}{2}$$

We see that the solutions to a quadratic equation may be complex numbers.

(c) Although this equation is not strictly of the form $ax^2 + c = 0$, we can use the same approach. We see that

$$(x - 5)^2 + 9 = 0$$
$$(x - 5)^2 = -9$$

which implies that

$$x - 5 = \pm\sqrt{-9}$$
$$x - 5 = \pm 3i \qquad \text{Since } (3i)^2 = (-3i)^2 = -9$$
$$x = 5 \pm 3i \qquad \text{add 5 to both sides.}$$

Thus, the solutions of the given equation are the complex numbers

$$x = 5 + 3i \quad \text{and} \quad x = 5 - 3i$$

Note that the solutions are complex conjugates; we will see that this situation applies in general.

✔ Progress Check 1

Solve each equation.

(a) $4x^2 - 9 = 0$ (b) $2x^2 - 15 = 0$

(c) $5x^2 + 13 = 0$ (d) $(2x - 7)^2 + 5 = 0$

Answers

(a) $\pm\dfrac{3}{2}$ (b) $\pm\dfrac{\sqrt{30}}{2}$ (c) $\pm\dfrac{i\sqrt{65}}{5}$ (d) $\dfrac{7 \pm i\sqrt{5}}{2}$

Solving by Factoring

Under what circumstances can the product of two numbers be 0? Stated more formally, if $ab = 0$, what must be true of a and b? A little thought will convince you that at least one of the numbers must be zero! In fact, this result is very easy to prove. If we assume that $a \neq 0$, then we can divide both sides by a.

$$ab = 0$$
$$\frac{ab}{a} = \frac{0}{a}$$
$$b = 0$$

Similarly, if we assumed $b \neq 0$, we would conclude that $a = 0$.

> If $ab = 0$, then $a = 0$ or $b = 0$ (or both $a = 0$ and $b = 0$).

This simple theorem provides us with a means for solving quadratic equations whenever we can factor the quadratic into linear factors.

EXAMPLE 2   SOLVING A QUADRATIC EQUATION BY FACTORING

Solve by factoring.

(a) $x^2 - 2x - 3 = 0$ (b) $2x^2 - 3x - 2 = 0$

(c) $3x^2 - 4x = 0$ (d) $x^2 + x + 1 = 0$

SOLUTIONS

(a) Factoring, we have

$$x^2 - 2x - 3 = 0$$
$$(x - 3)(x + 1) = 0$$

The product of two real numbers can equal 0 only if at least one of them is 0. Thus, either

$$x - 3 = 0 \qquad \text{or} \qquad x + 1 = 0$$

So

$$x = 3 \qquad \text{or} \qquad x = -1$$

You can verify that 3 and -1 are both roots of the equation by substituting each of these values back into the original equation.

(b) Factoring, we have

$$2x^2 - 3x - 2 = 0$$
$$(2x + 1)(x - 2) = 0$$

Either

$$2x + 1 = 0 \qquad \text{or} \qquad x - 2 = 0$$

Therefore,

$$x = -\frac{1}{2} \qquad \text{or} \qquad x = 2$$

(c) Factoring, we have

$$3x^2 - 4x = 0$$
$$x(3x - 4) = 0$$

Either

$$x = 0 \qquad \text{or} \qquad 3x - 4 = 0$$

Thus,

$$x = 0 \qquad \text{or} \qquad x = \frac{4}{3}$$

(d) If we attempt to factor $x^2 + x + 1$, we see that the only possible factors with integer coefficients are $(x + 1)$ and $(x - 1)$. However, trying all the possible combinations of these, $(x + 1)(x + 1)$ or $(x - 1)(x - 1)$ or $(x + 1)(x - 1)$, we find that none of them works. We will look at methods for handling this situation, following the progress check.

✔ Progress Check 2

Solve by factoring.

(a) $x^2 + 3x - 10 = 0$ (b) $3x^2 - 11x - 4 = 0$

(c) $4x^2 - x = 0$ (d) $2x^2 + 4x + 1 = 0$

Answers

(a) $-5, 2$ (b) $-\frac{1}{3}, 4$ (c) $0, \frac{1}{4}$ (d) cannot be factored

Completing the Square

We saw in Example 2d that the method of factoring doesn't always work if we restrict ourselves to integer coefficients. However, the following method will enable us to find solutions to *any* quadratic equation. Given an expression such as

$$x^2 + 10x$$

we seek a constant k such that the addition of k^2 will "complete" a perfect square on the left-hand side.

$$x^2 + 10x + k^2 = (x + k)^2 = x^2 + 2kx + k^2$$

Then we must have

$$10x = 2kx$$

from which we see that the constant k that we seek is exactly $\frac{1}{2}$ of the coefficient of x. Thus, in our example, $k = \frac{10}{2} = 5$ and $k^2 = 25$, so

$$x^2 + 10x + 25 = (x + 5)^2$$

This procedure is called **completing the square**.

EXAMPLE 3   COMPLETING THE SQUARE

Complete the square for each of the following.

(a) $x^2 - 6x$ (b) $x^2 + 3x$

SOLUTIONS

(a) The coefficient of x is -6 so $k^2 = (-\frac{6}{2})^2 = 9$. Then
$$x^2 - 6x + 9 = (x - 3)^2$$

(b) The coefficient of x is 3 and $k^2 = (\frac{3}{2})^2 = \frac{9}{4}$. Then
$$x^2 + 3x + \frac{9}{4} = \left(x + \frac{3}{2}\right)^2$$

✔ **Progress Check 3**

Complete the square for each of the following.

(a) $x^2 + 8x$ (b) $x^2 - 7x$

Answers

(a) $x^2 + 8x + 16 = (x + 4)^2$

(b) $x^2 - 7x + \dfrac{49}{4} = \left(x - \dfrac{7}{2}\right)^2$

When the coefficient of x^2 in a quadratic equation is 1, the process of completing the square can be used to solve the quadratic.

EXAMPLE 4   SOLVING A QUADRATIC EQUATION BY COMPLETING THE SQUARE

Solve the quadratic equation

$$x^2 + 8x - 1 = 0$$

by completing the square.

SOLUTION

Procedure	Example
Step 1. Isolate the constant on one side of the equation.	$x^2 + 8x = 1$
Step 2. Compute k, which is equal to half the coefficient of x.	$k = \frac{1}{2}(8) = 4$
Step 3. Complete the square by adding k^2 to both sides of the equation.	$x^2 + 8x + 16 = 1 + 16$ $(x + 4)^2 = 17$
Step 4. Solve for x.	$x + 4 = \pm\sqrt{17}$ $x = -4 \pm\sqrt{17}$

✔ **Progress Check 4**

Solve $x^2 - 3x + 2 = 0$ by completing the square.

Answer

1, 2

By modifying the procedure for completing the square to include the case where the coefficient of x^2 is *not* equal to 1, we can solve any quadratic equation. We now outline and explain each step of the process.

EXAMPLE 5 SOLVING A QUADRATIC EQUATION BY COMPLETING THE SQUARE

Solve the quadratic equation $2x^2 - 5x + 4 = 0$ by completing the square.

SOLUTION

Solving $ax^2 + bx + c = 0$ by Completing the Square	
Procedure	**Example**

Step 1. Isolate the constant on one side of the equation.

$$2x^2 - 5x = -4$$

Step 2. Factor out the coefficient a of x^2.

$$2\left(x^2 - \frac{5}{2}x\right) = -4$$

Step 3. Complete the square for the quadratic expression in parentheses

$x^2 + dx + k^2 = (x + k)^2$

where $k = d/2$. Balance the equation by adding

ak^2 to both sides. Simplify.

$$k = \frac{1}{2}\left(-\frac{5}{2}\right) = -\frac{5}{4}$$

$$2\left(x^2 - \frac{5}{2}x + \frac{25}{16}\right) = -4 + 2\left(\frac{25}{16}\right)$$

$$\left(x - \frac{5}{4}\right)^2 = -\frac{7}{16}$$

Step 4. Solve for x.

$$x - \frac{5}{4} = \pm\sqrt{\frac{-7}{16}} = \frac{\pm i\sqrt{7}}{4}$$

$$x = \frac{5}{4} \pm \frac{i\sqrt{7}}{4} = \frac{5 \pm i\sqrt{7}}{4}$$

✔ **Progress Check 5**

Solve by completing the square.

(a) $x^2 - 3x + 2 = 0$ (b) $3x^2 - 4x + 2 = 0$

Answers

(a) 1, 2   (b) $\dfrac{2 \pm i\sqrt{2}}{3}$

WARNING

In the equation

$$x^2 + 8x = -2$$

completing the square on the left-hand side produces $(x + 4)^2$, but this is $4^2 = 16$ more than the original left-hand side. *Don't* forget to balance the equation by adding 16 to the right-hand side.

$$x^2 + 8x + 16 = -2 + 16$$

$$(x + 4)^2 = 14$$

Exercise Set 9.1

In Exercises 1–20 solve the given equation.

1. $3x^2 - 27 = 0$
2. $4x^2 - 64 = 0$
3. $4x^2 - 25 = 0$
4. $49y^2 - 9 = 0$
5. $5y^2 - 25 = 0$
6. $6x^2 - 12 = 0$
7. $(x - 3)^2 = -2$
8. $(s + 3)^2 = 4$
9. $(2r + 5)^2 = 8$
10. $(3x - 4)^2 = -6$
11. $(2y + 4)^2 + 3 = 0$
12. $(3p - 2)^2 + 6 = 0$
13. $(3x - 5)^2 - 8 = 0$
14. $(4t + 1)^2 - 3 = 0$
15. $2x^2 + 8 = 0$
16. $6y^2 + 96 = 0$
17. $9x^2 + 64 = 0$
18. $81x^2 + 25 = 0$
19. $2y^2 + 12 = 0$
20. $9x^2 + 45 = 0$

In Exercises 21–34 solve by factoring.

21. $x^2 - 3x + 2 = 0$
22. $x^2 - 6x + 8 = 0$
23. $x^2 + x - 2 = 0$
24. $3r^2 - 4r + 1 = 0$
25. $x^2 + 6x = -8$
26. $x^2 + 6x + 5 = 0$
27. $y^2 - 4y = 0$
28. $2x^2 - x = 0$
29. $2x^2 - 5x = -2$
30. $2s^2 - 5s - 3 = 0$
31. $t^2 - 4 = 0$
32. $4x^2 - 9 = 0$
33. $6x^2 - 5x + 1 = 0$
34. $6x^2 - x = 2$

In Exercises 35–46 solve by completing the square.

35. $x^2 - 2x = 8$
36. $t^2 - 2t = 15$
37. $2r^2 - 7r = 4$
38. $9x^2 + 3x = 2$
39. $3x^2 + 8x = 3$
40. $2y^2 + 4y = 5$
41. $2y^2 + 2y = -1$
42. $3x^2 - 4x = -3$
43. $4x^2 - x = 3$
44. $2x^2 + x = 2$
45. $3x^2 + 2x = -1$
46. $3u^2 - 3u = -1$

In Exercises 47–60 solve by any method.

47. $x^2 + x - 12 = 0$
48. $x^2 - 2x - 8 = 0$
49. $3y^2 + y = 0$
50. $4x^2 - 4x - 3 = 0$
51. $2x^2 + 2x - 5 = 0$
52. $2t^2 + 2t + 3 = 0$
53. $3x^2 + 4x - 4 = 0$
54. $x^2 + 2x = 0$
55. $2x^2 + 5x + 4 = 0$
56. $2r^2 - 3r + 2 = 0$
57. $4u^2 - 1 = 0$
58. $x^2 + 2 = 0$
59. $4x^2 + 2x + 3 = 0$
60. $4s^2 + 4s - 15 = 0$

In Exercises 61–64 solve by completing the square, and verify the answer by substitution.

*61. $2x^2 + 3x - 1 = 0$
*62. $3x^2 - 4x - 4 = 0$
*63. $2x^2 - 3x - 9 = 0$
*64. $4x^2 + 4x - 3 = 0$

65. Find the solutions of $(3x - 1)^2 = 4$ by graphing both sides and looking for points of intersection. (See the figures below.)

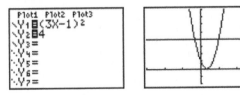

66. Find the solutions of $(1 - 5x)^2 = 1$ by graphing both sides and finding points of intersection.

67. Are there any solutions to $(0.2x + 2)^2 = -(0.3x - 1)^2$? Explain why or why not. Refer to the graphs of both sides of the equation.

68. Are there any solutions to $(0.2x + 1)^2 = (0.3x - 1)^2$? Explain why or why not. Refer to the graphs of both sides of the equation.

69. The following equation is an example of the "quarter squares rule" for finding the product of two numbers. In this case, 5 is one of the numbers and 3 is the other. Solve the equation below for x.

$$\left(\frac{x + 3}{2}\right)^2 - \left(\frac{5 - 3}{2}\right)^2 = 5(3)$$

(The chapter project reveals the complete formula.)

70. Solve for x:

$$\left(\frac{x + 7}{2}\right)^2 - \left(\frac{11 - 7}{2}\right)^2 = 7x$$

How does this equation provide a formula for finding the product of two integers?

9.2   The Quadratic Formula

Let's apply the method of completing the square to the general quadratic equation

$$ax^2 + bx + c = 0, \quad a > 0$$

where a, b, and c are real numbers. Following the steps we illustrated in the last section, we have

$$ax^2 + bx = -c$$

$$a\left(x^2 + \frac{b}{a}x\right) = -c$$

$$a\left[x^2 + \frac{b}{a}x + \left(\frac{b}{2a}\right)^2\right] = a\left(\frac{b}{2a}\right)^2 - c$$

$$a\left(x + \frac{b}{2a}\right)^2 = \frac{b^2}{4a} - c$$

$$\left(x + \frac{b}{2a}\right)^2 = \frac{b^2}{4a^2} - \frac{c}{a} = \frac{b^2 - 4ac}{4a^2}$$

$$x + \frac{b}{2a} = \pm\sqrt{\frac{b^2 - 4ac}{4a^2}} = \frac{\pm\sqrt{b^2 - 4ac}}{2a}$$

$$x = -\frac{b}{2a} \pm \frac{\sqrt{b^2 - 4ac}}{2a}$$

$$x = \frac{-b \pm \sqrt{b^2 - 4ac}}{2a}$$

By applying the method of completing the square to the standard form of the quadratic equation, we have derived a formula that gives us the roots, or solutions, of any quadratic equation in one variable.

If $ax^2 + bx + c = 0$, $a > 0$, then

$$x = \frac{-b \pm \sqrt{b^2 - 4ac}}{2a}$$

That is, the roots of the quadratic equation $ax^2 + bx + c = 0$ are

$$\frac{-b + \sqrt{b^2 - 4ac}}{2a} \quad \text{and} \quad \frac{-b - \sqrt{b^2 - 4ac}}{2a}$$

EXAMPLE 1   APPLYING THE QUADRATIC FORMULA

Solve by the quadratic formula.

(a) $2x^2 - 3x - 3 = 0$

(b) $-5x^2 + 3x = 2$

SOLUTIONS

(a) We begin by identifying a, b, and c.

$$a = 2$$
$$b = -3$$
$$c = -3$$

We can now write the quadratic formula and substitute.

$$x = \frac{-b \pm \sqrt{b^2 - 4ac}}{2a}$$

$$= \frac{-(-3) \pm \sqrt{(-3)^2 - 4(2)(-3)}}{2(2)}$$

$$= \frac{3 \pm \sqrt{33}}{4}$$

(b) We first rewrite the given equation as $5x^2 - 3x + 2 = 0$ so that $a > 0$ and the right-hand side equals 0. Now we can identify a, b, and c.

$$a = 5$$
$$b = -3$$
$$c = 2$$

Determining the Golden Ratio

When a point divides a line segment of length L into two parts of lengths a and b so that

$$\frac{L}{a} = \frac{a}{b}$$

then a/b is called the "golden ratio." (See Section 5.6.) To determine the golden ratio ϕ, assume that $b = 1$. Then we see from the accompanying figure that

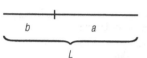

$$L = a + 1$$

In addition, the above proportion will simplify to

$$L = a^2$$

Equating the expressions for L, we have

$$a^2 = a + 1$$
$$a^2 - a - 1 = 0$$

The length a satisfies this quadratic equation. Using the quadratic formula, we have

$$a = \frac{1 \pm \sqrt{5}}{2}$$

You can use a calculator to verify that $(1 + \sqrt{5})/2$ yields an approximate value for the golden ratio ϕ of 1.61803. The negative number $(1 - \sqrt{5})/2$ is rejected because the segment has a positive length.

We write the quadratic formula and substitute.

$$x = \frac{-b \pm \sqrt{b^2 - 4(5)(2)}}{2a}$$

$$= \frac{-(-3) \pm \sqrt{(-3)^2 - 4(5)(2)}}{2(5)}$$

$$= \frac{3 \pm \sqrt{-31}}{10} = \frac{3 \pm i\sqrt{31}}{10}$$

✔ **Progress Check 1**

Solve by the quadratic formula.

(a) $x^2 - 8x = -10$ (b) $4x^2 - 2x + 1 = 0$

(c) $2x^2 - x - 1 = 0$ (d) $x^2 + \dfrac{5}{2}x + 1 = 0$

Answers

(a) $4 \pm \sqrt{6}$ (b) $\dfrac{1 \pm i\sqrt{3}}{4}$ (c) $1, -\dfrac{1}{2}$ (d) $-2, -\dfrac{1}{2}$

WARNING

There are a number of errors that students make in using the quadratic formula.

(a) To solve $x^2 - 3x = -4$, you must write the equation in the form

$$x^2 + (-3)x + 4 = 0$$

to properly identify a, b, and c.

(b) Since a, b, and c are coefficients, you must include the sign. If

$$x^2 - 3x + 4 = 0$$

then $b = -3$. *Don't* write $b = 3$.

(c) The quadratic formula is

$$x = \frac{-b \pm \sqrt{b^2 - 4ac}}{2a}$$

Don't write

$$x = -b \pm \frac{\sqrt{b^2 - 4ac}}{2a}$$

The term $-b$ must also be divided by $2a$.

Now that you have a formula that works for any quadratic equation, you may be tempted to use it all the time. However, if you see an equation of the form

$$x^2 = 15$$

it is certainly easier to immediately supply the answer: $x = \pm\sqrt{15}$. Similarly, if you are faced with

$$x^2 + 3x + 2 = 0$$

it is faster to solve if you see that

$$x^2 + 3x + 2 = (x + 1)(x + 2)$$

The method of completing the square is generally not used for solving quadratic equations once you have learned the quadratic formula. However, we will need to use this technique when we graph second-degree equations in Chapter 12. The technique of completing the square is occasionally helpful in a variety of areas of applications.

Exercise Set 9.2

In Exercises 1–4, a, b, and c denote the coefficients of the general quadratic equation $ax^2 + bx + c = 0$. Select the correct answer.

1. $2x^2 + 3x - 4 = 0$

   (a) $a = 2, b = 3, c = 4$

   (b) $a = 3, b = 2, c = 4$

   (c) $a = -2, b = 4, c = 3$

   (d) $a = 2, b = 3, c = -4$

2. $3x^2 - 2x = 5$

   (a) $a = 3, b = 2, c = 5$

   (b) $a = 2, b = 3, c = 5$

   (c) $a = 3, b = -2, c = -5$

   (d) $a = -3, b = 2, c = -5$

3. $r = 5r^2 - \frac{2}{3}$

   (a) $a = 1, b = 5, c = -\frac{2}{3}$

   (b) $a = -1, b = 5, c = \frac{2}{3}$

   (c) $a = 5, b = -1, c = -\frac{2}{3}$

   (d) $a = 5, b = 1, c = \frac{2}{3}$

4. $2r^2 + r = 0$

   (a) $a = -2, b = 1, c = 0$

   (b) $a = 0, b = 2, c = 1$

   (c) $a = 2, b = -1, c = 0$

   (d) $a = 2, b = 1, c = 0$

In Exercises 5–10 identify a, b, and c in the general quadratic equation $ax^2 + bx + c = 0$.

5. $3x^2 - 2x + 5 = 0$ 6. $2x^2 + x = 4$

7. $s = 2s^2 + 5$ 8. $2x^2 + 5 = 0$

9. $3x^2 - \frac{1}{3}x = 0$ 10. $4y^2 = 2y + 1$

In Exercises 11–32 solve, using the quadratic formula.

11. $x^2 + 5x + 6 = 0$ 12. $x^2 + 2x - 8 = 0$

13. $x^2 - 8x = -15$ 14. $6r^2 - r = 1$

15. $2x^2 + 3x = 0$ 16. $2x^2 + 3x + 3 = 0$

17. $5x^2 - 4x + 3 = 0$ 18. $2x^2 - 3x - 2 = 0$

19. $5y^2 - 4y + 5 = 0$ 20. $x^2 - 5x = 0$

21. $x^2 + x = 12$ 22. $2x^2 + 5x - 6 = 0$

23. $-3x^2 - x + 2 = 0$ 24. $-2x^2 - 4x + 3 = 0$

25. $x^2 - 9 = 0$ 26. $5x^2 + 2 = 0$

27. $3y^2 - 4 = 0$ 28. $2x^2 + 2x + 5 = 0$

29. $x^2 + \frac{7}{2}x - 2 = 0$ 30. $x^2 - \frac{4}{3}x + \frac{1}{3} = 0$

31. $4u^2 + 3u = 0$ 32. $4x^2 - 1 = 0$

*33. Show that if r_1 and r_2 are the roots of the equation $ax^2 + bx + c = 0$, then

   (a) $r_1 r_2 = \frac{c}{a}$, and

   (b) $r_1 + r_2 = -\frac{b}{a}$

   This result provides a quick check of the correctness of the roots.

*34. Show that if $b^2 - 4ac = 0$, then the two roots of the quadratic equation $ax^2 + bx + c = 0$, $a \neq 0$, are equal.

35.–66. Verify the answers you found to Exercises 1–32 by graphing. (See Exercise 65 in the last section for an example.)

9.3   Roots of a Quadratic Equation: The Discriminant

By analyzing the quadratic formula

$$x = \frac{-b \pm \sqrt{b^2 - 4ac}}{2a}$$

we can learn a great deal about the roots of the quadratic equation $ax^2 + bx + c = 0$. The key to the analysis is the **discriminant** $b^2 - 4ac$ found under the radical sign.

- If $b^2 - 4ac$ is negative, then we have the square root of a negative number and both values of x will be complex numbers; in fact, they will be complex conjugates of each other.

- If $b^2 - 4ac$ is positive, then we have the square root of a positive number and both values of x will be real.

- If $b^2 - 4ac$ is 0, then $x = -b/2a$, which we call a **double root** or **repeated root** of the quadratic equation. For example, if $x^2 - 10x + 25 = 0$, then $b^2 - 4ac = 0$ and $x = -b/2a = 10/2 = 5$. Moreover,

$$x^2 - 10x + 25 = (x - 5)(x - 5) = 0$$

We call $x = 5$ a double root because the factor $(x - 5)$ is a double factor of $x^2 - 10x + 25 = 0$.

If the roots of the quadratic equation are real and a, b, and c are rational numbers, the discriminant enables us to determine whether the roots are rational or irrational. Since $\sqrt{k}$ is a rational number only if k is a perfect square, we see that the quadratic formula produces a rational result only if $b^2 - 4ac$ is a perfect square. We summarize these results.

The quadratic equation $ax^2 + bx + c = 0$, $a > 0$, has exactly two roots, the nature of which is determined by the discriminant $b^2 - 4ac$.

Discriminant	Roots
Negative	Two conjugate complex roots
0	A double root (two equal roots)
Positive	Two real roots
a, b, c rational $\begin{cases} \text{A perfect square} \\ \text{Not a perfect square} \end{cases}$	Two rational roots Two irrational roots

EXAMPLE 1   USING THE DISCRIMINANT OF A QUADRATIC EQUATION

Without solving, determine the nature of the roots of the quadratic equation.

(a) $3x^2 - 4x + 6 = 0$ (b) $2x^2 - 7x = -1$ (c) $4x^2 + 12x + 9 = 0$

SOLUTIONS

(a) We evaluate $b^2 - 4ac$ using $a = 3$, $b = -4$, $c = 6$.

$$b^2 - 4ac = (-4)^2 - 4(3)(6) = 16 - 72 = -56$$

The discriminant is negative, and the equation has two conjugate complex roots.

(b) Rewrite the equation in the standard form.

$$2x^2 - 7x + 1 = 0$$

and then substitute $a = 2$, $b = -7$, $c = 1$ in the discriminant. Thus,

$$b^2 - 4ac = (-7)^2 - 4(2)(1) = 49 - 8 = 41$$

The discriminant is positive and is not a perfect square; thus, the roots are real and irrational.

(c) Setting $a = 4$, $b = 12$, $c = 9$, we evaluate the discriminant:

$$b^2 - 4ac = (12)^2 - 4(4)(9) = 144 - 144 = 0$$

The discriminant is 0, so there is a double real root.

✔ Progress Check 1

Without solving, determine the nature of the roots of the quadratic equation by using the discriminant.

(a) $4x^2 - 20x + 25 = 0$ (b) $5x^2 - 6x = -2$

(c) $10x^2 = x + 2$ (d) $x^2 + x - 1 = 0$

Answers

(a) double real root   (b) two conjugate complex roots

(c) two real, rational roots   (d) two real, irrational roots

---

Graph of a Quadratic Function

If we seek the zeros of the quadratic function

$$f(x) = ax^2 + bx + c, \quad a \neq 0 \tag{1}$$

we need only set $f(x) = 0$ and solve the resulting quadratic equation

$$ax^2 + bx + c = 0 \tag{2}$$

It is important to recognize that the solutions to Equation (2) are the same as the x-intercepts of the graph of the function in Equation (1) since these points have coordinates of the form $(x_1, 0)$.

In Section 6.3, we saw that the graph of a second-degree function is a parabola. The discriminant of the quadratic equation (2), therefore, tells us the number of x-intercepts of the parabola. The possibilities are two real roots (Figure 1a), a double root (Figure 1b) and two complex roots (Figure 1c). We can now summarize.

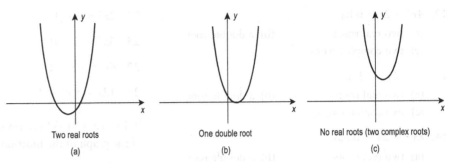

Figure 1   Possible Roots of a Quadratic Equation

The *x*-intercepts of the graph of a quadratic function are the real zeros of the function. The number of *x*-intercepts is related to the discriminant as follows:

Discriminant	Graph of the Function
Positive	Meets the *x*-axis at two distinct points
0	Meets the *x*-axis at one point
Negative	Does not meet the *x*-axis

Exercise Set 9.3

In Exercises 1–14 select the correct answer.

1. In $3x^2 - 2x + 4 = 0$, the discriminant is
   - (a) 52
   - (b) 44
   - (c) $\sqrt{44}$
   - (d) -52
   - (e) -44

2. In $x^2 - 6x + 9 = 0$, the discriminant is
   - (a) 72
   - (b) -72
   - (c) -36
   - (d) 0
   - (e) $\sqrt{72}$

3. In $3y^2 = 2y - 1$, the discriminant is
   - (a) $\sqrt{8}$
   - (b) -8
   - (c) 4
   - (d) $\sqrt{-8}$
   - (e) $-2\sqrt{3}$

4. In $3x^2 + 4x = 0$, the discriminant is
   - (a) 4
   - (b) -4
   - (c) 0
   - (d) 16
   - (e) 7

5. In $r = 5r^2 + 3$, the discriminant is
   - (a) -61
   - (b) 59
   - (c) 61
   - (d) -59
   - (e) $\sqrt{61}$

6. In $2t = -4t^2 - 3$, the discriminant is
   - (a) 44
   - (b) $2\sqrt{11}$
   - (c) -44
   - (d) -23
   - (e) 41

7. In $4x^2 - 8 = 0$, the discriminant is
   - (a) -64
   - (b) 64
   - (c) -128
   - (d) 128
   - (e) $\sqrt{128}$

8. In $4y^2 + 9 = 0$, the discriminant is
   - (a) 65
   - (b) -144
   - (c) -65
   - (d) 144
   - (e) 12

9. $4x^2 - 3x + 5 = 0$ has
   - (a) two real roots
   - (b) a double root
   - (c) two complex roots

10. $y^2 - 10y + 25 = 0$ has
    - (a) two real roots
    - (b) a double root
    - (c) two complex roots

11. $5x^2 = x + 1$ has
    - (a) two real roots
    - (b) a double root
    - (c) two complex roots

12. $4r^2 - 2r = 0$ has

   (a) two real roots   (b) a double root

   (c) two complex roots

13. $x = 2x^2 - 2$ has

   (a) two real roots   (b) a double root

   (c) two complex roots

14. $8x^2 + 24 = 0$ has

   (a) two real roots   (b) a double root

   (c) two complex roots

In Exercises 15–30 determine, without solving, the nature of the roots of each quadratic equation.

15. $x^2 - 2x + 3 = 0$ 16. $3x^2 + 2x - 5 = 0$

17. $4x^2 - 12x + 9 = 0$ 18. $2x^2 + x + 5 = 0$

19. $-3x^2 + 2x + 5 = 0$ 20. $-3y^2 + 2y - 5 = 0$

21. $3x^2 + 2x = 0$ 22. $4x^2 + 20x + 25 = 0$

23. $2r^2 = r - 4$ 24. $3x^2 = 5 - x$

25. $3x^2 + 6 = 0$ 26. $4x^2 - 25 = 0$

27. $6r = 3r^2 + 1$ 28. $4x = 2x^2 + 3$

29. $12x = 9x^2 + 4$ 30. $4s^2 = -4s - 1$

In Exercises 31–38 determine the number of x-intercepts of the graph of the function.

31. $f(x) = 3x^2 + 4x - 1$ 32. $f(x) = 2x^2 - 3x + 2$

33. $f(x) = x^2 + x + 3$ 34. $f(x) = 2x^2 - 6x + 1$

35. $f(x) = 4x^2 - 12x + 9$ 36. $f(x) = 9x^2 + 12x + 4$

37. $f(x) = 4x^2 + 3$ 38. $f(x) = -x^2 + 1$

*39. Show that if a, b, and c are rational numbers, and the discriminant of the equation $ax^2 + bx + c = 0$ is positive, then the quadratic has either two rational roots or two irrational roots.

9.4   Applications of Quadratic Equations

In earlier chapters we carefully avoided those work problems, number problems, business problems, geometric problems, and other applications that resulted in second-degree equations. Now that you can solve quadratic equations, we can look at these applications.

EXAMPLE 1   A WORK PROBLEM LEADING TO A QUADRATIC EQUATION

Working together, two cranes can unload a ship in 4 hours. The slower crane, working alone, requires 6 hours more than the faster crane to do the job. How long does it take each crane to do the job by itself?

SOLUTION

Let x = number of hours required by faster crane to do the job. Then $x + 6$ = number of hours required by slower crane to do the job.

Displaying the information in a table, we have

	Rate	×	Time	=	Fractional Part of the Work
Faster crane	$\dfrac{1}{x}$		4		$\dfrac{4}{x}$
Slower crane	$\dfrac{1}{x+6}$		4		$\dfrac{4}{x+6}$

Since the job is completed in 4 hours when the two cranes work together, we must have

| fractional part of the work done by faster crane | + | fractional part of the work done by slower crane | = | 1 whole job (sum of fractional parts) |

or

$$\frac{4}{x} + \frac{4}{x + 6} = 1$$

To solve, we multiply by the LCD, which is $x(x + 6)$.

$$x(x + 6)\left(\frac{4}{x} + \frac{4}{x + 6}\right) = x(x + 6)$$
$$4(x + 6) + 4x = x^2 + 6x$$
$$0 = x^2 - 2x - 24$$
$$0 = (x + 4)(x - 6)$$
$$x = -4 \quad \text{or} \quad x = 6$$

The solution $x = -4$ is rejected because it makes no sense to speak of negative hours of work. Thus,

$x = 6$ is the number of hours in which the faster crane can do the job alone.

$x + 6 = 12$ is the number of hours in which the slower crane can do the job alone.

To check our answer, we find that the rate of the faster crane is $\frac{1}{6}$ while that of the slower one is $\frac{1}{12}$. In 4 hours the sum of the fractional parts of the work done by the cranes is

$$\frac{4}{6} + \frac{4}{12} = \frac{12}{12} = 1$$

✔ Progress Check 1

A storage tank can be filled in 6 hours when two pipes are used. The larger-diameter pipe, used alone, requires 5 hours less to fill the tank than the smaller-diameter pipe. How many hours does each pipe require to fill the tank when working alone?

Answer

The larger pipe requires 10 hours. The smaller pipe requires 15 hours.

EXAMPLE 2   A PROBLEM IN AREA LEADING TO A QUADRATIC EQUATION

The length of a pool is 3 times its width, and the pool is surrounded by a grass walk 4 feet wide. If the area of the region consisting of the pool and the walk is 684 square feet, find the dimensions of the pool.

SOLUTION

A diagram is useful in solving geometric problems (see Figure 2). If we let $x =$ width of pool, then $3x =$ length of pool; and the region consisting of the pool and the walk has length $3x + 8$ and width $x + 8$. The area is then

$$\text{length} \times \text{width} = \text{area}$$
$$(3x + 8)(x + 8) = 684$$
$$3x^2 + 32x + 64 = 684$$
$$3x^2 + 32x - 620 = 0$$
$$(3x + 62)(x - 10) = 0$$
$$x = 10 \qquad \text{Reject } x = -\frac{62}{3}$$
$$3x = 30$$

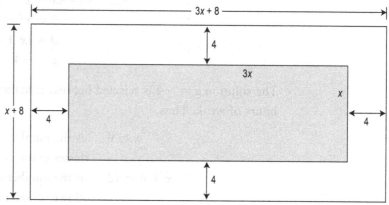

Figure 2   Diagram for Example 2

The dimensions of the pool are 10 feet by 30 feet.

To check our answer, we see that the dimensions of the region consisting of the pool and the walk are 18 feet by 38 feet, and the area is $(18)(38) = 684$ square feet.

✔ Progress Check 2

The altitude of a triangle is 2 centimeters less than the base. If the area of the triangle is 24 square centimeters, find the base and altitude of the triangle.

Answers

base $= 8$ cm; altitude $= 6$ cm

EXAMPLE 3   A NUMBER PROBLEM LEADING TO A QUADRATIC EQUATION

The larger of two numbers exceeds the smaller by 2. If the sum of the squares of the two numbers is 74, find the two numbers.

SOLUTION

If we let

$$x = \text{the smaller number}$$

then

$$x + 2 = \text{the larger number}$$

The sum of the squares is then

$$x^2 + (x + 2)^2 = 74$$
$$x^2 + x^2 + 4x + 4 = 74$$
$$2x^2 + 4x - 70 = 0$$
$$x^2 + 2x - 35 = 0$$
$$(x - 5)(x + 7) = 0$$
$$x = 5 \quad \text{or} \quad x = -7$$

The numbers are then 5 and 7, or −7 and −5. Verify that the sum of the squares is indeed 74.

✔ **Progress Check 3**

The sum of a number and its reciprocal is $\frac{17}{4}$. Find the number.

Answer

4 or $\frac{1}{4}$

EXAMPLE 4 AN INVESTMENT PROBLEM LEADING TO A QUADRATIC EQUATION

An investor purchased a number of shares of stock for a total of $600. If the investor had paid $2 less per share, the number of shares that could have been purchased for the same amount of money would have increased by 10. How many shares were bought?

SOLUTION

Let

$$n = \text{the number of shares purchased}$$

and

$$p = \text{the price paid per share}$$

Since

$$\begin{array}{ccc} \text{number of} & \times & \text{price per} & = & \text{total dollars} \\ \text{shares} & & \text{share} & & \text{invested} \end{array}$$

we must have

$$n \cdot p = 600 \qquad \text{Actual situation}$$

and

$$(n + 10)(p - 2) = 600 \qquad \text{Hypothetical situation}$$

Substituting $p = 600/n$ we obtain

$$(n + 10)\left(\frac{600}{n} - 2\right) = 600$$

$$600 + \frac{6000}{n} - 2n - 20 = 600$$

$$6000 - 2n^2 - 20n = 0 \qquad \text{Multiply by } n$$

$$n^2 + 10n - 3000 = 0 \qquad \text{Divide by } -2$$

$$(n - 50)(n + 60) = 0$$

$$n = 50 \qquad \text{Reject } n = -60$$

The investor purchased 50 shares of stock.

✔ Progress Check 4

A business machine dealer purchased a number of used printing calculators at an auction for a total expenditure of $240. After giving one of the calculators to his daughter, he sold the remaining calculators at a profit of $15 each, for a profit of $35 on the entire transaction. How many printing calculators did he buy?

Answer

6 calculators

Exercise Set 9.4

1. Working together, computers A and B can complete a data-processing job in 2 hours. Computer A working alone can do the job in 3 hours less than computer B working alone. How long does it take each computer to do the job by itself?

2. A graphic designer and her assistant working together can complete an advertising layout in 6 days. The assistant working alone could complete the job in 16 more days than the designer working alone. How long would it take each person to do the job alone?

3. A roofer and his assistant working together can finish a roofing job in 4 hours. The roofer working alone could finish the job in 6 hours less than the assistant working alone. How long would it take each person to do the job alone?

4. A mounting board 16 inches by 20 inches is used to mount a photograph. How wide is the uniform border if the photograph occupies $\frac{3}{5}$ of the area of the mounting board?

5. The length of a rectangle exceeds twice its width by 4 feet. If the area of the rectangle is 48 square feet, find the dimensions.

6. The length of a rectangle is 4 centimeters less than twice its width. Find the dimensions if the area of the rectangle is 96 square centimeters.

7. The area of a rectangle is 48 square centimeters. If the length and width are each increased by 4 centimeters, the area of the larger rectangle is 120 square centimeters. Find the dimensions of the original rectangle.

8. The base of a triangle is 2 feet more than twice its altitude. If the area is 12 square feet, find the base and altitude.

9. Find the width of a strip that has been mowed around a rectangular lawn 60 feet by 80 feet if $\frac{1}{2}$ of the lawn has not yet been mowed.

10. The sum of the reciprocals of two consecutive numbers is $\frac{7}{12}$. Find the numbers.

11. The sum of a number and its reciprocal is $\frac{26}{5}$. Find the numbers.

12. The difference between a number and its reciprocal is $\frac{35}{6}$. Find the number. (*Hint:* There are two answers.)

13. The smaller of the two numbers is 4 less than the larger. If the sum of their squares is 58, find the numbers.

14. The sum of the reciprocals of two consecutive odd numbers is $\frac{8}{15}$. Find the numbers.

15. The sum of the reciprocals of two consecutive even numbers is $\frac{7}{24}$. Find the numbers.

16. A number of students rented a car for a one-week camping trip for $160. If another student had joined the original group, each person's share of expenses would have been reduced by $8. How many students were in the original group?

17. An investor placed an order totaling $1200 for a certain number of shares of a stock. If the price of each share of stock was $2 more, the investor would get 30 shares less for the same amount of money. How many shares did the investor buy?

18. A fraternity charters a bus for a ski trip at a cost of $360. When 6 more students join the trip, each person's cost decreases by $2. How many students were in the original group of travelers?

19. A salesman worked a certain number of days to earn $192. If he had been paid $8 more per day, he would have earned the same amount of money in 2 fewer days. How many days did he work?

20. A freelance photographer worked a certain number of days for a newspaper to earn $480. If she had been paid $8 less per day, she would have earned the same amount in 2 more days. What was her daily rate of pay?

21. The square of one-half of the difference between eight and x is subtracted from the square of one-half of the sum of eight and x, and the result is equal to the product of eight and x. For what values of x is this true?

9.5 Forms Leading to Quadratics

Radical Equations

Certain types of equations that do not appear to be quadratic can be transformed into quadratic equations that can be solved by the methods discussed in this chapter. One such form that leads to a quadratic equation is the **radical equation**. To solve an equation such as

$$x = \sqrt{x + 12}$$

it seems natural to square both sides of the equation.

$$x^2 = x + 12$$

We now have a quadratic equation that is easily solved.

$$x^2 - x - 12 = 0$$
$$(x + 3)(x - 4) = 0$$
$$x = -3 \quad \text{or} \quad x = 4$$

Checking these solutions by substituting in the original equation, we have

$$-3 \overset{?}{=} \sqrt{-3 + 12} \qquad\qquad 4 \overset{?}{=} \sqrt{4 + 12}$$

$$-3 \overset{?}{=} \sqrt{9} \qquad\qquad\qquad 4 \overset{?}{=} \sqrt{16}$$

$$-3 \neq 3 \qquad\qquad\qquad\quad 4 \overset{\checkmark}{=} 4$$

(Remember: $\sqrt{9}$ is the principal square root of 9, which is 3.) Thus, 4 is a solution and -3 is not a solution of the original equation. We say that -3 is an **extraneous solution**, which was introduced when we raised each side of the original equation to the second power. This is an illustration of the following general theorem:

> The solution set of the equation
> $$f(x) = g(x)$$
> is a subset of the solution set of the equation
> $$[f(x)]^n = [g(x)]^n$$
> where n is a natural number.

This suggests that we can solve radical equations if we observe a precaution.

> If both sides of an equation are raised to the same power, the solutions of the resulting equation must be checked to see that they satisfy the original equation.

EXAMPLE 1   SOLVING A RADICAL EQUATION

Solve $x - \sqrt{x - 2} = 4$.

SOLUTION

Isolate the radical on one side of the equation before solving.

$$x - 4 = \sqrt{x - 2}$$
$$x^2 - 8x + 16 = x - 2 \qquad\qquad \text{Square both sides.}$$
$$x^2 - 9x + 18 = 0$$
$$(x - 3)(x - 6) = 0$$
$$x = 3 \quad \text{or} \quad x = 6$$

Checking by substituting in the original equation, we have

$$3 - \sqrt{3 - 2} \overset{?}{=} 4 \qquad\qquad 6 - \sqrt{6 - 2} \overset{?}{=} 4$$

$$3 - 1 \overset{?}{=} 4 \qquad\qquad 6 - \sqrt{4} \overset{?}{=} 4$$

$$2 \neq 4 \qquad\qquad 4 \overset{\checkmark}{=} 4$$

We conclude that 6 is a solution of the original equation, and 3 is rejected as an extraneous solution.

✔ **Progress Check 1**

Solve $x - \sqrt{1 - x} = -5$.

Answer

-3

EXAMPLE 2   SOLVING A RADICAL EQUATION

Solve $\sqrt{2x - 4} - \sqrt{3x + 4} = -2$.

SOLUTION

The algebraic manipulations are simpler if, before squaring, we rewrite the equation so that a radical is on each side of the equation.

$$\sqrt{2x - 4} = \sqrt{3x + 4} - 2$$

$$2x - 4 = (3x + 4) - 4\sqrt{3x + 4} + 4 \qquad \text{Square both sides (don't forget the middle term).}$$

$$-x - 12 = -4\sqrt{3x + 4} \qquad \text{Isolate the radical.}$$

$$x^2 + 24x + 144 = 16(3x + 4) \qquad \text{Square both sides.}$$

$$x^2 - 24x + 80 = 0$$

$$(x - 20)(x - 4) = 0$$

$$x = 20 \quad \text{or} \quad x = 4$$

Verify that both 20 and 4 are solutions of the original equation.

✔ **Progress Check 2**

Solve $\sqrt{5x - 1} - \sqrt{x + 2} = 1$.

Answer

2

Substitution of Variable

Although the equation

$$x^4 - x^2 - 2 = 0$$

is not a quadratic equation with respect to the variable x, it is a quadratic equation with respect to the variable x^2.

$$(x^2)^2 - (x^2) - 2 = 0$$

This may be seen more clearly by replacing x^2 with a new variable $u = x^2$, which gives us

$$u^2 - u - 2 = 0$$

a quadratic equation with respect to the variable u. Solving, we have

$$(u + 1)(u - 2) = 0$$

$$u = -1 \quad \text{or} \quad u = 2$$

Since $x^2 = u$, we must next solve the equations

$$x^2 = -1 \qquad x^2 = 2$$

$$x = \pm i \qquad x = \pm\sqrt{2}$$

The original equation has four solutions: i, $-i$, $\sqrt{2}$, and $-\sqrt{2}$.

The technique we have used is called a **substitution of variable**. Although simple in concept, it is a powerful method that is commonly used in calculus. We will apply this technique to a variety of examples.

EXAMPLE 3   CHOOSING AN APPROPRIATE SUBSTITUTION OF VARIABLE

Indicate an appropriate substitution of variable that will lead to a quadratic equation.

(a) $2x^6 + 7x^3 - 4 = 0$ (b) $y^{2/3} - 3y^{1/3} - 10 = 0$

SOLUTIONS

(a) The substitution $u = x^3$ results in the quadratic equation $2u^2 + 7u - 4 = 0$.
(b) The substitution $u = y^{1/3}$ results in the equation $u^2 - 3u - 10 = 0$.

✔ Progress Check 3

Indicate an appropriate substitution of variable that will lead to a quadratic equation.

(a) $3x^4 - 10x^2 - 8 = 0$ (b) $4x^{2/3} + 7x^{1/3} - 2 = 0$

Answers

(a) $u = x^2$; $3u^2 - 10u - 8 = 0$ (b) $u = x^{1/3}$; $4u^2 + 7u - 2 = 0$

EXAMPLE 4   USING A SUBSTITUTION OF VARIABLE

Indicate an appropriate substitution of variable that will lead to a quadratic equation, and solve each of the equations.

(a) $\dfrac{2}{z^2} - \dfrac{4}{z} + 1 = 0$ (b) $\left(\dfrac{1}{x} - 1\right)^2 + 6\left(\dfrac{1}{x} - 1\right) - 7 = 0$

SOLUTIONS

(a) Substituting $u = \dfrac{1}{z}$, we obtain $2u^2 - 4u + 1 = 0$.

Solving this quadratic equation by the quadratic formula, we have

$$u = \frac{4 \pm \sqrt{(-4)^2 - 4(2)(1)}}{2(2)} = \frac{4 \pm \sqrt{16 - 8}}{4}$$

$$= \frac{4 \pm 2\sqrt{2}}{4} = \frac{2 \pm \sqrt{2}}{2}$$

The solutions to the given equation are obtained by writing

$$u = \frac{2 \pm \sqrt{2}}{2} = \frac{1}{z}$$

and solving for z to get

$$z = \frac{2}{2 \pm \sqrt{2}}$$

which can be simplified as

$$z = 2 + \sqrt{2} \quad \text{and} \quad z = 2 - \sqrt{2}.$$

(b) Substituting $u = \dfrac{1}{x} - 1$, we have $u^2 + 6u - 7 = 0$.

Factoring this quadratic equation, we have

$$(u + 7)(u - 1) = 0$$
$$u = -7 \quad \text{and} \quad u = 1$$

The solutions to the given equation are obtained by solving the equations

$$u = -7 = \frac{1}{x} - 1 \quad \text{and} \quad u = 1 = \frac{1}{x} - 1$$

for x, yielding

$$x = -\frac{1}{6} \quad \text{and} \quad x = \frac{1}{2}$$

✔ Progress Check 4

Indicate an appropriate substitution of variable, and solve each of the following equations.

(a) $\dfrac{2}{x^2} + \dfrac{1}{x} - 10 = 0$ (b) $\left(1 + \dfrac{2}{x}\right)^2 - 8\left(1 + \dfrac{2}{x}\right) + 15 = 0$

Answers

(a) $u = \dfrac{1}{x}; -\dfrac{2}{5}, \dfrac{1}{2}$ (b) $u = 1 + \dfrac{2}{x}; 1, \dfrac{1}{2}$

Exercise Set 9.5

In Exercises 1–14 solve for x.

1. $x + \sqrt{x + 5} = 7$ 2. $x - \sqrt{13 - x} = 1$

3. $x + \sqrt{2x - 3} = 3$ 4. $x - \sqrt{4 - 3x} = -8$

5. $2x + \sqrt{x + 1} = 8$ 6. $3x - \sqrt{1 + 3x} = 1$

7. $\sqrt{3x + 4} - \sqrt{2x + 1} = 1$

8. $\sqrt{4x + 1} - \sqrt{x + 4} = 3$

9. $\sqrt{2x - 1} + \sqrt{x - 4} = 4$

10. $\sqrt{5x + 1} + \sqrt{4x - 3} = 7$

11. $\sqrt{x + 3} + \sqrt{2x - 3} = 6$

12. $\sqrt{x - 1} - \sqrt{3x - 2} = -1$

13. $\sqrt{8x + 20} - \sqrt{7x + 11} = 1$

14. $\sqrt{6x + 12} - \sqrt{5x + 5} = 1$

In Exercises 15–24 indicate an appropriate substitution that will lead to a quadratic equation. Do not attempt to solve.

15. $3x^4 + 5x^2 - 5 = 0$ 16. $-8y^8 + 5y^6 + 4 = 0$

17. $3x^{4/3} + 5x^{2/3} + 3 = 0$

18. $-3y^{6/5} + y^{3/5} - 8 = 0$

19. $\dfrac{5}{y^4} + \dfrac{2}{y^2} - 3 = 0$ 20. $\dfrac{2}{z^6} + \dfrac{5}{z^3} + 6 = 0$

21. $\dfrac{2}{x^{4/3}} + \dfrac{1}{x^{2/3}} + 4 = 0$ 22. $\dfrac{4}{x^{8/5}} - \dfrac{3}{x^{4/5}} + 2 = 0$

23. $\left(2 + \dfrac{3}{x}\right)^2 - 5\left(2 + \dfrac{3}{x}\right) - 5 = 0$

24. $\left(1 - \dfrac{2}{x}\right)^4 + 3\left(1 - \dfrac{2}{x}\right)^2 - 8 = 0$

In Exercises 25–32 indicate an appropriate substitution of variable, and solve the equation.

25. $3x^4 + 5x^2 - 2 = 0$ 26. $2x^6 + 15x^3 - 8 = 0$

27. $\dfrac{6}{x^2} + \dfrac{1}{x} - 2 = 0$ 28. $\dfrac{2}{x^4} - \dfrac{3}{x^2} - 9 = 0$

29. $2x^{2/5} + 5x^{1/5} + 2 = 0$ 30. $3x^{4/3} - 4x^{2/3} - 4 = 0$

31. $2\left(\dfrac{1}{x} + 1\right)^2 - 3\left(\dfrac{1}{x} + 1\right) - 20 = 0$

32. $3\left(\dfrac{1}{x} - 2\right)^2 + 2\left(\dfrac{1}{x} - 2\right) - 1 = 0$

9.6 Second-Degree Inequalities

To solve a second-degree inequality such as

$$x^2 - 2x > 15$$

we rewrite it as

$$x^2 - 2x - 15 > 0$$

When the left-hand side is factored as

$$(x + 3)(x - 5) > 0$$

we can solve the given inequality by determining under what circumstances the product of the factor $(x + 3)$ and the factor $(x - 5)$ will be positive. By the rules of algebra, a product of two real numbers is positive only if both factors have the same sign.

Let's form a table of the values of the linear factor $(x + 3)$.

x	-50	-10	-5	-4	-3	-2	0	5	10	50
$(x + 3)$	-47	-7	-2	-1	0	1	3	8	13	53

Something interesting has happened at $x = -3$: The factor $(x + 3)$ is negative when $x < -3$ and positive when $x > -3$. Similarly, the factor $(x - 5)$ is negative when $x < 5$ and positive when $x > 5$. In general,

Critical Value

> The linear factor $ax + b$ equals 0 at the **critical value** $x = -b/a$ and has opposite signs depending on whether x is to the left or right of the critical value on a number line.

Displaying these results for $(x + 3)$ and $(x - 5)$, using a real number line, we have

Recall that we want the values of x for which

$$(x + 3)(x - 5) > 0$$

that is, the values of x for which both factors have the same sign. From the graph we see that $(x + 3)$ and $(x - 5)$ have the same sign when $x < -3$ or $x > 5$. The solution of $x^2 - 2x > 15$ is the set

$$\{x \mid x < -3 \quad \text{or} \quad x > 5\}$$

⚠ **WARNING**

Don't write the above solution as

$$\{x \mid 5 < x < -3\}$$

since it states that x is simultaneously greater than 5 *and* less than -3, which is impossible.

EXAMPLE 1   SOLVING A QUADRATIC INEQUALITY

Solve the inequality $x^2 \le -3x + 4$, and then graph the solution set on a real number line.

SOLUTION

We rewrite the inequality and factor.

$$x^2 \le -3x + 4$$
$$x^2 + 3x - 4 \le 0$$
$$(x - 1)(x + 4) \le 0$$

The critical values are found by setting each factor equal to 0.

$$x - 1 = 0 \qquad\qquad x + 4 = 0$$
$$x = 1 \qquad\qquad\qquad x = -4$$

We mark the critical values on a real number line and analyze the *sign* of each factor to the left and to the right of each critical value.

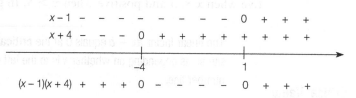

Since we are interested in values of x for which $(x - 1)(x + 4) \leq 0$, we seek values of x for which the factors $(x - 1)$ and $(x + 4)$ have opposite signs or are 0. From the graph, we see that when $-4 \leq x \leq 1$, the conditions are satisfied. Graphing the result, we have

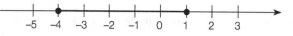

✔ **Progress Check 1**

Solve the inequality $2x^2 \geq 5x + 3$, and graph the solution set on a real number line.

Answer

$\left\{ x \mid x \leq -\dfrac{1}{2} \text{ or } x \geq 3 \right\}$

Although

$$\frac{ax + b}{cx + d} < 0$$

is not a second-degree inequality, the solution to this inequality is the same as the solution to the inequality $(ax + b)(cx + d) < 0$ since both expressions are negative (< 0) when $(ax + b)$ and $(cx + d)$ have opposite signs.

EXAMPLE 2   SOLVING AN INEQUALITY

Solve the inequality $\dfrac{y + 1}{2 - y} \leq 0$.

SOLUTION

The factors equal 0 at the critical value $y = -1$ and $y = 2$. Analyzing the signs of $y + 1$ and $2 - y$ we have

Since

$$\frac{y + 1}{2 - y}$$

can be negative (<0) only if the factors $(y + 1)$ and $(2 - y)$ have opposite signs, the solution set is $\{y | y \leq -1 \text{ or } y > 2\}$. Note that $y = 2$ would result in division by 0 and is therefore excluded from the solution set.

✔ Progress Check 2

Solve the inequality $\dfrac{2x - 3}{1 - 2x} \geq 0$.

Answers

$\left\{ x \left| \dfrac{1}{2} < x \leq \dfrac{3}{2} \right. \right\}$

EXAMPLE 3   SOLVING AN INEQUALITY

Solve the inequality $(x - 2)(2x + 5)(3 - x) < 0$.

SOLUTION

Although this is a third-degree inequality, the same approach will work. The critical values are $x = 2$, $x = -\frac{5}{2}$, and $x = 3$. Graphing, we have

The product of three factors is negative when one of the factors is negative or when all three factors are negative. The solution set is then

$$\{x | -\tfrac{5}{2} < x < 2 \text{ or } x > 3\}$$

✔ Progress Check 3

Solve the inequality $(2y - 9)(6 - y)(y + 5) \geq 0$.

Answers

$\left\{ y \left| y \leq -5 \text{ or } \dfrac{9}{2} \leq y \leq 6 \right. \right\}$

Exercise Set 9.6

In Exercises 1−6 select the values that are solutions to the given inequality.

1. $x^2 - 3x - 4 > 0$

   (a) $x = 3$ (b) $x = 5$ (c) $x = 0$
   (d) $x = -2$ (e) $x = 6$

2. $x^2 - 7x + 12 \leq 0$

   (a) $x = 3$ (b) $x = 3.5$ (c) $x = 5$
   (d) $x = 3.8$ (e) $x = 2$

3. $x^2 + 7x + 10 \geq 0$

   (a) $x = -2$ (b) $x = -3$ (c) $x = 0$
   (d) $x = -6$ (e) $x = 4$

4. $2x^2 - 3x - 2 < 0$

   (a) $x = 0$ (b) $x = -3$ (c) $x = 2$
   (d) $x = -1$ (e) $x = 3$

5. $2x^2 - x > 0$

   (a) $x = 0$ (b) $x = \dfrac{1}{2}$ (c) $x = -1$

   (d) $x = \dfrac{1}{4}$ (e) $x = 2$

6. $3x^2 + x \leq 0$

   (a) $x = 0$ (b) $x = 2$ (c) $x = -2$
   (d) $x = -4$ (e) $x = 1$

In Exercises 7−18 find the critical values of the factors in each given inequality. Do not solve.

7. $x^2 + 5x + 6 > 0$ 8. $x^2 + 3x + 4 \leq 0$

9. $2x^2 - x - 1 < 0$ 10. $3x^2 - 4x - 4 \geq 0$

11. $4x - 2x^2 < 0$ 12. $r^2 + 4r \geq 0$

13. $\dfrac{x + 5}{x + 3} < 0$ 14. $\dfrac{x - 6}{x + 4} \geq 0$

15. $\dfrac{2r + 1}{r - 3} \leq 0$ 16. $\dfrac{x - 1}{2x - 3} > 0$

17. $\dfrac{3s + 2}{2s - 1} > 0$ 18. $\dfrac{4x + 5}{x^2} < 0$

In Exercises 19−46 solve, and graph the solution set of the given inequality.

19. $x^2 + x - 6 > 0$ 20. $x^2 - 3x - 10 \geq 0$

21. $2x^2 - 3x - 5 < 0$ 22. $3x^2 - 4x - 4 \leq 0$

23. $2x^2 + 7x + 6 > 0$ 24. $2y^2 + 3y + 1 < 0$

25. $\dfrac{2r + 3}{1 - 2r} < 0$ 26. $\dfrac{3x + 2}{3 - 2x} \geq 0$

27. $\dfrac{x - 1}{x + 1} > 0$ 28. $\dfrac{2x - 1}{x + 2} \leq 0$

29. $6x^2 + 8x + 2 \geq 0$ 30. $2x^2 + 5x + 2 \leq 0$

31. $\dfrac{2x + 2}{x + 1} \geq 0$ 32. $\dfrac{3s + 1}{2s + 4} < 0$

33. $3x^2 - 5x + 2 \leq 0$ 34. $2x^2 - 9x + 10 > 0$

35. $\dfrac{5y - 2}{2 - 3y} \leq 0$ 36. $\dfrac{4x - 3}{3 - x} > 0$

37. $x^2 - 2x + 1 > 0$ 38. $4r^2 - 4r + 1 < 0$

39. $\dfrac{2x + 1}{2x - 3} \geq 0$ 40. $\dfrac{4x - 2}{2x} < 0$

41. $(x + 2)(3x - 2)(x - 1) > 0$

42. $(x - 4)(2x + 5)(2 - x) \leq 0$

43. $(y - 3)(2 - y)(2y + 4) \geq 0$

44. $(2x + 5)(3x - 2)(x + 1) < 0$

45. $(x - 3)(1 + 2x)(3x + 5) > 0$

46. $(1 - 2x)(2x + 1)(3 - x) \leq 0$

*47. $\dfrac{(x - 4)(2x - 3)}{x + 1} < 0$

*48. $\dfrac{(x + 1)(1 - 2x)}{x - 1} < 0$

*49. A manufacturer of solar heaters finds that when x units are made and sold per week, its profit (in thousands of dollars) is given by $x^2 - 50x - 5000$.

   (a) What is the minimum number of units that must be manufactured and sold each week to make a profit?

   (b) For what values of x is the firm losing money?

*50. Repeat Exercise 49, with the profit given by $x^2 - 180x - 4000$.

*51. A ball is thrown directly upward from level ground with an initial velocity such that the height d attained after t seconds is given by $d = 40t - 16t^2$. For what values of t is the ball at a height of at least 16 feet?

■ ■ ■

Chapter Summary

Terms and Symbols

completing the square	322	quadratic formula	326	second-degree inequality	344
critical value	345	quadratic function	318	solving by factoring	320
discriminant	330	radical equation	339	substitution of variable	342
double root	331	repeated root	331	zeros of a function	318
extraneous solution	340	second-degree equation in			
quadratic equation	318	one variable	318		

Key Ideas for Review

Topic	Page	Key Idea
Zero product rule	318	If the product of two real numbers is 0, at least one of the numbers must be 0. Thus, $ab = 0$ only if $a = 0$ or $b = 0$, or both $a = 0$ and $b = 0$.
Quadratic equation	318	A quadratic equation has the form $$ax^2 + bx + c = 0, a \neq 0.$$
solving when $b = 0$	318	When $b = 0$, the resulting quadratic equation $$ax^2 + c = 0$$ has solutions $x = \pm\sqrt{-c/a}$.
solving by factoring	320	If a quadratic equation can be written as a product of linear factors $$(rx + s)(ux + v) = 0$$ then $$x = -\frac{s}{r} \quad \text{and} \quad x = -\frac{v}{u}$$ are the roots of the quadratic equation.
Quadratic formula	326	The quadratic formula $$x = \frac{-b \pm \sqrt{b^2 - 4ac}}{2a}$$ provides us with a pair of solutions to the quadratic equation $ax^2 + bx + c = 0, a > 0$.
discriminant	330	The expression $b^2 - 4ac$ found under the radical in the quadratic formula is called the discriminant and determines the nature of the roots of the quadratic equation.
Power rule	340	If both sides of an equation are raised to the same power, then the resulting equation may have extraneous roots that are not solutions of the original equation.
Radical equations	339	Certain forms, such as radical equations, can be solved by raising both sides of the equation to a power. The solutions of the resulting equation must be checked to see that they satisfy the original equation.

(continues)

Topic	Page	Key Idea
Substitution of variable	342	The method of substitution of variable can be used to convert certain nonquadratic equations to quadratic equations.
Second-degree inequalities	344	
critical value	345	The linear factor $ax + b$ equals 0 at the critical value $$x = -\frac{b}{a}$$ and has opposite signs depending on whether x is to the left or right of the critical value on a number line.
solution process	345	To solve an inequality, write it as a product of linear factors with the right-hand side equal to 0. Analyze the signs to the left and right of each critical value. The product and quotient of linear factors can be negative (< 0) only if an odd number of factors is negative; they can be positive ($>$ 0) only if an even number of factors is negative.

Common Errors

1. The equation $2x^2 = 10$ has as its solutions $x = \pm\sqrt{5}$. Remember to write $\pm$ before the radical when solving a quadratic.

2. The quadratic equation $3x^2 + x = 0$ can be factored as
$$x(3x + 1) = 0$$
The solutions are then $x = 0$ and $x = -\frac{1}{3}$. Remember that each linear factor yields a root; in particular, the factor x yields the root $x = 0$.

3. When solving by factoring, make sure that one side of the equation is zero. Note that
$$(x + 1)(x - 2) = 2$$
does *not* imply that $x + 1 = 2$ or $x - 2 = 2$.

4. To complete the square for
$$4(x^2 + 6x \quad) = 7$$
we must add $(\frac{6}{2})^2 = 3^2 = 9$ within the parentheses. To balance the equation, we must add $4 \cdot 9 = 36$ to the right-hand side.
$$4(x^2 + 6x + 9) = 7 + 36$$

Don't write
$$4(x^2 + 6x + 9) = 7 + 9$$

5. The quadratic formula is
$$x = \frac{-b \pm \sqrt{b^2 - 4ac}}{2a}$$
Don't use the formula as
$$x = -b \pm \frac{\sqrt{b^2 - 4ac}}{2a}$$

6. Proper use of the quadratic formula requires that the equation be written in the form $ax^2 + bx + c = 0$. Remember that a, b, and c are coefficients and therefore include the sign.

7. To solve an inequality such as
$$x^2 + 2x \geq 3$$
you must make one side of the equation zero:
$$x^2 + 2x - 3 \geq 0$$
and then factor. *Don't* write
$$x(x + 2) \geq 3$$
and then attempt to analyze the signs. The inequality does *not* imply that $x \geq 3$ or that $x + 2 \geq 3$.

8. When solving

$$(x + 3)(2x - 1) < 0$$

don't write

$$(x + 3) < 0 \quad \text{or} \quad 2x - 1 < 0$$

You must analyze the linear factors $(x + 3)$ and $(2x - 1)$ and find the values of x for which the factors have opposite signs.

9. If both sides of an equation are raised to a power, some of the solutions of the resulting equation may be extraneous; that is, they may not satisfy the original equation. Always substitute all answers in the original equation to see if the answers are or are not solutions.

Review Exercises

Solutions to exercises whose numbers are in bold are in the Solutions section in the back of the book.

9.1 In Exercises 1–4 solve the given equation.

1. $8x^2 - 200 = 0$ 2. $4y^2 - 144 = 0$

3. $(x - 2)^2 = 9$ 4. $(2t + 1)^2 + 4 = 0$

In Exercises 5–8 solve the given equation by factoring.

5. $x^2 + x - 6 = 0$ 6. $2y^2 - 3y - 2 = 0$

7. $3r^2 - r = 0$ 8. $8x^2 - 50 = 0$

In Exercises 9 and 10 solve by completing the square.

9. $x^2 - 5x = 3$ 10. $3x^2 + 12x = 4$

9.2 In Exercises 11–16 solve by the quadratic formula.

11. $x^2 + 2x - 3 = 0$ 12. $6x^2 + 4x - 2 = 0$

13. $2x^2 + 4x + 1 = 0$ 14. $-3x^2 - 2x + 3 = 0$

15. $2x^2 - x + 1 = 0$ 16. $4x^2 + 2x + 3 = 0$

9.3 In Exercises 17–22 determine the nature of the roots of each quadratic equation.

17. $-4x^2 + x - 2 = 0$ 18. $3y^2 + y = 4$

19. $9r^2 + 1 = 6r$ 20. $3x^2 + 4 = 0$

21. $2y^2 = y$ 22. $2s^2 + s - 2 = 0$

In Exercises 23–26 determine the number of x-intercepts of the graph of the given function.

23. $f(x) = x^2 - 2x + 6$ 24. $f(x) = 3x^2 - x - 2$

25. $f(x) = x^2 - x + \dfrac{1}{4}$ 26. $f(x) = 6x^2 - x - 2$

9.4 27. The width of a rectangular field is 3 feet less than twice its length. If the area of the field is 54 square feet, find the dimensions of the field.

28. A charitable organization rented an auditorium at a cost of \$420 and split the cost among the attendees. If 10 additional persons had attended the meeting, the cost per person would have decreased by \$1. How many attendees were there in the original group?

9.5 In Exercises 29 and 30 solve for x.

29. $x + \sqrt{x + 10} = 10$

30. $\sqrt{5x + 6} - \sqrt{2x + 4} = 2$

In Exercises 31 and 32 indicate an appropriate substitution of variable that will change the given equation to a quadratic equation, and solve the given equation.

31. $2x^4 + x^2 - 6 = 0$ 32. $\dfrac{2}{x^4} - \dfrac{9}{x^2} + 10 = 0$

9.6 In Exercises 33 and 34 find the critical values for the given inequality.

33. $x^2 - 2x - 8 < 0$ 34. $\dfrac{x - 3}{x - 5} \geq 0$

In Exercises 35 and 36 solve, and graph the solution set of the given inequality.

35. $2x^2 - x - 3 \leq 0$ 36. $\dfrac{2s - 1}{3s + 2} > 0$

Progress Test 9A

1. Solve $3x^2 + 7 = 0$.

2. Solve $x - \sqrt{12 - 2x} = 2$.

3. Solve $(2x - 3)^2 = 16$.

4. Solve $\left(\dfrac{x}{2} - 1\right)^2 = -15$.

5. Solve $2x^2 - 7x = 4$ by factoring.

6. Solve $3x^2 - 5x = 2$ by factoring.

7. Solve $3x^2 - 6x = 8$ by completing the square.

8. Use the discriminant to determine the nature of the roots of the equation $3x^2 - 2x - 5 = 0$.

9. Use the discriminant to determine the nature of the roots of the equation $2x^2 - 4x = -7$.

10. Solve $2x^2 + 3x - \frac{1}{2} = 0$ by the quadratic formula.

11. Solve $3x^2 = -2x$ by the quadratic formula.

12. Solve $2x^2 + 5x \leq 3$.

13. Solve $\dfrac{x + 1}{x - 1} \leq 0$.

14. Solve $\dfrac{2x - 3}{4 - x} > 0$.

15. The length of a rectangle is 5 meters greater than its width. If the area of the rectangle is 546 square meters, find the dimensions of the rectangle.

16. A faster assembly line can fill an order in 6 fewer hours than it takes a slower assembly line to fill the same order. Working together, they can fill the order in 3 hours. How long would it take each assembly line to fill the order alone?

Progress Test 9B

1. Solve $4x^2 - 9 = 0$.

2. Solve $x - \sqrt{11 - 2x} = 4$.

3. Solve $\left(\dfrac{x}{3} - 2\right)^2 = 25$.

4. Solve $(3x + \frac{1}{2})^2 = -10$.

5. Solve $x^2 - x - 12 = 0$ by factoring.

6. Solve $2x^2 = -3x - 1$ by factoring.

7. Solve $2x^2 - 6x + 5 = 0$ by completing the square.

8. Use the discriminant to determine the nature of the roots of the equation $4x^2 - 12x + 9 = 0$.

9. Use the discriminant to determine the nature of the roots of the equation $3x^2 - 4x = -3$.

10. Solve $2x^2 - 5x + 4 = 0$ by the quadratic formula.

11. Solve $3x^2 = -5$ by the quadratic formula.

12. Solve $2x^2 + x \geq 10$.

13. Solve $\dfrac{2x - 1}{2x + 1} \geq 0$.

14. Solve $\dfrac{3x + 1}{x - 2} < 0$.

15. The length of one leg of a right triangle exceeds the length of the other by 3 meters. If the hypotenuse is 15 meters long, find the lengths of the legs of the triangle.

16. The formula

$$s = \frac{n(n + 1)}{2}$$

gives the sum of the first n natural numbers 1, 2, 3, ... How many consecutive natural numbers, starting with 1, must be added to obtain a sum of 325?

Chapter 9 Project

In the chapter opener, you were asked the question "How do you find the product of two numbers without multiplying them directly?"

One answer is, by using the "quarter squares rule."

Look at Exercises 69 and 70 in Section 9.1, and Exercise 21 in Section 9.4.

Here is the formula:

$$\left(\frac{a+b}{2}\right)^2 - \left(\frac{a-b}{2}\right)^2 = ab$$

Try it! Find the product of $a = 501$ and $b = 299$.

Now see if you can prove that this formula always works. Expand the two squared terms on the left-hand side, and combine like terms.

Make a list of pairs a and b for which you think it might be easier to use the quarter squares rule, rather than evaluating the product directly.

▪ ▪ ▪

10 Roots of Polynomials

> **"** *The most beautiful experience we can have is the mysterious. It is the fundamental emotion that stands at the cradle of true art and science.*
>
> —Albert Einstein

If a company which manufactures DVD players suddenly increases production levels, how will this affect the cost, revenue, or profit? Economists use mathematical models to answer questions like this, and they have found that finding the zeros of polynomial functions can be a big help. For instance, the marginal cost function may change from an increasing to a decreasing function at a certain production level. If the cost function is a polynomial function, then this level can be found by finding the zeros of another polynomial!

Learning more about concepts like marginal cost can help you see why concepts like finding roots of polynomials are important. While this course will enable you to analyze important economic models, developing those models (like marginal cost formulas) may require calculus.

In this chapter's project, we will see how far we can go to analyze a cost function without using calculus directly.

• • •

In Section 6.3 we observed that the polynomial function

$$f(x) = ax + b \tag{1}$$

is called a linear function, and the polynomial function

$$g(x) = ax^2 + bx + c, \quad a \neq 0 \tag{2}$$

is called a quadratic function. To facilitate the study of polynomial functions in general, we now introduce the notation

$$P(x) = a_n x^n + a_{n-1} x^{n-1} + \cdots + a_1 x + a_0, \quad a \neq 0 \tag{3}$$

to represent a **polynomial function of degree n**. The coefficients a_k may be real or complex numbers, and the subscript k of the coefficient a_k is the same as the exponent of x in x^k.

If $a \neq 0$ in Equation (1), we set the polynomial function equal to zero and obtain the linear equation

$$ax + b = 0$$

which has precisely one solution, $-\frac{b}{a}$. If we set the polynomial function in Equation (2) equal to zero, we have the quadratic equation

$$ax^2 + bx + c = 0$$

which has the two solutions given by the quadratic formula. If we set the polynomial function in Equation (3) equal to zero, we have the **polynomial equation of degree n:**

$$a_n x^n + a_{n-1} x^{n-1} + \cdots + a_1 x + a_0 = 0 \tag{4}$$

Our attention in this chapter will turn to finding the roots or solutions of Equation (4). These solutions are also known as the **zeros of the polynomial.** We will attempt to answer the following questions for a polynomial equation of degree n:

- How many zeros, including complex numbers, does a polynomial have?

- How many of the zeros of a polynomial are real numbers?

- If the coefficients of a polynomial are integers, how many of the zeros are rational numbers?

- Is there a relationship between the zeros and the factors of a polynomial?

10.1   Synthetic Division

Polynomial Division

We saw in Section 4.6 that when we divide the polynomial $P(x)$ by the polynomial $D(x)$, where $D(x) \neq 0$, we may write

$$\frac{P(x)}{D(x)} = Q(x) + \frac{R(x)}{D(x)} \tag{5}$$

where $R(x) = 0$ or where

$$\text{degree of } R(x) < \text{degree of } D(x)$$

We now also recall, by an example, the long division process from Section 2.6.

EXAMPLE 1   "LONG DIVISION"

Divide $3x^3 - 7x^2 + 1$ by $x - 2$.

SOLUTION

$$
\begin{array}{r}
3x^2 - x - 2 \\
x - 2 \overline{\smash{\big)}\ 3x^3 - 7x^2 + 0x + 1} \\
\underline{3x^3 - 6x^2} \\
-x^2 + 0x + 1 \\
\underline{-x^2 + 2x} \\
-2x + 1 \\
\underline{-2x + 4} \\
-3
\end{array}
$$

We can write this result in the form of Equation (5):

$$\frac{3x^3 - 7x^2 + 0x + 1}{x - 2} = 3x^2 - x - 2 + \frac{-3}{x - 2} = 3x^2 - x - 2 - \frac{3}{x - 2}$$

✔ Progress Check 1

Divide $4x^2 - 3x + 6$ by $x + 2$.

Answer

$$4x - 11 + \frac{28}{x + 2}$$

Synthetic Division

Our work in this chapter will frequently require division of a polynomial by a first-degree polynomial $x - r$, where r is a constant. Fortunately, there is a short-cut called **synthetic division** that simplifies this task. To demonstrate synthetic division we will do Example 1 again, writing only the coefficients.

$$
\begin{array}{r}
3 \quad -1 \quad +2 \\[2pt]
-2\overline{)3 \quad -7 \quad 0 \quad 1} \\[2pt]
3 \quad -6 \\ \hline
-1 \quad 0 \quad 1 \\
-1 \quad 2 \\ \hline
-2 \quad 1 \\
-2 \quad 4 \\ \hline
-3
\end{array}
$$

Note that the boldface numerals are duplicated. We can use this to our advantage and simplify the process as follows.

$$
\begin{array}{c|rrrr}
-2 & 3 & -7 & 0 & 1 \\
& & -6 & 2 & 4 \\ \hline
& 3 & -1 & -2 & -3
\end{array}
$$

$$\underbrace{}_{\substack{\text{coefficients of} \\ \text{the quotient}}} \quad \underset{\text{remainder}}{|}$$

In the third row we copied the leading coefficient (3) of the dividend, multiplied it by the divisor (-2), and wrote the result (-6) in the second row under the next coefficient. The numbers in the second column were subtracted to obtain $-7 - (-6) = -1$. The procedure is repeated until the third row is of the same length as the first row.

Since subtraction is more apt to produce errors than is addition, we can modify this process slightly. If the divisor is $x - 2$, we will write 2 instead of -2 in the box and use addition in each step instead of subtraction. Repeating our example, we have

$$
\begin{array}{c|rrrr}
2 & 3 & -7 & 0 & 1 \\
& & 6 & -2 & -4 \\ \hline
& 3 & -1 & -2 & -3
\end{array}
$$

EXAMPLE 2   SYNTHETIC DIVISION

Divide $4x^3 - 2x + 5$ by $x + 2$ using synthetic division.

SOLUTION

Synthetic Division
Procedure	**Example**

Step 1. If the divisor is $x - r$, write r in the box. Arrange the coefficients of the dividend by descending power of x, supplying a zero coefficient for every missing power of x.

$$\underline{-2}\rfloor \quad 4 \qquad 0 \qquad -2 \qquad 5$$

Step 2. Copy the leading coefficient in the third row.

$$\underline{-2}\rfloor \quad 4 \qquad 0 \qquad -2 \qquad 5$$
$$\overline{\qquad\qquad\qquad\qquad\qquad}$$
$$4$$

Step 3. Multiply the last entry in the third row by the number in the box and write the result in the second row under the next coefficient. Add the numbers in that column.

$$\underline{-2}\rfloor \quad 4 \qquad 0 \qquad -2 \qquad 5$$
$$\qquad\qquad -8$$
$$\overline{\quad 4 \quad -8}$$

Step 4. Repeat Step 3 until there is an entry in the third row for each entry in the first row. The last number in the third row is the remainder; the other numbers are the coefficients of the quotient in descending order. Notice that the degree of the quotient is one less than the degree of the dividend.

$$\underline{-2}\rfloor \quad 4 \qquad 0 \qquad -2 \qquad 5$$
$$\qquad\qquad -8 \qquad 16 \quad -28$$
$$\overline{\quad 4 \quad -8 \qquad 14 \quad -23}$$

$$\frac{4x^3 - 2x + 5}{x + 2}$$
$$= 4x^2 - 8x + 14 - \frac{23}{x + 2}$$

✔ Progress Check 2

Use synthetic division to obtain the quotient $Q(x)$ and the constant remainder R when $2x^4 - 10x^2 - 23x + 6$ is divided by $x - 3$.

Answer

$Q(x) = 2x^3 + 6x^2 + 8x + 1;\ R = 9$

WARNING

1. Synthetic division can be used only when the divisor is a linear factor. Don't forget to write a zero for the coefficient of each missing power of x.

2. When dividing by $x - r$, place r in the box. For example, when the divisor is $x + 3$, place -3 in the box, since $x + 3 = x - (-3)$. Similarly, when the divisor is $x - 3$, place $+3$ in the box since $x - 3 = x - (+3)$.

Exercise Set 10.1

In Exercises 1–16 use synthetic division to find the quotient $Q(x)$ and the constant remainder R when the first polynomial is divided by the second polynomial.

1. $x^3 - x^2 - 6x + 5, \quad x + 2$

2. $2x^3 - 3x^2 - 4, \quad x - 2$

3. $x^4 - 81, \quad x - 3$

4. $x^4 - 81, \quad x + 3$

5. $3x^3 - x^2 + 8, \quad x + 1$

6. $2x^4 - 3x^3 - 4x - 2, \quad x - 1$

7. $x^5 + 32, \quad x + 2$

8. $x^5 + 32, \quad x - 2$

9. $6x^4 - x^2 + 4, \quad x - 3$

10. $8x^3 + 4x^2 - x - 5, \quad x + 3$

11. $x^4 - x, \quad x + 2$

12. $x^5 + 2x^3 - 3x - 1, \quad x - 4$

13. $x^3 + 2x + 1, \quad x + 1$

14. $x^4 - x^2 + 3, \quad x - 2$

15. $x^5 + x, \quad x - 3$

16. $x^4 - x, \quad x - 1$

10.2 The Remainder and Factor Theorems

Remainder Theorem

From our work with the division process in the previous section, we may surmise that division of a polynomial $P(x)$ by $x - r$ results in a quotient $Q(x)$ and a constant remainder R, such that

$$P(x) = (x - r) \cdot Q(x) + R$$

Since this identity holds for all real values of x, it must hold when $x = r$. Consequently,

$$P(r) = (r - r) \cdot Q(r) + R$$

$$P(r) = 0 \cdot Q(r) + R$$

or

$$P(r) = R$$

We have proved the Remainder Theorem.

Remainder Theorem   If a polynomial $P(x)$ is divided by $x - r$, then the remainder is $P(r)$.

EXAMPLE 1   APPLYING THE REMAINDER THEOREM

Determine the remainder when $P(x) = 2x^3 - 3x^2 - 2x + 1$ is divided by $x - 3$.

SOLUTION

By the Remainder Theorem, the remainder is $R = P(3)$. We then have

$$R = P(3) = 2(3)^3 - 3(3)^2 - 2(3) + 1 = 22$$

We may verify this result by using synthetic division.

$$
\begin{array}{r|rrrr}
3 & 2 & -3 & -2 & 1 \\
  &   & 6 & 9 & 21 \\
\hline
  & 2 & 3 & 7 & \mathbf{22}
\end{array}
$$

The numeral in boldface is the remainder, so we have verified that $R = 22$.

✔ **Progress Check 1**

Determine the remainder when $3x^2 - 2x - 6$ is divided by $x + 2$.

Answer

10

Graphing

The Remainder Theorem can be used to tabulate values from which we can sketch the graph of a function. The most efficient scheme for performing the calculations is a streamlined form of synthetic division in which the addition is performed without writing the middle row. Repeating Example 1 in this condensed form, we have

$$
\begin{array}{r|rrrr}
  & 2 & -3 & -2 & 1 \\
3 & 2 & 3 & 7 & 22
\end{array}
$$

Then the point $(3, 22)$ lies on the graph of $y = 2x^3 - 3x^2 - 2x + 1$. In general, we may choose a value a of the independent variable and use synthetic division to find the remainder $P(a)$. Then $(a, P(a))$ is a point on the graph of $P(x)$.

EXAMPLE 2   USING SYNTHETIC DIVISION IN SKETCHING A GRAPH

Sketch the graph of $P(x) = x^3 - 3x + 3$ for $-2 \le x \le 2$.

SOLUTION

To sketch the graph of $y = P(x)$, we will allow x to assume integer values from -2 to $+2$. The remainder is found by using the condensed form of synthetic division and is the y-coordinate corresponding to the chosen value of x.

	1	0	−3	3	(x, y)
−2	1	−2	1	1	$(−2, 1)$
−1	1	−1	−2	5	$(−1, 5)$
0	1	0	−3	3	$(0, 3)$
1	1	1	−2	1	$(1, 1)$
2	1	2	1	5	$(2, 5)$

The ordered pairs shown at the right of each row are the coordinates of points on the graph shown in Figure 1.

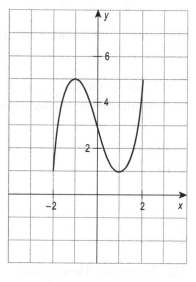

Figure 1   **Graph of $P(x) = x^3 − 3x + 3, \ −2 \leqslant x \leqslant 2$**

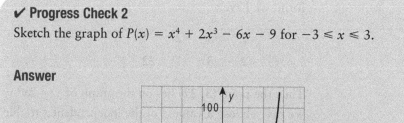

✔ Progress Check 2

Sketch the graph of $P(x) = x^4 + 2x^3 − 6x − 9$ for $−3 \leqslant x \leqslant 3$.

Answer

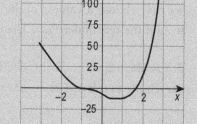

Factor Theorem

Let's assume that a polynomial $P(x)$ can be written as a product of polynomials; that is,

$$P(x) = D_1(x)D_2(x) \cdots D_n(x)$$

where $D_i(x)$ is a polynomial of degree greater than zero. Then $D_i(x)$ is called a **factor** of $P(x)$. If we focus on $D_1(x)$ and let

$$Q(x) = D_2(x)D_3(x) \cdots D_n(x)$$

then

$$P(x) = D_1(x)Q(x)$$

or

$$\frac{P(x)}{D_1(x)} = Q(x) + 0$$

which demonstrates the following rule:

> The polynomial $D(x)$ is a factor of a polynomial $P(x)$ if and only if the division of $P(x)$ by $D(x)$ results in a remainder of zero.

We can now combine this rule and the Remainder Theorem to prove the Factor Theorem.

Factor Theorem

> A polynomial $P(x)$ has a factor $x - r$ if and only if $P(r) = 0$.

If $x - r$ is a factor of $P(x)$, then division of $P(x)$ by $x - r$ must result in a remainder of 0. By the Remainder Theorem, the remainder is $P(r)$, and hence $P(r) = 0$. Conversely, if $P(r) = 0$, then the remainder is 0 and $P(x) = (x - r)Q(x)$ for some polynomial $Q(x)$ of degree one less than that of $P(x)$. By definition, $x - r$ is then a factor of $P(x)$.

EXAMPLE 3 APPLYING THE FACTOR THEOREM

Show that $x + 2$ is a factor of

$$P(x) = x^3 - x^2 - 2x + 8$$

SOLUTION

By the Factor Theorem, $x + 2$ is a factor if $P(-2) = 0$. Using synthetic division to evaluate $P(-2)$, we have

$$
\begin{array}{r|rrrr}
-2 & 1 & -1 & -2 & 8 \\
   &   & -2 & 6 & -8 \\
\hline
   & 1 & -3 & 4 & 0 \\
\end{array}
$$

Fermat's Last Theorem

a^n

$+$

b^n

$=$

c^n

If you were asked to find natural numbers a, b, and c that satisfy the equation

$$a^2 + b^2 = c^2$$

you would have no trouble coming up with "triplets" such as (3, 4, 5) and (5, 12, 13). In fact, there are an infinite number of solutions since any multiple of (3, 4, 5), such as (6, 8, 10), is also a solution.

Generalizing the above problem, suppose we seek natural numbers a, b, and c that satisfy the equation

$$a^n + b^n = c^n$$

for integer values of $n > 2$. Pierre Fermat, a great French mathematician of the seventeenth century, stated that there are no natural numbers a, b, and c that satisfy this equation for any integer $n > 2$. This seductively simple conjecture is known as Fermat's Last Theorem. Fermat wrote in his notebook that he had a proof but that it was too long to include in the margin. After 300 years, the elusive proof was finally found by Andrew Wiles of Princeton University. Wiles published his corrected results with Richard Taylor of Cambridge in 1995.

and we see that $P(-2) = 0$. Alternatively, we can evaluate

$$P(-2) = (-2)^3 - (2)^2 - 2(-2) + 8 = 0$$

We conclude that $x + 2$ is a factor of $P(x)$.

✔ **Progress Check 3**

Show that $x - 1$ is a factor of
$$P(x) = 3x^6 - 3x^5 - 4x^4 + 6x^3 - 2x^2 - x + 1$$

Exercise Set 10.2

In Exercises 1–6 use the Remainder Theorem and synthetic division to find $P(r)$.

1. $P(x) = x^3 - 4x^2 + 1$, $r = 2$

2. $P(x) = x^4 - 3x^2 - 5x$, $r = -1$

3. $P(x) = x^5 - 2$, $r = -2$

4. $P(x) = 2x^4 - 3x^3 + 6$, $r = 2$

5. $P(x) = x^6 - 3x^4 + 2x^3 + 4$, $r = -1$

6. $P(x) = x^6 - 2$, $r = 1$

In Exercises 7–12 use the Remainder Theorem to determine the remainder when $P(x)$ is divided by $x - r$.

7. $P(x) = x^3 - 2x^2 + x - 3$, $x - 2$

8. $P(x) = 2x^3 + x^2 - 5$, $x + 2$

9. $P(x) = -4x^3 + 6x - 2$, $x - 1$

10. $P(x) = 6x^5 - 3x^4 + 2x^2 + 7$, $x + 1$

11. $P(x) = x^5 - 30$, $x + 2$

12. $P(x) = x^4 - 16$, $x - 2$

In Exercises 13–18 use the Remainder Theorem and synthetic division to sketch the graph of the given polynomial for $-3 \leq x \leq 3$.

13. $P(x) = x^3 + x^2 + x + 1$

14. $P(x) = 3x^4 + 5x^3 + x^2 + 5x - 2$

15. $P(x) = 2x^3 + 3x^2 - 5x - 6$

16. $P(x) = x^3 + 3x^2 - 4x - 12$

17. $P(x) = x^4 - 10x^3 + 1$

18. $P(x) = 4x^4 + 4x^3 - 9x^2 - x + 2$

In Exercises 19–26 use the Factor Theorem to decide whether or not the first polynomial is a factor of the second polynomial.

19. $x - 2$, $x^3 - x^2 - 5x + 6$

20. $x - 1$, $x^3 + 4x^2 - 3x + 1$

21. $x + 2$, $x^4 - 3x - 5$

22. $x + 1$, $2x^3 - 3x^2 + x + 6$

23. $x + 3$, $x^3 + 27$ 24. $x + 2$, $x^4 + 16$

25. $x + 2$, $x^4 - 16$ 26. $x - 3$, $x^3 + 27$

In Exercises 27–30 use synthetic division to determine the values of k or r, as requested.

*27. Determine the values of r for which division of $x^2 - 2x - 1$ by $x - r$ has a remainder of 2.

*28. Determine the values of r so that

$$\frac{x^2 - 6x - 1}{x - r}$$

has a remainder of -9.

*29. Determine the values of k for which $x - 2$ is a factor of $x^3 - 3x^2 + kx - 1$.

*30. Determine the values of k for which $2k^2x^3 + 3kx^2 - 2$ is divisible by $x - 1$.

*31. Use the Factor Theorem to show that $x - 2$ is a factor of $P(x) = x^8 - 256$.

*32. Use the Factor Theorem to show that $P(x) = 2x^4 + 3x^2 + 2$ has no factor of the form $x - r$, where r is a real number.

*33. Use the Factor Theorem to show that $x - y$ is a factor of $x^n - y^n$, where n is a natural number.

10.3 Factors and Roots

Complex Numbers and Their Properties

In Chapter 9 we saw that the roots of quadratic equations may be complex numbers. Since complex numbers play a key role in providing solutions of polynomial equations, we will now review the material of Section 8.6 and explore further properties of this number system.

Recall that the complex number $a - bi$ is called the **complex conjugate** (or simply the **conjugate**) of the complex number $a + bi$. It is easy to verify that the product of a complex number and its conjugate is a real number, that is,

$$(a + bi)(a - bi) = a^2 + b^2$$

We have also seen that the quotient of two complex numbers

$$\frac{q + ri}{s + ti}$$

can be written in the form $a + bi$ by multiplying both the numerator and denominator by $s - ti$, the conjugate of the denominator. Of course, the reciprocal of the complex number $s + ti$ is the quotient $1/(s + ti)$, which can also be written as a complex number by using the same technique.

EXAMPLE 1   FINDING THE RECIPROCAL OF A COMPLEX NUMBER

Write the reciprocal of $2 - 5i$ in the form $a + bi$.

SOLUTION

The reciprocal is $1/(2 - 5i)$. Multiplying both numerator and denominator by the conjugate $2 + 5i$, we have

$$\frac{1}{2 - 5i} \cdot \frac{2 + 5i}{2 + 5i} = \frac{2 + 5i}{2^2 + 5^2} = \frac{2 + 5i}{29} = \frac{2}{29} + \frac{5}{29}i$$

Verify that $(2 - 5i)\left(\dfrac{2}{29} + \dfrac{5}{29}i\right) = 1$.

✔ Progress Check 1

Write the following in the form $a + bi$.

(a) $\dfrac{4 - 2i}{5 + 2i}$ (b) $\dfrac{1}{2 - 3i}$ (c) $\dfrac{-3i}{3 + 5i}$

Answers

(a) $\dfrac{16}{29} - \dfrac{18}{29}i$ (b) $\dfrac{2}{13} + \dfrac{3}{13}i$ (c) $-\dfrac{15}{34} - \dfrac{9}{34}i$

If we let $z = a + bi$, it is customary to write the conjugate $a - bi$ as $\bar{z}$. We will have need to use the following properties of complex numbers and their conjugates.

Properties of Complex Numbers

> If z and w are complex numbers, then
>
> 1. $\bar{z} = \bar{w}$ if, and only if, $z = w$.
>
> 2. $\bar{z} = z$ if, and only if, z is a real number.
>
> 3. $\overline{z + w} = \bar{z} + \bar{w}$
>
> 4. $\overline{z \cdot w} = \bar{z} \cdot \bar{w}$
>
> 5. $\overline{z^n} = \bar{z}^n$ n a positive integer

To prove Properties 1–5, let $z = a + bi$ and $w = c + di$. Properties 1 and 2 follow directly from the definition of equality of complex numbers. To prove Property 3, we note that $z + w = (a + c) + (b + d)i$. Then, by the definition of a complex conjugate,

$$\overline{z + w} = (a + c) - (b + d)i$$
$$= (a - bi) + (c - di)$$
$$= \bar{z} + \bar{w}$$

Properties 4 and 5 can be proved in a similar manner although a rigorous proof of Property 5 requires the use of mathematical induction, a concept taught in an advanced algebra course.

EXAMPLE 2 VERIFYING PROPERTIES OF COMPLEX NUMBERS

If $z = 1 + 2i$ and $w = 3 - i$, verify the following:

(a) $\overline{z + w} = \bar{z} + \bar{w}$ (b) $\overline{z \cdot w} = \bar{z} \cdot \bar{w}$ (c) $\overline{z^2} = \bar{z}^2$

SOLUTIONS

(a) Adding, we get $z + w = 4 + i$. Therefore, $\overline{z + w} = 4 - i$. Also,

$$\bar{z} + \bar{w} = (1 - 2i) + (3 + i) = 4 - i$$

Thus, $\overline{z + w} = \bar{z} + \bar{w}$.

(b) Multiplying, we get $z \cdot w = (1 + 2i)(3 - i) = 5 + 5i$. Therefore $\overline{z \cdot w} = 5 - 5i$. Also,

$$\bar{z} \cdot \bar{w} = (1 - 2i)(3 + i) = 5 - 5i$$

Thus, $\overline{z \cdot w} = \bar{z} \cdot \bar{w}$.

(c) Squaring, we get

$$z^2 = (1 + 2i)(1 + 2i) = -3 + 4i$$

Therefore, $\overline{z^2} = -3 - 4i$.
Also,

$$\bar{z}^2 = (1 - 2i)(1 - 2i) = -3 - 4i$$

Thus, $\overline{z^2} = \bar{z}^2$.

✔ Progress Check 2

If $z = 2 + 3i$ and $w = \frac{1}{2} - 2i$, verify the following.

(a) $\overline{z + w} = \bar{z} + \bar{w}$ (b) $\overline{z \cdot w} = \bar{z} \cdot \bar{w}$ (c) $\overline{z^2} = \bar{z}^2$ (d) $\overline{w^3} = \bar{w}^3$

Fundamental Theorem of Algebra

We are now in a position to answer some of the questions posed in the introduction to this chapter. By using the Factor Theorem, we can show that there is a close relationship between the factors and the zeros of the polynomial $P(x)$. By definition, r is a zero of $P(x)$ if, and only if, $P(r) = 0$, that is, if, and only if, r is a root of the equation $P(x) = 0$. However, the Factor Theorem tells us that $P(r) = 0$ if and only if $x - r$ is a factor of $P(x)$. This leads to the following alternate statement of the Factor Theorem:

Factor Theorem

A polynomial $P(x)$ has a zero r if and only if $x - r$ is a factor of $P(x)$.

EXAMPLE 3 DETERMINING A POLYNOMIAL WITH GIVEN ROOTS

Find a polynomial $P(x)$ of degree 3 whose zeros are -1, 1, and -2.

SOLUTION

By the Factor Theorem, $x + 1$, $x - 1$, and $x + 2$ are factors of $P(x)$. The product

$$P(x) = (x + 1)(x - 1)(x + 2) = x^3 + 2x^2 - x - 2$$

is a polynomial of degree 3 with the desired zeros. Note that multiplying $P(x)$ by any nonzero real number results in another polynomial that has the same zeros. For example, the polynomial

$$R(x) = 5x^3 + 10x^2 - 5x - 10$$

also has -1, 1, and -2 as its zeros. Thus, the answer is not unique.

✔ **Progress Check 3**

Find a polynomial $P(x)$ of degree 3 whose zeros are 2, 4, and -3.

Answer

$x^3 - 3x^2 - 10x + 24$

Does a polynomial always have a zero? The answer was supplied by Carl Friedrich Gauss in 1799. The proof of his theorem, however, is beyond the scope of this book.

The Fundamental Theorem of Algebra (Part I)

Every polynomial $P(x)$ of degree $n \geq 1$ has at least one complex zero.

Gauss, who is considered by many to have been the greatest mathematician of all time, supplied the proof at age 22. The importance of the theorem is reflected in its title. We now see that we need not create any other number system beyond the complex numbers in order to solve polynomial equations.

How many zeros does a polynomial of degree n have? The next theorem will bring us closer to an answer.

Linear Factor Theorem

A polynomial $P(x)$ of degree $n \geq 1$ can be written as the product of n linear factors:

$$P(x) = a(x - r_1)(x - r_2) \cdots (x - r_n)$$

where a is the leading coefficient of $P(x)$, and $r_1, r_2, \ldots, r_n$ are, in general, complex numbers.

To prove this theorem, we first note that the Fundamental Theorem of Algebra guarantees us the existence of a zero r_1. By the Factor Theorem, $x - r_1$ is a factor and consequently

$$P(x) = (x - r_1)Q_1(x) \tag{1}$$

where $Q_1(x)$ is a polynomial of degree $n - 1$. If $n - 1 \geq 1$, then $Q_1(x)$ must have a zero r_2. Thus,

$$Q_1(x) = (x - r_2)Q_2(x) \tag{2}$$

where $Q_2(x)$ is of degree $n - 2$. Substituting in Equation (1) for $Q_1(x)$, we have

$$P(x) = (x - r_1)(x - r_2)Q_2(x) \tag{3}$$

This process is repeated n times until $Q_n(x) = a$ is of degree 0. Hence,

$$P(x) = a(x - r_1)(x - r_2) \cdots (x - r_n) \tag{4}$$

Since a is the leading coefficient of the polynomial on the right side of Equation (4), it must also be the leading coefficient of $P(x)$.

It is now easy to establish the following, which may be thought of as an alternate form of the Fundamental Theorem of Algebra.

The Fundamental Theorem of Algebra (Part II)

If $P(x)$ is a polynomial of degree $n \geq 1$, then $P(x)$ has precisely n zeros among the complex numbers.

We may prove this theorem as follows. If we write $P(x)$ in the form of Equation (4) and set the polynomial equal to zero, we see that $r_1, r_2, \ldots, r_n$ are roots of the equation $P(x) = 0$ and hence there exist n roots. If there is an additional root r that is distinct from the roots $r_1, r_2, \ldots, r_n$, then $r - r_1, r - r_2, \ldots, r - r_n$ are all different from 0. Substituting r for x in Equation (4) yields

$$P(r) = a(r - r_1)(r - r_2) \cdots (r - r_n) \tag{5}$$

which cannot equal 0 since the product of nonzero numbers cannot equal 0. Thus, $r_1, r_2, \ldots, r_n$ are roots of $P(x)$, and there are no other roots. Hence, $P(x)$ has precisely n zeros.

It is important to recognize that the zeros of a polynomial need not be distinct from each other. The polynomial

$$P(x) = x^2 - 2x + 1$$

can be written in the factored form

$$P(x) = (x - 1)(x - 1)$$

which shows that the zeros of $P(x)$ are 1 and 1. Since a zero is associated with a factor and a factor may be repeated, we may have repeated zeros. If the factor $x - r$ appears k times, we say that r is a **zero of multiplicity** k.

Solving Polynomial Equations

Cardano's Formula

Cardano provided this formula for one root of the cubic equation

$$x^3 + bx + c = 0$$

$$x = \sqrt[3]{\sqrt{\frac{b^3}{27} + \frac{c^2}{4}} - \frac{c}{2}}$$

$$- \sqrt[3]{\sqrt{\frac{b^3}{27} + \frac{c^2}{4}} + \frac{c}{2}}$$

Try it for the cubics

$$x^3 - x = 0$$

$$x^3 - 1 = 0$$

$$x^3 - 3x + 2 = 0$$

The quadratic formula provides us with the solutions of a polynomial equation of second degree. How about polynomial equations of third degree? of fourth degree? of fifth degree?

The search for formulas expressing the roots of polynomial equations in terms of the coefficients of the equations intrigued mathematicians for hundreds of years. A method for finding the roots of polynomial equations of degree 3 was published around 1535 and is known as Cardano's formula, despite the possibility that Girolamo Cardano stole the result from his friend Nicolo Tartaglia. Shortly afterward a method that is attributed to Ferrari was published for solving polynomial equations of degree 4.

The next 250 years were spent in seeking formulas for the roots of polynomial equations of degree 5 or higher—without success. Finally, early in the nineteenth century, the Norwegian mathematician N. H. Abel and the French mathematician Evariste Galois proved that *no such formulas exist*. Galois's work on this problem was completed a year before his death in a duel at age 20. His proof, using the new concepts of group theory, was so advanced that his teachers wrote it off as being unintelligible gibberish.

EXAMPLE 4   FINDING THE REAL AND COMPLEX ZEROS OF A POLYNOMIAL

Find all zeros of the polynomial

$$P(x) = \left(x - \frac{1}{2}\right)^3 (x + i)(x - 5)^4$$

SOLUTION

The distinct zeros are $\frac{1}{2}$, $-i$, and 5. Further, $\frac{1}{2}$ is a zero of multiplicity 3; $-i$ is a zero of multiplicity 1; 5 is a zero of multiplicity 4.

> ✔ **Progress Check 4**
> Find all zeros of the polynomial $P(x) = (x + 3)^2(x - 1 + 2i)$.
>
> **Answer**
> -3 is a zero of multiplicity 2; $1 - 2i$ is a zero of multiplicity 1.

If we know that r is a zero of $P(x)$, then we may write

$$P(x) = (x - r)Q(x)$$

and note that the zeros of $Q(x)$ are also zeros of $P(x)$. We call $Q(x) = 0$ the **depressed equation** since $Q(x)$ is of lower degree than $P(x)$. The next example illustrates the use of the depressed equation in finding the zeros of a polynomial.

EXAMPLE 5   USING A KNOWN ZERO TO FIND OTHER ZEROS

If 4 is a zero of the polynomial $P(x) = x^3 - 8x^2 + 21x - 20$, find the other zeros.

SOLUTION

Since 4 is a zero of $P(x)$, $x - 4$ is a factor of $P(x)$. Therefore,

$$P(x) = (x - 4)Q(x)$$

To find the expressed equation, we compute $Q(x) = P(x)/(x - 4)$ by synthetic division.

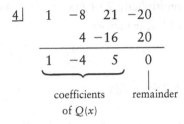

The depressed equation is

$$x^2 - 4x + 5 = 0$$

Using the quadratic formula, the roots of the depressed equation $Q(x) = 0$ are the zeros of the polynomial $Q(x)$ and are found to be $2 + i$ and $2 - i$. The zeros of $P(x)$ are then seen to be 4, $2 + i$, and $2 - i$.

> ✔ **Progress Check 5**
>
> If -2 is a zero of the polynomial $P(x) = x^3 - 7x - 6$, find the remaining zeros.
>
> **Answer**
> $-1, 3$

EXAMPLE 6   USING A KNOWN ZERO TO FIND OTHER ZEROS

If -1 is a zero of multiplicity 2 of $P(x) = x^4 + 4x^3 + 2x^2 - 4x - 3$, find the remaining zeros and write $P(x)$ as a product of linear factors.

SOLUTION

Since -1 is a double zero of $P(x)$, then $(x + 1)^2$ is a factor of $P(x)$. Therefore,

$$P(x) = (x + 1)^2 Q(x)$$

Repeated use of synthetic division with the divisor $x + 1$ (or polynomial division with the divisor $(x + 1)^2 = x^2 + 2x + 1$) results in

$$Q(x) = \frac{x^4 + 4x^3 + 2x^2 - 4x - 3}{(x + 1)^2}$$

$$= x^2 + 2x - 3$$

$$= (x - 1)(x + 3)$$

The roots of the depressed equation $Q(x) = 0$ are 1 and -3, and these are the remaining zeros of $P(x)$. By the Linear Factor Theorem,

$$P(x) = (x + 1)^2(x - 1)(x + 3)$$

✔ **Progress Check 6**

If -2 is a zero of multiplicity 2 of $P(x) = x^4 + 4x^3 + 5x^2 + 4x + 4$, write $P(x)$ as a product of linear factors.

Answer

$P(x) = (x + 2)(x + 2)(x + i)(x - i)$

We know from the quadratic formula that if a quadratic equation with real coefficients has a complex root $a + bi$, then the conjugate $a - bi$ is the other root. The following theorem extends this result to a polynomial of degree n with real coefficients.

Conjugate Zeros Theorem

> If $P(x)$ is a polynomial of degree $n \geq 1$ with real coefficients, and if $a + bi$, $b \neq 0$, is a zero of $P(x)$, then the complex conjugate $a - bi$ is also a zero of $P(x)$.

Proof of Conjugate Zeros Theorem (Optional)

To prove the Conjugate Zeros Theorem, we let $z = a + bi$ and make use of the properties of complex conjugates developed earlier in this section. We may write

$$P(x) = a_n x^n + a_{n-1} x^{n-1} + \cdots + a_1 x + a_0 \tag{6}$$

and, since z is a zero of $P(x)$,

$$a_n z^n + a_{n-1} z^{n-1} + \cdots + a_1 z + a_0 = 0 \tag{7}$$

But if $z = w$, then $\bar{z} = \bar{w}$. Applying this property of complex numbers to both sides of Equation (7), we have

$$\overline{a_n z^n + a_{n-1} z^{n-1} + \cdots + a_1 z + a_0} = \bar{0} = 0 \tag{8}$$

We also know that $\overline{z + w} = \bar{z} + \bar{w}$. Applying this property to the left side of Equation (8), we see that

$$\overline{a_n z^n} + \overline{a_{n-1} z^{n-1}} + \cdots + \overline{a_1 z} + \overline{a_0} = 0 \tag{9}$$

Further, $\overline{z \cdot w} = \bar{z} \cdot \bar{w}$ so that we may rewrite Equation (9) as

$$\overline{a_n} \overline{z^n} + \overline{a_{n-1}} \overline{z^{n-1}} + \cdots + \overline{a_1}\, \bar{z} + \overline{a_0} = 0 \tag{10}$$

Since a_i is all real numbers, we know that $\overline{a_i} = a_i$. Finally, we use the property $\overline{z^n} = \overline{z}^n$ to rewrite Equation (10) as

$$a_n \overline{z}^n + a_{n-1} \overline{z}^{n-1} + \cdots + a_1 \overline{z} + a_0 = 0$$

which establishes that $\overline{z}$ is a zero of $P(x)$.

EXAMPLE 7   APPLYING THE CONJUGATE ZEROS THEOREM

Find a polynomial $P(x)$ with real coefficients that is of degree 3 and whose zeros include -2 and $1 - i$.

SOLUTION

Since $1 - i$ is a zero, it follows from the Conjugate Zeros Theorem that $1 + i$ is also a zero of $P(x)$. By the Factor Theorem, $(x + 2)$, $[x - (1 - i)]$, and $[x - (1 + i)]$ are factors of $P(x)$. Therefore,

$$
\begin{aligned}
P(x) &= (x + 2)[x - (1 - i)][x - (1 + i)] \\
&= (x + 2)(x - 1 + i)(x - 1 - i) \\
&= (x + 2)(x^2 - 2x + 2) \\
&= x^3 - 2x + 4
\end{aligned}
$$

✔ Progress Check 7

Find a polynomial $P(x)$ with real coefficients that is of degree 4 and whose zeros include i and $-3 + i$.

Answer

$P(x) = x^4 + 6x^3 + 11x^2 + 6x + 10$

The following is a corollary of the Conjugate Zeros Theorem.

> A polynomial $P(x)$ of degree $n \geq 1$ with real coefficients can be written as a product of linear and quadratic factors with real coefficients, with the quadratic factors having no real zeros.

By the Linear Factor Theorem, we may write

$$P(x) = a(x - r_1)(x - r_2) \cdots (x - r_n)$$

where $r_1, r_2, \ldots, r_n$ are the n zeros of $P(x)$. Of course, some of these zeros may be complex numbers. A complex zero $a + bi$, $b \neq 0$, may be paired with its conjugate $a - bi$ to provide the quadratic factor

$$[x - (a + bi)][x - (a - bi)] = x^2 - 2ax + a^2 + b^2$$

that has real coefficients. Thus, a quadratic factor with real coefficients results from each pair of complex conjugate zeros; a linear factor with real coefficients results from each real zero. Further, the discriminant of the quadratic factor $x^2 - 2ax + a^2 + b^2$ is $-4b^2$ and is therefore always negative, which shows that the quadratic factor has no real zeros.

Exercise Set 10.3

In Exercises 1–4 perform the indicated operation and write the answer in the form $a + bi$.

1. $\dfrac{2 + 3i}{1 - 2i}$

2. $\dfrac{4 - 3i}{2 + 5i}$

3. $\dfrac{5 + 4i}{2 + 3i}$

4. $\dfrac{5 - 3i}{2 - 5i}$

In Exercises 5–8 find the reciprocal and write the answer in the form $a + bi$.

5. $5 + 2i$

6. $-2 + 3i$

7. $\frac{1}{4} - i$

8. $-1 - \frac{1}{2}i$

9. If z and w are complex numbers, show that $\overline{z \cdot w} = \overline{z} \cdot \overline{w}$.

10. If z is a complex number, verify that $\overline{z^2} = \overline{z}^2$ and $\overline{z^3} = \overline{z}^3$.

In Exercises 11–16 find a polynomial $P(x)$ of lowest degree that has the indicated zeros.

11. $2, -4, 4$

12. $5, -5, 1, -1$

13. $-1, -2, -3$

14. $-3, \sqrt{2}, -\sqrt{2}$

15. $4, 1 \pm \sqrt{3}$

16. $1, 2, 2 \pm \sqrt{2}$

In Exercises 17–20 find the polynomial $P(x)$ of lowest degree that has the indicated zeros and satisfies the given condition. (*Hint:* Write $P(x)$ in the form

$$P(x) = a(x - r_1)(x - r_2) \cdots (x - r_n)$$

where $r_1, r_2, \ldots, r_n$ are the indicated zeros, and a is a real number to be determined.)

17. $\frac{1}{2}, \frac{1}{2}, -2;\ \ P(2) = 3$

18. $3, 3, -2, 2;\ \ P(4) = 12$

19. $\sqrt{2}, -\sqrt{2}, 4;\ \ P(-1) = 5$

20. $\frac{1}{2}, -2, 5;\ \ P(0) = 5$

In Exercises 21–28 find the roots of the given equation.

21. $(x - 3)(x + 1)(x - 2) = 0$

22. $(x - 3)(x^2 - 3x - 4) = 0$

23. $(x + 2)(x^2 - 16) = 0$

24. $(x^2 - x)(x^2 - 2x + 5) = 0$

25. $(x^2 + 3x + 2)(2x^2 + x) = 0$

26. $(x^2 + x + 4)(x - 3)^2 = 0$

27. $(x - 5)^3(x + 5)^2 = 0$

28. $(x + 1)^2(x + 3)^4(x - 2) = 0$

In Exercises 29–32 find a polynomial that has the indicated zeros and no others.

29. -2 of multiplicity 3

30. 1 of multiplicity 2, -4 of multiplicity 1

31. $\frac{1}{2}$ of multiplicity 2, -1 of multiplicity 2

32. -1 of multiplicity 2, 0 and 2 each of multiplicity 1

In Exercises 33–38 use the given root(s) to help in finding the remaining roots of the equation.

33. $x^3 - 3x - 2 = 0;\ \ -1$

34. $x^3 - 7x^2 + 4x + 24 = 0;\ \ 3$

35. $x^3 - 8x^2 + 18x - 15 = 0;\ \ 5$

36. $x^3 - 2x^2 - 7x - 4 = 0;\ \ -1$

37. $x^4 + x^3 - 12x^2 - 28x - 16 = 0;\ \ -2$

38. $x^4 - 2x^2 + 1 = 0;\ \ 1$ is a double root

In Exercises 39–44 find a polynomial that has the indicated zeros and no others.

39. $1 + 3i, -2$

40. $1, -1, 2 - i$

41. $1 + i, 2 - i$

42. $-2, 3, 1 + 2i$

43. -2 is a root of multiplicity 2, $3 - 2i$

44. 3 is a triple root, $-i$

In Exercises 45–50 use the given root(s) to help in writing the given equation as a product of linear and quadratic factors with real coefficients.

45. $x^3 - 7x^2 + 16x - 10 = 0$; $3 - i$

46. $x^3 + x^2 - 7x + 65 = 0$; $2 + 3i$

47. $x^4 + 4x^3 + 13x^2 + 18x + 20 = 0$; $-1, -2i$

48. $x^4 + 3x^3 - 5x^2 - 29x - 30 = 0$; $-2 + i$

49. $x^5 + 3x^4 - 12x^3 - 42x^2 + 32x + 120 = 0$;
$-3 - i, -2$

50. $x^5 - 8x^4 + 29x^3 - 54x^2 + 48x - 16 = 0$;
$2 + 2i, 2$

*51. Write a polynomial $P(x)$ with *complex coefficients* that has the zero $a + bi$, $b \neq 0$, and does not have $a - bi$ as a zero.

*52. Show that a polynomial equation of degree 4 with real coefficients has either 4 real roots, 2 real roots, or no real roots.

*53. Show that a polynomial equation of odd degree with real coefficients has at least one real root.

54. A marketing firm tells the manufacturers of a brand of DVD players that the cost C of producing x thousand DVD players may be modeled by the equation

$$C = 0.01x^3 - 1.50x^2 + 50x$$

This cost function only makes sense if it yields positive values for the cost. Determine the zeros of the function, and use your graphing calculator to determine intervals where this function yields positive values.

55. Refer to Exercise 54. Using calculus, economists can show that the marginal cost function for the manufacturing process modeled above is

$$M = 0.03x^2 - 3x + 50$$

The zeros of this function reveal the production levels at which increasing production will begin to increase cost. Find the zeros.

56. MATHEMATICS IN WRITING: Refer to Exercises 54 and 55. Write a brief paragraph in which you interpret your results. Include sketches of the graphs of the cost and marginal cost functions. Suppose the marketing firm reveals that the model (that is, the equation) is only valid for production levels between 0 and 30,000 DVD players? (Remember that 30,000 players means $x = 3$, since x refers to the number of *tens of thousands* of players.)

10.4 Real and Rational Zeros

Descartes's Rule of Signs

In this section we will restrict our investigation to polynomials with real coefficients. Our first objective is to obtain some information concerning the number of positive real zeros and the number of negative real zeros of such polynomials.

If the terms of a polynomial with real coefficients are written in descending order, then a **variation in sign** occurs whenever two successive terms have opposite signs. In determining the number of variations in sign, we ignore terms with zero coefficients. The polynomial

$$4x^5 - 3x^4 - 2x^2 + 1$$

has two variations in sign. The French mathematician René Descartes (1596–1650), who provided us with the foundations of analytic geometry, also gave us a theorem that relates the nature of the real zeros of polynomials to the variations in sign.

> If $P(x)$ is a polynomial with real coefficients, then
>
> (I) the number of positive zeros of $P(x)$ is either equal to the number of variations in sign of $P(x)$, or is less than the number of variations in sign by an even number, and
>
> (II) the number of negative zeros of $P(x)$ is either equal to the number of variations in sign of $P(-x)$, or is less than the number of variations in sign by an even number.

Descartes's Rule of Signs

If it is determined that a polynomial of degree n has r real zeros, then the remaining $n - r$ zeros must be complex numbers.

To apply Descartes's Rule of Signs to the polynomial

$$P(x) = 3x^5 + 2x^4 - x^3 + 2x - 3$$

we first note that there are 3 variations in sign as indicated. Thus, either there are 3 positive zeros or there is 1 positive zero. Next, we form

$$P(-x) = 3(-x)^5 + 2(-x)^4 - (-x)^3 + 2(-x) - 3$$
$$= -3x^5 + 2x^4 + x^3 - 2x - 3$$

which can be obtained by negating the coefficients of the odd power terms. We see that $P(-x)$ has two variations in sign and conclude that $P(x)$ has either 2 negative zeros or no negative zeros.

EXAMPLE 1   APPLYING DESCARTES'S RULE OF SIGNS

Use Descartes's Rule of Signs to analyze the roots of the equation

$$2x^5 + 7x^4 + 3x^2 - 2 = 0$$

SOLUTION

Since

$$P(x) = 2x^5 + 7x^4 + 3x^2 - 2$$

has 1 variation in sign, there is precisely 1 positive zero. We form the polynomial

$$P(-x) = -2x^5 + 7x^4 + 3x^2 - 2$$

which is seen to have 2 variations in sign, so that $P(x)$ has either 2 negative zeros or no negative zeros. Since $P(x)$ has 5 zeros, $P(x) = 0$ has either

1 positive root, 2 negative roots, 2 complex roots

or

1 positive root, 0 negative roots, 4 complex roots

✔ Progress Check 1

Use Descartes's Rule of Signs to analyze the nature of the roots of the equation

$$x^6 + 5x^4 - 4x^2 - 3 = 0$$

Answer

1 positive root, 1 negative root, 4 complex roots

Rational Zeros

The following theorem provides the basis for a systematic search for the rational zeros of polynomials with *integer coefficients*.

Rational Zero Theorem

If the coefficients of the polynomial

$$P(x) = a_n x^n + a_{n-1} x^{n-1} + \cdots + a_1 x + a_0 \quad (a_n \neq 0)$$

are all integers and p/q is a rational zero, in lowest terms, then

(I) p is a factor of the constant term a_0, and

(II) q is a factor of the leading coefficient a_n.

Proof of Rational Zero Theorem (Optional)

Since p/q is a zero of P(x), then $P(p/q) = 0$. Thus,

$$a_n \left(\frac{p}{q}\right)^n + a_{n-1} \left(\frac{p}{q}\right)^{n-1} + \cdots + a_1 \left(\frac{p}{q}\right) + a_0 = 0 \qquad (1)$$

Multiplying Equation (1) by q^n, we have

$$a_n p^n + a_{n-1} p^{n-1} q + \cdots + a_1 p q^{n-1} + a_0 q^n = 0 \qquad (2)$$

or

$$a_n p^n + a_{n-1} p^{n-1} q + \cdots + a_1 p q^{n-1} = -a_0 q^n \qquad (3)$$

Factoring the common factor p out of the left-hand side of Equation (3) yields

$$p(a_n p^{n-1} + a_{n-1} p^{n-2} q + \cdots + a_1 q^{n-1}) = -a_0 q^n \qquad (4)$$

Since $a_1, a_2, \ldots, a_n, p,$ and q are all integers, the quantity in parentheses in the left-hand side of Equation (4) is an integer. Division of the left-hand side by p results in an integer, and we conclude that p must also be a factor of the right-hand side, $-a_0 q^n$. But p and q have no common factors, since, by hypothesis, p/q is in lowest terms. Hence, p must be a factor of a_0, which proves part (I) of the Rational Zero Theorem.

We may also rewrite Equation (2) in the form

$$q(a_{n-1}p^{n-1} + a_{n-2}p^{n-2}q + \cdots + a_1pq^{n-2} + a_0q^{n-1}) = -a_np^n \qquad (5)$$

An argument similar to the preceding one now establishes part (II) of the theorem.

EXAMPLE 2   APPLYING THE RATIONAL ROOT THEOREM

Find the rational roots of the following equation

$$8x^4 - 2x^3 + 7x^2 - 2x - 1 = 0$$

SOLUTION

If p/q is a rational root in lowest terms, then p is a factor of -1 and q is a factor of 8. We can now list the possibilities:

> possible numerators: ± 1 (the factors of -1)
> possible denominators: $\pm 1, \pm 2, \pm 4, \pm 8$ (the factors of 8)
> possible rational roots: $\pm 1, \pm\frac{1}{2}, \pm\frac{1}{4}, \pm\frac{1}{8}$

Synthetic division can be used to test if these numbers are roots. Trying $x = 1$ and $x = -1$, we find that they are not roots. Trying $\frac{1}{2}$, we have

$$
\begin{array}{r|rrrrr}
\frac{1}{2} & 8 & -2 & 7 & -2 & -1 \\
 & & 4 & 1 & 4 & 1 \\
\hline
 & 8 & 2 & 8 & 2 & 0
\end{array}
$$

which demonstrates that $\frac{1}{2}$ is a root, so

$$8x^4 - 2x^3 + 7x^2 - 2x - 1 = (x - \tfrac{1}{2})(8x^3 + 2x^2 + 8x + 2)$$

Similarly,

$$
\begin{array}{r|rrrr}
-\frac{1}{4} & 8 & 2 & 8 & 2 \\
 & & -2 & 0 & -2 \\
\hline
 & 8 & 0 & 8 & 0
\end{array}
$$

which shows that $-\frac{1}{4}$ is a root of the depressed equation $8x^3 + 2x^2 + 8x + 2 = 0$ and hence of the given equation. The student may verify that these roots are not repeated and that none of the other possible rational roots will result in a zero remainder when synthetic division is employed. We can conclude that the other two roots are a pair of complex conjugates, which can be found by solving the equation $8x^2 + 8 = 0$.

> ### ✔ Progress Check 2
>
> Find the rational roots of the following equation:
>
> $$9x^4 - 12x^3 + 13x^2 - 12x + 4 = 0$$
>
> **Answer**
>
> $\dfrac{2}{3}, \dfrac{2}{3}$

Finding Zeros Using a Graphing Calculator

Your graphing calculator can be a great help in locating zeros of polynomial functions. It is important to realize that irrational zeros will be displayed as decimals and therefore are naturally approximations. But when the calculator is able to locate a rational zero, this may be the start you need to find the other zeros using synthetic division, the quadratic formula, or other techniques which you have learned in this chapter.

Consider the polynomial $6x^3 + 17x^2 - 33x - 20$. Graphing this as a function in the graphing calculator (and selecting an appropriate viewing window) yields the following:

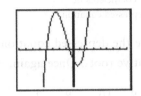

Now we can ask the calculator to locate a zero. Let's start with the leftmost zero. We have to pick an interval within which we expect the zero to be. It appears that $[-6, -2]$ is such an interval. When we ask the calculator to locate a zero, it will ask us for this information (can you see why it would need to ask this?) Here is the result:

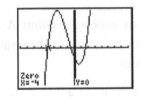

How can we tell when a zero found in this way is rational? One way is to make a list of all possible rational roots and then checking them against the zeros discovered by the calculator. For example, the calculator provides the zeros -2.236068, 2.236068, and -1.666667 for the polynomial $3x^3 + 5x^2 - 15x - 25$. Only the last is rational, because $-\frac{5}{3} \approx -1.666667$.

EXAMPLE 3   SYNTHESIZING THEOREMS ON ROOTS OF EQUATIONS
Find all roots of the following equation:

$$8x^5 + 12x^4 + 14x^3 + 13x^2 + 6x + 1 = 0$$

SOLUTION
We first list the possible numerators and denominators, and the possible rational roots they can form:

possible numerators: ± 1 (the factors of 1)
possible denominators: $\pm 1, \pm 2, \pm 4, \pm 8$ (the factors of 8)
possible rational roots: $\pm 1, \pm\frac{1}{2}, \pm\frac{1}{4}, \pm\frac{1}{8}$

We next employ Descartes's Rule of Signs. Since $P(x)$ has no variations in sign, there are no positive roots. $P(-x)$ has 5 variations in sign, indicating that there are either 5 negative roots, 3 negative roots, or 1 negative root. Using synthetic division to test the possible negative rational roots, we find that $-\frac{1}{2}$ is a root.

$$
\begin{array}{r|rrrrrr}
-\frac{1}{2} & 8 & 12 & 14 & 13 & 6 & 1 \\
 & & -4 & -4 & -5 & -4 & -1 \\
\hline
 & 8 & 8 & 10 & 8 & 2 & 0
\end{array}
$$

coefficients of
depressed equation

We can now use the depressed equation and continue testing with the same list of possible negative roots. Once again, $-\frac{1}{2}$ is seen to be a root.

$$
\begin{array}{r|rrrrr}
-\frac{1}{2} & 8 & 8 & 10 & 8 & 2 \\
 & & -4 & -2 & -4 & -2 \\
\hline
 & 8 & 4 & 8 & 4 & 0
\end{array}
$$

coefficients of
depressed equation

This illustrates an important point: A rational root may be a multiple root! Applying the same technique to the resulting depressed equation, we see that $-\frac{1}{2}$ is once again a root.

$$
\begin{array}{r|rrrr}
-\frac{1}{2} & 8 & 4 & 8 & 4 \\
 & & -4 & 0 & -4 \\
\hline
 & 8 & 0 & 8 & 0
\end{array}
$$

coefficients of
depressed equation

The final depressed equation

$$8x^2 + 8 = 0 \quad \text{or} \quad x^2 + 1 = 0$$

has the roots $\pm i$. Thus, the original equation has the roots

$$-\frac{1}{2}, -\frac{1}{2}, -\frac{1}{2}, i, \text{ and } -i$$

✔ Progress Check 3

Find all zeros of the following polynomial:

$$P(x) = 9x^4 - 3x^3 + 16x^2 - 6x - 4$$

Answer

$\frac{2}{3}, -\frac{1}{3}, \pm\sqrt{2}i$

Transcendental Numbers

Theorem: Every rational number p/q is algebraic.

Proof: The number p/q is a root of the equation

$$qx - p = 0$$

since

$$q\left(\frac{p}{q}\right) - p = p - p = 0$$

Further, by definition of a rational number, q and p are integers and $q \neq 0$. So p/q is a root of a polynomial equation with integer coefficients and is therefore algebraic.

A real number that is a root of some polynomial equation with integer coefficients is said to be **algebraic**. We see that $\frac{2}{3}$ is algebraic since it is the root of the equation $3x - 2 = 0$; $\sqrt{2}$ is also algebraic, since it satisfies the equation $x^2 - 2 = 0$.

Note that every real number a satisfies the equation $x - a = 0$; that is, it satisfies a polynomial equation with *real* coefficients. To be algebraic, the number a must satisfy a polynomial equation with *integer* coefficients. To show that a real number a is *not* algebraic we must demonstrate that there is *no* polynomial equation with integer coefficients that has a as one of its roots. Although this appears to be an impossible task, it was performed in 1844 when Joseph Liouville exhibited specific examples of such numbers, called **transcendental** numbers. Subsequently, Georg Cantor (1845−1918), in his brilliant work on infinite sets, provided a more general proof of the existence of transcendental numbers.

You are already familiar with at least one transcendental number: the number π is not a root of any polynomial equation with integer coefficients.

EXAMPLE 4   APPLYING THE RATIONAL ROOT THEOREM

Prove that $\sqrt{3}$ is not a rational number.

SOLUTION

If we let $x = \sqrt{3}$, then $x^2 = 3$, or $x^2 - 3 = 0$. By the Rational Zero Theorem, the only possible rational roots are ± 1, ± 3. Synthetic division can be used to show that none of these are roots. However, $\sqrt{3}$ is a root of $x^2 - 3 = 0$. Hence, $\sqrt{3}$ is not a rational number.

> ✔ **Progress Check 4**
>
> Prove that $\sqrt[3]{2}$ is not a rational number.

Exercise Set 10.4

In Exercises 1–12 use Descartes's Rule of Signs to analyze the nature of the roots of the given equation. List all possibilities.

1. $3x^4 - 2x^3 + 6x^2 + 5x - 2 = 0$

2. $2x^6 + 5x^5 + x^3 - 6 = 0$

3. $x^6 + 2x^4 + 4x^2 + 1 = 0$

4. $3x^3 - 2x + 2 = 0$

5. $x^5 - 4x^3 + 7x - 4 = 0$

6. $2x^3 - 5x^2 + 8x - 2 = 0$

7. $5x^3 + 2x^2 + 7x - 1 = 0$

8. $x^5 + 6x^4 - x^3 - 2x - 3 = 0$

9. $x^4 - 2x^3 + 5x^2 + 2 = 0$

10. $3x^4 - 2x^3 - 1 = 0$

11. $x^8 + 7x^3 + 3x - 5 = 0$

12. $x^7 + 3x^5 - x^3 - x + 2 = 0$

In Exercises 13–22 find only the rational roots of the given equation.

13. $x^3 - 2x^2 - 5x + 6 = 0$

14. $3x^3 - x^2 - 3x + 1 = 0$

15. $6x^4 - 7x^3 - 13x^2 + 4x + 4 = 0$

16. $36x^4 - 15x^3 - 26x^2 + 3x + 2 = 0$

17. $5x^6 - x^5 - 5x^4 + 6x^3 - x^2 - 5x + 1 = 0$

18. $16x^4 - 16x^3 - 29x^2 + 32x - 6 = 0$

19. $4x^4 - x^3 + 5x^2 - 2x - 6 = 0$

20. $6x^4 + 2x^3 + 7x^2 + x + 2 = 0$

21. $2x^5 - 13x^4 + 26x^3 - 22x^2 + 24x - 9 = 0$

22. $8x^5 - 4x^4 + 6x^3 - 3x^2 - 2x + 1 = 0$

In Exercises 23–30 find all roots of the given equation.

23. $4x^4 + x^3 + x^2 + x - 3 = 0$

24. $x^4 + x^3 + x^2 + 3x - 6 = 0$

25. $5x^5 - 3x^4 - 10x^3 + 6x^2 - 40x + 24 = 0$

26. $12x^4 - 52x^3 + 75x^2 - 16x - 5 = 0$

27. $6x^4 - x^3 - 5x^2 + 2x = 0$

28. $2x^4 - \frac{3}{2}x^3 + \frac{11}{2}x^2 + \frac{23}{2}x + \frac{5}{2} = 0$

29. $2x^4 - x^3 - 28x^2 + 30x - 8 = 0$

30. $12x^4 + 4x^3 - 17x^2 + 6x = 0$

In Exercises 31–34 find the integer value(s) of k for which each given equation has rational roots, and find the roots. (*Hint:* Use synthetic division.)

*31. $x^3 + kx^2 + kx + 2 = 0$

*32. $x^4 - 4x^3 - kx^2 + 6kx + 9 = 0$

*33. $x^4 - 3x^3 + kx^2 - 4x - 1 = 0$

*34. $x^3 - 3kx^2 + k^2x + 4 = 0$

*35. If $P(x)$ is a polynomial with real coefficients and has one variation in sign, prove that $P(x)$ has exactly one positive zero.

*36. If $P(x)$ is a polynomial with integer coefficients and the leading coefficient is $+1$ or -1, prove that the rational zeros of $P(x)$ are all integers and are factors of the constant term.

*37. Prove that $\sqrt{5}$ is not a rational number.

*38. If p is a prime, prove that $\sqrt{p}$ is not a rational number.

39. The polynomial below has only one rational zero. Use your graphing calculator to locate it. (You will need to adjust the viewing window.)

$$7x^5 - 20x^4 + 161x^3 - 460x^2 - 350x + 1000$$

40. The polynomial below has only one real zero. Use your graphing calculator to find it.

$$2x^3 + 12x^2 - 12x - 272$$

41. The polynomial below has two real, irrational roots. Find decimal approximations to these roots, then determine what the exact values are. (*Hint:* The answers are $\pm\sqrt{b}$, and b is a small positive integer.)

$$x^4 - 6x^2 - 7$$

42. The graph of a polynomial with a double root, like $x^2 + 2x + 1$ (see graph below), will appear to "rebound" at the zero.

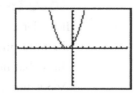

Graph the polynomial below and find all the double roots.

$$4x^4 + 20x^3 - 23x^2 - 120x + 144$$

■ ■ ■

Chapter Summary

Terms and Symbols

algebraic numbers	381	polynomial function of		variation in sign	375
complex conjugate $\bar{z}$	365	degree n	356	zero of multiplicity k	369
depressed equation	370	synthetic division	358	zeros of a polynomial	356
polynomial equation of		transcendental numbers	381		
degree n	356				

Key Ideas for Review

Topic	Page	Key Idea
Polynomial division	357	Division of two polynomials results in a quotient and a remainder, both of which are polynomials. The degree of the remainder must be less than the degree of the divisor.
Synthetic division	358	Synthetic division is a quick way to divide a polynomial by a first-degree polynomial $x - r$, where r is a real constant.
Remainder Theorem	360	If a polynomial $P(x)$ is divided by $x - r$, then the remainder is $P(r)$.
Factor Theorem	363	A polynomial $P(x)$ has a zero r if, and only if, $x - r$ is a factor of $P(x)$.
Linear Factor Theorem	368	A polynomial $P(x)$ of degree $n \geq 1$ can be written as the product of n linear factors $$P(x) = a(x - r_1)(x - r_2) \cdots (x - r_n)$$ where $r_1, r_2, \ldots, r_n$ are the complex zeros of $P(x)$ and a is the leading coefficient of $P(x)$.
Fundamental Theorem of Algebra	367	If $P(x)$ is a polynomial of degree $n \geq 1$, then $P(x)$ has precisely n zeros among the complex numbers, which are not necessarily distinct.
Conjugate Zeros Theorem	372	If $a + bi$, $b \neq 0$, is a zero of the polynomial $P(x)$ with real coefficients, then $a - bi$ is also a zero of $P(x)$.
Rational Zero Theorem	377	If p/q is a rational zero (in lowest terms) of the polynomial $P(x)$ with integer coefficients, then p is a factor of the constant term a_0 of $P(x)$ and q is a factor of the leading coefficient a_n of $P(x)$.
Depressed equation	370	If r is a real zero of the polynomial $P(x)$, then the zeros of the depressed equation are the other zeros of $P(x)$. The depressed equation can be found by using synthetic division.
Descartes's Rule of Signs	376	Descartes's Rule of Signs tells us the maximum number of positive zeros and the maximum number of negative zeros of a polynomial $P(x)$ with real coefficients.
Polynomials with integer coefficients	377	If $P(x)$ has integer coefficients, then the Rational Zero Theorem enables us to list all possible rational zeros of $P(x)$. Synthetic division can then be used to test these potential rational zeros, since r is a zero if and only if the remainder is zero, that is, if and only if $P(r) = 0$

Review Exercises

Solutions to exercises whose numbers are in bold are in the Solutions section in the back of the book.

10.1   In Exercises 1 and 2 use synthetic division to find the quotient $Q(x)$ and the constant remainder R when the first polynomial is divided by the second polynomial.

1. $2x^3 + 6x - 4$, $x - 1$

2. $x^4 - 3x^3 + 2x - 5$, $x + 2$

In Exercises 3 and 4 use synthetic division to find $P(2)$ and $P(-1)$.

3. $7x^3 - 3x^2 + 2$ 4. $x^5 - 4x^3 + 2x$

10.2   In Exercises 5 and 6 use the Factor Theorem to show that the second polynomial is a factor of the first polynomial.

5. $2x^4 + 4x^3 + 3x^2 + 5x - 2$, $x + 2$

6. $2x^3 - 5x^2 + 6x - 2$, $x - \dfrac{1}{2}$

10.3   In Exercises 7–9 write the given quotient in the form $a + bi$.

7. $\dfrac{3 - 2i}{4 + 3i}$ 8. $\dfrac{2 + i}{-5i}$ 9. $\dfrac{-5}{1 + i}$

In Exercises 10–12 write the reciprocal of the given complex number in the form $a + bi$.

10. $1 + 3i$ 11. $-4i$ 12. $2 - 5i$

In Exercises 13–15 find a polynomial of lowest degree that has the indicated zeros.

13. $-3, -2, -1$ 14. $3, \pm\sqrt{-3}$

15. $-2, \pm\sqrt{3}, 1$

In Exercises 16–18 find a polynomial that has the indicated zeros and no others.

16. $\frac{1}{2}$ of multiplicity 2, -1 of multiplicity 2

17. $i, -i$, each of multiplicity 2

18. -1 of multiplicity 3, 3 of multiplicity 1

In Exercises 19–21 use the given root to assist in finding the remaining roots of the equation.

19. $2x^3 - x^2 - 13x - 6 = 0$; -2

20. $x^3 - 2x^2 - 9x + 4 = 0$; 4

21. $2x^4 - 15x^3 + 34x^2 - 19x - 20 = 0$; $-\frac{1}{2}$

10.4   In Exercises 22–25 use Descartes's Rule of Signs to determine the maximum numbers of positive and negative real roots of the given equation.

22. $x^4 - 2x - 1 = 0$

23. $x^5 - x^4 + 3x^3 - 4x^2 + x - 5 = 0$

24. $x^3 - 5 = 0$

25. $3x^4 - 2x^2 + 1 = 0$

In Exercises 26–28 find all the rational roots of the given equation.

26. $6x^3 - 5x^2 - 33x - 18 = 0$

27. $6x^4 - 7x^3 - 19x^2 + 32x - 12 = 0$

28. $x^4 + 3x^3 + 2x^2 + x - 1 = 0$

In Exercises 29 and 30 find all roots of the given equations.

29. $6x^3 + 15x^2 - x - 10 = 0$

30. $2x^4 - 3x^3 - 10x^2 + 19x - 6 = 0$

Progress Test 10A

1. Find the quotient and remainder when $2x^4 - x^2 + 1$ is divided by $x^2 + 2$.

2. Use synthetic division to find the quotient and remainder when $3x^4 - x^3 - 2$ is divided by $x + 2$.

3. If $P(x) = x^3 - 2x^2 + 7x + 5$, use synthetic division to find $P(-2)$.

4. Determine the remainder when $4x^5 - 2x^4 - 5$ is divided by $x + 2$.

5. Use the Factor Theorem to show that $x - 3$ is a factor of $2x^4 - 9x^3 + 9x^2 + x - 3$.

In Problems 6 and 7 find a polynomial of lowest degree that has the indicated zeros.

6. $-2, 1, 3$ 7. $-1, 1, 3 \pm \sqrt{2}$

In Problems 8 and 9 find the roots of the given equation.

8. $(x^2 + 1)(x - 2) = 0$

9. $(x + 1)^2(x^2 - 3x - 2) = 0$

In Problems 10–12 find a polynomial that has the indicated zeros and no others.

10. -3 of multiplicity 2, 1 of multiplicity 3

11. $-\frac{1}{4}$ of multiplicity 2, i, $-i$, and 1

12. $i, 1 + i$

In Problems 13 and 14 use the given root(s) to help in finding the remaining roots of the given equation.

13. $4x^3 - 3x + 1 = 0;\ -1$

14. $x^4 - x^2 - 2x + 2 = 0;\ 1$

15. If $2 + i$ is a root of $x^3 - 6x^2 + 13x - 10 = 0$, write the equation as a product of linear and quadratic factors with real coefficients.

In Problems 16 and 17 determine the maximum number of roots, of the type indicated, of the given equation.

16. $2x^5 - 3x^4 + 1 = 0$; positive real roots

17. $3x^4 + 2x^3 - 2x^2 - 1 = 0$; negative real roots

In Problems 18 and 19 find all rational roots of the given equation.

18. $6x^3 - 17x^2 + 14x + 3 = 0$

19. $2x^5 - x^4 - 4x^3 + 2x^2 + 2x - 1 = 0$

20. Find all roots of the equation $3x^4 + 7x^3 - 3x^2 + 7x - 6 = 0$.

Progress Test 10B

1. Find the quotient and remainder when $3x^5 + 2x^3 - x^2 - 2$ is divided by $2x^2 - x - 1$.

2. Use synthetic division to find the quotient and remainder when $-2x^3 + 3x^2 - 1$ is divided by $x - 1$.

3. If $P(x) = 2x^4 - 2x^3 + x - 4$, use synthetic division to find $P(-1)$.

4. Determine the remainder when $3x^4 - 5x^3 + 3x^2 + 4$ is divided by $x - 2$.

5. Use the Factor Theorem to show that $x + 2$ is a factor of $x^3 - 4x^2 - 9x + 6$.

In Problems 6 and 7 find a polynomial of lowest degree that has the indicated zeros.

6. $-\frac{1}{2}, 1, 1, -1$ 7. $2, 1 \pm \sqrt{3}$

In Problems 8 and 9 find the roots of the given equation.

8. $(x^2 - 3x + 2)(x - 2)^2 = 0$

9. $(x^2 + 3x - 1)(x - 2)(x + 3)^2 = 0$

In Problems 10–12 find a polynomial that has the indicated zeros and no others.

10. $\frac{1}{2}$ of multiplicity 3, -2 of multiplicity 1

11. -3 of multiplicity 2, $1 + i$, $1 - i$

12. $3 \pm \sqrt{-1}$, -1 of multiplicity 2

In Problems 13 and 14 use the given root(s) to help in finding the remaining roots of the equation.

13. $x^3 - x^2 - 8x - 4 = 0;\ -2$

14. $x^4 - 3x^3 - 22x^2 + 68x - 40 = 0;\ 2, 5$

15. If $1 - i$ is a root of $2x^4 - x^3 - 4x^2 + 10x - 4 = 0$, write the equation as a product of linear and quadratic factors with real coefficients.

In Problems 16 and 17 determine the maximum number of roots, of the type indicated, of the given equation.

16. $3x^4 + 3x - 1 = 0$; positive real roots

17. $2x^4 + x^3 - 3x^2 + 2x + 1 = 0$; negative real roots

In Problems 18 and 19 find all rational roots of the given equation.

18. $3x^3 + 7x^2 - 4 = 0$

19. $4x^4 - 4x^3 + x^2 - 4x - 3 = 0$

20. Find all roots of the equation $2x^4 - x^3 - 4x^2 + 2x = 0$.

Chapter 10 Project

The zeros of polynomials can tell economists, marketers, and manufacturers the production levels where interesting things happen to cost, marginal cost, revenue, and profit. Using calculus in combination with economic principles, models of varying effectiveness can be designed, like those you explored in Exercises 54–56 in Section 10.3.

For this project, create a large-scale graph of the cost and marginal cost functions $C = 0.01x^3 - 1.50x^2 + 50x$, $M = 0.03x^2 - 3x + 50$. (Be sure to sketch both graphs on the same set of axes, so you can compare them more effectively.) Plot the zeros of the two functions and determine the value of C when M is zero, and the value of M when C is zero. Explain what one of the zeros of the function M tells you about the shape of the graph of C. What is happening to the cost at this production level?

Summarize your results, and include the definition of marginal cost.

■ ■ ■

11 Exponential and Logarithmic Functions

"There is no excellent beauty that hath not some strangeness in the proportion."

—Francis Bacon

On December 26, 2004, off the west coast of Northern Sumatra, an earthquake occurred that was felt in India, Myanmar, and Thailand, and caused landslides, mud volcanoes, and tsunami. The magnitude of the earthquake was measured at 9.0 on a special scale created in 1935 by Charles F. Richter at the California Institute of Technology, using data from seismograph stations in Southern California.

The Richter scale uses logarithms to compare the intensity of a given earthquake to the "standard intensity." Each integer step represents a tenfold increase in amplitude and about 31 times as much energy released. Look at the end of this chapter for a project dealing with this and other earthquakes.

http://earthquake.usgs.gov/

The story of measuring earthquakes has become a lot more complicated since Richter's time, including newer concepts like body-wave and surface-wave magnitude; but the Richter scale continues to be used. Discover the details of the mathematical methods employed at http://quake.usgs.gov/.

■   ■   ■

Thus far in our study of algebra, we have dealt primarily with functions that are polynomials or some combination of polynomials. In this chapter, we introduce another family: the exponential and logarithmic functions. These functions are inverses of each other.

Exponential functions are needed to help analyze the behavior of various phenomena found in biology, chemistry, physics and economics. For example, we shall observe how an exponential function can describe the growth of bacteria, as well as the increase in funds subject to compound interest.

Logarithms can be viewed as another way to write exponents. Historically, logarithms were used to simplify calculations. Prior to the availability of calculators, a device called a slide rule was used to perform various calculations. The design of the slide rule was based upon logarithms and their properties. Although the need for manipulating logarithms in calculations has diminished, the logarithmic functions are basic to developing more sophisticated mathematical ideas.

11.1   Combining Functions; Inverse Functions

We can combine two functions such as

$$f(x) = x^2 \quad g(x) = x - 1$$

by the operations of addition, subtraction, multiplication, and division. Using these functions f and g, we define new functions $f + g$, $f - g$, $f \cdot g$, and $\frac{f}{g}$ as follows:

$$(f + g)(x) = f(x) + g(x) = x^2 + x - 1$$
$$(f - g)(x) = f(x) - g(x) = x^2 - (x - 1) = x^2 - x + 1$$
$$(f \cdot g)(x) = f(x) \cdot g(x) = x^2(x - 1) = x^3 - x^2$$
$$\left(\frac{f}{g}\right)(x) = \frac{f(x)}{g(x)} = \frac{x^2}{x - 1}$$

In each case we have combined two functions f and g to form a new function. Note, however, that the domain of the new function need not be the same as the domain of the original functions. The function formed by division

$$\left(\frac{f}{g}\right)(x) = \frac{x^2}{x - 1}$$

has as its domain the set of all real numbers x except $x = 1$ since we cannot divide by 0. On the other hand, the functions $f(x) = x^2$ and $g(x) = x - 1$ are both defined at $x = 1$.

EXAMPLE 1   OPERATIONS WITH FUNCTIONS
Given $f(x) = x - 4$, $g(x) = x^2 - 4$, find the following:

(a) $(f + g)(x)$ (b) $(f - g)(x)$ (c) $(f \cdot g)(x)$

(d) $\left(\frac{f}{g}\right)(x)$ (e) the domain of $\left(\frac{f}{g}\right)(x)$

SOLUTIONS

(a) $(f + g)(x) = f(x) + g(x) = x - 4 + x^2 - 4 = x^2 + x - 8$

(b) $(f - g)(x) = f(x) - g(x) = x - 4 - (x^2 - 4) = -x^2 + x$

(c) $(f \cdot g)(x) = f(x) \cdot g(x) = (x - 4)(x^2 - 4) = x^3 - 4x^2 - 4x + 16$

(d) $\left(\dfrac{f}{g}\right)(x) = \dfrac{f(x)}{g(x)} = \dfrac{x - 4}{x^2 - 4}$

(e) The domain must exclude values of x for which $x^2 - 4 = 0$. Thus, the domain consists of all real numbers except 2 and -2.

✔ Progress Check 1

Given $f(x) = 2x^2$, $g(x) = x^2 - 5x + 6$, find:

(a) $(f + g)(x)$ (b) $(f - g)(x)$ (c) $(f \cdot g)(x)$

(d) $\left(\dfrac{f}{g}\right)(x)$ (e) the domain of $\left(\dfrac{f}{g}\right)(x)$

Answers

(a) $3x^2 - 5x + 6$ (b) $x^2 + 5x - 6$ (c) $2x^4 - 10x^3 + 12x^2$

(d) $\dfrac{2x^2}{x^2 - 5x + 6}$ (e) all real numbers except 2 and 3

EXAMPLE 2   PRACTICAL USES OF OPERATIONS WITH FRACTIONS

The treasurer of a corporation that manufactures tennis balls finds that the gross revenue R (in dollars) can be expressed as a function of the number of cans x (in millions sold) by

$$R(x) = -x^2 + 4x$$

Further, the total manufacturing cost C (in dollars) is given by

$$C(x) = \frac{5}{4}x + \frac{1}{2}$$

(a) Express the profit P in terms of the number of cans sold.

(b) Express the ratio of the profit P to the gross revenue R.

SOLUTIONS

(a) Since

$$\text{profit} = \text{revenue} - \text{cost}$$

$$P(x) = R(x) - C(x)$$

$$= -x^2 + 4x - \left(\frac{5}{4}x + \frac{1}{2}\right)$$

$$= -x^2 + \frac{11}{4}x - \frac{1}{2}$$

(b)　The ratio we seek is $\dfrac{\text{profit}}{\text{revenue}}$, or

$$\frac{P(x)}{R(x)} = \frac{-x^2 + \frac{11}{4}x - \frac{1}{2}}{-x^2 + 4x} = \frac{-4x^2 + 11x - 2}{-4x^2 + 16x}$$

✔ Progress Check 2

The Natural Fertilizer Company sets the price P (in dollars) per ton of fertilizer by

$$P(x) = \begin{cases} 200 - 10x, & 0 < x \le 5 \\ 150, & x > 5 \end{cases}$$

where x is the number of tons ordered.

(a)　Express the gross revenue R as a function of the quantity x.
Hint: gross revenue = price × quantity.

(b)　Find the gross revenue when the demand x is 4 tons.

Answers

(a)　$R(x) = \begin{cases} 200x - 10x^2, & 0 < x \le 5 \\ 150x, & x > 5 \end{cases}$ 　　(b)　$640

Composite Functions

There is another, important way in which two functions f and g can be combined to form a new function. In Figure 1, the function f assigns the value y in set Y to x in set X; then, function g assigns the value z in set Z to y in set Y. The net effect of this combination of f and g is a new function h, called the **composite function of g and f, $g \circ f$**, which assigns z in Z to x in X. We write this new function as

$$h(x) = (g \circ f)(x) = g[f(x)]$$

which is read "g of f of x."

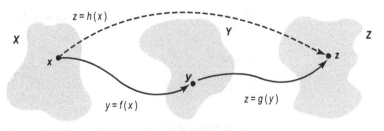

Figure 1　The Composite Function $(g \circ f)(x)$

EXAMPLE 3   COMPOSITE FUNCTION NOTATION

Given $f(x) = x^2$, $g(x) = x - 1$, find the following:

(a) $f[g(3)]$ (b) $g[f(3)]$ (c) $(f \circ g)(x)$ (d) $(g \circ f)(x)$

SOLUTIONS

(a) We begin by evaluating $g(3)$:

$$g(x) = x - 1$$
$$g(3) = 3 - 1 = 2$$

Therefore,

$$f[g(3)] = f(2)$$

Since

$$f(x) = x^2$$

then

$$f(2) = 2^2 = 4$$

Thus,

$$f[g(3)] = 4$$

(b) Beginning with $f(3)$, we have

$$f(3) = 3^2 = 9$$

Then we find by substituting $f(3) = 9$ that

$$g[f(3)] = g(9) = 9 - 1 = 8$$

(c) Since $g(x) = x - 1$, we make the substitution

$$(f \circ g)(x) = f[g(x)] = f(x - 1) = (x - 1)^2 = x^2 - 2x + 1$$

(d) Since $f(x) = x^2$, we make the substitution

$$(g \circ f)(x) = g[f(x)] = g(x^2) = x^2 - 1$$

Note that $f[g(x)] \neq g[f(x)]$.

✔ **Progress Check 3**

Given $f(x) = x^2 - 2x$, $g(x) = 3x$, find the following:

(a) $f[g(-1)]$ (b) $g[f(-1)]$ (c) $f[g(x)]$
(d) $g[f(x)]$ (e) $(f \circ g)(2)$ (f) $(g \circ f)(2)$

Answers

(a) 15   (b) 9   (c) $9x^2 - 6x$ (d) $3x^2 - 6x$ (e) 24   (f) 0

Sometimes it is useful to think of a function as a composite of functions. For example, if

$$h(x) = (3x + 1)^4$$

we can let

$$f(x) = 3x + 1 \quad \text{and} \quad g(x) = x^4$$

Then

$$h(x) = (3x + 1)^4 = g(3x + 1) = g[f(x)]$$

Thus, $h(x) = g[f(x)]$ is a way of writing the function h as a composite of the functions f and g. In general, there may be many ways of writing a function as a composite.

EXAMPLE 4   DECOMPOSITION OF A FUNCTION

Given

$$h(x) = \frac{\sqrt{x + 1}}{4}$$

write the function h as a composite of two functions f and g.

SOLUTIONS

There are many ways of writing h as a composite of two functions f and g. We illustrate two possibilities:

(a) The form $\sqrt{x + 1}$ suggests that we let $g(x) = x + 1$. If we then let

$$f(x) = \frac{\sqrt{x}}{4}$$

we have

$$h(x) = \frac{\sqrt{x + 1}}{4} = f(x + 1) = f[g(x)]$$

(b) Alternatively, let $g(x) = \sqrt{x + 1}$. If

$$f(x) = \frac{x}{4}$$

we have

$$h(x) = \frac{\sqrt{x + 1}}{4} = f(\sqrt{x + 1}) = f[g(x)]$$

✔ **Progress Check 4**

Given

$$h(x) = \frac{1}{(2x - 5)^{25}}$$

write the function h as a composite of two functions f and g.

Answers

$h(x) = f[g(x)]$, where $f(x) = \dfrac{1}{x^{25}}$, and $g(x) = 2x - 5$, or

$h(x) = f[g(x)]$, where $f(x) = x^{25}$, and $g(x) = \dfrac{1}{2x - 5}$

One-to-One Functions

An element in the range of a function may correspond to more than one element in the domain of the function. In Figure 2, we see that y in Y corresponds to both x_1 and x_2 in X.

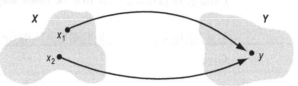

Figure 2   Schematic: A Function That is Not One-to-One

If we demand that every element in the domain be assigned to a *different* element of the range, then the function is called **one-to-one**. More formally

> A function *f* is one-to-one if whenever $a \neq b$, then $f(a) \neq f(b)$.

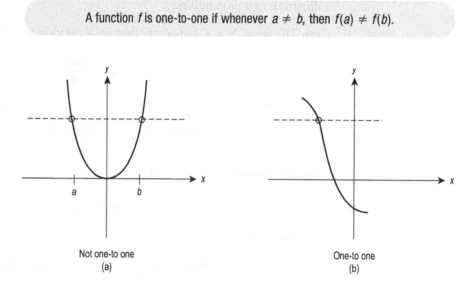

Not one-to one
(a)

One-to one
(b)

Figure 3   The Horizontal Line Test

There is a simple means of determining if a function $y = f(x)$ is one-to-one by examining the graph of the function. In Figure 3a, we see that a horizontal line meets the graph in more than one point. Thus, $f(a) = f(b)$ although $a \neq b$; hence, the function is not one-to-one. On the other hand, no horizontal line meets the graph in Figure 3b in more than one point; thus the graph is that of a one-to-one function. In summary, we have the following test.

Horizontal Line Test

> If no horizontal line meets the graph of a function $y = f(x)$ in more than one point, then the function is one-to-one.

EXAMPLE 5 APPLYING THE HORIZONTAL LINE TEST

Which of the graphs in Figure 4 are graphs of one-to-one functions?

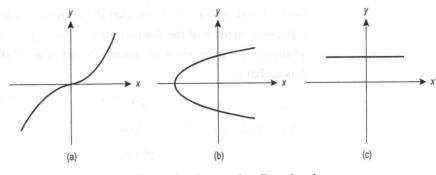

Figure 4 One-to-One Functions?

SOLUTIONS

(a) No *vertical* line meets the graph in more than one point; hence, it is the graph of a function. No *horizontal* line meets the graph in more than one point; hence, it is the graph of a one-to-one function.

(b) No *horizontal* line meets the graph in more than one point, but *vertical* lines do meet the graph in more than one point. It is therefore not the graph of a function and consequently cannot be the graph of a one-to-one function.

(c) No *vertical* line meets the graph in more than one point; hence it is the graph of a function. However, a *horizontal* line does meet the graph in more than one point. This is the graph a function but not of a one-to-one function.

✔ Progress Check 5

Which of the graphs in Figure 5 are graphs of one-to-one functions?

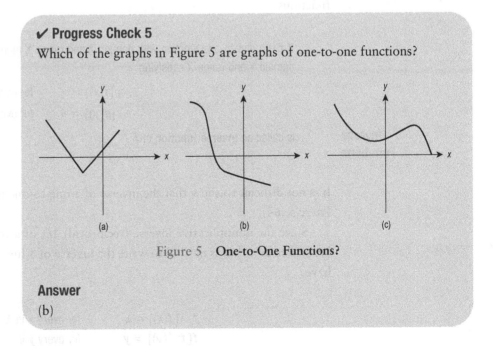

Figure 5 One-to-One Functions?

Answer

(b)

Inverse Functions

Suppose the function f in Figure 6a is a one-to-one function and that $y = f(x)$. Since f is one-to-one, we know that the correspondence is unique; that is, x in X is the *only* element of the domain for which $y = f(x)$. It is then possible to define a function g (Figure 6b) with domain Y and range X that reverses the correspondence, that is,

$$g(y) = x \qquad \text{for every } x \text{ in } X$$

If we substitute $y = f(x)$, we have

$$g[f(x)] = x \qquad \text{for every } x \text{ in } X \qquad (1)$$

Substituting $g(y) = x$ in the equation $f(x) = y$ yields

$$f[g(y)] = y \qquad \text{for every } y \text{ in } Y \qquad (2)$$

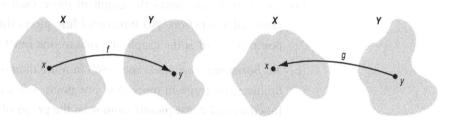

Figure 6   Schematic of Inverse Functions

Functions that satisfy the properties of Equations (1) and (2) are called inverse functions.

Inverse Functions

If f is a one-to-one function with domain X and range Y, then the function g with domain Y and range X satisfying

$$g[f(x)] = x \qquad \text{for every } x \text{ in } X$$
$$f[g(y)] = y \qquad \text{for every } y \text{ in } Y$$

is called an **inverse function** of f.

It is not difficult to show that the inverse of a one-to-one function is unique (see Exercise 64).

Since the multiplicative inverse (reciprocal) $1/x$ of a real number $x \neq 0$ can be written as x^{-1}, it is natural to write the inverse of a function f as f^{-1}. Thus we have

$$f^{-1}[f(x)] = x \qquad \text{for every } x \text{ in } X$$
$$f[f^{-1}(y)] = y \qquad \text{for every } y \text{ in } Y$$

See Figure 7 for a graphical representation.

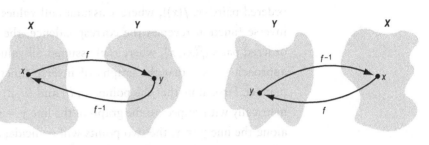

Figure 7   Schematic of an Inverse Function

In the following sections we will study a very important class of inverse functions, the exponential and logarithmic functions. Always remember that we can define an inverse function of f only if f is one-to-one.

EXAMPLE 6   APPLYING THE DEFINITION OF AN INVERSE FUNCTION

Let f be the function defined by

$$f(x) = x^2 - 2$$

Verify that the inverse of f is given by

$$f^{-1}(x) = \sqrt{x + 2}$$

SOLUTION

We must verify that $f[f^{-1}(x)] = x$ and $f^{-1}[f(x)] = x$. Thus,

$$f[f^{-1}(x)] = f(\sqrt{x + 2})$$
$$= (\sqrt{x + 2})^2 - 2$$
$$= x + 2 - 2 = x$$

and

$$f^{-1}[f(x)] = f^{-1}(x^2 - 2)$$
$$= \sqrt{(x^2 - 2) + 2}$$
$$= \sqrt{x^2} = x$$

We have verified that the equations defining inverse functions hold and conclude that the inverse of f is as given. The student should verify that the domain of f is the set of all real numbers and the range of f is also the set of all real numbers.

✔ **Progress Check 6**

Let f be the function defined by

$$f(x) = x^5 + 1$$

Verify that the inverse of f is given by

$$f^{-1}(x) = \sqrt[5]{x - 1}$$

We may also think of the function f defined by $y = f(x)$ as the set of all ordered pairs $(x, f(x))$, where x assumes all values in the domain of f. Since the inverse function reverses the correspondence, the function f^{-1} is the set of all ordered pairs $(f(x), x)$, where $f(x)$ assumes all values in the range of f. With this approach we see that the graphs of inverse functions are related in a distinct manner. First, note that the points (a, b) and (b, a) in Figure 8a are located symmetrically with respect to the graph of the line $y = x$. That is, if we fold the paper along the line $y = x$, the two points will coincide; and if (a, b) lies on the graph of a function f, then (b, a) must lie on the graph of f^{-1}. Thus, the graphs of a pair of inverse functions are reflections of each other about the line $y = x$. In Figure 8b we have sketched the graphs of a pair of inverse functions on the same coordinate axes to demonstrate this interesting relationship.

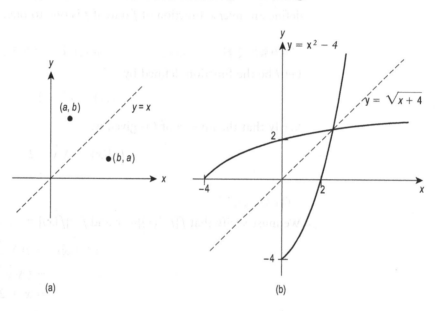

(a)   (b)

Figure 8   Symmetry of a Pair of Inverse Functions about the Line $y = x$

It is sometimes possible to find an inverse function by algebraic methods. Example 7 demonstrates a useful technique.

EXAMPLE 7   FINDING THE INVERSE OF A FUNCTION
Find the inverse function of $f(x) = 2x - 3$.

SOLUTION
By definition, $f[f^{-1}(x)] = x$. Then we must have

$$f[f^{-1}(x)] = 2[f^{-1}(x)] - 3 = x$$

$$f^{-1}(x) = \frac{x + 3}{2}$$

We then verify that

$$f^{-1}[f(x)] = \frac{2x - 3 + 3}{2} = x$$

✔ **Progress Check 7**

Given $f(x) = 3x + 5$, find $f^{-1}(x)$.

Answers

$$f^{-1}(x) = \frac{x - 5}{3}$$

EXAMPLE 8   FINDING THE INVERSE OF A FUNCTION

Given

$$h(x) = \frac{x - 3}{2}$$

find the following:

(a) $h^{-1}(x)$ (b) $h^{-1}(-1)$ (c) $h[h^{-1}(-1)]$ (d) $h^{-1}[h(-5)]$.

SOLUTIONS

(a) We find $h^{-1}(x)$ by following the procedure in Example 7.

$$h[h^{-1}(x)] = \frac{h^{-1}(x) - 3}{2} = x$$

$$h^{-1}(x) - 3 = 2x$$

$$h^{-1}(x) = 2x + 3$$

(b) $h^{-1}(-1) = 2(-1) + 3 = 1$

(c) $h[h^{-1}(-1)] = h(1) = \dfrac{1 - 3}{2} = -1$

(d) $h(-5) = \dfrac{-5 - 3}{2} = -4$

$$h^{-1}[h(-5)] = h^{-1}(-4) = 2(-4) + 3 = -5$$

Note that (c) and (d) illustrate the following rules:

$$h[h^{-1}(u)] = u$$

$$h^{-1}[h(x)] = x$$

✔ **Progress Check 8**

Given

$$g(x) = \frac{6 - x}{2}$$

find the following:

(a) $g^{-1}(x)$ (b) $g[g^{-1}(3)]$ (c) $g^{-1}[g(-2)]$

Answers

(a) $6 - 2x$ (b) 3 (c) -2

⚠️ **WARNING**

(a) In general,

$$f^{-1}(x) \neq \frac{1}{f(x)}$$

If $f(x) = x - 1$, *don't* write

$$f^{-1}(x) = \frac{1}{x - 1}$$

Use the methods of this section to show that

$$f^{-1}(x) = x + 1$$

(b) The inverse function notation is *not* to be thought of as a power.

Exercise Set 11.1

In Exercises 1–6, let $f(x) = x^2 + 1$, $g(x) = x - 2$.
Determine the following:

1. (a) $(f + g)(2)$ (b) $(f + g)(x)$ (c) $(f - g)(3)$

2. (a) $(f - g)(x)$ (b) $(f \cdot g)(1)$ (c) $(f \cdot g)(x)$

3. (a) $\left(\dfrac{f}{g}\right)(-2)$ (b) $\left(\dfrac{f}{g}\right)(x)$ (c) $(f \cdot g)(2)$

4. (a) $(g \cdot f)(2)$ (b) $(g \cdot f)(-3)$ (c) $(g \cdot f)(x)$

5. The domain of
   (a) $\left(\dfrac{f}{g}\right)(x)$ (b) $(f \circ g)(x)$

6. The domain of
   (a) $(g \circ f)(x)$ (b) $\left(\dfrac{g}{f}\right)(x)$

In Exercises 7–10, let $f(x) = 2x^2 - 1$, $g(x) = x + 1$.
Determine the following:

7. (a) $(f + g)(-1)$ (b) $(f + g)(x)$ (c) $(f \cdot g)(x)$

8. (a) $(f - g)(x)$ (b) $(f \cdot g)(-2)$ (c) $(f - g)(2)$

9. (a) $\left(\dfrac{f}{g}\right)(-3)$ (b) $(g \cdot f)(-3)$ (c) $(f \cdot g)(1)$

10. (a) $(f \cdot g)(a)$ (b) $\left(\dfrac{f}{g}\right)(x)$ (c) $(g \cdot f)(x)$

In Exercises 11–14 let $f(x) = 2x + 1$, $g(x) = 2x^2 + x$.
Determine the following:

11. (a) $(f \circ g)(2)$ (b) $(f \circ g)(x)$ (c) $(g \circ f)(3)$

12. (a) $(g \circ f)(x)$ (b) $(f \circ g)(x + 1)$
    (c) $(g \circ f)(x - 1)$

13. (a) $(f \circ f)(-2)$ (b) $(f \circ f)(x)$ (c) $(g \circ g)(2)$

14. (a) $(g \circ g)(x)$ (b) $(f \circ f)(x + 2)$
    (c) $(g \circ g)(x - 3)$

In Exercises 15–18 let $f(x) = x^2 + 4$, $g(x) = x + 2$.
Determine the following:

15. (a) $(f \circ g)(2)$ (b) $(f \circ g)(x)$ (c) $(g \circ f)(3)$

16. (a) $(g \circ f)(x)$ (b) $(f \circ f)(-1)$ (c) $(f \circ f)(x)$

17. The domain of

(a) $(f \circ g)(x)$ (b) $(g \circ f)(x)$

18. The domain of

(a) $(f \circ f)(x)$ (b) $(g \circ g)(x)$

In Exercises 19–22 compute $(f \circ g)(x)$ and $(g \circ f)(x)$.

19. $f(x) = x - 1, g(x) = x + 2$

20. $f(x) = \sqrt{x + 1}, g(x) = x + 2$

21. $f(x) = \dfrac{1}{x + 1}, g(x) = \dfrac{1}{x - 1}$

22. $f(x) = \dfrac{x + 1}{x - 1}, g(x) = x$

In Exercises 23–34 write the given function $h(x)$ as a composite of two functions f and g so that $h(x) = (f \circ g)(x)$.

23. $h(x) = (3x + 2)^8$

24. $h(x) = (x^3 + 2x^2 + 1)^{15}$

25. $h(x) = (x^3 - 2x^2)^{1/3}$ 26. $h(x) = \left(\dfrac{x^2 + 2x}{x^3 - 1}\right)^{3/2}$

27. $h(x) = (3x^2 + 1)^{20}$ 28. $h(x) = (3 - 2x^3)^{30}$

29. $h(x) = \sqrt{4 - x}$ 30. $h(x) = \sqrt{2x^2 - x + 2}$

31. $h(x) = (2 - 5x^2)^{-10}$ 32. $h(x) = \dfrac{1}{(3x^2 + 2x)^8}$

33. $h(x) = \sqrt{\dfrac{x - 2}{x + 5}}$

34. $h(x) = (5x^3 + 4x^2 - 2x + 4)^{1/5}$

In Exercises 35–40 verify that $g = f^{-1}$ for the given functions f and g by showing that $f[g(x)] = x$ and $g[f(x)] = x$.

35. $f(x) = 2x + 4; g(x) = \dfrac{1}{2}x - 2$

36. $f(x) = 3x - 2; g(x) = \dfrac{1}{3}x + \dfrac{2}{3}$

37. $f(x) = 2 - 3x; g(x) = -\dfrac{1}{3}x + \dfrac{2}{3}$

38. $f(x) = x^3; g(x) = \sqrt[3]{x}$

39. $f(x) = \dfrac{1}{x}; g(x) = \dfrac{1}{x}$

40. $f(x) = \dfrac{1}{x - 2}; g(x) = \dfrac{1}{x} + 2$

In Exercises 41–50 find the inverse function.

41. $f(x) = 2x + 3$ 42. $f(x) = 3x - 4$

43. $f(x) = 3 - 2x$ 44. $f(x) = \dfrac{1}{2}x + 1$

45. $f(x) = \dfrac{1}{3}x - 5$ 46. $f(x) = 2 - \dfrac{1}{5}x$

47. $f(x) = x^3 + 1$ 48. $f(x) = \dfrac{1}{x + 1}$

49. $f(x) = x^2, \; x \geq 0$ 50. $f(x) = (x + 3)^2$

51. If $f(x) = \dfrac{1}{3}x + 2$, find the following:

(a) $f^{-1}(x)$ (b) $f^{-1}(2)$

(c) $(f \circ f^{-1})(2)$ (d) $(f^{-1} \circ f)(3)$

52. If $g(x) = 2x - 5$, find the following:

(a) $g^{-1}(x)$ (b) $g^{-1}(3)$

(c) $(g \circ g^{-1})(2)$ (d) $(g^{-1} \circ g)(0)$

53. If $h(x) = 2 - 3x$, find the following:

(a) $h^{-1}(x)$ (b) $h^{-1}(-2)$

(c) $(h \circ h^{-1})(3)$ (d) $(h^{-1} \circ h)(-3)$

54. If $F(x) = 4 - \dfrac{1}{3}x$, find the following:

(a) $F^{-1}(x)$ (b) $F^{-1}(4)$

(c) $(F \circ F^{-1})(2)$ (d) $(F^{-1} \circ F)(-1)$

55. If $f(x) = x^3 - 2$, find the following:

(a) $f^{-1}(x)$ (b) $f^{-1}(3)$

(c) $(f \circ f^{-1})(1)$ (d) $(f^{-1} \circ f)(-2)$

In Exercises 56–63 graph the given function. Use the horizontal line test to determine whether it is a one-to-one function.

56. $f(x) = 2x - 1$ 57. $f(x) = 3 - 5x$

58. $f(x) = x^2 - 2x + 1$ 59. $f(x) = x^2 + 4x + 4$

60. $f(x) = -x^3 + 1$ 61. $f(x) = x^3 - 2$

62. $f(x) = \begin{cases} 2x, & x \leq -1 \\ x^2, & -1 < x \leq 0 \\ 3x - 1, & x > 0 \end{cases}$

63. $f(x) = \begin{cases} x^2 - 4x + 4, & x \leq 2 \\ x, & x > 2 \end{cases}$

*64. Prove that a one-to-one function can have at most one inverse function. (*Hint*: Assume that the functions g and h are both inverses of the function f. Show that $g(x) = h(x)$ for all real values x in the range of f.)

*65. Prove that the linear function $f(x) = ax + b$ is a one-to-one function if $a \neq 0$, and is not a one-to-one function if $a = 0$.

*66. Find the inverse of the linear function $f(x) = ax + b$, $a \neq 0$.

11.2   Exponential Functions

The function $f(x) = 2^x$ is very different from any of the functions we have worked with thus far. Previously, we defined functions by using the basic algebraic operations (addition, subtraction, multiplication, division, powers, and roots). However, $f(x) = 2^x$ has a variable in the exponent and doesn't fall into the class of algebraic functions. Rather, it is our first example of an exponential function.

> An **exponential function** has the form
> $$f(x) = a^x$$
> where $a > 0$, $a \neq 1$. The constant a is called the **base**, and the independent variable x may assume any real value.

Graphs of Exponential Functions

The best way to become familiar with exponential functions is to sketch their graphs.

EXAMPLE 1   GRAPHING AN EXPONENTIAL FUNCTION

Sketch the graph of $f(x) = 2^x$

SOLUTION

We let $y = 2^x$ and we form a table of values of x and y. Then we plot these points and sketch the smooth curve as in Figure 9.

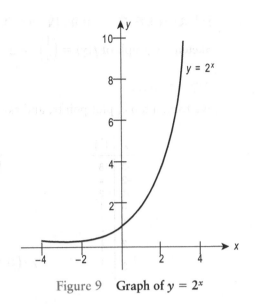

Figure 9   **Graph of $y = 2^x$**

✔ **Progress Check 1**

Sketch the graphs of $f(x) = 2^x$ and $g(x) = 3^x$ on the same coordinate axes.

Answer

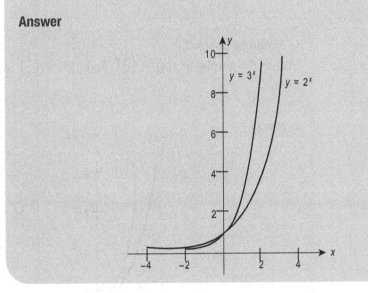

In a sense, we have cheated in our definition of $f(x) = 2^x$ and in sketching the graph in Figure 9. Since we have not explained the meaning of 2^x when x is irrational, we have no right to plot values such as $2^{\sqrt{2}}$. For our purposes, it will be adequate to think of $2^{\sqrt{2}}$ as the value we approach by taking successively closer approximations to $\sqrt{2}$, such as $2^{1.4}$, $2^{1.41}$, $2^{1.414}$, ... A precise definition is given in more advanced mathematics courses, where it is also shown that the laws of exponents hold for irrational exponents.

Let's look at $f(x) = a^x$ when $0 < a < 1$.

EXAMPLE 2   GRAPHING AN EXPONENTIAL FUNCTION

Sketch the graph of $f(x) = \left(\dfrac{1}{2}\right)^x = 2^{-x}$.

SOLUTION

We form a table, plot points, and sketch the graph. See Figure 10.

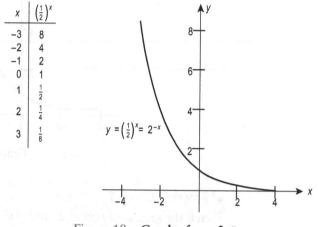

x	$\left(\frac{1}{2}\right)^x$
-3	8
-2	4
-1	2
0	1
1	$\frac{1}{2}$
2	$\frac{1}{4}$
3	$\frac{1}{8}$

$y = \left(\frac{1}{2}\right)^x = 2^{-x}$

Figure 10   Graph of $y = 2^{-x}$

✔ **Progress Check 2**

Sketch the graphs of $f(x) = \left(\dfrac{1}{2}\right)^x$ and $g(x) = \left(\dfrac{1}{3}\right)^x$ on the same coordinate axes.

Answer

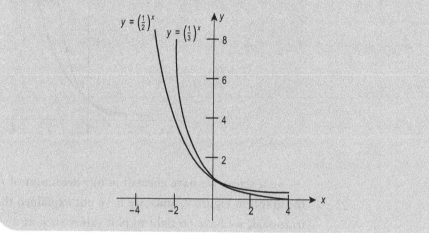

$y = \left(\frac{1}{2}\right)^x$ $y = \left(\frac{1}{3}\right)^x$

Properties of the Exponential Functions

There are a number of interesting observations we can make by examining the graphs in Figures 9 and 10, and the answers to Progress Checks 1 and 2. (Recall that the definition of the exponential functions $f(x) = a^x$ requires that $a > 0$ and $a \neq 1$.)

- The graph of $f(x) = a^x$ always passes through the point $(0, 1)$ since $a^0 = 1$.
- There are two basic types of exponential functions. The general shape of $f(x) = a^x$ when $a > 1$ can be seen in Figure 9 and in the answer to Progress Check 1; f is an increasing function. The general shape of $f(x) = a^x$ when $0 < a < 1$ can be seen in Figure 10 and in the answer to Progress Check 2; f is a decreasing function.
- The domain of $f(x) = a^x$ consists of the set of all real numbers; the range is the set of all positive real numbers.
- If $a < b$, then $a^x < b^x$ for all $x > 0$ and $a^x > b^x$ for all $x < 0$. Notice in the answers to Progress Checks 1 and 2 that the curves exchange positions as they cross the y-axis, that is, at $x = 0$.

Properties of Exponential Functions

Since a^x is either increasing or decreasing, it never assumes the same value twice. (Recall that $a \neq 1$.) This leads to a useful conclusion.

> If $a^u = a^v$ then $u = v$.

The graphs of a^x and b^x intersect only at $x = 0$. This observation provides us with the following result.

> If $a^u = b^u$ for $u \neq 0$, then $a = b$.

EXAMPLE 3   SOLVING EQUATIONS WITH EXPONENTS

Solve for x.

(a) $3^{10} = 3^{5x}$ (b) $2^7 = (x - 1)^7$ (c) $3^{3x} = 9^{x-1}$

SOLUTIONS

(a) Since $a^u = a^v$ implies $u = v$, we have

$$10 = 5x$$
$$2 = x$$

(b) Since $a^u = b^u$ implies $a = b$, we have

$$2 = x - 1$$
$$3 = x$$

(c) First,

$$3^{3x} = 9^{x-1} = (3^2)^{x-1} = 3^{2x-2}$$

Since $a^u = a^v$ implies $u = v$, we have

$$3x = 2x - 2$$
$$x = -2$$

✔ Progress Check 3

Solve for x.

(a) $2^8 = 2^{x+1}$ (b) $4^{2x+1} = 4^{11}$ (c) $8^{x+1} = 2$

Answers

(a) 7   (b) 5   (c) $-\dfrac{2}{3}$

The Number e

There is an irrational number, denoted by the letter e, that plays an important role in mathematics. In calculus, we show that the expression

$$\left(1 + \frac{1}{m}\right)^m$$

gets closer and closer to the number e as m gets larger and larger. We can evaluate this expression for different values of m, as shown in Table 1.

TABLE 1   Approximating the Value of e

m	1	2	10	100	1000	10,000	100,000	1,000,000
$\left(1 + \dfrac{1}{m}\right)^m$	2.0	2.25	2.5937	2.7048	2.7169	2.7181	2.7182	2.71828

From this table we see that as m gets larger and larger, the expression

$$\left(1 + \frac{1}{m}\right)^m$$

gets closer and closer to the irrational number e (to five decimal places), which is approximated as 2.71828. The number e was named by the Swiss mathematician Leonhard Euler (1707–1783), one of the greatest mathematicians of all time.

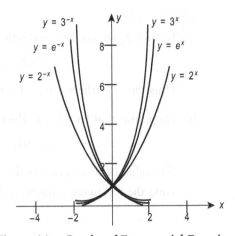

Figure 11   Graphs of Exponential Functions

The graphs of $y = e^x$ and $y = e^{-x}$ are shown in Figure 11.

Applications

Exponential functions occur in a wide variety of applied problems. We will look at problems dealing with population growth, such as the growth of bacteria in a culture medium; radioactive decay, such as determining the half-life in strontium 90; and interest earned when the interest rate is compounded.

Exponential Growth

The function Q defined by

$$Q(t) = q_0 e^{kt} \quad (k > 0)$$

where the variable t represents time, is called an **exponential growth model**; k is a constant and t is the independent variable. We may think of $Q(t)$ as the quantity of a substance available at any given time t. Note that when $t = 0$ we have

$$Q(0) = q_0 e^0 = q_0$$

which says that q_0 is the initial quantity. (It is customary to use the subscript 0 to denote an initial value.) The constant k is called the **growth constant**.

EXAMPLE 4   APPLICATIONS: EXPONENTIAL GROWTH MODEL

The number of bacteria in a culture after t hours is described by the exponential growth model

$$Q(t) = 50e^{0.7t}$$

(a) Find the initial number of bacteria, q_0, in the culture.

(b) How many bacteria are there in the culture after 10 hours?

SOLUTIONS

(a) To find q_0 we need to evaluate $Q(t)$ at $t = 0$.

$$Q(0) = 50e^0 = 50 = q_0$$

Thus, initially there are 50 bacteria in the culture.

(b) The number of bacteria in the culture after 10 hours is given by

$$Q(10) = 50e^{0.7(10)} = 50e^7$$

The value of e^7 can be obtained with a calculator that has an "e^x" key by using the following sequence of keystrokes:

$$7 \quad \boxed{e^x}$$

The displayed answer is

$$1096.6$$

On a calculator that doesn't have an "e^x" key but has a "y^x" key, we use the following sequence of keystrokes:

$$2.71828 \quad \boxed{y^x} \quad 7 \quad \boxed{=}$$

(2.71828 is the approximate value of e.) The displayed answer is again 1096.6. Then

$$Q(10) = 50(1096.6) = 54{,}830$$

Thus, there are 54,830 bacteria in the culture after 10 hours.

In Section 11.3 we will show another way of computing e^7, using a calculator without a "y^x" key.

✔ **Progress Check 4**

The number of bacteria in a culture after t minutes is described by the exponential growth model $Q(t) = q_0 e^{0.005t}$. If there were 100 bacteria present initially, how many bacteria will be present after one hour has elapsed?

Answer

135

Exponential Decay

The model defined by the function

$$Q(t) = q_0 e^{-kt} \quad (k > 0)$$

is called an **exponential decay model**; k is a constant, called the **decay constant**, and t is the independent variable representing time.

In exponential growth and decay models, the growth (or decay) constant k is often given as a percentage. Thus, if the growth constant is 3%, then $k = 0.03$; and if the growth constant is 30%, then $k = 0.30$. Moreover, the growth (or decay) constant is also called the **growth** (or **decay**) **rate**.

EXAMPLE 5   APPLICATION: EXPONENTIAL DECAY MODEL

A substance has a decay rate of 5% per hour. If 500 grams is present initially, how much of the substance will remain after 4 hours?

SOLUTION

The general equation of an exponential decay model is

$$Q(t) = q_0 e^{-kt}$$

In our model, $q_0 = 500$ grams (since the quantity available initially is 500 grams) and $k = 0.05$ (since the decay rate is 5% per hour). After 4 hours

$$Q(4) = 500e^{-0.05(4)} = 500e^{-0.2} \approx 500(0.8187) \approx 409.4$$

(You will find the value $e^{-2} \approx 0.8187$ on a calculator.) Thus, 409.4 grams of the substance will remain.

✔ Progress Check 5

The number of grams Q of a certain radioactive substance present after t seconds is given by the exponential decay model $Q(t) = q_0 e^{-0.4t}$. If 200 grams of the substance is present initially, find how much will remain after 6 seconds.

Answer

18.1 grams

Compound Interest

In Section 3.2 we studied simple interest as an application of linear equations. Recall that if the principal P is invested at a simple annual interest rate r for t years, then the amount or sum S that we will have on hand is given by

$$S = P + Prt$$

or

$$S = P(1 + rt)$$

In many business transactions the interest that is added to the principal at regular time intervals also earns interest. This is called the **compound interest** process.

The time period between successive additions of interest is known as the **conversion period**. Thus, if interest is compounded quarterly, the conversion period is three months; if interest is compounded semiannually, the conversion period is six months.

Suppose now that a principal P is invested at an annual interest rate r, compounded k times a year. Then each conversion period lasts $1/k$ years. Thus, the amount S_1 at the end of the first conversion period is

$$S_1 = P + Prt = P + P \cdot r \cdot \frac{1}{k} = P\left(1 + \frac{r}{k}\right)$$

The amount S_2 at the end of the second conversion period is

$$S_2 = S_1 + \text{interest earned by } S_1$$

$$= P\left(1 + \frac{r}{k}\right) + P\left(1 + \frac{r}{k}\right) \cdot r \cdot \frac{1}{k}$$

$$= \left[P\left(1 + \frac{r}{k}\right)\right]\left(1 + \frac{r}{k}\right)$$

or

$$S_2 = P\left(1 + \frac{r}{k}\right)^2$$

In this way, we see that the amount S after n conversion periods is given by

$$S = P\left(1 + \frac{r}{k}\right)^n$$

which is usually written

$$S = P(1 + i)^n$$

where $i = r/k$. Values of $(1 + i)^n$ can be obtained by using a calculator with a "y^x" or "x^x" key.

EXAMPLE 6   APPLICATION: COMPOUND INTEREST

Suppose that $6000 is invested at an annual interest rate of 8% compounded quarterly. What will the value of the investment be after 3 years?

SOLUTION

We are given $P = 6000$, $r = 0.08$, $k = 4$, and $n = 12$ (since there are four conversion periods per year for three years). Thus,

$$i = \frac{r}{k} = \frac{0.08}{4} = 0.02$$

and

$$S = P(1 + i)^n = 6000(1 + 0.02)^{12}$$

Using a calculator, with $i = 0.02$ and $n = 12$, we obtain

$$S \approx 6000(1.26824179) \approx 7609.45$$

Thus, the sum at the end of the three-year period will be $7609.45.

✔ **Progress Check 6**

Suppose that $5000 is invested at an annual interest rate of 6% compounded semiannually. What is the value of the investment after 12 years?

Answer

$10,163.97

Continuous Compounding

When P, r, and t are held fixed and the frequency of compounding is increased, the return on the investment is increased. We wish to determine the effect of making the number of conversions per year larger and larger.

Suppose a principal P is invested at an annual rate r, compounded k times per year. After t years, the number of conversions is $n = tk$. Then the value of the investment after t years is

$$S = P\left(1 + \frac{r}{k}\right)^{tk}$$

Letting $m = k/r$, we can rewrite this equation as

$$S = P\left(1 + \frac{1}{m}\right)^{tmr}$$

or

$$S = P\left[\left(1 + \frac{1}{m}\right)^{m}\right]^{rt}$$

If the number of conversions k per year gets larger and larger, then m gets larger and larger. Since we saw in Table 1 of this chapter that the expression

$$\left(1 + \frac{1}{m}\right)^{m}$$

gets closer and closer to e as m gets larger and larger, we conclude that

$$S = Pe^{rt} \tag{1}$$

As the number of conversions increases, so does the value of the investment. However, there is a limit, or bound, to this value, and it is given by Equation (1). We say that Equation (1) represents the result of **continuous compounding**.

EXAMPLE 7   APPLICATION: CONTINUOUS COMPOUNDING

Suppose that $20,000 is invested at an annual interest rate of 7% compounded continuously. What is the value of the investment after 4 years?

SOLUTION

We have $P = 20,000$, $r = 0.07$, and $t = 4$, and we substitute in Equation (1):

$$S = Pe^{rt}$$
$$= 20,000e^{0.07(4)}$$
$$= 20,000e^{0.28}$$
$$\approx 20,000(1.3231) \qquad \text{from a calculator}$$
$$= 26,462$$

The sum available after 4 years is $26,462.

✔ Progress Check 7

Suppose that $10,000 is invested at an annual interest rate of 10% compounded continuously. What is the value of the investment after 6 years?

Answer

$18,221

By solving Equation (1) for P, we can determine the principal P that must be invested at continuous compounding to have a certain amount S at some future time. The values of e^{-x} will be used in this connection.

EXAMPLE 8   APPLICATION: CONTINUOUS COMPOUNDING

Suppose that a principal P is to be invested at continuous compound interest of 8% per year to yield $10,000 in 5 years. Approximately how much should be invested?

SOLUTION

Using Equation (1) with $S = 10,000$, $r = 0.08$, and $t = 5$, we have

$$S = Pe^{rt}$$
$$10,000 = Pe^{0.08(5)} = Pe^{0.40}$$
$$P = \frac{10,000}{e^{0.40}}$$
$$= 10,000e^{-0.40}$$
$$= 10,000(0.6703) \qquad \text{from a calculator}$$
$$\approx 6703$$

Thus, approximately $6703 should be invested initially.

✔ **Progress Check 8**

Approximately how much money should a 35-year-old woman invest now at continuous compound interest of 10% per year to obtain the sum of $20,000 upon her retirement at age 65?

Answer

$996

Exercise Set 11.2

In Exercises 1–18 sketch the graph of the given function f.

1. $f(x) = 4^x$

2. $f(x) = 4^{-x}$

3. $f(x) = \left(\frac{1}{4}\right)^x$

4. $f(x) = \left(\frac{1}{4}\right)^{-x}$

5. $f(x) = \left(\frac{1}{2}\right)2^x$

6. $f(x) = \left(-\frac{1}{3}\right)2^x$

7. $f(x) = 2(3^x)$

8. $f(x) = -2(3^x)$

9. $f(x) = 2^{x+1}$

10. $f(x) = 2^{x-1}$

11. $f(x) = 2^{2x}$

12. $f(x) = 3^{-2x}$

13. $f(x) = e^{2x}$

14. $f(x) = e^{-2x}$

15. $f(x) = e^{x+1}$

16. $f(x) = e^{x-2}$

17. $f(x) = 40e^{0.20x}$

18. $f(x) = 50e^{-0.40x}$

In Exercises 19–32 solve for x.

19. $2^x = 2^3$

20. $2^{x-1} = 2^4$

21. $2^{2x-1} = 2^5$

22. $3^{-x+1} = 3^4$

23. $3^x = 9^{x-2}$

24. $2^x = 8^{x+2}$

25. $2^{3x} = 4^{x+1}$

26. $3^{4x} = 9^{x-1}$

27. $e^x = e^3$

28. $e^{x-1} = e^3$

29. $e^{2x+1} = e^3$

30. $e^{-2x-3} = e^9$

31. $e^x = e^{2x+1}$

32. $e^{x-1} = 1$

In Exercises 33–36 solve for a.

33. $(a + 1)^x = (2a - 1)^x$

34. $(2a + 1)^x = (a + 4)^x$

35. $(a + 1)^x = (2a)^x$

36. $(2a + 3)^x = (3a + 1)^x$

37. The number of bacteria in a culture after t hours is described by the exponential growth model $Q(t) = 200e^{0.25t}$.

   (a) What is the initial number of bacteria in the culture?

   (b) What is the growth constant?

   (c) Find the number of bacteria in the culture after 20 hours.

   (d) Use a calculator to help you complete the following table.

t	1	4	8	10
$Q(t)$				

38. The number of bacteria in a culture after t hours is described by the exponential growth model $Q(t) = q_0 e^{0.01t}$. If there were 500 bacteria present initially, how many bacteria will be present after 2 *days*?

39. At the beginning of 1975, the world population was approximately 4 billion. Suppose that the population is described by an exponential growth model and that the growth rate is 2% per year. Give the approximate world population in the year 2000.

40. The number of grams of potassium 42 present after t hours is given by the exponential decay model $Q(t) = q_0 e^{-0.055t}$. If 400 grams of the substance is present initially, how much will remain after 10 hours?

41. A radioactive substance has a decay rate of 4% per hour. If 100 grams is present initially, how much of the substance will remain after 10 hours?

42. An investor purchases a $12,000 savings certificate paying 10% annual interest compounded semiannually. Find the amount that will be received when the savings certificate is redeemed at the end of 8 years.

43. The parents of a newborn infant place $10,000 in an investment that pays 8% annual interest compounded quarterly. What sum will be available at the end of 18 years to finance the child's college education?

44. A widow is offered a choice of two investments. Investment A pays 5% annual interest compounded semiannually, and investment B pays 6% compounded annually. Which investment will yield a greater return?

45. A firm intends to replace its present computer in 5 years. The treasurer suggests that $25,000 be set aside in an investment paying 6% compounded monthly. What sum will be available for the purchase of the new computer?

In Exercises 46–50 use a calculator to assist in the computations.

46. If $5000 is invested at an annual interest rate of 9% compounded continuously, how much will be available after 5 years?

47. If $100 is invested at an annual interest rate of 5.5% compounded continuously, how much will be available after 10 years?

48. A principal P is to be invested at continuous compound interest of 9% to yield $50,000 in 20 years. What is the approximate value of P to be invested?

49. A 40-year-old executive plans to retire at age 65. How much should be invested at 12% annual interest compounded continuously to provide the sum of $50,000 upon retirement?

50. Investment A offers 8% annual interest compounded semiannually, and investment B offers 8% annual interest compounded continuously. If $1000 were invested in each, what would be the approximate difference in value after 10 years?

In Exercises 51 and 52 use a calculator to determine which number is greater.

51. 2^{π}, π^2

52. 3^{π}, π^3

53. MATHEMATICS IN WRITING: Write a PROGRAM in your calculator that will enable the user to enter the principal, interest rate, and time for an investment, and will return the value of the investment. You may be able to find such a program at your calculator manufacturer's website.

54. Under what circumstances is an exponential function increasing (rising) or decreasing? Compare Exercises 2, 3, and 4. How can you rewrite

$$f(x) = \left(\frac{1}{4}\right)^x$$

so that $a > 1$? What conclusions can you draw?

11.3 Logarithmic Functions

The two forms of the graph of $f(x) = a^x$ are shown in Figure 12. We have previously noted that the range of the function $f(x) = a^x$ is the set of all positive real numbers. When we combine this fact with the observation that $f(x) = a^x$ is either increasing or decreasing (since $a \neq 1$), we can conclude that the exponential function is a one-to-one function.

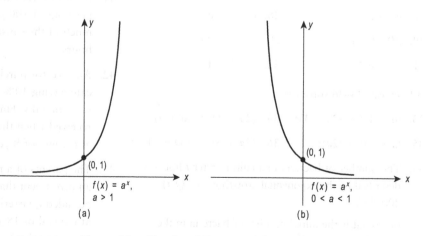

Figure 12   **Graphs of Exponential Functions**

Logarithms as Exponents

In Figure 13a, we see the function $f(x) = 2^x$ assigning values in the set Y to various values of x in the domain X. Since $f(x) = 2^x$ is a one-to-one function, it makes sense to seek a function f^{-1} that will return the values of the range of f back to their corresponding domain values, as in Figure 13b. That is,

$$f \text{ maps 3 into 8, } f^{-1} \text{ maps 8 into 3}$$

$$f \text{ maps 4 into 16, } f^{-1} \text{ maps 16 into 4}$$

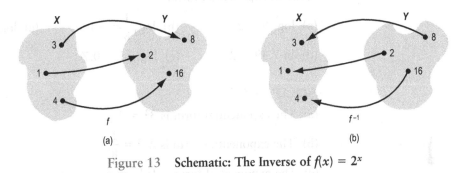

Figure 13   Schematic: The Inverse of $f(x) = 2^x$

and so on. We saw in Section 11.2 that the domain of $f(x) = 2^x$ is the set of real numbers, hence the range of f^{-1} is the set of real numbers. The range of $f(x) = 2^x$ is the set of positive real numbers, so the *domain* of f^{-1} is the set of positive real numbers.

The function f^{-1} of Figure 13b has a special name, the **logarithmic function base 2**, which we write as $\log_2$. It is also possible to generalize and define the logarithmic function as the inverse of the exponential function with any base a such that $a > 0$ and $a \neq 1$.

Logarithmic Function Base a

$$y = \log_a x \quad \text{if and only if} \quad x = a^y, a > 0, a \neq 1$$

Examination of this definition shows that a *logarithm* is an *exponent*. If a is a positive number, then $\log_a x$ represents that power to which a must be raised to obtain x. Thus,

$$\log_2 16 = 4$$

since 2 must be raised to the fourth power to obtain 16. Similarly,

$$\log_{10} 100 = 2$$

since $10^2 = 100$. In short, when $a > 0$ and $a \neq 1$,

$$y = \log_a x \quad \text{and} \quad x = a^y$$

are equivalent statements. Also, since a^y is always positive, it follows that $\log_a x$ is defined only when x is positive. When no base is indicated, the notation $\log x$ is interpreted to mean $\log_{10} x$, which is called a **common logarithm**.

The notation $\ln x$ is used to indicate logarithms to the base e. Since $\ln x$ is the inverse of the natural exponential function e^x, it is called the **natural logarithm of x**. Thus, we have

Natural Logarithm

$$\ln x = \log_e x$$

EXAMPLE 1   LOGARITHMS AS EXPONENTS

Write in exponential form.

(a) $\log_3 9 = 2$ 　　　(b) $\log_2 \dfrac{1}{8} = -3$ 　　　(c) $\log_{16} 4 = \dfrac{1}{2}$

(d) $\ln 7.39 = 2$ 　　　(e) $\log_{10} 5 = 0.70$

SOLUTIONS

(a) The exponential form is $3^2 = 9$.

(b) The exponential form is $2^{-3} = \dfrac{1}{8}$.

(c) The exponential form is $16^{1/2} = 4$.

(d) The exponential form is $e^2 = 7.39$.

(e) The exponential form is $10^{0.70} = 5$.

✔ Progress Check 1

Write in exponential form.

(a) $\log_4 64 = 3$ 　(b) $\log_{10}\left(\dfrac{1}{10,000}\right) = -4$ 　(c) $\log_{25} 5 = \dfrac{1}{2}$ 　(d) $\ln 0.05 = -3$

Answers

(a) $4^3 = 64$ 　　(b) $10^{-4} = \dfrac{1}{10,000}$ 　　(c) $25^{1/2} = 5$ 　(d) $e^{-3} = 0.05$

EXAMPLE 2   LOGARITHMS AS EXPONENTS

Write in logarithmic form.

(a) $36 = 6^2$ 　　(b) $7 = \sqrt{49}$ 　　(c) $\dfrac{1}{16} = 4^{-2}$ 　　(d) $0.1353 = e^{-2}$

SOLUTIONS

(a) The logarithmic form is $\log_6 36 = 2$.

(b) The logarithmic form is $\log_{49} 7 = \dfrac{1}{2}$.

(c) The logarithmic form is $\log_4 \dfrac{1}{16} = -2$.

(d) The logarithmic form is $\ln 0.1353 = -2$.

✔ **Progress Check 2**

Write in logarithmic form.

(a) $64 = 8^2$ (b) $6 = 36^{1/2}$ (c) $\dfrac{1}{7} = 7^{-1}$ (d) $20.09 = e^3$

Answers

(a) $\log_8 64 = 2$ (b) $\log_{36} 6 = \dfrac{1}{2}$ (c) $\log_7 \dfrac{1}{7} = -1$ (d) $\ln 20.09 = 3$

Logarithmic equations can often be solved by changing to an equivalent exponential form.

EXAMPLE 3   SOLVING LOGARITHMIC EQUATIONS

Solve for x:

(a) $\log_3 x = -2$ (b) $\log_5 125 = x$ (c) $\log_x 81 = 4$ (d) $\ln x = \dfrac{1}{2}$

SOLUTIONS

(a) The equivalent exponential form is

$$x = 3^{-2}$$

Thus

$$x = \frac{1}{9}$$

(b) In exponential form, we have

$$5^x = 125$$

Writing 125 in exponential form to the base 5, we have

$$5^x = 5^3$$

and since $a^x = a^y$ implies $x = y$, we conclude that

$$x = 3$$

(c) The equivalent exponential form is

$$x^4 = 81 = 3^4$$

and thus

$$x = 3$$

(d) The equivalent exponential form is

$$x = e^{1/2}$$

or

$$x \approx 1.65$$

which we obtain by using a calculator with a "y^x" key.

Measuring an Earthquake

Richter Scale Readings

Here's what you can anticipate from an earthquake of various Richter scale readings.

2.0 not noticed

4.5 some damage in a very limited area

6.0 hazardous; serious damage with destruction of buildings in a limited area

7.0 felt over a wide area with significant damage

8.0 great damage

9.5 maximum recorded

The great San Francisco earthquake of 1906 is estimated to have had a Richter scale reading of 8.3.

Radio and television newscasts often describe earthquakes in this way: "A minor earthquake in China registered 3.0 on the Richter scale," or, "A major earthquake in Chile registered 8.0 on the Richter scale." From statements like these we know that 3.0 is a "low" value and 8.0 is a "high" value, but just what is the Richter scale?

On the Richter scale, the magnitude of R of an earthquake is defined as

$$R = \log \frac{l}{l_o}$$

where l_o is a constant that represents a standard intensity and l is the intensity of the earthquake being measured. The Richter scale is a means of measuring a given earthquake against a "standard earthquake" of intensity l_o.

What does 3.0 on the Richter scale mean? Substituting $R = 3$ in the above equation, we have

$$3 = \log \frac{l}{l_o}$$

or in the equivalent exponential form,

$$1000 = \frac{l}{l_o}$$

Solving for l, we have

$$l = 1000 l_o$$

which states that an earthquake with a Richter scale reading of 3.0 is 1000 times as intense as the standard. No wonder, then, that an earthquake registering 8.0 on the Richter scale is serious: it has an intensity 100,000,000 times that of the standard!

✔ **Progress Check 3**

Solve for x:

(a) $\log_x 1000 = 3$ (b) $\log_2 x = 5$ (c) $x = \log_7 \frac{1}{49}$

Answers

(a) 10   (b) 32   (c) -2

Logarithmic Identities

If $f(x) = a^x$, then $f^{-1}(x) = \log_a x$. Recall that inverse functions have the property that

$$f[f^{-1}(x)] = x \quad \text{and} \quad f^{-1}[f(x)] = x$$

Substituting $f(x) = a^x$ and $f^{-1}(x) = \log_a x$, we have

$$f[f^{-1}(x)] = x \qquad\qquad f^{-1}[f(x)] = x$$
$$f(\log_a x) = x \qquad\qquad f^{-1}(a^x) = x$$
$$a^{\log_a x} = x \qquad\qquad \log_a a^x = x$$

These two identities are useful in simplifying expressions and should be remembered.

$$a^{\log_a x} = x$$
$$\log_a a^x = x$$

Here is another pair of identities that can be verified by converting to the equivalent exponential form:

$$\log_a a = 1$$
$$\log_a 1 = 0$$

EXAMPLE 4   APPLYING THE LOGARITHMIC IDENTITIES

Evaluate.

(a) $8^{\log_8 5}$ (b) $\log 10^{-3}$ (c) $\log_7 7$ (d) $\log_4 1$

SOLUTIONS

(a) $8^{\log_8 5} = 5$ (b) $\log 10^{-3} = -3$ (c) $\log_7 7 = 1$ (d) $\log_4 1 = 0$

✔ Progress Check 4

Evaluate.

(a) $\log_3 3^4$ (b) $6^{\log_6 9}$ (c) $\log_5 1$ (d) $\log_8 8$

Answers

(a) 4   (b) 9   (c) 0   (d) 1

Graphs of Logarithmic Functions

An easy way to graph $y = \log_a x$ is to convert to the equivalent exponential form $x = a^y$ and graph the second equation.

EXAMPLE 5   GRAPH OF A LOGARITHMIC FUNCTION

Sketch the graph of $f(x) = \log_2 x$.

SOLUTION

To obtain the equivalent exponential equation, let

$$y = \log_2 x$$

Then solve for x by converting to the equivalent exponential form.

$$x = 2^y$$

Now we form a table of values of $x = 2^y$.

y	-3	-2	-1	0	1	2	3
$x = 2^y$	$\dfrac{1}{8}$	$\dfrac{1}{4}$	$\dfrac{1}{2}$	1	2	4	8

We can now plot these points and sketch a smooth curve, as in Figure 14. We have included the graph of $y = 2^x$ to illustrate that the graphs of a pair of inverse functions are reflections of each other about the line $y = x$.

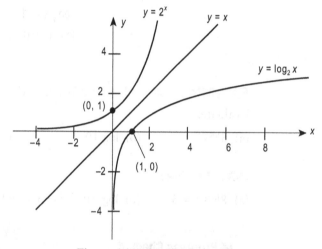

Figure 14   **Graph of $y = \log_2 x$**

✔ Progress Check 5

Sketch the graphs of $y = \log_3 x$ and $y = \log_{1/3} x$ on the same coordinate axes.

Answer

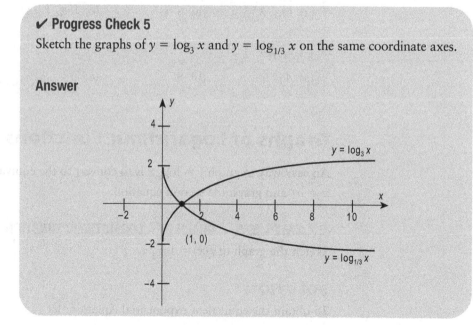

Properties of Logarithmic Functions

We can reach several conclusions by examining the graph in Figure 14 and the answer to Progress Check 5.

Properties of Logarithmic Functions

- The point $(1, 0)$ lies on the curve $y = \log_a x$ for any positive real number a. This is another way of saying $\log_a 1 = 0$.

- The domain of $f(x) = \log_a x$ is the set of all positive real numbers; the range is the set of all real numbers.

- When $a > 1$, $f(x) = \log_a x$ is an increasing function; when $0 < a < 1$, $f(x) = \log_a x$ is a decreasing function.

Since $\log_a x$ is either increasing or decreasing, the same value cannot be assumed more than once. Thus,

$$\text{If } \log_a x = \log_a y, \text{ then } x = y.$$

Since the graphs of $\log_a x$ and $\log_b x$ intersect only at $x = 1$, we have

$$\text{If } \log_a x = \log_b x \text{ and } x \neq 1, \text{ then } a = b.$$

EXAMPLE 6   SOLVING LOGARITHMIC EQUATIONS

Solve for x.

(a) $\log_5(x + 1) = \log_5 25$ (b) $\log_{x-1} 31 = \log_5 31$

SOLUTIONS

(a) $\log_5(x + 1) = \log_5 25$

$\quad\quad\quad x + 1 = 25$ If $\log_a x = \log_a y$, then $x = y$.

$\quad\quad\quad\quad\quad x = 24$

(b) $\log_{x-1} 31 = \log_5 31$

$\quad\quad\quad x - 1 = 5$ If $\log_a x = \log_b x$ and $x \neq 1$, then $a = b$.

$\quad\quad\quad\quad\quad x = 6$

✔ Progress Check 6

Solve for x.

(a) $\log_2 x^2 = \log_9 9$

(b) $\log_7 14 = \log_{2x} 14$

Answers

(a) $3, -3$

(b) $\dfrac{7}{2}$

In Section 11.2, we showed an easy way to calculate the value of an expression such as e^7, using a calculator and an "e^x" key. When a calculator doesn't have such a key but has an "ln" and a "y^x" key, we use the following sequence of keystrokes to calculate e^7:

$$7 \quad \boxed{\text{INV}} \quad \boxed{\text{ln}}$$

The displayed answer is

$$1096.6$$

The above sequence of keystrokes does the following: the number 7 is assigned to x. Since the inverse of $\ln x$ is e^x, the calculator now computes $e^x = e^7$.

Exercise Set 11.3

In Exercises 1–12 write the expression in exponential form.

1. $\log_2 4 = 2$

2. $\log_5 125 = 3$

3. $\log_9 \dfrac{1}{81} = -2$

4. $\log_{64} 4 = \dfrac{1}{3}$

5. $\ln 20.09 = 3$

6. $\ln \dfrac{1}{739} = -2$

7. $\log 1000 = 3$

8. $\log \dfrac{1}{1000} = -3$

9. $\ln 1 = 0$

10. $\log 0.01 = -2$

11. $\log_3 \dfrac{1}{27} = -3$

12. $\log_{125} \dfrac{1}{5} = -\dfrac{1}{3}$

In Exercises 13–26 write the expression in logarithmic form.

13. $25 = 5^2$

14. $27 = 3^3$

15. $10{,}000 = 10^4$

16. $\dfrac{1}{100} = 10^{-2}$

17. $\dfrac{1}{8} = 2^{-3}$

18. $\dfrac{1}{27} = 3^{-3}$

19. $1 = 2^0$

20. $1 = e^0$

21. $6 = \sqrt{36}$

22. $2 = \sqrt[3]{8}$

23. $64 = 16^{3/2}$

24. $81 = 27^{4/3}$

25. $\dfrac{1}{3} = 27^{-1/3}$

26. $\dfrac{1}{2} = 16^{-1/4}$

In Exercises 27–48 solve for x.

27. $\log_5 x = 2$

28. $\log_4 x = 2$

29. $\log_{16} x = \dfrac{1}{2}$

30. $\log_{25} x = -\dfrac{1}{2}$

31. $\log_{1/2} x = 3$

32. $\log_2 x = 1$

33. $\ln x = 2$

34. $\ln x = -3$

35. $\ln x = \dfrac{1}{3}$

36. $\ln x = -\dfrac{1}{2}$

37. $\log_4 64 = x$

38. $\log_5 \dfrac{1}{25} = x$

39. $\log_x 4 = \dfrac{1}{2}$

40. $\log_x \dfrac{1}{8} = -\dfrac{1}{3}$

41. $\log_3 (x - 1) = 2$

42. $\log_5 (x + 1) = 3$

43. $\log_3 (x + 1) = \log_3 27$

44. $\log_2 (x - 1) = \log_2 10$

45. $\log_{x+1} 24 = \log_3 24$

46. $\log_3 x^3 = \log_3 64$

47. $\log_{x+1} 17 = \log_4 17$

48. $\log_{3x} 18 = \log_4 18$

In Exercises 49–72 compute the given expression.

49. $3^{\log_3 6}$

50. $2^{\log_2 (2/3)}$

51. $e^{\ln 2}$

52. $e^{\ln 1/2}$

53. $\log_5 5^3$

54. $\log_4 4^{-2}$

55. $\log_8 8^{1/2}$

56. $\log_{64} 64^{-1/3}$

57. $\log_7 49$

58. $\log_7 \sqrt{7}$

59. $\log_5 5$

60. $\ln e$

61. $\ln 1$

62. $\log_4 1$

63. $\log_3 \dfrac{1}{3}$

64. $\log_2 \dfrac{1}{4}$

65. $\log_{16} 4$

66. $\log_{36}\left(\dfrac{1}{6}\right)$

67. $\log 10{,}000$

68. $\log 0.001$

69. $\ln e^2$

70. $\ln e^{1/3}$

71. $\ln e^{-2/3}$

72. $\ln e^{-3}$

In Exercises 73–80 sketch the graph of the given function.

73. $f(x) = \log_4 x$

74. $f(x) = \log_{1/2} x$

75. $f(x) = \log 2x$

76. $f(x) = \dfrac{1}{2} \log x$

77. $f(x) = \ln \dfrac{x}{2}$

78. $f(x) = \ln 3x$

79. $f(x) = \log_3 (x - 1)$

80. $f(x) = \log_3 (x + 1)$

81. When are the values of $y = 3\log(x - 2)$ greater than zero? Graph the function in your graphing calculator and copy the graph carefully onto a sheet of paper. Make the part of the graph above the x-axis bolder.

82. Using calculus, an advanced mathematics student can show that $\ln x \approx x - 1$ for values of x near 1. Try it out: compare $\ln 1.002$ with $1.002 - 1$. Graph both functions, as shown below, and then select a viewing window that reveals that the two graphs are very similar near $x = 1$.

```
Plot1 Plot2 Plot3
\Y1▆ln(X)
\Y2▆X-1
\Y3=
·\Y4=
·\Y5=
·\Y6=
·\Y7=
```

11.4 Fundamental Properties of Logarithms

There are fundamental properties of logarithms that have made them a powerful computational aid.

Fundamental Properties of Logarithms

Property 1. $\log_a(x \cdot y) = \log_a x + \log_a y$

Property 2. $\log_a\left(\dfrac{x}{y}\right) = \log_a x - \log_a y$

Property 3. $\log_a x^r = r \log_a x, \quad r$ a real number

These properties can be proved by using equivalent exponential forms. To prove the first property, $\log_a(x \cdot y) = \log_a x + \log_a y$, we let

$$\log_a x = u \quad \text{and} \quad \log_a y = v$$

Then the equivalent exponential forms are

$$a^u = x \quad \text{and} \quad a^v = y$$

Multiplying the left-hand and right-hand sides of these equations, we have

$$a^u \cdot a^v = x \cdot y$$

or

$$a^{u+v} = x \cdot y$$

Writing this statement in equivalent logarithmic form gives

$$\log_a(x \cdot y) = u + v$$
$$= \log_a x + \log_a y$$

Properties 2 and 3 can be established in much the same way.

EXAMPLE 1   USING THE FUNDAMENTAL PROPERTIES OF LOGARITHMS
Write in terms of simpler logarithmic forms:

(a) $\log(225 \cdot 478)$ (b) $\log_8\left(\dfrac{422}{735}\right)$ (c) $\log_2(2^5)$

(d) $\log_3(x \cdot y \cdot z)$ (e) $\log_a\left(\dfrac{x \cdot y}{z}\right)$

SOLUTIONS
(a) $\log(225 \cdot 478) = \log 225 + \log 478$

(b) $\log_8\left(\dfrac{422}{735}\right) = \log_8 422 - \log_8 735$

(c) $\log_2(2^5) = 5\log_2 2 = 5 \cdot 1 = 5$, since $\log_2 2 = 1$

(d) $\log_3(x \cdot y \cdot z) = \log_3 x + \log_3 y + \log_3 z$

(e) $\log_a\left(\dfrac{x \cdot y}{z}\right) = \log_a x + \log_a y - \log_a z$

✔ **Progress Check 1**
Write in terms of simpler logarithmic forms:

(a) $\log_4(1.47 \cdot 22.3)$ (b) $\log_5\left(\dfrac{149}{37.62}\right)$

(c) $\log_6 8^4$ (d) $\log_a\left(\dfrac{m \cdot n}{p \cdot q}\right)$

Answers
(a) $\log_4 1.47 + \log_4 22.3$ (b) $\log_5 149 - \log_5 37.62$
(c) $4\log_6 8$ (d) $\log_a m + \log_a n - \log_a p - \log_a q$

EXAMPLE 2   USING THE FUNDAMENTAL PROPERTIES OF LOGARITHMS

Write in terms of simpler logarithmic forms:

(a) $\log_a(xy^2)$ (b) $\log_a\left[\dfrac{x^2y^{3/2}}{(z+1)^5}\right]$

SOLUTIONS

(a) $\log_a(xy^2) = \log_a x + \log_a y^2$ Property 1

$\qquad\qquad\quad = \log_a x + 2\log_a y$ Property 3

(b) $\log_a\left[\dfrac{x^2y^{3/2}}{(z+1)^5}\right] = \log_a(x^2y^{3/2}) - \log_a(z+1)^5$ Property 2

$\qquad\qquad\qquad = \log_a x^2 + \log_a y^{3/2} - \log_a(z+1)^5$ Property 1

$\qquad\qquad\qquad = 2\log_a x + \dfrac{3}{2}\log_a y - 5\log_a(z+1)$ Property 3

✔ Progress Check 2

Write in terms of simpler logarithmic forms:

(a) $\log_a\dfrac{x-1}{\sqrt{x}}$

(b) $\log_a\dfrac{(x+1)^5(x-1)^4}{x^2}$

Answers

(a) $\log_a(x-1) - \dfrac{1}{2}\log_a x$ (b) $5\log_a(x+1) + 4\log_a(x-1) - 2\log_a x$

Simplifying Logarithms

The next example illustrates steps that simplify the handling of logarithmic forms.

EXAMPLE 3   USING THE FUNDAMENTAL PROPERTIES OF LOGARITHMS

Write $\log_a\dfrac{(x-1)^{-2}(y+2)^3}{\sqrt{x}}$ in terms of simpler logarithmic forms.

SOLUTION

$\log_a\dfrac{(x-1)^{-2}(y+2)^3}{x^{1/2}}$

$\qquad = \log_a\left[(x-1)^{-2}(y+2)^3\right] - \log_a x^{1/2}$ Property 2

$\qquad = \log_a(x-1)^{-2} + \log_a(y+2)^3 - \log_a x^{1/2}$ Property 1

$\qquad = -2\log_a(x-1) + 3\log_a(y+2) - \dfrac{1}{2}\log_a x$ Property 3

✔ **Progress Check 3**

Write $\log_a \dfrac{(2x-3)^{1/2}(y+2)^{2/3}}{z^4}$ in terms of simpler logarithmic forms.

Answer

$\dfrac{1}{2}\log_a(2x-3) + \dfrac{2}{3}\log_a(y+2) - 4\log_a z$

EXAMPLE 4   USING THE FUNDAMENTAL PROPERTIES OF LOGARITHMS

If $\log_a 1.5 = 0.37$, $\log_a 2 = 0.63$, and $\log_a 5 = 1.46$, find the following:

(a) $\log_a 7.5$ (b) $\log_a\left[(1.5)^3 \cdot \sqrt[5]{\dfrac{2}{5}}\right]$

SOLUTIONS

(a) Since

$$7.5 = 1.5 \cdot 5$$

then

$$
\begin{aligned}
\log_a 7.5 &= \log_a(1.5 \cdot 5) \\
&= \log_a 1.5 + \log_a 5 &&\text{Property 1}\\
&= 0.37 + 1.46 &&\text{Substitution}\\
&= 1.83
\end{aligned}
$$

(b) We write this as

$$\log_a(1.5)^3 + \log_a\left(\frac{2}{5}\right)^{1/5} \qquad\text{Property 1}$$

$$= 3\log_a 1.5 + \frac{1}{5}\log_a\left(\frac{2}{5}\right) \qquad\text{Property 3}$$

$$= 3\log_a 1.5 + \frac{1}{5}(\log_a 2 - \log_a 5) \qquad\text{Property 2}$$

$$= 3(0.37) + \frac{1}{5}(0.63 - 1.46) \qquad\text{Substitution}$$

$$= 0.944$$

✔ **Progress Check 4**

If $\log_a 2 = 0.43$ and $\log_a 3 = 0.68$, find the following:

(a) $\log_a 18$ (b) $\log_a \sqrt[3]{\dfrac{9}{2}}$

Answers

(a) 1.79   (b) 0.31

WARNING

(a) *Don't* write

$$\log_a(x + y) = \log_a x + \log_a y$$

Property 1 tells us that

$$\log_a(x \cdot y) = \log_a x + \log_a y$$

Don't try to apply this property to $\log_a(x + y)$, which cannot be simplified.

(b) *Don't* write

$$\log_a x^n = (\log_a x)^n$$

By Property 3,

$$\log_a x^n = n \log_a x$$

We can also apply the properties of logarithms to combine terms involving logarithms.

EXAMPLE 5   COMBINING LOGARITHMIC FORMS

Write as a single logarithm:

$$2 \log_a x - 3 \log_a(x + 1) + \log_a \sqrt{x - 1}$$

SOLUTIONS

$$2 \log_a x - 3 \log_a(x + 1) + \log_a \sqrt{x - 1}$$

$$= \log_a x^2 - \log_a(x + 1)^3 + \log_a \sqrt{x - 1} \qquad \text{Property 3}$$

$$= \log_a x^2 \sqrt{x - 1} - \log_a(x + 1)^3 \qquad \text{Property 1}$$

$$= \log_a \frac{x^2 \sqrt{x - 1}}{(x + 1)^3} \qquad \text{Property 2}$$

✔ Progress Check 5

Write as a single logarithm:

$$\frac{1}{3}[\log_a(2x - 1) - \log_a(2x - 5)] - 4 \log_a x$$

Answers

$$\log_a\left(\frac{1}{x^4} \sqrt[3]{\frac{2x - 1}{2x - 5}}\right)$$

WARNING

(a) Don't write

$$\frac{\log_a x}{\log_a y} = \log_a(x - y)$$

Property 2 tells us that

$$\log_a\left(\frac{x}{y}\right) = \log_a x - \log_a y$$

Don't try to apply this property to

$$\frac{\log_a x}{\log_a y}$$

which cannot be simplified in this way.

(b) The expressions

$$\log_a x + \log_b x$$

and

$$\log_a x - \log_b x$$

cannot be simplified. Logarithms with different bases cannot readily be written as a single logarithm.

Change of Base

Sometimes it is convenient to be able to write a logarithm that is given in terms of a base a in terms of another base b, that is, to convert $\log_a x$ to $\log_b x$. (As always, we must require a and b to be positive real numbers other than 1.) For example, some calculators can compute $\log x$ but not $\ln x$, and vice versa.

To compute $\log_b x$ given $\log_a x$ let $y = \log_b x$. The equivalent exponential form is then

$$b^y = x$$

Taking logarithms to the base a of both sides of this equation, we have

$$\log_a b^y = \log_a x$$

We now apply the fundamental properties of logarithms developed earlier in this section. By Property 3,

$$y \log_a b = \log_a x$$

Solving for y, we obtain

$$y = \frac{\log_a x}{\log_a b}$$

Since $y = \log_b x$, we have the following formula:

Change of Base Forumla

$$\log_b x = \frac{\log_a x}{\log_a b}$$

EXAMPLE 6   USING THE CHANGE OF BASE FORMULA

A calculator has a key labeled "log" (for $\log_{10}$) but doesn't have a key labeled "$\log_3$." The calculator is used to find that

$$\log 27 \approx 1.4314$$
$$\log 3 \approx 0.4771$$

Find $\log_3 27$.

SOLUTION

We use the change of base formula

$$\log_b x = \frac{\log_a x}{\log_a b}$$

With $b = 3$, $a = 10$, and $x = 27$, we have

$$\log_3 27 = \frac{\log 27}{\log 3}$$

$$\approx \frac{1.4314}{0.4771} \approx 3.0002$$

Since $3^3 = 27$, $\log_3 27 = 3$. Our computed answer differs from the exact answer because of the rounded values of log 27 and log 3.

✔ Progress Check 6

Use the change of base formula to find $\log_5 16$.

Answer

1.7227

A calculator that has a "log" key can be used efficiently to find logarithms to other bases, including natural logarithms. The conversions involving natural logarithms are summarized as follows:

$$\ln x = \frac{\log x}{\log e} = \frac{\log x}{0.4343}$$

$$\log x = \frac{\ln x}{\ln 10} = \frac{\ln x}{2.3026}$$

Exercise Set 11.4

In Exercises 1–12 find the error.

1. $\log_2 12 = \log_2 3 - \log_2 4$

2. $\log_2\left(\dfrac{7}{4}\right) = \log_3 7 + \log_3 4$

3. $\log_4(8.4 + 1.5) = \log_4 8.4 + \log_4 1.5$

4. $\log_3(7.6 - 4.2) = \log_3 7.6 - \log_3 4.2$

5. $\log_2 5^3 = (\log_2 5)^3$

6. $\log_3 \sqrt{5} = \sqrt{\log_3 5}$

7. $\ln 15 = \ln 5 - \ln 3$

8. $\ln \dfrac{8}{5} = \ln 8 + \ln 5$

9. $\ln(4 + 7) = \ln 4 + \ln 7$

10. $\ln(12.3 - 8.4) = \ln 12.3 - \ln 8.4$

11. $\ln 4^4 = (\ln 4)^4$

12. $\ln \sqrt[3]{5} = \sqrt[3]{\ln 5}$

In Exercises 13–34 express in terms of simpler logarithmic forms.

13. $\log_{10}(120 \cdot 36)$

14. $\log_6\left(\dfrac{187}{39}\right)$

15. $\log_3(3^4)$

16. $\log_3(4^3)$

17. $\log_a(2xy)$

18. $\ln(4x \cdot y \cdot z)$

19. $\log_a\left(\dfrac{x}{yz}\right)$

20. $\ln\left(\dfrac{2x}{y}\right)$

21. $\ln x^5$

22. $\log_3 y^{2/3}$

23. $\log_a(x^2 y^3)$

24. $\log_a(xy)^3$

25. $\log_a \sqrt{xy}$

26. $\log_a \sqrt[3]{xy^4}$

27. $\ln(x^2 y^3 z^4)$

28. $\log_a(xy^3 z^2)$

29. $\ln(\sqrt{x}\sqrt[3]{y})$

30. $\ln(\sqrt[3]{xy^2}\sqrt[4]{z})$

31. $\log_a\left(\dfrac{x^2 y^3}{z^4}\right)$

32. $\ln\left(\dfrac{x^4 y^2}{z^{1/2}}\right)$

33. $\ln\left(\dfrac{1}{a^2}\right)$

34. $\ln\sqrt{\dfrac{xz^2}{y}}$

In Exercises 35–46, if $\log_a 2 = 0.46$, $\log_a 3 = 0.73$, and $\log_a 5 = 1.07$, compute the given expression.

35. $\log_a 6$

36. $\log_a \dfrac{2}{3}$

37. $\log_a 9$

38. $\log_a \sqrt{5}$

39. $\log_a 12$

40. $\log_a 18$

41. $\log_a \dfrac{6}{5}$

42. $\log_a \dfrac{15}{2}$

43. $\log_a 0.30$

44. $\log_a \sqrt{7.5}$

45. $\log_a \dfrac{125}{36}$

46. $\log_a \sqrt[4]{30}$

In Exercises 47–60 write the given expression as a single logarithm.

47. $2 \log x + \dfrac{1}{2}\log y$

48. $3 \log_a x - 2 \log_a z$

49. $\dfrac{1}{3}\ln x + \dfrac{1}{3}\ln y$

50. $\dfrac{1}{3}\ln x - \dfrac{2}{3}\ln y$

51. $\dfrac{1}{3}\log_a x + 2 \log_a y - \dfrac{3}{2}\log_a z$

52. $\dfrac{2}{3}\log_a x + \log_a y - 2 \log_a z$

53. $\dfrac{1}{2}(\log_a x + \log_a y)$

54. $\dfrac{2}{3}(4 \ln x - 5 \ln y)$

55. $\dfrac{1}{3}(2 \ln x + 4 \ln y) - 3 \ln z$

56. $\ln x - \dfrac{1}{2}(3 \ln x + 5 \ln y)$

57. $\dfrac{1}{2}\log_a(x - 1) - 2 \log_a(x + 1)$

58. $2 \log_a(x + 2) - \dfrac{1}{2}(\log_a y + \log_a z)$

59. $3 \log_a x - 2 \log_a(x - 1) + \dfrac{1}{2}\log_a \sqrt[3]{x + 1}$

60. $4 \ln(x - 1) + \dfrac{1}{2}\ln(x + 1) - 3 \ln y$

The key labeled "ln" on a calculator is used to compute $\ln 10 \approx 2.3026$, $\ln 6 \approx 1.7918$, and $\ln 3 \approx 1.0986$. In Exercises 61–66 use the first given value to find the required value.

61. $\ln 17 \approx 2.8332$; find $\log 17$

62. $\ln 141 \approx 4.9488$; find $\log_3 141$

63. $\ln 245 \approx 5.5013$; find $\log 245$

64. $\ln 22 \approx 3.0910$; find $\log_6 22$

65. $\ln 78 \approx 4.3567$; find $\log_6 78$

66. $\ln 7 \approx 1.9459$; find $\log_3 7$

In Exercises 67–70 use either the "ln" key or the "log" key of a calculator to find the required value.

67. $\log_2 7$

68. $\log_5 326$

69. $\log_8 75$

70. $\log_{14} 108$

11.5 Exponential and Logarithmic Equations

The following approach will often help in solving exponential and logarithmic equations:

- To solve an exponential equation, take logarithms of both sides of the equation.
- To solve a logarithmic equation, form a single logarithm on one side of the equation, and then convert the equation to the equivalent exponential form.

EXAMPLE 1   SOLVING AN EXPONENTIAL EQUATION

Solve $3^{2x-1} = 17$.

SOLUTION

Taking logarithms to the base 3 of both sides of the equation, we have

$$\log_3 3^{2x-1} = \log_3 17$$
$$(2x-1)\log_3 3 = \log_3 17 \qquad \text{Property 3}$$
$$(2x-1)(1) = \log_3 17 \qquad \log_3 3 = 1$$
$$2x = 1 + \log_3 17$$
$$x = \frac{1}{2} + \frac{1}{2}\log_3 17$$

If a numerical answer is required, we can use the change of base formula to rewrite $\log_3 17$ in terms of common logarithms:

$$\log_3 17 = \frac{\log 17}{\log 3}$$

Then

$$x = \frac{1}{2} + \frac{1}{2}\left(\frac{\log 17}{\log 3}\right)$$

Now we use a calculator to approximate $\log 17$ and $\log 3$, and find that x is approximately 3.0789.

✔ **Progress Check 1**

Solve $2^{x+1} = 3^{2x-3}$.

Answer

$$\frac{\log 2 + 3\log 3}{2\log 3 - \log 2} \approx 2.6521$$

EXAMPLE 2 SOLVING A LOGARITHMIC EQUATION

Solve $\log(2x + 8) = 1 + \log(x - 4)$.

SOLUTION

If we rewrite the equation in the form

$$\log(2x + 8) - \log(x - 4) = 1$$

then we can apply Property 2 to form a single logarithm:

$$\log \frac{2x + 8}{x - 4} = 1$$

Now we can convert to the equivalent exponential form:

$$\frac{2x + 8}{x - 4} = 10^1 = 10$$

$$2x + 8 = 10x - 40$$

$$x = 6$$

Note that this is a proper solution since both expressions $2x + 8$ and $x - 4$ are positive when $x = 6$, a condition that is required for the logarithm function to be defined.

✔ **Progress Check 2**

Solve $\log(x + 1) = 2 + \log(3x - 1)$.

Answer

$$\frac{101}{299}$$

EXAMPLE 3 SOLVING A LOGARITHMIC EQUATION

Solve $\log_2 x = 3 - \log_2(x + 2)$.

SOLUTION

Rewriting the equation with a single logarithm, we have

$$\log_2 x + \log_2(x + 2) = 3$$
$$\log_2[x(x + 2)] = 3 \qquad \text{Why?}$$
$$x(x + 2) = 2^3 = 8 \quad \text{Equivalent exponential form}$$
$$x^2 + 2x - 8 = 0$$
$$(x - 2)(x + 4) = 0 \qquad \text{Factor}$$
$$x = 2 \quad \text{or} \quad x = -4$$

The "solution" $x = -4$ must be rejected since the original equation contains $\log_2 x$, which requires that x be positive.

Dating the Latest Ice Age

$$Q(t) = q_0 e^{-kt}$$

$$0.254 q_0 = q_0 e^{-0.00012t}$$

$$0.254 = e^{-0.0012t}$$

$$\ln 0.254 = \ln e^{-0.00012t}$$

$$-1.3704 = -0.00012t$$

$$t = 11{,}420$$

All organic forms of life contain radioactive carbon 14. In 1947 the chemist Willard Libby (who the Nobel prize in 1960) found that the percentage of carbon 14 in the atmosphere equals the percentage found in the living tissues of all organic forms of life. When an organism dies, it stops replacing carbon 14 in its living tissues. Yet the carbon 14 continues decaying at the rate of 0.012% per year. By measuring the amount of carbon 14 in the remains of an organism, it is possible to estimate fairly accurately when the organism died.

In the late 1940s, radiocarbon dating was used to date the last ice sheet to cover the North American and European continents. Remains of trees in the Two Creeks Forest in northern Wisconsin were found to have lost 74.6 of their carbon 14 content. The remaining carbon 14, therefore, was 25.4% of the original quantity q_0 that was present when the descending ice sheet felled the trees. The accompanying computations use the general equation of an exponential decay model to find the age t of the wood. Conclusion: The latest ice age occurred approximately 11,420 years before the measurements were taken.

✔ **Progress Check 3**

Solve $\log_3(x - 8) = 2 - \log_3 x$.

Answer

$x = 9$

EXAMPLE 4   APPLICATION: EXPONENTIAL GROWTH MODEL

Suppose that world population is described by an exponential growth model in which the growth rate is 2.5% per year. In how many years will the population double?

SOLUTION

The exponential growth model

$$Q(t) = q_0 e^{0.025t}$$

describes the population Q as a function of time t. Since the initial population is $Q(0) = q_0$, we seek the time t required for the population to double or become $2q_0$. We wish to solve the equation

$$Q(t) = 2q_0 = q_0 e^{0.025t}$$

for t. We then have

$$2q_0 = q_0 e^{0.025t}$$
$$2 = e^{0.025t} \qquad \text{Divide by } q_0.$$
$$\ln 2 = \ln e^{0.025t} \qquad \text{Take natural logs of both sides,}$$
$$\qquad\qquad\qquad\qquad \text{since the base is } e.$$
$$\ln 2 = 0.025t \qquad \text{Since } \ln e^x = x$$
$$t = \frac{\ln 2}{0.025} \approx \frac{0.6931}{0.025} \approx 27.7$$

or approximately 28 years.

✔ **Progress Check 4**

In a nuclear power plant accident, strontium 90 has been deposited outside the plant and nearby residents have been evacuated. The decay constant of strontium 90 is 2.77% per year. Public officials will not allow the residents to return to their homes until 90% of the radioactivity has disappeared. Assuming that no cleanup efforts are made, how long will it be before the nearby area is once again fit for human habitation?

Answer

83 years

EXAMPLE 5   APPLICATION: CONTINUOUS COMPOUNDING

A trust fund invests $8000 at an annual interest rate of 8% compounded continuously. How long will it take for the initial investment to grow to $12,000?

SOLUTION

Using Equation (1) of Section 11.2

$$S = Pe^{rt}$$

we have $S = 12,000$, $P = 8000$, $r = 0.08$; and we must solve for t. Thus,

$$12,000 = 8000e^{0.08t}$$

$$\frac{12,000}{8000} = e^{0.08t}$$

$$e^{0.08t} = 1.5$$

Taking natural logarithms of both sides, we have

$$0.08t = \ln 1.5$$

$$t = \frac{\ln 1.5}{0.08} \approx \frac{0.4055}{0.08} \qquad \text{from your calculator}$$

$$\approx 5.07$$

It will take approximately 5.07 years for the initial $8000 to grow to $12,000.

✔ **Progress Check 5**

A woman invests $10,000 in her Individual Retirement Account at an annual interest rate of 9% compounded continuously. How long will it take for the initial investment to grow to $16,000?

Answer

approximately 5.22 years

Exercise Set 11.5

In Exercises 1−29 solve for x.

1. $5^x = 18$

2. $2^x = 24$

3. $2^{x-1} = 7$

4. $3^{x-1} = 12$

5. $3^{2x} = 46$

6. $2^{2x-1} = 56$

7. $5^{2x-5} = 564$

8. $3^{3x-2} = 23.1$

9. $3^{x-1} = 2^{2x+1}$

10. $4^{2x-1} = 3^{2x+3}$

11. $2^{-x} = 15$

12. $3^{-x+2} = 103$

13. $4^{-2x+1} = 12$

14. $3^{-3x+2} = 2^{-x}$

15. $e^x = 18$

16. $e^{x-1} = 2.3$

17. $e^{2x+3} = 20$

18. $e^{-3x+2} = 40$

19. $\log x + \log 2 = 3$

20. $\log x - \log 3 = 2$

21. $\log_x(3 - 5x) = 1$

22. $\log_x(8 - 2x) = 2$

23. $\log x + \log(x - 3) = 1$

24. $\log x + \log(x + 21) = 2$

25. $\log(3x + 1) - \log(x - 2) = 1$

26. $\log(7x - 2) - \log(x - 2) = 1$

27. $\log_2 x = 4 - \log_2(x - 6)$

28. $\log_2(x - 4) = 2 - \log_2 x$

29. $\log_2(x + 4) = 3 - \log_2(x - 2)$

30. Suppose that world population is described by an exponential growth model, with a growth rate of 2% per year. In how many years will the population double?

31. Suppose that the population of a certain city is described, by an exponential growth model, with a growth rate of 3% per year. In how many years will the population triple?

32. The population P of a certain city t years from now is given by

$$P = 20{,}000e^{0.05t}$$

How many years from now will the population be 50,000?

33. Potassium 42 has a decay rate of approximately 5.5% per hour. Assuming an exponential decay model, in how many hours will the original quantity of potassium 42 have been halved?

34. Consider an exponential decay model given by

$$Q = q_0 e^{-0.4t}$$

where t is in weeks. How many weeks does it take for Q to decay to one fourth of its original amount?

35. How long does it take an amount of money to double if it is invested at a rate of 8% per year compounded semiannually? Use an exponential growth model.

36. At what rate of annual interest, compounded semiannually, should a certain amount of money be invested so it will double in 8 years? Use an exponential growth model.

37. The number N of radios that an assembly-line worker can assemble daily after t days of training is given by

$$N = 60 - 60e^{-0.04t}$$

After how many days of training will the worker be able to assemble 40 radios daily?

38. The quantity Q (in grams) of a radioactive substance that is present after t days of decay is given by

$$Q = 400e^{-kt}$$

If $Q = 300$ when $t = 3$, find k, the decay rate.

39. A person on an assembly line produces P items per day after t days of training. If

$$P = 400(1 - e^{-t})$$

how many days of training will it take this person to be able to produce 300 items per day?

40. Suppose that the number N of mopeds sold when x thousands of dollars are spent on advertising is given by

$$N = 4000 + 1000 \ln(x + 2)$$

How much advertising money must be spent to sell 6000 mopeds?

41. The Richter scale discussed in the chapter opener, and in the "measuring an earthquake" sidebar in section 11.3, is described by the model

$$M = \log_{10} \frac{I}{S}$$

where I is the intensity of the earthquake measured in microns (the amplitude of a seismograph reading taken 100 km from the epicenter) and S represents a standard intensity of 1 micron.

a. Convert the Richter model to an exponential equation.

b. Given any two earthquakes with intensities I_1 and I_2, with Richter scale intensities M_1 and M_2, find a formula for the ratio of the intensities.

42. Use your results from Exercise 41 b to find the ratio of the intensity of the Indonesia earthquake to each of the following earthquakes (all data found at http://earthquake.usgs.gov/earthquakes/eqarchives/year/):

    a. November 28, 2004, in Hokkaido, Japan $M = 7.0$
    b. June 9, 1994, in northern Bolivia, $M = 8.2$
    c. November 17, 2003, Rat Islands, $M = 7.8$

43. Refer back to Exercises 41 and 42. On May 22, 1960 in Chile, there was an earthquake that was

about 3.162 times as intense as the Indonesia earthquake. What was its magnitude on the Richter scale?

44. Set up a table including the intensities of various earthquakes and the ratio of their intensities to that of the Indonesia earthquake. Use data from http://earthquake.usgs.gov/activity/past.html.

45. MATHEMATICS IN WRITING: How are logarithms useful in comparing the intensities of earthquakes? How might the Richter scale be confusing to someone who did not understand that it is a logarithmic, rather than a linear, scale?

■ ■ ■

Chapter Summary

Terms and Symbols

base	402	Euler's constant, e	406	horizontal line test	394
composite function, $g \circ f$, $g[f(x)]$	391	exponential decay model	408	inverse function, $f^{-1}(x)$	396
compound interest	409	exponential function, a^x	402	logarithmic function, $\log_a x$	415
continuous compounding	411	exponential growth model	407	natural logarithm, $\ln x$	416
conversion period	409	growth constant	407	one-to-one function	394

Key Ideas for Review

Topic	Page	Key Idea
Exponential function	402	An exponential function has a variable in the exponent and has a base that is a positive constant.
graph	402	The graph of the exponential function $f(x) = a^x$, where $a > 0$ and $a \neq 1$, • passes through the points $(0, 1)$ and $(1, a)$ for any value of x; • is increasing if $a > 1$ and decreasing if $0 < a < 1$.
domain and range	405	The domain of the exponential function is the set of all real numbers; the range is the set of all positive numbers.
properties	405	If $a^x = a^y$, then $x = y$ (assuming $a > 0$, $a \neq 1$). If $a^x = b^x$ for all $x \neq 0$, then $a = b$ (assuming $a > 0$, $b > 0$).

Topic	Page	Key Idea
applications	407	Exponential functions play a key role in the following important applications: • Exponential growth model: $Q(t) = q_0 e^{kt}$, $k > 0$ • Exponential decay model: $Q(t) = q_0 e^{-kt}$, $k > 0$ • Compound interest: $S = P(1 + i)^n$ • Continuous compounding: $S = P e^{rt}$
Logarithmic function	414	The logarithmic function $\log_a x$ is the inverse of the function a^x.
graph	419	The graph of the logarithmic function $f(x) = \log_a x$, where $x > 0$, • passes through the points $(1, 0)$ and $(a, 1)$ for any $a > 0$, $a \neq 1$; • is increasing if $a > 1$ and decreasing if $0 < a < 1$.
domain and range	415	The domain of the logarithmic function is the set of all positive real numbers; the range is the set of all positive real numbers
equations	421	If $\log_a x = \log_a y$, then $x = y$. If $\log_a x = \log_b x$ and $x \neq 1$, then $a = b$.
fundamental properties	423	The fundamental properties of logarithms are as follows: *Property 1.* $\log_a(xy) = \log_a x + \log_a y$ *Property 2.* $\log_a\left(\dfrac{x}{y}\right) = \log_a x - \log_a y$ *Property 3.* $\log_a x^n = n \log_a x$
Logarithmic identities	418	The following identities are useful in simplifying expressions and in solving equations: $a^{\log_a x} = x \qquad \log_a a = 1$ $\log_a a^x = x \qquad \log_a 1 = 0$
Logarithms and exponents	419	The logarithmic form $y = \log_a x$ and the exponential form $x = a^y$ are two ways of expressing the same relationship. In short, logarithms are exponents. Consequently, it is always possible to convert from one to the other.
Calculating with logarithms	423	The fundamental properties of logarithms, used in conjunction with tables of logarithms, are a powerful tool in performing calculations. It is these properties that make the study of logarithms worthwhile.
Change of base formula	429	The change of base formula is $\log_b x = \dfrac{\log_a x}{\log_a b}$

Common Errors

1. In general, $f^{-1}(x) \neq \dfrac{1}{f(x)}$

2. In general,

$$\log_a(x + y) \neq \log_a x + \log_a y$$
$$\log_a(x - y) \neq \log_a x - \log_a y$$

3. *Don't write*

$$\log_a x^n = (\log_a x)^n$$

Instead, note that

$$\log_a x^n = n \log_a x$$

4. *Don't write*

$$\frac{\log_a x}{\log_a y} = \log_a\!\left(\frac{x}{y}\right)$$

You cannot simplify

$$\frac{\log_a x}{\log_a y}$$

5. *Don't write*

$$\frac{\log_a x}{\log_a y} = \log_a(x - y)$$

Recall that

$$\log_a\!\left(\frac{x}{y}\right) = \log_a x - \log_a y$$

Review Exercises

Solutions to exercises whose numbers are in bold are in the Solutions section in the back of the book.

11.1 In Exercises 1–6 $f(x) = x + 1$ and $g(x) = x^2 - 1$. Determine the following:

1. $(f + g)(x)$ 2. $(f \cdot g)(-1)$

3. $\left(\dfrac{f}{g}\right)(x)$ 4. the domain of $\left(\dfrac{f}{g}\right)(x)$

5. $(g \circ f)(x)$ 6. $(f \circ g)(2)$

In Exercises 7–10 $f(x) = \sqrt{x} - 2$ and $g(x) = x^2$. Determine the following:

7. $(f \circ g)(x)$ 8. $(g \circ f)(x)$

9. $(f \circ g)(-2)$ 10. $(g \circ f)(-2)$

In Exercises 11 and 12 $f(x) = 2x + 4$ and $g(x) = \dfrac{x}{2} - 2$.

11. Prove that f and g are inverse functions of each other.

12. Sketch the graphs of $y = f(x)$ and $y = g(x)$ on the same coordinate axes.

11.2 13. Sketch the graph of $f(x) = \left(\dfrac{1}{3}\right)^x$. Label the point $(-1, f(-1))$.

14. Solve $2^{2x} = 8^{x-1}$ for x.

15. Solve $(2a + 1)^x = (3a - 1)^x$ for a.

16. The sum of \$8000 is invested in a certificate paying 12% annual interest compounded semiannually. What sum will be available at the end of 4 years?

11.3 In Exercises 17–20 write each logarithmic form in exponential form and vice versa.

17. $27 = 9^{3/2}$ 18. $\log_{64} 8 = \dfrac{1}{2}$

19. $\log_2 \dfrac{1}{8} = -3$ 20. $6^0 = 1$

In Exercises 21–24 solve for x.

21. $\log_x 16 = 4$ 22. $\log_5 \dfrac{1}{125} = x - 1$

23. $\ln x = -4$ 24. $\log_3(x + 1) = \log_3 27$

In Exercises 25–28 evaluate the given expression.

25. $\log_3 3^5$ 26. $\ln e^{-1/3}$

27. $\log_3\!\left(\dfrac{1}{3}\right)$ 28. $e^{\ln 3}$

29. Sketch the graph of $f(x) = \log_3 x + 1$.

11.4 In Exercises 30–33 write the given expression in terms of simpler logarithmic forms.

30. $\log_a \dfrac{\sqrt{x - 1}}{2x}$ 31. $\log_a\!\left[\dfrac{x(2 - x)^2}{(y + 1)^{12}}\right]$

32. $\ln [(x + 1)^4(y - 1)^2]$ 33. $\log \sqrt[5]{\dfrac{y^2 z}{z + 3}}$

34. If $\ln 10 = 2.3026$ and $\ln 5 = 1.6094$, find $\log 5$.

35. If $\ln 10 = 2.3026$ and $\ln 20 = 2.9957$, find $\log 20$.

In Exercises 36 and 37 use the change of base formula to find the required value.

36. $\log_5 75$

37. $\log_{15} 95$

In Exercises 38–41 use the values $\log 2 = 0.30$, $\log 3 = 0.50$, and $\log 7 = 0.85$ to evaluate the given expression.

38. $\log 14$

39. $\log 3.5$

40. $\log \sqrt{6}$

41. $\log 0.7$

In Exercises 42–45 write the given expression as a single logarithm.

42. $\dfrac{1}{3}\log_a x - \dfrac{1}{2}\log_a y$

43. $\dfrac{4}{3}[\log x + \log(x - 1)]$

44. $\ln 3x + 2\left(\ln y - \dfrac{1}{2}\ln z\right)$

45. $2\log_a(x + 2) - \dfrac{3}{2}\log_a(x + 1)$

In Exercises 46 and 47 use the values $\log 32 = 1.5$, $\log 8 = 0.9$, and $\log 5 = 0.7$ to find the requested value.

46. $\log_8 32$

47. $\log_5 32$

11.5 In Exercises 48–50 solve for x.

48. $2^{3x-1} = 14$

49. $2\log x - \log 5 = 3$

50. $\log(2x - 1) = 2 + \log(x - 2)$

51. A substance is known to have a decay rate of 6% per hour. Approximately how many hours are required for the substance to decay to half of the original quantity?

Progress Test 11A

1. If $f(x) = x - 1$ and $g(x) = -x^2 + x$, compute the following:

   (a) $\left(\dfrac{f}{g}\right)(2)$ (b) $(g \circ g)(-2)$

2. Verify that $f(x) = 2x + 4$ and $g(x) = \dfrac{x}{2} - 2$ are inverse functions.

3. Sketch the graph of $f(x) = 2^{x+1}$. Label the point $(1, f(1))$.

4. Solve $\left(\dfrac{1}{2}\right)^x = \left(\dfrac{1}{4}\right)^{2x+1}$.

In Problems 5 and 6 convert from logarithmic form to exponential form or vice versa.

5. $\log_3 \dfrac{1}{9} = -2$

6. $64 = 16^{3/2}$

In Problems 7 and 8 solve for x.

7. $\log_x 27 = 3$

8. $\log_6\left(\dfrac{1}{36}\right) = 3x + 1$

In Problems 9 and 10 evaluate the given expression.

9. $\ln e^{5/2}$

10. $\log_5 \sqrt{5}$

In Problems 11 and 12 write the given expression in terms of simpler logarithmic forms.

11. $\log_a \dfrac{x^3}{y^2 z}$

12. $\log \dfrac{x^2\sqrt{2y - 1}}{y^3}$

In Problems 13 and 14 use the values $\log 2.5 = 0.4$ and $\log 2 = 0.3$ to evaluate the given expression.

13. $\log 5$

14. $\log 2\sqrt{2}$

In Problems 15 and 16 write the given expression as a single logarithm.

15. $2\log x - 3\log(y + 1)$

16. $\dfrac{2}{3}[\log_a(x + 3) - \log_a(x - 3)]$

17. If $\ln 10 = 2.3026$ and $\ln 16 = 2.7726$, find $\log 16$.

18. Use the change of base formula to find $\log_3 35$.

In Problems 19 and 20 solve for x.

19. $\log x - \log 2 = 2$

20. $\log_4(x - 3) = 1 - \log_4 x$

21. The number of bacteria in a culture is described by the exponential growth model

$$Q(t) = q_0 e^{0.02t}$$

Approximately how many hours are required for the number of bacteria to double?

Progress Test 11B

1. If $f(x) = x^2 + 3$ and $g(x) = 2x - 1$, compute the following:

   (a) $\left(\dfrac{g}{f}\right)(x)$ 　　　　　(b) $(f \circ f)(-1)$

2. Verify that $f(x) = -3x + 1$ and $g(x) = -\frac{1}{3}x + \frac{1}{3}$ are inverse functions.

3. Sketch the graph of $f(x) = \left(\frac{1}{2}\right)^{x-1}$. Label the point $(0, f(0))$.

4. Solve $(a + 3)^x = (2a - 5)^x$ for a.

In Problems 5 and 6 convert from logarithmic form to exponential form and vice versa.

5. $\dfrac{1}{1000} = 10^{-3}$ 　　　　6. $\log_3 1 = 0$

In Problems 7 and 8 solve for x.

7. $\log_2(x - 1) = -1$ 　　8. $\log_{2x} 27 = \log_3 27$

In Problems 9 and 10 evaluate the given expression.

9. $\log_3 3^{10}$ 　　　　　　10. $e^{\ln 4}$

In Problems 11 and 12 write the given expression in terms of simpler logarithmic forms.

11. $\log_a[(x - 1)(y + 3)]^{5/4}$ 　　12. $\ln\left(\sqrt{xy}\,\sqrt[4]{2z}\right)$

In Problems 13 and 14 use the values log 2.5 = 0.4, log 2 = 0.3, and log 6 = 0.75 to evaluate the given expression.

13. $\log 7.5$ 　　　　　　　14. $\log 36$

In Problems 15 and 16 write the given expression as a single logarithm.

15. $\dfrac{3}{5}\ln(x - 1) + \dfrac{2}{5}\ln y - \dfrac{1}{5}\ln z$

16. $\log \dfrac{x}{y} - \log \dfrac{y}{x}$

17. If $\ln 10 = 2.3026$ and $\ln 70 = 4.2485$, find log 70.

18. Use the change of base formula to find log 55.

In Problems 19 and 20 solve for x.

19. $\log_x(x + 6) = 2$ 　　20. $\log(x - 9) = 1 - \log x$

21. Suppose that $500 is invested in a certificate at an annual interest rate of 12% compounded monthly. What will the value of the investment be after 6 months?

Chapter 11 Project

In 1865, in Memphis, Tennessee, there was a earthquake that measured 5.0 on the Richter scale. Memphis is part of a region which the United States Geological Survey refers to as the New Madrid Seismic Zone. Many buildings in this part of the country were never designed with large earthquakes in mind, but seismologists consider the likelihood of a large earthquake in this region within the next 50 years to be high. Tennessee schools have had Earthquake Awareness Week since 1995. (This information comes from http://www.cusec.org/).

What is the likelihood of a large earthquake in your area? What precautions exist, if any, against the possibility of damage or loss of life from seismic activity?

For this project, first refer back to Exercises 41–45 in Section 11.5.

On your graphing calculator, display the graph of $y = \log x$ and set the viewing window large enough so that you can TRACE a point on the graph all the way up to $y = 9.0$. What is the range of x values? Write a brief essay comparing this graph to the Richter scale and describing how the y values are related to the x values. (Hint: the independent variable represents the ratio I/S.)

Copy your graph, and label the points on the graph which give information about the earthquakes in Bolivia, Indonesia, Memphis, Alaska, and Japan.

■ ■ ■

12 Analytic Geometry: The Conic Sections

It is impossible not to feel stirred at the thought of the emotions of men at certain historic moments of adventure and discovery. Such moments are also granted to students in the abstract regions of thought, and high among them must be placed the morning when Descartes lay in bed and invented the method of coordinate geometry.

—Alfred North Whitehead

When NASA scientists want to launch a probe to study the planets of our solar system, how do they plot the path of the probe through space? For example, the *Voyager* probe (which discovered the presence of active volcanoes on the moon Io) crashed into the giant planet Jupiter after traveling almost three billion miles! How did NASA scientists know where Jupiter would be when the probe arrived?

Scientists can accurately predict the location of any planet in our solar system at any future time because they know that the planets follow elliptical orbits around the Sun. In fact,

http://www.jpl.nasa.gov/

the Sun is one of the two foci of each ellipse. An ellipse can look a lot like a circle, or it can appear longer and flatter. Which planets in our solar system have orbits which are most nearly circular? In this chapter's project, you will learn how to answer that question.

Learn more about the planets and the probes that have been sent out to study them at http://www.jpl.nasa.gov/.

■ ■ ■

In 1637 the great French philosopher and scientist René Descartes developed an idea that the nineteenth-century British philosopher John Stuart Mill described as "the greatest single step ever made in the progress of the exact sciences." Descartes combined the techniques of algebra with those of geometry and created a new field of study called **analytic geometry**. Analytic geometry enables us to apply algebraic methods and equations to the solution of problems in geometry and, conversely, to obtain geometric representations of algebraic equations.

We will first develop two simple but powerful devices: a formula for the distance between two points and a formula for the coordinates of the midpoint of a line segment. With these tools, we will demonstrate the power of analytic geometry by proving a number of general theorems from plane geometry.

The power of the methods of analytic geometry is also very well demonstrated, as we shall see in this chapter, in a study of the conic sections. We will find in the course of that study that (a) a geometric definition can be converted into an algebraic equation, and (b) an algebraic equation can be classified by the type of graph it represents.

12.1   The Distance and Midpoint Formulas

There is a useful formula that gives the distance $\overline{PQ}$ between two points $P(x_1, y_1)$ and $Q(x_2, y_2)$. In Figure 1a, we have shown the x-coordinate of a point as the distance of the point from the y-axis and the y-coordinate as its distance from the x-axis. Thus, we have labeled the horizontal segments x_1 and x_2 and the vertical segments y_1 and y_2. In Figure 1b we use the lengths from Figure 1a to indicate that $\overline{PR} = x_2 - x_1$ and $\overline{QR} = y_2 - y_1$. Since triangle PRQ is a right triangle, we can apply the Pythagorean theorem.

$$d^2 = (x_2 - x_1)^2 + (y_2 - y_1)^2$$

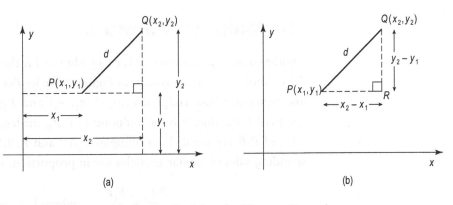

(a)   (b)

Figure 1   Deriving the Distance Formula

Although the points in Figure 1 are both in quadrant I, the same result will be obtained for any two points. Since distance cannot be negative, we have

<table>
<tr><td>**The Distance Formula**</td><td>The distance d between two points $P_1(x_1, y_1)$ and $P_2(x_2, y_2)$ is given by

$$d = \sqrt{(x_2 - x_1)^2 + (y_2 - y_1)^2}$$</td></tr>
</table>

The student should verify that the formula is true regardless of the quadrants in which P_1 and P_2 are located.

EXAMPLE 1 FINDING THE DISTANCE BETWEEN TWO POINTS

Find the distance between points $(3, -2)$ and $(-1, -5)$.

SOLUTION

We let $(x_1, y_1) = (3, -2)$ and $(x_2, y_2) = (-1, -5)$. Substituting these values in the distance formula, we have

$$d = \sqrt{(x_2 - x_1)^2 + (y_2 - y_1)^2}$$
$$= \sqrt{(-1 - 3)^2 + \left[-5 - (-2)\right]^2}$$
$$= \sqrt{(-4)^2 + (-3)^2} = \sqrt{25} = 5$$

If we had let $(x_1, y_1) = (-1, -5)$ and $(x_2, y_2) = (3, -2)$, we would have obtained the same result for d. Verify this.

✔ **Progress Check 1**

Find the distance between the points.
(a) $(-4, 3), (-2, 1)$ (b) $(-6, -7), (3, 0)$

Answers
(a) $2\sqrt{2}$ (b) $\sqrt{130}$

The Midpoint Formula

Another useful expression that is easily obtained is the one for the coordinates of the midpoint of a line segment. In Figure 2, we let $P(x, y)$ be the midpoint of the line segment whose endpoints are $P_1(x_1, y_1)$ and $P_2(x_2, y_2)$. Let d denote the length of P_1P_2. Since P is the midpoint of P_1P_2, the length of P_1P is $d/2$. The lines PA and P_2B are parallel, so triangles P_1AP and P_1BP_2 are similar. Since corresponding sides of similar triangles are in proportion, we can write

$$\frac{\overline{P_1P_2}}{\overline{P_2B}} = \frac{\overline{P_1P}}{\overline{PA}} \qquad \text{where } \overline{P_1P_2} \text{ denotes the length of the segment } P_1P_2$$

or

$$\frac{d}{y_2 - y_1} = \frac{\dfrac{d}{2}}{(y - y_1)}$$

This gives

$$\frac{d}{2}(y_2 - y_1) = d(y - y_1)$$

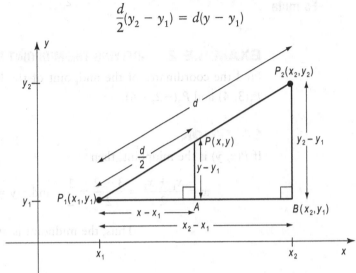

Figure 2 **Deriving the Midpoint Formula**

Dividing both sides by d, we have

$$\frac{1}{2}(y_2 - y_1) = (y - y_1)$$

$$\frac{1}{2}y_2 - \frac{1}{2}y_1 = y - y_1$$

$$y = \frac{y_1 + y_2}{2}$$

Similarly, from

$$\frac{\overline{P_1P_2}}{\overline{P_1B}} = \frac{\overline{P_1P}}{\overline{P_1A}}$$

we obtain

$$\frac{d}{x_2 - x_1} = \frac{\dfrac{d}{2}}{x - x_1}$$

so that

$$x = \frac{x_1 + x_2}{2}$$

We have the following general result:

The Midpoint Formula

If $P(x, y)$ is the midpoint of the line segment whose endpoints are $P_1(x_1, y_1)$ and $P_2(x_2, y_2)$, then

$$x = \frac{x_1 + x_2}{2} \quad \text{and} \quad y = \frac{y_1 + y_2}{2}$$

EXAMPLE 2   APPLYING THE MIDPOINT FORMULA

Find the coordinates of the midpoint of the line segment whose endpoints are $P_1(3, 4)$ and $P_2(-2, -6)$.

SOLUTION

If $P(x, y)$ is the midpoint, then

$$x = \frac{x_1 + x_2}{2} = \frac{3 - 2}{2} = \frac{1}{2} \quad \text{and} \quad y = \frac{y_1 + y_2}{2} = \frac{4 - 6}{2} = -1$$

Thus, the midpoint is at $\left(\frac{1}{2}, -1\right)$.

✔ **Progress Check 2**

Find the coordinates of the midpoint of the line segment whose endpoints are given.

(a) $(0, -4), (-2, -2)$ (b) $(-10, 4), (7, -5)$

Answers

(a) $(-1, -3)$ (b) $\left(-\frac{3}{2}, -\frac{1}{2}\right)$

The formulas for distance, midpoint of a line segment, and slope of a line are adequate to allow us to demonstrate some of the beauty and power of analytic geometry. With these tools, we can prove many theorems from plane geometry by placing the figures on a rectangular coordinate system.

EXAMPLE 3   PROVING A THEOREM

Prove that the line joining the midpoints of two sides of a triangle is parallel to the third side and has length equal to one half the length of the third side.

SOLUTION

We place the triangle OAB in a convenient location, namely, with one vertex at the origin and one side on the positive x-axis (Figure 3). If Q and R are the midpoints of OB and AB, respectively, then by the midpoint formula the coordinates of Q are

$$\left(\frac{b}{2}, \frac{c}{2}\right)$$

and the coordinates of R are

$$\left(\frac{a + b}{2}, \frac{c}{2}\right)$$

We see that the line joining

$$Q\left(\frac{b}{2}, \frac{c}{2}\right) \quad \text{and} \quad R\left(\frac{a + b}{2}, \frac{c}{2}\right)$$

has slope 0 since the difference of the y-coordinates is

$$\frac{c}{2} - \frac{c}{2} = 0$$

Side OA also has slope 0, which proves that QR is parallel to OA.

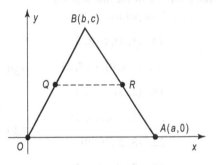

Figure 3   **Diagram for Example 3**

Applying the distance formula to QR, we have

$$d = \sqrt{(x_2 - x_1)^2 + (y_2 - y_1)^2}$$

$$= \sqrt{\left(\frac{a + b}{2} - \frac{b}{2}\right)^2 + \left(\frac{c}{2} - \frac{c}{2}\right)^2}$$

$$= \sqrt{\left(\frac{a}{2}\right)^2} = \frac{a}{2}$$

Since OA has length a, we have shown that $\overline{QR}$ is one half of $\overline{OA}$.

✔ Progress Check 3
Prove that the midpoint of the hypotenuse of a right triangle is equidistant from all three vertices.

Answer
Hint: Place the triangle so that two legs coincide with the positive x- and y-axes. Find the coordinates of the midpoint of the hypotenuse by the midpoint formula. Finally, compute the distance from the midpoint to each vertex by the distance formula.

Exercise Set 12.1

In Exercises 1–12 find the distance between the given points.

1. $(5, 4), (2, 1)$
2. $(-4, 5), (-2, 3)$
3. $(-1, -5), (-5, -1)$
4. $(2, -4), (3, -1)$
5. $(3, 1), (-4, 5)$
6. $(2, 4), (-3, 3)$
7. $(-2, 4), (-4, -2)$
8. $(-3, 0), (2, -4)$
9. $\left(-\frac{1}{2}, 3\right), \left(-1, -\frac{3}{4}\right)$
10. $(3, 0), (0, 4)$
11. $(2, -4), (0, -1)$
12. $\left(\frac{2}{3}, \frac{3}{2}\right), (-2, -4)$

In Exercises 13–24 find the midpoint of the line segment whose endpoints are the given pair of points.

13. $(2, 6), (3, 4)$
14. $(1, 1), (-2, 5)$
15. $(2, 0), (0, 5)$
16. $(-3, 0), (-5, 2)$
17. $(-2, 1), (-5, -3)$
18. $(2, 3), (-1, 3)$
19. $(0, -4), (0, 3)$
20. $(1, -3), (3, 2)$
21. $(-1, 3), (-1, 6)$
22. $(3, 2), (0, 0)$
23. $(1, -1), (-1, 1)$
24. $(2, 4), (2, -4)$

*25. Show that the medians from the equal angles of an isosceles triangle are of equal length. (*Hint*: Place the triangle so that its vertices are at the points $A(-a, 0)$, $B(a, 0)$, and $C(0, b)$.)

*26. Show that the midpoints of the sides of a rectangle are the vertices of a rhombus (a quadrilateral with four equal sides). (*Hint*: Place the rectangle so that its vertices are at the points $(0, 0)$, $(a, 0)$, $(0, b)$, and (a, b).)

*27. Show that a triangle with two equal medians is isosceles.

*28. Show that the sum of the squares of the lengths of the medians of a triangle equals three fourths the sum of the squares of the lengths of the sides. (*Hint*: Place the triangle so that its vertices are the points $(-a, 0)$, $(b, 0)$, and $(0, c)$.)

*29. Show that the diagonals of a rectangle are equal in length. (*Hint*: Place the rectangle so that its vertices are the points $(0, 0)$, $(a, 0)$, $(0, b)$, and (a, b).)

*30. Find the length of the longest side of the triangle whose vertices are $A(3, -4)$, $B(-2, -6)$, and $C(-1, 2)$.

12.2 Symmetry

If we fold the graph in Figure 4a along the x-axis, the portion of the graph lying above the x-axis will coincide with the portion lying below. Similarly, if we fold the graph in Figure 4b along the y-axis, the portion to the left of the y-axis will coincide with the portion to the right. These properties illustrate the notion of symmetry, which we now define more carefully.

A curve in the xy-plane is **symmetric with respect to the**

    (a) **x-axis** if for every point (x_1, y_1) on the curve, the point $(x_1, -y_1)$ is also on the curve;

    (b) **y-axis** if for every point (x_1, y_1) on the curve, the point $(-x_1, y_1)$ is also on the curve;

    (c) **origin** if for every point (x_1, y_1) on the curve, the point $(-x_1, -y_1)$ is also on the curve.

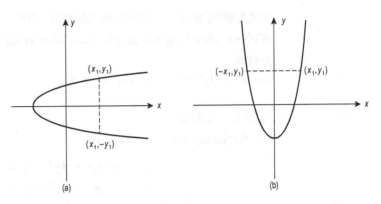

Figure 4   Symmetry with Respect to the Coordinate Axes

Thus, a curve is symmetric with respect to the x-axis if the portion of the curve lying below the x-axis is the mirror image in the x-axis of the portion above the x-axis. Similarly, a curve is symmetric with respect to the y-axis if the portion of the curve lying to the left of the y-axis is the mirror image in the y-axis of the portion to the right of the y-axis. Thus, the curve in Figure 4a is symmetric with respect to the x-axis, and the curve in Figure 4b is symmetric with respect to the y-axis. The curve in Figure 5 is symmetric with respect to the origin.

The symmetries of a curve can be discovered by looking at the curve. However, it is sometimes helpful to discover the symmetries of the graph by examining the equation and to use these symmetries as aids in sketching the graph. Thus, we have the following tests for symmetry:

Tests for Symmetry

The graph of an equation is **symmetric with respect to the**

(a) **x-axis** if replacing y with $-y$ results in an equivalent equation;

(b) **y-axis** if replacing x with $-x$ results in an equivalent equation;

(c) **origin** if replacing x with $-x$ and y with $-y$ results in an equivalent equation.

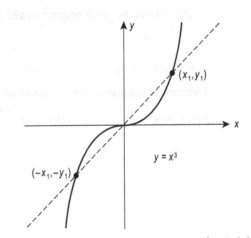

Figure 5   Symmetry with Respect to the Origin

EXAMPLE 1   DETERMINING SYMMETRY

Without sketching the graph, determine symmetry with respect to the x- and y-axes.

(a) $x^2 + 4y^2 - y = 1$ (b) $xy = 5$

SOLUTIONS

(a) Replacing x by $-x$, we have

$$(-x)^2 + 4y^2 - y = 1$$
$$x^2 + 4y^2 - y = 1$$

Since this is an equivalent equation, the curve is symmetric with respect to the y-axis. Now, replacing y by $-y$, we have

$$x^2 + 4(-y)^2 - (-y) = 1$$
$$x^2 + 4y^2 + y = 1$$

which is *not* an equivalent equation. Thus, the curve is not symmetric with respect to the x-axis.

(b) Replacing x by $-x$, we have $-xy = 5$, which is not an equivalent equation. Replacing y by $-y$, we have $-xy = 5$, which is not an equivalent equation. Thus, the curve is not symmetric with respect to either axis.

✔ Progress Check 1

Without graphing, determine symmetry with respect to the coordinate axes.

(a) $x^2 - y^2 = 1$ (b) $x + y = 10$ (c) $y = \dfrac{1}{x^2 + 1}$

Answers

(a) symmetric with respect to both x- and y-axes

(b) not symmetric with respect to either axis

(c) symmetric with respect to the y-axis

EXAMPLE 2   DETERMINING SYMMETRY

Determine symmetry with respect to the origin.

(a) $y = x^3 - 1$ (b) $y^2 = \dfrac{x^2 + 1}{x^2 - 1}$

SOLUTIONS

(a) Replacing x by $-x$ and y by $-y$, we have

$$-y = (-x)^3 - 1$$
$$-y = -x^3 - 1$$
$$y = x^3 + 1$$

Since the equation is not an equivalent equation, the curve is not symmetric with respect to the origin.

(b) Replacing x by $-x$ and y by $-y$, we have

$$(-y)^2 = \frac{(-x)^2 + 1}{(-x)^2 - 1}$$

$$y^2 = \frac{x^2 + 1}{x^2 - 1}$$

The equation is an equivalent equation, so we conclude that the curve is symmetric with respect to the origin.

✔ **Progress Check 2**

Determine symmetry with respect to the origin.

(a) $x^2 + y^2 = 1$ (b) $y^2 = x - 1$ (c) $y = x + \dfrac{1}{x}$

Answers

(a) symmetric with respect to the origin
(b) not symmetric with respect to the origin
(c) symmetric with respect to the origin

Note that in Example 2b and Progress Check 2a, the given curves are symmetric with respect to *both* the x- and y-axes, as well as the origin. In fact, we have the following general rule:

> A curve that is symmetric with respect to both coordinate axes is also symmetric with respect to the origin. The converse, however, is not true.

The curve $y = x^3$ in Figure 5 is an example of one that is symmetric with respect to the origin, but not with respect to the coordinate axes.

Exercise Set 12.2

In Exercises 1–34 determine, without graphing, whether the given curve is symmetric with respect to the *x*-axis, the *y*-axis, or the origin, or is not symmetric with respect to any of these.

1. $y = x + 3$

2. $x - 2y = 5$

3. $2x - 5y = 0$

4. $3x + 2y = 5$

5. $y = 4x^2$

6. $x = 2y^2$

7. $y^2 = x - 4$

8. $x^2 - y = 2$

9. $y = 4 - 9x^2$

10. $y = x(x - 4)$

11. $y = 1 + x^3$

12. $y^2 = 1 + x^3$

13. $y = (x - 2)^2$

14. $y^2 = (x - 2)^2$

15. $y^2 = x^2 - 9$

16. $y^2x + 2x = 4$

17. $y + yx^2 = x$

18. $y^2x + 2x^2 = 4x^2y$

19. $y^3 = x^2 - 9$

20. $y^3 = x^3 + 9$

21. $y = \dfrac{1}{x^2}$

22. $y = \dfrac{x^2 + 4}{x^2 - 4}$

23. $y = \dfrac{1}{x^2 + 1}$

24. $y^2 = \dfrac{x^2 + 1}{x^2 - 1}$

25. $4y^2 - x^2 = 1$

26. $4x^2 + 9y^2 = 36$

27. $9y^2 - 4x^2 = 36$

28. $4 + x^2y = x^2$

29. $y^2 = \dfrac{1}{x^2}$

30. $y = \dfrac{1}{x^3}$

31. $y = x + \dfrac{1}{x^2}$

32. $y^2 = \dfrac{x}{x - 1}$

33. $xy = 4$

34. $x^2y = 4$

*35. Show that the graph of an even function is symmetric with respect to the *y*-axis. (See Exercise 61 in Section 6.2.)

*36. Show that the graph of an odd function is symmetric with respect to the origin. (See Exercise 61 in Section 6.2.)

12.3   The Circle

The conic sections provide us with an outstanding opportunity to demonstrate the double-edged power of analytic geometry. We will see that a geometric figure defined as a set of points can often be described analytically by an algebraic equation; conversely, we can start with an algebraic equation and use graphing procedures to study the properties of the curve.

First, let's see how the term "conic section" originates. If we pass a plane through a cone at various angles, the intersections are called conic sections. Figure 6 shows four conic sections: a circle, a parabola, an ellipse, and a hyperbola.

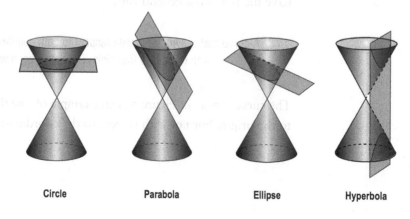

Circle   Parabola   Ellipse   Hyperbola

Figure 6   The Conic Sections

Let's begin with the geometric definition of a circle.

> A **circle** is the set of all points in a plane that are at a given distance from a fixed point. The fixed point is called the **center** of the circle, and the given distance is called the **radius**.

Using the methods of analytic geometry, we place the center at a point (h, k), as in Figure 7. If $P(x, y)$ is a point on the circle, then the distance from P to the center (h, k) must be equal to the radius r. By the distance formula

$$\sqrt{(x - h)^2 + (y - k)^2} = r$$

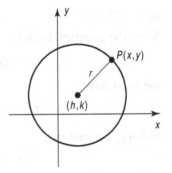

Figure 7   Deriving the Equation of the Circle

Squaring both sides provides us with an important form of the equation of the circle.

Standard Form of the Equation of a Circle

> $$(x - h)^2 + (y - k)^2 = r^2$$
>
> is the standard form of the equation of the circle with center at (h, k) and radius r.

EXAMPLE 1   FINDING THE EQUATION OF A CIRCLE

Write the standard form of the equation of the circle with center at $(2, -5)$ and radius 3.

SOLUTION

Substituting $h = 2$, $k = -5$, and $r = 3$ in the equation

$$(x - h)^2 + (y - k)^2 = r^2$$

yields

$$(x - 2)^2 + (y + 5)^2 = 9$$

✔ Progress Check 1

Write the standard form of the equation of the circle with center at $(-4, -6)$ and radius 5.

Answer

$(x + 4)^2 + (y + 6)^2 = 25$

EXAMPLE 2   USING THE STANDARD FORM FOR A CIRCLE

Find the coordinates of the center and the radius of the circle whose equation is

$$(x + 1)^2 + (y - 3)^2 = 4$$

SOLUTION

Since the standard form is

$$(x - h)^2 + (y - k)^2 = r^2$$

we must have

$$x - h = x + 1, \quad y - k = y - 3, \quad r^2 = 4$$

Solving, we find that

$$h = -1, \quad k = 3, \quad r = 2$$

Thus, the center is at $(-1, 3)$ and the radius is 2.

✔ Progress Check 2

Find the coordinates of the center and the radius of the circle whose equation is $(x - \frac{1}{2})^2 + (y + 5)^2 = 15$.

Answer

center: $(\frac{1}{2}, -5)$;   radius: $\sqrt{15}$

General Form

It is also possible to begin with the equation of a circle in the **general form**

$$Ax^2 + Ay^2 + Dx + Ey + F = 0, \quad A \neq 0$$

and to rewrite the equation in standard form. The process involves completing the square in each variable.

EXAMPLE 3   WRITING AN EQUATION IN STANDARD FORM

Write the equation of the circle $2x^2 + 2y^2 - 12x + 16y - 31 = 0$ in standard form.

SOLUTION

Grouping the terms in x and y and factoring produces

$$2(x^2 - 6x) + 2(y^2 + 8y) = 31$$

Completing the square in both x and y, we have

$$2(x^2 - 6x + 9) + 2(y^2 + 8y + 16) = 31 + 18 + 32$$
$$2(x - 3)^2 + 2(y + 4)^2 = 81$$

Note that the quantities 18 and 32 were added to the right-hand side because each factor is multiplied by 2. The last equation can be written as

$$(x - 3)^2 + (y + 4)^2 = \frac{81}{2}$$

This is the standard form of the equation of the circle with center at $(3, -4)$ and radius $\dfrac{9\sqrt{2}}{2}$.

✔ **Progress Check 3**

Write the equation of the circle $4x^2 + 4y^2 - 8x + 4y = 103$ in standard form, and determine the center and radius.

Answer

$(x - 1)^2 + (y + \frac{1}{2})^2 = 27$; center: $(1, -\frac{1}{2})$; radius: $\sqrt{27}$

EXAMPLE 4   WRITING AN EQUATION IN STANDARD FORM

Write the equation $3x^2 + 3y^2 - 6x + 15 = 0$ in standard form.

SOLUTION

Grouping and factoring, we have

$$3(x^2 - 2x) + 3y^2 = -15$$

We then complete the square in x and y:

$$3(x^2 - 2x + 1) + 3y^2 = -15 + 3$$
$$3(x - 1)^2 + 3y^2 = -12$$
$$(x - 1)^2 + y^2 = -4$$

Since $r^2 = -4$ is an impossible situation, the graph of the equation is not a circle. Note that the left-hand side of the equation in standard form is a sum of squares and is therefore nonnegative, while the right-hand side is negative. Thus, there are no real values of x and y that satisfy the equation. This is an example of an equation that does not have a graph.

> **✔ Progress Check 4**
>
> Write the equation $x^2 + y^2 - 12y + 36 = 0$ in standard form, and analyze its graph.
>
> **Answer**
>
> The standard form is $x^2 + (y - 6)^2 = 0$. The equation is that of a "circle" with center at $(0, 6)$ and radius 0. The "circle" is actually the point $(0, 6)$.

EXERCISE SET 12.3

In Exercises 1–8 write an equation of the circle with center at (h, k) and radius r.

1. $(h, k) = (2, 3)$, $r = 2$

2. $(h, k) = (-3, 0)$, $r = 3$

3. $(h, k) = (-2, -3)$, $r = \sqrt{5}$

4. $(h, k) = (2, -4)$, $r = 4$

5. $(h, k) = (0, 0)$, $r = 3$

6. $(h, k) = (0, -3)$, $r = 2$

7. $(h, k) = (-1, 4)$, $r = 2\sqrt{2}$

8. $(h, k) = (2, 2)$, $r = 2$

In Exercises 9–16 find the coordinates of the center and radius of the circle with the given equation.

9. $(x - 2)^2 + (y - 3)^2 = 16$ 10. $(x + 2)^2 + y^2 = 9$

11. $(x - 2)^2 + (y + 2)^2 = 4$

12. $\left(x + \dfrac{1}{2}\right)^2 + (y - 2)^2 = 8$

13. $(x + 4)^2 + \left(y + \dfrac{3}{2}\right)^2 = 18$ 14. $x^2 + (y - 2)^2 = 4$

15. $\left(x - \dfrac{1}{3}\right)^2 + y^2 = -\dfrac{1}{9}$ 16. $x^2 + \left(y - \dfrac{1}{2}\right)^2 = 3$

In Exercises 17–24 write the equation of the given circle in standard form and determine the radius and the coordinates of the center, if possible.

17. $x^2 + y^2 + 4x - 8y + 4 = 0$

18. $x^2 + y^2 - 2x + 6y - 15 = 0$

19. $2x^2 + 2y^2 - 6x - 10y + 6 = 0$

20. $2x^2 + 2y^2 + 8x - 12y - 8 = 0$

21. $2x^2 + 2y^2 - 4x - 5 = 0$

22. $4x^2 + 4y^2 - 2y + 7 = 0$

23. $3x^2 + 3y^2 - 12x + 18y + 15 = 0$

24. $4x^2 + 4y^2 + 4x + 4y - 4 = 0$

In Exercises 25–32 write the equation in standard form, and determine if the graph of the equation is a circle, a point, or neither.

25. $x^2 + y^2 - 6x + 8y + 7 = 0$

26. $x^2 + y^2 + 4x + 6y + 5 = 0$

27. $x^2 + y^2 + 3x - 5y + 7 = 0$

28. $x^2 + y^2 - 4x - 6y - 13 = 0$

29. $2x^2 + 2y^2 - 12x - 4 = 0$

30. $2x^2 + 2y^2 + 4x - 4y + 25 = 0$

31. $2x^2 + 2y^2 - 6x - 4y - 2 = 0$

32. $2x^2 + 2y^2 - 10y + 6 = 0$

*33. Find the area of the circle whose equation is
$$x^2 + y^2 - 2x + 4y - 4 = 0$$

*34. Find the circumference of the circle whose equation is
$$x^2 + y^2 - 6x + 8 = 0$$

*35. Show that the circles whose equations are
$$x^2 + y^2 - 4x + 9y - 3 = 0$$
and
$$3x^2 + 3y^2 - 12x + 27y - 27 = 0$$
are concentric (have the same centers).

*36. Find an equation of the circle that has its center at $(3, -1)$ and that passes through the point $(-2, 2)$.

*37. Find an equation of the circle that has its center at $(-5, 2)$ and that passes through the point $(-3, 4)$.

*38. The two points $(-2, 4)$ and $(4, 2)$ are the endpoints of a diameter of a circle. Write the equation of the circle in standard form.

*39. The two points $(3, 5)$ and $(7, -3)$ are the endpoints of a diameter of a circle. Write the equation of the circle in standard form.

12.4   The Parabola

We begin our study of the parabola with the geometric definition.

> A **parabola** is the set of all points that are equidistant from a given point and a given line.

The given point is called the **focus** and the given line is called the **directrix** of the parabola. In Figure 8, all points P on the parabola are equidistant from the focus F and the directrix L; that is, $\overline{PF} = \overline{PQ}$. The line through the focus that is perpendicular to the directrix is called the **axis of the parabola** (or simply the **axis**), and the parabola is seen to be symmetric with respect to the axis. The point V (Figure 8), where the parabola intersects its axis, is called the **vertex** of the parabola. The vertex, then, is the point from which the parabola opens. Note that the vertex is the point on the parabola that is closest to the directrix.

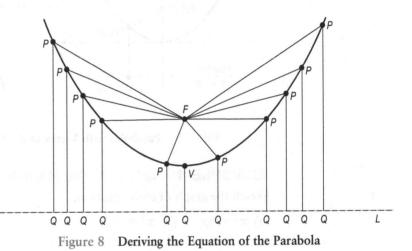

Figure 8   **Deriving the Equation of the Parabola**

We can apply the methods of analytic geometry to find an equation of the parabola. We choose the y-axis as the axis of the parabola and the origin as the vertex (Figure 9). Since the vertex is on the parabola, it is equidistant from the focus and the directrix. Thus, if the coordinates of the focus F are $(0, p)$, then the equation of the directrix is $y = -p$. We then let $P(x, y)$ be any point on the parabola, and we equate the distance from P to the focus F and the distance from P to the directrix L. Using the distance formula, we have

$$\overline{PF} = \overline{PQ}$$

$$\sqrt{(x - 0)^2 + (y - p)^2} = \sqrt{(x - x)^2 + (y + p)^2}$$

Squaring both sides, and expanding, we have

$$x^2 + y^2 - 2py + p^2 = y^2 + 2py + p^2$$

$$x^2 = 4py$$

We have obtained an important form of the equation of a parabola.

$$x^2 = 4py$$

is the equation of a parabola whose vertex is at the origin,
whose focus is at $(0, p)$, and whose axis is vertical.

Conversely, it can be shown that the graph of the equation $x^2 = 4py$ is a parabola. Note that substituting $-x$ for x leaves the equation unchanged, verifying symmetry with respect to the y-axis. If $p > 0$, the parabola opens upward, as shown in Figure 9a; if $p < 0$, the parabola opens downward, as shown in Figure 9b.

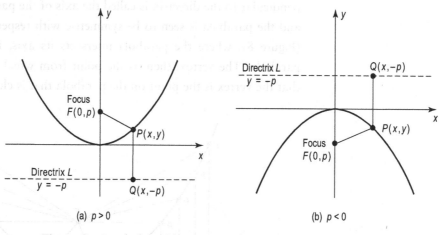

(a) $p > 0$ (b) $p < 0$

Figure 9   Parabolas with Vertex at the Origin and a Vertical Axis

EXAMPLE 1   SKETCHING THE GRAPH OF A PARABOLA

Sketch the graph of each equation.

(a) $x^2 = 8y$ (b) $x^2 = -2y$

SOLUTIONS

We form tables of values giving points on the graphs and draw smooth curves. See Figure 10.

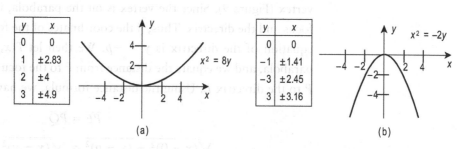

y	x
0	0
1	±2.83
2	±4
3	±4.9

(a)

y	x
0	0
-1	±1.41
-3	±2.45
3	±3.16

(b)

Figure 10   Diagram for Example 1

✔ **Progress Check 1**

Sketch the graph of each equation.

(a) $x^2 = 3y$ (b) $x^2 = -y$

Answers

(a) (b)

If we place the parabola as shown in Figure 11, we can proceed as before to obtain the following result:

$$y^2 = 4px$$

is the equation of a parabola whose vertex is at the origin, whose focus is at $(p, 0)$, and whose axis is horizontal.

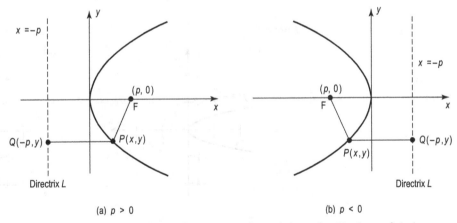

(a) $p > 0$ (b) $p < 0$

Figure 11   **Parabolas with Vertex at the Origin and a Horizontal Axis**

Note that substituting $-y$ for y leaves this equation unchanged, verifying symmetry with respect to the x-axis. If $p > 0$, the parabola opens to the right, as shown in Figure 11a; if $p < 0$, the parabola opens to the left, as shown in Figure 11b.

EXAMPLE 2   SKETCHING THE GRAPH OF A PARABOLA

Sketch the graph of each equation.

(a) $y^2 = \dfrac{x}{2}$ (b) $y^2 = -2x$

SOLUTIONS

We form tables of values giving points on the graphs and draw smooth curves.
See Figure 12.

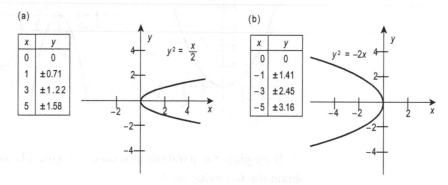

x	y
0	0
1	±0.71
3	±1.22
5	±1.58

x	y
0	0
−1	±1.41
−3	±2.45
−5	±3.16

Figure 12   Diagram for Example 2

✔ Progress Check 2

Sketch the graph of each equation.

(a) $y^2 = -\dfrac{x}{2}$ (b) $y^2 = \dfrac{1}{4}x$

Answers

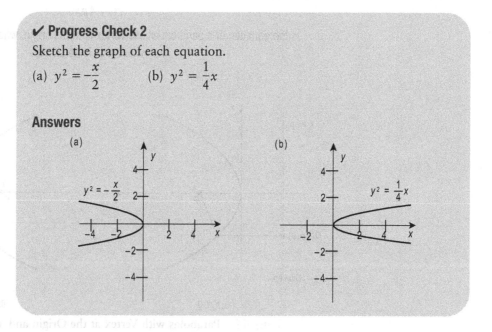

EXAMPLE 3   FINDING THE EQUATION OF A PARABOLA

Find the equation of the parabola that has the x-axis as its axis, has vertex at $(0, 0)$, and passes through the point $(-2, 3)$.

SOLUTION

Since the axis of the parabola is the x-axis, the equation of the parabola is $y^2 = 4px$. The parabola passes through the point $(-2, 3)$, so the coordinates of this point must satisfy the equation of the parabola. Thus,

$$y^2 = 4px$$
$$(3)^2 = 4p(-2)$$
$$4p = -\frac{9}{2}$$

and the equation of the parabolas is

$$y^2 = 4px = -\frac{9}{2}x$$

> ✔ **Progress Check 3**
>
> Find the equation of the parabola that has the x-axis as its axis, has vertex at $(0, 0)$, and passes through the point $(-2, 1)$.
>
> **Answer**
>
> $y^2 = -\frac{1}{2}x$

Vertex at (h, k)

It is also possible to determine an equation of the parabola when the vertex is at some arbitrary point (h, k). The form of the equation depends on whether the axis of the parabola is parallel to the x-axis or to the y-axis. The situations are summarized in Table 1. Note that if the point (h, k) is the origin, then $h = k = 0$, and we arrive at the equations we derived previously, $x^2 = 4py$ and $y^2 = 4px$.

TABLE 1   Standard Forms of the Equations of the Parabola

Equation	Vertex	Axis
$(x - h)^2 = 4p(y - k)$	(h, k)	$x = h$
$(y - k)^2 = 4p(x - h)$	(h, k)	$y = k$

EXAMPLE 4   GRAPHING FROM STANDARD FORM

Sketch the graph of the equation $(y - 3)^2 = -2(x + 2)$.

SOLUTION

The equation is the standard form of a parabola, with vertex at $(-2, 3)$ and axis of symmetry $y = 3$. See Figure 13.

y	x
5	-4
3	-2
1	-4
0	$-\dfrac{13}{2}$

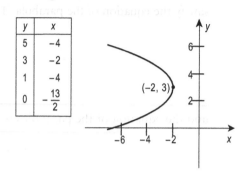

Figure 13   Diagram for Example 4

✔ Progress Check 4

Sketch the graph of the equation $(x + 1)^2 = 2(y + 2)$. Locate the vertex and the axis of symmetry.

Answer

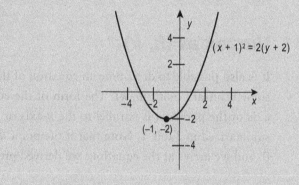

vertex: $(-1, -2)$; axis of symmetry: $x = -1$

From the graphs in Figures 10 and 13 and the answers to Progress Checks 1 and 4, we can make the following observations:

The graph of a parabola whose equation is

$$(x - h)^2 = 4p(y - k)$$

opens upward if $p > 0$ and downward if $p < 0$, and the axis of symmetry is $x = h$.
See Figures 14a and 14b.

Devices with a Parabolic Shape

The properties of the parabola are used in the design of some important devices. For example, by rotating a parabola about its axis, we obtain a **parabolic reflector,** a shape used in the headlight of an automobile. In the accompanying figure, the light source (the bulb) is placed at the focus of the parabolic reflector. The headlight is coated with a reflecting material, and the rays of light bounce back in lines that are parallel to the axis of the parabola. This permits a headlight to disperse light in front of the auto where it is needed.

A reflecting telescope reverses the use of these same properties. Here, the rays of light from a distant star, which are nearly parallel to the axis of the parabola, are reflected by the mirror to the focus (see accompanying figure). The eyepiece is placed at the focus, where the rays of light are gathered.

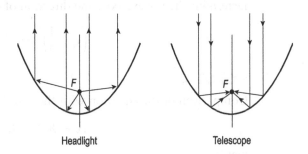

Headlight   Telescope

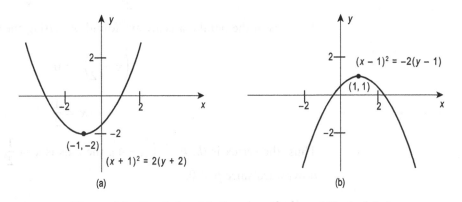

(a)   (b)

Figure 14   **Parabola with Center at (h, k) and Vertical Axis**

The graph of a parabola whose equation is

$$(y - k)^2 = 4p(x - h)$$

opens to the right if $p > 0$ and to the left if $p < 0$, and the axis of symmetry is $y = k$.
See Figures 15a and 15b.

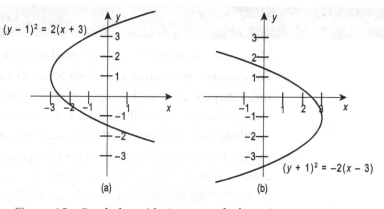

Figure 15   Parabolas with Center at (h, k) and Horizontal Axis

EXAMPLE 5   WORKING WITH THE STANDARD FORM

Determine the vertex, axis, and direction of opening of the graph of the parabola

$$\left(x - \frac{1}{2}\right)^2 = -\frac{1}{2}(y + 4)$$

SOLUTION

Comparison of the equation with the standard form

$$(x - h)^2 = 4p(y - k)$$

yields

$$h = \frac{1}{2}, k = -4, p = -\frac{1}{8}$$

The axis of the parabola is always found by setting the square term equal to 0.

$$\left(x - \frac{1}{2}\right)^2 = 0$$

$$x = \frac{1}{2}$$

Thus, the vertex is $(h, k) = \left(\frac{1}{2}, -4\right)$, the axis is $x = \frac{1}{2}$, and the parabola opens downward since $p < 0$.

> ✔ **Progress Check 5**
>
> Determine the vertex, axis, and direction of opening of the graph of the parabola
>
> $$(y + 1)^2 = 4\left(x - \frac{1}{3}\right)$$
>
> **Answer**
> vertex: $(\frac{1}{3}, -1)$; axis: $y = -1$; opens to the right

Any second-degree equation in x and y that has a square term in one variable but only first-degree terms in the other, represents a parabola. We can put such an equation in standard form by completing the square.

EXAMPLE 6   WRITING AN EQUATION IN STANDARD FORM

Determine the vertex, axis, and direction of opening of the parabola

$$2y^2 - 12y + x + 19 = 0$$

SOLUTION

First, we complete the square in y.

$$2y^2 - 12y + x + 19 = 0$$
$$2(y^2 - 6y) = -x - 19$$
$$2(y^2 - 6y + 9) = -x - 19 + 18$$
$$2(y - 3)^2 = -x - 1 = -(x + 1)$$
$$(y - 3)^2 = -\frac{1}{2}(x + 1)$$

With the equation in standard form, we see that $(h, k) = (-1, 3)$ is the vertex, $y = 3$ is the axis, and the curve opens to the left.

✔ **Progress Check 6**

Write the equation of the parabola $x^2 + 4x + y + 9 = 0$ in standard form. Determine the vertex, axis, and direction of opening.

Answer

$(x + 2)^2 = -(y + 5)$; vertex: $(-2, -5)$; axis: $x = -2$; opens downward

---

Exercise Set 12.4

In Exercises 1–16 sketch the graph of the given equation.

1. $x^2 = 4y$

2. $x^2 = -4y$

3. $y^2 = 2x$

4. $y^2 = -\frac{3}{2}x$

5. $x^2 = y$

6. $y^2 = x$

7. $x^2 + 5y = 0$

8. $2y^2 - 3x = 0$

9. $(x - 2)^2 = 2(y + 1)$

10. $(x + 4)^2 = 3(y - 2)$

11. $(y - 1)^2 = 3(x - 2)$

12. $(y - 2)^2 = -2(x + 1)$

13. $(x + 4)^2 = -\frac{1}{2}(y + 2)$

14. $(y - 1)^2 = -3(x - 2)$

15. $y^2 = -2(x + 1)$

16. $x^2 = \frac{1}{2}(y - 3)$

In Exercises 17–30 determine the vertex, axis, and direction of opening of the given parabola.

17. $x^2 - 2x - 3y + 7 = 0$

18. $x^2 + 4x + 2y - 2 = 0$

19. $y^2 - 8y + 2x + 12 = 0$

20. $y^2 + 6y - 3x + 12 = 0$

21. $x^2 - x + 3y + 1 = 0$

22. $y^2 + 2y - 4x - 3 = 0$

23. $y^2 - 10y - 3x + 24 = 0$

24. $x^2 + 2x - 5y - 19 = 0$

25. $x^2 - 3x - 3y + 1 = 0$

26. $y^2 + 4y + x + 3 = 0$

27. $y^2 + 6y + \frac{1}{2}x + 7 = 0$

28. $x^2 + 2x - 3y + 19 = 0$

29. $x^2 + 2x + 2y + 3 = 0$

30. $y^2 - 6y + 2x + 17 = 0$

In Exercises 31–40 determine the equation of the parabola that has its vertex at the origin and that satisfies the given conditions.

*31. focus at $(1, 0)$

*32. focus at $(0, -3)$

*33. directrix $x = -\dfrac{3}{2}$

*34. directrix $y = \dfrac{5}{2}$

*35. axis is the x-axis, and parabola passes through the point $(2, 1)$

*36. axis is the y-axis, and parabola passes through the point $(4, -2)$

*37. axis is the x-axis, and $p = -\dfrac{5}{4}$

*38. axis is the y-axis, and $p = 2$

*39. focus at $(-1, 0)$ and directrix $x = 1$

*40. focus at $(0, -\dfrac{5}{2})$ and directrix $y = \dfrac{5}{2}$

12.5   The Ellipse and the Hyperbola

The Ellipse

The geometric definition of an ellipse is as follows:

> An **ellipse** is the set of all points the sum of whose distances from two fixed points is a constant.

The fixed points are called the **foci** of the ellipse. An ellipse may be constructed in the following way. Place a thumbtack at each of the foci F_1 and F_2, and attach one end of a string to each of the thumbtacks. Hold a pencil tight against the string, as shown in Figure 16, and move the pencil. The point P will describe an ellipse since the sum of the distances from P to the foci is always a constant, namely, the length of the string.

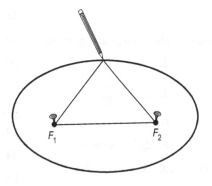

Figure 16   Sketching an Ellipse

The ellipse is in **standard position** if the foci are on either the x-axis or the y-axis and are equidistant from the origin. If the focus F_2 is at $(c, 0)$, then the other focus F_1 is at $(-c, 0)$, as in Figure 17. Let $P(x, y)$ be a point on the ellipse, and let the constant sum of the distances from P to the foci be denoted by $2a$. Then we have

$$\overline{PF_1} + \overline{PF_2} = 2a$$

Using the distance formula, we can obtain the equation of an ellipse in standard position as follows:

Standard Form of the Equation of an Ellipse

$$\frac{x^2}{a^2} + \frac{y^2}{b^2} = 1, \quad b \leq a$$

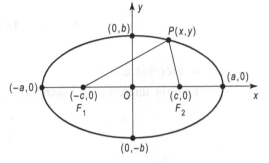

Figure 17   **Deriving the Equation of the Ellipse**

If we let $x = 0$ in the standard form, we find $y = \pm b$; if we let $y = 0$, we find $x = \pm a$. Thus, the ellipse whose equation is

$$\frac{x^2}{a^2} + \frac{y^2}{b^2} = 1$$

has intercepts $(\pm a, 0)$ and $(0, \pm b)$. See Figure 17.

EXAMPLE 1   USING THE STANDARD FORM FOR AN ELLIPSE

Find the intercepts and sketch the graph of the ellipse whose equation is

$$\frac{x^2}{16} + \frac{y^2}{9} = 1$$

SOLUTION

The intercepts are found by setting $x = 0$ and solving, then setting $y = 0$ and solving. Thus, the intercepts are $(\pm 4, 0)$ and $(0, \pm 3)$. The graph is then easily sketched (Figure 18).

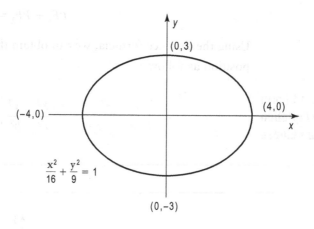

Figure 18   Diagram for Example 1

✔ **Progress Check 1**

Find the intercepts and sketch the graph of

$$\frac{x^2}{9} + \frac{y^2}{16} = 1$$

Answer

$(\pm 3, 0), (0, \pm 4)$

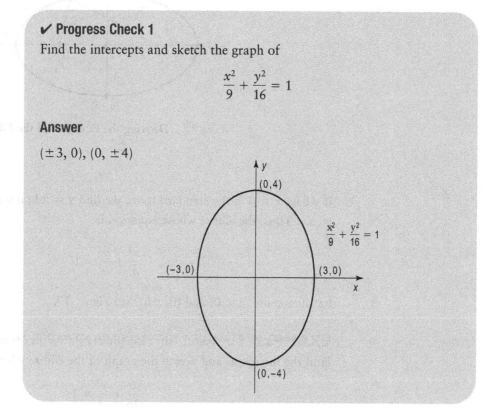

EXAMPLE 2   WRITING AN EQUATION IN STANDARD FORM

Write the equation of the ellipse in standard form and determine the intercepts.

(a) $4x^2 + 3y^2 = 12$ (b) $9x^2 + y^2 = 10$

Whispering Galleries

The domed roof in the accompanying figure has the shape of an ellipse that has been rotated about its major axis. It can be shown, using basic laws of physics, that a sound uttered at one focus will be reflected to the other focus, where it will be clearly heard. This property of such rooms is known as the "whispering gallery effect."

Famous whispering galleries include the dome of St. Paul's Cathedral, London; St. John Lateran, Rome; the Salle des Cariatides in the Louvre, Paris; and the original House of Representatives (now the National Statuary Hall in the United States Capitol), Washington, D.C.

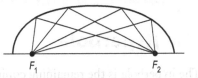

SOLUTIONS

(a) Dividing by 12 to make the right-hand side equal to 1, we have

$$\frac{x^2}{3} + \frac{y^2}{4} = 1$$

The x-intercepts are $(\pm\sqrt{3}, 0)$; the y-intercepts are $(0, \pm2)$.

(b) Dividing by 10, we have

$$\frac{9x^2}{10} + \frac{y^2}{10} = 1$$

But this is not standard form. However, if we write

$$\frac{9x^2}{10} \quad \text{as} \quad \frac{x^2}{\frac{10}{9}}$$

then

$$\frac{x^2}{\frac{10}{9}} + \frac{y^2}{10} = 1$$

is the standard form of an ellipse. The intercepts are

$$\left(\frac{\pm\sqrt{10}}{3}, 0\right) \quad \text{and} \quad (0, \pm\sqrt{10})$$

✔ **Progress Check 2**

Find the standard form and determine the intercepts of the ellipse.

(a) $2x^2 + 3y^2 = 6$ (b) $3x^2 + y^2 = 5$

Answers

(a) $\dfrac{x^2}{3} + \dfrac{y^2}{2} = 1$ $(\pm\sqrt{3}, 0), (0, \pm\sqrt{2})$

(b) $\dfrac{x^2}{\dfrac{5}{3}} + \dfrac{y^2}{5} = 1$ $\left(\pm\dfrac{\sqrt{15}}{3}, 0\right), (0, \pm\sqrt{5})$

The Hyperbola

The hyperbola is the remaining conic section that we will consider in this chapter.

A **hyperbola** is the set of all points the difference of whose distances from two fixed points is a positive constant.

The two fixed points are called the foci of the hyperbola, and the hyperbola is in **standard position** if the foci are on either the x-axis or the y-axis and are equidistant from the origin. If the foci lie on the x-axis and one focus F_2 is at $(c, 0)$, $c > 0$, then the other focus F_1 is at $(-c, 0)$. (See Figures 19a and 19b.)

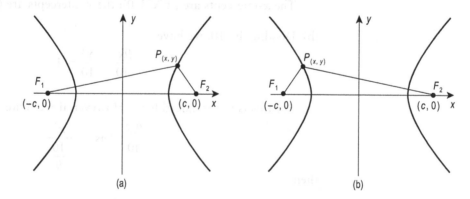

Figure 19   Deriving the Equation of the Hyperbola

Let P(x, y) be a point on the hyperbola, and let the constant difference of the distances from P to the foci be denoted by $2a$. If P is on the right branch, we have

$$\overline{PF_1} - \overline{PF_2} = 2a$$

whereas if P is on the left branch, we have

$$\overline{PF_2} - \overline{PF_1} = 2a$$

Both of these equations can be expressed by the single equation

$$\left| \overline{PF_1} - \overline{PF_2} \right| = 2a$$

Using the distance formula, we can obtain the equation of a hyperbola in standard position as follows:

Standard Form of the Equation of a Hyperbola (Foci on the x-axis)

$$\frac{x^2}{a^2} - \frac{y^2}{b^2} = 1 \qquad (1)$$

If the foci lie on the y-axis and one focus F_2 is at $(0, c)$, $c > 0$, then the other focus F_1 is at $(0, -c)$. In this case, we obtain the following equation of a hyperbola in standard position:

Standard Form of the Equation of a Hyperbola (Foci on the y-axis)

$$\frac{y^2}{a^2} - \frac{x^2}{b^2} = 1 \qquad (2)$$

Letting $y = 0$, we see that the x-intercepts of the graph of Equation (1) are $\pm a$. Letting $x = 0$, we find there are no y-intercepts since the equation $y^2 = -b^2$ has no real roots. (See Figure 20.) Similarly, the graph of Equation (2) has y-intercepts $\pm a$ and no x-intercepts.

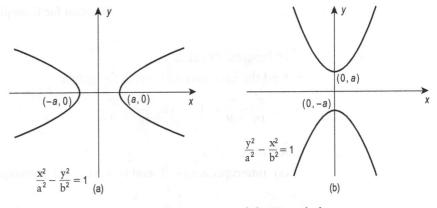

Figure 20   Intercepts of the Hyperbola

EXAMPLE 3   GRAPHING A HYPERBOLA

Find the intercepts and sketch the graph of the equation.

(a) $\dfrac{x^2}{9} - \dfrac{y^2}{4} = 1$ \qquad (b) $\dfrac{y^2}{4} - \dfrac{x^2}{3} = 1$

SOLUTIONS

(a) When $y = 0$, we have $x^2 = 9$, or $x = \pm 3$. The intercepts are $(3, 0)$ and $(-3, 0)$. With the assistance of a few plotted points, we can sketch the graph (Figure 21).

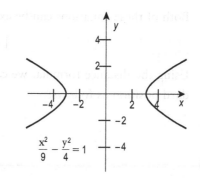

Figure 21   **Diagram for Example 3a**

(b) When $x = 0$, we have $y^2 = 4$, or $y = \pm 2$. The intercepts are $(0, 2)$ and $(0, -2)$.
Plotting a few points, we can sketch the graph (Figure 22).

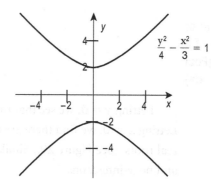

Figure 22   **Diagram for Example 3b**

✔ Progress Check 3
Find the intercepts and sketch the graph.

(a) $\dfrac{x^2}{16} - \dfrac{y^2}{9} = 1$ (b) $\dfrac{y^2}{16} - \dfrac{x^2}{9} = 1$

Answers
(a) intercepts are $(4, 0)$ and $(-4, 0)$ (b) intercepts are $(0, 4)$ and $(0, -4)$

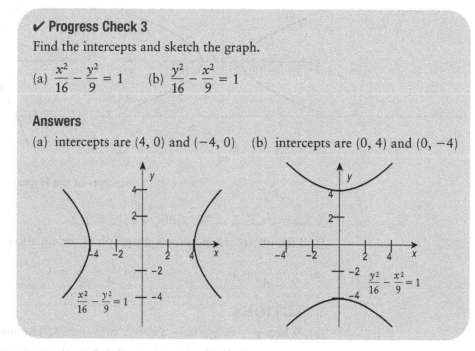

EXAMPLE 4   WRITING AN EQUATION IN STANDARD FORM

Write the equation of the hyperbola in standard form and determine the intercepts.

(a) $9y^2 - 4x^2 = 36$ (b) $8x^2 - 9y^2 = 18$

SOLUTIONS

(a) Dividing by 36 to produce a 1 on the right-hand side, we have

$$\frac{y^2}{4} - \frac{x^2}{9} = 1$$

The y-intercepts are $(0, \pm 2)$. There are no x-intercepts.

(b) Dividing by 18, we have

$$\frac{4x^2}{9} - \frac{y^2}{2} = 1$$

Rewritten in standard form, the equation becomes

$$\frac{x^2}{\frac{9}{4}} - \frac{y^2}{2} = 1$$

The x-intercepts are

$$\left(\pm\frac{3}{2}, 0\right)$$

There are no y-intercepts.

✔ **Progress Check 4**

Write the equation of the hyperbola in standard form and determine the intercepts.

(a) $2x^2 - 5y^2 = 6$ (b) $4y^2 - x^2 = 5$

Answers

(a) $\dfrac{x^2}{3} - \dfrac{y^2}{\frac{6}{5}} = 1$ $(\pm\sqrt{3}, 0)$ (b) $\dfrac{y^2}{\frac{5}{4}} - \dfrac{x^2}{5} = 1$ $\left(0, \dfrac{\pm\sqrt{5}}{2}\right)$

Asymptotes

There is a way of sketching the graph of a hyperbola without the need for plotting points of the curve. Given the equation of the hyperbola

$$\frac{x^2}{a^2} - \frac{y^2}{b^2} = 1$$

in standard form, we plot the four points $(\pm a, \pm b)$, as in Figure 23, and draw the diagonals of the rectangle formed by the four points. The hyperbola opens from the intercepts $(\pm a, 0)$ and *approaches the lines formed by the diagonals of the rectangle.* We call these lines the asymptotes of the hyperbola. Since one asymptote passes through the points $(0, 0)$ and (a, b), its equation is

$$y = \frac{b}{a}x$$

The equation of the other asymptote is found to be

$$y = -\frac{b}{a}x$$

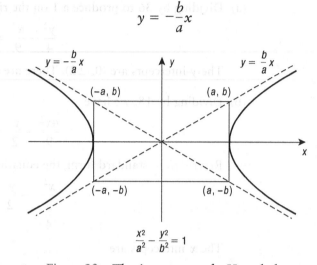

$$\frac{x^2}{a^2} - \frac{y^2}{b^2} = 1$$

Figure 23   **The Asymptotes of a Hyperbola**

Of course, a similar argument can be made about the standard form

$$\frac{y^2}{a^2} - \frac{x^2}{b^2} = 1$$

In this case, the four points $(\pm b, \pm a)$ determine the rectangle and the equations of the asymptotes are

$$y = \pm \frac{a}{b}x$$

To summarize:

Asymptotes of the Hyperbola

$\dfrac{x^2}{a^2} - \dfrac{y^2}{b^2} = 1$	has asymptotes	$y = \pm \dfrac{b}{a}x$
$\dfrac{y^2}{a^2} - \dfrac{x^2}{b^2} = 1$	has asymptotes	$y = \pm \dfrac{a}{b}x$

EXAMPLE 5   USING THE ASYMPTOTES TO GRAPH A HYPERBOLA

Using asymptotes, sketch the graph of the equation

$$\frac{y^2}{4} - \frac{x^2}{9} = 1$$

SOLUTION

The points $(\pm 3, \pm 2)$ form the vertices of the rectangle. See Figure 24. Using the fact that $(0, \pm 2)$ are intercepts, we can sketch the graph opening from these points and approaching the asymptotes.

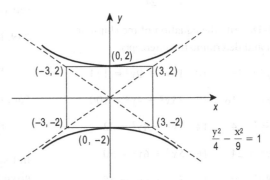

Figure 24   Graph for Example 5

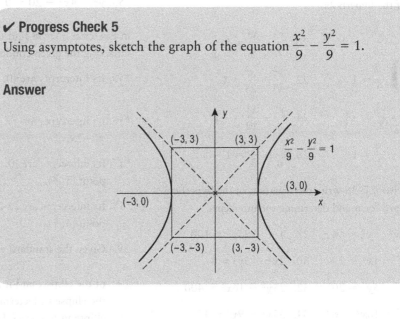

✔ **Progress Check 5**
Using asymptotes, sketch the graph of the equation $\dfrac{x^2}{9} - \dfrac{y^2}{9} = 1$.

Answer

Exercise Set 12.5

In Exercises 1–8 find the intercepts and sketch the graph of the ellipse.

1. $\dfrac{x^2}{25} + \dfrac{y^2}{4} = 1$ 2. $\dfrac{x^2}{4} + \dfrac{y^2}{16} = 1$

3. $\dfrac{x^2}{9} + \dfrac{y^2}{4} = 1$ 4. $\dfrac{x^2}{12} + \dfrac{y^2}{18} = 1$

5. $\dfrac{x^2}{16} + \dfrac{y^2}{25} = 1$ 6. $\dfrac{x^2}{1} + \dfrac{y^2}{3} = 1$

7. $\dfrac{x^2}{20} + \dfrac{y^2}{10} = 1$ 8. $\dfrac{x^2}{6} + \dfrac{y^2}{24} = 1$

In Exercises 9–18 write the equation of the ellipse in standard form and determine the intercepts.

9. $4x^2 + 9y^2 = 36$ 10. $16x^2 + 9y^2 = 144$

11. $4x^2 + 16y^2 = 16$ 12. $25x^2 + 4y^2 = 100$

13. $4x^2 + 16y^2 = 4$ 14. $8x^2 + 4y^2 = 32$

15. $8x^2 + 6y^2 = 24$ 16. $5x^2 + 6y^2 = 50$

17. $36x^2 + 8y^2 = 9$ 18. $5x^2 + 4y^2 = 45$

In Exercises 19–26 find the intercepts and sketch the graph of the hyperbola.

19. $\dfrac{x^2}{25} - \dfrac{y^2}{16} = -1$ 20. $\dfrac{y^2}{9} - \dfrac{x^2}{4} = 1$

21. $\dfrac{x^2}{36} - \dfrac{y^2}{9} = 1$ 22. $\dfrac{y^2}{49} - \dfrac{x^2}{25} = 1$

23. $\dfrac{x^2}{6} - \dfrac{y^2}{8} = -1$ 24. $\dfrac{y^2}{8} - \dfrac{x^2}{10} = -1$

25. $\dfrac{x^2}{12} - \dfrac{y^2}{2} = 1$ 26. $\dfrac{y^2}{6} - \dfrac{x^2}{5} = 1$

In Exercises 27–36 write the equation of the hyperbola in standard form and determine the intercepts.

27. $16x^2 - y^2 = 64$ 28. $4x^2 - 25y^2 = 100$

29. $4y^2 - 4x^2 = 1$ 30. $2x^2 - 3y^2 = 6$

31. $4x^2 - 5y^2 = 20$ 32. $25y^2 - 16x^2 = 400$

33. $4y^2 - 16x^2 = 64$ 34. $35x^2 - 9y^2 = 45$

35. $8x^2 - 4y^2 = 32$ 36. $4y^2 - 36x^2 = 9$

In Exercises 37–48, using asymptotes, sketch the graph of the given hyperbola.

37. $\dfrac{x^2}{16} - \dfrac{y^2}{4} = 1$ 38. $\dfrac{y^2}{4} - \dfrac{x^2}{25} = 1$

39. $\dfrac{y^2}{4} - \dfrac{x^2}{4} = 1$ 40. $\dfrac{x^2}{4} - \dfrac{y^2}{16} = 1$

41. $16x^2 - 4y^2 = 144$ 42. $16y^2 - 25x^2 = 400$

43. $9y^2 - 9x^2 = 1$ 44. $25x^2 - 9y^2 = 225$

45. $\dfrac{x^2}{25} - \dfrac{y^2}{36} = 1$ 46. $y^2 - 4x^2 = 4$

47. $y^2 - x^2 = 1$ 48. $\dfrac{x^2}{36} - \dfrac{y^2}{36} = 1$

In Exercises 49 and 50 find an equation of the ellipse satisfying the given conditions.

*49. Its intercepts are $(\pm 7, 0)$, and it passes through the point $\left(1, \dfrac{6\sqrt{3}}{7}\right)$.

*50. Its intercepts are $(0, \pm 1)$, and it passes through the point $\left(\dfrac{1}{4}, \dfrac{\sqrt{3}}{2}\right)$.

In Exercises 51–54 determine whether the foci of the given hyperbola lie on the x-axis or on the y-axis.

*51. $2x^2 - 3y^2 - 5 = 0$ *52. $3x^2 - 3y^2 + 4 = 0$

*53. $y^2 - 4x^2 - 20 = 0$ *54. $4y^2 - 9x^2 + 36 = 0$

In Exercises 55–58 find the equation of the hyperbola satisfying the given conditions.

*55. Its intercepts are $(0, \pm 3)$, and it has asymptote $y = x$.

*56. Its intercepts are $(\pm 2, 0)$, and it has asymptote $y = -2x$.

*57. Its intercepts are $(0, \pm 4)$, and it passes through the point $(5, 5)$.

*58. Its intercepts are $(\pm 2, 0)$, and it passes through the point $(3, 1)$.

59. Given the standard equation for an ellipse, define $c = \sqrt{a^2 - b^2}$. The ratio $\dfrac{c}{a}$ is called the eccentricity of the ellipse, and it measures how nearly circular the ellipse is. Determine the eccentricity of each ellipse in Exercises 1–8.

60. The planets in our solar system travel in elliptical orbits around the sun. The eccentricity of the Earth's orbit is about 0.017, and that of the orbit of Mars is 0.093. What does this tell you about the shapes of the two planets' orbits?

12.6   Identifying the Conic Sections

Each of the conic sections we have studied in this chapter has one or more axes of symmetry. We studied the circle and parabola when their axes of symmetry were the coordinate axes or lines parallel to them. Although our study of the ellipse and hyperbola was restricted to those that have the coordinate axes as their axes of symmetry, the same method of completing the square allows us to transform the general equation of the conic section

$$Ax^2 + Cy^2 + Dx + Ey + F = 0$$

into standard form. This transformation is very helpful in sketching the graph of the conic section. It is easy, also, to identify the conic section from the general equation (see Table 2).

TABLE 2   The General Second-Degree Equation and the Conic Sections

$Ax^2 + Cy^2 + Dx + Ey + F = 0$	Conic Section	Remarks
$A = 0$ or $C = 0$ (A and C not both 0)	Parabola	Second degree in one variable, first degree in the other
$A = C$ ($\neq 0$)	Circle	Coefficients A and C are the same. *Caution:* Complete the square and check that $r > 0$.
$A \neq C$ $AC > 0$	Ellipse	A and C are unequal but have the same sign. *Caution:* Complete the square and check that the right-hand side is a positive constant.
$A \neq C$ $AC < 0$	Hyperbola	A and C have opposite signs.

EXAMPLE 1   IDENTIFYING THE CONIC SECTIONS

Identify the conic section.

(a) $3x^2 + 3y^2 - 2y = 4$ (b) $3x^2 - 9y^2 + 2x - 4y = 7$
(c) $2x^2 + 5y^2 - 7x + 3y - 4 = 0$ (d) $3y^2 - 4x + 17y = -10$

SOLUTIONS

(a) Since the coefficients of x^2 and y^2 are the same, the graph will be a circle if the standard form yields $r > 0$. Completing the square, we have

$$3x^2 + 3\left(y - \frac{1}{3}\right)^2 = \frac{13}{3}$$

which is the equation of a circle.

(b) Since the coefficients of x^2 and y^2 are of opposite sign, the graph is a hyperbola.

(c) The coefficients of x^2 and y^2 are unequal but of like sign, so the graph is an ellipse. (Verify that the right-hand side is positive.)

(d) The graph is a parabola since the equation is of the second degree in y and of first degree in x.

✔ **Progress Check 1**

Identify the conic section.

(a) $\dfrac{x^2}{5} - 3y^2 - 2x + 2y - 4 = 0$ 　　　 (b) $x^2 - 2y - 3x = 2$

(c) $x^2 + y^2 - 4x - 6y = -11$ 　　　 (d) $4x^2 + 3y^2 + 6x - 10 = 0$

Answers

(a) hyperbola 　　 (b) parabola 　　 (c) circle 　　 (d) ellipse

A summary of the characteristics of the conic sections is given in Table 3.

TABLE 3 Standard Forms of the Conic Sections

Curves and Standard Equation	Characteristics	Example
Circle $(x - h)^2 + (y - k)^2 = r^2$	Center: (h, k) Radius: r	$(x - 2)^2 + (y + 4)^2 = 25$ Center: $(2, -4)$ Radius: 5
Parabola $(x - h)^2 = 4p(y - k)$ or	Vertex: (h, k) Axis: $x = h$ $p > 0$: Opens up $p < 0$: Opens down	$(x + 1)^2 = 2(y - 3)$ Vertex: $(-1, 3)$ Axis: $x = -1$ Opens up
$(y - k)^2 = 4p(x - h)$	Vertex: (h, k) Axis: $y = k$ $p > 0$: Opens to the right $p < 0$: Opens to the left	$(y + 4)^2 = -3(x + 5)$ Vertex: $(-5, -4)$ Axis: $y = -4$ Opens to the left
Ellipse $\dfrac{x^2}{a^2} + \dfrac{y^2}{b^2} = 1$	Intercepts: $(\pm a, 0), (0, \pm b)$	$\dfrac{x^2}{4} + \dfrac{y^2}{6} = 1$ Intercepts: $(\pm 2, 0), (0, \pm \sqrt{6})$

continues

TABLE 3 *continued*

Curves and Standard Equation	Characteristics	Example
Hyperbola $\dfrac{x^2}{a^2} - \dfrac{y^2}{b^2} = 1$ or $\dfrac{y^2}{a^2} - \dfrac{x^2}{b^2} = 1$	Intercepts: $(\pm a, 0)$ Asymptotes: $y = \pm \dfrac{b}{a}x$ Opens to left and right Intercepts: $(0, \pm a)$ Asymptotes: $y = \pm \dfrac{a}{b}x$ Opens up and down	$\dfrac{x^2}{4} - \dfrac{y^2}{9} = 1$ Intercepts: $(\pm 2, 0)$ Asymptotes: $y = \pm \dfrac{3}{2}x$ Opens to left and right $\dfrac{y^2}{9} - \dfrac{x^2}{4} = 1$ Intercepts: $(0, \pm 3)$ Asymptotes: $y = \pm \dfrac{3}{2}x$ Opens up and down

Exercise Set 12.6

In Exercises 1–30 identify the conic section.

1. $2x^2 + y - x + 3 = 0$

2. $4y^2 - x^2 + 2x - 3y + 5 = 0$

3. $4x^2 + 4y^2 - 2x + 3y - 4 = 0$

4. $3x^2 + 6y^2 - 2x + 8 = 0$

5. $36x^2 - 4y^2 + x - y + 2 = 0$

6. $x^2 + y^2 - 6x + 4y + 13 = 0$

7. $16x^2 + 4y^2 - 2y + 3 = 0$

8. $2y^2 - 3x + y + 4 = 0$

9. $x^2 + y^2 - 4x - 2y + 8 = 0$

10. $x^2 + y^2 - 2x - 2y + 6 = 0$

11. $4x^2 + 9y^2 - x + 2 = 0$

12. $3x^2 + 3y^2 - 3x + y = 0$

13. $4x^2 - 9y^2 + 2x + y + 3 = 0$

14. $x^2 + y^2 + 6x - 2y + 10 = 0$

15. $x^2 + y^2 - 4x + 4 = 0$

16. $2x^2 + 3x - 5y^2 + 4y - 6 = 0$

17. $4x^2 + y^2 - 2x + y + 4 = 0$

18. $x^2 - \dfrac{1}{2}y^2 + 2x - y + 3 = 0$

19. $4x^2 + 4y^2 - x + 2y - 1 = 0$

20. $x^2 + y^2 + 6x - 6y + 18 = 0$

21. $4x^2 + y + 2x - 3 = 0$

22. $y^2 - \dfrac{1}{4}x^2 + 2x + 6 = 0$

23. $x^2 + y^2 + 4x - 2y + 7 = 0$

24. $y^2 + 2y - \dfrac{1}{2}x + 3 = 0$

25. $x^2 + y^2 - 2x - 10y - 26 = 0$

26. $3x^2 + 2y^2 - y + 2 = 0$

27. $\dfrac{1}{2}x^2 + y - x - 3 = 0$

28. $3x^2 - 2y^2 + 2x - 5y + 5 = 0$

29. $2x^2 + y^2 - 3x + 2y - 5 = 0$

30. $x^2 - 2x - y + 1 = 0$

■ ■ ■

Chapter Summary

Terms and Symbols

asymptotes of a hyperbola	474	foci of a hyperbola	470	standard equation of a circle	453
axis of a parabola	457	focus of a parabola	457	standard equation of an ellipse	467
center	453	general equation of a circle	454	standard equations of a hyperbola	471
circle	452	general equation of the conic sections	477		
conic sections	452			standard equation of a parabola	458
directrix	457	hyperbola	470		
distance formula	444	midpoint formula	444	symmetry	448
ellipse	466	parabola	457	vertex	457
foci of an ellipse	466	radius	453		

Key Ideas for Review

Topic	Page	Key Idea
Distance and midpoint formulas	443	If $P_1(x_1, y_1)$ and $P_2(x_2, y_2)$ are any two points, then the distance d between the points is given by the formula $$d = \sqrt{(x_2 - x_1)^2 + (y_2 - y_1)^2}$$ and the midpoint Q has coordinates $$\left(\frac{x_1 + x_2}{2}, \frac{y_1 + y_2}{2}\right)$$
Analytic geometry: proving theorems	446	Theorems from plane geometry can be proven using the methods of analytic geometry. In general, place the given geometric figure in a convenient position relative to the origin and axes. The distance formula, the midpoint formula, and the computation of slope are the tools to apply in proving such theorems.
Symmetry	448	Symmetry about a line or a point means that the curve is its own reflection about that line or that point. The graph of an equation in x and y will be symmetric with respect to the (a) x-axis if an equivalent equation results when y is replaced by $-y$; (b) y-axis if an equivalent equation results when x is replaced by $-x$; (c) origin if an equivalent equation results when both x and y are replaced by $-x$ and $-y$, respectively
Conic sections	452	The conic sections are the circle, the parabola, the ellipse, and the hyperbola. In some special cases, these reduce to a point, a line, two lines, or no graph. The conic sections represent the possible intersections of a cone and a plane.
geometric definition	452	Each conic section has a geometric definition as a set of points satisfying certain given conditions.

continues

Topic	Page	Key Idea
Graph of a second-degree equation		
standard form	478	A second-degree equation in x and y can be written in standard form by completing the square in the variables. It is much easier to sketch the graph when the equation is in standard form than it is when the equation is in general form.
general form	477	It is often possible to distinguish the various conic sections even when the equation is given in the general form.

Common Errors

1. When completing the square, be careful to balance both sides of the equation.

2. The first step in writing the equation

$$4x^2 + 25y^2 = 9$$

in standard form is to divide both sides of the equation by 9. The result,

$$\frac{4x^2}{9} + \frac{25y^2}{9} = 1$$

is *not* in standard form. You must rewrite this as

$$\frac{x^2}{\frac{9}{4}} + \frac{y^2}{\frac{9}{25}} = 1$$

to obtain standard form and to determine the intercepts

$$\left(\pm\frac{3}{2},\ 0\right), \left(0,\ \pm\frac{3}{5}\right).$$

3. The graph of the equation $3y^2 - 4x - 6 = 0$ is *not* a hyperbola. If only one variable appears to the second degree, the equation is that of a parabola.

4. The safest way to find the intercepts is to let one variable equal 0 and solve for the other variable. If

you attempt to memorize the various forms, you might conclude that the intercepts of

$$\frac{y^2}{16} - \frac{x^2}{9} = 1$$

are $(\pm 4, 0)$. However, when $x = 0$, we see that $y^2 = 16$ or $y = \pm 4$ and the intercepts are $(0, \pm 4)$. To find the intercepts of

$$\frac{y^2}{16} - \frac{x^2}{9} = -1$$

don't conclude that the intercepts are $(0, \pm 4)$. When $x = 0$, $y^2 = -16$ has no solution. When $y = 0$, $x^2 = 9$ leads to the intercepts $(\pm 3, 0)$.

5. When analyzing the type of conic section from the general form of the second-degree equation, remember that the circle and ellipse have degenerate cases in which the graph turns out to be a point, a line, or a pair of lines. The equation

$$2x^2 + y^2 - 8x + 6y + 21 = 0$$

is equivalent to

$$2(x - 2)^2 + (y + 3)^2 = -4$$

which is impossible. There are no points we can graph that will satisfy this equation.

Review Exercises

Solutions to exercises whose numbers are in bold are in the Solutions section in the back of the book.

12.1 In Exercises 1–3 find the distance between the given pair of points.

1. $(-4, -6), (2, -1)$ **2.** $(3, 4), (3, -2)$

3. $(4, 5), (1, 3)$

In Exercises 4–6 find the midpoint of the line segment whose endpoints are given.

4. $(-5, 4), (3, -6)$ **5.** $(-2, 0), (-3, 5)$

6. $(2, -7), (-3, -2)$

7. Find the coordinates of the point P_2 if $(2, 2)$ are the coordinates of the midpoint of the line segment joining $P_1(-6, -3)$ and P_2.

8. Use the distance formula to show that $P_1(-1, 2)$, $P_2(4, 3)$, $P_3(1, -1)$, and $P_4(-4, -2)$ are the coordinates of a parallelogram.

9. Show that the points $A(-8, 4)$, $B(5, 3)$, and $C(2, -2)$ are the vertices of a right triangle.

10. Find an equation of the perpendicular bisector of the line segment joining the points $A(-4, -3)$ and $B(1, 3)$. (The perpendicular bisector passes through the midpoint of AB and is perpendicular to AB.)

12.2 In Exercises 11 and 12 analyze the given equation for symmetry with respect to the x-axis, y-axis, and origin.

11. $y^2 = 1 - x^3$ **12.** $y^2 = \dfrac{x^2}{x^2 - 5}$

12.3 13. Write an equation of the circle with center at $(-5, 2)$ and a radius of 4.

14. Write an equation of the circle with center at $(-3, -3)$ and radius 2.

In Exercises 15–20 determine the center and radius of the circle with the given equation.

15. $(x - 2)^2 + (y + 3)^2 = 9$

16. $\left(x + \dfrac{1}{2}\right)^2 + (y - 4)^2 = \dfrac{1}{9}$

17. $x^2 + y^2 + 4x - 6y = -10$

18. $2x^2 + 2y^2 - 4x + 4y = -3$

19. $x^2 + y^2 - 6y + 3 = 0$

20. $x^2 + y^2 - 2x - 2y = 8$

12.4 In Exercises 21 and 22 determine the vertex and axis of the given parabola. Sketch the graph.

21. $(y + 5)^2 = 4\left(x - \dfrac{3}{2}\right)$ **22.** $(x - 1)^2 = 2 - y$

In Exercises 23–28 determine the vertex, axis, and direction of the given parabola.

23. $y^2 + 3x + 9 = 0$

24. $y^2 + 4y + x + 2 = 0$

25. $2x^2 - 12x - y + 16 = 0$

26. $x^2 + 4x + 2y + 5 = 0$

27. $y^2 - 2y - 4x + 1 = 0$

28. $x^2 + 6x + 4y + 9 = 0$

12.5 In Exercises 29–34 write the given equation in standard form and determine the intercepts of its graph.

29. $9x^2 - 4y^2 = 36$ **30.** $9x^2 + y^2 = 9$

31. $5x^2 + 7y^2 = 35$ **32.** $9x^2 - 16y^2 = 144$

33. $3x^2 + 4y^2 = 9$ **34.** $3y^2 - 5x^2 = 20$

In Exercises 35 and 36 use the intercepts and asymptotes of the hyperbola to sketch the graph.

35. $4x^2 - 4y^2 = 1$ **36.** $9y^2 - 4x^2 = 36$

12.6 In Exercises 37–40 identify the conic section whose equation is given.

37. $2y^2 + 6y - 3x + 2 = 0$

38. $6x^2 - 7y^2 - 5x + 6y = 0$

39. $2x^2 + y^2 + 12x - 2y + 17 = 0$

40. $9x^2 + 4y^2 = -36$

Progress Test 12A

1. Find the distance between the points $P_1(-3, 4)$ and $P_2(4, -3)$.

2. Find the midpoint of the line segment whose endpoints are $P_1(\frac{1}{2}, -1)$ and $P_2(2, \frac{3}{4})$.

3. Given the points $A(1, -2)$, $B(5, -1)$, $C(2, 7)$, and $D(6, 8)$, show that AC is equal and parallel to BD.

4. Show that $A(-1, 7)$, $B(-3, 2)$, and $C(4, 5)$ are the coordinates of the vertices of an isosceles triangle.

5. Without sketching, determine symmetry with respect to the x-axis, y-axis, and origin:
$$3x^2 - 2x - 4y^2 = 6$$

6. Without sketching, determine symmetry with respect to the x-axis, y-axis, and origin:
$$y^2 = \frac{2x}{x^2 - 1}$$

7. Find the center and radius of the circle whose equation is $x^2 - 8x + y^2 + 6y + 15 = 0$. Sketch.

8. Find the vertex and axis of symmetry of the parabola whose equation is $4y^2 - 4y + 12x = -13$. Sketch.

9. Find the intercepts and asymptotes of the hyperbola whose equation is
$$4y^2 - \frac{x^2}{9} = 1.$$
Sketch.

10. Find the equation of the circle having center at $(\frac{2}{3}, -3)$ and radius $\sqrt{3}$.

11. Find the intercepts and vertex and sketch the graph of the parabola whose equation is $y = x^2 - x - 6$.

12. Find the intercepts and sketch the graph of the equation
$$\frac{x^2}{36} + \frac{y^2}{9} = 1$$

13. Identify the conic section whose equation is
$$3x^2 + 2x - 7y^2 + 3y - 14 = 0$$

14. Identify the conic section whose equation is
$$y^2 - 3y - 5x = 20$$

15. Identify the conic section whose equation is
$$x^2 - 6x + y^2 = 0$$

Progress Test 12B

1. Find the distance between the points $P_1(6, -7)$ and $P_2(2, -5)$.

2. Find the midpoint of the line segment whose endpoints are $P_1(-\frac{3}{2}, -\frac{1}{2})$ and $P_2(-2, 1)$.

3. The point $(3, 2)$ is the midpoint of a line segment having the point $(4, -1)$ as an endpoint. Find the other endpoint.

4. Show that the points $A(-8, 4)$, $B(5, 3)$, and $C(2, -2)$ are the vertices of a right triangle.

5. Without sketching, determine symmetry with respect to the x-axis, y-axis, and origin:
$$y = 3x^3 - 8x$$

6. Without sketching, determine symmetry with respect to the x-axis, y-axis, and origin:
$$y = \frac{1}{4 - x^2}$$

7. Find the center and radius of the circle whose equation is $x^2 + x + y^2 - 6y = -9$. Sketch.

8. Find the vertex and axis of symmetry of the parabola whose equation is $16x^2 - 8x + 32y + 65 = 0$. Sketch.

9. Find the intercepts and asymptotes of the hyperbola whose equation is $3x^2 - 8y^2 = 2$. Sketch.

10. Find the equation of the circle having center at $(-1, -\frac{1}{2})$ and radius $\sqrt{5}$.

11. Find the intercepts and vertex and sketch the graph of the parabola whose equation is $y = -x^2 + 16x - 14$.

12. Find the intercepts and sketch the graph of the equation
$$4x^2 + y^2 = 9$$

13. Identify the conic section whose equation is
$$x^2 - 4x + y^2 - 6y + 12 = 0$$

14. Identify the conic section whose equation is
$$x^2 + 2x - 5y + 4 = 0$$

15. Identify the conic section whose equation is
$$x^2 + 2y^2 - 4x + 3 = 0$$

Chapter 12 Project

The planet that is usually farthest from the sun is Pluto. The orbit of Pluto, like that of all the planets in our Solar System, is an ellipse. The ellipse that Pluto traces, however, is much less nearly circular than that of any other planet. The eccentricity of the orbit of Pluto is about 0.25, which is almost fifteen times as great as that of Earth.

Review Exercises 59 and 60 in Section 12.5.

For this project, we will imagine ourselves to be NASA scientists, planning to launch a probe to study Pluto. We must try to determine an equation for the orbit of Pluto, given the following facts: The eccentricity of the ellipse is 0.25, and the value of a is about 3,670 million miles. Recall that $e = \frac{c}{a}$.

From this information, set up and solve an equation for c. Now use the fact that $c = \sqrt{a^2 - b^2}$ to solve a radical equation for b. Then write out an equation for the ellipse that is the orbit of Pluto.

Do some more research into the mathematics of space and space travel. How accurate is your equation?

■ ■ ■

13 Systems of Equations and Inequalities

The mathematician's patterns, like the painter's or poet's must be beautiful; the ideas, like the colours or the words, must fit together in a harmonious way. Beauty is the first test; there is no permanent place in the world for ugly mathematics.

—G. H. Hardy

Mathematics students become accustomed to seeing equations. However, if you look at the world around you, you rarely see equations! What you do see is relationships that can be modeled by equations. One way to do this is by polynomial curve fitting. This is a process whereby we find the equation of a polynomial that passes through any point we are given (perhaps these points represent paired data, like heights and weights). The process of finding an equation in standard form for a polynomial that passes through a given set of points requires that we solve a system of equations. You will get some practice doing this in this chapter's project.

Continue your investigation of mathematics on the Web by checking out the following site: www.cut-the-knot.org/.

www.cut-the-knot.org/

485

Many problems in business and engineering require the solution of systems of equations and inequalities. In fact, systems of linear equations and inequalities occur with such frequency that mathematicians and computer scientists have devoted considerable energy to devising methods for their solution. With the aid of large-scale computers, it is possible to solve systems involving thousands of equations or inequalities, containing thousands of variables.

We begin with the study of the methods of substitution and elimination, methods that are applicable to all types of systems. We then introduce graphical methods for solving systems of linear inequalities and apply this technique to linear programming problems, a type of optimization problem.

13.1   Systems of Equations

A pile of 9 coins consists of nickels and quarters. If the total value of the coins is $1.25, how many of each type of coin are in the pile?

This type of word problem was handled in earlier chapters by using one variable. A more natural way to approach this problem is to let

$$x = \text{the number of nickels}$$

and

$$y = \text{the number of quarters}$$

that is, to use two variables. The requirements can then be expressed as

$$x + y = 9$$
$$5x + 25y = 125$$

This is an example of a **system of equations**, and we seek values of x and y that satisfy both equations. An ordered pair (a, b) such that $x = a$, $y = b$ that satisfies both equations is called a **solution** of the system. Thus,

$$x = 5, \qquad y = 4$$

is a solution because substituting in the equations of the system gives

$$5 + 4 = 9$$
$$5(5) + 25(4) = 125$$

Solving by Graphing

The coordinates of every point on the graph of an equation must satisfy the equation. If we sketch the graphs of a pair of equations on the same coordinate axes, it follows that the *points of intersection* must satisfy *both* equations. Thus, we have a graphical means of solving a system of equations.

EXAMPLE 1   SOLVING A SYSTEM OF EQUATIONS BY GRAPHING

Solve the system of equations by graphing.

$$x^2 + y^2 = 25$$
$$x + y = -1$$

SOLUTION

The graphs of the equations are a circle and a line, as shown in Figure 1. The points of intersection are seen to be $(-4, 3)$ and $(3, -4)$. The solutions of the system are $x = -4$, $y = 3$ and $x = 3$, $y = -4$.

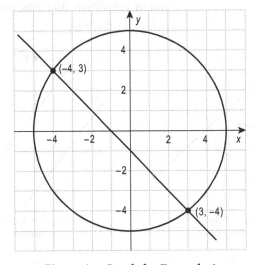

Figure 1   Graph for Example 1

✔ Progress Check 1

Solve the system of equations by graphing.

$$x^2 + y^2 + 2y = 9$$
$$y - 2x = 4$$

Answers

$x = -1, y = 2; x = -3, y = -2$

It is possible for a system of equations to have no solutions. Surprisingly, a system of equations may even have an infinite number of solutions. The following terminology is used to distinguish these situations.

Consistent and Inconsistent Systems

- A **consistent** system of equations has one or more solutions.
- An **inconsistent** system of equations has no solutions.

A system consisting only of equations that are of the first degree in x and y is called a **system of linear equations** or simply a **linear system**. When we graph a linear system of two equations on the same set of coordinate axes, there are three possibilities:

1. The two lines intersect at a point (Figure 2a). The system is consistent and has a unique solution, the point of the intersection.

2. The two lines are parallel (Figure 2b). Since the lines do not intersect, the linear system is inconsistent.

3. The equations are different forms of the same line (Figure 2c). The system is consistent and has an infinite number of solutions, namely, all points on the line.

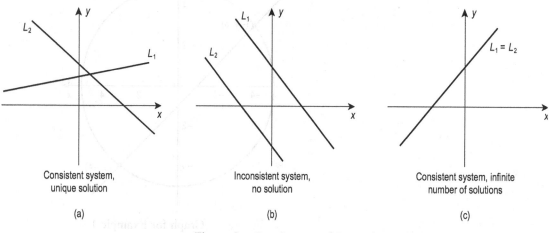

Consistent system,
unique solution

(a)

Inconsistent system,
no solution

(b)

Consistent system, infinite
number of solutions

(c)

Figure 2   **Consistent and Inconsistent Systems**

The following example illustrates the latter two cases.

EXAMPLE 2   GRAPHING LINEAR SYSTEMS
Solve by graphing.

(a) $6x - 2y = 9$
$3x - y = 12$

(b) $2x + 3y = 5$
$6x + 9y = 15$

SOLUTIONS

(a) See Figure 3a. The graphs are those of parallel lines. Therefore, since the lines do not intersect, the system has no solution.

(b) See Figure 3b. The system yields only one line because the two equations are equivalent. Since any point on the line is a solution, we can say that the solution set is

$$\{(x, y) \mid 2x + 3y = 5\}$$

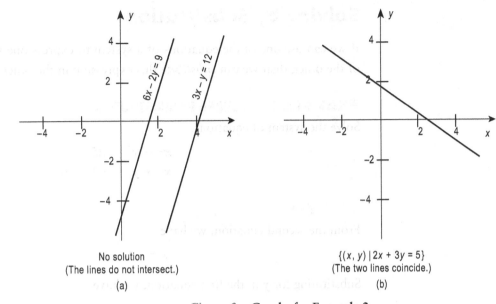

No solution
(The lines do not intersect.)
(a)

$\{(x, y) \mid 2x + 3y = 5\}$
(The two lines coincide.)
(b)

Figure 3   Graphs for Example 2

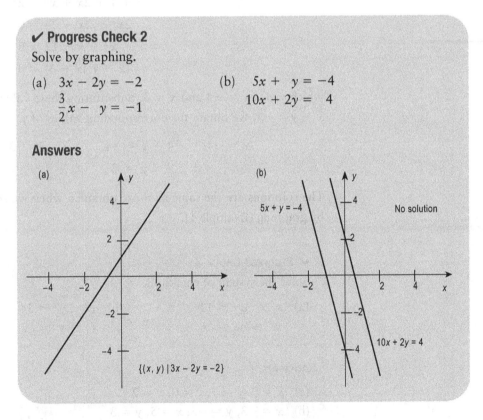

✔ **Progress Check 2**

Solve by graphing.

(a) $3x - 2y = -2$
    $\dfrac{3}{2}x - y = -1$

(b) $5x + y = -4$
    $10x + 2y = 4$

Answers

(a)

$\{(x, y) \mid 3x - 2y = -2\}$

(b)

$5x + y = -4$

No solution

$10x + 2y = 4$

The method of graphing has severe limitations since the accuracy of the solutions depends on the accuracy of the graph. The algebraic methods that follow avoid this limitation.

Solving by Substitution

If we can use one of the equations of a system to express one variable in terms of the other, then we can *substitute* this expression in the other equation.

EXAMPLE 3   SOLVING BY SUBSTITUTION

Solve the system of equations.

$$x^2 + y^2 = 25$$
$$x + y = -1$$

SOLUTION

From the second equation, we have

$$y = -1 - x$$

Substituting for y in the first equation, we have

$$x^2 + (-1 - x)^2 = 25$$
$$x^2 + 1 + 2x + x^2 = 25$$
$$2x^2 + 2x - 24 = 0$$
$$x^2 + x - 12 = 0$$
$$(x + 4)(x - 3) = 0$$

which yields $x = -4$ and $x = 3$. Substituting these values for x in the equation $x + y = -1$, we obtain the corresponding values of y.

$$x = -4: \quad -4 + y = -1 \qquad x = 3: \quad 3 + y = -1$$
$$y = 3 \qquad\qquad\qquad y = -4$$

The solutions are the same as those obtained when we solved this same system by graphing (Example 1).

✔ **Progress Check 3**

Solve the system of equations.

(a) $x^2 + 3y^2 = 12$
  $x + 3y = 6$

(b) $x^2 + y^2 = 34$
  $x - y = 2$

Answers

(a) $x = 3, y = 1; x = 0, y = 2$

(b) $x = -3, y = -5; x = 5, y = 3$

WARNING

The expression for x or y obtained from an equation *must not be substituted in the same equation*. From the first equation of the system

$$x + 2y = -1$$
$$3x^2 + y = 2$$

we obtain

$$x = -1 - 2y$$

Substituting (*incorrectly*) in the same equation would result in

$$(-1 - 2y) + 2y = -1$$
$$-1 = -1$$

The substitution $x = -1 - 2y$ must be made in the *second* equation.

EXAMPLE 4   SOLVING BY SUBSTITUTION

Solve the system of equations.

(a) $x^2 - 2x - y + 3 = 0$ (b) $x + 4y = 10$
       $x + y - 1 = 0$ $-2x - 8y = -20$

SOLUTIONS

(a) Solving the second equation for y, we have

$$y = 1 - x$$

and substituting in the first equation yields

$$x^2 - 2x - (1 - x) + 3 = 0$$
$$x^2 - x + 2 = 0$$

Since the discriminant of this quadratic equation is negative, the equation has no real roots. Any solution of the system of equations must satisfy this quadratic equation. We can therefore conclude that the system is inconsistent. The graphs of the equations are a parabola and a line that do not intersect (see Figure 4).

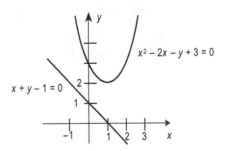

Figure 4   Graph for Example 4a

(b) Solving the first equation for x, we have

$$x = 10 - 4y$$

and substituting in the second equation gives

$$-2(10 - 4y) - 8y = -20$$
$$-20 + 8y - 8y = -20$$
$$-20 = -20$$

The substitution procedure has resulted in an identity, indicating that any solution of the first equation will also satisfy the second equation. Since there are an infinite number of ordered pairs $x = a$, $y = b$ satisfying the first equation, the system is consistent and has an infinite number of solutions.

✔ Progress Check 3

Solve by substitution.

(a) $3x - y = 7$
     $-9x + 3y = -22$

(b) $-5x + 2y = -4$
     $\dfrac{5}{2}x - y = 2$

Answers

(a) no solution

(b) any point on the line $-5x + 2y = -4$

Exercise Set 13.1

In Exercises 1–10 find appropriate solutions of the given system by graphing.

1. $x + y = 1$
   $x - y = 3$

2. $x - y = 1$
   $x + y = 5$

3. $3x - y = 4$
   $6x - 2y = -8$

4. $x^2 + 4y^2 = 32$
   $x + 2y = 0$

5. $xy = -4$
   $4x - y = 8$

6. $4x^2 + y^2 = 4$
   $x^2 - y^2 = 9$

7. $4x^2 + 9y^2 = 72$
   $4x - 3y^2 = 0$

8. $2y^2 - x^2 = -1$
   $4y^2 + x^2 = 25$

9. $x^2 + y^2 = 1$
   $y^2 - 3x^2 = 5$

10. $3x^2 + 8y^2 = 21$
    $x^2 + 4y^2 = 10$

In Exercises 11–20 solve the system of equations by the method of substitution.

11. $x + y = 1$
    $x - y = 3$

12. $x + 2y = 8$
    $3x - 4y = 4$

13. $x^2 + y^2 = 13$
    $2x - y = 4$

14. $x^2 + 4y^2 = 32$
    $x + 2y = 0$

15. $y^2 - x = 0$
    $y - 4x = -3$

16. $xy = -4$
    $4x - y = 8$

17. $x^2 - 2x + y^2 = 3$
    $2x + y = 4$

18. $4x^2 + y^2 = 4$
    $x - y = 3$

19. $xy = 1$
    $x - y + 1 = 0$

20. $\dfrac{1}{2}x - \dfrac{3}{2}y = 4$
    $\dfrac{3}{2}x + y = 1$

21. Recall that the standard form for a linear polynomial is

$$y = a_1 x + a_0$$

Suppose you want to model the following data by a linear function: $(1, -3)$, $(3, 5)$. Proceed by substituting the given values for x and y into the standard form. This will give you two equations with the two unknowns a_1, a_0. Solve this system; then use your solution to write the quadratic polynomial that fits this data.

22. Use the method described in Exercise 21 to redo Exercises 57 and 58 in Section 7.2.

13.2 Solving by Elimination

If we require answers to a system of linear equations accurate to, say, five decimal places, then the estimates obtained by graphing won't suffice. The method of substitution provides exact answers, but is not suitable for a computer.

The **method of elimination** overcomes these difficulties. The strategy of the method is to replace the original system of equations by a simpler, equivalent system that has the same solution set. The following operations are used to obtain an equivalent system:

    (a) An equation may be multiplied by a nonzero constant.

    (b) An equation may be replaced by the sum of itself and another equation.

WARNING

When multiplying an equation by a constant, be sure to multiply each term of both sides of the equation by the constant.

    When checking answers, be sure to check in *both* equations. Values of x and y may satisfy one equation but not the other.

The procedure will be illustrated with the linear system

$$3x + y = 7$$
$$2x - 4y = 14$$

Method of Elimination

Step 1. Multiply each equation by a constant so that the coefficients of either x or y will differ only in sign.

Multiply the first equation by 4 and the second equation by 1, so that the coefficients of y will be 4 and -4.

$$12x + 4y = 28$$
$$2x - 4y = 14$$

Step 2. Add the equations. The resulting equation will contain (at most) one variable.

$$
\begin{array}{r}
12x + 4y = 28 \\
2x - 4y = 14 \\
\hline
14x = 42
\end{array}
$$

continues

Method of Elimination *continued*

Step 3. Solve the resulting linear equation in one variable.

$$14x = 42$$
$$x = 3$$

Step 4. Substitute in either of the *original* equations to solve for the second variable.

Substituting $x = 3$ in the first equation of the original system, we have

$$3x + y = \quad 7$$
$$3(3) + y = \quad 7$$
$$9 + y = \quad 7$$
$$y = \quad -2$$

Step 5. Check in both equations.

$$3x + y = 7 \qquad\qquad 2x - 4y = 14$$
$$3(3) + (-2) \overset{?}{=} 7 \qquad\qquad 2(3) - 4(-2) \overset{?}{=} 14$$
$$9 - 2 \overset{?}{=} 7 \qquad\qquad 6 + 8 \overset{?}{=} 14$$
$$7 \overset{✔}{=} 7 \qquad\qquad 14 \overset{✔}{=} 14$$

EXAMPLE 1   SOLVING BY ELIMINATION

Solve by elimination.

$$2x + 5y = \quad -5$$
$$3x - 2y = -17$$

SOLUTION

We choose to eliminate x. If we multiply the first equation by 3 and the second equation by -2, we will have coefficients of 6 and -6 as desired. We add the resulting equations.

$$6x + 15y = -15$$
$$\underline{-6x + 4y = 34}$$
$$19y = 19$$
$$y = 1$$

Substituting in the first equation, we have

$$2x + 5y = -5$$
$$2x + 5(1) = -5$$
$$2x = -10$$
$$x = -5$$

Check that the solution $x = -5$, $y = 1$ satisfies both equations.

✔ Progress Check 1

Solve by elimination.

(a) $2x - y = 2$

$-4x - 2y = 8$

(b) $5x + 2y = 5$

$-2x + 3y = -21$

Answers

(a) $x = -\dfrac{1}{2}$, $y = -3$

(b) $x = 3$, $y = -5$

In Section 13.1, we saw that the graphs of the equations

$$6x - 2y = 9$$
$$3x - y = 12$$

are parallel lines and that the system of equations has no solution. If we attempt to solve this system by elimination, we can multiply the second equation by -2 to eliminate y.

$$
\begin{array}{rr}
6x - 2y = & 9 \\
-6x + 2y = & -24 \\
\hline
0x + 0y = & -15 \\
0 = & -15 \qquad \text{Impossible!}
\end{array}
$$

We see that the elimination method signals us when there is no solution by yielding an impossibility. In general,

> If the elimination method results in an equation of the form
>
> $$0x + 0y = c$$
>
> where $c \neq 0$, then there is no solution of the original system of linear equations, and the system is inconsistent.

We also saw in Section 13.1 that the system of equations

$$2x + 3y = 5$$
$$6x + 9y = 15$$

is really two forms of the same equation. If we eliminate x by multiplying the first equation by -3, we have

$$
\begin{array}{rr}
-6x - 9y = & -15 \\
6x + 9y = & 15 \\
\hline
0x + 0y = & 0 \qquad \text{Always true}
\end{array}
$$

Again, the elimination method has signaled us that any pair of numbers satisfying either equation is a solution. In general,

> If the elimination method results in an equation of the form
>
> $$0x + 0y = 0$$
>
> then the equations in the original system are equivalent.

You may have noticed that the special cases are signaled in essentially the same way by both the method of elimination and the method of substitution. The case of an inconsistent system is signaled by a contradiction; the case of a consistent system composed of equivalent equations is indicated by an identity.

EXAMPLE 2   SOLVING BY ELIMINATION

Solve by elimination.

(a) $6x - 2y = 7$
$3x - y = 16$

(b) $5x + 6y = 4$
$-10x - 12y = -8$

SOLUTIONS

(a) If we multiply the second equation by -2, we have

$$
\begin{array}{r}
6x - 2y = 7 \\
-6x + 2y = -32 \\
\hline
0x + 0y = -25
\end{array}
$$

We can conclude that the system of equations represents a pair of parallel lines and that there is no solution.

(b) Multiplying the first equation by 2, we have

$$
\begin{array}{r}
10x + 12y = 8 \\
-10x - 12y = -8 \\
\hline
0x + 0y = 0
\end{array}
$$

We can conclude that the equations are equivalent and that the solution set is given by $y = -\frac{5}{6}x + \frac{2}{3}$.

✔ Progress Check 2

Solve by elimination.

(a) $x - y = 2$
$3x - 3y = -6$

(b) $4x + 6y = 3$
$-2x - 3y = -\dfrac{3}{2}$

Answers

(a) no solution

(b) $y = -\dfrac{2}{3}x + \dfrac{1}{2}$

Exercise Set 13.2

In Exercises 1–20 solve by elimination and check.

1. $x + y = -1$
   $x - y = 3$

2. $x - 2y = 8$
   $2x + y = 1$

3. $x + 4y = -1$
   $2x - 4y = 4$

4. $2x - 2y = 4$
   $x - y = 8$

5. $x + 2y = 6$
   $2x + 4y = 12$

6. $x - 2y = 4$
   $2x + y = 3$

7. $x + 3y = 2$
   $3x - 5y = -6$

8. $x + 2y = 0$
   $5x - y = 22$

9. $2x + 2y = 6$
   $3x + 3y = 6$

10. $2x + y = 2$
    $3x - y = 8$

11. $x + 2y = 1$
    $5x + 2y = 13$

12. $x - 4y = -7$
    $2x + 3y = -8$

13. $x - 3y = 9$
    $x + 5y = 11$

14. $2x - 3y = 8$
    $4x - 6y = 16$

15. $x - y = 3$
    $3x + 2y = 14$

16. $4x + y = 3$
    $2x - y = 3$

17. $2x + y = 7$
    $3x - 2y = 0$

18. $2x + 3y = 4$
    $4x + 6y = 6$

19. $2x + 3y = 13$
    $3x - 4y = 1$

20. $3x - 2y = 5$
    $\dfrac{3}{2}x - y = \dfrac{5}{2}$

13.3   Applications

In Section 13.1, we saw that many of the word problems that we previously solved by using one variable can be recast as a system of linear equations. There are, in addition, many word problems that are difficult to handle with one variable but are easily formulated by using two variables.

EXAMPLE 1   APPLYING LINEAR SYSTEMS

If 3 sulfa pills and 4 penicillin pills cost 69 cents while 5 sulfa pills and 2 penicillin pills cost 73 cents, what is the cost of each kind of pill?

SOLUTION

Using two variables, we let

$$x = \text{the cost of each sulfa pill}$$
$$y = \text{the cost of each penicillin pill}$$

Then

$$3x + 4y = 69$$
$$5x + 2y = 73$$

Multiplying the second equation by -2 and adding to eliminate y, we have

$$3x + 4y = 69$$
$$-10x - 4y = -146$$
$$\overline{-7x = -77}$$
$$x = 11$$

Substituting in the first equation, we have

$$3(11) + 4y = 69$$
$$33 + 4y = 69$$
$$4y = 36$$
$$y = 9$$

Thus, each sulfa pill costs 11 cents and each penicillin pill costs 9 cents. (Could you have set up this problem using only one variable? Unlikely!)

✔ Progress Check 1

If 2 pounds of rib steak and 6 pounds of hamburger meat cost $12.30 and 3 pounds of rib steak and 2 pounds of hamburger meat cost $9.70, what is the cost per pound of each type of meat?

Answer

steak: $2.40; hamburger: $1.25

EXAMPLE 2   APPLYING LINEAR SYSTEMS

Swimming downstream, a swimmer can cover 2 kilometers in 15 minutes; the return trip upstream requires 20 minutes. What is the rate of the swimmer and what is the rate of the current? (The rate of the swimmer is the speed at which he would swim if there were no current.)

SOLUTION

Let

$$x = \text{rate of the swimmer (in km per hour)}$$
$$y = \text{rate of the current (in km per hour)}$$

When swimming downstream, the rate of the current is added to the rate of the swimmer so that $x + y$ is the rate downstream. Similarly, $x - y$ is the rate while swimming upstream. We display the information we have, expressing time in hours.

	Rate ×	Time =	Distance
Downstream	$x + y$	$\dfrac{1}{4}$	$\dfrac{1}{4}(x + y)$
Upstream	$x - y$	$\dfrac{1}{3}$	$\dfrac{1}{3}(x - y)$

Since distance upstream = distance downstream = 2 kilometers,

$$\frac{1}{4}(x + y) = 2$$

$$\frac{1}{3}(x - y) = 2$$

or, equivalently,

$$x + y = 8$$

$$x - y = 6$$

Solving, we have

$$x = 7 \quad \text{Rate of the swimmer}$$

$$y = 1 \quad \text{Rate of the current}$$

Thus, the rate of the swimmer is 7 kilometers per hour, and the rate of the current is 1 kilometer per hour. (The student is urged to verify the solution.)

✔ **Progress Check 2**

Rowing downstream, a boat can travel a distance of 16 miles in 2 hours. If the return trip upstream requires 8 hours, what is the rate of the boat in still water and what is the rate of the current?

Answer

boat: 5 miles per hour; current: 3 miles per hour

EXAMPLE 3   APPLYING LINEAR SYSTEMS

The sum of a two-digit number and its units digit is 64; the sum of the number and its tens digit is 62. Find the number.

SOLUTION

The basic idea in solving digit problems is to note that if we let

$$t = \text{tens digit}$$

and

$$u = \text{units digit}$$

then

$$10t + u = \text{the two-digit number}$$

Our word problem then translates into

$$(10t + u) + u = 64 \qquad \text{or} \qquad 10t + 2u = 64$$

and

$$(10t + u) + t = 62 \qquad \text{or} \qquad 11t + u = 62$$

Solving, we find that $t = 5$, $u = 7$ (verify), and the number we seek is 57.

✔ Progress Check 3

The sum of twice the tens digit and the units digit of a two-digit number is 16; the sum of the tens digit and twice the units digit is 14. Find the number.

Answer

64

EXAMPLE 4   APPLYING LINEAR SYSTEMS

A landscaping firm prepares two plans for a homeowner. Plan A uses 8 hemlocks and 12 junipers at a cost of $520. If Plan B uses 6 hemlocks and 15 junipers at a cost of $510, what is the cost of each hemlock and of each juniper?

SOLUTION

Let

$$x = \text{the cost of each hemlock}$$

and

$$y = \text{the cost of each juniper}$$

Then Plan A results in the equation

$$8x + 12y = 520$$

while Plan B yields the equation

$$6x + 15y = 510$$

Solving, we find that $x = 35$ and $y = 20$, so each hemlock costs $35 and each juniper costs $20.

✔ Progress Check 4

A manufacturer of children's toys is producing two types of model airplanes. Model A requires 7 minutes on the jigsaw and 10 minutes on the lathe, while model B requires 15 minutes on the jigsaw and 6 minutes on the lathe. If the jigsaw and lathe are each used 15 hours per day, what is the daily production of each type of model airplane?

Answer

75 of model A and 25 of model B

Applications in Business and Economics: Break-Even Analysis

One of the problems faced by a manufacturer is that of determining the **level of production**; that is, how many units of the product should be manufactured during a given fixed time period such as a day, a week, or a month? Suppose that

$$C = 400 + 2x \qquad\qquad (1)$$

is the total cost (in thousands of dollars) of producing x units of the product and that

$$R = 4x \qquad\qquad (2)$$

is the total revenue (in thousands of dollars) when x units of the product are sold. This would happen, for example, if, after setting up production at a cost of $400,000, there is an additional cost of $2000 to make each unit [Equation (1)], and a revenue of $4000 is earned from the sale of each unit [Equation (2)]. If all the units that are manufactured are sold, then the total profit P is the difference between total revenue and total cost.

$$
\begin{aligned}
P &= R - C \\
&= 4x - (400 + 2x) \\
&= 2x - 400
\end{aligned}
$$

The value of x for which $R = C$, so that the profit is zero, is called the **break-even point**. When that many units of the product have been produced and sold, the manufacturer neither makes money nor loses money. To find the break-even point, we set $R = C$. Using Equations (1) and (2), we obtain

$$400 + 2x = 4x$$

or

$$400 = 2x$$

$$x = \frac{400}{2} = 200$$

Thus, the break-even point is 200 units.

The break-even point can also be obtained graphically as follows. Observe that Equations (1) and (2) are linear equations, and therefore, equations whose graphs are straight lines. The break-even point is the x-coordinate of the point where the lines given by Equations (1) and (2) intersect. Figure 5 shows the lines and their point of intersection (200, 800). When 200 units of the product are made, the cost ($800,000) is exactly equal to the revenue, and the profit is $0. If $x > 200$, then $R > C$, so that the manufacturer is making a profit. If $x < 200$, $R < C$, and the manufacturer is losing money.

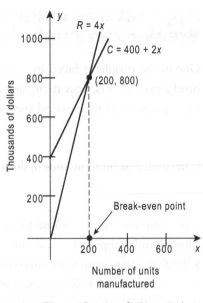

Figure 5   **Break-Even Point**

EXAMPLE 5   FINDING THE BREAK-EVEN POINT

A steel producer finds that when x million tons of steel are made, the total cost and total revenue are given (in millions of dollars) by

$$C = 20 + 0.4x$$
$$R = 0.8x$$

(a) Find the break-even point graphically.

(b) What is the total revenue at the break-even point?

SOLUTIONS

(a) See Figure 6. The break-even point is $x = 50$ million tons.

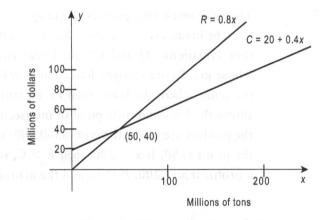

Figure 6   **Diagram for Example 5**

(b) When the level of production is 50 million tons, the total revenue is

$$R = 0.8x$$
$$= (0.8)(50)$$
$$= 40 \text{ million dollars}$$

Notice that this is also the total cost of producing the 50 million tons of steel.

$$C = 20 + 0.4(50) = 40 \text{ million dollars}$$

✔ Progress Check 5

A producer of photographic developer finds that the total weekly cost of producing x liters of developer is given (in dollars) by $C = 550 + 0.40x$. The manufacturer sells the product at $0.50 per liter.

(a) What is the total revenue received when x liters of developer is sold?

(b) Find the break-even point graphically.

(c) What is the total revenue at the break-even point?

Answers

(a) $R = 0.50x$ (b) 5500 liters   (c) $2750

Applications in Business and Economics: Supply and Demand

A manufacturer of a product is free to set any price p (in dollars) for each unit of the product. Of course, if the price is too high, not enough people will buy the product; if the price is too low, so many people will rush to buy the product that the producer will not be able to satisfy demand. Thus, in setting price, the manufacturer must take into consideration the demand for the product.

Let S be the number of units that the manufacturer is willing to supply at the price p; S is called the **supply**. Generally, the value of S will increase as p increases; that is, the manufacturer is willing to supply more of the product as the price p increases. Let D be the number of units of the product that consumers are willing to buy at price p; D is called the **demand**. Generally, the value of D will decrease as p increases; that is, consumers are willing to buy fewer units of the product as the price rises. For example, suppose that S and D are related to price p (in dollars) as follows:

$$S = 2p + 3 \tag{3}$$
$$D = -p + 12 \tag{4}$$

Equations (3) and (4) are linear equations, so they are equations of straight lines (see Figure 7). The price at which supply S and demand D are equal is called the **equilibrium price**. At this price, every unit that is supplied is purchased. Thus, there is neither a surplus nor a shortage. In Figure 7, the equilibrium price is $p = 3$. At this price, the number of units supplied equals the number of units demanded and is given by substituting in Equation (3) to obtain $S = 9$. This value can also be obtained by finding the y-coordinate at the point of intersection in Figure 7.

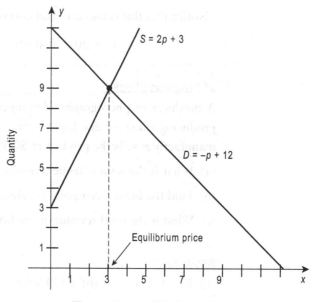

Figure 7   **Equilibrium Price**

If we are in an economic system in which there is pure competition, then the law of supply and demand states that the selling price of a product will be its equilibrium price. That is, if the selling price were higher than the equilibrium price, then the consumers' reduced demand would leave the manufacturer with an unsold surplus. This would force the manufacturer to reduce the selling price. If the selling price is below the equilibrium price, then the increased demand would cause a shortage of the product. This would lead the manufacturer to raise the selling price. Of course, in actual practice, the marketplace does not operate under pure competition since manufacturers consult with each other on selling prices, governments try to influence selling prices, and many other factors are present. In addition, deeper mathematical analysis of economic systems requires the use of more sophisticated equations.

EXAMPLE 6   FINDING THE EQUILIBRIUM PRICE

Suppose that supply and demand for ball-point pens are related to price p (in dollars) as follows:

$$S = p + 5$$
$$D = -p + 7$$

(a) Find the equilibrium price.

(b) Find the number of pens sold at that price.

SOLUTIONS

(a) Figure 8 illustrates the graphical solution. Thus, the equilibrium price is $p = 1$. (Algebraic methods will, of course, yield the same solution.)

(b) When $p = 1$, the number of pens sold is $S = 1 + 5 = 6$, the y-coordinate of the point of intersection. This number is also the number of pens in demand.

$$D = -1 + 7 = 6$$

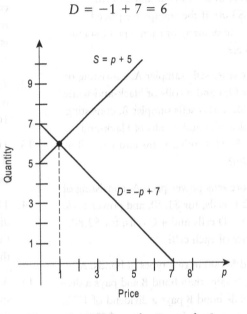

Figure 8   **Diagram for Example 6**

✔ Progress Check 6

Suppose that supply and demand for radios are related to price p (in dollars) as follows:

$$S = 3p + 120$$
$$D = -p + 200$$

(a) Find the equilibrium price.

(b) Find the number of radios sold at this price.

Answers

(a) $20   (b) 180

Exercise Set 13.3

1. A pile of 40 coins consists of nickels and dimes. If the total value of the coins is $2.75, how many of each type of coin are in the pile?

2. An automatic vending machine in the post office provides a packet of 27 10-cent and 20-cent stamps worth $3.00. If the stamps are priced at their face value, how many of each type of stamp are in the packet?

3. A photography store sells sampler A, consisting of 6 rolls of color film and 4 rolls of black-and-white film, for $21.00. It also sells sampler B, consisting of 4 rolls of color film and 6 rolls of black-and-white film, for $19.00. What is the cost per roll of each type of film?

4. A hardware store sells power pack A, consisting of 4 D cells and 2 C cells, for $1.70, and power pack B, consisting of 6 D cells and 4 C cells, for $2.80. What is the price of each cell?

5. A fund invested $6000 in two types of bonds, A and B. Bond A is safer than bond B and pays a dividend of 8%, while bond B pays a dividend of 10%. If the total return on both investments is $520, how much was invested in each type of bond?

6. A trash removal company carries waste material in two sizes of sealed containers weighing 4 and 3 kilograms, respectively. On a certain trip there are a total of 30 containers weighing 100 kilograms. How many of each type of container are there?

7. A paper firm makes rolls of paper in two widths, 12" and 15", by cutting a sheet that is 180" wide. Suppose that a total of 14 rolls of paper need to be cut without any waste. How many of each type of roll will be made?

8. An animal-feed producer mixes two types of grain, A and B. Each unit of grain A contains 2 grams of fat and 80 calories, while each unit of grain B contains 3 grams of fat and 60 calories. If the producer wants the final product to provide 18 grams of fat and 480 calories, how much of each type of grain should be used?

9. A supermarket mixes coffee that sells for $1.20 per pound with coffee selling for $1.80 per pound, to obtain 24 pounds of coffee selling for $1.60 per pound. How much of each type of coffee should be used?

10. An airplane flying against the wind covers a distance of 3000 kilometers in 6 hours, and the return trip with the aid of the wind takes 5 hours. What is the speed of the airplane in still air, and what is the speed of the wind?

11. A cyclist who is traveling against the wind can cover a distance of 45 miles in 4 hours. The return trip with the aid of the wind takes 3 hours. What is the speed of the bicycle in still air, and what is the speed of the wind?

12. The sum of a two-digit number and its units digit is 20; the sum of the number and its tens digit is 16. Find the number.

13. The sum of the digits of a two-digit number is 7. If the digits are reversed, the resulting number exceeds the given number by 9. Find the number.

14. The sum of three times the tens digit and the units digit of a two-digit number is 14, while the sum of the tens digit and twice the units digit is 18. Find the number.

15. A health food shop mixes nuts and raisins into a snack pack. How many pounds of nuts, selling for $2 per pound, and how many pounds of raisins, selling for $1.50 per pound, must be mixed to produce a 50-pound mixture selling for $1.80 per pound?

16. A movie theater charges $3 admission for an adult and $1.50 for a child. If 600 tickets were sold and the total revenue received was $1350, how many tickets of each type were sold?

17. A moped dealer selling model A and model B mopeds has $18,000 in inventory. The profit on selling a model A moped is 12%, and the profit on a model B moped is 18%. If the profit on selling the entire stock would be 16%, how much is invested in each type of model?

18. The cost of sending a telegram is determined by a flat charge for the first 10 words and a uniform rate for each additional word. Suppose that an 18-word telegram costs $1.94, and a 22-word telegram costs $2.16. Find the cost of the first 10 words and the rate for each additional word.

19. A certain epidemic disease is treated by a combination of the drugs Epiline I and Epiline II. Suppose that each unit of Epiline I contains 1 milligram of factor X and 2 milligrams of factor Y, and each unit of Epiline II contains 2 milligrams of factor X

and 3 milligrams of factor Y. Successful treatment of the disease calls for 13 milligrams of factor X and 22 milligrams of factor Y. How many units of each drug, Epiline I and Epiline II, should be administered to a patient?

20. (**Break-even analysis**) An animal-feed manufacturer finds that the weekly cost of making x kilograms of feed is given (in dollars) by $C = 2000 + 0.50x$, and the revenue received from selling the feed is given by $R = 0.75x$.

    (a) Find the break-even point graphically.
    (b) What is the total weekly revenue received at the break-even point?

21. (**Break-even analysis**) A small manufacturer of a new solar device finds that the annual cost of making x units is given (in dollars) by $C = 24,000 + 55x$. Each device sells for $95.

    (a) What is the total annual revenue received when x devices are sold?
    (b) Find the break-even point graphically.
    (c) What is the total annual revenue received at the break-even point?

22. (**Break-even analysis**) An ice cream vendor finds that her weekly operating cost is $300 plus $0.60 per ice cream portion served. If each ice cream portion retails for $0.80, what is the break-even point?

23. (**Break-even analysis**) A newspaper vendor finds that his monthly operating cost is $400 plus $0.15 per newspaper sold. If each newspaper is sold for $0.25, what is the break-even point?

24. (**Supply and demand**) A manufacturer of calculators finds that supply and demand are related to price p (in dollars) as follows:

$$S = 4p + 120$$
$$D = -2p + 180$$

(a) Find the equilibrium price.
(b) Find the number of calculators sold at this price.

25. (**Supply and demand**) A manufacturer of mopeds finds that supply and demand are related to price p (in dollars) as follows:

$$S = 2p + 1000$$
$$D = -p + 1900$$

(a) Find the equilibrium price.
(b) Find the number of mopeds sold at this price.

26. (**Supply and demand**) A record manufacturer finds that when a record is priced at p dollars, he is willing to supply (in thousands)

$$4p + 10$$

records per week. Market research shows that consumers are willing to buy (in thousands)

$$-2p + 52$$

records per week at this price.

(a) Find the equilibrium price.
(b) Find the number of records sold weekly at this price.

27. (**Supply and demand**) A manufacturer of jeans has decided that is he able to supply (in thousands)

$$3p + 60$$

pairs of jeans per month, when each pair is priced at p dollars. Market research shows that at this price consumers are willing to buy (in thousands)

$$-4p + 200$$

pairs of jeans per month.

(a) Find the equilibrium price.
(b) Find the number of jeans sold monthly at this price.

13.4 Systems of Linear Equations in Three Unknowns

Gaussian Elimination and Triangular Form

The method of substitution and the method of elimination can both be applied to systems of linear equations in three unknowns and, more generally, to systems of linear equations in any number of unknowns. There is yet another method, ideally suited for computers, which we will now apply to solving linear systems in three unknowns.

In solving equations, we found it convenient to transform an equation into an equivalent equation having the same solution set. Similarly, we can attempt to transform a system of equations into another system, called an **equivalent system**, that has the same solution set. In particular, the objective of **Gaussian elimination** is to transform a linear system into an equivalent system in triangular form, such as

$$3x - y + 3z = -11$$
$$2y + z = 2$$
$$2z = -4$$

A linear system is in **triangular form** when the only nonzero coefficient of x appears in the first equation, the only nonzero coefficients of y appear in the first and second equations, and so on.

Note that when a linear system is in triangular form, the last equation immediately yields the value of an unknown. In our example, we see that

$$2z = -4$$
$$z = -2$$

Substituting $z = -2$ in the second equation yields

$$2y + (-2) = 2$$
$$y = 2$$

Finally, substituting $z = -2$ and $y = 2$ in the first equation yields

$$3x - (2) + 3(-2) = -11$$
$$3x = -3$$
$$x = -1$$

This process of **back-substitution** thus allows us to solve a linear system quickly when it is in triangular form.

The challenge, then, is to find a means of transforming a linear system into triangular form. We now offer (without proof) a list of operations that transform a system of linear equations into an equivalent system.

1. Interchange any two equations.

2. Multiply an equation by a nonzero constant.

3. Replace an equation with the sum of itself plus a constant times another equation.

Using these operations, we can now demonstrate the method of Gaussian elimination.

EXAMPLE 1 SOLVING A LINEAR SYSTEM IN THREE UNKNOWNS

Solve the linear system.

$$2y - z = -5$$
$$x - 2y + 2z = 9$$
$$2x - 3y + 3z = 14$$

SOLUTION

Gaussian Elimination

Step 1. (a) If necessary, interchange equations to obtain a nonzero coefficient of x in the first equation.

(a) Interchanging the first two equations yields

$$x - 2y + 2z = 9$$
$$2y - z = -5$$
$$2x - 3y + 3z = 14$$

(b) Replace the second equation with the sum of itself and an appropriate multiple of the first equation, which will result in a zero coefficient for x.

(b) The coefficient of x in the second equation is already 0.

(c) Replace the third equation with the sum of itself and an appropriate multiple of the first equation, which will result in a zero coefficient for x.

(c) Replace the third equation with the sum of itself and -2 times the first equation.

$$x - 2y + 2z = -9$$
$$2y - z = -5$$
$$y - z = -4$$

Step 2. Apply the procedures of Step 1 to the second and third equations.

Replace the third equation with the sum of itself and $-\frac{1}{2}$ times the second equation.

$$x - 2y + 2z = 9$$
$$2y - z = -5$$
$$-\frac{1}{2}z = -\frac{3}{2}$$

Step 3. The system is now in triangular form. The solution is obtained by back-substitution.

From the third equation, we obtain

$$-\frac{1}{2}z = -\frac{3}{2}$$
$$z = 3$$

Substituting this value of z in the second equation, we have

$$2y - (3) = -5$$
$$y = -1$$

Substituting for y and z in the first equation, we obtain

$$x - 2(-1) + 2(3) = 9$$
$$x + 8 = 9$$
$$x = 1$$

The solution is $x = 1$, $y = -1$, $z = 3$.

✔ Progress Check 1

Solve by Gaussian elimination.

(a) $2x - 4y + 2z = 1$
$ 3x + y + 3z = 5$
$ x - y - 2z = -8$

(b) $-2x + 3y - 12z = -17$
$ 3x - y - 15z = 11$
$ -x + 5y + 3z = -9$

Answers

(a) $x = -\dfrac{3}{2}, y = \dfrac{1}{2}, z = 3$

(b) $x = 5, y = -1, z = \dfrac{1}{3}$

Consistent and Inconsistent Systems

The graph of a linear equation in three unknowns is a plane in three-dimensional space. A system of three linear equations in three unknowns corresponds to three planes (Figure 9). If the planes intersect in a point P (Figure 9a), the coordinates of the point P are a solution of the system and can be found by Gaussian elimination. The cases of no solution and of an infinite number of solutions are signaled as follows:

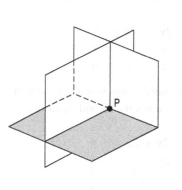

(a)

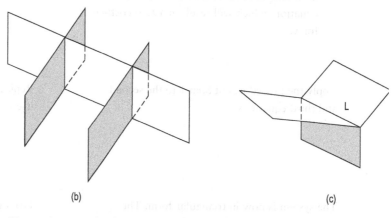

(b)

(c)

Figure 9   **Graph of a Linear System in Three Unknowns**

- If Gaussian elimination results in an equation of the form
$$0x + 0y + 0z = c, \quad c \neq 0$$
then the system is inconsistent (Figure 9b).

- If Gaussian elimination results in no equation of the type above but results in an equation of the form
$$0x + 0y + 0z = 0$$
then the system is consistent and has an infinite number of solutions (Figure 9c).

Consistent and Inconsistent Systems

- Otherwise, the system is consistent and has a unique solution.

EXAMPLE 2   SOLVING A LINEAR SYSTEM IN THREE UNKNOWNS

Solve the linear system.

$$\begin{aligned} x - 2y + 2z &= -4 \\ x + y - 7z &= 8 \\ -x - 4y + 16z &= -20 \end{aligned}$$

SOLUTION

Replacing the second equation with itself minus the first equation, and replacing the third equation with itself plus the first equation, we have

$$\begin{aligned} x - 2y + 2z &= -4 \\ 3y - 9z &= 12 \\ -6y + 18z &= -24 \end{aligned}$$

Replacing the third equation of this system with itself plus 2 times the second equation results in the system

$$\begin{aligned} x - 2y + 2z &= -4 \\ 3y - 9z &= 12 \\ 0x + 0y + 0z &= 0 \end{aligned}$$

in which the last equation indicates that the system is consistent and has an infinite number of solutions. If we solve the second equation of the last system for y, we have

$$y = 3z + 4$$

Then, solving the first equation for x, we have

$$\begin{aligned} x &= 2y - 2z - 4 \\ &= 2(3z + 4) - 2z - 4 \qquad \text{Substitute for } y \\ &= 4z + 4 \end{aligned}$$

The equations

$$\begin{aligned} x &= 4z + 4 \\ y &= 3z + 4 \end{aligned}$$

yield a solution of the original system for every real value of z. For example, if $z = 0$, then $x = 4$, $y = 4$, $z = 0$ satisfies the original system; if $z = -2$, then $x = -4$, $y = -2$, $z = -2$ is another solution.

✔ Progress Check 2

(a) Verify that the linear system

$$\begin{aligned} x - 2y + z &= 3 \\ 2x + y - 2z &= -1 \\ -x - 8y + 7z &= 5 \end{aligned}$$

is consistent.

(b) Verify that the linear system

$$\begin{aligned} 2x + y + 2z &= 1 \\ x - 4y + 7z &= -4 \\ x - y + 3z &= -1 \end{aligned}$$

has an infinite number of solutions.

Exercise Set 13.4

In Exercises 1–20 solve by Gaussian elimination and check.

1. $x + 2y + 3z = -6$
    $2x - 3y - 4z = 15$
    $3x + 4y + 5z = -8$

2. $2x + 3y + 4z = -12$
    $x - 2y + z = -5$
    $3x + y + 2z = 1$

3. $x + y + z = 1$
    $x + y - 2z = 3$
    $2x + y + z = 2$

4. $2x - y + z = 3$
    $x - 3y + z = 4$
    $-5x - 2z = -5$

5. $x + y + z = 2$
    $x - y + 2z = 3$
    $3x + 5y + 2z = 6$

6. $x + y + z = 0$
    $x + y = 3$
    $y + z = 1$

7. $x + 2y + z = 7$
    $x + 2y + 3z = 11$
    $2x + y + 4z = 12$

8. $4x + 2y - z = 5$
    $3x + 3y + 6z = 1$
    $5x + y - 8z = 8$

9. $x + y + z = 2$
    $x + 2y + z = 3$
    $x + y - z = 2$

10. $x + y - z = 2$
    $x + 2y + z = 3$
    $x + y + 4z = 3$

11. $2x + y + 3z = 8$
    $-x + y + z = 10$
    $x + y + z = 12$

12. $2x - y + z = 2$
    $3x + y + 2z = 3$
    $x + y - z = -1$

13. $x + 2y - 2z = 8$
    $5y - z = 6$
    $-2x + y + 3z = -2$

14. $x - 2y + z = -5$
    $2x + z = -10$
    $y - z = 15$

15. $3x - y + 4z = 6$
    $x + y + z = 8$
    $2x - y - 2z = 12$

16. $2x - y + z = 4$
    $3x + y - z = 8$
    $x - y - z = 6$

17. $x + y - 2z = 6$
    $x - y = -12$
    $y - z = 8$

18. $x + 2y - 3z = 10$
    $5x + y - z = -12$
    $3x - 3y + 5z = 15$

19. $2x - y + 2z = 6$
    $2x - y + 3z = -5$
    $x + y = -4$

20. $x - y - z = 3$
    $y + z = 5$
    $x + y - z = 8$

*21. A special low-calorie diet consists of dishes A, B, and C. Each unit of A has 2 grams of fat, 1 gram of carbohydrate, and 3 grams of protein. Each unit of B has 1 gram of fat, 2 grams of carbohydrate, and 1 gram of protein. Each unit of C has 1 gram of fat, 2 grams of carbohydrate, and 3 grams of protein. The diet must provide exactly 10 grams of fat, 14 grams of carbohydrate, and 18 grams of protein. How many units of each dish should be used?

*22. A furniture manufacturer makes chairs, coffee tables, and dining room tables. Each chair requires 2 minutes of sanding, 2 minutes of staining, and 4 minutes of varnishing. Each coffee table requires 5 minutes of sanding, 4 minutes of staining, and 3 minutes of varnishing. Each dining room table requires 5 minutes of sanding, 4 minutes of staining, and 6 minutes of varnishing. The sanding benches, staining benches, and varnishing benches are available 6, 5, and 6 hours per day, respectively. How many of each type of furniture can be made if all facilities are used to capacity?

*23. A manufacturer produces 12", 16", and 19" television sets that require assembly, testing, and packing. The 12" sets each require 45 minutes to assemble, 30 minutes to test, and 10 minutes to package. The 16" sets each require 1 hour to assemble, 45 minutes to test, and 15 minutes to package. The 19" sets each require $1\frac{1}{2}$ hours to assemble, 1 hour to test, and 15 minutes to package. If the assembly line operates for $17\frac{3}{4}$ hours per day, the test facility is available for $12\frac{1}{2}$ hours per day, and the packing equipment is available for $3\frac{3}{4}$ hours per day, how many of each type of set can be produced?

24. Recall that a second degree polynomial can be written as

$$y = a_2x^2 + a_1x + a_0$$

Suppose you want to model the following data by a quadratic function: (0, 1), (3, 16), and (−1, 8). Proceed by substituting the given values for x and y into the standard form. This will give you three equations with the three unknowns a_2, a_1, a_0. Solve this system; then use your solution to write the quadratic polynomial that fits this data.

25. Repeat Exercise 24 for the following data points: (1, 11), (2, 24), (−2, −4).

13.5   Systems of Linear Inequalities

In Section 7.4, we developed a method for graphing a linear inequality. We can use this same method in solving a **system of linear inequalities** in two variables, x and y. Examples of such systems are

$$2x - 3y > 6 \quad 2x - 5y \leqslant 12$$
$$x + 2y < 2 \quad\ \ 2x + y \leqslant 18$$
$$x \geqslant 0$$
$$y \geqslant 0$$

The **solution of a system of linear inequalities** consists of all ordered pairs (a, b) such that the substitution $x = a$, $y = b$ satisfies *all* the inequalities. Thus, the ordered pair $(2, 1)$ is a solution of the system

$$2x - 3y \leqslant 2$$
$$x +\ \ y \leqslant 6$$

because the substitution $x = 2$, $y = 1$ satisfies both inequalities

$$(2)(2) - (3)(1) = 1 \leqslant 2$$
$$2 + 1 = 3 \leqslant 6$$

We can graph the solution set of a system of linear inequalities by graphing the solution set of each inequality and marking that portion of the graph that satisfies all the inequalities.

EXAMPLE 1   SOLVING A SYSTEM OF LINEAR INEQUALITIES BY GRAPHING
Graph the solution set of the system.

$$2x - 3y \leqslant 2$$
$$x +\ \ y \leqslant 6$$

SOLUTION
In Figure 10, we have graphed the solution set of each of the inequalities. The cross-hatched region indicates those points that satisfy both inequalities and is therefore the solution set of the system of inequalities.

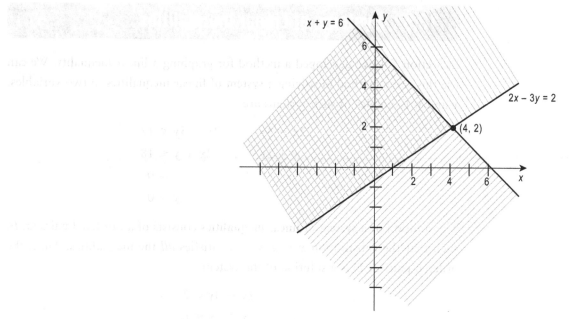

Figure 10   **Graph for Example 1**

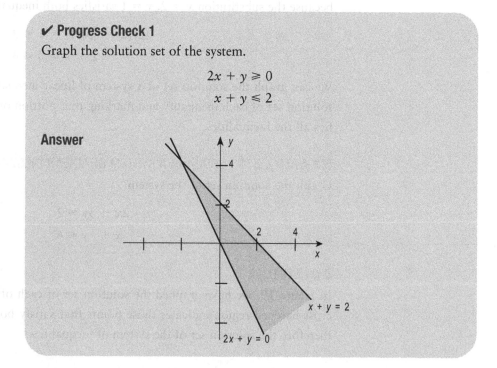

✔ Progress Check 1

Graph the solution set of the system.

$$2x + y \geq 0$$
$$x + y \leq 2$$

Answer

EXAMPLE 2   **SOLVING A SYSTEM OF LINEAR INEQUALITIES BY GRAPHING**

Graph the solution set of the system.

$$x + y < 2$$
$$2x + 3y \geq 9$$
$$x \geq 1$$

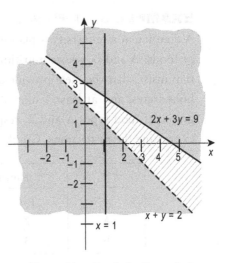

Figure 11 Graph for Example 2

SOLUTION

See Figure 11. Since there are no points satisfying *all* the inequalities, we conclude that the system is inconsistent and has no solutions.

✔ Progress Check 2

Graph the solution set of the given system.

(a) $x + y \geq 3$
    $x + 2y < 8$

(b) $2x + y \leq 4$
    $x + y \leq 3$
    $x \geq 0$
    $y \geq 0$

Answers

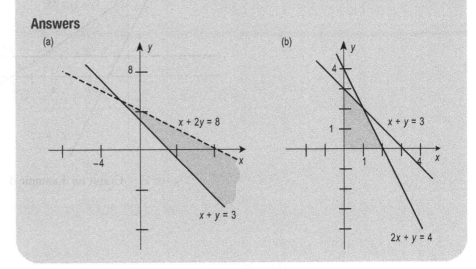

EXAMPLE 3   APPLYING SYSTEMS OF LINEAR INEQUALITIES

A dietitian at a university is planning a menu for a meal to consist of two primary foods, A and B, whose nutritional contents are shown in the table. The dietitian insists that the meal provide at most 12 units of fat, at least 2 units of carbohydrates, and at least 1 unit of protein. If x and y represent the number of grams of food types A and B, respectively, write a system of linear inequalities expressing the restrictions. Graph the solution set.

	Nutritional Content in Units per Gram		
	Fat	Carbohydrate	Protein
A	2	2	0
B	3	1	1

SOLUTION

The number of units of fat contained in the meal is $2x + 3y$, so x and y must satisfy the inequality

$$2x + 3y \leq 12 \qquad \text{fat requirement}$$

Similarly, the requirements for carbohydrate and protein result in the inequalities

$$2x + y \geq 2 \qquad \text{carbohydrate requirement}$$
$$y \geq 1 \qquad \text{protein requirement}$$

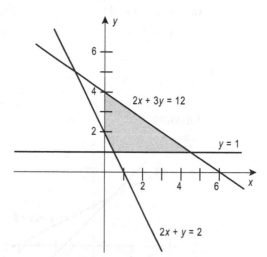

Figure 12   Graph for Example 3

Of course, we must also have $x \geq 0$, since negative quantities of food type A would make no sense. The system of linear inequalities is then

$$2x + 3y \leq 12$$
$$2x + y \geq 2$$
$$x \geq 0$$
$$y \geq 1$$

and the graph is shown in Figure 12.

✔ Progress Check 3

A 2000-seat theater prices the better seats at $25 per ticket and the less desirable seats at $15 per ticket. A local drama company seeking to rent the theater is told that a minimum of 1000 tickets must be sold, that at least half of these must be at the higher price, and that the gross revenue must exceed $25,000. If x represents the number of higher-priced tickets sold and y the number of lower-priced tickets, write a system of linear inequalities that expresses the restrictions.

Answer

$$x + y \geq 1000$$
$$x + y \leq 2000$$
$$25x + 15y \geq 25,000$$
$$x \geq 500$$
$$y \geq 0$$

Exercise Set 13.5

Graph the solution set of the system of linear inequalities.

1. $2x - y \leq 3$
   $2x + 3y \geq -3$

2. $x - y \leq 4$
   $2x + y \geq 6$

3. $3x - y \geq -7$
   $3x + y \leq -2$

4. $3x - 2y \geq 1$
   $2x + 3y \leq 18$

5. $3x - 2y \geq -4$
   $2x - y \leq 5$
   $y \geq 1$

6. $2x - y \geq -3$
   $x + y \leq 5$
   $y \geq 1$

7. $2x - y \leq 5$
   $x + 2y \geq 1$
   $x \geq 0$
   $y \geq 0$

8. $-x + 3y \leq 2$
   $4x + 3y \leq 18$
   $x \geq 0$
   $y \geq 0$

9. $3x + y \leq 6$
   $x - 2y \leq -1$
   $x \geq 2$

10. $x - y \geq -2$
    $x + y \geq -5$
    $y \geq 0$

11. $3x - 2y \leq -6$
    $8x + 3y \leq 24$
    $5x + 4y \geq 20$
    $x \geq 0$
    $y \geq 0$

12. $2x + 3y \geq 18$
    $x + 3y \geq 12$
    $4x + 3y \geq 24$
    $x \geq 0$
    $y \geq 0$

13. A farmer has 10 quarts of milk and 15 quarts of cream, which he will use to make ice cream and ice milk. Each quart of ice cream requires 0.4 quart of milk and 0.2 quart of cream, and each quart of ice milk requires 0.2 quart of milk and 0.4 quart of cream. Graph the set of points representing the possible production of ice cream and of ice milk.

14. A coffee packer uses Jamaican and Colombian coffee to prepare a mild blend and a strong blend. Each pound of mild blend contains $\frac{1}{2}$ pound of Jamaican coffee and $\frac{1}{2}$ pound of Colombian coffee, and each pound of the strong blend requires $\frac{1}{4}$ pound of Jamaican coffee and $\frac{3}{4}$ pound of

Colombian coffee. The packer has available 100 pounds of Jamaican coffee and 125 pounds of Colombian coffee. Graph the set of points representing the possible production of the two blends.

15. A trust fund of $100,000 that has been established to provide university scholarships must adhere to certain restrictions.

   • No more than half of the fund may be invested in common stocks.

   • No more than $35,000 may be invested in preferred stocks.

   • No more than $60,000 may be invested in all types of stocks.

   • The amount invested in common stocks may not be more than twice the amount invested in preferred stocks.

   Graph the solution set representing the possible investments in common and preferred stocks.

16. An institution serves a luncheon consisting of two dishes, A and B, whose nutritional content in grams per unit served is given in the accompanying table.

	Fat	Carbohydrate	Protein
A	1	1	2
B	2	1	6

   The meal is to provide no more than 10 grams of fat, no more than 7 grams of carbohydrate, and at least 6 grams of protein. Graph the solution set of possible quantities of dishes A and B.

In Exercise 17–20, write the inequality whose solution set is graphed (all windows are set to the default setting):

17.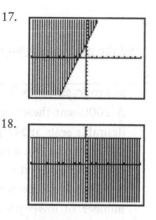

18.

19.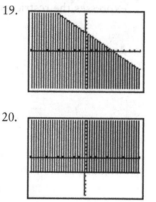

20.

13.6   Linear Programming (Optional)

Let's pose the following problem:

A lot is zoned for an apartment building to consist of no more than 40 apartments, totaling no more than 45,000 square feet. A builder is planning to construct 1-bedroom apartments, each of which will require 1000 square feet and will rent for $200 per month, and 2-bedroom apartments, each of which will utilize 1500 square feet and will rent for $280 per month. If all available apartments can be rented, how many apartments of each type should be built to maximize the builder's monthly revenue?

If we let x denote the number of 1-bedroom units and y denote the number of 2-bedroom units, the accompanying table displays the information given in the problem.

	Number of Units	Square Feet	Rental
1-bedroom	x	1000	$200
2-bedroom	y	1500	$280
Total	40	45,000	z

Using the methods of the previous section, we can translate the **constraints** or requirements on the variables x and y into a system of inequalities. The total number of apartments is $x + y$, so we have

$$x + y \leq 40 \qquad \text{number of units constraint}$$

Since each 1-bedroom apartment occupies 1000 square feet of space, x apartments will occupy $1000x$ square feet of space. Similarly, the 2-bedroom apartments will require $1500y$ square feet of space. The total amount of space needed is $1000x + 1500y$, so we must have

$$1000x + 1500y \leq 45{,}000 \qquad \text{square footage constraint}$$

Moreover, since x and y denote the number of apartments to be built, we must have $x \geq 0$, $y \geq 0$. Thus, we have obtained the following system of inequalities:

$$
\begin{aligned}
x + \quad y &\leq \quad 40 &&\text{number of units constraint} \\
1000x + 1500y &\leq 45{,}000 &&\text{square footage constraint} \\
x &\geq \quad\ 0 &&\left\{\begin{array}{l}\text{need for number of apartments} \\ \text{to be nonnegative}\end{array}\right. \\
y &\geq \quad\ 0 &&
\end{aligned}
$$

We can graph the solution set of this system of linear inequalities as shown in Figure 13.

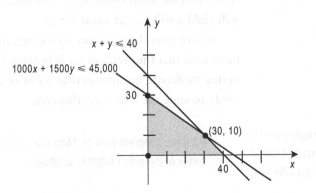

Figure 13   **Feasible Solutions to a Linear Programming Problem**

But the problem as stated asks that we *maximize* the monthly rental

$$z = 200x + 280y$$

a requirement that we have never before seen in a mathematical problem of this sort! It is this requirement to **optimize**, that is, to seek a maximum or a minimum value of a linear expression, that characterizes a linear programming problem.

Linear Programming Problem

A **linear programming problem** seeks the optimal (either the largest or the smallest) value of a linear expression called the **objective function** while satisfying constraints that can be formulated as a system of linear inequalities.

Returning to our apartment building, we can state the linear programming problem in the following way:

$$\text{maximize} \quad z = 200x + 280y$$
$$\text{subject to} \qquad x + y \leq 40$$
$$1000x + 1500y \leq 45{,}000$$
$$x \geq 0$$
$$y \geq 0$$

Then the coordinates of each point of the solution set shown in Figure 13 are a **feasible solution**; that is, the coordinates give us ordered pairs (a, b) that satisfy the system of linear inequalities. Which points provide us with values of x and y that maximize the rental income z? For example, the points $(40, 0)$ and $(15, 20)$ are feasible solutions, yielding these results for z:

x	y	$z = 200x + 280y$
40	0	8000
15	20	8600

Clearly, building 15 one-bedroom and 20 two-bedroom units yields a higher rental revenue than building 40 one-bedroom units, but is there a solution that will yield a still higher value for z?

Before providing the key to solving linear programming problems, we first must note that the solution set is bounded by straight lines, and we use the term **vertex** to denote an intersection point of any two boundary lines. We are then ready to state the following theorem:

Fundamental Theorem of Linear Programming

If a linear programming problem has an optimal solution, that solution occurs at a vertex of the set of feasible solutions.

With this result, the builder need only examine the vertices of the solution set of Figure 13, rather than considering each of the infinite number of feasible solutions—a bewildering task! We then evaluate the objective function $z = 200x + 280y$ for the coordinates of the vertices $(0, 0)$, $(0, 30)$, $(40, 0)$, and $(30, 10)$.

x	y	$z = 200x + 280y$
0	0	0
0	30	8400
40	0	8000
30	10	8800

Since the largest value of z is 8800 and this value corresponds to $x = 30$, $y = 10$, the builder finds that the optimal strategy is to build 30 one-bedroom and 10 two-bedroom units.

We can now illustrate the steps in solving a linear programming problem.

EXAMPLE 1   SOLVING A LINEAR PROGRAMMING PROBLEM

Solve the linear programming problem

$$\text{minimize } z = x - 4y$$
$$\text{subject to} \quad x + 2y \leq 10$$
$$-x + 4y \leq 8$$
$$x \geq 0$$
$$y \geq 1$$

SOLUTION

Linear Programming

Step 1. Sketch the solution set of the system of linear inequalities.

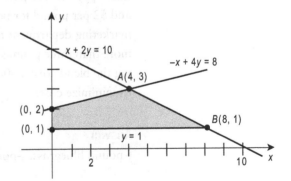

Figure 14   **Vertices of the Solution Set**

continues

Linear Programming *continued*

Step 2. Determine all vertices of the solution set.

The vertices $(0, 1)$ and $(0, 2)$ are the y-intercepts of the lines whose equations are $y = 1$ and $-x + 4y = 8$, respectively. The vertex B in Figure 14 is the intersection of the lines $y = 1$ and $x + 2y = 10$ and is seen to be $(8, 1)$. The vertex A of Figure 14 is the intersection of the lines whose equations are

$$-x + 4y = 8$$

and

$$x + 2y = 10$$

Solving the system of equations (try elimination) yields the vertex $A(4, 3)$.

Step 3. Evaluate the objective function for the coordinates of each vertex.

Vertex	x	y	$z = x - 4y$
$(0, 1)$	0	1	-4
$(0, 2)$	0	2	-8
$(8, 1)$	8	1	4
$(4, 3)$	4	3	-8

Step 4. The point or points providing the optimal value of the objective function are solutions of the linear programming problem.

The minimum value of the objective function is -8, which occurs at the vertices $(0, 2)$ and $(4, 3)$. Thus, $x = 0$, $y = 2$ and $x = 4$, $y = 3$ are both solutions of the linear programming problem.

✔ Progress Check 1

A grass seed mixture is comprised of bluegrass and perennial rye. The producer pays $3 per pound for bluegrass (which will cover 2000 square feet) and $2 per pound for perennial rye (which will cover 1000 square feet). The marketing department requires that the blend be sold in boxes weighing no more than three pounds with a minimum 75% ryegrass and a statement saying the blend covers 3000 square feet. How should the blend be formulated to minimize cost?

Answer

$\frac{3}{5}$-pound bluegrass, $\frac{9}{5}$-pound ryegrass

Linear programming problems occur in real-life situations with great frequency. In certain industries these problems can involve thousands of variables and hundreds of constraints. Obviously, the method of graphical solution we presented for two variables cannot be used. A solution method known as the simplex algorithm was first devised by George Dantzig in 1947. Despite the sophistication of this approach, the number of calculations required becomes unmanageably large for hand computation even for relatively small numbers of constraints. Fortunately, the discovery of the simplex algorithm occurred at the time electronic computers made their initial appearance. Since then industries such as oil refining and steel production have used linear programming to determine the optimum use of their facilities.

Exercise Set 13.6

In Exercises 1–8 find the minimum value and the maximum value of the linear expression, subject to the given constraints. Indicate coordinates of the vertices at which the minimum and maximum values occur.

1. $x - \dfrac{1}{2}y$ subject to

$$3x - y \geq 1$$
$$x \geq 0$$
$$x \leq 5$$
$$y \geq 0$$

2. $2x + y$ subject to

$$x + y \leq 4$$
$$x \geq 1$$
$$y \geq 2$$

3. $\dfrac{1}{2}x - 2y$ subject to

$$x + 2y \leq 6$$
$$-2x + 3y \leq 2$$
$$x \geq 0$$
$$y \geq 0$$

4. $0.2x + 0.8y$ subject to

$$x + 3y \leq 8$$
$$x - 4y \geq 1$$
$$x \geq 0$$
$$y \geq 0$$

5. $2x - y$ subject to

$$-x + y \leq 0$$
$$3x + 4y \geq 6$$
$$x \leq 4$$

6. $x + 3y$ subject to

$$2x + y \geq 2$$
$$4x + 5y \leq 40$$
$$x \geq 0$$
$$y \geq 1$$
$$y \leq 6$$

7. $2x - y$ subject to

$$-x + 2y \leq 8$$
$$x + 2y \geq 12$$
$$5x + 2y \leq 44$$
$$x \geq 3$$

8. $y - x$ subject to

$$-5x + 2y \leq 10$$
$$5x + 6y \leq 50$$
$$5x + y \leq 20$$
$$x \geq 0$$
$$y \geq 1$$

9. A firm has budgeted $1500 for display space at a toy show. Two types of display booths are available: "preferred space" costs $18 per square foot, with a minimum rental of 60 square feet; "regular space" costs $12 per square foot, with a minimum rental of 30 square feet. It is estimated that there will be 120 visitors for each square foot of "preferred space" and 60 visitors for each square foot of "regular space." How should the firm allot its budget to maximize the number of potential clients that will visit the booths?

10. A company manufactures a 16-bit computer and a 32-bit computer. To meet existing orders, it must schedule at least 50 16-bit computers for the next production cycle and can produce no more than 150 16-bit computers. The manufacturing facilities are adequate to produce no more than 300 32-bit computers, but the total number of computers that can be produced cannot exceed 400. The profit on each 16-bit computer is $310; on each 32-bit computer the profit is $275. Find the number of computers of each type that should be manufactured to maximize profit.

11. Swift Truckers is negotiating a contract with Better Spices, which uses two sizes of containers: large, 4-cubic-foot containers weighing 10 pounds and small, 2-cubic-foot containers weighing 8 pounds. Swift Truckers will use a vehicle that can handle a maximum load of 3280 pounds of cargo size of up to 1000 cubic feet. The firms have agreed on a shipping rate of 50 cents for each large container and 30 cents for each small container. How many containers of each type should Swift place on a truck to maximize income?

12. A bakery makes both yellow cake and white cake. Each pound of yellow cake requires $\frac{1}{4}$ pound of flour and $\frac{1}{4}$ pound of sugar; each pound of white cake requires $\frac{1}{3}$ pound of flour and $\frac{1}{5}$ pound of sugar. The baker finds that 100 pounds of flour and 80 pounds of sugar are available. If yellow cake sells for $3 per pound and white cake sells for $2.50 per pound, how many pounds of each cake should the bakery produce to maximize income, assuming that all cakes baked can be sold?

13. A shop sells a mixture of Java and Colombian coffee beans for $4 per pound. The shopkeeper has allocated $1000 for buying fresh beans and finds that he must pay $1.50 per pound for Java beans

and $2 per pound for Colombian beans. In a satis-factory mixture, the weight of Colombian beans will be at least twice and no more than four times the weight of the Java beans. How many pounds of each type of coffee bean should be ordered to maximize the profit if all the mixture can be sold?

14. A pension fund plans to invest up to $50,000 in U.S. Treasury bonds yielding 12% interest per year and corporate bonds yielding 15% interest per year. The fund manager is told to invest a minimum of $25,000 in the Treasury bonds and a minimum of $10,000 in the corporate bonds, with no more than $\frac{1}{4}$ of the total investment to be in corporate bonds. How much should the manager invest in each type of bond to achieve a maximum amount of annual interest? What is the maximum interest?

15. A farmer intends to plant crops A and B on all or part of a 100-acre field. Seed for crop A costs $6 per acre, and labor and equipment costs $20 per acre. For crop B, seed costs $9 per acre, and labor and equipment costs $15 per acre. The farmer cannot spend more than $810 for seed and $1800 for labor and equipment. If the income per acre is $150 for crop A and $175 for crop B, how many acres of each crop should be planted to maximize total income?

16. The farmer in Exercise 15 finds that a worldwide surplus in crop B reduces the income to $140 per acre while the income for crop A remains steady at $150 per acre. How many acres of each crop should be planted to maximize total income?

17. In preparing food for the college cafeteria, a dietician will combine Volume Pack A and Volume Pack B. Each pound of Volume Pack A costs $2.50 and contains 4 units of carbohydrate, 3 units of protein, and 5 units of fat. Each pound of Volume Pack B costs $1.50 and contains 3 units of carbohydrate, 4 units of protein, and 1 unit of fat. If minimum monthly requirements are 60 units of carbohydrates, 52 units of protein, and 42 units of fat, how many pounds of each food pack will the dietician use to minimize costs?

18. A lawn service uses a riding mower that cuts a 5000-square-foot area per hour and a smaller mower that cuts a 3000-square-foot area per hour. Surprisingly, each mower uses 0.5 gallon of gasoline per hour. Near the end of a long summer day, the supervisor finds that both mowers are empty and that there remains 0.6 gallon of gasoline in the storage cans. To conclude the day at a sensible point, at least 4000 square feet of lawn must still be mowed. If the cost of operating the riding mower is $9 per hour and the cost of operating the smaller mower is $5 per hour, how much of the remaining gasoline should be allocated to each mower to do the job at the least possible cost?

■   ■   ■

Chapter Summary

Terms and Symbols

Key Ideas for Review

Topic	Page	Key Idea
Solving a system of equations	486	To solve a system of equations, we must find a set of values for the unknowns that satisfies all of the equations.
method of graphing	486	The coordinates of each point common to the graphs of the equations is a solution of the system.
method of substitution	490	The method of substitution involves solving an equation for one variable and substituting the result into another equation.
method of elimination	493	The method of elimination involves multiplying an equation by a nonzero constant so that, when the equation is added to a second equation, a variable drops out.
Consistent and inconsistent systems	487	A consistent system of equations has one or more real solutions; an inconsistent system has no real solutions.
Linear systems	488	The graph of a pair of linear equations in two variables is two straight lines that may either (a) intersect in a point, (b) be parallel, or (c) be the same line. If the two straight lines intersect, the coordinates of the point of intersection are a solution of the system of linear equations. If the lines do not intersect, the system is inconsistent. If the lines coincide, then the coordinates of any point on the graph of either equation is a solution of the system.
special cases	496	When using the method of elimination or the method of substitution, it is possible to detect the special cases in which the lines are parallel or reduce to the same line.
applications	497	It is often easier and more natural to set up word problems by using two or more variables.
Gaussian elimination	507	Gaussian elimination is a systematic way of transforming a linear system into triangular form. A system of equations in triangular form is easily solved by back-substitution.

continues

Topic	Page	Key Idea
Solving linear inequalities	513	The solution of a system of linear inequalities can be found graphically as the region satisfying all the inequalities.
Linear programming	518	To solve a linear programming problem, it is only necessary to consider the vertices of the region of feasible solutions.

Common Errors

1. When multiplying an equation by a nonzero constant, you must multiply each term of both sides of the equation by the constant.

2. When using the method of substitution, the expression obtained for a variable from one equation must be substituted into a *different* equation.

3. Don't be frustrated if the method of substitution or method of elimination doesn't yield a solution to a linear system. A linear system need not have a solution, and these methods will call your attention to this situation.

4. Given the linear system

$$x + 3y - 2z = 5$$
$$2x - 2y + 5z = -4$$
$$-3x + y - 6z = 13$$

the variable x is eliminated from the *second* equation by replacing the *second* equation with the sum of itself plus -2 times the first equation. This yields

$$x + 3y - 2z = 5$$
$$-8y + 9z = -14$$
$$-3x + y - 6z = 13$$

Remember that the triangular form requires zero coefficients of x in all equations other than the first. This will help you to avoid the common error of replacing the wrong equation.

Review Exercises

Solutions to exercises whose numbers are in bold are in the Solutions section in the back of the book.

13.1   In Exercises 1 and 2 solve the given system by graphing.

1. $2x + 3y = 2$
   $4x + 5y = 3$

2. $y^2 = x - 1$
   $x + y = 7$

In Exercises 3–8 solve the given system by the method of substitution.

3. $x + 6y = -11$
   $2x + 5y = 5$

4. $2x - 4y = -14$
   $-x - 6y = -5$

5. $2x + y = 0$
   $x - 3y = \dfrac{7}{4}$

6. $x^2 + y^2 = 25$
   $x + 3y = 5$

7. $x^2 - 4y^2 = 9$
   $y - 2x = 0$

8. $y^2 = 4x$
   $y^2 + x - 2y = 12$

13.2   In Exercises 9–14 solve the given system by the method of elimination.

9. $x + 4y = 17$
   $2x - 3y = -21$

10. $5x - 2y = 14$
    $-x - 3y = 4$

11. $-3x + y = -13$
    $2x - 3y = 11$

12. $7x - 2y = -20$
    $3x - y = -9$

13. $y^2 = 2x - 1$
    $x - y = 2$

14. $x^2 + y^2 = 9$
    $y = x^2 + 3$

13.3 **15.** The sum of the digits of a two-digit number is 10. If the sum of the number and its tens digit is 50, find the number.

16. The sum of a two-digit number and its units digit is 36. If we reverse the digits of the number, the resulting number is 54 more than the original number. Find the number.

17. Five pounds of hamburger and 4 pounds of steak cost $22, and 3 pounds of hamburger and 7 pounds of steak cost $28.15. Find the cost per pound of hamburger and of steak.

18. A jogger running with the wind covers a 4-mile course in 20 minutes; it takes her 30 minutes to cover the same course against the wind. Find the jogger's speed and the speed of the wind.

19. A video recorder manufacturer finds that supply S and demand D are related to price p (in dollars) as follows:

$$S = 5p + 300$$
$$D = -3p + 3500$$

Find the equilibrium price and the number of recorders sold at this price.

20. A small book publisher finds that its monthly expenditure (in dollars) is given by $C = 3300 + 5x$, where x is the number of books produced during the month. Each book is sold by the publisher for $8. If all books that are produced can be sold, find the break-even point and the total revenue received at that point.

13.4 In Exercises 21–24 use Gaussian elimination to solve the given linear system.

21. $\begin{aligned} -3x - y + z &= 12 \\ 2x + 5y - 2z &= -9 \\ -x + 4y + 2z &= 15 \end{aligned}$

22. $\begin{aligned} 3x + 2y - z &= -8 \\ 2x \quad + 3z &= 5 \\ x - 4y \quad &= -4 \end{aligned}$

23. $\begin{aligned} 5x - y + 2z &= 10 \\ -2x + 3y - z &= -7 \\ 3x \quad + 2z &= 7 \end{aligned}$

24. $\begin{aligned} x + 4y \quad &= 4 \\ -x \quad + 3z &= -4 \\ 2x + 2y - z &= \frac{41}{6} \end{aligned}$

In Exercises 25–28 solve by any method.

25. $\begin{aligned} 2x + 3y &= 6 \\ 3x - y &= -13 \end{aligned}$

26. $\begin{aligned} x + 2y &= 0 \\ -x + 4y &= 5 \end{aligned}$

27. $\begin{aligned} 2x + 3y - z &= -4 \\ x - 2y + 2z &= -6 \\ 2x \quad - 3z &= 5 \end{aligned}$

28. $\begin{aligned} 2x + 2y - 3z &= -4 \\ 3y - z &= -4 \\ 4x - y + z &= 4 \end{aligned}$

13.5 In Exercises 29–34 graph the solution set of the linear inequality or system of linear inequalities.

29. $x - 2y \leq 5$

30. $2x + y > 4$

31. $\begin{aligned} 2x + 3y &\leq 2 \\ x - y &\geq 1 \end{aligned}$

32. $\begin{aligned} x - 2y &\geq 4 \\ 2x - y &\leq 2 \end{aligned}$

33. $\begin{aligned} 2x + 3y &\leq 6 \\ x &\geq 0 \\ y &\geq 1 \end{aligned}$

34. $\begin{aligned} 2x + y &\leq 4 \\ 2x - y &\leq 3 \\ x &\geq 0 \\ y &\geq 0 \end{aligned}$

13.6 In Exercises 35 and 36 solve the given linear programming problem.

35. maximize $z = 5y - x$

subject to $\begin{aligned} 8y - 3x &\leq 36 \\ 6x + y &\leq 30 \\ y &\geq 1 \\ x &\geq 0 \end{aligned}$

36. minimize $z = x + 4y$

subject to $\begin{aligned} 4x - y &\geq 8 \\ 4x + y &\leq 24 \\ 5y + 4x &\geq 32 \end{aligned}$

Progress Test 13A

1. Solve by graphing.

$$2x + 2y = 2$$
$$-4x - 5y = -3$$

2. Solve by substitution.

$$-x + 6y = -11$$
$$2x + 5y = 5$$

3. Solve by substitution.

$$2x - 4y = -14$$
$$-x - 6y = -5$$

4. Solve by elimination.

$$x + y = 1$$
$$3x - 6y = -3$$

5. Solve by elimination.

$$2x - 5y = 15$$
$$-4x + 10y = 7$$

6. Solve by any method.

$$4x - 3y = 0$$
$$6x + y = -\frac{11}{6}$$

7. Solve by any method.

$$y^2 = 5x$$
$$y^2 - x^2 = 6$$

8. Solve by any method.

$$x^2 + y^2 = 25$$
$$4x^2 - y^2 = 20$$

9. Solve by Gaussian elimination.

$$-3x - y + z = 12$$
$$2x + 5y - 2z = 1$$
$$-x + 4y + 2z = 8$$

10. The sum of a two-digit number and its tens digit is 49. If we reverse the digits of the number, the resulting number is 9 more than the original number. Find the number.

11. An airplane flying with a tail wind can complete a journey of 3500 kilometers between two cities in 5 hours. Flying back, the plane travels the same distance in 7 hours. What is the speed of the plane in still air, and what is the wind speed?

12. Two bottles of Brand A aspirin and 3 bottles of Brand B aspirin cost $2.80. The cost of 4 bottles of Brand A aspirin and 2 bottles of Brand B is $3.20. What is the cost per bottle of each brand of aspirin?

13. An auto repair shop finds that the monthly expenditures (in dollars) is given by $C = 4025 + 9x$, where x is the total number of hours worked by all employees. If the monthly revenue received (in dollars) is given by $R = 16x$, find the break-even point in number of work hours and the total monthly revenue received at that point.

14. A manufacturer of faucets finds that supply S and demand D are given by

$$S = 3p + 10$$
$$D = -2p + 130$$

Find the equilibrium price and the number of faucets sold at this price.

In Problems 15 and 16 graph the solution set of the system of linear inequalities.

15. $x - 2y \leq 1$
$3x + 2y \geq 4$

16. $2x + y \leq 10$
$-x + 3y \leq 12$
$x \geq 0$
$y \geq 0$

Progress Test 13B

1. Solve by graphing.

$$3x - y = -17$$
$$x + 2y = -1$$

2. Solve by substitution.

$$2x + y = 4$$
$$3x - 2y = -15$$

3. Solve by substitution.

$$3x + 6y = -1$$
$$6x - 3y = 3$$

4. Solve by substitution

$$4x - 4y = -3$$
$$-2x + 8y = 3$$

5. Solve by elimination

$$7x - 2y = 3$$
$$-21x + 6y = -9$$

6. Solve by any method.

$$3x + y = -11$$
$$-2x + 2y = 2$$

7. Solve by any method.

$$x^2 + 3y^2 = 12$$
$$x + 3y = 6$$

8. Solve by any method.

$$x^2 - y^2 = 9$$
$$x^2 + y^2 = 41$$

9. Solve by Gaussian elimination.

$$x + 2y - 3z = -2$$
$$-x + 3y + 6z = 15$$
$$2x + 3y + 6z = 0$$

10. The sum of the digits of a two-digit number is 10, and the units digit exceeds the tens digit by 4. Find the number.

11. A motorboat can travel 60 kilometers downstream in 3 hours, and the return trip requires 4 hours. What is the rate of the boat in still water and what is the rate of the current?

12. If a dozen pencils and 5 pens cost 96 cents, and 8 pencils and 10 pens cost $1.44, what is the cost of each pencil and of each pen?

13. A school cafeteria manager finds that the weekly cost of operation is $1375, plus $1.25 for every meal served. If the average meal produces a revenue of $2.50, find the break-even point.

14. Suppose that supply and demand for a particular tennis racket are given by

$$S = 5p + 10$$
$$D = -2p + 430$$

Find the equilibrium price and the number of rackets sold at this price.

In Problems 15 and 16 graph the solution set of the system of linear inequalities.

15. $2x - 3y \geqslant 6$
    $3x + y \leqslant 4$

16. $2x + y \leqslant 4$
    $2x - 5y \leqslant 5$
    $y \geqslant 1$

Chapter 13 Project

In the chapter opener you read about polynomial curve fitting and how it can be used to model (that is, design equations for) data from the real world. Solving systems of equations, both "two-by-two" (two equations and two unknowns) and "three-by-three," was necessary to complete this task. Review Exercises 21—22 in Section 13.1 and Exercises 24—25 in Section 13.4.

Now use the method outlined in those exercises to model the following data with a quadratic polynomial:

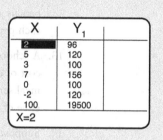

X	Y_1	
2	96	
5	120	
3	100	
7	156	
0	100	
-2	120	
100	19500	
X=2		

(This table gives you many more data points than are needed. Use the "extra" data points to check your answer.)

Not all data perfectly matches a polynomial function. Your graphing calculator probably has regression capabilities. This means that you can enter your own data, select a type of function, and your calculator will give you the coefficients to complete the function. Try it!

■ ■ ■

14 Matrices and Determinants

"Mathematics, rightly viewed, possesses not only truth, but supreme beauty—a beauty cold and austere, like that of sculpture."

—Bertrand Russell

Have you recently sent or received a picture of a friend by email or cell phone? Or perhaps you plan on watching a DVD with friends tonight. The pictures you will see are digital images, which are made up of pixels. For a black-and-white image, each pixel has a value representing the gray-level intensity. If we replace each pixel in the image with its value, a number, we get a rectangular array that looks like this:

$$\begin{bmatrix} 5 & 6 & 8 \\ 4 & 0 & 1 \\ 2 & 1 & 10 \end{bmatrix}$$

This array is called a matrix. By multiplying each entry by 3, we would increase the contrast. Other matrix operations (Section 14.2) can be applied to alter the image in other ways. The chapter project explores some possibilities.

Explore some mathematical topics, including this one, in the *Journal of Online Mathematics* at http://www.joma.org/, which is part of the Mathematical Association of America's Mathematical Sciences Digital Library.

http://www.joma.org/

The material on matrices and determinants presented in this chapter serves as an introduction to linear algebra, a mathematical subject that is used in the natural sciences, business and economics, and the social sciences. Since methods involving matrices may require millions of numerical computations, computers have played an important role in expanding the use of matrix techniques to a wide variety of practical problems.

Our study of matrices and determinants will focus on their application to the solution of systems of linear equations. We will see that the method of Gaussian elimination studied in the previous chapter can be readily implemented using matrices. We will show that matrix notation provides a convenient means for writing linear systems and that the inverse of a matrix enables us to solve such a system. Determinants will also provide us with an additional technique, known as Cramer's Rule, for the solution of certain linear systems.

It should be emphasized that this material is a very brief introduction to matrices and determinants. Their properties and applications are both extensive and important.

14.1   Matrices and Linear Systems

Definitions

In Chapter 13 we studied methods for solving a system of linear equations such as

$$2x + 3y = -7$$
$$3x - y = 17$$

This system can be displayed by a matrix, which is simply a rectangular array of $m \times n$ real numbers arranged in m horizontal rows and n vertical columns. The numbers are called the entries or elements of the matrix and are enclosed within brackets. Thus,

$$A = \begin{bmatrix} 2 & 3 & -7 \\ 3 & -1 & 17 \end{bmatrix} \leftarrow \text{rows}$$

$$\underset{\text{columns}}{\uparrow \quad \uparrow \quad \uparrow}$$

is the matrix consisting of two rows and three columns, whose entries are obtained from the two given equations. We shall soon see that this matrix represents the linear system.

In general, a matrix of m rows and n columns has mn elements and is said to be of *dimension m by n*, written $m \times n$. The matrix A is seen to be of dimension 2×3. If the numbers of rows and columns of a matrix are both equal to n, the matrix is called a **square** matrix of *order n*.

EXAMPLE 1   EXPLORING MATRICES

(a)
$$A = \begin{bmatrix} -1 & 4 \\ 0.1 & -2 \end{bmatrix}$$

is a 2×2 matrix. Since matrix A has two rows and two columns, it is a square matrix of order 2.

(b)
$$B = \begin{bmatrix} 4 & -5 \\ -2 & 1 \\ 3 & 0 \end{bmatrix}$$

has three rows and two columns and is a 3×2 matrix.

(c)
$$C = \begin{bmatrix} -8 & 6 & 1 \end{bmatrix}$$

is a 1×3 matrix and is called a **row matrix** since it has precisely one row.

(d)
$$D = \begin{bmatrix} 2 \\ -4 \end{bmatrix}$$

is a 2×1 matrix and is called a **column matrix** since it has precisely one column.

✔ Progress Check 1

Determine the dimensions of each matrix.

(a) $A = \begin{bmatrix} -0.25 & -5 & 6 \\ 10 & 0.1 & -3 \\ -2 & 4 & 6 \end{bmatrix}$ (b) $B = \begin{bmatrix} 2 & 3 \end{bmatrix}$

(c) $C = \begin{bmatrix} -1 & 2 \\ 20 & 0 \\ 4 & -3 \end{bmatrix}$

Answers

(a) 3×3 (b) 1×2 (c) 3×2

Subscript Notation

There is a convenient way of denoting a general $m \times n$ matrix, using "double subscripts."

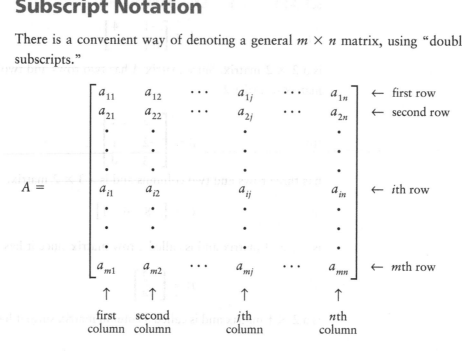

$$A = \begin{bmatrix} a_{11} & a_{12} & \cdots & a_{1j} & \cdots & a_{1n} \\ a_{21} & a_{22} & \cdots & a_{2j} & \cdots & a_{2n} \\ \vdots & \vdots & & \vdots & & \vdots \\ a_{i1} & a_{i2} & & a_{ij} & & a_{in} \\ \vdots & \vdots & & \vdots & & \vdots \\ a_{m1} & a_{m2} & \cdots & a_{mj} & \cdots & a_{mn} \end{bmatrix} \begin{array}{l} \leftarrow \text{first row} \\ \leftarrow \text{second row} \\ \\ \leftarrow i\text{th row} \\ \\ \leftarrow m\text{th row} \end{array}$$

first   second jth nth
column   column   column   column

Thus, a_{ij} is the entry in the ith row and jth column of the matrix A. It is customary to write $A = [a_{ij}]$ to indicate that a_{ij} is the entry in row i and column j of matrix A.

EXAMPLE 2   SUBSCRIPT NOTATION

Let

$$A = \begin{bmatrix} 3 & -2 & 4 & 5 \\ 9 & 1 & 2 & 0 \\ -3 & 2 & -4 & 8 \end{bmatrix}$$

Matrix A is of dimension 3×4. The element a_{12} is found in the first row and second column and is seen to be -2. Similarly, we see that $a_{31} = -3$, $a_{33} = -4$, and $a_{34} = 8$.

✔ Progress Check 2

Let

$$B = \begin{bmatrix} 4 & 8 & 1 \\ 2 & -5 & 3 \\ -8 & 6 & -4 \\ 0 & 1 & -1 \end{bmatrix}$$

Find

(a) b_{11} (b) b_{23} (c) b_{31} (d) b_{42}

Answers

(a) 4   (b) 3   (c) -8 (d) 1

Coefficient and Augmented Matrices

If we begin with the system of linear equations

$$2x + 3y = -7$$
$$3x - y = 17$$

then the matrix

$$\begin{bmatrix} 2 & 3 \\ 3 & -1 \end{bmatrix}$$

in which the first column is formed from the coefficients of x and the second column is formed from the coefficients of y is called the **coefficient matrix**. The matrix

$$\begin{bmatrix} 2 & 3 & | & -7 \\ 3 & -1 & | & 17 \end{bmatrix}$$

which includes the column consisting of the right-hand sides of the equations separated by a dashed line is called the **augmented matrix**.

In writing the augmented matrix of a linear system, be sure to enter a zero whenever a variable is missing in an equation since the coefficient of the variable is zero.

EXAMPLE 3   THE AUGMENTED MATRIX

The augmented matrix of the linear system

$$3x - y + 2z = 4$$
$$x - 2y \qquad = 6$$
$$-5x \qquad + 3z = 4$$

is

$$\begin{bmatrix} 3 & -1 & 2 & | & 4 \\ 1 & -2 & 0 & | & 6 \\ -5 & 0 & 3 & | & 4 \end{bmatrix}$$

✔ Progress Check 3

Write the augmented matrix of the linear system

$$2x \qquad - 3z = 5$$
$$-x + y + 5z = 2$$
$$x - 2y + 4z = 6$$

Answer

$$\begin{bmatrix} 2 & 0 & -3 & | & 5 \\ -1 & 1 & 5 & | & 2 \\ 1 & -2 & 4 & | & 6 \end{bmatrix}$$

Conversely, any matrix with more than one column can be thought of as the augmented matrix of a linear system.

EXAMPLE 4   THE AUGMENTED MATRIX

Write the system of linear equations that corresponds to the augmented matrix

$$\begin{bmatrix} -5 & 2 & -1 & \vdots & 15 \\ 0 & -2 & 1 & \vdots & -7 \\ \frac{1}{2} & 1 & -1 & \vdots & 3 \end{bmatrix}$$

SOLUTION

We attach the unknown x to the first column, the unknown y to the second column, and the unknown z to the third column; and we use the numbers to the right of the dashed line as the right-hand sides of the equations. The resulting system is

$$-5x + 2y - z = 15$$
$$-2y + z = -7$$
$$\frac{1}{2}x + y - z = 3$$

✔ Progress Check 3

Write the system of linear equations that corresponds to the augmented matrix

$$\begin{bmatrix} 3 & -2 & 5 & \vdots & -1 \\ 3 & 0 & \frac{1}{3} & \vdots & 2 \\ -1 & 4 & 2 & \vdots & 5 \end{bmatrix}$$

Answer

$$3x - 2y + 5z = -1$$
$$3x + \tfrac{1}{3}z = 2$$
$$-x + 4y + 2z = 5$$

Now that we have seen how a matrix can be used to represent a system of linear equations, we next proceed to show how routine operations on that matrix can yield the solution of the system. These "matrix methods" are simply a clever streamlining of the methods already studied in the previous chapter.

In Section 13.4, we used three elementary operations to transform a system of linear equations into triangular form. When applying the same procedures to a matrix, we speak of rows, columns, and elements instead of equations, variables, and coefficients. The three elementary operations that yield an equivalent system now become the **elementary row operations.**

The following elementary row operations transform an augmented matrix representing a linear system into a matrix representing an equivalent system.

1. Interchange any two rows.
2. Multiply each element of any row by a constant $k \neq 0$.
3. Replace each element of a given row by the sum of itself plus k times the corresponding element of any other row.

Elementary Row Operations

Gaussian Elimination

The method of Gaussian elimination introduced in Section 13.4 can now be restated in terms of matrices. By use of elementary row operations, we seek to transform an augmented matrix into a matrix for which $a_{ij} = 0$ when $i > j$. The resulting matrix will have the following appearance for a system of three linear equations in three unknowns:

$$\left[\begin{array}{ccc|c} * & * & * & * \\ 0 & * & * & * \\ 0 & 0 & * & * \end{array} \right]$$

Since this matrix represents a linear system in triangular form, back-substitution will provide a solution of the original system. We will illustrate the process with an example.

EXAMPLE 5   GAUSSIAN ELIMINATION
Solve the system.

$$\begin{array}{rcl} x - y + 4z &=& 4 \\ 2x + 2y - z &=& 2 \\ 3x - 2y + 3z &=& -3 \end{array}$$

SOLUTION
We describe and illustrate the steps of the procedure on the next page.

Gaussian Elimination

Step 1. Form the augmented matrix.

The augmented matrix is

$$\left[\begin{array}{ccc|c} 1 & -1 & 4 & 4 \\ 2 & 2 & -1 & 2 \\ 3 & -2 & 3 & -3 \end{array}\right]$$

Step 2. If necessary, interchange rows to make sure that a_{11}, the first element of the first row, is nonzero. We call a_{11} the **pivot element** and row 1 the **pivot row**.

We see that $a_{11} = 1 \neq 0$. The pivot element is a_{11} and is shown in bold.

Step 3. Arrange to have 0 as the first element of every row below row 1. This is done by replacing row 2, row 3, and so on by the sum of itself and an appropriate multiple of row 1.

To make $a_{21} = 0$, replace row 2 by the sum of itself and (-2) times row 1; to make $a_{31} = 0$, replace row 3 by the sum of itself and (-3) times row 1.

$$\left[\begin{array}{ccc|c} 1 & -1 & 4 & 4 \\ 0 & 4 & -9 & -6 \\ 0 & 1 & -9 & -15 \end{array}\right]$$

Step 4. Repeat the process defined by Steps 2 and 3, allowing row 2, row 3, and so on to play the role of the first row. Thus row 2, row 3, and so on serve as the pivot rows.

Since $a_{22} = 4 \neq 0$, it will serve as the next pivot element and is shown in bold. To make $a_{32} = 0$, replace row 3 by the sum of itself and $\left(-\frac{1}{4}\right)$ times row 2.

$$\left[\begin{array}{ccc|c} 1 & -1 & 4 & 4 \\ 0 & 4 & -9 & -6 \\ 0 & 0 & -\frac{27}{4} & -\frac{27}{2} \end{array}\right]$$

Step 5. The corresponding linear system is in triangular form. Solve by back-substitution.

The third row of the final matrix yields

$$-\frac{27}{4}z = -\frac{27}{2}$$

$$z = 2$$

Substituting $z = 2$, we obtain from the second row of the final matrix

$$\begin{aligned} 4y - 9z &= -6 \\ 4y - 9(2) &= -6 \\ y &= 3 \end{aligned}$$

Substituting $y = 3$, $z = 2$, we obtain from the first row of the final matrix

$$\begin{aligned} x - y + 4z &= 4 \\ x - 3 + 4(2) &= 4 \\ x &= -1 \end{aligned}$$

The solution is $x = -1$, $y = 3$, $z = 2$.

✔ **Progress Check 5**

Solve the following linear system by matrix methods.

$$\begin{aligned} 2x + 4y - z &= 0 \\ x - 2y - 2z &= 2 \\ -5x - 8y + 3z &= -2 \end{aligned}$$

Answers

$x = 6, y = -2, z = 4$

Note that we have described the process of Gaussian elimination in a manner that will apply to any augmented matrix that is $n \times (n + 1)$; that is, Gaussian elimination may be used on any system of n linear equations in n unknowns.

It is also permissible to perform elementary row operations in clever ways to simplify the arithmetic. For instance, you may wish to interchange rows, or to multiply a row by a constant to obtain a pivot element equal to 1. We will illustrate these ideas with an example.

EXAMPLE 6   MATRIX METHODS FOR SOLVING LINEAR SYSTEMS

Solve by matrix methods:

$$\begin{aligned} 2y + 3z \qquad\quad &= 4 \\ 4x + y + 8z + 15w &= -14 \\ x - y + 2z \qquad\quad &= 9 \\ -x - 2y - 3z - 6w &= 10 \end{aligned}$$

SOLUTION

We begin with the 4×5 augmented matrix and perform a sequence of elementary row operations. The pivot element is shown in bold.

$$\left[\begin{array}{cccc|c} 0 & 2 & 3 & 0 & 4 \\ 4 & 1 & 8 & 15 & -14 \\ 1 & -1 & 2 & 0 & 9 \\ -1 & -2 & -3 & -6 & 10 \end{array}\right] \quad \begin{array}{l}\text{Augmented matrix} \\ \text{Note that } a_{11} = 0.\end{array}$$

$$\left[\begin{array}{cccc|c} \mathbf{1} & -1 & 2 & 0 & 9 \\ 4 & 1 & 8 & 15 & -14 \\ 0 & 2 & 3 & 0 & 4 \\ -1 & -2 & -3 & -6 & 10 \end{array}\right] \quad \text{Interchanged rows 1 and 3 so that } a_{11} = 1.$$

$$\begin{bmatrix} 1 & -1 & 2 & 0 & | & 9 \\ 0 & 5 & 0 & 15 & | & -50 \\ 0 & 2 & 3 & 0 & | & 4 \\ 0 & -3 & -1 & -6 & | & 19 \end{bmatrix}$$

To make $a_{21} = 0$, replaced row 2 by the sum of itself and (-4) times row 1.

To make $a_{41} = 0$, replaced row 4 by the sum of itself and row 1.

$$\begin{bmatrix} 1 & -1 & 2 & 0 & | & 9 \\ 0 & 1 & 0 & 3 & | & -10 \\ 0 & 2 & 3 & 0 & | & 4 \\ 0 & -3 & -1 & -6 & | & 19 \end{bmatrix}$$

Multiplied row 2 by $\frac{1}{5}$ so that $a_{22} = 1$.

$$\begin{bmatrix} 1 & -1 & 2 & 0 & | & 9 \\ 0 & 1 & 0 & 3 & | & -10 \\ 0 & 0 & 3 & -6 & | & 24 \\ 0 & 0 & -1 & 3 & | & -11 \end{bmatrix}$$

To make $a_{32} = 0$, replaced row 3 by the sum of itself and (-2) times row 2.

To make $a_{42} = 0$, replaced row 4 by the sum of itself and 3 times row 2.

$$\begin{bmatrix} 1 & -1 & 2 & 0 & | & 9 \\ 0 & 1 & 0 & 3 & | & -10 \\ 0 & 0 & -1 & 3 & | & -11 \\ 0 & 0 & 3 & -6 & | & 24 \end{bmatrix}$$

Interchanged rows 3 and 4 so that the next pivot will be $a_{33} = -1$.

$$\begin{bmatrix} 1 & -1 & 2 & 0 & | & 9 \\ 0 & 1 & 0 & 3 & | & -10 \\ 0 & 0 & -1 & 3 & | & -11 \\ 0 & 0 & 0 & 3 & | & -9 \end{bmatrix}$$

To make $a_{43} = 0$, replaced row 4 by the sum of itself and 3 times row 3.

The last row of the matrix indicates that

$$3w = -9$$
$$w = -3$$

The remaining variables are found by back-substitution.

Third row of final matrix	Second row of final matrix	First row of final matrix
$-z + 3w = -11$	$y + 3w = -10$	$x - y + 2z = 9$
$-z + 3(-3) = -11$	$y + 3(-3) = -10$	$x - (-1) + 2(2) = 9$
$z = 2$	$y = -1$	$x = 4$

The solution is $x = 4$, $y = -1$, $z = 2$, $w = -3$.

✔ **Progress Check 6**
Solve by matrix methods:

$$2x \quad\quad - 3z + 2w = -7$$
$$2y + 2z - 3w = 1$$
$$-2x + y - 2z + w = -9$$
$$4x - 3y \quad\quad + 5w = 6$$

Answer

$x = \dfrac{1}{2}, y = -3, z = 2, w = -1$

Gauss-Jordan Elimination

There is an important variant of Gaussian elimination known as **Gauss-Jordan elimination**. The objective is to transform a linear system into a form that yields a solution without back-substitution. For a 3×3 system that has a unique solution, the final matrix and equivalent linear system will look like this.

$$\begin{bmatrix} 1 & 0 & 0 & | & c_1 \\ 0 & 1 & 0 & | & c_2 \\ 0 & 0 & 1 & | & c_3 \end{bmatrix} \quad \begin{matrix} x + 0y + 0z = c_1 \\ 0x + y + 0z = c_2 \\ 0x + 0y + z = c_3 \end{matrix}$$

The solution is then seen to be $x = c_1$, $y = c_2$, and $z = c_3$.

The execution of the Gauss-Jordan method is essentially the same as that of Gaussian elimination except that

(a) the pivot elements are always required to be equal to 1, and

(b) all elements in a column, other than the pivot element, are forced to be 0.

These objectives are accomplished by the use of elementary row operations, as illustrated in the following example.

EXAMPLE 7   GAUSS-JORDAN ELIMINATION

Solve the following linear system by the Gauss-Jordan method:

$$x - 3y + 2z = 12$$
$$2x + y - 4z = -1$$
$$x + 3y - 2z = -8$$

SOLUTION

We begin with the augmented matrix. At each stage, the pivot element is shown in bold and is used to force all elements in that column (other than the pivot element itself) to be zero.

$$\begin{bmatrix} 1 & -3 & 2 & | & 12 \\ 2 & 1 & -4 & | & -1 \\ 1 & 3 & -2 & | & -8 \end{bmatrix}$$ Pivot element is a_{11}.

$$\begin{bmatrix} 1 & -3 & 2 & | & 12 \\ 0 & 7 & -8 & | & -25 \\ 0 & 6 & -4 & | & -20 \end{bmatrix}$$ To make $a_{21} = 0$, replaced row 2 by the sum of itself and -2 times row 1.

To make $a_{31} = 0$, replaced row 3 by the sum of itself and -1 times row 1.

$$\begin{bmatrix} 1 & -3 & 2 & | & 12 \\ 0 & 1 & -4 & | & -5 \\ 0 & 6 & -4 & | & -20 \end{bmatrix}$$ Replaced row 2 by the sum of itself and -1 times row 3 to yield the next pivot, $a_{22} = 1$.

$$\begin{bmatrix} 1 & 0 & -10 & | & -3 \\ 0 & 1 & -4 & | & -5 \\ 0 & 0 & 20 & | & 10 \end{bmatrix}$$ To make $a_{12} = 0$, replaced row 1 by the sum of itself and 3 times row 2.

To make $a_{32} = 0$, replaced row 3 by the sum of itself and -6 times row 2.

$$\begin{bmatrix} 1 & 0 & -10 & | & -3 \\ 0 & 1 & -4 & | & -5 \\ 0 & 0 & 1 & | & \frac{1}{2} \end{bmatrix}$$ Multiplied row 3 by $\frac{1}{20}$ so that $a_{33} = 1$.

$$\begin{bmatrix} 1 & 0 & 0 & | & 2 \\ 0 & 1 & 0 & | & -3 \\ 0 & 0 & 1 & | & \frac{1}{2} \end{bmatrix}$$ To make $a_{13} = 0$, replaced row 1 by the sum of itself and 10 times row 3.

To make $a_{23} = 0$, replaced row 2 by the sum of itself and 4 times row 3.

We can see the solution directly from the final matrix: $x = 2$, $y = -3$, and $z = \frac{1}{2}$.

✔ **Progress Check 7**

Solve the following linear system by the Gauss-Jordan method:

$$x + 2y - 3z = -12$$
$$-2x - y + 2z = 6$$
$$3x + y + 4z = 13$$

Answer

$x = 1, y = -2, z = 3$

Exercise Set 14.1

In Exercises 1–6 state the dimensions of each matrix.

1. $\begin{bmatrix} 3 & -1 \\ 2 & 4 \end{bmatrix}$

2. $\begin{bmatrix} 1 & 2 & 3 & -1 \end{bmatrix}$

3. $\begin{bmatrix} 4 & 2 & 3 \\ 5 & -1 & 4 \\ 2 & 3 & 6 \\ -8 & -1 & 2 \end{bmatrix}$

4. $\begin{bmatrix} -1 \\ 3 \\ 2 \end{bmatrix}$

5. $\begin{bmatrix} 4 & 2 & 1 \\ 3 & 1 & 5 \\ -4 & -2 & 3 \end{bmatrix}$

6. $\begin{bmatrix} 3 & -1 & 2 & 6 \\ 2 & 8 & 4 & 1 \end{bmatrix}$

In Exercises 7 and 8 find the indicated element in the given matrix.

7. $A = \begin{bmatrix} 3 & -4 & -2 & 5 \\ 8 & 7 & 6 & 2 \\ 1 & 0 & 9 & -3 \end{bmatrix}$

   (a) a_{12} (b) a_{22} (c) a_{23} (d) a_{34}

8. $B = \begin{bmatrix} -5 & 6 & 8 \\ 4 & 1 & 3 \\ 0 & 2 & -6 \\ -3 & 9 & 7 \end{bmatrix}$

   (a) b_{13} (b) b_{21} (c) b_{33} (d) b_{42}

In Exercises 9–12 write the coefficient matrix and the augmented matrix for each given linear system.

9. $3x - 2y = 12$
   $5x + y = -8$

10. $3x - 4y = 15$
    $4x - 3y = 12$

11. $\frac{1}{2}x + y + z = 4$
    $2x - y - 4z = 6$
    $4x + 2y - 3z = 8$

12. $2x + 3y - 4z = 10$
    $3x + y = 12$
    $5x - 2y + z = -8$

In Exercises 13–16 write the linear system whose augmented matrix is given.

13. $\begin{bmatrix} \frac{3}{2} & 6 & | & -1 \\ 4 & 5 & | & 3 \end{bmatrix}$

14. $\begin{bmatrix} 4 & 0 & | & 2 \\ -7 & 8 & | & 3 \end{bmatrix}$

15. $\begin{bmatrix} 1 & 1 & 3 & | & -4 \\ -3 & 4 & 0 & | & 8 \\ 2 & 0 & 7 & | & 6 \end{bmatrix}$

16. $\begin{bmatrix} 4 & 8 & 3 & | & 12 \\ 1 & -5 & 3 & | & -14 \\ 0 & 2 & 7 & | & 18 \end{bmatrix}$

In Exercises 17–20 decide whether the given augmented matrix represents a linear system in triangular form. If it does not, transform it, using elementary row operations, into an augmented matrix representing a linear system in triangular form.

17. $\begin{bmatrix} 1 & 0 & 2 & | & 4 \\ 0 & 1 & -3 & | & 5 \\ 0 & 0 & 1 & | & 6 \end{bmatrix}$

18. $\begin{bmatrix} 1 & 0 & -3 & | & -4 \\ 0 & 1 & 2 & | & 5 \\ 0 & 0 & 1 & | & 2 \end{bmatrix}$

19. $\begin{bmatrix} -2 & -1 & 3 & | & -1 \\ 4 & 1 & 4 & | & 2 \\ 6 & 0 & 1 & | & 5 \end{bmatrix}$

20. $\begin{bmatrix} 1 & 0 & 4 & | & 2 \\ 2 & -1 & -1 & | & 5 \\ 0 & 0 & 1 & | & 6 \end{bmatrix}$

In Exercises 21–24 the augmented matrix corresponding to a linear system has been transformed into the given matrix by elementary row operations. Find a solution of the original linear system.

21. $\begin{bmatrix} 1 & 2 & 0 & | & 3 \\ 0 & 1 & -2 & | & 4 \\ 0 & 0 & 1 & | & 2 \end{bmatrix}$

22. $\begin{bmatrix} 1 & 0 & 2 & | & -1 \\ 0 & 1 & 3 & | & 2 \\ 0 & 0 & 1 & | & 5 \end{bmatrix}$

23. $\begin{bmatrix} 1 & -2 & 1 & | & 3 \\ 0 & 1 & 3 & | & 2 \\ 0 & 0 & 1 & | & -4 \end{bmatrix}$

24. $\begin{bmatrix} 1 & -4 & 2 & | & -4 \\ 0 & 1 & 3 & | & -2 \\ 0 & 0 & 1 & | & 5 \end{bmatrix}$

In Exercises 25–28 transform the given augmented matrix so that the corresponding linear system is in triangular form.

25. $\begin{bmatrix} 2 & -4 & -2 & | & 1 \\ 2 & -2 & -4 & | & 4 \\ 2 & 4 & 2 & | & 2 \end{bmatrix}$

26. $\begin{bmatrix} 1 & -2 & 0 & | & 1 \\ 2 & -3 & -1 & | & 3 \\ 1 & 3 & 2 & | & 4 \end{bmatrix}$

27. $\begin{bmatrix} 1 & 2 & 1 & | & 0 \\ 1 & -3 & 2 & | & 1 \\ 1 & 4 & 3 & | & 2 \end{bmatrix}$

28. $\begin{bmatrix} 1 & 3 & 2 & | & 10 \\ -2 & 2 & 2 & | & 8 \\ -1 & 1 & 3 & | & 9 \end{bmatrix}$

In Exercises 29–38 solve the given linear system by applying Gaussian elimination to the augmented matrix.

29. $x - 2y = -4$
    $2x + 3y = 13$

30. $2x + y = -1$
    $3x - y = -7$

31. $x + y + z = 4$
    $2x - y + 3z = 14$
    $x + 2y + z = 3$

32. $x - y + z = -5$
    $3x + y + 2z = -5$
    $2x - y - z = -2$

33. $2x + y - z = 9$
    $x - 2y + 2z = -3$
    $3x + 3y + 4z = 11$

34. $2x + y - z = -2$
    $-2x - 2y + 3z = 2$
    $3x + y - z = -4$

35. $\begin{aligned}-x - y + 2z &= 9\\ x + 2y - 2z &= -7\\ 2x - y + z &= -9\end{aligned}$ 36. $\begin{aligned}4x + y - z &= -1\\ x - y + 2z &= 3\\ -x + 2y - z &= 0\end{aligned}$

37. $\begin{aligned}x + y - z + 2w &= 0\\ 2x + y \quad\quad - w &= -2\\ 3x \quad\quad + 2z \quad\quad &= -3\\ -x + 2y \quad\quad + 3w &= 1\end{aligned}$

38. $\begin{aligned}2x + y \quad\quad - 3w &= -7\\ 3x \quad\quad + 2z + w &= 0\\ -x + 2y \quad\quad + 3w &= 10\\ -2x - 3y + 2z - w &= 7\end{aligned}$

In Exercises 39–48 solve the linear systems of Exercises 29–38 by Gauss–Jordan elimination applied to the augmented matrix.

49. A black-and-white digital image has 30 rows of 18 pixels each. If the image is represented as a matrix with each entry the value of the corresponding pixel, what are the dimensions of the matrix?

50. A square black-and-white digital image with 9 pixels may be represented as a matrix, like matrix A in Exercise 23. Suppose the image has 4 bits per pixel. Each bit has a value of zero or one. So each entry in A must be an integer between zero (dark-

est black) to $2^4 - 1$, or 15 (whitest white). (Note: The integers from 0 to 15 represent 16 possible values.)

Suppose

$$A = \begin{bmatrix} 0 & 4 & 6 \\ 5 & 0 & 1 \\ 7 & 2 & 3 \end{bmatrix}$$

The *contrast* is increased by multiplying each entry by a scaling factor. Find the matrix $2A$, representing an image with increased contrast.

51. The *digital negative image* of an image is found by subtracting each element of the image matrix from its maximum possible value. So the i,j entry of the matrix N for the digital negative of A in Exercise 37 is

$$n_{ij} = 15 - a_{ij}$$

Find the matrix N.

52. We can add one image to another and represent the resulting image by the matrix sum of the image matrix for each. Find the matrix for the image that results from adding the image represented by A to its negative N. Describe the image qualitatively. What would it look like?

14.2   Determinants

In this section we will define a determinant and will develop manipulative skills for evaluating determinants. In the next section we will show you that determinants have important applications and can be used to solve linear systems.

Associated with every square matrix A is a number called the **determinant** of A, denoted by $|A|$. If A is the 2×2 matrix

$$A = \begin{bmatrix} a_{11} & a_{12} \\ a_{21} & a_{22} \end{bmatrix}$$

then $|A|$ is said to be a **determinant of second order** and is defined by the rule

$$|A| = \begin{vmatrix} a_{11} & a_{12} \\ a_{21} & a_{22} \end{vmatrix} = a_{11}a_{22} - a_{21}a_{12}$$

EXAMPLE 1   DETERMINANT OF SECOND ORDER

Compute the real number represented by

$$\begin{vmatrix} 4 & -5 \\ 3 & -1 \end{vmatrix}$$

SOLUTION

We apply the rule for a determinant of second order.

$$\begin{vmatrix} 4 & -5 \\ 3 & -1 \end{vmatrix} = (4)(-1) - (3)(-5) = 11$$

✔ **Progress Check 1**

Compute the real numbers represented by

(a) $\begin{vmatrix} -6 & 2 \\ -1 & -2 \end{vmatrix}$ (b) $\begin{vmatrix} \frac{1}{2} & \frac{1}{4} \\ -4 & -\frac{1}{2} \end{vmatrix}$

Answers

(a) 14   (b) 0

To simplify matters, when we want to compute the determinant of a matrix we will say "evaluate the determinant." This is not technically correct, however, since a determinant *is* a real number.

Minors and Cofactors

The rule for evaluating a determinant of order 3 is

$$\begin{vmatrix} a_{11} & a_{12} & a_{13} \\ a_{21} & a_{22} & a_{23} \\ a_{31} & a_{32} & a_{33} \end{vmatrix} = a_{11}a_{22}a_{33} - a_{11}a_{32}a_{23} - a_{12}a_{21}a_{33} \\ + a_{12}a_{31}a_{23} + a_{13}a_{21}a_{32} - a_{13}a_{31}a_{22}$$

The situation becomes even more cumbersome for determinants of higher order! Fortunately, we don't have to memorize this rule; instead, we shall see that it is possible to evaluate a determinant of order 3 by reducing the problem to that of evaluating three determinants of order 2.

The **minor of an element** a_{ij} is the determinant of the matrix remaining after deleting the row and column in which the element a_{ij} appears. Given the matrix

$$\begin{bmatrix} 4 & 0 & -2 \\ 1 & 6 & 7 \\ -3 & 2 & 5 \end{bmatrix}$$

the minor of the element in row 2, column 3, is

$$\begin{vmatrix} 4 & 0 & -2 \\ 1 & 6 & 7 \\ -3 & 2 & 5 \end{vmatrix} = \begin{vmatrix} 4 & 0 \\ -3 & 2 \end{vmatrix} = 8 - 0 = 8$$

The **cofactor** of the element a_{ij} is the minor of the element a_{ij} multiplied by $(-1)^{i+j}$. Since $(-1)^{i+j}$ is $+1$ if $i + j$ is even and -1 if $i + j$ is odd, we see that the cofactor is the minor with a sign attached. The cofactor attaches to the minor the sign found in row i and column j in the following pattern:

$$\begin{matrix} + & - & + & - & \cdots \\ - & + & - & + & \cdots \\ + & - & + & - & \cdots \\ - & + & - & + & \cdots \\ \vdots & \vdots & \vdots & \vdots \end{matrix}$$

In the above matrix, the cofactor of 7 is

$$(-1)^{2+3} \begin{vmatrix} 4 & 0 \\ -3 & 2 \end{vmatrix} = -8$$

EXAMPLE 2   COMPUTING COFACTORS

Find the cofactor of each element in the first row of the matrix:

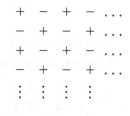

$$\begin{bmatrix} -2 & 0 & 12 \\ -4 & 5 & 3 \\ 7 & 8 & -6 \end{bmatrix}$$

SOLUTION

The cofactor of $a_{11} = -2$ is

$$(-1)^{1+1} \begin{vmatrix} -2 & 0 & 12 \\ -4 & 5 & 3 \\ 7 & 8 & -6 \end{vmatrix} = \begin{vmatrix} 5 & 3 \\ 8 & -6 \end{vmatrix} = -30 - 24 = -54$$

The cofactor of $a_{12} = 0$ is

$$(-1)^{1+2} \begin{vmatrix} -2 & 0 & 12 \\ -4 & 5 & 3 \\ 7 & 8 & -6 \end{vmatrix} = -\begin{vmatrix} -4 & 3 \\ 7 & -6 \end{vmatrix} = -(24 - 21) = -3$$

The cofactor of $a_{13} = 12$ is

$$(-1)^{1+3} \begin{vmatrix} -2 & 0 & 12 \\ -4 & 5 & 3 \\ 7 & 8 & -6 \end{vmatrix} = \begin{vmatrix} -4 & 5 \\ 7 & 8 \end{vmatrix} = -32 - 35 = -67$$

✔ **Progress Check 2**

Find the cofactor of each entry in the second column of the matrix:

$$\begin{bmatrix} 16 & -9 & 3 \\ -5 & 2 & 0 \\ -3 & 4 & -1 \end{bmatrix}$$

Answer

cofactor of -9 is -5; cofactor of 2 is -7; cofactor of 4 is -15

The cofactor is the key to the process of evaluating determinants of order 3 or higher.

Expansion by Cofactors

To evaluate a determinant, form the sum of the products obtained by multiplying each entry of any row or any column by its cofactor. This process is called **expansion by cofactors**. Let's illustrate the process with an example.

EXAMPLE 3 EVALUATING A DETERMINANT OF THIRD ORDER

Evaluate the following determinant by cofactors:

$$\begin{vmatrix} -2 & 7 & 2 \\ 6 & -6 & 0 \\ 4 & 10 & -3 \end{vmatrix}$$

SOLUTION

Expansion by Cofactors

Step 1. Choose a row or column about which to expand. In general, a row or column containing zeros will simplify the work.

We will expand about column 3.

Step 2. Expand about the cofactors of the chosen row or column by multiplying each entry of the row or column by its cofactor.

The expansion about column 3 is

$$(2)(-1)^{1+3} \begin{vmatrix} 6 & -6 \\ 4 & 10 \end{vmatrix}$$

$$+ (0)(-1)^{2+3} \begin{vmatrix} -2 & 7 \\ 4 & 10 \end{vmatrix}$$

$$+ (-3)(-1)^{3+3} \begin{vmatrix} -2 & 7 \\ 6 & -6 \end{vmatrix}$$

Step 3. Evaluate the cofactors and form their sum.

Using the rule for evaluating a determinant of order 2, we have

$$(2)(1)[(6)(10) - (4)(-6)] + 0$$
$$+ (-3)(1)[(-2)(-6) - (6)(7)]$$
$$= 2(60 + 24) - 3(12 - 42)$$
$$= 258$$

Note that expansion by cofactors of *any row or any column* will produce the same result. This important property of determinants can be used to simplify the arithmetic. The best choice of a row or column about which to expand is the one that has the most zero entries. The reason for this is that if any entry is zero the entry times its cofactor will be zero, so we don't have to evaluate that cofactor.

✔ **Progress Check 3**

Evaluate the determinant of Example 3 by expanding about the second row.

Answer

258

EXAMPLE 4   EVALUATING A DETERMINANT OF THIRD ORDER

Verify the rule for evaluating a determinant of order 3.

$$\begin{vmatrix} a_{11} & a_{12} & a_{13} \\ a_{21} & a_{22} & a_{23} \\ a_{31} & a_{32} & a_{33} \end{vmatrix} = \begin{aligned} &a_{11}a_{22}a_{33} - a_{11}a_{32}a_{23} - a_{12}a_{21}a_{33} \\ &+ a_{12}a_{31}a_{23} + a_{13}a_{12}a_{32} - a_{13}a_{31}a_{22} \end{aligned}$$

SOLUTION

Expanding about the first row, we have

$$\begin{vmatrix} a_{11} & a_{12} & a_{13} \\ a_{21} & a_{22} & a_{23} \\ a_{31} & a_{32} & a_{33} \end{vmatrix} = a_{11}\begin{vmatrix} a_{22} & a_{23} \\ a_{32} & a_{33} \end{vmatrix} - a_{12}\begin{vmatrix} a_{21} & a_{23} \\ a_{31} & a_{33} \end{vmatrix} + a_{13}\begin{vmatrix} a_{21} & a_{22} \\ a_{31} & a_{32} \end{vmatrix}$$

$$= a_{11}(a_{22}a_{33} - a_{32}a_{23}) - a_{12}(a_{21}a_{33} - a_{31}a_{23}) + a_{13}(a_{21}a_{32} - a_{31}a_{22})$$

$$= a_{11}a_{22}a_{33} - a_{11}a_{32}a_{23} - a_{12}a_{21}a_{33} + a_{12}a_{31}a_{23} + a_{13}a_{21}a_{32} - a_{13}a_{31}a_{22}$$

✔ **Progress Check 4**

Show that the determinant is equal to zero.

$$\begin{vmatrix} a & b & c \\ a & b & c \\ d & e & f \end{vmatrix}$$

The process of expanding by cofactors works for determinants of any order. If we apply the method to a determinant of order 4, we will produce determinants of order 3; applying the method again will result in determinants of order 2.

EXAMPLE 5 EVALUATING A DETERMINANT OF FOURTH ORDER

Evaluate the determinant:

$$\begin{vmatrix} -3 & 5 & 0 & -1 \\ 1 & 2 & 3 & -3 \\ 0 & 4 & -6 & 0 \\ 0 & -2 & 1 & 2 \end{vmatrix}$$

SOLUTION

Expanding about the cofactors of the first column, we have

$$\begin{vmatrix} -3 & 5 & 0 & -1 \\ 1 & 2 & 3 & -3 \\ 0 & 4 & -6 & 0 \\ 0 & -2 & 1 & 2 \end{vmatrix} = -3\begin{vmatrix} 2 & 3 & -3 \\ 4 & -6 & 0 \\ -2 & 1 & 2 \end{vmatrix} - 1\begin{vmatrix} 5 & 0 & -1 \\ 4 & -6 & 0 \\ -2 & 1 & 2 \end{vmatrix}$$

Each determinant of order 3 can then be evaluated.

$$-3\begin{vmatrix} 2 & 3 & -3 \\ 4 & -6 & 0 \\ -2 & 1 & 2 \end{vmatrix} = (-3)(-24) = 72$$

$$-1\begin{vmatrix} 5 & 0 & -1 \\ 4 & -6 & 0 \\ -2 & 1 & 2 \end{vmatrix} = (-1)(-52) = 52$$

The original determinant has the value $72 + 52 = 124$.

✔ Progress Check 5

Evaluate.

$$\begin{vmatrix} 0 & -1 & 0 & 2 \\ 3 & 0 & 4 & 0 \\ 0 & 5 & 0 & -3 \\ 1 & 0 & 1 & 0 \end{vmatrix}$$

Answer

7

Exercise Set 14.2

In Exercises 1–4 let

$$A = \begin{bmatrix} 3 & -1 & 2 \\ 4 & 1 & -3 \\ 5 & -2 & 0 \end{bmatrix}$$

1. Compute the minor of each of the following elements:

   (a) a_{11} (b) a_{23} (c) a_{31} (d) a_{33}

2. Compute the minor of each of the following elements:

   (a) a_{12} (b) a_{22} (c) a_{13} (d) a_{32}

3. Compute the cofactor of each of the following elements:

   (a) a_{11} (b) a_{23} (c) a_{31} (d) a_{33}

4. Compute the cofactor of each of the following elements:

   (a) a_{12} (b) a_{22} (c) a_{13} (d) a_{32}

In Exercises 5–8 let

$$A = \begin{bmatrix} -1 & 0 & 3 \\ -2 & 4 & 5 \\ -3 & -4 & 2 \end{bmatrix}$$

5. Compute the minor of each of the following elements:

   (a) a_{12} (b) a_{21} (c) a_{23} (d) a_{31}

6. Compute the minor of each of the following elements:

   (a) a_{11} (b) a_{13} (c) a_{22} (d) a_{33}

7. Compute the cofactor of each of the following elements:

   (a) a_{12} (b) a_{21} (c) a_{23} (d) a_{31}

8. Compute the cofactor of each of the following elements:

   (a) a_{11} (b) a_{13} (c) a_{22} (d) a_{33}

In Exercises 9–14 let

$$A = \begin{bmatrix} 3 & -2 & 5 \\ 0 & 1 & 2 \\ -4 & 3 & 4 \end{bmatrix}$$

and mark each statement as true (T) or false (F).

9. The cofactor of a_{11} is 2.

10. The cofactor of a_{22} is 32.

11. The cofactor of a_{13} is -4.

12. The cofactor of a_{13} is 3.

13. The cofactor of a_{23} is -1.

14. The cofactor of a_{33} is 3.

In Exercises 15–30 evaluate the given determinant.

15. $\begin{vmatrix} 2 & -3 \\ 4 & 5 \end{vmatrix}$

16. $\begin{vmatrix} 3 & 4 \\ -1 & 2 \end{vmatrix}$

17. $\begin{vmatrix} -4 & 1 \\ 0 & 2 \end{vmatrix}$

18. $\begin{vmatrix} 2 & 2 \\ 3 & 3 \end{vmatrix}$

19. $\begin{vmatrix} 0 & 0 \\ 1 & 3 \end{vmatrix}$

20. $\begin{vmatrix} -4 & -1 \\ -2 & 3 \end{vmatrix}$

21. $\begin{vmatrix} 4 & -2 & 5 \\ 5 & 2 & 0 \\ 2 & 0 & 4 \end{vmatrix}$

22. $\begin{vmatrix} 4 & 1 & 2 \\ 0 & 2 & 3 \\ 0 & 0 & -4 \end{vmatrix}$

23. $\begin{vmatrix} -1 & 2 & 0 \\ 3 & 4 & 1 \\ 6 & 5 & 2 \end{vmatrix}$

24. $\begin{vmatrix} -1 & 3 & 2 \\ 0 & 7 & 7 \\ 2 & 1 & 3 \end{vmatrix}$

25. $\begin{vmatrix} 2 & 2 & 4 \\ 3 & 8 & 1 \\ 1 & 1 & 2 \end{vmatrix}$

26. $\begin{vmatrix} 0 & 1 & 3 \\ 2 & 5 & -1 \\ 4 & 2 & -2 \end{vmatrix}$

27. $\begin{vmatrix} 3 & 2 & 1 & 0 \\ -1 & -3 & -1 & 0 \\ 0 & 0 & 2 & 2 \\ 4 & 1 & 3 & 3 \end{vmatrix}$

28. $\begin{vmatrix} -1 & 2 & 4 & 0 \\ 3 & -2 & -3 & 0 \\ 0 & 4 & 2 & 5 \\ 0 & -3 & 1 & 4 \end{vmatrix}$

29. $\begin{vmatrix} 2 & -3 & 2 & -4 \\ 0 & 4 & -1 & 9 \\ 0 & 1 & 2 & 0 \\ 0 & 1 & 3 & -1 \end{vmatrix}$

30. $\begin{vmatrix} 1 & 1 & 0 & 1 \\ 0 & -1 & 4 & -1 \\ -2 & 3 & 1 & -4 \\ 0 & 2 & 0 & 2 \end{vmatrix}$

In Exercises 31–36 solve for x.

31. $\begin{vmatrix} x & 3 \\ -2 & 1 \end{vmatrix} = 8$

32. $\begin{vmatrix} -2 & x \\ 3 & 1 \end{vmatrix} = 7$

33. $\begin{vmatrix} x & 3 \\ 1 & x \end{vmatrix} = -1$

34. $\begin{vmatrix} x & 2 \\ -4 & x \end{vmatrix} = 24$

35. $\begin{vmatrix} -2 & 0 & 5 \\ 1 & 1 & 1 \\ 2 & 0 & x \end{vmatrix} = 3$

36. $\begin{vmatrix} 1 & -1 & x \\ 0 & 1 & 1 \\ -1 & 0 & 2 \end{vmatrix} = 5$

*37. Show that

$$\begin{vmatrix} a_1+b_1 & a_2+b_2 \\ c & d \end{vmatrix} = \begin{vmatrix} a_1 & a_2 \\ c & d \end{vmatrix} + \begin{vmatrix} b_1 & b_2 \\ c & d \end{vmatrix}$$

*38. Show that

$$\begin{vmatrix} ka_{11} & ka_{12} \\ a_{21} & a_{22} \end{vmatrix} = \begin{vmatrix} a_{11} & a_{12} \\ ka_{21} & ka_{22} \end{vmatrix} = k\begin{vmatrix} a_{11} & a_{12} \\ a_{21} & a_{22} \end{vmatrix}$$

*39. Show that if a row or column of a square matrix consists entirely of zeros, then the determinant of the matrix is zero. (*Hint*: Expand by cofactors.)

*40. Show that if matrix B is obtained by multiplying each element of a row of a square matrix A by a constant k, then $|B| = k|A|$.

41. Finding the determinants by using your graphing calculator's MATRIX menu, investigate what happens to the determinant of the matrix in Exercise 27 if you

   a. Interchange row 2 and row 3.

   b. Interchange row 2 and row 3, then the new row 3 and row 4.

   What can you conclude from these results?

14.3 Cramer's Rule

Determinants provide a convenient way of expressing formulas in many areas of mathematics, particularly in geometry. One of the best known uses of determinants is in solving systems of linear equations, using a procedure known as **Cramer's rule.**

In Chapter 13 we solved systems of linear equations by the method of elimination. Let's apply this method to the general system of two equations in two unknowns.

$$a_{11}x + a_{12}y = c_1 \qquad (1)$$
$$a_{21}x + a_{22}y = c_2 \qquad (2)$$

If we multiply Equation (1) by a_{22} and Equation (2) by $-a_{12}$, and add the resulting equations, we will eliminate y:

$$a_{11}a_{22}x + a_{12}a_{22}y = c_1 a_{22}$$
$$\underline{-a_{21}a_{12}x - a_{12}a_{22}y = -c_2 a_{12}}$$
$$a_{11}a_{22}x - a_{21}a_{12}x = c_1 a_{22} - c_2 a_{12}$$

Thus,

$$x(a_{11}a_{22} - a_{21}a_{12}) = c_1 a_{22} - c_2 a_{12}$$

or

$$x = \frac{c_1 a_{22} - c_2 a_{12}}{a_{11}a_{22} - a_{21}a_{12}}$$

Similarly, multiplying Equation (1) by a_{21} and Equation (2) by $-a_{11}$ and then adding, we can eliminate x and solve for y:

$$y = \frac{c_2 a_{11} - c_1 a_{21}}{a_{11}a_{22} - a_{21}a_{12}}$$

The denominators in the expressions for x and y are identical and can be written as the determinant of the matrix

$$A = \begin{bmatrix} a_{11} & a_{12} \\ a_{21} & a_{22} \end{bmatrix}$$

If we apply this same idea to the numerators, we have

$$x = \frac{\begin{vmatrix} c_1 & a_{12} \\ c_2 & a_{22} \end{vmatrix}}{|A|} \quad \text{and} \quad y = \frac{\begin{vmatrix} a_{11} & c_1 \\ a_{21} & c_2 \end{vmatrix}}{|A|}, \quad |A| \neq 0$$

What we have arrived at is Cramer's rule, which is a means of expressing the solution of a system of linear equations in determinant form.

The following example outlines the steps for using Cramer's rule.

EXAMPLE 1   SOLVING A LINEAR SYSTEM BY CRAMER'S RULE

Solve by Cramer's rule.

$$3x - y = 9$$
$$x + 2y = -4$$

SOLUTION

Cramer's Rule

Step 1. Write the determinant of the coefficient matrix A.

$$|A| = \begin{vmatrix} 3 & -1 \\ 1 & 2 \end{vmatrix}$$

Step 2. The numerator for x is the determinant of the matrix obtained from A by replacing the column of coefficients of x with the column of right-hand sides of the equations.

$$x = \frac{\begin{vmatrix} 9 & -1 \\ -4 & 2 \end{vmatrix}}{|A|}$$

Step 3. The numerator for y is the determinant of the matrix obtained from A by replacing the column of coefficients of y with the column of right-hand sides of the equation.

$$y = \frac{\begin{vmatrix} 3 & 9 \\ 1 & -4 \end{vmatrix}}{|A|}$$

Step 4. Evaluate the determinants to obtain the solution. If $|A| = 0$, Cramer's rule cannot be used.

$$|A| = 6 + 1 = 7$$
$$x = \frac{18 - 4}{7} = \frac{14}{7} = 2$$
$$y = \frac{-12 - 9}{7} = -\frac{21}{7} = -3$$

✔ Progress Check 1

Solve by Cramer's rule.

$$2x + 3y = -4$$
$$3x + 4y = -7$$

Answer

$x = -5, y = 2$

The steps outlined in Example 1 can be applied to solve any system of linear equations in which the number of equations is the same as the number of variables and in which $|A| \neq 0$. Here is an example with three equations and three unknowns.

EXAMPLE 2   SOLVING A LINEAR SYSTEM BY CRAMER'S RULE

Solve by Cramer's rule:

$$
\begin{aligned}
3x \quad\quad + 2z &= -2 \\
2x - y \quad\quad &= 0 \\
2y + 6z &= -1
\end{aligned}
$$

SOLUTION

We form the determinant of coefficients.

$$
|A| = \begin{vmatrix} 3 & 0 & 2 \\ 2 & -1 & 0 \\ 0 & 2 & 6 \end{vmatrix}
$$

Then

$$
x = \frac{|A_1|}{|A|} \qquad y = \frac{|A_2|}{|A|} \qquad z = \frac{|A_3|}{|A|}
$$

where A_1 is obtained from A by replacing its first column with the column of right-hand sides, A_2 is obtained from A by replacing the second column of A with the column of right-hand sides, and A_3 is obtained from A by replacing its third column with the column of right-hand sides. Thus

$$
x = \frac{\begin{vmatrix} -2 & 0 & 2 \\ 0 & -1 & 0 \\ -1 & 2 & 6 \end{vmatrix}}{|A|} \qquad y = \frac{\begin{vmatrix} 3 & -2 & 2 \\ 2 & 0 & 0 \\ 0 & -1 & 6 \end{vmatrix}}{|A|} \qquad z = \frac{\begin{vmatrix} 3 & 0 & -2 \\ 2 & -1 & 0 \\ 0 & 2 & -1 \end{vmatrix}}{|A|}
$$

Expanding by cofactors, we calculate $|A| = -10$, $|A_1| = 10$, $|A_2| = 20$, and $|A_3| = -5$, obtaining

$$
x = \frac{10}{-10} = -1 \qquad y = \frac{20}{-10} = -2 \qquad z = \frac{-5}{-10} = \frac{1}{2}
$$

✔ Progress Check 2

Solve by Cramer's rule.

$$
\begin{aligned}
3x \quad\quad - z &= 1 \\
-6x + 2y \quad\quad &= -5 \\
-4y + 3z &= 5
\end{aligned}
$$

Answer

$$
x = \frac{2}{3}, \, y = -\frac{1}{2}, \, z = 1
$$

WARNING

(a) Each equation of the linear system must be written in the form

$$ax + by + cz = k$$

before using Cramer's rule.

(b) If $|A| = 0$, Cramer's rule cannot be used. The system does not have a unique solution.

Determinants have significant theoretical importance but are not of much use for computational purposes. The matrix methods discussed in this chapter provide the basis for techniques better suited for computer implementation.

Exercise Set 14.3

In Exercises 1–16 solve the given linear system by Cramer's rule, if possible.

1. $x + 2y = 5$
    $2x - y = 0$

2. $x - y = 5$
    $3x + 4y = -6$

3. $x - y = 4$
    $3x - 3y = 6$

4. $3x + y = -5$
    $2x - 3y = -18$

5. $3x + 2y = 9$
    $4x - 3y = 29$

6. $2x - 3y = -4$
    $-6x + 9y = 12$

7. $x - y + 2z = 10$
    $2x + y - 2z = -4$
    $3x + y + z = 7$

8. $x + 2y + z = 9$
    $x - y + 2z = 2$
    $x + y - z = 2$

9. $x - y + z = 2$
    $2x + y - 3z = 10$
    $x - y + 2z = 2$

10. $2x - 2y - 2z = 2$
    $-2x + 2y + 2z = -2$
    $3x + y - z = 3$

11. $2x + y = 2$
    $3x - y + 5z = 3$
    $x + y - z = 4$

12. $x - 2y + 2z = -7$
    $2x + 2y - z = -2$
    $3x + y + z = -7$

13. $x - y + 3z = 6$
    $-x + 2y - 2z = -10$
    $2x + 3y - z = 4$

14. $2x + 4y - 3z = -10$
    $x - 2y + z = 7$
    $3x - 2y - 3z = -5$

15. $2x + y + 5z = -5$
    $x - y + z = 0$
    $5x + y - 2z = 3$

16. $x + 2y + z = 0$
    $3x - y + 2z = 18$
    $5x + 3y = 6$

■ ■ ■

Chapter Summary

Terms and Symbols

augmented matrix	535	dimension	532	minor	545
coefficient matrix	535	element	532	pivot row	538
cofactor	546	elementary row operations	536	row (of a matrix)	532
column (of a matrix)	532	entry	534	square matrix	532
Cramer's rule	551	expansion by cofactors	547		
determinant	544	matrix	532		

Key Ideas for Review

Topic	Page	Key Idea
Matrix	532	A matrix is a rectangular array of numbers.
systems of linear equations	532	Systems of linear equations can be conveniently handled in matrix notation. By dropping the names of the variables, matrix notation focuses on the coefficients and the right-hand side of the system. The elementary row operations are then seen to be a restatement of those operations that produce equivalent systems of equations.
application	544	Matrices have much broader use than simply solving linear systems. In more advanced mathematics courses (such as linear algebra), properties of matrices are studied and are applied to problems in many disciplines.
Determinant	544	The rule for evaluating a determinant of order 2 is $$\begin{vmatrix} a & b \\ c & d \end{vmatrix} = ad - bc$$ For determinants of higher order, the method of expansion by cofactors may be used to reduce the problem to that of evaluating determinants of order 2.
cofactors	546	When expanding by cofactors, choose the row or column that contains the greatest number of zeros. This will ease the arithmetic burden. When expanding by cofactors, remember to attach the proper sign to each minor.
Cramer's rule	551	Cramer's rule expresses the value of each unknown of a system of linear equations as a quotient of determinants.

Common Errors

1. After the first stage of Gaussian elimination, the elements in the first column, except a_{11}, are all zero. Subsequent elementary row operations must *not* use row 1. This will insure that the zeros will remain, that is, that $a_{i1} = 0$ for all $i > 1$.

2. Remember that the cofactor of an element a_{ij} is a determinant multiplied by $(-1)^{i+j}$. When evaluating

a determinant by expanding by cofactors of a row or column, remember that the multipliers of the minors will alternate in sign.

3. Do not use Cramer's rule if the determinant of the coefficient matrix is 0.

Review Exercises

Solutions to exercises whose numbers are in bold are in the Solutions section in the back of the book.

14.1 In Exercises 1–4 refer to the matrix

$$A = \begin{bmatrix} -1 & 4 & 2 & 0 & 8 \\ 2 & 0 & -3 & -1 & 5 \\ 4 & -6 & 9 & 1 & -2 \end{bmatrix}$$

1. Determine the dimension of the matrix A.

2. Find a_{24}.

3. Find a_{31}.

4. Find a_{15}.

Exercises 5 and 6 refer to the linear system

$$3x - 7y = 14$$
$$x + 4y = 6$$

5. Write the coefficient matrix of the linear system.

6. Write the augmented matrix of the linear system.

In Exercises 7 and 8 write a linear system corresponding to the augmented matrix.

7. $\begin{bmatrix} 4 & -1 & | & 3 \\ 2 & 5 & | & 0 \end{bmatrix}$ 8. $\begin{bmatrix} -2 & 4 & 5 & | & 0 \\ 6 & -9 & 4 & | & 0 \\ 0 & 2 & -1 & | & 0 \end{bmatrix}$

In Exercises 9–12 use back-substitution to solve the linear system corresponding to the given augmented matrix.

9. $\begin{bmatrix} 1 & -2 & | & 7 \\ 0 & 1 & | & -4 \end{bmatrix}$ 10. $\begin{bmatrix} 1 & 2 & | & 4 \\ 0 & 1 & | & 5 \end{bmatrix}$

11. $\begin{bmatrix} 1 & -4 & 2 & | & -18 \\ 0 & 1 & -2 & | & 5 \\ 0 & 2 & 1 & | & -1 \end{bmatrix}$ 12. $\begin{bmatrix} 1 & -2 & 2 & | & -9 \\ 0 & 1 & 3 & | & -8 \\ 0 & 0 & 1 & | & -3 \end{bmatrix}$

In Exercises 13–16 solve the given linear system by applying Gaussian elimination to the augmented matrix.

13. $\begin{aligned} x + y &= 2 \\ 2x - 4y &= -5 \end{aligned}$ 14. $\begin{aligned} 3x - y &= -17 \\ 2x + 3y &= -4 \end{aligned}$

15. $\begin{aligned} x + 3y + 2z &= 0 \\ -2x \quad\quad + 3z &= -12 \\ 2x - 6y - z &= 6 \end{aligned}$

16. $\begin{aligned} 2x - y - 2z &= 3 \\ -2x + 3y + z &= 3 \\ 2y - z &= 6 \end{aligned}$

In Exercises 17–20 solve the given linear system by applying Gauss-Jordan elimination to the augmented matrix.

17. $\begin{aligned} x - y &= 1 \\ 3x + 2y &= 13 \end{aligned}$ 18. $\begin{aligned} 2x + y &= 2 \\ 5x + 3y &= 7 \end{aligned}$

19. $\begin{aligned} x - 2y + 3z &= -9 \\ 2x - y + 4z &= -9 \\ 3x - 2y + z &= 1 \end{aligned}$

20. $\begin{aligned} 2x - y + z &= 7 \\ -2x + 3y - z &= -11 \\ 4x - 2y + 2z &= 14 \end{aligned}$

14.2 In Exercises 21–29 evaluate the given determinant.

21. $\begin{vmatrix} 3 & 1 \\ -4 & 2 \end{vmatrix}$

22. $\begin{vmatrix} -1 & 2 \\ 0 & 6 \end{vmatrix}$

23. $\begin{vmatrix} 2 & -1 \\ 6 & -3 \end{vmatrix}$

24. $\begin{vmatrix} 1 & 0 & -1 \\ 2 & 3 & -5 \\ 0 & 4 & 0 \end{vmatrix}$

25. $\begin{vmatrix} 1 & -1 & 2 \\ 0 & 5 & 4 \\ 2 & 3 & 8 \end{vmatrix}$

26. $\begin{vmatrix} 1 & 2 & -1 \\ 0 & 3 & 4 \\ 0 & 0 & -1 \end{vmatrix}$

27. $\begin{vmatrix} 2 & 0 & -1 & 3 \\ 1 & -1 & 0 & 0 \\ 0 & 2 & 3 & 4 \\ 5 & 1 & 0 & 1 \end{vmatrix}$

28. $\begin{vmatrix} 1 & -1 & 0 & 0 \\ 0 & 0 & 3 & 4 \\ 1 & -1 & 1 & 0 \\ 0 & 3 & 5 & 2 \end{vmatrix}$

14.3 In Exercises 29–34 use Cramer's rule to solve the given linear system.

29. $2x - y = -3$
$-2x + 3y = 11$

30. $3x - y = 7$
$2x + 5y = -18$

31. $x + 2y = 2$
$2x - 7y = 48$

32. $2x + 3y - z = -3$
$-3x + 4z = 16$
$2y + 5z = 9$

33. $3x + z = 0$
$x + y + z = 0$
$-3y + 2z = -4$

34. $2x + 3y + z = -5$
$2y + 2z = -3$
$4x + y - 2z = -2$

Progress Test 14A

1. Given the matrix

$$A = \begin{bmatrix} -2 & 0.5 \\ 1.1 & -3 \\ 14 & 7 \end{bmatrix}$$

(a) Determine the dimension of A.

(b) Find a_{22}.

2. Write the augmented matrix that corresponds to the linear system

$$\begin{array}{rcl} -2x + y & = & 4 \\ 3x - y + z & = & 2 \\ x + 2y - 3z & = & -2 \end{array}$$

3. Write a system of linear equations that corresponds to the augmented matrix

$$\begin{bmatrix} 3 & -5 & | & 4 \\ 4 & 2 & | & -1 \end{bmatrix}$$

4. Solve the system of linear equations that corresponds to the augmented matrix

$$\begin{bmatrix} 2 & 1 & 3 & | & -6 \\ 0 & -1 & 2 & | & -3 \\ 0 & 0 & 1 & | & -2 \end{bmatrix}$$

5. Given the matrix

$$B = \begin{bmatrix} 2 & 0 & 4 & -3 \\ 4 & 3 & -2 & -8 \\ -1 & 1 & 5 & 4 \end{bmatrix}$$

(a) Replace row 2 of B by the sum of itself and a multiple of row 1 so that $b_{21} = 0$.

(b) Replace row 3 of B by the sum of itself and a multiple of row 1 so that $b_{31} = 0$.

6. Solve by matrix methods.

$$\begin{array}{rcl} 3x - y & = & -17 \\ 2x + 3y & = & -4 \end{array}$$

7. Solve by matrix methods.

$$\begin{array}{rcl} x + 3y + 2z & = & 0 \\ -2x + 3z & = & -12 \\ 2x - 6y - z & = & 6 \end{array}$$

8. Find the value of the determinant

$$\begin{vmatrix} 2 & 2 \\ 4 & -1 \end{vmatrix}$$

9. Find the cofactor of each element in the first column of the determinant

$$\begin{vmatrix} 1 & 2 & -1 \\ 3 & 0 & -3 \\ 4 & 5 & 1 \end{vmatrix}$$

10. Evaluate the given determinant by expanding by cofactors

(a) about row 1   (b) about column 2

$$\begin{vmatrix} 4 & -1 & 2 \\ -3 & 0 & 5 \\ -2 & 1 & 6 \end{vmatrix}$$

11. Evaluate by expanding by cofactors.

$$\begin{vmatrix} 3 & 0 & -4 & 5 \\ -4 & 6 & -2 & 1 \\ 0 & 2 & -1 & 0 \\ 8 & 4 & 1 & -1 \end{vmatrix}$$

12. Solve by Cramer's rule.

$$9x - 3y = 7$$
$$x + 8y = -2$$

13. Solve by Cramer's rule.

$$2x + 2y - z = -3$$
$$x \qquad + 2z = 13$$
$$3x - 2y - z = 8$$

Progress Test 14B

1. Given the matrix

$$A = \begin{bmatrix} 4 & -1.5 & 0.6 \\ 1.2 & 15 & -3 \end{bmatrix}$$

(a) Determine the dimension of A.

(b) Find a_{13}.

2. Write the augmented matrix that corresponds to the linear system

$$3x - y + 5z = 6$$
$$-2x \qquad + z = -3$$
$$5x + 2y - 3z = 0$$

3. Write a system of linear equations that corresponds to the augmented matrix

$$\begin{bmatrix} 2.6 & 1.5 & | & -13 \\ 0.2 & -3.7 & | & 7 \end{bmatrix}$$

4. Solve the system of linear equations that corresponds to the augmented matrix

$$\begin{bmatrix} 2 & 1 & -4 & | & 13 \\ 0 & -3 & 2 & | & 0 \\ 0 & 0 & 4 & | & -6 \end{bmatrix}$$

5. Given the matrix

$$B = \begin{bmatrix} -1 & 2 & 4 & 0 \\ 3 & 0 & -4 & -3 \\ -\frac{1}{2} & -5 & -2 & 7 \end{bmatrix}$$

(a) Replace row 2 of B by the sum of itself and a multiple of row 1 so that $b_{21} = 0$.

(b) Replace row 3 of B by the sum of itself and a multiple of row 1 so that $b_{31} = 0$.

6. Solve by matrix methods.

$$\frac{1}{2}x + y = 0$$
$$x - y = 10$$

7. Solve by matrix methods.

$$-2x + y - z = -3$$
$$x + 2y \qquad = -1$$
$$3x + 4y + 2z = -9$$

8. Find the value of the determinant

$$\begin{vmatrix} -3 & 4 \\ \frac{1}{2} & -2 \end{vmatrix}$$

9. Find the cofactor of each element in the second row of the determinant

$$\begin{vmatrix} 4 & 0 & 2 \\ 2 & 1 & -5 \\ -2 & 3 & -1 \end{vmatrix}$$

10. Evaluate the given determinant by expanding by cofactors

   (a) about column 1   (b) about row 3

$$\begin{vmatrix} -1 & 4 & 5 \\ 0 & -2 & 4 \\ 2 & -3 & 0 \end{vmatrix}$$

11. Evaluate by expanding by cofactors.

$$\begin{vmatrix} -1 & 3 & 4 & -2 \\ 5 & 2 & -1 & 0 \\ 2 & 1 & 1 & 0 \\ -4 & 0 & 3 & 1 \end{vmatrix}$$

12. Solve by Cramer's rule.

$$3x - y = 2$$
$$2x + 3y = 5$$

13. Solve by Cramer's rule.

$$x + 2y + 4z = 3$$
$$3x \qquad - 2z = 8$$
$$-2x + y \qquad = -7$$

Chapter 14 Project

Manipulating images using computer technology is a major component of special effects in some of today's most popular films. The mathematics of matrices can help us see how images can be altered by increasing the contrast or adding two images together. One interesting use of the latter technique is a process called blue-screen chromakey, by which a character may appear to be in an environment that was actually photographed separately.

For this project, do the following exercises from this chapter: Section 14.1, 49–52, and Section 14.2, 37–39.

Now make up your own image matrix. Make it 20 pixels by 15 pixels, and let each pixel have 6 bits. (This means each entry will be an integer between 0 and 63.) Repeat the exercises using this matrix. Use your calculator to help you. If increasing the contrast results in an entry greater than 63, what should you do?

■ ■ ■

15 Topics in Algebra

"Mathematics is the queen of the sciences and number theory the queen of mathematics."

—Carl Friedrich Gauss

There is a famous story from antiquity in which a grateful king offers a wise subject (a mathematician, no doubt!) any reward he can name. The subject requests to be given a chessboard with 64 squares and to be given one grain of rice on the first square, two grains on the second square, four grains on the third, and so on, doubling the number of grains upon each square. The king readily agrees, imagining that he will need only a few bushels to satisfy the request.

Imagine his surprise when the Royal Mathematician showed him how much grain would be needed for the last square of the chessboard! This problem is similar to Exercise 40 of Section 15.2. You are asked to find the answer at the end of the chapter.

If mathematical recreations interest you, take a look at some illusions and other fun items by visiting http://www.mathworld.wolfram.com and clicking "Recreational Mathematics." Check out the Parallelogram Illusion!

http://www.mathworld
.wolfram.com

■ ■ ■

The topics in this chapter are related in that they all involve the set of natural numbers. As you might expect, despite our return to a simpler number system, the approach and results will be more advanced than in earlier chapters. For example, in discussing sequences, we will be dealing with functions whose domain is the set of natural numbers. Yet, sequences lead to considerations of series, and the underlying concepts of infinite series can be used as an introduction to calculus.

Another of the topics, mathematical induction, provides a means of proving certain theorems involving the natural numbers. As an example, we will use mathematical induction to prove that the sum of the first n consecutive positive integers is

$$\frac{n(n + 1)}{2}$$

Yet another topic is the binomial theorem, which gives us a way to expand the expression $(a + b)^n$, where n is a natural number. One of the earliest results obtained in a calculus course requires the binomial theorem in its derivation.

Probability theory enables us to state the likelihood of the occurrence of a given event and has obvious applications to games of chance. The theory of permutations and combinations, which enables us to count the number of arrangements of a set of objects under various conditions, is a useful background to the study of probability theory.

15.1   Arithmetic Sequences

Can you see a pattern or relationship that describes the following string of numbers?

$$1, 4, 9, 16, 25, \ldots$$

If we rewrite this string as

$$1^2, 2^2, 3^2, 4^2, 5^2, \ldots$$

it is clear that these are the squares of successive natural numbers. Each number in the string is called a **term**. We could write the nth term of the list as a function a such that

$$a(n) = n^2$$

where n is a natural number. Such a string of numbers is called an **infinite sequence** since the list is infinitely long.

Infinite Sequence   An infinite sequence is a function whose domain is the set of natural numbers.

The range of the function a is

$$a(1), a(2), a(3), \ldots$$

which we write as

$$a_1, a_2, a_3, \ldots$$

That is, we indicate a sequence by using subscript notation rather than function notation. We say that a_1 is the first term of the sequence, a_2 is the second term, and so on, and write the nth term as a_n.

EXAMPLE 1 WORKING WITH SUBSCRIPT NOTATION

Write the first four terms of a sequence whose nth term is

$$a_n = \frac{n}{n+1}$$

SOLUTION

To find a_1, we substitute $n = 1$ in the formula

$$a_1 = \frac{1}{1+1} = \frac{1}{2}$$

Similarly, we have

$$a_2 = \frac{2}{2+1} = \frac{2}{3}, \quad a_3 = \frac{3}{3+1} = \frac{3}{4}, \quad a_4 = \frac{4}{4+1} = \frac{4}{5}$$

✔ **Progress Check 1**

Write the first four terms of a sequence whose nth term is

$$a_n = \frac{n-1}{n^2}$$

Answer

$0, \dfrac{1}{4}, \dfrac{2}{9}, \dfrac{3}{16}$

Now let's try to find a pattern or relationship for the sequence

$$2, 5, 8, 11, 14, 17, \ldots$$

You may notice that the nth term can be written as $a_n = 3n - 1$. But there is another way to describe this sequence. Each term after the first can be obtained by adding 3 to the preceding term.

$$a_1 = 2, \quad a_2 = a_1 + 3, \quad a_3 = a_2 + 3, \quad \ldots$$

A sequence in which each successive term is obtained by adding a fixed number to the previous term is called an **arithmetic sequence**.

<table>
<tr><td>

Arithmetic Sequence

</td><td>

In an **arithmetic sequence** there is a real number d such that

$$a_n = a_{n-1} + d$$

for all $n > 1$. The number d is called the **common difference**.

</td></tr>
</table>

An arithmetic sequence is also called an **arithmetic progression**. Returning to the sequence

$$2, 5, 8, 11, 14, 17, \ldots$$

the nth term can be defined by

$$a_n = a_{n-1} + 3, \quad a_1 = 2$$

This is an arithmetic sequence with the first term equal to 2 and a common difference of 3. The formula $a_n = a_{n-1} + 3$ is said to be a **recursive formula** since it defines the nth term by means of preceding terms. Beginning with $a_1 = 2$, the formula is used "recursively" (over and over) to obtain a_2, then a_3, then a_4, and so on.

EXAMPLE 2   TEST FOR AN ARITHMETIC SEQUENCE

Which of the following are arithmetic sequences?

(a) $5, 7, 9, 11, \ldots$ (b) $4, 8, 11, 13, \ldots$ (c) $3, -1, -5, -9, \ldots$

(d) $1, \dfrac{3}{2}, 2, \dfrac{5}{2}, \ldots$

SOLUTIONS

(a) Since each term can be obtained from the preceding by adding 2, this is an arithmetic sequence with first term equal to 5 and a common difference of 2.

(b) This is not an arithmetic sequence since there is not a common difference between terms. The difference between the first and second term is 4, while that between the next two terms is 3.

(c) The difference between terms is -4, that is,

$$a_n = a_{n-1} - 4$$

This is an arithmetic sequence with first term equal to 3 and a common difference of -4.

(d) This is an arithmetic sequence with a common difference of $\frac{1}{2}$.

✔ **Progress Check 2**
Which of the following are arithmetic sequences?

(a) 16, 17, 16, 17, ...   (b) −2, −1, 0, 1, ...

(c) $6, \frac{9}{2}, 3, \frac{3}{2}, ...$ (d) 2, 4, 8, 12, ...

Answers
b and c

EXAMPLE 3   TERMS OF AN ARITHMETIC SEQUENCE

Write the first four terms of an arithmetic sequence whose first term is −4 and whose common difference is −3.

SOLUTION

The arithmetic sequence is defined by

$$a_n = a_{n-1} - 3, \quad a_1 = -4$$

which leads to the terms

$$a_1 = -4, \quad a_2 = -7, \quad a_3 = -10, \quad a_4 = -13$$

✔ **Progress Check 3**
Write the first four terms of an arithmetic sequence whose first term is 4 and whose common difference is $-\frac{1}{3}$.

Answer
$4, \frac{11}{3}, \frac{10}{3}, 3$

For a given arithmetic sequence it's easy to find a formula for the nth term, a_n, in terms of n and the first term a_1. Since

$$a_2 = a_1 + d$$

and

$$a_3 = a_2 + d$$

we see that

$$a_3 = (a_1 + d) + d = a_1 + 2d$$

Similarly, we can show that

$$a_4 = a_3 + d = (a_1 + 2d) + d = a_1 + 3d$$
$$a_5 = a_4 + d = (a_1 + 3d) + d = a_1 + 4d$$

and, in general,

$$a_n = a_{n-1} + d = [a_1 + (n-2)d] + d = a_1 + (n-1)d$$

> The nth term a_n of an arithmetic sequence is given by
>
> $$a_n = a_1 + (n-1)d$$

EXAMPLE 4 FINDING A SPECIFIED TERM OF AN ARITHMETIC SEQUENCE

Find the 7th term of the arithmetic sequence whose first term is 2 and whose common difference is 4.

SOLUTION

We substitute $n = 7$, $a_1 = 2$, and $d = 4$ in the formula

$$a_n = a_1 + (n-1)d$$

obtaining

$$a_7 = 2 + (7-1)4 = 2 + 24 = 26$$

> ✔ **Progress Check 4**
>
> Find the 16th term of the arithmetic sequence whose first term is -5 and whose common difference is $\frac{1}{2}$.
>
> **Answer**
>
> $\dfrac{5}{2}$

EXAMPLE 5 FINDING A SPECIFIED TERM OF AN ARITHMETIC SEQUENCE

Find the 25th term of an arithmetic sequence whose first and 20th terms are -7 and 31, respectively.

SOLUTION

We can apply the given information to find d:

$$a_n = a_1 + (n-1)d$$
$$a_{20} = a_1 + (20-1)d$$
$$31 = -7 + 19d$$
$$d = 2$$

Now we use the formula for a_n to find a_{25}:

$$a_n = a_1 + (n-1)d$$
$$a_{25} = -7 + (25-1)2$$
$$a_{25} = 41$$

✔ **Progress Check 5**

Find the 60th term of an arithmetic sequence whose first and 10th terms are 3 and $-\frac{3}{2}$, respectively.

Answer

$-\dfrac{53}{2}$

Arithmetic Series

In many applications of sequences, we wish to *add* the terms. A sum of the terms of a sequence is called a **series**. When we are dealing with an arithmetic sequence, the associated series is called an **arithmetic series**.

We denote the sum of the first n terms of the arithmetic sequence a_1, a_2, a_3, ... by S_n:

$$S_n = a_1 + a_2 + a_3 + \ldots + a_{n-2} + a_{n-1} + a_n$$

Since an arithmetic sequence has a common difference d, we may write

$$S_n = a_1 + (a_1 + d) + (a_1 + 2d) + \ldots + (a_n - 2d) + (a_n - d) + a_n \qquad (1)$$

where we write a_2, a_3, ... in terms of a_1 and we write a_{n-1}, a_{n-2}, ... in terms of a_n. Rewriting the right-hand side of Equation (1) in reverse order, we have

$$S_n = a_n + (a_n - d) + (a_n - 2d) + \ldots + (a_1 + 2d) + (a_1 + d) + a_1 \qquad (2)$$

Summing the corresponding sides of Equations (1) and (2), we obtain

$$2S_n = (a_1 + a_n) + (a_1 + a_n) + (a_1 + a_n) + \ldots$$
$$= n(a_1 + a_n)$$

since $(a_1 + a_n)$ occurs n times. Thus,

$$S_n = \frac{n}{2}(a_1 + a_n)$$

Since $a_n = a_1 + (n-1)d$, we see that

$$S_n = \frac{n}{2}[a_1 + a_1 + (n-1)d] \qquad \text{Substitute for } a_n.$$

$$= \frac{n}{2}[2a_1 + (n-1)d]$$

We now have two useful formulas.

Arithmetic Series

For an arithmetic series, the sum S_n is given by

$$S_n = \frac{n}{2}(a_1 + a_n)$$

or by

$$S_n = \frac{n}{2}[2a_1 + (n-1)d]$$

The choice of which formula to use depends on the available information. The following examples illustrate the use of the formulas.

EXAMPLE 6   WORKING WITH AN ARITHMETIC SERIES

Find the sum of the first 30 terms of an arithmetic sequence whose first term is -20 and whose common difference is 3.

SOLUTION

We know that $n = 30$, $a_1 = -20$, and $d = 3$. Since we don't know the value of a_n, we substitute in the formula

$$S_n = \frac{n}{2}[2a_1 + (n-1)d]$$

which gives us

$$
\begin{aligned}
S_{30} &= \frac{30}{2}[2(-20) + (30-1)3] \\
&= 15(-40 + 87) \\
&= 705
\end{aligned}
$$

 Progress Check 6

Find the sum of the first 10 terms of the arithmetic sequence whose first term is 2 and whose common difference is $-\frac{1}{2}$.

Answer

$-\dfrac{5}{2}$

EXAMPLE 7   WORKING WITH AN ARITHMETIC SERIES

The first term of an arithmetic sequence is 2, the last term is 58, and the sum of the corresponding series is 450. Find the number of terms and the common difference.

SOLUTION

We have $a_1 = 2$, $a_n = 58$, and $S_n = 450$. Since we know the value of a_n, we substitute in the simpler formula:

$$S_n = \frac{n}{2}(a_1 + a_n)$$

We obtain

$$450 = \frac{n}{2}(2 + 58)$$

$$900 = 60n$$

$$n = 15$$

Now we use this value of n to find d by substituting in the following formula:

$$a_n = a_1 + (n - 1)d$$

$$58 = 2 + (14)d$$

$$56 = 14d$$

$$d = 4$$

✔ Progress Check 7

The first term of an arithmetic sequence is 6, the last term is 1, and the sum of the corresponding series is 77/2. Find the number of terms and the common difference.

Answer

$n = 11$, $d = -\dfrac{1}{2}$

Exercise Set 15.1

In Exercises 1–12 write the first four terms of the sequence whose nth term is given as a_n.

1. $a_n = 2n$

2. $a_n = 2n + 1$

3. $a_n = 2n + 3$

4. $a_n = 2n - 2$

5. $a_n = 3n - 1$

6. $a_n = \dfrac{2n + 5}{2}$

7. $a_n = \dfrac{n + 3}{3}$

8. $a_n = \dfrac{n - 1}{2n}$

9. $a_n = \dfrac{n^2 + n}{n + 1}$

10. $a_n = \dfrac{n^2 - 1}{n^2 + 1}$

11. $a_n = \dfrac{n^2}{2n + 1}$

12. $a_n = \dfrac{2n + 1}{n^2}$

In Exercises 13–24 determine whether or not the given sequence is an arithmetic sequence.

13. $3, 6, 9, 12, \ldots$

14. $4, \dfrac{11}{2}, 7, \dfrac{17}{2}, \ldots$

15. $1, -2, -6, -10, \ldots$

16. $-\dfrac{1}{2}, -1, -\dfrac{3}{2}, -2, \ldots$

17. $0, \frac{1}{4}, \frac{1}{2}, \frac{3}{4}, \ldots$

18. $2, 0, 1, 4, \ldots$

19. $-3, -\frac{8}{3}, -\frac{7}{3}, -2, \ldots$

20. $2, 0, -2, -4, \ldots$

21. $-1, 2, 6, 11, \ldots$

22. $18, 15, 12, 9, \ldots$

23. $-1, 2, 5, 8, \ldots$

24. $12, 8, 4, 1, \ldots$

In Exercises 25–34 write the first four terms of an arithmetic sequence whose first term is a_1 and whose common difference is d.

25. $a_1 = 2, d = 4$

26. $a_1 = -2, d = -5$

27. $a_1 = 3, d = -\frac{1}{2}$

28. $a_1 = \frac{1}{2}, d = 2$

29. $a_1 = -4, d = 4$

30. $a_1 = 17, d = \frac{3}{2}$

31. $a_1 = 21, d = -4$

32. $a_1 = -7, d = 2$

33. $a_1 = \frac{1}{3}, d = -\frac{1}{3}$

34. $a = 6, d = \frac{5}{2}$

In Exercises 35–38 find the specified term of the arithmetic sequence whose first term is a_1 and whose common difference is d.

35. $a_1 = 4, d = 3$; 8th term

36. $a_1 = -3, d = \frac{1}{4}$; 14th term

37. $a_1 = 14, d = -2$; 12th term

38. $a_1 = 6, d = -\frac{1}{3}$; 9th term

In Exercises 39–44, given two terms of an arithmetic sequence, find the specified term.

39. $a_1 = -2, a_{20} = -2$; 24th term

40. $a_1 = \frac{1}{2}, a_{12} = 6$; 30th term

41. $a_1 = 0, a_{61} = 20$; 20th term

42. $a_1 = 23, a_{15} = -19$; 6th term

43. $a_1 = -\frac{1}{4}, a_{41} = 10$; 22th term

44. $a_1 = -3, a_{18} = 65$; 30th term

In Exercises 45–50 find the sum of the specified number of terms of an arithmetic sequence whose first term is a_1 and whose common difference is d.

45. $a_1 = 3, d = 2$; 20 terms

46. $a_1 = -4, d = \frac{1}{2}$; 24 terms

47. $a_1 = \frac{1}{2}, d = -2$; 12 terms

48. $a_1 = -3, d = -\frac{1}{3}$; 18 terms

49. $a_1 = 82, d = -2$; 40 terms

50. $a_1 = 6, d = 4$; 16 terms

*51. How many terms of the arithmetic sequence 2, 4, 6, 8, ... add up to 930?

*52. How many terms of the arithmetic sequence 44, 41, 38, 35, ... add up to 340?

*53. The first term of an arithmetic sequence is 3, the last term is 90, and the sum of the corresponding series is 1395. Find the number of terms and the common difference.

*54. The first term of an arithmetic sequence is -3, the last term is $\frac{5}{2}$, and the sum of the corresponding series is -3. Find the number of terms and the common difference.

*55. The first term of an arithmetic sequence is $\frac{1}{2}$, the last term is $\frac{7}{4}$, and the sum of the corresponding series is $\frac{27}{4}$. Find the number of terms and the common difference.

*56. The first term of an arithmetic sequence is 20, the last term is -14, and the sum of the corresponding series is 54. Find the number of terms and the common difference.

*57. Find the sum of the first 16 terms of an arithmetic sequence whose 4th and 10th terms are $-\frac{5}{4}$ and $\frac{1}{4}$, respectively.

*58. Find the sum of the first 12 terms of an arithmetic sequence whose 3rd and 6th terms are 9 and 18, respectively.

*59. Suppose a depositor opens a Christmas Club savings account with an initial deposit of $50 and agrees to deposit $5 per week.

(a) How much money will have been saved after 10 additional weeks?

(b) Write an expression for the amount saved after n weeks.

15.2   Geometric Sequences

The sequence

$$3, 6, 12, 24, 48, \ldots$$

has a distinct pattern. Each term after the first is obtained by multiplying the preceding one by 2. Thus, we could rewrite the sequence as

$$3, 3 \cdot 2, (3 \cdot 2) \cdot 2, (3 \cdot 2 \cdot 2) \cdot 2, \ldots$$

Such a sequence is called a **geometric sequence.** Each successive term is found by multiplying the previous term by a fixed number.

Geometric Sequence

> In a **geometric sequence** there is a real number r such that
>
> $$a_n = r a_{n-1}$$
>
> for all $n > 1$. The number r is called the **common ratio**.

A geometric sequence is also called a **geometric progression.** The common ratio r can be found by dividing any term a_k by the preceding term, a_{k-1}.

> In a geometric sequence, the common ratio r is given by
>
> $$r = \frac{a_k}{a_{k-1}}$$

EXAMPLE 1   TEST FOR A GEOMETRIC SEQUENCE

If the sequence is a geometric sequence, find the common ratio.

(a) $2, -4, 8, -16, \ldots$ (b) $1, 2, 6, 24, \ldots$ (c) $\dfrac{1}{4}, \dfrac{1}{8}, \dfrac{1}{16}, \dfrac{1}{32}, \ldots$

SOLUTIONS

(a) Since each term can be obtained by multiplying the preceding one by -2, this is a geometric sequence with common ratio of -2.

(b) The ratio between successive terms is not constant. This is not a geometric sequence.

(c) This is a geometric sequence with common ratio of $\frac{1}{2}$.

> ### ✔ Progress Check 1
>
> For each sequence that is a geometric sequence, find the common ratio.
>
> (a) $3, -9, 27, -81, \ldots$ (b) $4, 1, -2, -5, \ldots$
>
> (c) $6, 2, \dfrac{2}{3}, \dfrac{2}{9}, \ldots$ (d) $4, 16, 48, 96, \ldots$
>
> ### Answers
>
> Sequence (a) is a geometric sequence with $r = -3$.
>
> Sequence (c) is a geometric sequence with $r = \frac{1}{3}$.

Let's look at successive terms of a geometric sequence whose first term is a_1 and whose common ratio is r. We have

$$a_2 = ra_1$$
$$a_3 = ra_2 = r(ra_1) = r^2 a_1$$
$$a_4 = ra_3 = r(r^2 a_1) = r^3 a_1$$

The pattern suggests that the exponent of r is one less than the subscript of a in the left-hand side. Thus,

> The nth term of a geometric sequence is given by
>
> $$a_n = a_1 r^{n-1}$$

EXAMPLE 2   FINDING A SPECIFIED TERM OF A GEOMETRIC SEQUENCE

Find the seventh term of the geometric sequence $-4, -2, -1, \ldots$.

SOLUTION

Since

$$r = \frac{a_k}{a_{k-1}}$$

we see that

$$r = \frac{a_3}{a_2} = \frac{-1}{-2} = \frac{1}{2}$$

Substituting $a_1 = -4$, $r = \frac{1}{2}$, and $n = 7$, we have

$$a_n = a_1 r^{n-1}$$

$$a_7 = (-4)\left(\frac{1}{2}\right)^{7-1} = (-4)\left(\frac{1}{2}\right)^6$$

$$= (-4)\left(\frac{1}{64}\right) = -\frac{1}{16}$$

✔ **Progress Check 2**
Find the sixth term of the geometric sequence 2, −6, 18, ...

Answer
−486

Geometric Mean

In a geometric sequence, the terms between the first term and the nth term are called **geometric means**. We will illustrate the method of calculating such means.

EXAMPLE 3   INSERTING GEOMETRIC MEANS

Insert three geometric means between 3 and 48.

SOLUTION

The geometric sequence must look like this:

$$3, a_2, a_3, a_4, 48, ...$$

Thus, $a_1 = 3$, $a_5 = 48$, and $n = 5$. Substituting in

$$a_n = a_1 r^{n-1}$$

we have

$$48 = 3r^4$$
$$r^4 = 16$$
$$r = \pm 2$$

Thus there are two geometric sequences with three geometric means between 3 and 48.

$$3, 6, 12, 24, 48, ... \qquad \text{for } r = 2$$
$$3, -6, 12, -24, 48, ... \quad \text{for } r = -2$$

✔ **Progress Check 3**
Insert two geometric means between 5 and $\frac{8}{25}$.

Answer
$2, \dfrac{4}{5}$

Fibonacci Counts the Rabbits

Here is a problem that was first published in the year 1202.

A pair of newborn rabbits begins breeding at age one month and thereafter produces one pair of offspring per month. If we start with a newborn pair of rabbits, how many rabbits will there be at the beginning of each month?

Month	Pairs of Rabbits
0	P_1
1	P_1
2	$P_1 \rightarrow P_2$
3	$P_1 \rightarrow P_3$ P_2
4	$P_1 \rightarrow P_4$ $P_2 \rightarrow P_5$ P_3
5	$P_1 \rightarrow P_6$ $P_2 \rightarrow P_7$ $P_3 \rightarrow P_8$ P_4 P_5

The problem was posed by Leonardo Fibonacci of Pisa, and the resulting sequence is known as a **Fibonacci sequence**.

The accompanying figure helps in analyzing the problem. At the beginning of month zero, we have the pair of newborn rabbits P_1. At the beginning of month 1, we still have the pair P_1, since the rabbits do not breed until age 1 month. At the beginning of month 2, the pair P_1 has the pair of offspring P_2. At the beginning of month 3, P_1 again has offspring, P_3, but P_2 does not breed during its first month. At the beginning of month 4, P_1 has offspring P_4, P_2 has offspring P_5, and P_3 does not breed during its first month.

If we let a_n denote the number of pairs of rabbits at the beginning of the month n, we see that

$$a_0 = 1, a_1 = 1, a_2 = 2, a_3 = 3, a_4 = 5, a_5 = 8, \ldots$$

The sequence has the interesting property that each term is the sum of the two preceding terms; that is,

$$a_n = a_{n-1} + a_{n-2}$$

Strange as it seems, nature appears to be aware of the Fibonacci sequence. For example, arrangements of seeds on sunflowers and leaves on some trees are related to Fibonacci numbers. Stranger still, some researchers believe that cycle analysis, such as analysis of stock market prices, is also related in some way to Fibonacci numbers.

Geometric Series

If $a_1, a_2, \ldots$ is a geometric sequence, then the series

$$S = a_1 + a_2 + \ldots$$

is called a **geometric series**. The sum of the first n terms of the geometric sequence $a_1, a_2, a_3, \ldots$ is denoted by S_n:

$$S_n = a_1 + a_2 + \ldots + a_n \tag{1}$$

Since each term of a geometric sequence can be written as $a_k = a_1 r^{k-1}$, we can rewrite Equation (1) as

$$S_n = a_1 + a_1 r + a_1 r^2 + \ldots + a_1 r^{n-2} + a_1 r^{n-1} \tag{2}$$

Multiplying each term in Equation (2) by r, we have

$$rS_n = a_1r + a_1r^2 + a_1r^3 + \ldots + a_1r^{n-1} + a_1r^n \qquad (3)$$

Subtracting Equation (3) from Equation (2) yields

$$S_n - rS_n = a_1 - a_1r^n$$
$$S_n(1 - r) = a_1(1 - r^n) \qquad \text{Factor.}$$
$$S_n = \frac{a_1(1 - r^n)}{1 - r} \qquad \text{Divide by } 1 - r \text{ (if } r \neq 1\text{)}.$$

Geometric Series: *n*th Partial Sum

In a geometric series with first term a_1 and common ratio $r \neq 1$,

$$S_n = \frac{a_1(1 - r^n)}{1 - r}$$

EXAMPLE 4   WORKING WITH A GEOMETRIC SERIES

Find the sum of the first six terms of the geometric sequence whose first three terms are 12, 6, 3.

SOLUTION

Since we have a geometric sequence, the common ratio can be found by dividing any term by the preceding term.

$$r = \frac{a_k}{a_{k-1}} = \frac{a_2}{a_1} = \frac{6}{12} = \frac{1}{2}$$

Substituting $a_1 = 12$, $r = \frac{1}{2}$, $n = 6$ in the formula for S_n, we have

$$S_n = \frac{a_1(1 - r^n)}{1 - r} = \frac{12\left[1 - \left(\frac{1}{2}\right)^6\right]}{1 - \frac{1}{2}} = \frac{189}{8}$$

✔ Progress Check 4

Find the sum of the first five terms of the geometric sequence whose first three terms are $2, -\frac{4}{3}, \frac{8}{9}$.

Answer

$$\frac{110}{81}$$

EXAMPLE 5   APPLICATION: GEOMETRIC SERIES

A father promises to give each child 2 cents on the first day and 4 cents on the second day and to continue doubling the amount each day for a total of 8 days.

How much will each child receive on the last day? How much will each child have received in total after 8 days?

SOLUTION

The daily payout to each child forms a geometric sequence 2, 4, 8, ... , a_8, with $a_1 = 2$ and $r = 2$. The term a_8 is given by substituting in

$$a_n = a_1 r^{n-1}$$
$$a_8 = a_1 r^{8-1} = 2 \cdot 2^7 = 256$$

Thus, each child will receive $2.56 on the last day. The total received by each child is given by

$$S_n = \frac{a_1(1 - r^n)}{1 - r}$$
$$S_8 = \frac{a_1(1 - r^8)}{1 - r} = \frac{2(1 - 2^8)}{1 - 2}$$
$$= \frac{2(1 - 256)}{-1} = 510$$

Each child will receive a total of $5.10 after 8 days.

✔ **Progress Check 5**

A ball is dropped from a height of 64 feet. On each bounce, it rebounds half the height it fell (Figure 1). How high is the ball at the top of the fifth bounce? What is the total distance the ball has traveled at the top of the fifth bounce?

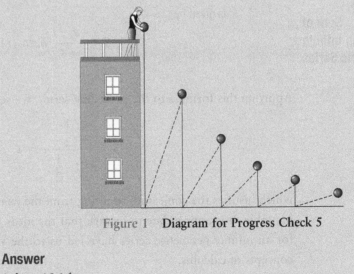

Figure 1   Diagram for Progress Check 5

Answer
2 feet; 186 feet

Infinite Geometric Series

We now want to focus on a geometric series for which $|r| < 1$, say,

$$\frac{1}{2} + \frac{1}{4} + \frac{1}{8} + \ldots + \frac{1}{2^n} + \ldots$$

To see how the sum increases as n increases, let's form a table of values of S_n.

n	1	2	3	4	5	6	7	8	9
S_n	0.500	0.750	0.875	0.938	0.969	0.984	0.992	0.996	0.998

We begin to suspect that S_n gets closer and closer to 1 as n increases. To see that this is really so, let's look at the formula

$$S_n = \frac{a_1(1 - r^n)}{1 - r}$$

when $|r| < 1$. When a number r that is less than 1 in absolute value is raised to higher and higher positive integer powers, the absolute value of r^n gets smaller and smaller. Thus, the term r^n can be made as small as we like by choosing n sufficiently large. Since we are dealing with an infinite series, we say that "r^n approaches zero as n approaches infinity." We can then replace r^n with 0 in the formula and denote the sum by S.

Sum of an Infinite Geometric Series

The sum S of the **infinite geometric series**

$$a_1 + a_1 r + a_1 r^2 + \ldots + a_1 r^n + \ldots$$

is given by

$$S = \frac{a_1}{1 - r} \quad \text{when } |r| < 1$$

Applying this formula to the preceding series, we see that

$$S = \frac{\dfrac{1}{2}}{1 - \dfrac{1}{2}} = 1$$

which justifies the conjecture resulting from the examination of the accompanying table. It is appropriate to remark that the ideas used in deriving the formula for an infinite geometric series have led us to the very border of the beginning concepts of calculus.

EXAMPLE 6   FINDING THE SUM OF AN INFINITE GEOMETRIC SERIES

Find the sum of the infinite geometric series

$$\frac{3}{2} + 1 + \frac{2}{3} + \frac{4}{9} + \ldots$$

SOLUTION

The common ratio $r = \frac{2}{3}$. The sum of the infinite geometric series, with $|r| < 1$, is given by

$$S = \frac{a_1}{1-r} = \frac{\dfrac{3}{2}}{1-\dfrac{2}{3}} = \frac{9}{2}$$

✔ Progress Check 6

Find the sum of the infinite geometric series

$$4 - 1 + \frac{1}{4} - \frac{1}{16} + \cdots$$

Answer

$\dfrac{16}{5}$

Exercise Set 15.2

In Exercises 1–10 determine whether the given sequence is a geometric sequence. If it is, find the common ratio.

1. $3, 6, 12, 24, \ldots$
2. $-4, 12, -36, 108, \ldots$

3. $-2, 4, 12, -36, \ldots$
4. $27, 18, 12, 8, \ldots$

5. $-4, 3, -\frac{9}{4}, \frac{27}{16}, \ldots$
6. $3, -1, \frac{1}{2}, -\frac{1}{4}, \ldots$

7. $1.2, 0.24, 0.048, 0.0096, \ldots$

8. $\frac{2}{3}, 1, \frac{3}{2}, \frac{9}{4}, \ldots$
9. $\frac{1}{4}, \frac{1}{2}, 2, 8, \ldots$

10. $\frac{1}{2}, \frac{3}{2}, \frac{9}{4}, \frac{27}{8}, \ldots$

In Exercises 11–18 write the first four terms of the geometric sequence whose first term is a_1 and whose common ratio is r.

11. $a_1 = 3, r = 3$
12. $a_1 = -4, r = 2$

13. $a_1 = 4, r = \frac{1}{2}$
14. $a_1 = 16, r = -\frac{3}{2}$

15. $a_1 = \frac{1}{2}, r = 4$
16. $a_1 = \frac{3}{2}, r = -\frac{2}{3}$

17. $a_1 = -3, r = 2$
18. $a_1 = 3, r = -\frac{2}{3}$

In Exercises 19–32 use the information given about a geometric sequence to find the requested value.

19. $a_1 = 3$ and $r = -2$; find a_8

20. $a_1 = 18$ and $r = -\frac{1}{2}$; find a_6

21. $a_1 = 24$ and $r = -\frac{1}{4}$; find a_5

22. $a_1 = 16$ and $r = \frac{1}{2}$; find a_7

23. $a_1 = 15$ and $r = -\frac{2}{3}$; find a_6

24. $a_1 = 10$ and $r = \frac{3}{2}$; find a_6

25. $a_1 = 3$ and $a_5 = \frac{1}{27}$; find a_7

26. $a_1 = 2$ and $a_6 = \frac{1}{16}$; find a_3

27. $a_1 = \frac{16}{81}$ and $a_6 = \frac{3}{2}$; find a_8

28. $a_4 = \frac{1}{4}$ and $a_7 = 1$; find r

29. $a_2 = 4$ and $a_8 = 256$; find r

30. $a_3 = 3$ and $a_6 = -81$; find a_8

31. $a_1 = \dfrac{1}{2}$, $r = 2$, and $a_n = 32$; find n

32. $a_1 = -2$, $r = 3$, and $a_n = 162$; find n

33. Insert two geometric means between 3 and 96.

34. Insert two geometric means between -3 and 192.

35. Insert two geometric means between 1 and $\dfrac{1}{64}$.

36. Insert three geometric means between $\dfrac{2}{3}$ and $\dfrac{32}{243}$.

37. Find the sum of the first seven terms of the geometric sequence whose first three terms are 3, 1, $\frac{1}{3}$.

38. Find the sum of the first six terms of the geometric sequence whose first three terms are $\frac{1}{3}$, 1, 3.

39. Find the sum of the first five terms of the geometric sequence whose first three terms are -3, $\frac{6}{5}$, $-\frac{12}{25}$.

40. Find the sum of the first six terms of the geometric sequence whose first three terms are 2, $\frac{4}{3}$, $\frac{8}{9}$.

41. If $a_1 = 4$ and $r = 2$, find S_8.

42. If $a_1 = -\dfrac{1}{2}$ and $r = -3$, find S_{10}.

43. If $a_1 = 2$ and $a_4 = \dfrac{-54}{8}$, find S_5.

44. If $a_1 = 64$ and $a_7 = 1$, find S_6.

In Exercises 45–53 evaluate the sum of the geometric series.

45. $1 + \dfrac{1}{2} + \dfrac{1}{4} + \dfrac{1}{8} + \ldots$ 46. $\dfrac{4}{5} + \dfrac{1}{5} + \dfrac{1}{20} + \dfrac{1}{80} + \ldots$

47. $1 - \dfrac{1}{3} + \dfrac{1}{9} - \dfrac{1}{27} + \ldots$ 48. $\dfrac{1}{2} - \dfrac{1}{4} + \dfrac{1}{8} - \dfrac{1}{16} + \ldots$

49. $2 + \dfrac{1}{2} + \dfrac{1}{8} + \dfrac{1}{32} + \ldots$

50. $1 + 0.1 + 0.01 + 0.001 + \ldots$

51. $0.5 + (0.5)^2 + (0.5)^3 + (0.5)^4 + \ldots$

52. $\dfrac{2}{5} + \dfrac{4}{25} + \dfrac{8}{125} + \dfrac{16}{625} + \ldots$

53. $\dfrac{1}{3} - \dfrac{2}{9} + \dfrac{4}{27} - \dfrac{8}{81} + \ldots$

*54. A Christmas Club calls for savings of $5 in January, and twice as much on each successive month as in the previous month. How much money will have been saved by the end of November?

*55. A city has a population of 20,000 people in 1980. If the population increases 5% per year, what will the population be in 1990?

*56. A city has a population of 30,000 in 1980. If the population increases 25% every ten years, what will the population be in the year 2010?

*57. For good behavior a child is offered a reward consisting of 1 cent on the first day, 2 cents on the second day, 4 cents on the third day, and so on. If the child behaves properly for two weeks, what is the total amount that the child will receive?

*58. The rational number 0.1111 … can be viewed as the sum of $0.1 + 0.01 + 0.001 + \ldots$ which is an infinite geometric series with $a = 0.1$ and $r = 0.1$. Find the corresponding rational number in the form p/q, where p and q are integers.

*59. Repeat Exercise 58 with the rational number $0.0909\overline{09}$, where the bar means that these two integers are repeated indefinitely.

*60. Repeat Exercise 58 with the rational number $0.2727\overline{27}$.

*61. Repeat Exercise 58 with the rational number $0.999\overline{9} \ldots$. (Don't be surprised if you obtain an integer answer.)

15.3 The Binomial Theorem

By sequential multiplication by $(a + b)$ you may verify that

$$(a + b)^0 = 1$$
$$(a + b)^1 = a + b$$
$$(a + b)^2 = a^2 + 2ab + b^2$$
$$(a + b)^3 = a^3 + 3a^2b + 3ab^2 + b^3$$
$$(a + b)^4 = a^4 + 4a^3b + 6a^2b^2 + 4ab^3 + b^4$$
$$(a + b)^5 = a^5 + 5a^4b + 10a^3b^2 + 10a^2b^3 + 5ab^4 + b^5$$

The expression on the right-hand side of the equation is called the **expansion** of the left-hand side. If we have to predict the form of the expansion of $(a + b)^n$, where n is a natural number, the preceding examples would lead us to conclude that it has the following properties:

(a) The expansion has $n + 1$ terms.

(b) The first term is $a^nb^0 = a^n$ and the last term is $a^0b^n = b^n$.

(c) The sum of the exponents of a and b in each term is n.

(d) In each successive term after the first, the power of a decreases by 1 and the power of b increases by 1.

(e) The coefficients may be obtained from the following array, which is known as Pascal's triangle. (See Figure 2). Each number, with the exception of those at the ends of the rows, is the sum of the two nearest numbers in the row above. The numbers at the ends of the rows are always 1.

```
              1
            1   1
          1   2   1
        1   3   3   1
      1   4   6   4   1
    1   5   10  10  5   1
```

Figure 2   **Pascal's Triangle**

Pascal's triangle is not a convenient means for determining the coefficients of the expansion when n is large. Here is an alternative method:

(e′) The coefficient of any term (after the first) can be found by the following rule: In the preceding term, multiply the coefficient by the exponent of a and then divide by one more than the exponent of b.

EXAMPLE 1   EXPANDING A BINOMIAL

Write the expansion of $(a + b)^6$.

SOLUTION

From Property (b) we know that the first term is a^6. Thus,

$$(a + b)^6 = a^6 + \dots$$

From Property (e') the next coefficient is

$$\frac{1 \cdot 6}{1} = 6$$

(since the exponent of b is 0). By Property (d) the exponents of a and b in this term are 5 and 1, respectively, so we have

$$(a + b)^6 = a^6 + 6a^5b + \dots$$

Applying Property (e') again, we find that the next coefficient is

$$\frac{6 \cdot 5}{2} = 15$$

and by Property (d) the exponents of a and b in this term are 4 and 2, respectively. Thus,

$$(a + b)^6 = a^6 + 6a^5b + 15a^4b^2 + \dots$$

Continuing in this manner, we see that

$$(a + b)^6 = a^6 + 6a^5b + 15a^4b^2 + 20a^3b^3 + 15a^2b^4 + 6ab^5 + b^6$$

✔ **Progress Check 1**

Write the first five terms in the expansion of $(a + b)^{10}$.

Answer

$a^{10} + 10a^9b + 45a^8b^2 + 120a^7b^3 + 210a^6b^4$

The expansion of $(a + b)^n$ that we have described is called the **binomial theorem** or **binomial formula** and can be written as

The Binomial Formula

$$(a + b)^n = a^n + \frac{n}{1}a^{n-1}b + \frac{n(n-1)}{1 \cdot 2}a^{n-2}b^2 + \frac{n(n-1)(n-2)}{1 \cdot 2 \cdot 3}a^{n-3}b^3$$

$$+ \dots + \frac{n(n-1)(n-2)\cdots(n-r+1)}{1 \cdot 2 \cdot 3 \cdot \dots \cdot r}a^{n-r}b^r + \dots + b^n$$

EXAMPLE 2   USING THE BINOMIAL FORMULA

Find the expansion of $(2x - 1)^4$.

SOLUTION

Let $a = 2x$ and $b = -1$, and apply the binomial formula.

$$(2x - 1)^4 = (2x)^4 + \frac{4}{1}(2x)^3(-1) + \frac{4 \cdot 3}{1 \cdot 2}(2x)^2(-1)^2 + \frac{4 \cdot 3 \cdot 2}{1 \cdot 2 \cdot 3}(2x)(-1)^3 + (-1)^4$$

$$= 16x^4 - 32x^3 + 24x^2 - 8x + 1$$

✔ **Progress Check 2**

Find the expansion of $(x^2 - 2)^4$.

Answer

$x^8 - 8x^6 + 24x^4 - 32x^2 + 16$

Factorial Notation

Note that the denominator of the coefficient in the binomial formula is always the product of the first n natural numbers. We use the symbol $n!$, which is read as **n factorial**, to indicate this type of product. For example,

$$4! = 4 \cdot 3 \cdot 2 \cdot 1 = 24$$

$$6! = 6 \cdot 5 \cdot 4 \cdot 3 \cdot 2 \cdot 1 = 720$$

and, in general,

n Factorial

$$n! = n(n - 1)(n - 2) \cdot \ldots \cdot 4 \cdot 3 \cdot 2 \cdot 1, \quad n \geqslant 1$$

Since

$$(n - 1)! = (n - 1)(n - 2)(n - 3) \cdot \ldots \cdot 4 \cdot 3 \cdot 2 \cdot 1$$

we see that for $n > 1$

$$n! = n(n - 1)!$$

For convenience, we define 0! by

$$0! = 1$$

EXAMPLE 3 WORKING WITH FACTORIAL NOTATION

Evaluate each of the following.

(a) $\dfrac{5!}{3!}$

Since $5! = 5 \cdot 4 \cdot 3!$, we may write

$$\frac{5!}{3!} = \frac{5 \cdot 4 \cdot 3!}{3!} = 5 \cdot 4 = 20$$

(b) $\dfrac{9!}{8!} = \dfrac{9 \cdot 8!}{8!} = 9$

(c) $\dfrac{10!4!}{12!} = \dfrac{10!4!}{12 \cdot 11 \cdot 10!} = \dfrac{4!}{12 \cdot 11} = \dfrac{4 \cdot 3 \cdot 2 \cdot 1}{12 \cdot 11} = \dfrac{2}{11}$

(d) $\dfrac{n!}{(n-2)!} = \dfrac{n(n-1)(n-2)!}{(n-2)!} = n(n-1) = n^2 - n$

(e) $\dfrac{(2-2)!}{3!} = \dfrac{0!}{3 \cdot 2} = \dfrac{1}{6}$

✔ Progress Check 3

Evaluate each of the following:

(a) $\dfrac{12!}{10!}$

(b) $\dfrac{6!}{4!2!}$

(c) $\dfrac{10!8!}{9!7!}$

(d) $\dfrac{n!(n-1)!}{(n+1)!(n-2)!}$

(e) $\dfrac{8!}{6!(3-3)!}$

Answers

(a) 132   (b) 15   (c) 80   (d) $\dfrac{n-1}{n+1}$ (e) 56

Here is what the binomial formula looks like in factorial notation.

$$(a+b)^n = a^n + \frac{n!}{1!(n-1)!}a^{n-1}b + \frac{n!}{2!(n-2)!}a^{n-2}b^2$$

$$+ \frac{n!}{3!(n-3)!}a^{n-3}b^3 + \cdots + \frac{n!}{r!(n-r)!}a^{n-r}b^r$$

$$+ \cdots + b^n$$

The symbol $\binom{n}{r}$, called the **binomial coefficient**, is defined in this way:

Binomial Coefficient

$$\binom{n}{r} = \frac{n!}{r!(n-r)!}$$

This symbol is useful in denoting the coefficients of the binomial expansion. Using this notation, the binomial formula can be written as

$$(a + b)^n = a^n + \binom{n}{1}a^{n-1}b + \binom{n}{2}a^{n-2}b^2 + \binom{n}{3}a^{n-3}b^3$$

$$+ \cdots + \binom{n}{r}a^{n-r}b^r + \cdots + b^n$$

Sometimes we merely want to find a certain term in the expansion of $(a + b)^n$. We shall use the following observation to answer this question. In the binomial formula for the expansion of $(a + b)^n$, b occurs in the second term, b^2 occurs in the third term, b^3 occurs in the fourth term, and, in general, b^r occurs in the $(r + 1)$th term. The exponents of a and b must add up to n in each term. Since the exponent of b in the $(r + 1)$th term is r, we conclude that the exponent of a must be $n - r$. Thus, we see that the $(r + 1)$th term in the expansion of $(a + b)^n$ is

$$\binom{n}{r}a^{n-r}b^r$$

EXAMPLE 4   FINDING A SPECIFIED TERM OF A BINOMIAL EXPANSION

Find the fourth term in the expansion of $(x - 1)^5$.

SOLUTION

The exponent of b in the fourth term is 3, and the exponent of a is then $5 - 3 = 2$. From the binomial formula we see that the coefficient of the term a^2b^3 is

$$\binom{n}{3} = \binom{5}{3} = \frac{5!}{3!2!}$$

Since $a = x$ and $b = -1$, the fourth term is

$$\frac{5!}{3!2!}x^2(-1)^3 = -10x^2$$

✔ **Progress Check 4**

Find the third term in the expansion of

$$\left(\frac{x}{2} - 1\right)^8$$

Answer

$\frac{7}{16}x^6$

EXAMPLE 5   FINDING A SPECIFIED TERM OF A BINOMIAL EXPANSION

Find the term in the expansion of $(x^2 - y^2)^6$ that involves y^8.

SOLUTION

Here $b = -y^2$, so $y^8 = (-y^2)^4 = b^4$. The term containing b^4 is the fifth term in the expansion. In this term the exponent of a is $6 - 4 = 2$. By the binomial formula the corresponding coefficient is

$$\binom{6}{4} = \frac{6!}{4!2!} = 15$$

Since $a = x^2$ and $b = -y^2$, the desired term is

$$15(x^2)^2(-y^2)^4 = 15x^4y^8$$

✔ Progress Check 5

Find the term in the expansion of $(x^3 - \sqrt{2})^5$ that involves x^6.

Answer

$-20\sqrt{2}x^6$

Exercise Set 15.3

In Exercises 1–12 expand and simplify.

1. $(3x + 2y)^5$

2. $(2a - 3b)^6$

3. $(4x - y^4)$

4. $\left(3 + \frac{1}{2}x\right)^4$

5. $(2 - xy)^5$

6. $(3a^2 + b)^4$

7. $(a^2b + 3)^4$

8. $(x - y)^7$

9. $(a - 2b)^8$

10. $\left(\frac{x}{y} + y\right)^6$

11. $\left(\frac{1}{3}x + 2\right)^3$

12. $\left(\frac{x}{y} + \frac{y}{x}\right)^5$

In Exercises 13–20 find the first four terms in the given expansion and simplify.

13. $(2 + x)^{10}$

14. $(x - 3)^{12}$

15. $(3 - 2a)^9$

16. $(a^2 + b^2)^{11}$

17. $(2x - 3y)^{14}$

18. $\left(a - \frac{1}{a^2}\right)^8$

19. $(2x - yz)^{13}$

20. $\left(x - \frac{1}{y}\right)^{15}$

In Exercises 21–32 evaluate.

21. $5!$

22. $7!$

23. $\dfrac{12!}{11!}$

24. $\dfrac{13!}{12!}$

25. $\dfrac{11!}{8!}$

26. $\dfrac{7!}{9!}$

27. $\dfrac{10!}{6!}$

28. $\dfrac{9!}{6!}$

29. $\dfrac{6!}{3!}$

30. $\binom{8}{5}$

31. $\binom{10}{6}$

32. $\dfrac{(n + 1)!}{(n - 1)!}$

In Exercises 33–46 find only the term specified in the given expansion.

*33. The fourth term in $(2x - 4)^7$

*34. The third term in $(4a + 3b)^{11}$

*35. The fifth term in $\left(\frac{1}{2}x - y\right)^{12}$

*36. The sixth term in $(3x - 2y)^{10}$

*37. The fifth term in $\left(\frac{1}{x} - 2\right)^9$

*38. The next to last term in $(a + 4b)^5$

*39. The middle term in $(x - 3y)^6$

*40. The middle term in $\left(2a + \frac{1}{2}b\right)^6$

*41. The term involving x^4 in $(3x + 4y)^7$

*42. The term involving x^6 in $(2x^2 - 1)^9$

*43. The term involving x^6 in $(2x^3 - 1)^9$

*44. The term involving x^8 in $\left(x^2 + \frac{1}{y}\right)^8$

*45. The term involving x^{12} in $\left(x^3 + \frac{1}{2}\right)^7$

*46. The term involving x^{-4} in $\left(y + \frac{1}{x^2}\right)^8$

*47. Evaluate $(1.3)^6$ to four decimal places by writing it as $(1 + 0.3)^6$ and using the binomial formula.

*48. Using the method of Example 47, evaluate the following:

(a) $(3.4)^4$ (b) $(48)^5$ (Hint: $48 = 50 - 2$)

15.4 Counting: Permutations and Combinations

How many arrangements can be made using the letters a, b, c, and d three at a time? One way to solve this problem is to enumerate all the possible arrangements. The tree diagram shown in Figure 3 is a graphic device that yields precisely what we need. The letters a, b, c, and d are listed at the top and represent the candidates for the first letter. The three branches emanating from these lead to the possible choices for the second letter, and so on. For example, the portion of the tree shown in Figure 4 illustrates the arrangements bda and bdc. In this way we determine that there are a total of 24 arrangements.

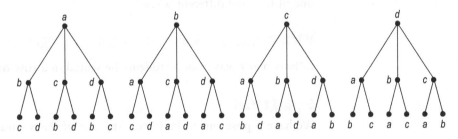

Figure 3   Arrangements of the Letters a, b, c, d

Figure 4   Arrangements bda and bdc

There is a more efficient way to solve this problem. Each arrangement consists of a choice of letters to fill the 3 positions in Figure 5. Any one of the 4 letters a, b, c, or d can be assigned to the first position; once a letter is assigned to the first position, any one of the 3 remaining letters can be assigned to the second position; finally, either one of the remaining 2 letters can be assigned to the third position. Since each candidate for a position can be associated with any other candidate in the other position, the product

$$4 \cdot 3 \cdot 2 = 24$$

yields the total number of arrangements. This simple example illustrates a very important principle.

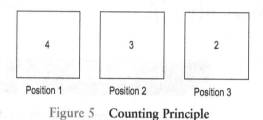

Figure 5   **Counting Principle**

Counting Principle

> If one event can occur in *m* different ways and, after it has happened in one of these ways, a second event can occur in *n* different ways, then both events can occur in *mn* different ways.

Note that the order of events is significant since each arrangement is counted as one of the "*mn* different ways."

EXAMPLE 1   APPLYING THE COUNTING PRINCIPLE

In how many ways can 5 students be seated in a row of 5 seats?

SOLUTION

We have 5 positions to be filled. Any one of the 5 students can occupy the first position, after which any one of the remaining 4 students can occupy the next position. Reapplying the counting principle to the other positions, we see that the number of arrangements is

$$5 \cdot 4 \cdot 3 \cdot 2 \cdot 1 = 120$$

> **✔ Progress Check 1**
> How many different 4-digit numbers can be formed using the digits 2, 4, 6, and 8? (Don't repeat any of the digits.)
>
> **Answer**
> 24

EXAMPLE 2 REPEATING AND NONREPEATING ARRANGEMENTS

How many different 3-letter arrangements can be made using the letters *A, B, C, X, Y,* and *Z*

(a) if no letter may be repeated in an arrangement?

(b) if letters may be repeated?

SOLUTIONS

(a) We need to fill 3 positions. Any one of the 6 letters may occupy the first position; then, any one of the remaining 5 letters may occupy the second position (since repetitions are not allowed). Finally, any one of the remaining 4 letters may occupy the third position. Thus, the total number of arrangements is $6 \cdot 5 \cdot 4 = 120$.

(b) Any one of the 6 letters may fill any of the 3 positions (since repetitions are allowed). The total number of arrangements is $6 \cdot 6 \cdot 6 = 216$.

✔ **Progress Check 2**

The positions of president, secretary, and treasurer are to be filled from a class of 15 students. In how many ways can these positions be filled if no student may hold more than 1 position?

Answer
2730

Permutations

Each arrangement that can be made by using all or some of the elements of a set of objects without repetition is called a **permutation**. The phrase "without repetition" means that no element of the set appears more than once. For example, the permutations of the letters *a, b,* and *c* taken 3 at a time include *b a c* but exclude *a a b.*

We will use the notation $P(n, r)$ to indicate the number of permutations of *n* distinct objects taken *r* at a time. If $r = n$, then using the counting principle, we see that

$$P(n, n) = n(n - 1)(n - 2) \cdots 2 \cdot 1$$

since any one of the *n* objects may fill the first position, any one of the remaining $(n - 1)$ objects may fill the second position, and so on. Using factorial notation, we have

$$P(n, n) = n!$$

Let's try to calculate $P(n, r)$, that is, the number of permutations of n distinct objects taken r at a time when r is less than n. We may think of this as the number of ways of filling r positions with n candidates. Once again, we may fill the first position with any one of the n candidates, the second position with any one of the remaining $(n - 1)$ candidates, and so on, obtaining

$$P(n, r) = n(n - 1)(n - 2) \ldots (n - r + 1) \tag{1}$$

since $(n - r + 1)$ will be the rth factor. If we multiply the right-hand side of Equation (1) by

$$\frac{(n - r)!}{(n - r)!} = 1$$

we have

$$P(n, r) = \frac{n(n - 1)(n - 2) \cdots (n - r + 1)(n - r)(n - r - 1) \cdots 2 \cdot 1}{(n - r)!}$$

or

Number of Permutations of n Distinct Objects Taken r at a Time

$$P(n, r) = \frac{n!}{(n - r)!}$$

EXAMPLE 3   USING PERMUTATION NOTATION

Evaluate.

(a) $P(5, 5)$ 　　　　(b) $P(5, 2)$ 　　　　(c) $\dfrac{P(6, 2)}{3!}$

SOLUTIONS

(a) $P(5, 5) = \dfrac{5!}{(5 - 5)!} = \dfrac{5!}{0!} = \dfrac{5 \cdot 4 \cdot 3 \cdot 2 \cdot 1}{1} = 120$

(b) $P(5, 2) = \dfrac{5!}{(5 - 2)!} = \dfrac{5!}{3!} = \dfrac{5 \cdot 4 \cdot 3!}{3!} = 20$

(c) $\dfrac{P(6, 2)}{3!} = \dfrac{6!}{3!(6 - 2)!} = \dfrac{6!}{3!4!} = \dfrac{6 \cdot 5 \cdot 4!}{3 \cdot 2 \cdot 4!} = 5$

✔ **Progress Check 3**

Evaluate.

(a) $P(4, 4)$ 　　　　(b) $P(6, 3)$ 　　　　(c) $\dfrac{2P(6, 4)}{2!}$

Answers

(a) 24 　　　　(b) 120 　　　　(c) 360

EXAMPLE 4 WORKING WITH PERMUTATIONS

How many different arrangements can be made by taking 5 of the letters of the word *relation*?

SOLUTION

Since the word *relation* has 8 different letters, we are seeking the number of permutations of 8 objects taken 5 at a time, or $P(8, 5)$. Thus,

$$P(n, r) = \frac{n!}{(n - r)!}$$

$$P(8, 5) = \frac{8!}{(8 - 5)!} = \frac{8!}{3!} = 6720$$

> ✔ **Progress Check 4**
>
> There is space on a bookshelf for displaying 4 books. If there are 6 different novels available, how many arrangements can be made?
>
> **Answer**
> 360

EXAMPLE 5 WORKING WITH PERMUTATIONS

How many arrangements can be made using all the letters of the word *quartz* if the vowels are always to remain adjacent to each other?

SOLUTION

If we treat the vowel pair *ua* (or *au*) as a unit, then there are five "letters" (q, *ua*, r, t, z) that can be arranged in $P(5, 5)$ ways. But the vowels can themselves be arranged in $P(2, 2)$ ways. By the counting principle, the total number of arrangements is

$$P(5, 5) \cdot P(2, 2)$$

Since $P(5, 5) = 120$ and $P(2, 2) = 2$, the total number of arrangements is 240.

> ✔ **Progress Check 5**
>
> A bookshelf is to be used to display 5 new textbooks. There are 7 mathematics textbooks and 4 biology textbooks available. If we wish to put 3 mathematics books and 2 biology books on display, how many arrangements can be made if the books in each discipline must be kept together?
>
> **Answer**
> 5040

Not all permutations of the word *state* are distinct since the letter *t* appears more than once. The next example illustrates the procedure for finding the number of distinct or *distinguishable* permutations.

EXAMPLE 6   DISTINGUISHABLE PERMUTATIONS

Find the number of permutations of the letters in the word *remember*.

SOLUTION

The number of permutations of the eight letters is 8!. However, permutations in which the two *r*'s exchange places are not distinguishable. Similarly, permutations in which the three *e*'s exchange places are not distinguishable, and neither are those in which the two *m*'s exchange places. Since there are 2! permutations of the two *r*'s, 3! permutations of the three *e*'s, and 2! permutations of the two *m*'s, the number of distinguishable permutations of the letters in the word *remember* is

$$\frac{8!}{2!3!2!} = 1680$$

✔ **Progress Check 6**

Find the number of distinguishable permutations of the letters in the word ALASKA.

Answer
120

Combinations

Let's take another look at the arrangements of the letters *a*, *b*, and *c* taken two at a time:

ab	*ba*	*ca*
ac	*bc*	*cb*

Now let's ask a different question: In how many ways can we select 2 letters from the letters *a*, *b*, and *c*? In answering this question, we disregard the order in which the letters are chosen. The result is then

ab	*ac*	*bc*

In general, a set of *r* objects chosen from a set of *n* objects is called a **combination**. We denote the number of combinations of *r* objects chosen from *n* objects by $C(n, r)$.

EXAMPLE 7   WORKING WITH COMBINATIONS

List the combinations of the letters a, b, c, and d taken three at a time.

SOLUTION

The combinations are seen to be

$$abc \qquad abd \qquad acd \qquad bcd$$

✔ Progress Check 7

List the combinations of the letters a, b, c, and d taken two at a time.

Answers

ab, ac, ad, bc, bd, cd

Here is a rule that is helpful in determining whether a problem calls for the number of permutations or the number of combinations:

> If we are interested in calculating the number of arrangements in which different orderings of the same objects are counted, we use permutations.
>
> If we are interested in calculating the number of ways of selecting objects, and the order of the selected objects does not matter, we use combinations.

$P(n, r)$ or $C(n, r)$

For example, suppose we want to determine the number of different 4-card hands that can be dealt from a deck of 52 cards. Since a hand consisting of 4 cards is the same hand regardless of the order of the cards, we must use combinations.

Let's find a formula for $C(n, r)$. There are three combinations of the letters a, b, and c taken 2 at a time, namely

$$ab \qquad ac \qquad bc$$

so that $C(3, 2) = 3$. Now, each of these combinations can be arranged in 2! ways to yield the total list of permutations

$$ab \quad ba \quad ac \quad ca \quad bc \quad cb$$

Thus, $P(3, 2) = 6 = 2!C(3, 2)$. In general, each of the $C(n, r)$ combinations can be permutated in $r!$ ways, so by the counting principle the total number of permutations is $P(n, r) = r!C(n, r)$. Solving for $C(n, r)$, we derive the following formula:

Number of Combinations of n Distinct Objects Taken r at a Time

$$C(n, r) = \frac{P(n, r)}{r!} = \frac{n!}{r!(n - r)!}$$

The 15 Puzzle

The 15 puzzle was created in 1878 by Sam Lloyd. A square frame consisting of 16 compartments contains 15 numbered blocks, each occupying a compartment; one compartment is vacant. The object is to move the numbered blocks from a given arrangement to a specified arrangement by sliding numbered blocks into the empty compartment. The accompanying figure shows a starting arrangement and a desired ending arrangement.

1	2	3	4
5	6	7	8
9	10	11	12
13	14	15	

starting arrangement

The 15 puzzle was the rage of Europe and the United States in the late 1800s, and contests were held with substantial prizes being offered. The prizes were never collected since the specified arrangements could not be achieved.

Since there are 16 locations on the board, there are 16! possible arrangements of the 15 numbered blocks. (Consider that, for each arrangement of the 15 numbers, the empty position can occur in any of the 16 compartments.) If you compute 16!, you will find that this number is more than 20,000,000,000,000 (20 trillion).

A permutation, or arrangement, of the set of numbers from 1 to n is said to have an **inversion** each time a larger number precedes a smaller one. Thus the permutation 54,132 of the numbers 1, 2, 3, 4, 5 has 8 inversions:

1	5	9	13
2	6	10	14
3	7	11	15
4	8	12	

final arrangement

5 before 4	5 before 1	5 before 3	5 before 2
4 before 1	4 before 3	4 before 2	3 before 2

A permutation is said to be **even** if it has an even number of inversions, and **odd** if it has an odd number of inversions. Thus the permutation 54,132 is an even permutation. In 1879 the American mathematicians W. W. Johnson and W. E. Story showed that if the empty position remains fixed, then it is possible to go from any even (odd) arrangement to any other even (odd) arrangement and it is impossible to go from an even to an odd or from an odd to an even arrangement.

In the accompanying figure, the starting arrangement consists of the permutation

$$1 \quad 2 \quad 3 \quad 4 \quad 5 \quad 6 \quad 7 \quad 8 \quad 9 \quad 10 \quad 11 \quad 12 \quad 13 \quad 14 \quad 15$$

which has no inversions and is thus an even permutation.

The desired final arrangement is the permutation

$$1 \quad 5 \quad 9 \quad 13 \quad 2 \quad 6 \quad 10 \quad 14 \quad 3 \quad 7 \quad 11 \quad 15 \quad 4 \quad 8 \quad 12$$

which has 36 inversions (count them!) and thus is also an even permutation. It is therefore possible to go from the starting arrangement to the final arrangement.

EXAMPLE 8   NOTATION FOR PERMUTATIONS AND COMBINATIONS

Evaluate.

(a) $C(5, 2)$

(b) $C(4, 4)$

(c) $\dfrac{P(6, 3)}{C(6, 3)}$

SOLUTIONS

(a) $C(5, 2) = \dfrac{5!}{2!(5 - 2)!} = \dfrac{5!}{2!3!} = \dfrac{5 \cdot 4 \cdot 3!}{2 \cdot 3!} = 10$

(b) $C(4, 4) = \dfrac{4!}{4!(4 - 4)!} = \dfrac{4!}{4!0!} = 1$

(c) $P(6, 3) = \dfrac{6!}{(6 - 3)!} = \dfrac{6!}{3!} = 6 \cdot 5 \cdot 4 = 120$

$C(6, 3) = \dfrac{6!}{3!(6 - 3)!} = \dfrac{6!}{3!3!} = \dfrac{6 \cdot 5 \cdot 4}{3 \cdot 2 \cdot 1} = 20$

$\dfrac{P(6, 3)}{C(6, 3)} = \dfrac{120}{20} = 6$

✔ **Progress Check 8**

Evaluate.

(a) $C(6, 2)$ (b) $C(10, 10)$ (c) $\dfrac{P(3, 2)}{3!C(5, 4)}$

Answers

(a) 15   (b) 1   (c) $\dfrac{1}{5}$

EXAMPLE 9   AN APPLICATION OF COMBINATIONS

In how many ways can a committee of 4 be selected from a group of 10 people?

SOLUTION

If A, B, C, and D constitute a committee, is the arrangement B, A, C, D a different committee? Of course not—the order does not matter. We are therefore interested in computing $C(10, 4)$:

$$C(10, 4) = \frac{10!}{4!6!} = \frac{10 \cdot 9 \cdot 8 \cdot 7}{4 \cdot 3 \cdot 2 \cdot 1} = 210$$

✔ **Progress Check 9**

In how many ways can a 5-card hand be dealt from a deck of 52 cards?

Answer

2,598,960

EXAMPLE 10   AN APPLICATION OF COMBINATIONS

In how many ways can a committee of 3 girls and 2 boys be selected from a class of 8 girls and 7 boys?

SOLUTION

The girls can be selected in $C(8, 3)$ ways, and the boys can be selected in $C(7, 2)$ ways. By the counting principle, each choice of boys can be associated with each choice of girls:

$$C(8, 3) \cdot C(7, 2) = \frac{8!}{3!5!} \cdot \frac{7!}{2!5!} = (56)(21) = 1176$$

✔ **Progress Check 10**

In how many ways can 4 persons be chosen from 5 representatives of District A and 8 representatives of District B, if only 1 representative from District A is to be included?

Answer

280

EXAMPLE 11   AN APPLICATION OF COMBINATIONS AND PERMUTATIONS

A bookstore has 12 French and 9 German books. In how many ways can a group of 6 books, consisting of 4 French and 2 German books, be placed on a shelf?

SOLUTION

The French books can be selected in $C(12, 4)$ ways and the German books in $C(9, 2)$ ways. The 6 books can then be selected in $C(12, 4) \cdot C(9, 2)$ ways. Each *selection* of 6 books can then be *arranged* on the shelf in $P(6, 6)$ ways, so the total number of arrangements is

$$C(12, 4) \cdot C(9, 2) \cdot P(6, 6)$$

$$= \frac{12!}{4!8!} \cdot \frac{9!}{2!7!} \cdot \frac{6!}{(6 - 6)!} = 495 \cdot 36 \cdot 720 = 12{,}830{,}400$$

✔ **Progress Check 11**

From 6 different consonants and 4 different vowels, how many 5-letter words can be made consisting of 3 consonants and 2 vowels? (Assume every arrangement is a "word.")

Answer

14,400

Exercise Set 15.4

1. How many different five-digit numbers can be formed using the digits 1, 3, 4, 6, and 8?

2. How many different ways are there to arrange the letters in the word *study*?

3. An employee identification number consists of two letters of the alphabet followed by a sequence of three digits selected from the digits 2, 3, 5, 6, 8, and 9. If repetitions are allowed, how many different identification numbers are possible?

4. In a psychological experiment, a subject has to arrange a cube, a square, a triangle, and a rhombus in a row. How many different arrangements are possible?

5. A coin is tossed eight times, and the result of each toss is recorded. How many different sequences of heads and tails are possible?

6. A die (from a pair of dice) is tossed four times, and the result of each toss is recorded. How many different sequences are possible?

7. A concert is to consist of 3 guitar pieces, 2 vocal numbers, and 2 jazz selections. In how many ways can the program be presented?

In Exercises 8–19 compute the given expression.

8. $P(6, 6)$

9. $P(6, 5)$

10. $P(4, 2)$

11. $P(8, 3)$

12. $P(5, 2)$

13. $P(10, 2)$

14. $P(8, 4)$

15. $\dfrac{P(9, 3)}{3!}$

16. $\dfrac{4P(12, 3)}{2!}$

17. $P(3, 1)$

18. $\dfrac{P(7, 3)}{2!}$

19. $\dfrac{P(10, 4)}{4!}$

20. Find the number of ways in which 5 men and 5 women can be seated in a row

    (a) if any person may sit next to any other person.

    (b) if the men and women must be seated alternately.

21. Find the number of permutations of the letters of the word *money*.

22. Find the number of distinguishable permutations of the letters of the word *goose*. (Hint: Permutations in which the letters *o* and *o* exchange places are not distinguishable.)

23. Find the number of distinguishable permutations of the letters of the word *needed*.

24. How many permutations of the letters *a, b, e, g, h, k,* and *m* are there when taken

    (a) two at a time?

    (b) three at a time?

25. How many three-letter labels of new chemical products can be formed from the letters *a, b, c, d, f, g, l,* and *m*?

26. Find the number of distinguishable permutations that can be formed from the letters of the word *Mississippi.*

27. A family consisting of a mother, a father, and three children is having a picture taken. If all 5 people are arranged in a row, how many different photographs can be taken?

28. List all the combinations of the numbers 4, 3, 5, 8, and 9 taken three at a time.

In Exercises 29–37 evaluate the given expression.

29. $C(9, 3)$

30. $C(7, 3)$

31. $C(10, 2)$

32. $C(7, 1)$

33. $C(7, 7)$

34. $C(5, 4)$

35. $C(n, n - 1)$

36. $C(n, n - 2)$

37. $C(n + 1, n - 1)$

38. In how many ways can a committee of 2 faculty members and 3 students be selected from 8 faculty members and 10 students?

39. In how many ways can a basketball team of 5 players be selected from among 15 candidates?

40. In how many ways can a 4-card hand be dealt from a deck of 52 cards?

41. How many three-letter moped plates on a local campus can be formed for each of the following results?

    (a) if no letters can be repeated

    (b) if letters can be repeated

42. In a certain city each police car is staffed by two officers: one male and one female. A police captain, who needs to staff 8 cars, has 15 male officers and 12 female officers available. How many different teams can be formed?

43. How many different 10-card hands with 4 aces can be dealt from a deck of 52 cards?

44. A car manufacturer makes three different models, each of which is available in five different colors and with two different engines. How many cars must a dealer stock in the showroom to display the full line?

45. A penny, a nickel, a dime, a quarter, a half-dollar, and a silver dollar are to be arranged in a row. How many different arrangements can be formed if the penny and the dime must always be next to each other?

46. An automobile manufacturer who is planning an advertising campaign is considering seven newspapers, two magazines, three radio stations, and four television stations. In how many ways can five advertisements be placed?

    (a) if all five are to be in newspapers

    (b) if two are to be in newspapers, two on radio, and one on television

*47. In a certain police station there are 12 prisoners and 10 police officers. How many possible line-ups consisting of 4 prisoners and 3 officers can be formed?

*48. The notation

$$\binom{n}{r}$$

is often used in place of $C(n, r)$. Show that

$$\binom{n}{r} = \binom{n}{n-r}$$

*49. How many different 10-card hands with 6 red cards and 4 black cards can be dealt from a deck of 52 cards?

*50. A bin contains 12 transistors, 7 of which are defective. In how many ways can four transistors be chosen?

    (a) so that all four are defective

    (b) so that two are good and two are defective

    (c) so that all four are good

    (d) so that three are defective and one is good

*51. Find the number of distinguishable permutations that can be formed from the letters of the word *Mississippi* taken four at a time.

15.5   Probability

Definition

There is a vast difference between the statements "It will probably rain today" and "It is equally probable that a tossed coin will come up heads or tails." The first statement conveys an expectation but only in a vague sense; the latter statement is much more useful because it quantifies the notion of probability.

Let's take a closer look at what happens when we toss a coin. The event has only 2 possible outcomes: heads and tails. Since heads represents 1 of 2 possible outcomes, we say that the probability of a head is 1/2. Thus, we can define probability in the following way: If an event can occur in a total of t ways and s of these are considered successful, the probability of success is s/t. In short,

$$\text{probability} = \frac{\text{number of successful outcomes}}{\text{total number of outcomes}}$$

EXAMPLE 1   CALCULATING THE PROBABILITY OF AN EVENT

A container holds 1 red ball, 2 white balls, and 2 blue balls. If 1 ball is drawn, what is the probability that it will be white?

SOLUTION

The selection of a ball represents a possible outcome, so there are a total of 5 possible outcomes. Since there are 2 ways of achieving a successful outcome (a white ball),

$$\begin{matrix}\text{probability of} \\ \text{selecting a white ball}\end{matrix} = \frac{\text{number of successful outcomes}}{\text{total number of outcomes}} = \frac{2}{5}$$

✔ Progress Check 1

One card is drawn from an ordinary deck of 52 cards. What is the probability it is an ace?

Answer

$\dfrac{1}{13}$

EXAMPLE 2   CALCULATING THE PROBABILITY OF AN EVENT

A single die (whose faces contain the numbers 1, 2, 3, 4, 5, and 6) is tossed. What is the probability that the result is less than 5?

SOLUTION

There are 4 successful outcomes, occurring when the die shows a 1, 2, 3, or 4. Since there are 6 possible outcomes, we see that

$$\text{probability} = \frac{\text{number of successful outcomes}}{\text{total number of outcomes}}$$

$$= \frac{4}{6} = \frac{2}{3}$$

✔ Progress Check 2

A bag of coins contains 4 nickels, 5 dimes, and 10 quarters. If 1 coin is withdrawn, what is the probability that it will be worth less than 25 cents?

Answer

$\dfrac{9}{19}$

Principles of Probability

Let's consider a bag containing 3 red marbles and 5 brown marbles. It is easy to verify that the probability of drawing a red marble in a single draw is 3/8 and that the probability of drawing a brown marble is $5/8 = 1 - 3/8$. What is the probability of drawing either a red marble or a brown marble? Since any of the 8 possible outcomes is considered a success, the probability is $8/8 = 1$. What is the probability of drawing a black marble? Since there are no successful outcomes, the probability is $0/8 = 0$. Generalizing these results, we can state the following principles:

- A probability of 1 indicates certainty.
- A probability of 0 indicates impossibility.
- If p is the probability that an event will happen, $1 - p$ is the probability that it will not happen.

EXAMPLE 3   PROBABILITY OF EVENT NOT OCCURRING

While shuffling an ordinary deck of 52 cards, you drop 1 card. What is the probability that it is not a king?

SOLUTION

Since there are 4 kings in a deck, the probability of a king is $p = 4/52 = 1/13$. Then the probability that it is not a king is $1 - p = 12/13$.

> ✔ **Progress Check 3**
>
> Two people throw a single die. If player A rolls a 4, what is the probability that player B will not also roll a 4?
>
> **Answer**
>
> $\dfrac{5}{6}$

Applications

The rules for computing permutations and combinations are useful in solving probability problems.

EXAMPLE 4   COMBINATIONS AND PROBABILITY

A bag contains 3 green, 5 white, and 7 yellow balls. If 3 balls are drawn at random, what is the probability that they will all be white?

SOLUTION

We can select 3 white balls from 5 white balls in $C(5, 3)$ ways; we can select 3 balls from the bag of 15 balls in $C(15, 3)$ ways. Then

$$\text{probability of selecting} \atop \text{three white balls} = \frac{C(5, 3)}{C(15, 3)} = \frac{10}{455} = \frac{2}{91}$$

✔ Progress Check 4

Three cards are drawn from an ordinary deck of 52 cards. What is the probability that they are all aces?

Answer

$\dfrac{1}{5525}$

Many problems in probability involve the tossing of a pair of dice. Since the faces of the dice contain the numbers 1, 2, 3, 4, 5, and 6, the sum of the numbers on the 2 dice can be any of the numbers 2 through 12. The outcomes, however, are not equally probable. In Table 1 we display the possible outcomes of tossing a pair of dice. In Table 2 we then summarize the number of ways in which each sum can be obtained. The probability of tossing a 3 with a pair of dice is therefore 2/36, or 1/18; the probability of tossing a 7 is 6/36, or 1/6.

TABLE 1 *Possible Outcomes of Tossing a Pair of Dice*

Die 1	Die 2					
	1	2	3	4	5	6
1	2	3	4	5	6	7
2	3	4	5	6	7	8
3	4	5	6	7	8	9
4	5	6	7	8	9	10
5	6	7	8	9	10	11
6	7	8	9	10	11	12

TABLE 2 *Frequency of Outcomes of Tossing a Pair of Dice*

Sum of 2 dice	2	3	4	5	6	7	8	9	10	11	12
Number of ways	1	2	3	4	5	6	5	4	3	2	1

EXAMPLE 5   CALCULATING PROBABILITY WITH DICE

What is the probability of throwing a 10 or higher with a single throw of a pair of dice?

SOLUTION

The favorable outcomes are 10, 11, and 12, which, by Table 2, can occur in a total of 6 ways. Then

$$\text{probability} = \frac{\text{number of successful outcomes}}{\text{total number of outcomes}}$$

$$= \frac{6}{36} = \frac{1}{6}$$

✔ **Progress Check 5**

What is the probability of throwing no higher than a 5 with a single throw of a pair of dice?

Answer

$\dfrac{5}{18}$

Independent Events

We conclude our introduction to probability by considering the probability of successive, independent events. For example, if a card is drawn from a deck of 52 cards, that card is replaced in the deck, and a second card is drawn, what is the probability that both cards will be aces? Note that these events are independent since the second outcome in no way depends on the first outcome. Here is the principle that permits us to solve this type of problem:

> If p_1 is the probability that an event will occur and p_2 is the probability that a second, independent event will occur, then $p_1 p_2$ is the probability that both events will occur.

In our example, the probability that the first card drawn will be an ace is $p_1 = 4/52 = 1/13$; the probability that the second card drawn will be an ace is also $1/13 = p_2$. Then the probability of drawing aces successively is $p_1 p_2 = (1/13)(1/13) = 1/169$. Of course, we can extend this principle to more than two events by forming the product of the probabilities of the independent events.

EXAMPLE 6   CALCULATING PROBABILITY OF MULTIPLE EVENTS

What is the probability of throwing a 7 twice in succession with a pair of dice?

SOLUTION

From Table 2 we see that a 7 can occur in 6 ways, so the probability of throwing a 7 is $p_1 = 6/36 = 1/6$. The probability of throwing a 7 on the second roll is again $p_2 = 1/6$, so the probability of throwing a 7 on both rolls is $p_1p_2 = (1/6)(1/6) = 1/36$.

✔ **Progress Check 6**

What is the probability of throwing an 11 twice in succession with a pair of dice?

Answer

$\dfrac{1}{324}$

EXAMPLE 7   CALCULATING PROBABILITY OF MULTIPLE EVENTS

What is the probability of drawing an ace 3 times in succession from a deck of 52 cards if the drawn cards are not replaced?

SOLUTION

On the first draw, the probability of obtaining an ace is $p_1 = 4/52$. Since the ace is not replaced in the deck, there remain 3 aces and a total of 51 cards, so the probability of obtaining a second ace is $p_2 = 3/51$. Arguing the same way, we see that there now remain 2 aces and 50 cards, so the probability of drawing a third ace is $p_3 = 2/50$. Thus, the probability of drawing aces 3 times in succession without replacement is

$$p_1p_2p_3 = \frac{4}{52} \cdot \frac{3}{51} \cdot \frac{2}{50} = \frac{1}{5525}$$

✔ **Progress Check 7**

What is the probability of drawing a spade 3 times in succession from a deck of 52 cards if the drawn cards are not replaced?

Answer

$\dfrac{11}{850}$

EXAMPLE 8   CALCULATING PROBABILITY OF MULTIPLE EVENTS

What is the probability of throwing a 5 only on the first of 2 successive throws with a single die?

SOLUTION

The probability of throwing a 5 on the first toss is $p_1 = 1/6$. A success on the second toss consists of *not* throwing a 5 and has a probability $p_2 = 1 - p_1 = 5/6$. The probability of the desired result is

$$p_1p_2 = \frac{1}{6} \cdot \frac{5}{6} = \frac{5}{36}$$

✔ **Progress Check 8**

What is the probability of throwing a 7 or an 11 on the first of two successive throws with a pair of dice but not on the second throw?

Answer

$\dfrac{14}{81}$

EXAMPLE 9   EMPIRICAL PROBABILITY AND MULTIPLE EVENTS

A transistor manufacturer finds that 81 of every 1000 transistors made are defective. What is the probability that 2 transistors selected at random will both prove to be defective?

SOLUTION

This problem is an example of **empirical probability**, that is, probability obtained from experience or measurement rather than by theoretical means. The probability that a transistor is defective is $p_1 = 81/1000$. The probability that a second transistor is defective is $p_2 = 81/1000$. Thus, the probability that both transistors will be defective is

$$p_1 p_2 = \frac{81}{1000} \cdot \frac{81}{1000} = \frac{6561}{1,000,000}$$

✔ **Progress Check 9**

The probability of rain in a certain town on any given day is 1/4. What is the probability of having a rainy Monday, a dry Tuesday, and a rainy Wednesday?

Answer

$\dfrac{3}{64}$

Exercise Set 15.5

1. If a single die is tossed, what is the probability that an odd number will appear?

2. If two dice are tossed, what is the probability of having at least one 5 showing on the top faces of the dice?

3. If a card is randomly selected from an ordinary deck of 52 cards, what is the probability for each of the following results?

   (a) a red card   (b) a spade   (c) a king

4. Suppose that 2 coins are tossed. What is the probability for each of the following results?

   (a) both tails   (b) at least 1 heads

   (c) neither tails   (d) 1 heads and 1 tails

5. If 2 dice are tossed, what is the probability for each of the following results?

   (a) at least 1 of the dice will show a 4 on its top face

   (b) the sum of the numbers on the dice will be 8

   (c) neither a 3 nor a 4 will appear on the top face of a die

6. If a card is picked at random from a standard deck of 52 cards, what is the probability for each of the following results?

(a) a club (b) a 4

(c) not an ace (d) a 4 of spades

(e) either an ace or a king

(d) neither an ace nor a king

7. The quality control department of a calculator manufacturer determines that 1 percent of all calculators made are defective. What is the probability that a buyer of a calculator will get the following?

(a) a good calculator

(b) a defective calculator

8. A photography club consisting of 18 women and 12 men wishes to elect a steering committee composed of 3 members. If every member is equally likely to be elected, what is the probability for each of the following results?

(a) all 3 members will be women

(b) none of the members will be a woman

(c) exactly 1 member will be a woman

(d) at least 1 member will be a woman

9. A box contains 97 good bulbs and 5 defective bulbs. If 3 bulbs are chosen at random, what is the probability for each of the following results?

(a) all three bulbs will be defective

(b) exactly one of the bulbs will be defective

(c) none of the bulbs will be defective

10. Suppose that 2 cards are to be drawn in succession from a deck of 52 cards. What is the probability that both cards will be aces for each of the following?

(a) drawn cards are replaced

(b) drawn cards are not replaced

11. Suppose that 4 cards are selected, without replacement, from a deck of 52 cards. What is the probability that they are all hearts?

12. If the probability of getting an A in this course is 0.2, what is the probability of not getting an A?

13. The board of trustees of a university consists of 14 women and 12 men. Suppose that an executive committee of 6 persons is to be elected and that every trustee is equally likely to be elected. Find the probability that the committee will consist of 3 men and 3 women.

14. Suppose that the probability of a cloudy day in a certain town in England is 0.6.

(a) What is the probability of a clear day?

(b) What is the probability of 2 consecutive clear days?

15. A bag contains 6 blue marbles, 5 green marbles, and 7 yellow marbles. If 5 marbles are chosen without replacement, what is the probability that 2 will be blue, 2 will be green, and 1 will be yellow?

16. Suppose that 2 cards have been chosen at random from a deck of 52 cards. What is the probability that 1 card is an ace and the other card is not a king?

17. If 2 percent of cameras made on a production line are defective, what is the probability that 4 cameras chosen at random will be the following

(a) all good (b) all defective

18. A fraternity consists of 12 seniors, 10 juniors, and 14 sophomores. A steering committee of 7 members is randomly chosen. What is the probability that it consists of 3 seniors, 2 juniors, and 2 sophomores?

■ ■ ■

Chapter Summary

Terms and Symbols

arithmetic progression	565	empirical probability	604	infinite geometric series	578
arithmetic sequence	565	expansion of $(a + b)^n$	581	infinite sequence	563
arithmetic series	568	factorial, $n!$	583	Pascal's triangle	581
binomial formula	582	geometric means	574	permutation, $P(n, r)$	589
binomial theorem	581	geometric progression	572	probability	598
combination, $C(n, r)$	592	geometric sequence	572	recursive formula	565
common difference	565	geometric series	575	series	568
common ratio	572	independent events	602	term	563

Key Ideas for Review

Topic	Page	Key Idea
Sequence	563	A sequence is a function whose domain is restricted to the set of natural numbers. We generally write a sequence by using subscript notation; that is, a_n replaces $a(n)$.
arithmetic	565	An arithmetic sequence has a common difference d between terms. We can define an arithmetic sequence recursively by writing $a_n = a_{n-1} + d$ and specifying a_1 and d.
geometric	572	A geometric sequence has a common ratio r between terms. We can define a geometric sequence recursively by writing $a_n = ra_{n-1}$ and specifying a_1 and r.
nth terms	567	The formulas for the nth term of an arithmetic or geometric sequence are $$a_n = a_1 + (n - 1)d \qquad \text{Arithmetic}$$ $$a_n = a_1 r^{n-1} \qquad \text{Geometric}$$
Series	568	A series is the sum of the terms of a sequence.
sum	568	The formulas for the sums S_n of the first n terms of arithmetic and geometric sequences are $$S_n = \frac{n}{2}(a_1 + a_n) \qquad \text{Arithmetic}$$ $$S_n = \frac{n}{2}[2a_1 + (n - 1)d] \quad \text{Arithmetic}$$ $$S_n = \frac{a_1(1 - r^n)}{1 - r} \qquad \text{Geometric}$$
Infinite geometric series	578	If the common ratio r satisfies $-1 < r < 1$, then the infinite geometric series has the sum S given by $$S = \frac{a_1}{1 - r}$$
Factorial notation	583	The notation $n!$ indicates the product of the natural numbers 1 through n: $$n! = n(n - 1)(n - 2) \cdots 2 \cdot 1 \qquad \text{for } n \geq 1$$ $$0! = 1$$

Topic	Page	Key Idea
Binomial coefficient $\binom{n}{r}$	584	The notation $\binom{n}{r}$ is defined by the formula $$\binom{n}{r} = \frac{n!}{r!(n-r)!}$$ and is useful in writing out the binomial formula.
Binomial formula	582	The binomial formula provides the terms of the expansion of $(a + b)^n$: $$(a+b)^n = a^n + \frac{n!}{1!(n-1)!}a^{n-1}b + \frac{n!}{2!(n-2)!}a^{n-2}b^2$$ $$+ \frac{n!}{3!(n-3)!}a^{n-3}b + \cdots + \frac{n!}{r!(n-r)!}a^{n-r}b^r + \cdots + b^n$$
Permutations	589	Permutations involve arrangements of the order of objects; thus, abc and bac are distinct permutations of the letters a, b, and c. The number $P(n, r)$ of permutations of n objects taken r at a time is $$P(n, r) = \frac{n!}{(n-r)!}$$
Combinations	592	Combinations involve selection of objects; the order is not significant. If we are selecting three letters from a box containing the letters a, b, c, and d, then abc and bac are the same combination. The number $C(n, r)$ of combinations of n objects taken r at a time is $$C(n, r) = \frac{n!}{r!(n-r)!}$$
Probability	598	Probability is a means of expressing the likelihood of the occurrence of an event. It is the ratio of the number of successful outcomes to the total number of outcomes.
certainty	600	A probability of 1 indicates that an event is certain to occur, whereas a probability of impossibility 0 indicates that an event cannot possibly occur.
independent events	602	If p_1 and p_2 are the probabilities of the occurrence of two independent events, then $p_1 p_2$ is the probability that both events will occur.

Common Errors

1. The sum of the first n terms of a geometric sequence is given by

$$S_n = \frac{a_1(1 - r^n)}{1 - r}$$

Don't write

$$S_n = \frac{a_1(1 - r)^n}{1 - r}$$

2. The formula for the sum of the terms of an infinite geometric sequence can only be used if $|r| < 1$.

Review Exercises

Solutions to exercises whose numbers are in bold are in the Solutions section in the back of the book.

15.1 In Exercises 1 and 2 write the first three terms and the tenth term of the sequence whose nth term is given.

1. $a_n = n^2 + n + 1$ 2. $a_n = \dfrac{n^3 - 1}{n + 1}$

In Exercises 3 and 4 find the specified term of the arithmetic sequence whose first term is a_1 and whose common difference is d.

3. $a_1 = -2, d = 2$; 21st term

4. $a_1 = 6, d = -1$; 16th term

In Exercises 5 and 6, given two terms of an arithmetic sequence, find the specified term.

5. $a_1 = 4, a_{16} = 9$; 13th term

6. $a_1 = -4, a_{23} = -15$; 26th term

In Exercises 7 and 8 find the sum of the first 25 terms of the arithmetic sequence whose first term is a_1 and whose common difference is d.

7. $a_1 = -\dfrac{1}{3}, d = \dfrac{1}{3}$

8. $a_1 = 6, d = -2$

15.2 In Exercises 9 and 10 determine the common ratio of the given geometric sequence.

9. $2, -6, 18, -54, \ldots$ 10. $-\dfrac{1}{2}, \dfrac{3}{4}, -\dfrac{9}{8}, \dfrac{27}{16}, \ldots$

In Exercises 11 and 12, write the first four terms of the geometric sequence whose first term is a_1 and whose common ratio is r.

11. $a_1 = 5, r = \dfrac{1}{5}$ 12. $a_1 = -2, r = -1$

13. Find the sixth term of the geometric sequence $-4, 6, -9, \ldots$

14. Find the eighth term of a geometric sequence for which $a_1 = -2$ and $a_5 = -32$.

15. Insert two geometric means between 3 and 1/72.

16. Find the sum of the first six terms of the geometric sequence whose first three terms are $\frac{1}{3}, \frac{1}{6}, \frac{1}{12}$.

17. Find the sum of the first six terms of the geometric sequence for which $a_1 = -2$ and $r = 3$.

In Exercises 18 and 19 find the sum of the infinite geometric series.

18. $5 + \dfrac{5}{2} + \dfrac{5}{4} + \cdots$

19. $3 - 2 + \dfrac{4}{3} - \cdots$

15.3 In Exercises 20−22 expand and simplify.

20. $(2x - y)^4$ 21. $\left(\dfrac{x}{2} - 2\right)^4$

22. $(x^2 + 1)^3$

In Exercises 23−28 evaluate the expression.

23. $6!$ 24. $\dfrac{13!}{11!2!}$

25. $\dfrac{(n - 1)!(n + 1)!}{n!n!}$ 26. $\dbinom{6}{4}$

27. $\dbinom{3}{0}$ 28. $\dbinom{10}{8}$

15.4 29. Four novels have been selected for display on a shelf. How many different arrangements are possible?

30. Find the number of distinguishable permutations of the letters in the word *soothe*.

31. In how many ways can a tennis team of 6 players be selected from 10 candidates?

32. In how many ways can a consonant and a vowel be chosen from the letters in the word *fouled*?

15.5 33. If 2 dice are tossed, what is the probability that the sum of the numbers on the dice will be 7 or 11?

34. A box contains 3 red pens and 4 white pens. If 2 pens are selected at random, what is the probability that they will both be white?

35. Two cards are drawn in succession from a deck of 52 cards. What is the probability that the cards will be a king and an ace if the first card drawn is not replaced?

36. If 10 percent of the trees in a region are found to be diseased, what is the probability that 2 trees chosen at random are both free of disease?

37. Six husband-wife teams volunteer for an experiment in parapsychology. If 4 persons are selected at random to participate in the experiment, what is the probability that they will be two husband-wife teams?

Progress Test 15A

1. Write the first four terms of the sequence whose nth term is
$$a_n = \frac{n + 2}{n^2 - 2}$$

2. Find the 8th term of the arithmetic sequence $3, \frac{5}{2}, 2, \dots$.

3. Find the 16th term of the arithmetic sequence whose first and 30th terms are 2 and 60, respectively.

4. Find the sum of the first 12 terms of an arithmetic sequence whose fist term is -1 and whose common difference is $\frac{1}{2}$.

5. The first term of an arithmetic sequence is -5, the last term is 35, and the sum of the corresponding series is 165. Find the number of terms and the common difference.

6. Find the 7th term of the geometric sequence $16, 8, 4, \dots$.

7. Find the sum of the first six terms of the geometric sequence whose first term is 6 and whose common ratio is $\frac{1}{2}$.

8. Find the sum of the infinite geometric series
$$5 + \frac{5}{2} + \frac{5}{4} \dots$$

9. Expand and simplify $\left(x - \frac{y}{2}\right)^4$.

10. Evaluate $\frac{9!6!}{10!5!}$.

11. Five paintings are to be hung on a wall in a side-by-side arrangement. If seven paintings are available, how many arrangements are possible?

12. A row in a stamp album provides space for 5 postage stamps. There are 6 airmail and 5 regular postage stamps available. How many arrangements can be made consisting of 3 airmail and 2 regular postage stamps if the stamps of each type must be kept together?

13. In how many ways can a committee of 5 be selected from a group of 10 people if the past chairperson must serve on the committee?

14. An army task requires 2 privates, 2 sergeants, and a major. If 5 privates, 4 sergeants, and 3 majors are available, in how many ways can a team be formed?

15. The telephone company uses white, black, and green telephones, which are distributed to new customers at random. If an apartment dweller requests 2 telephones, what is the probability that they will be the same color?

16. Four marbles are removed at random from a box containing 4 purple, 3 blue, and 3 red marbles. What is the probability that these are 2 purple and 2 blue marbles?

Progress Test 15B

1. Write the first four terms of the sequence whose nth term is

$$a_n = n^2 + \frac{1}{n}$$

2. Find the 11th term of the arithmetic sequence $4, \frac{17}{4}, \frac{9}{2}, \dots$.

3. Find the 40th term of the arithmetic sequence whose first and 21st terms are 5 and 15, respectively.

4. Find the sum of the first 15 terms of an arithmetic sequence whose first term is 4 and whose common difference is $-\frac{1}{4}$.

5. The first term of an arithmetic sequence is -3, the last term is -39, and the sum of the corresponding series is -525. Find the number of terms and the common difference.

6. Find the 6th term of the geometric sequence 1, 3, 9, ...

7. Find the sum of the first five terms of the geometric sequence whose first term is 8 and whose common ratio is $-\frac{1}{2}$.

8. Find the sum of the infinite geometric series

$$3 - 2 + \frac{4}{3} - \dots$$

9. Expand and simplify $\left(\frac{x^2}{2} - y\right)^4$.

10. Simplify $\dfrac{7!(n-2)!}{6!n!}$.

11. There is a space available for three books on a shelf. If there are six books from which to select, how many arrangements can be made?

12. A store clerk wants to display 3 symphonic and 3 jazz records on a shelf. There are 6 symphonic and 5 jazz records available. How many arrangements of the records are possible if the records of each type must be kept together?

13. In how many different ways can a committee of 6 persons be chosen if 9 people are available?

14. The capitals A, B, C, consonants m, n, p, r, and vowels a, e, i, o, u can be used for making words. If each word must begin with a capital and must contain 3 consonants and 2 vowels, how many "words" can be made?

15. A manufacturer finds that 2 percent of his products are defective. If 3 items are selected at random, what is the probability that they will all be defective?

16. What is the probability that a throw of two dice will result in a sum of 7 or greater?

Chapter 15 Project

Read the chapter opener about the grateful king. How many grains of wheat were on that final square of the chessboard?

Let your graphing calculator help you. Use the SEQUENCE options to set this problem up as a sequence.

Now use the cumulative sum option to find the total number of grains on the board.

■ ■ ■

Answers to Odd-Numbered Exercises, Review Exercises, and Progress Tests

Chapter 1

Exercise Set 1.1, page 7

1. a, b, c, d

3. a, c

5. a, b, c, d

7. a, c, d

9. c, e

11. c, e

13. F

15. F

17. F

19. T

21. T

23.

25. (a) 10   (b) −20   (c) 20   (d) −5

27. 0

29. −4

31. −5

33. 3

35. 0

37. 5

39.

41. Although pi is irrational, the calculator rounds it off in order to display an approximate value.

Exercise Set 1.2, page 19

1. 4

3. 27

5. 0

7. 8/33

9. 10/3

11. 4/3

13. 3/2

15. 12

17. 7

19. 25

21. 60

23. 180

25. 17/12

27. 5/12

29. 8/23

31. 20/39

33. 1/5, 0.2

35. 131/200, 0.655

37. 6/125, 0.048

39. 6/5, 1.2

41. 1/500, 0.002

43. 5%

45. 42.5%

47. 628%

49. 60%

51. 225%

53. 28.57%

55. 21

57. 42

59. 0.2

73. $115,200

75. $32.20

61. 5/32

63. 125/144

77. 8%

79. $8649.60

65. 52/89

67. 850/304

81. $399,000

69. $58

71. $6480

Exercise Set 1.3, page 23

1. T

3. T

29. 18.84

31. 9.4

5. 11

7. 2

33. 3.76

35. 1.06

9. 64

11. 1/11

37. (a) $2160   (b) $2480   (c) $2080   (d) $2106.67

13. 10

15. 5

39. $3(1.25) + 2(1.10) + 1.5(2.29)$

17. 33

19. 1/2

41. $0.85d + 1.35h + 0.8f$

21. 12

23. 8/3

43. -0.358; approximately -0.343

25. 5/4

27. 1/3

Exercise Set 1.4, page 28

1. 8

3. -7

41. 0

43. -3

5. 2

7. -2

45. -4

47. -12

9. 3

11. 2

49. $2x - 3y$

51. x/y

13. 8

15. -5

53. $-4/x$

55. -7

17. -13

19. -2

57. 2/3

59. 1

21. -3

23. 10

61. -1

63. 216

25. $-1/2$

27. 4

65. 8/125

67. 625/81

29. -3

31. $-3/5$

69. -8

71. 3

33. 18

35. $-9/2$

73. 12°C

75. $1200

37. 6

39. 0

77. $y - x$

79. average profit $= \$500$

Exercise Set 1.5, page 34

1. commutative (addition)

13. associative (multiplication)

3. commutative (multiplication)

15. commutative and associative (multiplication)

5. distributive

17. commutative and associative (addition)

7. distributive

19. $1 - 2 \neq 2 - 1; 1 - (3 - 2) \neq (1 - 3) - 2$

9. associative (addition)

21. $2(a + 2) = 2a + 4$

11. commutative (addition)

23. $(a - b)2 = 2a - 2b$

25. $(2a + 3) + a = 3(a + 1)$ 27. $4 - x$

29. $-x - 5$ 31. $12x$

33. $6abc$ 35. $6 + 8a - 4b$

37. $-\dfrac{1}{2x}$ 39. $-\dfrac{4}{3}xy$

41. $2ab$ 43. $\dfrac{5}{4}x - \dfrac{1}{4}y$

45. $3a - \dfrac{5}{2}b + \dfrac{15}{2}c$

47. $4x + 4y - 2z + 4w$ 49. $x + 2y + 2u - 8$

51. 1.31 53. 2.01

55. $a = 2, b = 3, c = 4$ 57. $a = 3, b = 2, c = 5$

Exercise Set 1.6, page 43

1. 2 3. 1.5

5. -2 7. 1

9. 4 11. 2

13. $1/5$ 15. -1

17. 6 19. -7

21. 1 23. 0.31

25. 3 27. 2

29. $8/5$ 31. $4 > 1$

33. $2 \leqslant 3$ 35. $3 \geqslant 0$

37. $<$ 39. $>$

41. $<$ 43. $<$

45. $>$ 47. $<$

49. $>$ 51. $<$

53. $>$ 55. $>$

57. $>$ 59. $x \geqslant -1$

61. $-3 \leqslant x < 4$

63.

65.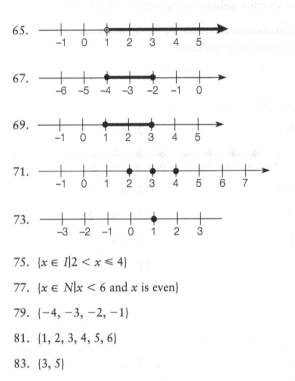

67.

69.

71.

73.

75. $\{x \in I | 2 < x \leqslant 4\}$

77. $\{x \in N | x < 6 \text{ and } x \text{ is even}\}$

79. $\{-4, -3, -2, -1\}$

81. $\{1, 2, 3, 4, 5, 6\}$

83. $\{3, 5\}$

85. The distance from a to b equals the distance from b to a.

Review Exercises, page 46

1. $\{1, 2, 3, 4\}$ 2. $\{-3, -2, -1\}$

3. $\{2\}$ 4. T

5. F   6. F

7. F

8.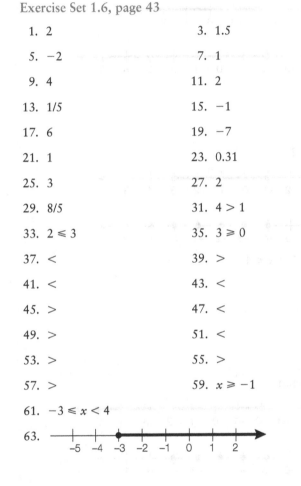

9. 3 10. -4

11. 0 12. 14

13. $-5/2$ 14. $16/35$

15. $6/5$ 16. $6/5$

17. $-15/23$ 18. $7/100, 0.07$

19. $9/400, 0.0225$ 20. 452%

21. 2.1%

22. 2%

23. T

24. F

25. F

26. T

27. $51

28. −2

29. −2

30. −8

31. −1

32. 1

33. 8

34. 11

35. $y − x + 1000$

36. distributive

37. associative (addition), commutative (addition)

38. distributive, commutative (multiplication), commutative (addition)

39. associative (multiplication), commutative (multiplication)

40. $2(a + 3) = 2a + 6$

41. $\dfrac{4 + a}{2} = 2 + a/2$

42. $−2(a − 3) = −2a + 6$

43. $2(ab) = (2b)a$

44. −1/7

45. 3/2

46. $a = 3, b = −3$

47. 5

48. 4

49. $x \geq −1$

50. $x < 2$

51.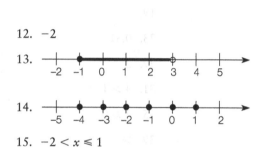

52.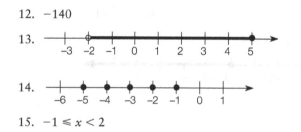

Progress Test 1A, page 48

1. b

2. c

3.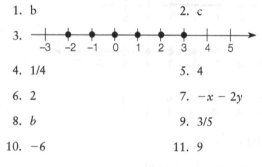

4. 1/4

5. 4

6. 2

7. $−x − 2y$

8. b

9. 3/5

10. −6

11. 9

12. −2

13.

14.

15. $−2 < x \leq 1$

Progress Test 1B, page 48

1. c

2. c

3.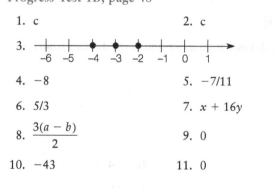

4. −8

5. −7/11

6. 5/3

7. $x + 16y$

8. $\dfrac{3(a − b)}{2}$

9. 0

10. −43

11. 0

12. −140

13.

14.

15. $−1 \leq x < 2$

Chapter 2

Exercise Set 2.1, page 59

1. T
3. F
5. T
7. T
9. 4
11. −5/4
13. −2
15. 1
17. −4/3
19. 2
21. 6
23. 3
25. 4
27. 3/2
29. −10/3
31. −2
33. 3
35. 5
37. −7/2
39. −7
41. 1
43. $8/(5 - k)$
45. $(6 + k)/5$
47. C
49. I
51. C
53. 4
55. 20
57. 10.25
61. $x = 2050$. x represents the number of calories the man should eat each day to lose one pound per week.

Exercise Set 2.2, page 66

1. $250
3. 50
5. 8.5 cents
7. 260
9. 80
11. no
13. $1.20
15. 8
17. 38
19. 6
21. 9 and 12
23. 11, 3
25. 24, 27
27. 15, 45
29. 16, 28
31. 8
33. 5, 13
35. 68°F
37. $12.30
39. 4 m and 8 m
41. 9.5 m by 27.5 m
43. 9 cm
45. 65°, 65°, and 50°
47. $W = 5, L = 15$
49. $W = 27, L = 43$
51. 5, 8, 11

Exercise Set 2.3, page 71

1. $\dfrac{C}{2\pi}$
3. $\dfrac{S}{2\pi r}$
5. $\dfrac{2A}{h} - b'$
7. $\dfrac{A - p}{Pr}$
9. $\dfrac{a_n - a_1}{d} + 1$
11. $\dfrac{S - a_1}{S}$
13. $\dfrac{A}{2\pi r} - r$
15. $\dfrac{3V}{\pi r^2}$
17. $\dfrac{2s}{t^2}$
19. $\dfrac{S}{(l + r)^t}$
21. $\dfrac{A - c}{b}$
23. $-\dfrac{2kt}{5A + 3bt}$
25. (a) $\dfrac{A - P}{Pt}$ (b) $\dfrac{A - P}{Pr}$
27. $\dfrac{a(1 + A)}{1 - A}$
29. $\dfrac{a - St}{t - S}$

Exercise Set 2.4, page 76

1. c, d, e

3. a, c, d, e

5. $x < 4$

7. $x < -6$

9. $x \geq 5$

11. $a > -1$

13. $y < -1/2$

15. $x \geq 0$

17. $r < 2$

19. $x \geq 1$

21. $y \leq 8$

23. $x \geq 1$

25. $x \geq -2$

27. $x < 3/2$

29. $x > -12$

31. $a > 9/2$

33. $x \leq 7$

35. $-1/2 < x \leq 5/4$

37. $-10/3 < x < -4/3$

39. $-3 \leq x \leq -2$

41. $-3 < x \leq -1$

43. $-1 \leq x < 2$

45. over 300 miles

47. $2000

49. $4 \leq h \leq 16$

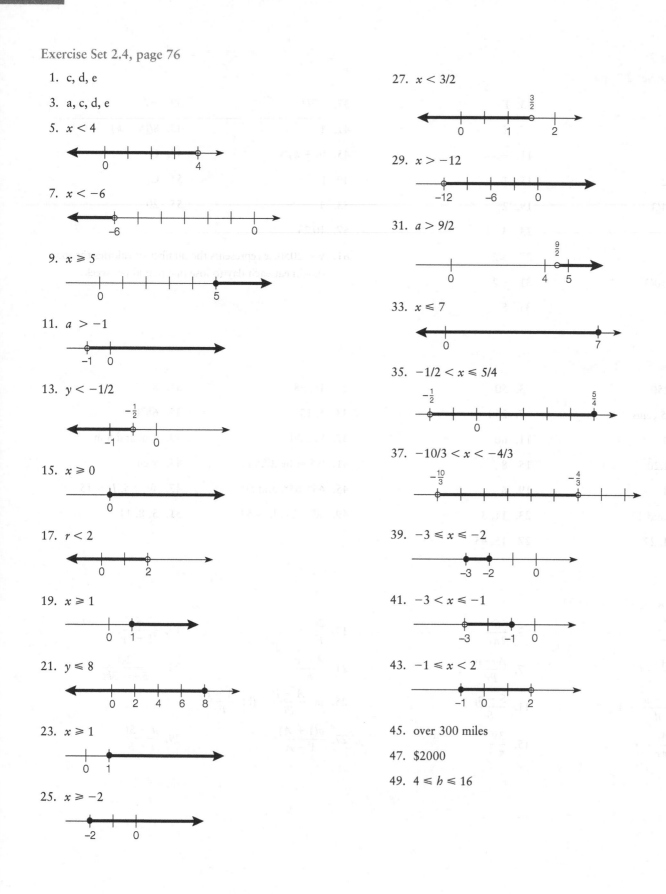

Exercise Set 2.5, page 81

1. b, d

3. b, d

5. b, c

7. e

9. 1, −5

11. 11/2, 9/2

13. 1, −2

15. 2, −2/3

17. 2, −4/3

19. −5/2, 1/2

21. −5 < x < 5

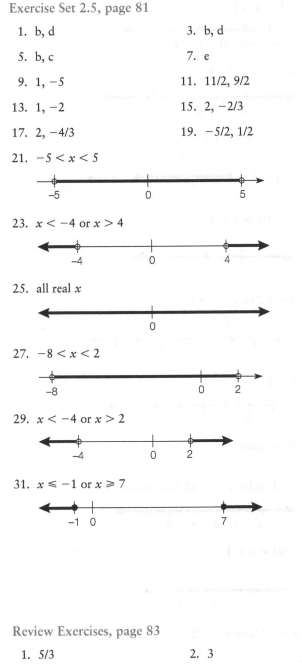

23. x < −4 or x > 4

25. all real x

27. −8 < x < 2

29. x < −4 or x > 2

31. x ≤ −1 or x ≥ 7

33. −6 ≤ x ≤ 2

35. all real x

37. −1 ≤ x ≤ 2

39. x > 5/3 or x < −1

41. x < −1 or x > 0

43. −5 < x < 7

45. −7/2 < x < 9/2

47. $|x − 100| ≤ 2$; x = 98, 99, 100, 101, 102

49. 3, −7

51. 0 < a < 3

53. a < 3, a > 7

Review Exercises, page 83

1. 5/3

2. 3

3. 6

4. 2

5. 1/2

6. 1/2

7. The domestic profit is 14 million dollars; the foreign profit is 5 million dollars.

8. One book costs $25; the other costs $19.

9. 20 sec

10. 12 in by 11 in

11. $\dfrac{r − 2s}{4t}$

12. $\dfrac{2B + C + D}{3}$

13. $\dfrac{3A + C − D}{2}$

14. $\dfrac{ef − g − 2a}{3d}$

15. x < 3

16. x ≤ 6

17. x > 1

18. x ≥ 5/3

19. x > 7

20. no real x

21. 3/2 < x < 3

22. −5/3 < x ≤ 2/3

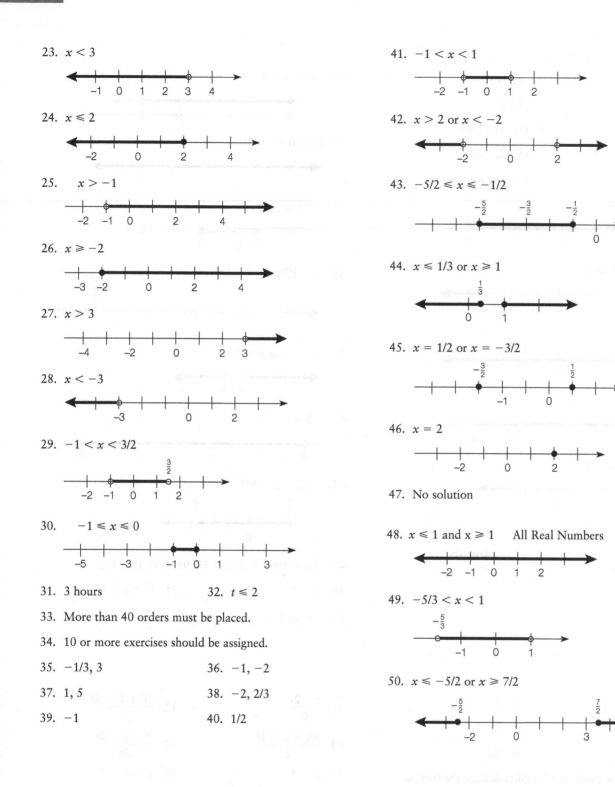

23. $x < 3$

24. $x \leq 2$

25. $x > -1$

26. $x \geq -2$

27. $x > 3$

28. $x < -3$

29. $-1 < x < 3/2$

30. $-1 \leq x \leq 0$

31. 3 hours   32. $t \leq 2$

33. More than 40 orders must be placed.

34. 10 or more exercises should be assigned.

35. $-1/3$, 3   36. -1, -2

37. 1, 5   38. -2, 2/3

39. -1 40. 1/2

41. $-1 < x < 1$

42. $x > 2$ or $x < -2$

43. $-5/2 \leq x \leq -1/2$

44. $x \leq 1/3$ or $x \geq 1$

45. $x = 1/2$ or $x = -3/2$

46. $x = 2$

47. No solution

48. $x \leq 1$ and $x \geq 1$ All Real Numbers

49. $-5/3 < x < 1$

50. $x \leq -5/2$ or $x \geq 7/2$

Progress Test 2A, page 84

1. 15/4

2. −4

3. F

4. $h = V/\pi r^2$

5. $x = \dfrac{-1}{k+2}$

6. 70

7. 3200

8. $L = 21/2$, $W = 15/2$

9. 14, 16, 18

10. $3000 at 6%, $2000 at 7%

11. $x > -2$

12. $x \geqslant 1$

13. 7/2, −3/2

14. $-10 \leqslant x \leqslant 14$

15. $x > 1$ or $x < -6$

Progress Test 2B, page 84

1. −2

2. 5

3. F

4. $\dfrac{1}{h}(2A - ch) = b$

5. $\dfrac{1}{2(k-1)}$

6. 40

7. 80

8. $W = 7$, $L = 4$

9. 25, 21

10. $4000 at 5%, $4000 at 8%

11. $x < -5/2$

12. $x \leqslant -1$

13. 3, −1/3

14. $x \geqslant 15/2$ or $x \leqslant -9/2$

15. $-1/3 < x < 1$

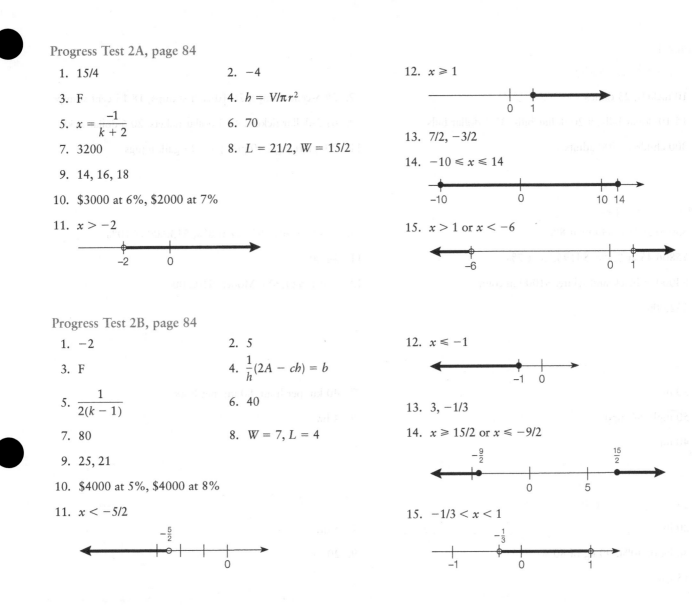

Chapter 3

Exercise Set 3.1, page 93

1. 10 nickels, 25 dimes

3. 14 10-dollar bills, 8 20-dollar bills, 32 5-dollar bills

5. 300 children, 400 adults

7. 28 5-cent stamps, 26 10-cent stamps, 18 15-cent stamps

9. 61 3-dollar tickets, 40 5-dollar tickets, 20 6-dollar tickets

11. 20 quart jugs, 40 pint jugs, 12 gallon jugs

Exercise Set 3.2, page 97

1. $5000 at 7%, $3000 at 8%

3. $5806.45 at 8.5%, $4193.55 at 7%

5. $3000 in black-and-white, $1000 in color

7. $32,000

9. $3400 at 6%, $3700 at 8%, $13,600 at 10%

11. $4.80

13. Goya: $24,900; Monet: $10,800

Exercise Set 3.3, page 102

1. 20 hr.

3. 50 mph, 54 mph

5. 40 mi

7. 40 km per hour, 80 km per hour

9. 4 hr.

Exercise Set 3.4, page 108

1. 20 lb.

3. 30 kg of 40%, 90 kg of 80%

5. 15 gal.

7. 5 qt.

9. 20 lb.

Review Exercises, page 109

1. 3 quarters, 6 dimes, 8 half-dollars

2. 4 16-transistor components, 2 48-transistor components, 5 64-transistor components

3. 29 2-ton slabs, 9 5-ton slabs, 59 8-ton slabs

4. 4 20-cent stamps, 7 40-cent stamps, 2 1-dollar stamps

5. $15,000 at 10%, $25,000 at 8%

6. $4000 in classical, $8000 in popular

7. $4500 at 10% profit, $2500 at 5% loss

8. $5000 to the AB company, $5500 to the CD company, $4600 to the EF company

9. 200 mph, 100 mph   10. .6 hr. or 36 min.   17. 0.0000013%   18. 0.08755 mL

11. .57 hr.   12. 400 mph, 500 mph   19. There are 172 L of gas in the mixture, and 17% is the final concentration of the mixture.

13. 2 lbs.   14. 20 gal.

15. 5 lbs.   16. 5 lb.

Progress Test 3A, page 111

1. $C = 4T - 3$

2. 17, 23

3. $L = 10/3$ cm, $W = 8/3$ cm

4. 3 quarters, 10 dimes, 17 nickels

5. six 30-pound, six 50-pound, eleven 60-pound crates

6. $8000

7. $6000 at 6.5%, $6200 at 7.5%, $12,300 at 9%

8. moped: 15 mph; car: 45 mph

9. 240 miles

10. 30 oz. of 60%, 90 oz. of 80%

11. 37.5 cc

Progress Test 3B, page 111

1. $D = \frac{1}{3}R + 4$

2. 16, 32

3. first side: 3.6 cm; second side: 5.8 cm; third side: 5.6 cm

4. fourteen $1, four $5, two $10 coupons

5. six 1-oz., five 2-oz., three 3-oz. samples

6. $3000 at 6%, $15,000 at 7.2%

7. $8000 at 6%, $6000 at 8%

8. 6 P.M.   9. 12 hr.

10. 3.75 lb.   11. 20 gal.

Chapter 4

Exercise Set 4.1, page 120

1. base: 2; exponent: 5

3. base: t; exponent: 4

5. bases: 3, y; exponents: 1, 5

7. bases: 3, x, y; exponents: 1, 2, 3

9. 3^3

11. $\left(\dfrac{1}{3}\right)^4$

13. $3y^4$

15. (a) 36   (b) -36

17. b^7

19. $6x^6$

21. $-20y^9$

23. $\dfrac{20}{21}v^8$

25. $-3x^4$

27. c, d

29.

Term	$4x^4$	$-2x^2$	x	-3
Coefficient	4	-2	1	-3

31.

Term	$\frac{2}{3}x^3y$	$\frac{1}{2}xy$	$-y$	2
Coefficient	$\frac{2}{3}$	$\frac{1}{2}$	-1	2

33.

Term	$\frac{1}{3}x^3$	$\frac{1}{2}x^2y$	$-2x$	y	7
Coefficient	$\frac{1}{3}$	$\frac{1}{2}$	-2	1	7

35.

Term	$3x^3$	$-2x^2$	3
Degree	3	2	0

37.

Term	$4x^4$	$-5x^3$	$2x^2$	$-5x$	1
Degree	4	3	2	1	0

39.

Term	$\frac{3}{2}x^4$	$2xy^2$	y^3	$-y$	2
Degree	4	3	3	1	0

41. 3

43. 3

45. 4

47. b

49. 13

51. 11

53. 176.2

55. πr^2

57. (a) the area of the field
    (b) the perimeter of the rectangle
    (c) the perimeter of the square
    (d) the total amount of fencing

Exercise Set 4.2, page 123

1. $7x$

3. $3x^3 - 6x^2$

5. $4x^2 - x + 4$

7. $7x^2 + 3$

9. $-3rs$

11. $\dfrac{6}{5}rs^3 - 2r^2s^2 - r^2s + 2r^2 + 7$

13. $-x^2 - 4x + 14$

15. $y^2 - 2x^2 - xy + 7y$

17. $24y$

19. $6x^2 - 3$

21. $x^2y^2 + 3xy - 3y - x - 3$

23. $\dfrac{19}{10}x^3 - 3x^2 + x + 2$

25. $3rs^3 - 2rs + r - s + 3$

27. $2x^2 - 6x + 9$

29. $4xy + 2y + 3$

31. $5r^2s^2 + rs^2 - r^2s - rs + r + s + 1$

33. $2s^2t^3 - 3s^2t^2 + 2s^2t + 3st^2 + st - s + 2t - 3$

35. $-2a^2bc + ab^2c - 2ab^3 + 3$

37. $-110x + 13y + 17z$

Exercise Set 4.3, page 129

1. $6x^5$

3. $6a^2b^3$

5. $2x^3 + 6x^2 - 10x$

7. $-4s^4t^2 + 4s^4t - 12s^3$

9. $8a^4b^2 + 4a^3b^3 - 4a^2b^4$

11. $x^2 - x - 6$

13. $y^2 + 7y + 10$

15. $x^2 + 6x + 9$

17. $s^2 - 9$

19. $3x^2 - x - 2$

21. $2a^2 + a - 10$

23. $6y^2 + 13y + 6$

25. $4a^2 + 12a + 9$

27. $4y^2 - 25$

29. $9x^2 - 16$

31. $x^4 + 4x^2 + 4$

33. $x^4 - 4$

35. $x^3 + 3x^2 - x - 3$

37. $2s^4 - 3s^3 - 2s^2 + 7s - 6$

39. $3a^3 + 5a^2 + 3a + 10$

41. $2x^4 - x^3 + 8x^2 - 3x + 6$

43. $2x^4 + x^3 - 6x^2 + 7x - 2$

45. $6x^5 - 4x^4 - 8x^3 + 14x^2 - 12x + 4$

47. $6a^3 + 2a^2 + 3a^2b - 2a^2b^2 + 3ab^2 - ab^3 + ab + b^2 - b^4$

49. $20x^2 - 60x + 45$

51. $2x^3 + 3x^2 - 2x$

53. $x^3 + 4x^2 + x - 6$

55. (a) -3 (b) 5

57. (a) 1 (b) 6

59. $4x^3y + 2x^2y$

61. $2x - 3$

63. $-2x^2 - 6x + 16$

65. $4x - 20$

67. c

69. $1.56x^2 - 9.18x + 13.5$

71. $22.73y^4 - 4.57y^2 - 3.24$

73. $21.68x^3 - 2.90x^2 - 6.88x + 0.28$

75. no

77. $a = 1, b = 2$

Exercise Set 4.4, page 137

1. $2(x + 3)$

3. $3(x - 3y)$

5. $-2(x + 4y)$

7. $2(2x^2 + 4y - 3)$

9. $5b(c + 5)$

11. $y(1 - 3y^2)$

13. $-y^2(3 + 4y^3)$

15. $3bc(a + 4)$

17. $5r^3s^3(s - 8rt)$

19. $4(2a^3b^5 - 3a^5b^2 + 4)$

21. $(x + 1)(x + 3)$

23. $(y - 5)(y - 3)$

25. $(a - 3b)(a - 4b)$

27. $(y + 3)(y + 3)$

29. $(5 - x)(5 - x)$

31. $(x - 7)(x + 2)$

33. $(2 + y)(2 - y)$

35. $(x - 3)^2$

37. $(x - 10)(x - 2)$

39. $(x + 8)(x + 3)$

41. $(2x + 1)(x - 2)$

43. $(3a - 2)(a - 3)$

45. $(3x + 2)(2x + 3)$

47. $(2m - 3)(4m + 3)$

49. $(2x - 3)(5x + 1)$

51. $(2a - 3b)(3a + 2b)$

53. $(5rs + 2t)(2rs + t)$

55. $(3 + 4x)(2 - x)$

57. $25r^2 + 4s^2$

59. $2(x - 3)(x + 2)$

61. $2(5x - 2)(3x + 4)$

63. $2b^2(3x - 4)(2x + 3)$

65. $3m(3x + 1)(2x + 3)$

67. $5m^2n(5n^2 - 1)$

69. $xy\left(1 + \frac{1}{4}x^2y^2\right)$

71. $(x^2 + y^2)(x^2 + y^2)$

73. $(b^2 + 4)(b^2 - 2)$

75. $(3b^2 - 1)(2b^2 + 3)$

77. $(x - 1)(2x + 7)$

79. $3(x + 1)(y - 2)$

81. $(x^2 - y)(2xy - 3)$

83. $(2x - 1)^2(x + 2)^2[4(x + 2)(x + 1) - 3(2x - 1)^3(x + 3)]$

85. $10(5x)(7 - 5x)(7 - 2x)^2$

89. $(2x - 3)(x + 4)$

91. $(3x + 1)(2x - 3)$

Exercise Set 4.5, page 141

1. $8x^3 + y^3$

3. $x^3 - 8y^3$

5. $27r^3 + 8s^3$

7. $8m^3 - 125n^3$

9. $\frac{1}{8}x^3 - 8y^3$

11. $(x - 7)(x + 7)$

13. $\left(y + \frac{1}{3}\right)\left(y - \frac{1}{3}\right)$

15. $(2b + a)(2b - a)$

17. $(xy + 3)(xy - 3)$

19. $(x + 3y)(x^2 - 3xy + 9y^2)$

21. $(3x - y)(9x^2 + 3xy + y^2)$

23. $(a + 2)(a^2 - 2a + 4)$

25. $\left(\frac{1}{2}m - 2n\right)\left(\frac{1}{4}m^2 + mn + 4n^2\right)$

27. $(x + y - 2)(x^2 + 2xy + y^2 + 2x + 2y + 4)$

29. $(2x^2 - 5y^2)(4x^4 + 10x^2y^2 + 25y^4)$

31. $(x^3 - y^3)(x^3 + y^3); (x^2 - y^2)(x^4 + x^2y^2 + y^4)$

Exercise Set 4.6, page 144

1. $2x + 5$

3. $4x - \frac{4}{3}$

5. $4x^2 - 2x + 1$

7. $6x - 4$

9. $-3a^2 + \frac{5}{2}$

11. $x^2 - 3x + 4$

13. $x - 4$

15. $a - \frac{8}{a - 2}$

17. $x - 2 + \frac{2}{x - 5}$

19. $x + 2 + \frac{1}{2x + 1}$

21. $3a + 2 + \frac{1}{2a - 1}$

23. $2x - \frac{1}{5} - \frac{14}{25x + 5}$

25. $2s - 3$

27. $2s - 3 + \frac{18}{2s + 3}$

29. $3y^2 - 1$

31. $x^2 - 2x + 4 - \frac{16}{x + 2}$

33. $x^2 - 2x + 1$

35. $-a - 3 + \frac{14}{4 - a^2}$

37. $1.27x + \frac{-19.88x + 3.05}{x^2 - 2}$

39. c

Review Exercises, page 146

1. yes

2. yes

3. no

4. yes

5.

Term	$3x^3$	$-4x$	2
Coefficient	3	-4	2

6.

Term	$4x^4$	$-x^2$	$2x$	-3
Coefficient	4	-1	2	-3

7.

Term	$-4x^2y^2$	$3x^2y$	$-xy^2$	xy	-1
Coefficient	-4	3	-1	1	-1

8.

Term	$2xy^2$	$-3xy$	x	3
Coefficient	2	-3	1	3

9. 7

10. 5

11. 2

12. 4

13. 35

14. 8

15. 17

16. 63

17. $5x^3 + 2x^2 - 3x - 2$

18. $2a^3b^3 + 3a^2b^3 - 2a^2b - ab^2 + 3ab - a - b$

19. $x^2y + 2xy^2 - x + y + 2$

20. $4x^4 - 5x^3 + x^2 - x + 2$ 21. $6x^2 - x - 2$

22. $4x^3 - 4x^2 + x$ 23. $6y^2 + 4y - 2$

24. $6y^3 - 2y^2 + 6y - 2$ 25. $a^4b + 3a^3b - 4ab$

26. $a^4 + a^3 - 5a - 3$

27. $x^4 - 2x^3 - x^2 + 8x - 12$

28. $4b^4 + 4b^3 - 3b^2 - 2b + 1$

29. 3

30. 0

31. -12

32. 0

33. $x(x + 2)(x - 1)$

34. $y^2(y - 3)(y + 2)$

35. $x(x + 3)(x - 1)$

36. $(2x + 1)(x - 3)$

37. $(2x - 1)(3x - 2)$

38. $(4x + y)(4x - y)$

39. $6(3x - 1)(x - 1)$

40. $(2r + 1)(s - 1)$

41. $(3a^2 + 1)^2$

42. $(2x - y)(x + y)$

43. $\left(y + \dfrac{1}{2}x\right)\left(y - \dfrac{1}{2}x\right)$

44. $(3a + 2b)(a - 1)$

45. $(a - 1)(2b + c)$

46. $(a^2 - 1)^2$

47. $\left(a + \dfrac{1}{2}b\right)\left(a - \dfrac{1}{2}b\right)$

48. $(xy + 3)(xy - 3)$

49. $(2a + 3b)(4a^2 - 6ab + 9b^2)$

50. $(2x + 5y)(4x^2 - 10xy + 25y^2)$

51. $(2a - 3b)(4a^2 + 6ab + 9b^2)$

52. $(2x - 5y)(4x^2 + 10xy + 25y^2)$

53. $4x - 2$

54. $2 - 6x^2$

55. $2y^3 - 3y^2 + y$

56. $4y - 20 + \dfrac{75}{y + 5}$

57. $x^2 - 3x + 9$

58. $x^2 - 3x + 9 - \dfrac{54}{x + 3}$

59. $y^2 + 2y + 1 + \dfrac{4}{y - 2}$

60. $a - 3 + \dfrac{-4a + 12}{a^2 + 2}$

Progress Test 4A, page 147

1. base: $-1/5$; exponent: 4

2. 5

3. 31

4. s^3

5. $-3x^3 + 3x^2 + x - 2$

6. $2x^2y - x + 6y - 2$

7. $-x^3 + x^2 - 6x + 3$

8. $3x^2y + 3xy^2 - x^2 + 4y - 2$

9. $4x^2 - 20xy + 25y^2$

10. $3x^4 - 2x^3 + 11x^2 - 4x + 10$

11. $(x + 6)(x - 2)$

12. $2y(x - 3)(x - 1)$

13. $(2a + 7)(2a - 7)$

14. $(x - 5y)(3x + 2y)$

15. $\left(\dfrac{x}{5} - 5y\right)\left(\dfrac{x^2}{25} + xy + 25y^2\right)$

16. $x^2 + 4x + 6 + \dfrac{13}{x - 2}$

17. $2a^2 - 3a - 4$

18. 7

Progress Test 4B, page 148

1. base: $-2/3$; exponent: 5

2. 5

3. 2

4. $\dfrac{1}{2}s^2$

5. $6x^5 + 4x^4 + 2x^3 - x^2 + 1$

6. $x^2y + 6x^2 - 3y^2 - 10$

7. $-5x^3 + 2x^2 + 3x - 8$

8. $4x^2y^2 - xy^2 + xy + 2$

9. $9x^2 - 24x + 16$

10. $2x^2 - 3y^2 - xy - 2x - 2y$

11. $(r + 7)(r + 2)$

12. $3(x + 1)(x + 1)$

13. $16(y + 2x)(y - 2x)$

14. $(3x - 2)(x - 5)$

15. $\left(2a + \dfrac{b}{2}\right)\left(4a^2 - ab + \dfrac{b^2}{4}\right)$

16. $4x^2 + 10x + 36 + \dfrac{103}{x - 3}$

17. $r^2 - 3r + 1 + \dfrac{r - 1}{r^2 - 1}$

18. 10

Chapter 5

Exercise Set 5.1, page 155

1. $\dfrac{1}{8}$

3. -7

5. $-\dfrac{2}{7}$

7. $\dfrac{3}{13}$

9. -3

11. $3b^2$

13. $-\dfrac{2(z+3)}{3x}$

15. $-\dfrac{8s(r+4)}{3(s-1)}$

17. $-\dfrac{y^2+z^2}{4}$

19. $\dfrac{2(z^2+z+1)}{17}$

21. $-\dfrac{1}{3}x$

23. $\dfrac{1}{3}x^2$

25. $2x^2$

27. $\dfrac{1}{5}b$

29. $\dfrac{1}{2}(x-1)$

31. $\dfrac{t^2-t+1}{t}$

33. $\dfrac{2a-3}{a-3}$

35. 4

37. $\dfrac{3}{2}t(t+3)$

39. $a(3b+1)$

41. $-\dfrac{2x+3}{x-3}$

43. $3-a$

45. -4

47. $-\dfrac{2}{3t+1}$

49. $\dfrac{x+3}{x}$

Exercise Set 5.2, page 159

1. T

3. F

5. T

7. F

9. $2x+1$

11. $\dfrac{3x+2}{3}$

13. $\dfrac{1}{2x^2-3}$

15. $a^2/5$

17. $\dfrac{1}{x-4}$

19. $x-4$

21. $\dfrac{3x+1}{x+2}$

23. $\dfrac{2x^2+5x+3}{12}$

25. $\dfrac{3(a^2-16)}{b}$

27. $a/2$

29. $4/9$

31. $\dfrac{2(3x+1)}{(x+2)^2}$

33. $-2b(5+a)$

35. $\dfrac{x+3}{3x(x-3)}$

37. $\dfrac{-x(2y+3)}{x+1}$

39. $\dfrac{2(x+2)(x-2)^2}{(x+1)(2x+3)}$

41. $\dfrac{5y}{x-4}$

43. $\dfrac{(2x+1)(x-2)}{(x-1)(x+1)}$

45. $\dfrac{(x-2)^2}{(x+3)(x-3)}$

47. $\dfrac{(x+2)(2x+3)}{x+4}$

49. $b(b+1)$

51. $\dfrac{(x+3)(x^2+1)}{x-2}$

53. $\dfrac{x+4}{(x+1)(x-5)}$

55. $x(x-3)$

Exercise Set 5.3, page 164

1. xy

3. $2a$

5. $(b-1)^2$

7. $(x-2)(x+3)$

9. $x(x+1)(x-1)$

11. $7/x$

13. $3x/y$

15. 1

17. $x-3$

19. $\dfrac{y-14}{(y-4)(y+4)}$

21. $\dfrac{4}{a-2}$

23. $\dfrac{14y}{3(2-y)}$

25. 2

27. $\dfrac{10+x}{5x}$

29. $\dfrac{5x-2}{x}$

31. $\dfrac{3x-4}{(x-1)(x-2)}$

33. $\dfrac{3a^2-2b^2}{24ab}$

35. $\dfrac{8x-1}{6x^3}$

37. $\dfrac{2(x+1)}{3(x-3)}$

39. $\dfrac{x^2+y^2}{x^2-y^2}$

41. $\dfrac{x^2+2xy-y^2}{x^2-y^2}$

43. $\dfrac{r+8}{r(r+2)}$

45. $\dfrac{3x^2 - 4x - 1}{(x-1)(x-2)(x+1)}$

47. $-\dfrac{2a^3 - 3a^2 - 3a - 2}{a(a-1)(a+1)}$

53. $\dfrac{17x + 26}{(x+2)(x-2)(x+3)}$

49. $\dfrac{3x^2 - 4x - 12}{(x-2)(x+2)(x-3)}$

55. $\dfrac{2y^2 + y + 1}{y(y+1)(y-1)}$

57. $\dfrac{x+3}{x-1}$

51. $-\dfrac{x^3 - 4x^2 + 3x - 1}{x(x-2)(x+2)(x-1)}$

Exercise Set 5.4, page 169

1. $\dfrac{x+2}{x-3}$

3. $\dfrac{3x-4}{5x^2}$

13. $a - b$

15. $\dfrac{1-y}{y}$

5. $\dfrac{x(x+1)}{x-1}$

7. $4x(x+4)$

17. $\dfrac{5-a}{a}$

19. $\dfrac{b}{2(2-b)}$

9. $\dfrac{x}{x-1}$

11. $\dfrac{x+3}{(3x-7)(x+2)}$

21. $\dfrac{4}{5}$

23. $-\dfrac{1}{2}$

Exercise Set 5.5, page 173

1. 10/3

3. 1

21. 12/7

23. $x < 7$

5. 9/2

7. 4

25. $x \le -1$

27. $x \ge 1$

9. 4

11. no solution

29. no solution

31. $\dfrac{3a - 14}{3a - 2}$

13. 1/4

15. 12

17. 5/19

19. 2

33. $r \le \dfrac{a+2}{a-2}$

Exercise Set 5.6, page 179

1. 18

3. 3/8, 3/4

17. 9 hr.

19. 8 hr.

5. 3/4

7. 4

21. 25 km per hour

9. 6/5 hr.

11. 12/13 hr.

23. 100 km per hour, 120 km per hour

13. 6 hr.

15. 60/7 hr.

Exercise Set 5.7, page 185

1. $\dfrac{5.08 \text{ cm}}{2 \text{ in}}$ or 5.08 cm:2 in

3. $\dfrac{16}{5}$ or 8:2.5

17. $500

19. 60 ft.

21. 55,000

23. 962

5. 3/4 or 3:4

7. 20 cm, 16 cm

25. 24 cm^3

27. $\dfrac{3a + 4}{4}$

9. 18/5

11. 3/10

13. 5

15. 9, 21

Review Exercises, page 187

1. $x + 2$

2. $\dfrac{2x - 3}{2}$

3. $x - 4$

4. $2x^2 - x + 3$

5. $\dfrac{x^2 - 3x + 2}{6}$

6. $\dfrac{4x^2 - 1}{6}$

7. $\dfrac{2x - 2}{x^2 + x}$

8. $\dfrac{2x^2 + 2x - 4}{x - 4}$

9. $\dfrac{4x^2 + 4x - 3}{6x^2 - x - 2}$

10. $\dfrac{x^2 - 3x + 2}{x^2 + 5x + 6}$

11. $x^2 - 4$

12. $(x - 2)^2$

13. $y^3 - 4y$

14. $3y^2(y - 1)$

15. $\dfrac{10 - x^2}{3x}$

16. $\dfrac{4a^2 - a - 1}{a^2 - 1}$

17. $\dfrac{a - 6}{a - 2}$

18. $\dfrac{3y - yx + x - 1}{2x^2 + x - 3}$

19. $\dfrac{-4x^2 + 21x - 15}{6(x^2 - 9)}$

20. $\dfrac{6x^2 - 7x - 1}{2(x^2 - 1)}$

21. $\dfrac{2x - 1}{x + 5}$

22. $\dfrac{a^2 - a - 1}{3a^2 - 3a - 1}$

23. $\dfrac{1 - a}{1 + a}$

24. $\dfrac{3(10 - y^2)(y + 1)}{2(y + 3)}$

25. $\dfrac{x^2 - x - 1}{x^2 + x + 1}$

26. $\dfrac{(x + 1)(x + 3)}{x + 9}$

27. $4/7$

28. $x = 3/2$

29. $a = -5/8$

30. $y = -2$

31. $x = -1/10$

32. $r = -5$

33. $5/3$

34. $3, -3$

35. 2

36. 6 days

37. 7.5 hr.

38. 12 mo.

39. 24/13 hr.

40. 16 km per hour

41. Computer A carries out 25 million operations; computer B carries out 15 million operations.

42. 30 mph

43. $x = 2$

44. $y = 3$

45. $r = 1/2$

46. $r = -13$

47. 10 smokers

48. $3.125

49. $800.00

50. 19.2 oz.

Progress Test 5A, page 189

1. $\dfrac{12x^2(x + 2)}{y}$

2. $-\dfrac{(2x + 3)(3x - 1)}{(x + 4)^2}$

3. $-\dfrac{(2x - 1)(x - 2)(x - 1)}{3x}$

4. $5y^2(x - 1)^2$

5. $\dfrac{13}{x - 5}$

6. $\dfrac{7 - 5y^2}{2y(y + 1)}$

7. $3x$

8. $\dfrac{(x + 4)(x - 2)}{x - 3}$

9. -2

10. $x \leq -33/5$

11. 2 hr.

12. 4

13. $291.67

Progress Test 5B, page 189

1. $\dfrac{-6(y - 1)}{y^2(x - y)}$

2. $-\dfrac{(2x - 1)}{(3x - 1)(x + 1)}$

3. $-\dfrac{2x(x + 1)}{x + 2}$

4. $4x^2(y + 1)^2(y - 1)$

5. $\dfrac{2}{3 - x}$

6. $\dfrac{-2v^3 + 3v^2 + 6v + 8}{4v^2(v - 1)}$

7. $-2x$

8. $\dfrac{(x - 1)(x - 3)}{2(2 - x)}$

9. $11/12$

10. $x \leq 24/5$

11. 7/3 hr.

12. 7

13. 81

Chapter 6
Exercise Set 6.1, page 199

1. $A(2, 3)$, $B(-2, -1)$, $C(4, -1)$, $D(0, 5)$, $E(-4, 0)$, $F(-3, 4)$, $G(1, 1/2)$, $H(-1, 7/2)$

3.
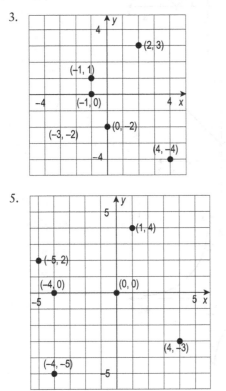

5.

7.
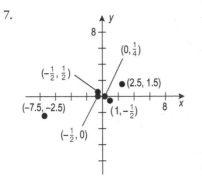

9. (a) $(-4, 0)$ (b) $(6, -2)$

11. I   13. IV

15. III   17. I

19. III   21. I

23. a, d   25. a, c

27.

x	1	$\frac{9}{2}$	0	3	-3	$\frac{3}{2}$
y	$\frac{8}{3}$	-2	4	0	8	2

29.
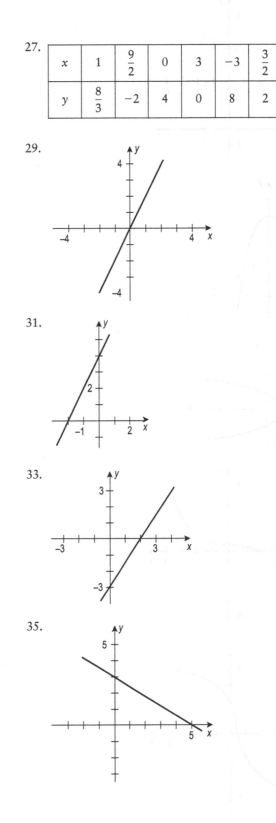

31.

33.

35.

37.

39.

41.

43.

45.

47.

49.

51.

53.

55.

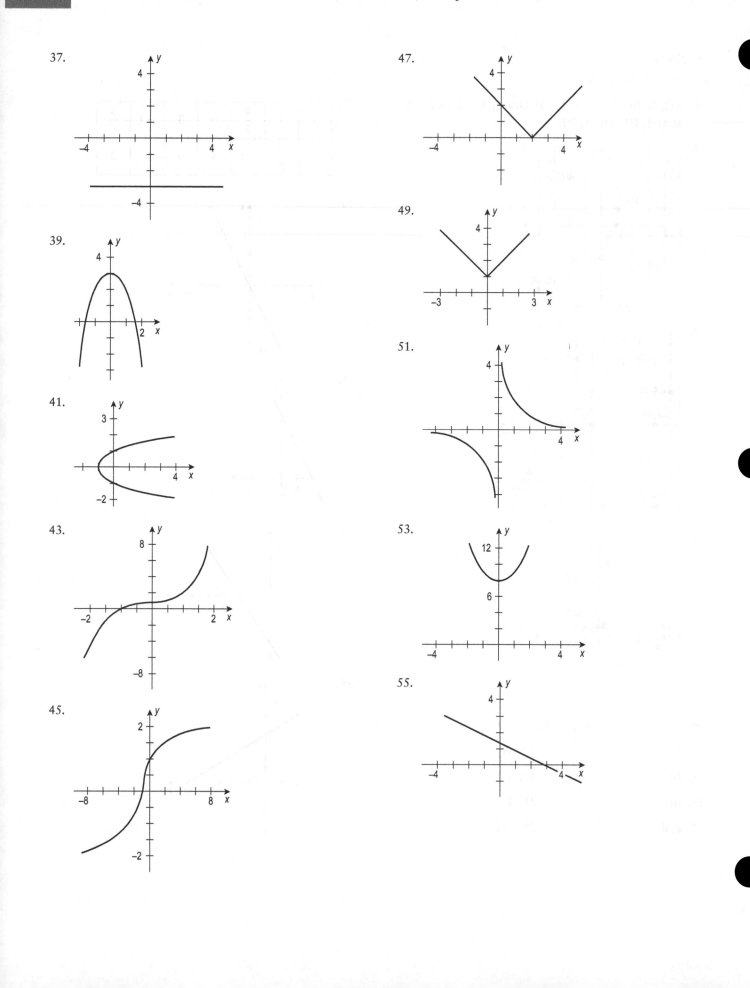

57.

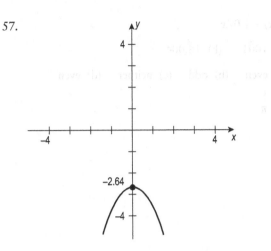

59.

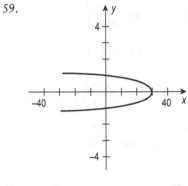

61. $x = 6$ 63. $(2, 8)$

Exercise Set 6.2, page 208

1.

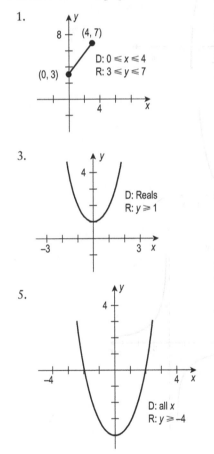

$D: 0 \leqslant x \leqslant 4$
$R: 3 \leqslant y \leqslant 7$

3.

D: Reals
$R: y \geqslant 1$

5.

D: all x
$R: y \geqslant -4$

7.

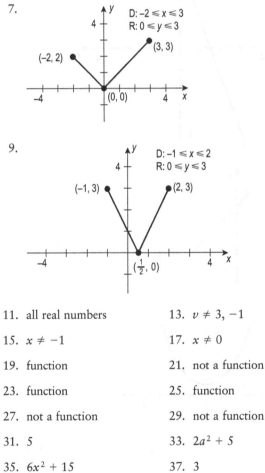

$D: -2 \leqslant x \leqslant 3$
$R: 0 \leqslant y \leqslant 3$

9.

$D: -1 \leqslant x \leqslant 2$
$R: 0 \leqslant y \leqslant 3$

11. all real numbers   13. $v \neq 3, -1$

15. $x \neq -1$ 17. $x \neq 0$

19. function   21. not a function

23. function   25. function

27. not a function   29. not a function

31. 5   33. $2a^2 + 5$

35. $6x^2 + 15$ 37. 3

39. $\dfrac{1}{x^2 + 2x}$

41. $a^2 + b^2 + 2ab + 2a + 2b$

43. −0.92

45. $\dfrac{3x - 1}{x^2 + 1}$

47. $\dfrac{8x^2 + 2}{6x - 1}$

49. −0.21

51. $\dfrac{2(a - 1)}{4a^2 + 4a - 3}$

53. $\dfrac{a - 1}{a(a + 4)}$

55. $R(x) = \begin{cases} 300x, & 0 \leq x \leq 100 \\ 30{,}000 + 250(x - 100), & 100 < x < 150 \end{cases}$

57. $A(x) = 1.07x$

59. (a) 1001   (b) 16,004

61. (a) even   (b) odd   (c) neither   (d) even

63. $d = \dfrac{c}{\pi}$

Exercise Set 6.3, page 218

1.

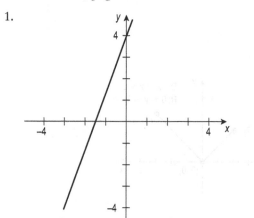

3.

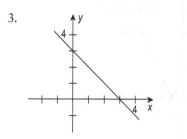

5.

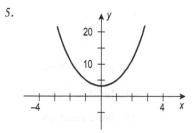

7.

9.

11.

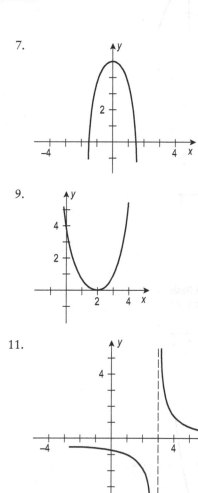

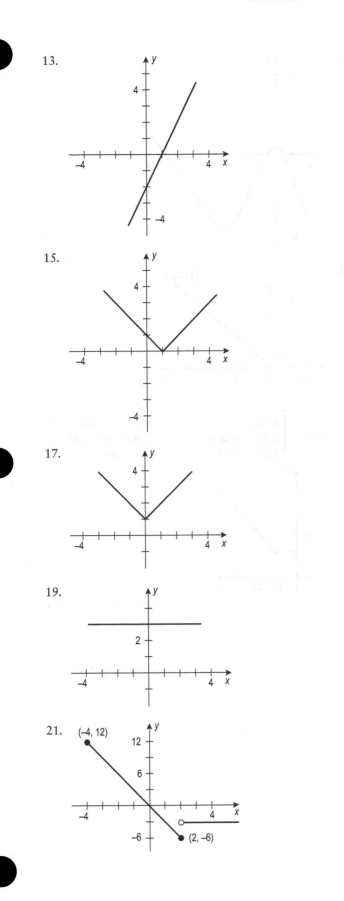

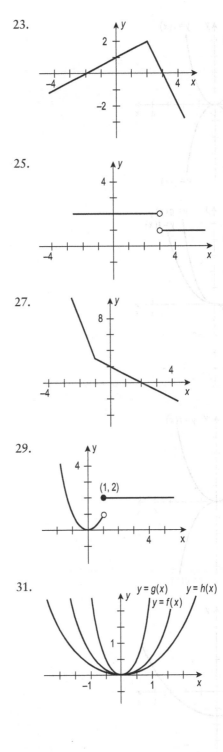

33.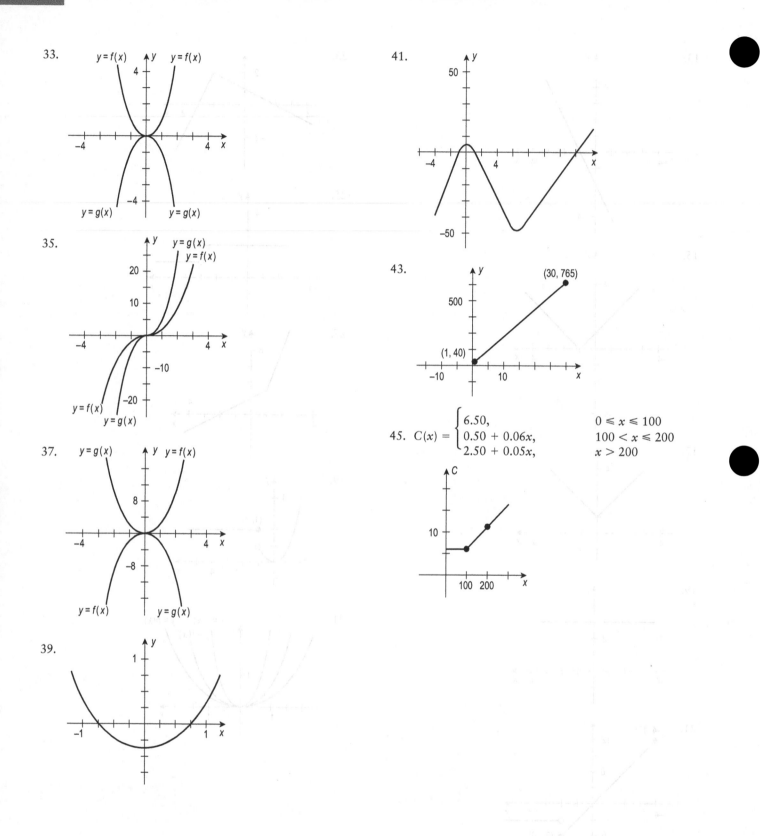

35.

37.

39.

41.

43.

45. $C(x) = \begin{cases} 6.50, & 0 \le x \le 100 \\ 0.50 + 0.06x, & 100 < x \le 200 \\ 2.50 + 0.05x, & x > 200 \end{cases}$

Exercise Set 6.4, page 223

1. always increasing

3. decreasing for $x \leq 0$; increasing for $x \geq 0$

5. decreasing for $x \geq 0$; increasing for $x \leq 0$

7. decreasing for $x \geq 2$; increasing for $x \leq 2$

9. decreasing for $x \leq 0$; increasing for $x \geq 0$

11. decreasing for $x \leq 2$; increasing for $x \geq 2$

13. decreasing for $x \leq -1/2$; increasing for $x \geq -1/2$

15. decreasing for $x \leq -1$; increasing for $x > -1$

17. always increasing

19. always increasing

21. decreasing for $x \leq 1$; increasing for $x \geq 1$

23. decreasing for all $x \neq 1$

25. decreasing for $x \geq 40$; increasing for $x \leq 40$

27. decreasing for $2 \leq x \leq 5$; increasing for $0 \leq x \leq 2$, $5 \leq x \leq 6$

Exercise Set 6.5, page 228

1. (a) 4   (b) $y = 4x$ (c)

x	8	12	20	30
y	32	48	80	120

3. (a) $-1/32$ (b) $-3/8$

5. (a) $1/10$ (b) $5/2$

7. (a) -3 (b) $-1/4$

9. (a) 512   (b) 512/125

11. (a) $M = r^2/s^2$ (b) 36/25

13. (a) $T = 16pv^3/u^2$ (b) 2/3

15. (a) 256 ft.   (b) 5 sec.

17. 80/9 ohms

19. (a) 89 candlepower   (b) 64 ft.

21. 6

23. 120 candlepower/ft^2

Review Exercises, page 231

1. $(-2, -4)$

2. $(-3, 1)$

3. II

4. a, d

5. d

6.

x	2	$\dfrac{25}{2}$	0	10	3	0
y	$\dfrac{16}{5}$	-1	4	0	$\dfrac{14}{5}$	4

7.

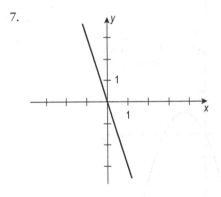

8.

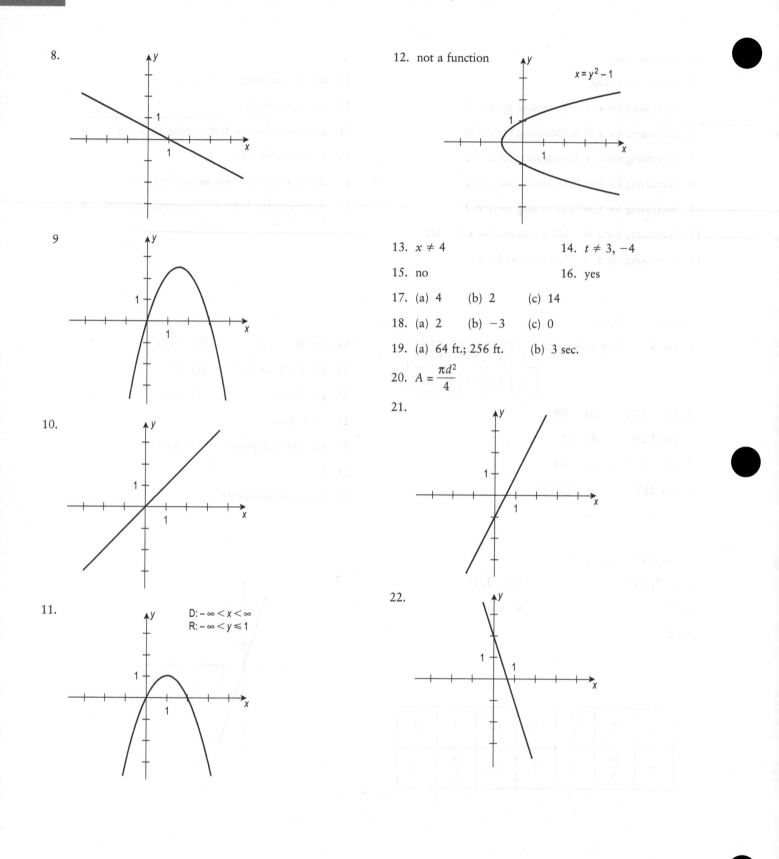

9

10.

11.
D: $-\infty < x < \infty$
R: $-\infty < y \leq 1$

12. not a function

$x = y^2 - 1$

13. $x \neq 4$ 14. $t \neq 3, -4$

15. no   16. yes

17. (a) 4   (b) 2   (c) 14

18. (a) 2   (b) -3 (c) 0

19. (a) 64 ft.; 256 ft.   (b) 3 sec.

20. $A = \dfrac{\pi d^2}{4}$

21.

22.

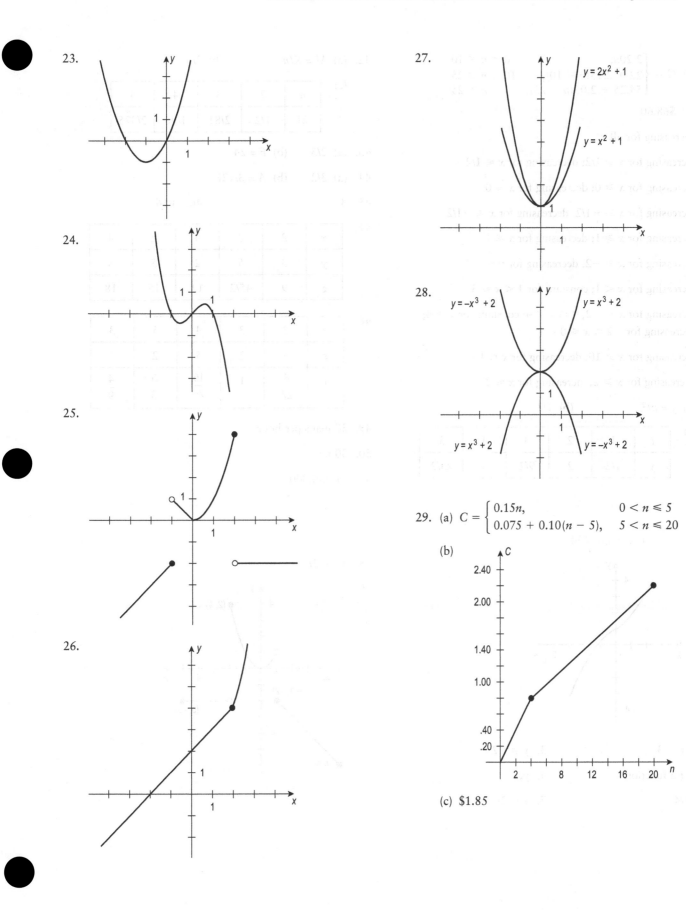

23.

24.

25.

26.

27. $y = 2x^2 + 1$
$y = x^2 + 1$

28. $y = -x^3 + 2$ $y = x^3 + 2$
$y = x^3 + 2$ $y = -x^3 + 2$

29. (a) $C = \begin{cases} 0.15n, & 0 < n \le 5 \\ 0.075 + 0.10(n - 5), & 5 < n \le 20 \end{cases}$

(b)

(c) $1.85

30. (a) $C = \begin{cases} 2.20n, & 0 < n \leq 10 \\ 22 + 2.15(n - 10), & 10 < n \leq 25 \\ 54.25 + 2.05(n - 25), & n > 25 \end{cases}$

(b) $68.60

31. decreasing for all x

32. increasing for $x \geq 1/2$; decreasing for $x \leq 1/2$

33. increasing for $x \geq 0$; decreasing for $x \leq 0$

34. increasing for $x \geq -1/2$; decreasing for $x \leq -1/2$

35. increasing for $x \geq 1$; decreasing for $x \leq 1$

36. increasing for $x \geq -2$; decreasing for $x \leq -2$

37. increasing for $x < 1$; constant for $1 < x \leq 3$

38. increasing for $x < -2$, $0 \leq x < 4$; constant for $x \geq 4$; decreasing for $-2 \leq x \leq 0$

39. increasing for $x \geq 10$; decreasing for $x \leq 10$

40. decreasing for $x \geq 2$; increasing for $x \leq 2$

41. (a) $y = kt^2$ (b) 1/2

(c)

t	1	2	3	4	5
y	1/2	2	9/2	8	25/2

42. (a) $M = K/n^3$ (b) 2/3

(c)

n	2	3	4	5
M	1/2	2/81	1/96	2/375

43. (a) 2/3   (b) $F = 24$

44. (a) 3/2   (b) $A = 3/128$

45. 3   46. 3/16

47.

x	2	3	4	2	4
y	3	5	2	5	3
z	9	45/2	12	15	18

48.

r	2	3	4	5	3
s	3	2	5	2	3
t	$\frac{8}{27}$	1	$\frac{16}{75}$	$\frac{5}{3}$	$\frac{4}{9}$

49. 30 items per hour

50. 30 min.

51. $1,250,000

Progress Test 6A, page 234

1.

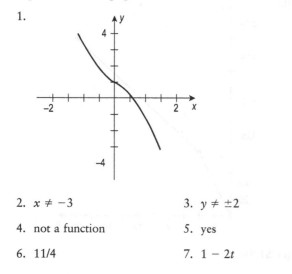

8. $4a + 2h$

9.

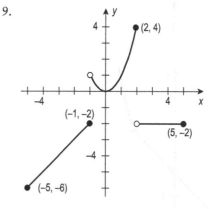

2. $x \neq -3$

3. $y \neq \pm 2$

4. not a function

5. yes

6. 11/4

7. $1 - 2t$

10.

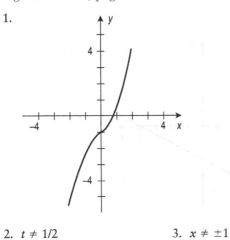

11. 160

12. 1

13. $-1/4$

14. increasing for $x \geq 1$; decreasing for $x \leq 1$

15. increasing for $1 \leq x \leq 3$; decreasing for $x \leq 1$; constant for $x \geq 3$

Progress Test 6B, page 234

1.

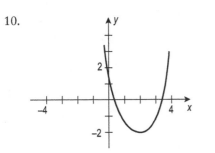

2. $t \neq 1/2$

3. $x \neq \pm 1$

4. function

5. yes

6. -3

7. $1 + a + \dfrac{a^2}{4}$

8. $-2a - h$

9.

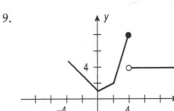

10.

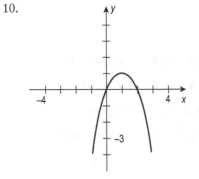

11. -1024

12. $-32/9$

13. 65,536

14. increasing for $x \geq 2$; decreasing for $x \leq 2$

15. increasing for $0 \leq x \leq 3$; decreasing for $-1 \leq x \leq 0$; constant for $x < -1$ and $x > 3$

Chapter 7

Exercise Set 7.1, page 242

1. 2; rising   3. −1; falling   21. $C = -2$

5. −3/2; falling   7. 0

9. P   11. N

13. T   15. F

17. 1   19. undefined

Exercise Set 7.2, page 251

1. a, d   17.

3. $2x - y - 3 = 0; A = 2, B = -1, C = -3$

5. $0x + y - 3 = 0; A = 0, B = 1, C = -3$

7. $3x - 2y - 7 = 0; A = 3, B = -2, C = -7$

9. $x + 0y - 1/2 = 0; A = 1, B = 0, C = -1/2$

11. yes

13.

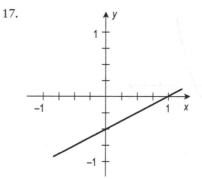

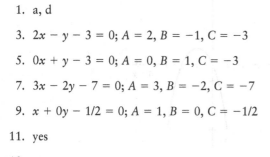

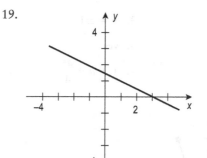

19.

15.

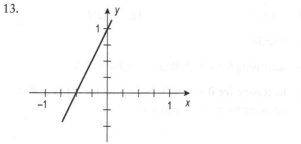

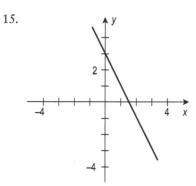

21.

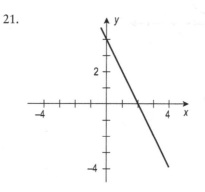

23.

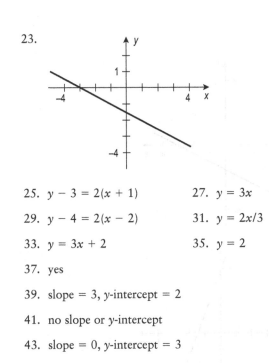

25. $y - 3 = 2(x + 1)$ 27. $y = 3x$

29. $y - 4 = 2(x - 2)$ 31. $y = 2x/3$

33. $y = 3x + 2$ 35. $y = 2$

37. yes

39. slope = 3, y-intercept = 2

41. no slope or y-intercept

43. slope = 0, y-intercept = 3

45. slope = $-3/4$, y-intercept = 5/4

47. slope = 2/5, y-intercept = 3/5

49. slope = 3/2, y-intercept = -3

51. rises   53. falls

55. rises   57. $y = \frac{3}{4}x + \frac{11}{4}$

59. $y = -0.98x + 14.57$ 61. $y = 0.83x - 7.04$

63. $y = -\frac{3}{4}x + \frac{5}{2}$

65. $c = 8 + 1.5h$; c = charge in dollars, h = hours

67. $c = 25 + 0.12s$; c = charge in dollars, s = number of shares

69. (a) $F = \frac{9}{5}C + 32$ (b) 68°F

71. $1,000,000   73. 5

75. $f(x) = 8x + 13$

Exercise Set 7.3, page 259

1. $y = 2$ 3. $x = -2$

5. (a) $y = 3$ (b) $x = -6$

7. (a) $y = -5$ (b) $x = 4$

9. (a) $y = 0$ (b) $x = 0$

11. (a) $y = 0$ (b) $x = -7$

13. (a) $y = 5$ (b) $x = 0$

15. $y = 3$

17.

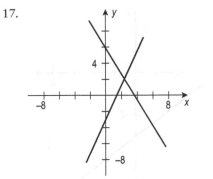

Lines are not parallel.

19.

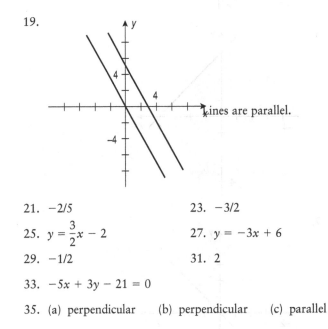

Lines are parallel.

21. $-2/5$ 23. $-3/2$

25. $y = \frac{3}{2}x - 2$ 27. $y = -3x + 6$

29. $-1/2$ 31. 2

33. $-5x + 3y - 21 = 0$

35. (a) perpendicular   (b) perpendicular   (c) parallel

Exercise Set 7.4, page 266

1.

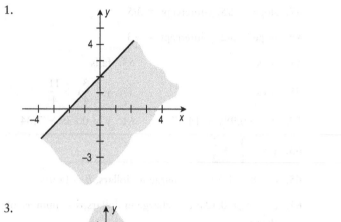

9.

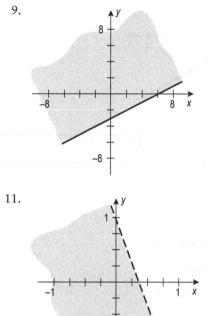

3.

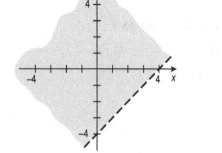

11.

5.

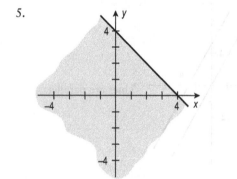

13.

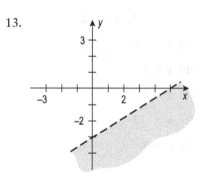

7.

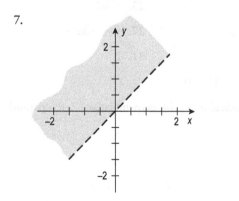

15.

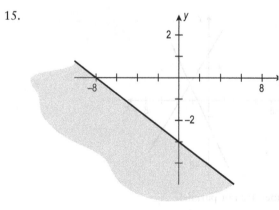

17.

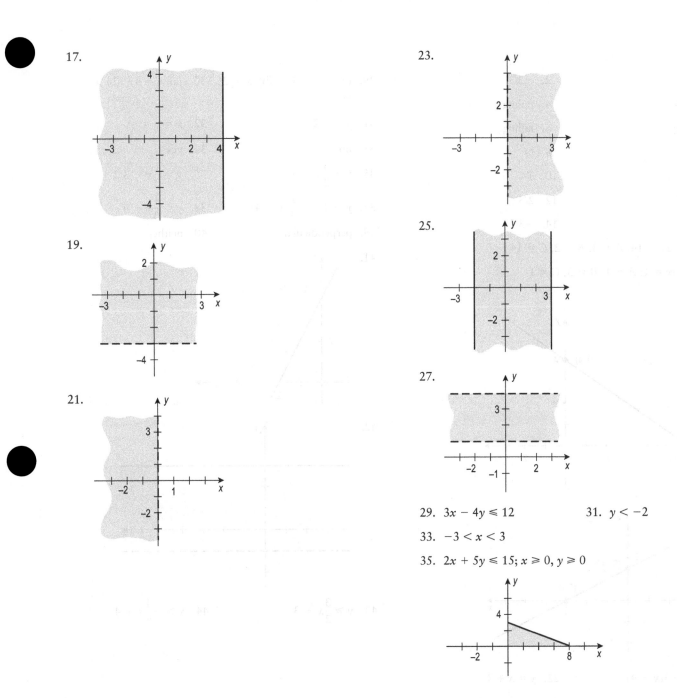

19.

21.

23.

25.

27.

29. $3x - 4y \leq 12$ 31. $y < -2$

33. $-3 < x < 3$

35. $2x + 5y \leq 15; x \geq 0, y \geq 0$

Review Exercises, page 268

1. 1/2

2. −2/3

3. rising

4. falling

5. falling

6. falling

7. P

8. N

9. F

10. T

11. −3/4

12. 2/3

13. −6

14. −3/2

15. $3x + 2y = 14; A = 3, B = 2, C = 14$

16. $x + 3y = 1; A = 1, B = 3, C = 1$

17. yes

19.

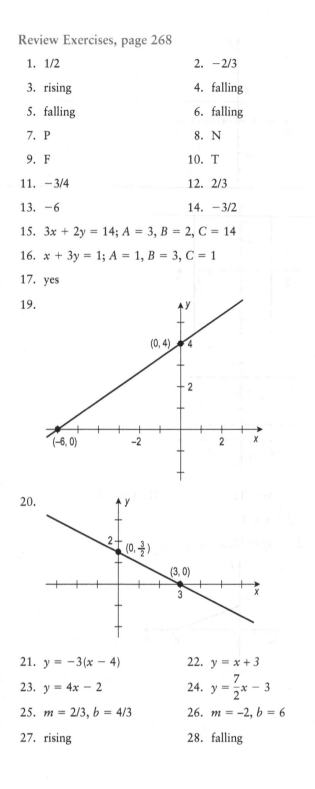

20.

21. $y = -3(x - 4)$

22. $y = x + 3$

23. $y = 4x - 2$

24. $y = \dfrac{7}{2}x - 3$

25. $m = 2/3, b = 4/3$

26. $m = -2, b = 6$

27. rising

28. falling

29. (a) $y = -3$ (b) $x = 2$

30. (a) $y = 4$ (b) $x = -3$

31. $y = -2$

32. $x = -4$

33. no

34. yes

35. $y = \dfrac{3}{2}x + 5$

36. $y = \dfrac{1}{2}x - 3/2$

37. $y - 1 = -\dfrac{2}{5}(x - 4)$

38. $y = \dfrac{4}{3}x + 4$

39. perpendicular

40. neither

41.

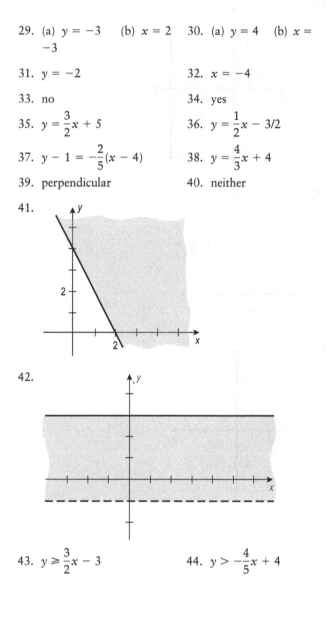

42.

43. $y \geq \dfrac{3}{2}x - 3$

44. $y > -\dfrac{4}{5}x + 4$

Progress Test 7A, page 271

1. 0

2. $-2/3$

3. $7x + y + 5 = 0$

4. $x - 10y + 74 = 0$

5. slope $= -5/2$, y-intercept $= 3$

6. slope $= 2/3$; rising

7. slope $= -1/4$; falling

8. $c = 20t + 5$

9. $x = -11$

10. $y = -7/3$

11. $y = 3x + 2$, same line

12. $2/7$

13. $3x + 4y + 11 = 0$

14.

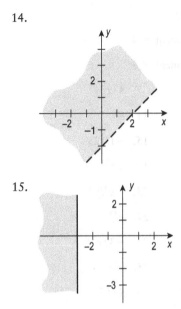

15.

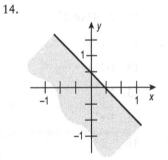

Progress Test 7B, page 271

1. no slope

2. -2

3. $y - 5x - 23 = 0$

4. $2x + 3y + 12 = 0$

5. slope $= 4$, y-intercept $= -5/3$

6. slope $= 7/2$; rising

7. slope $= -5/4$; falling

8. $C = 17n + 5$

9. $y = 5/4$

10. $x = 3$

11. $y - 2x - 3 = 0$

12. $-5/3$

13. $y = -3x$

14.

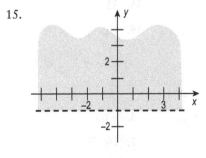

15.

Chapter 8

Exercise Set 8.1, page 279

1. $1/81$, base $= 1/3$, exponent $= 4$

3. -32, base $= -2$, exponent $= 5$

5. $(-5)^4$ 7. $4^2x^2y^3$

9. x^6 11. b^4

13. $16x^4$ 15. $-1/128$

17. x^{3m^2} 19. $x^{(m^2 + m)}$

21. 81 23. $-x^3/y^3$

25. y^8 27. x^{19}

29. $-a^5/b^5$ 31. $-32x^{10}$

33. 3^{3m} 35. x^{4n}

37. 3^8 39. 5^{n+1}

41. $1/x^2$ 43. $3^5x^{15}/y^{10}$

45. $-30x^8$ 47. $x^{27}y^8$

49. 1 51. $(3b + 1)^{25}$

53. $1/(2a + b)^2$ 55. $-27x^9y^3$

57. $2^n a^{n^2}/b^{2n^2}$ 59. $-27x^3/8$

61. $(2x + 1)^{10}$ 63. $1/y^9$

65. $2^{2n}a^{4n}b^{6n}$ 67. $-8a^6b^9/c^6$

69. 21.49 71. -2.57

73. 302.90 75. 888.73

79. $10^{12} \times 10^{12} \times 10^{12};\ 10^{36}$

Exercise Set 8.2, page 284

1. 1 3. 1

5. 3 7. $-5x$

9. $-1/3^3$ 11. $2 \cdot 4^3$ or 2^7

13. $-x^3$ 15. $-1/16$

17. y^6 19. $1/2^6a^6$

21. $-4(5a - 3b)^2$ 23. 25

25. $4y^3$ 27. $1/x^7$

29. $1/3^6$ 31. -2^9

33. x^9 35. 32

37. x^{18} 39. $4/x$

41. 2 43. $b^9/8a^6$

45. ab 47. $a^4b^6/9$

49. a^9/b^9c^6 51. a^2/b^4c

53. $a^9/3b^4$ 55. x

57. $4a^{10}c^6/b^8$ 59. $2y^5$

61. $1/y$ 63. $a^4/4b^6c^4$

65. x^9z^9/y^3 67. $4b^6c^6/a^4$

69. $(a - b)^2/a + b$ 71. $xy/(x + y)^2$

73. 0.69 75. 0.00000499

77. 1.9 79. 3.20

Exercise Set 8.3, page 291

1. 8 3. $-1/5$

5. $4/25$ 7. $1/c^{5/12}$

9. $2x^{13/12}$ 11. $1/x^{17}$

13. 25 15. $x^{2/3}y$

17. $64a^6b^3$ 19. $a^{9/2}/b^3$

21. $-4x^{2n}$ 23. x^9/y^6

25. $x^{12}y^4$ 27. $1/x^4y^8$

29. $-32x^{15}y^{5/2}/243$ 31. $64^{1/4}x^{3/2}/y^3$

33. $\sqrt[5]{1/16}$ 35. $\sqrt[3]{x^2}$

37. $\sqrt[5]{64x^4}$ 39. $\sqrt[3]{(x^2 - 1)^2}$

41. $8^{3/4}$

43. $1/(-8)^{2/5}$

57. $1/3$

59. -5

45. $1/(\frac{4}{9}a^3)^{1/4}$

47. $(2y^3)^{7/2}/x^{14}$

61. $1/2$

63. $-7/2$

49. c

51. c

65. 54.82

67. 4.78

53. $2/3$

55. not real

69. 0.15

71. 27.4

Exercise Set 8.4, page 296

1. $4\sqrt{3}$

3. $3\sqrt[3]{2}$

37. $\sqrt{5}/5$

39. $4\sqrt{11}/33$

5. $2\sqrt[3]{5}$

7. $2/3$

41. $\sqrt{3}/3$

43. $\sqrt{3y}/3y$

9. $2/5$

11. x^4

45. $2x\sqrt{2x}$

47. $3y\sqrt{2x}$

13. $a^3\sqrt[3]{a^2}$

15. x^3

49. $-5x^3y^4\sqrt[3]{xy}$

51. $5\sqrt[3]{4a^2b}/2$

17. $7b^5\sqrt{2}$

19. $3y^5\sqrt[3]{4y}$

53. $2x^2\sqrt{5xy}/y^2$

55. $x\sqrt[3]{x^2y}/y$

21. $2x^2\sqrt{5}$

23. $a^5b^3\sqrt{b}$

57. $\sqrt[4]{216x^2y^3}/3y$

59. $x^3y^2\sqrt{xy}$

25. $x^2y^2\sqrt[3]{y^2}$

27. $ab^2\sqrt[4]{ab^2}$

61. $2x^2y\sqrt[4]{2y^2}$

63. $2x^2y\sqrt[4]{3y^2z^2}$

29. $6x^3y^5\sqrt{2xy}$

31. $2b^3c^4\sqrt[3]{3bc^2}$

65. $7y\sqrt[4]{27xy}/6x$

67. $\sqrt[4]{216x^2y^3}/12xy^3$

33. $2b^2c^3\sqrt[4]{3b^2}$

35. $2a^2bc\sqrt[3]{5a^2bc^2}$

69. $\frac{4}{5}a\sqrt[3]{b^2}$

Exercise Set 8.5, page 301

1. $7\sqrt{3}$

3. $-2\sqrt[3]{11}$

43. 0

45. $3x - 4y - \sqrt{6xy}$

5. $7\sqrt{x}$

7. $6\sqrt{2}$

47. $\sqrt[3]{4x^2} - 9$

9. $\frac{9}{2}\sqrt{y}$

11. $5\sqrt{6}$

49. $a^2 - 2b^2 - 2ab\sqrt[3]{ab} + \sqrt[3]{a^2b^2}$

13. $4\sqrt{3}$

15. $11\sqrt{5} - \sqrt[3]{5}$

51. $\frac{3}{7}(3 - \sqrt{2})$

53. $\dfrac{3(9 + \sqrt{7})}{74}$

17. $5\sqrt[3]{xy^2} - 4\sqrt[3]{x^2y}$

19. $\frac{3}{2}a\sqrt[3]{ab} + \frac{5}{2}\sqrt{ab}$

55. $\dfrac{2(\sqrt{x} - 3)}{x - 9}$

57. $\dfrac{3(1 - 3\sqrt{a})}{9a - 1}$

21. $2\sqrt[5]{2x^3y^2}$

23. $-3y\sqrt[3]{xy} - \frac{1}{2}y^2\sqrt{x}$

25. $-5\sqrt{5}$

59. $\dfrac{2(2 + \sqrt{2y})}{2 - y}$

61. $2(\sqrt{2} - 1)$

27. $x(x\sqrt[3]{xy} - \sqrt[3]{x^2y} + 2x^2\sqrt{y})$

63. $3 + 2\sqrt{2}$

65. $4 + \sqrt{15}$

29. $3 + 4\sqrt{3}$

31. $2\sqrt{3} + 6\sqrt{2}$

67. $\dfrac{x - \sqrt{xy}}{x - y}$

33. $3xy$

35. $-4xy\sqrt[5]{x}$

37. $\sqrt{2} - 4$

69. $\dfrac{2a + \sqrt{ab} + 2\sqrt{a} + \sqrt{b}}{4a - b}$

39. $6\sqrt{6} + 4\sqrt{3} - 9\sqrt{2} - 6$ 41. $5 - 2\sqrt{6}$

71. $\dfrac{2x\sqrt{2} + 2\sqrt{xy} + \sqrt{2xy} + y}{2x - y}$

Exercise Set 8.6, page 310

1. 1

3. $-i$

5. -1

7. $-i$

9. i

11. 1

13. i

15. $2 + 0i$

17. $-\dfrac{1}{2} + 0i$

19. $0 + 4i$

21. $0 - \sqrt{5}i$

23. $0 - 6i$

25. $2 + 4i$

27. $-\dfrac{3}{2} - 6i\sqrt{2}$

29. $0.3 - 7i\sqrt{2}$

31. $3 + i$

33. $8 - i$

35. $5 + i$

37. $-5 - 4i$

39. $-8 + 0i$

41. $2 - 6i$

43. $-1 - \dfrac{1}{2}i$

45. $-5 + 12i$

47. $5 + 0i$

49. $2 + 14i$

51. $4 - 7i$

53. $5 + 12i$

55. $8 - 6i$

57. $-2 + 0i$

59. $4 + 0i$

61. $5 + 0i$

63. 25

65. 20

67. $-\dfrac{13}{10} + \dfrac{11}{10}i$

69. $-\dfrac{7}{25} - \dfrac{24}{25}i$

71. $\dfrac{8}{5} - \dfrac{1}{5}i$

73. $\dfrac{5}{3} - \dfrac{2}{3}i$

75. $\dfrac{4}{5} + \dfrac{8}{5}i$

77. $\dfrac{3}{13} - \dfrac{2}{13}i$

79. $\dfrac{2}{5} + \dfrac{4}{5}i$

81. $0 + \dfrac{1}{7}i$

83. $\dfrac{\sqrt{2}}{3} + \dfrac{1}{3}i$

85. $\dfrac{1}{s+ti} = \dfrac{1}{s+ti} \cdot \dfrac{s-ti}{s-ti} = \dfrac{s-ti}{s^2+t^2} = \dfrac{s}{s^2+t^2} - \dfrac{t}{s^2+t^2}i$

Review Exercises, page 313

1. x^{6n}

2. y^9

3. $-a^5/b^5$

4. x^{22}

5. b^4

6. $(2a - 1)^{10}$

7. $(2x + y)^5$

8. $27/16a^7b^6$

9. $-1/32$

10. $3x^3$

11. $2/y^2$

12. a^2

13. 1

14. $4b^3/a^2$

15. $16x^{12}y^4/81$

16. $-8/27x^3y^3$

17. 4

18. $x^{1/3}$

19. $a^{11/12}$

20. $1/81$

21. $x^{1/2}y^{2/3}$

22. $1/x^2y^{1/5}$

23. $1/x^{1/6}$

24. $1/x^3y^{1/5}$

25. $2\sqrt{15}$

26. $5x^2\sqrt[3]{x^2}/3$

27. $\dfrac{\sqrt{x}}{x}$

28. $4\sqrt[3]{3^2ab^2}/3$

29. $2a^7\sqrt{3b}/b$

30. $\dfrac{2x^2\sqrt[4]{125y^2}}{5y}$

31. $3\sqrt{5}$

32. $3\sqrt[4]{x^2y^2}$

33. $\sqrt[3]{xy^2}(\sqrt[3]{3} + \sqrt[3]{5})$

34. $(\sqrt{2} + 2)\sqrt{xy}$

35. $(-9 - 3\sqrt{x})/(9 - x)$

36. $(\sqrt{3x} - 1)^2/(3x - 1)$

37. $2\sqrt{x - y}/(x - y)$

38. $(a\sqrt{2ab} + b\sqrt{2a})/(a - b)$

39. 1

40. $0 - i$

41. $0 + 2\sqrt{5}i$

42. $2 - 3\sqrt[3]{2} + 0i$

43. $-4 + 8i$

44. 25

45. $10 + 15i$

46. $7 - 24i$

47. $\dfrac{\sqrt{3}}{7} - \dfrac{2}{7}i$

48. $-\dfrac{1}{2} - \dfrac{5}{2}i$

49. $0 - i$

50. $-\dfrac{1}{2} + \dfrac{1}{2}i$

Progress Test 8A, page 314

1. $(x + 1)^{n-2}$
2. $x^{12}y^8/16$
3. $-8y^6/125x^3$
4. $5x^6$
5. $1/64x^{8/5}$
6. $x^{4/3}y^2$
7. $25x^4/9y$
8. $\sqrt{(2y-1)^5}$
9. $(6y^5)^{1/3}$
10. $-4x^2y^4\sqrt{2y}$
11. $\sqrt{5x}/5$
12. $-4a^4b^3$
13. $-7\sqrt[3]{3}$
14. $5y\sqrt{x} - 8x\sqrt{y}$
15. $3(4x - 9y)$
16. $4 - 2i$
17. 2
18. i
19. $\dfrac{-4}{25} - \dfrac{22}{25}i$
20. $\dfrac{4}{25} - \dfrac{3}{25}i$

Progress Test 8B, page 315

1. x^{6n-2}
2. $-a^6b^3/27$
3. $-y^6/27x^9$
4. $4/(x + 1)$
5. $-1/216y^{3/2}$
6. $x^{5/2}/y^{4/5}$
7. $x^{8/5}/27^{2/5}y^{6/25}$
8. $\sqrt[3]{(3x + 1)^2}$
9. $(4x^3)^{1/5}$
10. $-6x\sqrt[4]{x^2z^2}$
11. $x\sqrt{2xy}/y$
12. $-2x^5y^4\sqrt{y}$
13. $-2\sqrt[3]{2}$
14. $-3b\sqrt{a-1} - (a-1)\sqrt{b(a-1)}$
15. $-2(6a + 3b - 11\sqrt{ab})$
16. $2 + 2\sqrt{2}i$
17. -3
18. $-3i$
19. $\dfrac{7}{13} + \dfrac{4}{13}i$
20. $\dfrac{3}{34} + \dfrac{5}{34}i$

Chapter 9

Exercise Set 9.1, page 325

1. ± 3
3. $\pm 5/2$
5. $\pm\sqrt{5}$
7. $3 \pm i\sqrt{2}$
9. $-5/2 \pm \sqrt{2}$
11. $-2 \pm \dfrac{\sqrt{3}}{2}i$
13. $(5 \pm 2\sqrt{2})/3$
15. $\pm 2i$
17. $\pm\dfrac{8}{3}i$
19. $\pm i\sqrt{6}$
21. $1, 2$
23. $-2, 1$
25. $-4, -2$
27. $0, 4$
29. $1/2, 2$
31. ± 2
33. $1/3, 1/2$
35. $4, -2$
37. $-1/2, 4$
39. $1/3, -3$
41. $-\dfrac{1}{2} \pm \dfrac{1}{2}i$
43. $1, -3/4$
45. $-\dfrac{1}{3} \pm \dfrac{\sqrt{2}}{3}i$
47. $3, -4$
49. $0, -1/3$
51. $(-1 \pm \sqrt{11})/2$
53. $-2, 2/3$
55. $-\dfrac{5}{4} \pm \dfrac{\sqrt{7}}{4}i$
57. $\pm 1/2$
59. $-\dfrac{1}{4} \pm \dfrac{\sqrt{11}}{4}i$
61. $-\dfrac{3}{4} \pm \dfrac{\sqrt{17}}{4}$
63. $3, -3/2$
65. $1, -1/3$
69. $x = 5$

Exercise Set 9.2, page 330

1. d

3. c

5. $a = 3, b = -2, c = 5$

7. $a = 2, b = -1, c = 5$

9. $a = 3, b = -1/3, c = 0$

11. $-2, -3$

13. $3, 5$

15. $0, -3/2$

17. $\dfrac{2}{5} \pm \dfrac{\sqrt{11}}{5} i$

19. $\dfrac{2}{5} \pm \dfrac{\sqrt{21}}{5} i$

21. $3, -4$

23. $2/3, -1$

25. ± 3

27. $\pm 2\sqrt{3}/3$

Exercise Set 9.3, page 333

29. $1/2, -4$

31. $u = 0, u = -\dfrac{3}{4}$

1. e

3. b

5. d

7. d

9. c

11. a

13. a

15. two complex roots

17. a double root

19. two real roots

21. two real roots

23. two complex roots

25. two complex roots

27. two real roots

29. a double root

31. 2

33. 0

35. 1

37. 0

Exercise Set 9.4, page 338

1. A: 3 hr.; B: 6 hr.

3. roofer: 6 hr.; assistant: 12 hr.

5. $L = 12$ ft., $W = 4$ ft.

7. $L = 8$ cm, $W = 6$ cm

9. 10 ft.

11. 5 or 1/5

13. $3, 7$ or $-3, -7$

15. $6, 8$

17. 150

19. 8

21. true for all x

Exercise Set 9.5, page 344

1. 4

3. 2

5. 3

7. $0, 4$

9. 5

11. 6

13. $2, 10$

15. $u = x^2$

17. $u = x^{2/3}$

19. $u = 1/y^2$

21. $u = 1/x^{2/3}$

23. $u = 2 + 3/x$

25. $u = x^2; \pm\sqrt{3}/3, \pm i\sqrt{2}$

27. $u = 1/x; -3/2, 2$

29. $u = x^{1/5}; -1/32, -32$

31. $u = 1 + 1/x; -2/7, 1/3$

Exercise Set 9.6, page 348

1. b, d, e

3. a, c, d, e

5. c, e

7. $-2, -3$

9. $-1/2, 1$

11. $0, 2$

13. $-5, -3$

15. $-1/2, 3$

17. $-2/3, 1/2$

19. $x < -3, x > 2$

21. $x < -1, x < 5/2$

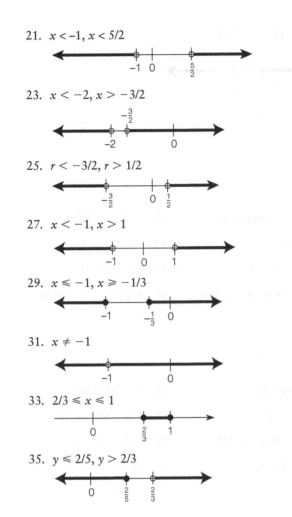

23. $x < -2, x > -3/2$

25. $r < -3/2, r > 1/2$

27. $x < -1, x > 1$

29. $x \leq -1, x \geq -1/3$

31. $x \neq -1$

33. $2/3 \leq x \leq 1$

35. $y \leq 2/5, y > 2/3$

37. $x \neq 1$

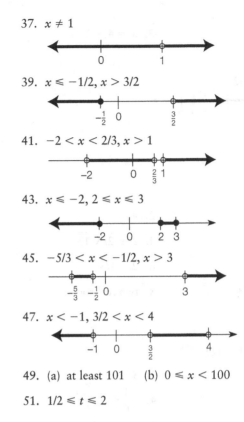

39. $x \leq -1/2, x > 3/2$

41. $-2 < x < 2/3, x > 1$

43. $x \leq -2, 2 \leq x \leq 3$

45. $-5/3 < x < -1/2, x > 3$

47. $x < -1, 3/2 < x < 4$

49. (a) at least 101   (b) $0 \leq x < 100$

51. $1/2 \leq t \leq 2$

Review Exercises, page 351

1. $x = \pm 5$

2. $y = \pm 6$

3. $x = -1, 5$

4. $t = -\dfrac{1}{2} \pm i$

5. $x = -3, 2$

6. $y = 2, -1/2$

7. $r = 0, 1/3$

8. $x = \pm 5/2$

9. $x = (\sqrt{37} + 5)/2, (-\sqrt{37} + 5)/2$

10. $x = -2 + 4\sqrt{3}/3, -2 - 4\sqrt{3}/3$

11. $x = -3, 1$

12. $x = -1, 1/3$

13. $x = -1 + \sqrt{2}/2, -1 - \sqrt{2}/2$

14. $x = -1 + \sqrt{10}/3, -1 - \sqrt{10}/3$

15. $x = \dfrac{1}{4} \pm \dfrac{\sqrt{7}}{4} i$

16. $x = -\dfrac{1}{4} \pm \dfrac{\sqrt{11}}{4} i$

17. 2 complex roots

18. 2 real roots

19. double real root

20. 2 complex roots

21. 2 real roots

22. 2 real roots

23. no x-intercepts

24. 2 x-intercepts

25. 1 x-intercept

26. No x-intercepts

27. length = 6 ft; width = 9 ft

28. 60

29. $x = 6$

30. $x = 6$

31. $x = \pm i\sqrt{2}, \pm \dfrac{\sqrt{6}}{2}$

32. $u = \dfrac{1}{x^2}$

33. $x = 4, -2$

34. $x = 3, 5$

35. $-1 \leqslant x \leqslant 3/2$

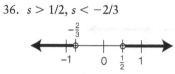

36. $s > 1/2$, $s < -2/3$

Progress Test 9A, page 352

1. $\pm \dfrac{\sqrt{21}}{3} i$

2. 4

3. $7/2, -1/2$

4. $2 \pm 2i\sqrt{15}$

5. $4, -1/2$

6. $2, -1/3$

7. $(3 \pm \sqrt{33})/3$

8. two real roots

9. two complex roots

10. $(-3 \pm \sqrt{13})/4$

11. $0, -2/3$

12. $-3 \leqslant x \leqslant 1/2$

13. $-1 \leqslant x < 1$

14. $3/2 < x < 4$

15. $L = 26$ m, $W = 21$ m

16. $3\sqrt{2}$, $3\sqrt{2} + 6$ hr

Progress Test 9B, page 352

1. $\pm 3/2$

2. 5

3. $-9, 21$

4. $-\dfrac{1}{6} \pm \dfrac{i\sqrt{10}}{3}$

5. $4, -3$

6. $-1/2, -1$

7. $\dfrac{3}{2} \pm \dfrac{1}{2}i$

8. a double root

9. two real roots

10. $(5 \pm i\sqrt{7})/4$

11. $\pm \dfrac{\sqrt{15}}{3} i$

12. $x \leqslant -5/2$, $x \geqslant 2$

13. $x \leqslant -1/2$, $x \geqslant 1/2$

14. $-1/3 < x < 2$

15. 9 m, 12 m

16. 25

Chapter 10

Exercise Set 10.1, page 360

1. $Q(x) = x^2 - 3x$, $R(x) = 5$

3. $Q(x) = x^3 + 3x^2 + 9x + 27$, $R(x) = 0$

5. $Q(x) = 3x^2 - 4x + 4$, $R(x) = 4$

7. $Q(x) = x^4 - 2x^3 + 4x^2 - 8x + 16$, $R(x) = 0$

9. $Q(x) = 6x^3 + 18x^2 + 53x + 159$, $R(x) = 481$

11. $Q(x) = x^3 - 2x^2 + 4x - 9$, $R(x) = 18$

13. $Q(x) = x^2 - x + 3$, $R(x) = -2$

15. $Q(x) = x^4 + 3x^3 + 9x^2 + 27x + 82$, $R(x) = 246$

Exercise Set 10.2, page 364

1. −7

3. −34

5. 0

7. −1

9. 0

11. −62

13.

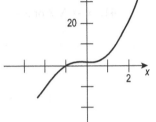

15.

17.

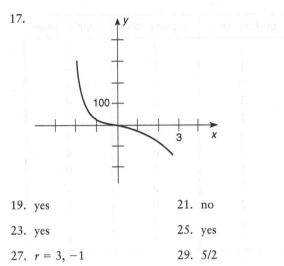

19. yes

21. no

23. yes

25. yes

27. $r = 3, -1$

29. 5/2

Exercise Set 10.3, page 374

1. $-\dfrac{4}{5} + \dfrac{7}{5}i$

3. $\dfrac{22}{13} - \dfrac{7}{13}i$

5. $\dfrac{5}{29} - \dfrac{2}{29}i$

7. $\dfrac{4}{17} + \dfrac{16}{17}i$

11. $x^3 - 2x^2 - 16x + 32$

13. $x^3 + 6x^2 + 11x + 6$

15. $x^3 - 6x^2 + 6x + 8$

17. $x^3/3 + x^2/3 - 7x/12 + 1/6$

19. $x^3 - 4x^2 - 2x + 8$

21. 3, −1, 2

23. −2, 4, −4

25. −2, −1, 0, −1/2

27. 5, 5, 5, −5, −5

29. $x^3 + 6x^2 + 12x + 8$

31. $4x^4 + 4x^3 - 3x^2 - 2x + 4$

33. 2, −1

35. $(3 \pm i\sqrt{3})/2, 5$

37. −1, −2, 4

39. $x^2 + (1 - 3i)x - (2 + 6i)$

41. $x^2 - 3x + (3 + i)$

43. $x^3 + (1 + 2i)x^2 + (-8 + 8i)x + (-12 + 8i)$

45. $(x^2 - 6x + 10)(x - 1)$

47. $(x^2 + 2x + 5)(x^2 + 2x + 4)$

49. $(x - 2)(x + 2)(x - 3)(x^2 + 6x + 10)$

51. $x - (a + bi)$

Exercise Set 10.4, page 381

	positive roots	negative roots	complex roots
1.	3	1	0
	1	1	2
3.	0	0	6
5.	3	2	0
	1	2	2
	3	0	2
	1	0	4
7.	1	2	0
	1	0	2
9.	2	0	2
	0	0	4
11.	1	1	6

13. $1, -2, 3$

15. $2, -1, -1/2, 2/3$

17. $1, -1, -1, 1/5$

19. $1, -3/4$

21. $3, 3, 1/2$

23. $-1, 3/4, \pm i$

25. $3/5, \pm 2, \pm i\sqrt{2}$

27. $0, 1/2, 2/3, -1$

29. $1/2, -4, 2 \pm \sqrt{2}$

31. $k = 3, r = -2$

33. $k = 7, r = 1$

41. $x = \sqrt{7}$ or $x = -\sqrt{7}$

Review Exercises, page 384

1. $Q(x) = 2x^2 + 2x + 8, R = 4$

2. $Q(x) = x^3 - 5x^2 + 10x - 18, R = 31$

3. $46, -8$

4. $4, 1$

7. $6/25 - 17i/25$

8. $-1/5 + 2i/5$

9. $-5/2 + 5i/2$

10. $1/10 - 3i/10$

11. $i/4$

12. $2/29 + 5i/29$

13. $x^3 + 6x^2 + 11x + 6$

14. $x^3 - 3x^2 + 3x - 9$

15. $x^3 - 6x^2 + 11x - 6$

16. $4x^4 + 4x^3 - 3x^2 - 2x + 1$

17. $x^4 + 2x^2 + 1$

18. $x^4 - 6x^2 - 8x - 3$

19. $-1/2, 3$

20. $-1 \pm \sqrt{2}$

21. $4, 2 + i, 2 - i$

22. 1 positive, 1 negative

23. 5 positive, 0 negative

24. 1 positive, 0 negative

25. 2 positive, 2 negative

26. $3, -2/3, -3/2$

27. $1, -2, 2/3, 3/2$

28. none

29. $-1, (-9 \pm \sqrt{321})/12$

30. $2, 3/2, -1 \pm \sqrt{2}$

Progress Test 10A, page 385

1. $Q(x) = 2x^2 - 5, R(x) = 11$

2. $Q(x) = 3x^3 - 7x^2 + 14x - 28, R(x) = 54$

3. -25

4. -165

6. $x^3 - 2x^2 - 5x + 6$

7. $x^4 - 6x^3 + 6x^2 + 6x - 7$ 8. $2, \pm i$

9. $-1, -1, (3 \pm \sqrt{17})/2$

10. $x^5 + 3x^4 - 6x^3 - 10x^2 + 21x - 9$

11. $16x^5 - 8x^4 + 9x^3 - 9x^2 - 7x - 1$

12. $x^2 - (1 + 2i)x + (-1 + i)$

13. $1/2, 1/2$

14. $1, -1 \pm i$

15. $(x^2 - 4x + 5)(x - 2)$

16. 2

17. 1

18. none

19. $1, 1, -1, -1, 1/2$

20. $2/3, -3, \pm i$

Progress Test 10B, page 385

1. $Q(x) = 3x^3/2 + 3x^2/4 + 17x/8 + 15/16$,
   $R(x) = 49x - 17$

2. $Q(x) = -2x^2 + x + 1$, $R(x) = 0$

3. -1 4. 24

6. $2x^4 - x^3 - 3x^2 + x + 1$ 7. $x^3 - 4x^2 + 2x + 4$

8. $1, 2, 2, 2$ 9. $(-3 \pm \sqrt{13})/2, -3,$
   -3

10. $8x^4 + 4x^3 - 18x^2 + 11x - 2$

11. $x^4 + 4x^3 - x^2 - 6x + 18$

12. $x^4 - 4x^3 - x^2 + 14x + 10$ 13. $(3 \pm \sqrt{17})/2$

14. $-2 \pm 2\sqrt{2}$

15. $(x^2 - 2x + 2)(2x^2 + 3x - 2)$

16. 1 17. 2

18. $-1, 2/3, -2$ 19. $-1/2, 3/2, \pm i$

20. $0, 1/2, \pm \sqrt{2}$

Chapter 11

Exercise Set 11.1, page 400

1. (a) 5 (b) $x^2 + x - 1$ (c) 9

3. (a) $-5/4$ (b) $\dfrac{x^2 + 1}{x - 2}$ (c) 0

5. (a) $x \neq 2$ (b) all real numbers

7. (a) 1 (b) $2x^2 + x$ (c) $2x^3 + 2x^2 - x - 1$

9. (a) $-17/2$ (b) -34 (c) 2

11. (a) 21 (b) $4x^2 + 2x + 1$ (c) 105

13. (a) -5 (b) $4x + 3$ (c) 210

15. (a) 20 (b) $x^2 + 4x + 8$ (c) 15

17. (a) all real numbers   (b) all real numbers

19. (a) $x + 1$ (b) $x + 1$

21. $\dfrac{x - 1}{x}, -\dfrac{x + 1}{x}$

23. $f(x) = x^8; g(x) = 3x + 2$

25. $f(x) = x^{1/3}; g(x) = x^3 - 2x^2$

27. $f(x) = x^{20}; g(x) = 3x^2 + 1$

29. $f(x) = \sqrt{x}; g(x) = 4 - x$

31. $f(x) = x^{-10}; g(x) = 2 - 5x^2$

33. $f(x) = \sqrt{x}; g(x) = \dfrac{x - 2}{x + 5}$

41. $f^{-1}(x) = \dfrac{x - 3}{2}$ 43. $f^{-1}(x) = -\dfrac{x - 3}{2}$

45. $f^{-1}(x) = 3x + 15$ 47. $f^{-1}(x) = \sqrt[3]{x - 1}$

49. $f^{-1}(x) = \sqrt{x}$

51. (a) $f^{-1}(x) = 3x - 6$
    (b) 0
    (c) 2
    (d) 3

53. (a) $h^{-1}(x) = -\dfrac{x - 2}{3}$
    (b) $4/3$
    (c) 3
    (d) -3

55. (a) $f^{-1}(x) = \sqrt[3]{x + 2}$
    (b) $\sqrt[3]{5}$
    (c) 1
    (d) -2

57. yes   59. no

61. yes   63. no

Exercise Set 11.2, page 413

1.

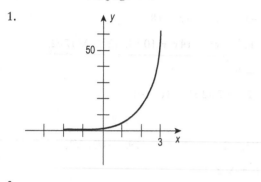

3.

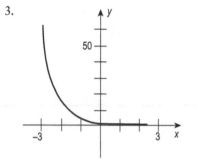

5.

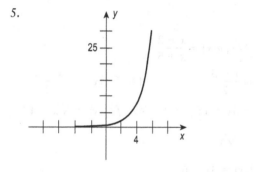

7.

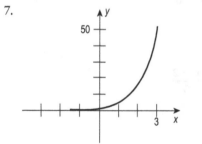

9.

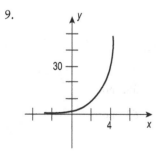

11.

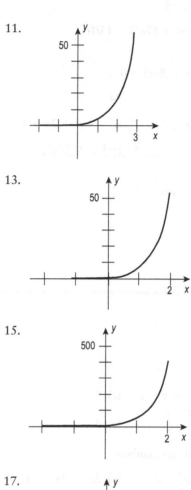

13.

15.

17.

19. 3   21. 3

23. 4   25. 2

27. 3   29. 1

31. −1   33. 2

35. 1

37. (a) 200   (b) 0.25   (c) 29,682
    (d) 256.8, 543.7, 1478, 2436

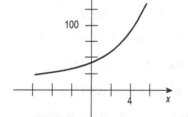

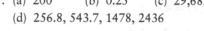

39. 6.59 billion

41. 67 grams

47. $173

49. $2489

43. $41,611

45. $33,721.25

51. π^2

Exercise Set 11.3, page 422

1. $2^2 = 4$

3. $9^{-2} = 1/81$

5. $e^3 = 20.09$

7. $10^3 = 1000$

9. $e^0 = 1$

11. $3^{-3} = 1/27$

13. $\log_5 25 = 2$

15. $\log 10{,}000 = 4$

17. $\log_2 \dfrac{1}{8} = -3$

19. $\log_2 1 = 0$

21. $\log_{36} 6 = 1/2$

23. $\log_{16} 64 = 3/2$

25. $\log_{27} \dfrac{1}{3} = -\dfrac{1}{3}$

27. 25

29. 4

31. $\dfrac{1}{8}$

33. $e^2 \approx 7.39$

35. $e^{1/3} \approx 1.40$

37. 3

39. 16

41. 10

43. 26

45. 2

47. 3

49. 6

51. 2

53. 3

55. 1/2

57. 2

59. 1

61. 0

63. −1

65. 1/2

67. 4

69. 2

71. −2/3

75.

77.

79.

73.

Exercise Set 11.4, page 430

1. $\log_2 12 = \log_2 3 + \log_2 4$

3. $\log_4(8.4 \cdot 1.5) = \log_4 8.4 + \log_4 1.5$

5. $\log_2 5^3 = 3 \log_2 5$ 7. $\ln 15 = \ln 5 + \ln 3$

9. $\ln(4 \cdot 7) = \ln 4 + \ln 7$ 11. $\ln 4^4 = 4 \ln 4$

13. $\log 120 + \log 36$ 15. 4

17. $\log_a 2 + \log_a x + \log_a y$ 19. $\log_a x - \log_a y - \log_a$
    z

21. $5 \ln x$ 23. $2 \log_a x + 3 \log_a y$

25. $\dfrac{1}{2}(\log_a x + \log_a y)$ 27. $2 \ln x + 3 \ln y + 4 \ln$
    z

29. $\dfrac{1}{2} \ln x + \dfrac{1}{3} \ln y$

31. $2 \log_a x + 3 \log_a y - 4 \log_a z$

33. $-2 \ln a$ 35. 1.19

37. 1.46 39. 1.65

41. 0.12 43. -0.8

45. $.83$ 47. $\log(x^2 \sqrt{y})$

49. $\ln \sqrt[3]{xy}$ 51. $\log_a \dfrac{\sqrt[3]{xy^2}}{\sqrt{z^3}}$

53. $\log_a \sqrt{xy}$ 55. $\ln \dfrac{\sqrt[3]{x^2 y^4}}{z^3}$

57. $\log_a \dfrac{\sqrt{x-1}}{(x+1)^2}$ 59. $\log_a \dfrac{x^3 \sqrt[6]{x+1}}{(x-1)^2}$

61. 1.2304 63. 2.3892

65. 2.3892 67. 2.8074

69. 2.0763

Exercise Set 11.5, page 435

1. $\log_5 18$ 3. $1 + \log_2 7$

5. $(\log_3 46)/2$ 7. $(5 + \log_5 564)/2$

9. $(\log 2 + \log 3)/(\log 3 - 2 \log 2)$

11. $-\log_2 15$ 13. $(1 - \log_4 12)/2$

15. $\ln 18$ 17. $(-3 + \ln 20)/2$

19. 500 21. $1/2$

23. 5 25. 3

27. 8 29. $-1 + \sqrt{17}$

31. 36.62 years   33. 12.6 hours

35. 8.8 years   37. 27.47 days

39. 1.386 days

Review Exercises, page 438

1. $x^2 + x$ 2. 0

3. $(x + 1)/(x^2 - 1)$ 4. $x \neq \pm 1$

5. $x^2 + 2x$ 6. 4

7. $|x| - 2$ 8. $x + 4 - 4\sqrt{x}$

9. 0 10. not defined

12.

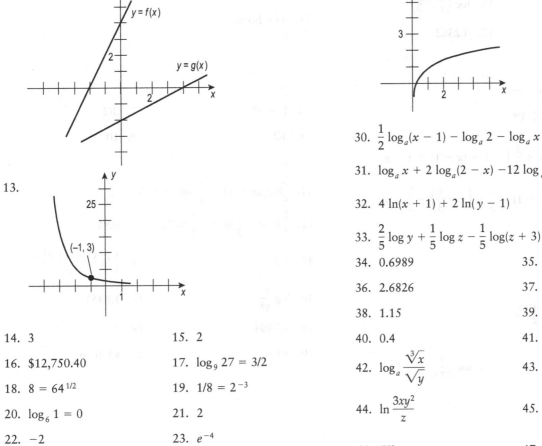

13.

14. 3

15. 2

16. $12,750.40

17. $\log_9 27 = 3/2$

18. $8 = 64^{1/2}$

19. $1/8 = 2^{-3}$

20. $\log_6 1 = 0$

21. 2

22. -2

23. e^{-4}

24. 26

25. 5

26. $-1/3$

27. -1

28. 3

29.

30. $\frac{1}{2} \log_a(x - 1) - \log_a 2 - \log_a x$

31. $\log_a x + 2 \log_a(2 - x) - 12 \log_a(y + 1)$

32. $4 \ln(x + 1) + 2 \ln(y - 1)$

33. $\frac{2}{5} \log y + \frac{1}{5} \log z - \frac{1}{5} \log(z + 3)$

34. 0.6989

35. 1.3010

36. 2.6826

37. 1.6816

38. 1.15

39. 0.55

40. 0.4

41. -0.15

42. $\log_a \dfrac{\sqrt[3]{x}}{\sqrt{y}}$

43. $\log(x^2 - x)^{4/3}$

44. $\ln \dfrac{3xy^2}{z}$

45. $\log_a \dfrac{(x + 2)^2}{(x + 1)^{3/2}}$

46. 5/3

47. 15/7

48. $\dfrac{1}{3} + \dfrac{\log 14}{3 \log 2}$

49. $\sqrt{5000}$

50. $\dfrac{199}{98}$

51. 11.5 hours

Progress Test 11A, page 439

1. (a) $-1/2$ (b) -6

2. $g[f(x)] = \dfrac{(2x + 4)}{2} - 2 = (x + 2) - 2 = x$

3.

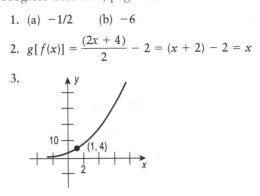

4. $-2/3$

5. $1/9 = 3^{-2}$

6. $\log_{16} 64 = 3/2$

7. 3

8. -1

9. 5/2

10. 1/2

11. $3 \log_a x - 2 \log_a y - \log_a z$

12. $2 \log x + \dfrac{1}{2} \log(2y - 1) - 3 \log y$

13. 0.7

14. 0.45

15. $\log \dfrac{x^2}{(y+1)^3}$

16. $\log \left(\dfrac{x+3}{x-3}\right)^{2/3}$

17. 1.2041

18. 3.2362

19. 200

20. 4

21. 34.6 hours

Progress Test 11B, page 440

1. (a) $\dfrac{2x-1}{x^2+3}$ (b) 19

2. $f[g(x)] = -3\left(-\dfrac{1}{3}x + \dfrac{1}{3}\right) + 1 = (x-1) + 1 = x$

$g[f(x)] = -\dfrac{1}{3}(-3x+1) + \dfrac{1}{3} = \left(x - \dfrac{1}{3}\right) + \dfrac{1}{3} = x$

3.

(0, 2)   10   2   x

4. 8

5. $\log \dfrac{1}{1000} = -3$

6. $1 = 3^0$

7. 3/2

8. 3/2

9. 10

10. 4

11. $\dfrac{5}{4}\log_a(x-1) + \dfrac{5}{4}\log_a(y+3)$

12. $\dfrac{1}{2}\ln x + \dfrac{1}{2}\ln y + \dfrac{1}{4}\ln 2z$ 13. 0.85

14. 1.5

15. $\dfrac{1}{5}\ln \dfrac{(x-1)^3 y^2}{z}$

16. $\log \dfrac{x^2}{y^2}$

17. 1.8451

18. 1.7404

19. 3

20. 10

21. $530.76

Chapter 12

Exercise Set 12.1, page 448

1. $3\sqrt{2}$

3. $4\sqrt{2}$

5. $\sqrt{65}$

7. $2\sqrt{10}$

9. $\sqrt{229}/4$

11. $\sqrt{13}$

13. (5/2, 5)

15. (1, 5/2)

17. (−7/2, −1)

19. (0, −1/2)

21. (−1, 9/2)

23. (0, 0)

Exercise Set 12.2, page 452

1. none

3. none

5. y-axis

7. x-axis

9. y-axis

11. none

13. none

15. all

17. origin

19. y-axis

21. y-axis

23. y-axis

25. all

27. all

29. all

31. none

33. origin

Exercise Set 12.3, page 456

1. $(x - 2)^2 + (y - 3)^2 = 4$

3. $(x + 2)^2 + (y + 3)^2 = 5$

5. $x^2 + y^2 = 9$

7. $(x + 1)^2 + (y - 4)^2 = 8$

9. $(h, k) = (2, 3); r = 4$ 11. $(h, k) = (2, -2); r = 2$

13. $(h, k) = \left(-4, -\dfrac{3}{2}\right); r = 3\sqrt{2}$

15. no graph

17. $(x + 2)^2 + (y - 4)^2 = 16;$
    $(h, k) = (-2, 4); r = 4$

19. $\left(x - \dfrac{3}{2}\right)^2 + \left(y - \dfrac{5}{2}\right)^2 = \dfrac{11}{2};$

    $(h, k) = \left(\dfrac{3}{2}, \dfrac{5}{2}\right); r = \dfrac{\sqrt{22}}{2}$

21. $(x - 1)^2 + y^2 = \dfrac{7}{2};$

    $(h, k) = (1, 0); r = \dfrac{\sqrt{14}}{2}$

23. $(x - 2)^2 + (y + 3)^2 = 8;$
    $(h, k) = (2, -3); r = 2\sqrt{2}$

25. $(x - 3)^2 + (y + 4)^2 = 18;$
    $(h, k) = (3, -4); r = 3\sqrt{2}$
    circle

27. $\left(x + \dfrac{3}{2}\right)^2 + \left(y - \dfrac{5}{2}\right)^2 = \dfrac{3}{2};$

    $(h, k) = \left(-\dfrac{3}{2}, \dfrac{5}{2}\right); r = \dfrac{\sqrt{6}}{2}$
    circle

29. $(x - 3)^2 + y^2 = 11;$
    $(h, k) = (3, 0); r = \sqrt{11}$
    circle

31. $\left(x - \dfrac{3}{2}\right)^2 + (y - 1)^2 = \dfrac{17}{4};$

    $(h, k) = \left(\dfrac{3}{2}, 1\right); r = \dfrac{\sqrt{17}}{2}$
    circle

33. 9π

37. $(x + 5)^2 + (y - 2)^2 = 8$

39. $(x - 5)^2 + (y - 1)^2 = 20$

Exercise Set 12.4, page 465

1.

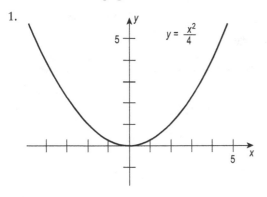

3.

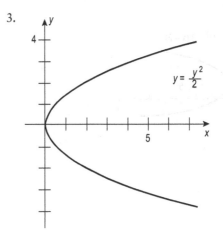

5.

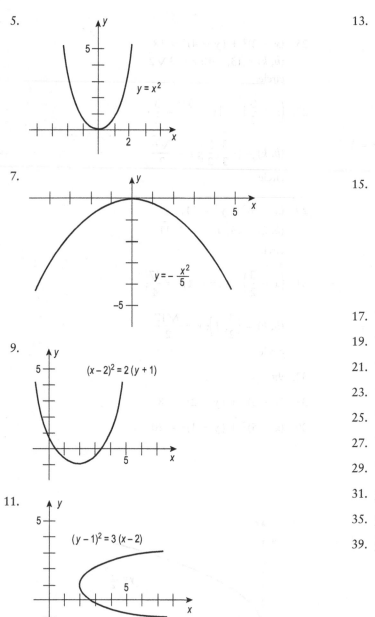

7.

9.

11.

13.

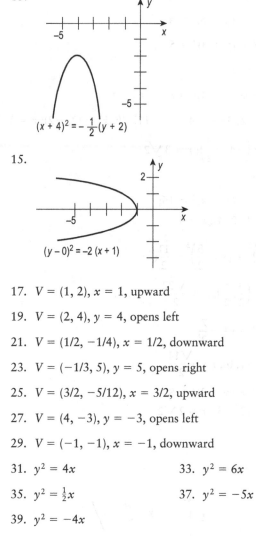

15.

17. $V = (1, 2)$, $x = 1$, upward

19. $V = (2, 4)$, $y = 4$, opens left

21. $V = (1/2, -1/4)$, $x = 1/2$, downward

23. $V = (-1/3, 5)$, $y = 5$, opens right

25. $V = (3/2, -5/12)$, $x = 3/2$, upward

27. $V = (4, -3)$, $y = -3$, opens left

29. $V = (-1, -1)$, $x = -1$, downward

31. $y^2 = 4x$ 33. $y^2 = 6x$

35. $y^2 = \frac{1}{2}x$ 37. $y^2 = -5x$

39. $y^2 = -4x$

Exercise Set 12.5, page 476

1.

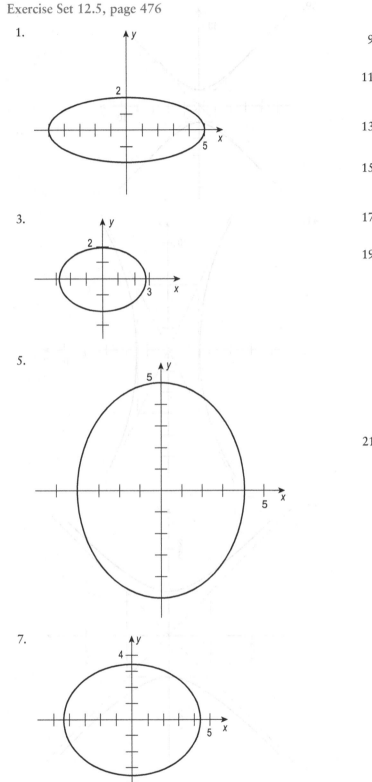

3.

5.

7.

9. $\dfrac{x^2}{9} + \dfrac{y^2}{4} = 1$; $(0, \pm 2)$, $(\pm 3, 0)$

11. $\dfrac{x^2}{4} + \dfrac{y^2}{1} = 1$; $(0, \pm 1)$, $(\pm 2, 0)$

13. $\dfrac{x^2}{1} + \dfrac{y^2}{\frac{1}{4}} = 1$; $\left(0, \pm\dfrac{1}{2}\right)$, $(\pm 1, 0)$

15. $\dfrac{x^2}{3} + \dfrac{y^2}{4} = 1$; $(0, \pm 2)$, $(\pm \sqrt{3}, 0)$

17. $\dfrac{x^2}{\frac{1}{4}} + \dfrac{y^2}{\frac{9}{8}} = 1$; $\left(0, \pm\dfrac{3\sqrt{2}}{4}\right)$, $\left(\pm\dfrac{1}{2}, 0\right)$

19.

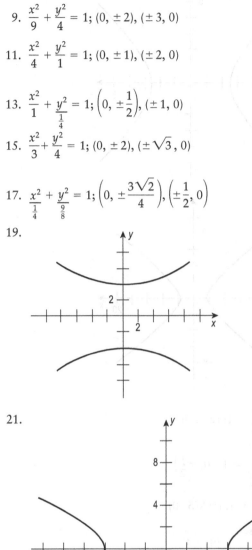

21.

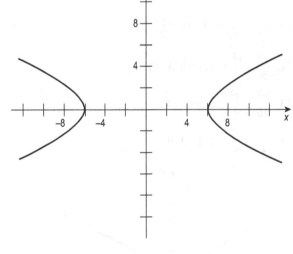

23.

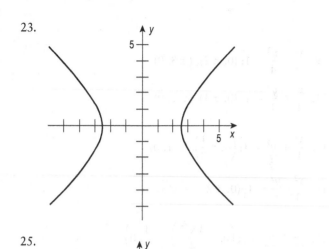

25.

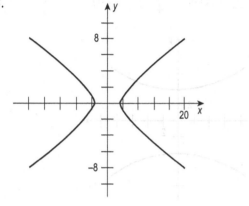

27. $\dfrac{x^2}{4} - \dfrac{y^2}{64} = 1; \, (\pm 2, 0)$

29. $\dfrac{y^2}{\frac{1}{4}} - \dfrac{x^2}{\frac{1}{4}} = 1; \, \left(0, \pm\dfrac{1}{2}\right)$

31. $\dfrac{x^2}{5} - \dfrac{y^2}{4} = 1; \, (\pm\sqrt{5}, 0)$

33. $\dfrac{y^2}{16} - \dfrac{x^2}{4} = 1; \, (0, \pm 4)$

35. $\dfrac{x^2}{4} - \dfrac{y^2}{8} = 1; \, (\pm 2, 0)$

37.

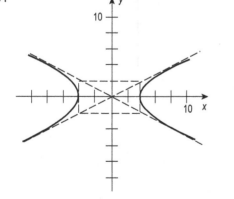

39.

41.

43.

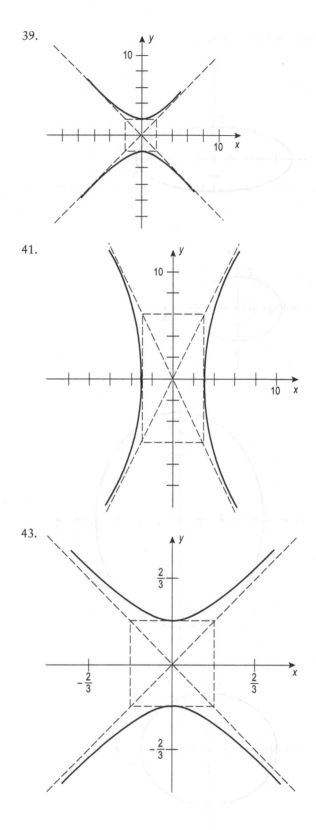

45.

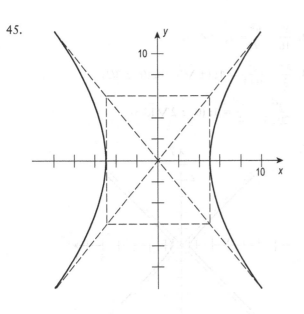

47.

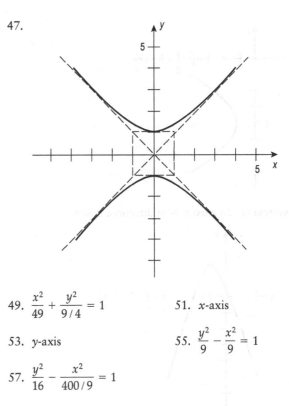

49. $\dfrac{x^2}{49} + \dfrac{y^2}{9/4} = 1$ 51. x-axis

53. y-axis   55. $\dfrac{y^2}{9} - \dfrac{x^2}{9} = 1$

57. $\dfrac{y^2}{16} - \dfrac{x^2}{400/9} = 1$

Exercise Set 12.6, page 479

1. parabola   3. circle

5. hyperbola   7. ellipse

9. no graph   11. ellipse

13. hyperbola   15. point

17. ellipse   19. circle

21. parabola   23. no graph

25. circle   27. parabola

29. ellipse

Review Exercises, page 481

1. $\sqrt{61}$ 2. 6

3. $\sqrt{13}$ 4. $(-1, -1)$

5. $(-5/2, 5/2)$ 6. $(-1/2, -9/2)$

7. $(10, 7)$

8. $\overline{P_1P_2} = \overline{P_3P_4} = \sqrt{26}$, $\overline{P_1P_4} = \overline{P_2P_3} = 5$

9. $\overline{AB} = \sqrt{170}$, $\overline{AC} = \sqrt{136}$, $\overline{BC} = \sqrt{34}$, $\overline{AB}^2 = \overline{AC}^2 + \overline{BC}^2$

10. $10x + 12y + 15 = 0$ 11. x-axis

12. all

13. $(x + 5)^2 + (y - 2)^2 = 16$

14. $(x + 3)^3 + (y + 3)^2 = 4$

15. $(h, k) = (2, -3)$; $r = 3$

16. $(h, k) = (-1/2, 4)$; $r = 1/3$

17. $(h, k) = (-2, 3)$; $r = \sqrt{3}$

18. $(h, k) = (1, -1)$; $r = \sqrt{2}/2$

19. $(h, k) = (0, 3)$; $r = \sqrt{6}$

20. $(h, k) = (1, 1)$; $r = \sqrt{10}$

21. vertex: $(3/2, -5)$; axis: $y = -5$; direction: right

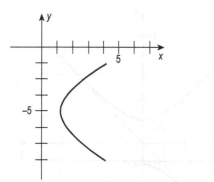

22. vertex: $(1, 2)$; axis: $x = 1$; direction: down

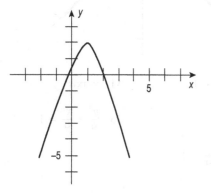

	Vertex	Axis	Direction
23.	$(-3, 0)$	$y = 0$	left
24.	$(2, -2)$	$y = -2$	left
25.	$(3, -2)$	$x = 3$	up
26.	$(-2, -1/2)$	$x = -2$	down
27.	$(0, 1)$	$y = 1$	right
28.	$(-3, 0)$	$x = -3$	down

29. $\dfrac{x^2}{4} - \dfrac{y^2}{9} = 1$; $(\pm 2, 0)$

30. $\dfrac{x^2}{1} + \dfrac{y^2}{9} = 1$; $(\pm 1, 0)$, $(0, \pm 3)$

31. $\dfrac{x^2}{7} + \dfrac{y^2}{5} = 1$; $(\pm \sqrt{7}, 0)$, $(0, \pm \sqrt{5})$

32. $\dfrac{x^2}{16} - \dfrac{y^2}{9} = 1$; $(\pm 4, 0)$

33. $\dfrac{x^2}{3} + \dfrac{y^2}{9/4} = 1$; $(\pm \sqrt{3}, 0)$, $(0, \pm 3/2)$

34. $\dfrac{y^2}{20/3} - \dfrac{x^2}{4} = 1$; $(0, \pm 2\sqrt{15}/3)$

35.

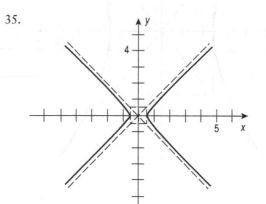

36.

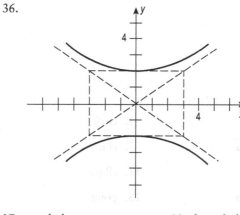

37. parabola

38. hyperbola

39. ellipse

40. no graph

Progress Test 12A, page 482

1. $7\sqrt{2}$

2. $(5/4, -1/8)$

5. x-axis

6. x-axis

7. $(h, k) = (4, -3); r = \sqrt{10}$

8. $V = (-1, 1/2); y = 1/2$

9. intercepts: $\left(0, \pm\dfrac{1}{2}\right)$; asymptotes: $y = \pm 6x$

10. $\left(x - \dfrac{2}{3}\right)^2 + (y + 3)^2 = 3$

11.

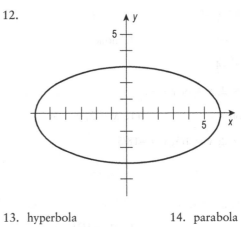

12.

13. hyperbola   14. parabola

15. circle

Progress Test 12B, page 483

1. $2\sqrt{5}$

2. $(-7/4, 1/4)$

3. $(2, 5)$

5. none

6. y-axis

7. $(h, k) = (-1/2, 3); r = 1/2$

8. $V = (1/4, -2); x = 1/4$

9. intercepts: $\left(\pm\dfrac{\sqrt{6}}{3}, 0\right)$; asymptotes: $y = \pm\dfrac{\sqrt{6}}{4}x$

10. $(x + 1)^2 + \left(y + \dfrac{1}{2}\right)^2 = 5$

11.

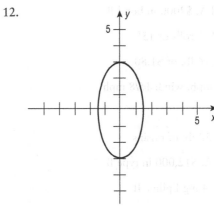

12.

13. circle   14. parabola

15. ellipse

Chapter 13

Exercise Set 13.1, page 492

1. $x = 2, y = -1$ 3. none

5. $x = 1, y = -4$

7. $x = 3, y = 2; x = 3, y = -2$

9. no solution   11. $x = 2, y = -1$

13. $x = 3, y = 2; x = 1/5, y = -18/5$

15. $x = 1, y = 1; x = 9/16, y = -3/4$

17. $x = 1, y = 2; x = 13/5, y = -6/5$

19. $x = \dfrac{-1 + \sqrt{5}}{2}, y = \dfrac{1 + \sqrt{5}}{2}; x = \dfrac{-1 - \sqrt{5}}{2}, y = \dfrac{1 - \sqrt{5}}{2}$

Exercise Set 13.2, page 497

1. $(1, -2)$ 3. $(1, -1/2)$

5. all points on the line $y = -\dfrac{1}{2}x + 3$

7. $(-4/7, 6/7)$ 9. no solution

11. $(3, -1)$ 13. $(39/4, 1/4)$

15. $(4, 1)$ 17. $(2, 3)$

19. $(55/17, 37/17)$

Exercise Set 13.3, page 507

1. 25 nickels, 15 dimes

3. color: $2.50; black-and-white: $1.50

5. $4000 in bond A, $2000 in bond B

7. 10 rolls of 12", 4 rolls of 15"

9. 8 lb. of $1.20, 16 lb. of $1.80

11. bicycle: 105/8 mph; wind: 15/8 mph

13. 34

15. 30 lb. of nuts, 20 lb. of raisins

17. $6000 in type A, $12,000 in type B

19. 5 mg Epiline I, 4 mg Epiline II

21. (a) $R = 95x$

(b)

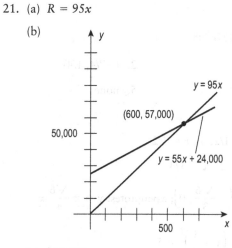

(c) $57,000

23. 4000 newspapers sold
revenue = profit = $1000
(4000, 1000)

25. (a) $p = $300
(b) 1600

27. (a) $p = 20
(b) 120,000

Exercise Set 13.4, page 512

1. $x = 2, y = -1, z = -2$ 3. $x = 1, y = 2/3, z = -2/3$

5. no solution   7. $x = 1, y = 2, z = 2$

9. $x = 1, y = 1, z = 0$ 11. $x = 1, y = 27/2, z = -5/2$

13. no solution   15. $x = 6, y = 4, z = -2$

17. no solution   19. $x = 8, y = -12, z = -11$

21. 2 units of A, 3 units of B, 3 units of C

23. three 12" sets, eight 16" sets, five 19" sets

Exercise Set 13.5, page 517

1.
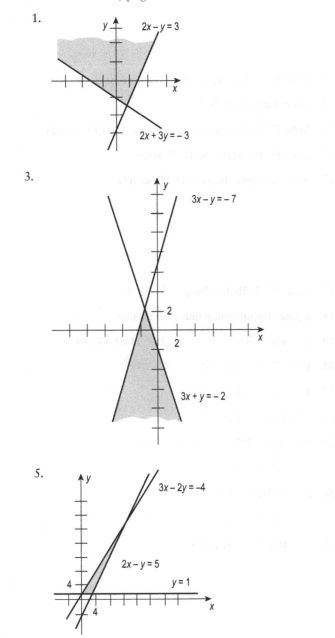

3.

5.

7.
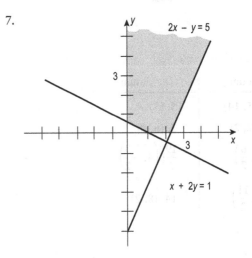

9. no solution

11.
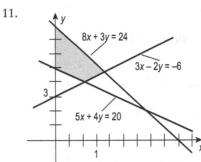

13.
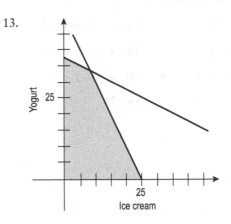

15.

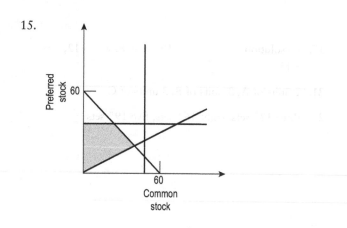

17. $y > 4x + 4$

19. $y < -x + 5$

Exercise Set 13.6, page 523

Minimum	Maximum
1. -2; $(5, 14)$	5; $(5, 0)$
3. -3; $(2, 2)$	3; $(6, 0)$
5. $\frac{6}{7}$; $\left(\frac{6}{7}, \frac{6}{7}\right)$	$\frac{19}{2}$; $\left(4, -\frac{3}{2}\right)$
7. $\frac{1}{2}$; $\left(3, \frac{11}{2}\right)$	14; $(8, 2)$

9. preferred: 190/3 square feet; regular: 30 square feet

11. large: 120; small: 260

13. Java: 2000/11 pounds; Colombian: 4000/11 pounds

15. crop A: 30 acres; crop B: 70 acres

17. pack A: 6 pounds; pack B: 12 pounds

Review Exercises, page 526

1. $x = -1/2, y = 1$

2. $x = 5, y = 2$; $x = 10, y = -3$

3. $x = 5, y = -1$ 4. $x = -4, y = 3/2$

5. $x = 1/4, y = -1/2$

6. $x = 5, y = 0$; $x = -4, y = 3$

7. none

8. $x = 4, y = 4$; $x = 36/25, y = -12/5$

9. $x = -3, y = 5$ 10. $x = 2, y = -2$

11. $x = 4, y = -1$ 12. $x = -2, y = 3$

13. $x = 1, y = -1$; $x = 5, y = 3$ 14. $x = 0, y = 3$

15. 46   16. 28

17. steak: \$3.25/lb; hamburger: \$1.80/lb

18. jogger: 1/6 mi/min; wind: 1/30 mi/min

19. $p = 400$; 2300   20. 1100, \$8800

21. $x = -3, y = 1, z = 4$

22. $x = -2, y = 1/2, z = 3$

23. $x = 1, y = -1, z = 2$

24. $x = 3, y = 1/4, z = -1/3$

25. $x = -3, y = 4$

26. $x = -5/3, y = 5/6$

27. $x = -2, y = -1, z = -3$

28. $x = 1/2, y = -1, z = 1$

29.

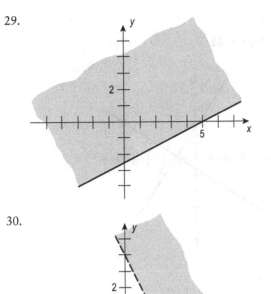

30.

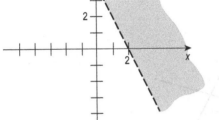

31.

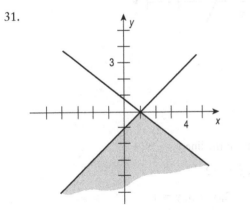

32.

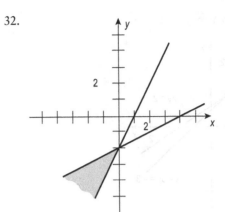

33.

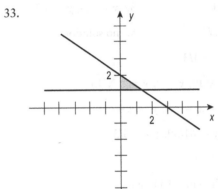

34.

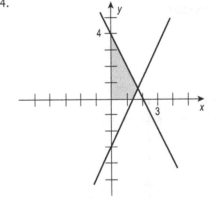

35. $x = 4, y = 6, z = 26$

36. $x = 11/2, y = 2, z = 27/2$

Progress Test 13A, page 527

1.
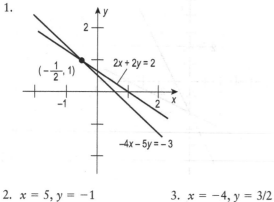

2. $x = 5, y = -1$ 3. $x = -4, y = 3/2$

4. $x = 1/3, y = 2/3$ 5. no solution

6. $x = -1/4, y = -1/3$

7. $x = 2, y = \pm\sqrt{10}; x = 3, y = \pm\sqrt{15}$

8. $x = 3, y = \pm 4; x = -3, y = \pm 4$

9. $x = -66/13, y = 61/39, z = -5/3$

10. 45

11. plane: 600 kph; wind: 100 kph

12. A: 50 cents; B: 60 cents

13. $x = 575, R = \$9200$

14. $p = 24, S = 82$

15.
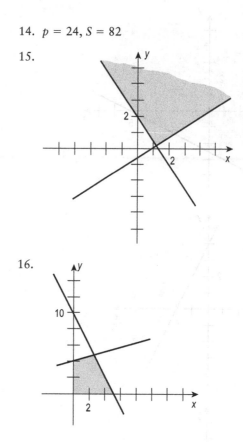

16.
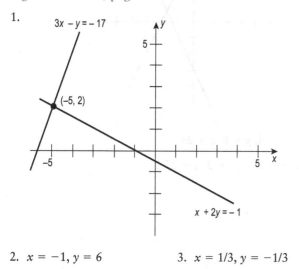

Progress Test 13B, page 528

1.

2. $x = -1, y = 6$ 3. $x = 1/3, y = -1/3$

4. $x = -1/2, y = 1/4$

5. all points on the line $y = \dfrac{7}{2}x - \dfrac{3}{2}$

6. $x = -3, y = -2$

7. $x = 0, y = 2; x = 3, y = 1$

8. $x = 5, y = \pm 4; x = -5, y = \pm 4$

9. $x = -5, y = 16/7, z = 11/21$

10. 37

11. boat: $\dfrac{35}{2}$ kph; current: $\dfrac{5}{2}$ kph

12. pencil: 3 cents; pen: 12 cents

13. 1100

14. $p = 60, S = 310$

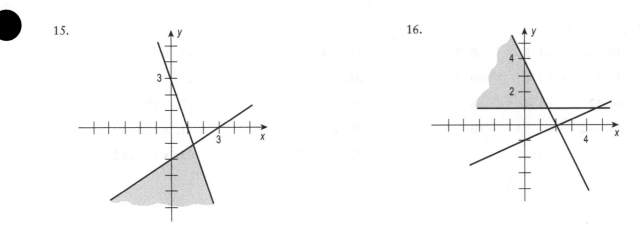

15.

16.

Chapter 14
Exercise Set 14.1, page 543

1. 2×2

3. 4×3

5. 3×3

7. (a) -4 (b) 7 (c) 6 (d) -3

9. $\begin{bmatrix} 3 & -2 \\ 5 & 1 \end{bmatrix}, \begin{bmatrix} 3 & -2 & 12 \\ 5 & 1 & -8 \end{bmatrix}$

11. $\begin{bmatrix} \frac{1}{2} & 1 & 1 \\ 2 & -1 & -4 \\ 4 & 2 & -3 \end{bmatrix}, \begin{bmatrix} \frac{1}{2} & 1 & 1 & 4 \\ 2 & -1 & -4 & 6 \\ 4 & 2 & -3 & 8 \end{bmatrix}$

13. $\frac{3}{2}x + 6y = -1$
$4x + 5y = 3$

15. $x + y + 3z = -4$
$-3x + 4y = 8$
$2x + 7z = 6$

17. yes

19. No—the answer is not unique. A possible answer is:

$\begin{bmatrix} 1 & \frac{1}{2} & -\frac{3}{2} & \vdots & \frac{1}{2} \\ 0 & 1 & -10 & \vdots & 0 \\ 0 & 0 & 1 & \vdots & \frac{1}{10} \end{bmatrix}$

21. $x = -13, y = 8, z = 2$

23. $x = 35, y = 14, z = -4$

25. The answer is not unique. A possible answer is:

$\begin{bmatrix} 1 & -2 & -1 & \vdots & \frac{1}{2} \\ 0 & 1 & -1 & \vdots & \frac{3}{2} \\ 0 & 0 & 12 & \vdots & -11 \end{bmatrix}$

27. The answer is not unique. A possible answer is:

$\begin{bmatrix} 1 & 2 & 1 & \vdots & 0 \\ 0 & 1 & -\frac{1}{5} & \vdots & -\frac{1}{5} \\ 0 & 0 & 1 & \vdots & 1 \end{bmatrix}$

29. $x = 2, y = 3$ 31. $x = 2, y = -1, z = 3$

33. $x = 3, y = 2, z = -1$ 35. $x = -5, y = 2, z = 3$

37. $x = -5/7, y = -2/7, z = -3/7, w = 2/7$

39. $x = 2, y = 3$ 41. $x = 2, y = -1, z = 3$

43. $x = 3, y = 2, z = -1$ 45. $x = -5, y = 2, z = 3$

47. $x = -5/7, y = -2/7, z = -3/7, w = 2/7$

Exercise Set 14.2, page 549

1. (a) -6 (b) -1 (c) 1 (d) 7 17. -8 19. 0

3. (a) -6 (b) 1 (c) 1 (d) 7 21. 52 23. -3

5. (a) 11 (b) 12 (c) 4 (d) -12 25. 0 27. -12

7. (a) -11 (b) -12 (c) -4 (d) -12 29. 0 31. $x = 2$

9. F   11. F   33. $x = \pm\sqrt{2}$ 35. $x = -13/2$

13. T   15. 22

Exercise Set 14.3, page 554

1. $x = 1, y = 2$ 3. impossible   13. $x = 6, y = -3, z = -1$

5. $x = 5, y = -3$ 7. $x = 2, y = -2, z = 3$ 15. $x = 1/3, y = -2/3, z = -1$

9. $x = 4, y = 2, z = 0$ 11. no solution

Review Exercises, page 556

1. 3×5 2. -1 16. $x = 3 + 5t/4, y = 3 + t/2, z = t$

3. 4 4. 8 17. $x = 3, y = 2$ 18. $x = -1, y = 4$

5. $\begin{bmatrix} 3 & -7 \\ 1 & 4 \end{bmatrix}$ 6. $\begin{bmatrix} 3 & -7 & | & 14 \\ 1 & 4 & | & 6 \end{bmatrix}$ 19. $x = 2, y = 1, z = -3$ 20. $x = 1/2, y = -2, z = 4$

21. 10 22. -6

7. $\begin{aligned} 4x - 9y &= 3 \\ 2x + 5y &= 0 \end{aligned}$ 23. 0 24. 12

25. 0 26. -3

8. $\begin{aligned} -2x + 4y + 5z &= 0 \\ 6x - 9y + 4z &= 0 \\ 3x + 2y - z &= 0 \end{aligned}$ 27. 70 28. -12

29. $x = 1/2, y = 4$ 30. $x = 1, y = -4$

9. $x = -1, y = -4$ 10. $x = -6, y = 5$ 31. $x = 10, y = -4$ 32. $x = -4, y = 2, z = 1$

11. $x = -4, y = 3, z = -1$ 12. $x = -1, y = 1, z = -3$ 33. $x = 1/3, y = 2/3, z = -1$

13. $x = 1/2, y = 3/2$ 14. $x = -5, y = 2$ 34. $x = 1/4, y = -2, z = 1/2$

15. $x = 3, y = 1/3, z = -2$

Progress Test 14A, page 557

1. (a) 3×2 (b) -3

2. $\begin{bmatrix} -2 & 1 & 0 & \vert & 4 \\ 3 & -1 & 1 & \vert & 2 \\ 1 & 2 & -3 & \vert & -2 \end{bmatrix}$

3. $3x - 5y = 4$
   $4x + 2y = -1$

4. $x = 1/2, y = -1, z = -2$

5. (a) $\begin{bmatrix} 2 & 0 & 4 & -3 \\ 0 & 3 & -10 & -2 \\ -1 & 1 & 5 & 4 \end{bmatrix}$ (b) $\begin{bmatrix} 2 & 0 & 4 & -3 \\ 4 & 3 & -2 & -8 \\ 0 & 1 & 7 & \frac{5}{2} \end{bmatrix}$

6. $x = -5, y = 2$

7. $x = 3, y = 1/3, z = -2$

8. -10

9. $15, -7, -6$

10. (a) -34 (b) -34

11. 256

12. $x = 2/3, y = -1/3$

13. $x = 3, y = -2, z = 5$

Progress Test 14B, page 558

1. (a) 2×3 (b) 0.6

2. $\begin{bmatrix} 3 & -1 & 5 & \vert & 6 \\ -2 & 0 & 1 & \vert & -3 \\ 5 & 2 & -3 & \vert & 0 \end{bmatrix}$

3. $2.6x + 1.5y = -13$
   $0.2x - 3.7y = 7$

4. $x = 4, y = -1, z = -3/2$

5. (a) $\begin{bmatrix} -1 & 2 & 4 & 0 \\ 0 & 6 & 8 & -3 \\ -\frac{1}{2} & -5 & -2 & 7 \end{bmatrix}$ (b) $\begin{bmatrix} -1 & 2 & 4 & 0 \\ 3 & 0 & -4 & -3 \\ 0 & -6 & -4 & 7 \end{bmatrix}$

6. $x = 20/3, y = -10/3$

7. $x = 3, y = -2, z = -5$

8. 4

9. $6, 0, -12$

10. (a) 40 (b) 40

11. -38

12. $x = 1, y = 1$

13. $x = 3, y = -1, z = 1/2$

Chapter 15

Exercise Set 15.1, page 570

1. $2, 4, 6, 8$

3. $5, 7, 9, 11$

5. $2, 5, 8, 11$

7. $4/3, 5/3, 2, 7/3$

9. $1, 2, 3, 4$

11. $1/3, 4/5, 9/7, 16/9$

13. yes

15. no

17. yes

19. yes

21. no

23. yes

25. $2, 6, 10, 14$

27. $3, 5/2, 2, 3/2$

29. $-4, 0, 4, 8$

31. $21, 17, 13, 9$

33. $1/3, 0, -1/3, -2/3$

35. 25

37. -8

39. -2

41. $19/3$

43. $821/160$

45. 440

47. -126

49. 1720

51. 30

53. $n = 30, d = 3$

55. $n = 6, d = 1/4$

57. -2

59. (a) $\$100$ (b) $50 + 5n$

Exercise Set 15.2, page 579

1. yes, $r = 2$

3. no

5. yes, $r = -3/4$

7. yes, $r = 1/5$

9. no

11. 3, 9, 27, 81

13. 4, 2, 1, 1/2

15. 1/2, 2, 8, 32

17. $-3, -6, -12, -24$

19. -384

21. 3/32

23. $-160/81$

25. 1/243

27. 27/8

29. ± 2

31. 7

33. $2\sqrt[3]{4}, 24\sqrt[3]{2}$

35. 1/4, 1/16

37. 1093/243

39. $-1353/625$

41. 1020

43. 55/8

45. 2

47. 3/4

49. 8/3

51. 1

53. 1/5

55. 32,578

57. \$163.83

59. 1/11

61. 1

Exercise Set 15.3, page 586

1. $243x^5 + 810x^4y + 1080x^3y^2 + 720x^2y^3 + 240xy^4 + 32y^5$

3. $256x^4 - 256x^3y + 96x^2y^2 - 16xy^3 + y^4$

5. $32 - 80xy + 80x^2y^2 - 40x^3y^3 + 10x^4y^4 - x^5y^5$

7. $a^8b^4 + 12a^6b^3 + 54a^4b^2 + 108a^2b + 81$

9. $a^8 - 16a^7b + 112a^6b^2 - 448a^5b^3 + 1120a^4b^4 - 1792a^3b^5 + 1792a^2b^6 - 1024ab^7 + 256b^8$

11. $\dfrac{1}{27}x^3 + \dfrac{2}{3}x^2 + 4x + 8$

13. $1024 + 5120x + 11,520x^2 + 15,360x^3$

15. $19,683 - 118,098a + 314,928a^2 - 489,888a^3$

17. $16,384x^{14} - 344,064x^{13}y + 3,354,624x^{12}y^2 - 20,127,744x^{11}y^3$

19. $8192x^{13} - 53,248x^{12}yz + 159,744x^{11}y^2z^2 - 292,864x^{10}y^3z^3$

21. 120

23. 12

25. 990

27. 5040

29. 120

31. 210

33. $-35,840x^4$

35. $\dfrac{495}{256}x^8y^4$

37. $2016x^{-5}$

39. $-540x^3y^3$

41. $181,440x^4y^3$

43. $-144x^6$

45. $\dfrac{35}{8}x^{12}$

47. 4.8268

Exercise Set 15.4, page 597

1. 120

3. 146,016

5. 256

7. 5040

9. 720

11. 336

13. 90

15. 84

17. 3

19. 210

21. 120

23. 60

25. 336

27. 120

29. 84

31. 45

33. 1

35. n

37. $\dfrac{n^2 + n}{2}$

39. 3003

41. (a) 15,600   (b) 17,576

43. 12, 271, 512

45. 240

47. 59,400

49. $\dfrac{(26!)^2}{6!4!22!20!}$

Exercise Set 15.5, page 604

1. 1/2

3. (a) 1/2   (b) 1/4   (c) 1/13

5. (a) 11/36   (b) 5/36   (c) 4/9

7. (a) 99/100   (b) 1/100

9. (a) 1/17170   (b) 1164/8585   (c) 7372/8585

11. 11/4165   13. 8008/23023

15. 75/612

17. (a) 0.922   (b) 1.6×10^{-7}

Review Exercises, page 608

1. 3, 7, 13; 111

2. 0, 7/3, 13/2; 999/11

3. 38

4. −9

5. 8

6. −33/2

7. 275/3

8. −450

9. −3

10. −3/2

11. 5, 1, 1/5, 1/25

12. −2, 2, −2, 2

13. 243/8

14. ±256

15. 1/2, 1/12

16. 21/32

17. −728

18. 10

19. 9/5

20. $16x^4 - 32x^3y + 24x^2y^2 - 8xy^3 + y^4$

21. $x^4/16 - x^3 + 6x^2 - 16x + 16$

22. $x^6 + 3x^4 + 3x^2 + 1$ 23. 720

24. 78   25. $(n + 1)/n$

26. 15   27. 1

28. 45   29. 24

30. 360   31. 210

32. 9   33. 2/9

34. 2/7   35. 4/663

36. 0.81   37. 1/33

Progress Test 15A, page 609

1. −3, 2, 5/7, 3/7

2. −1/2

3. 32

4. 21

5. $n = 11, d = 4$

6. 1/4

7. 189/16

8. 10

9. $x^4 - 2x^3y + \frac{3}{2}x^2y^2 - \frac{1}{2}xy^3 + \frac{1}{16}y^4$

10. 3/5

11. 2520

12. 4800

13. 126

14. 180

15. 1/3

16. 3/35

Progress Test 15B, page 610

1. 2, 9/2, 28/3, 65/4

2. 13/2

3. 49/2

4. 135/4

5. $n = 25, d = -3/2$

6. 243

7. 11/2

8. 9/5

9. $\frac{x^8}{16} - \frac{1}{2}x^6y + \frac{3}{2}x^4y^2 - 2x^2y^3 + y^4$

10. $\frac{7}{n^2 - n}$

11. 120

12. 14,400

13. 84

14. 14,400

15. 0.8×10^{-5}

16. 7/12

Photo Credits

Page iv – Shutterstock photo

Page xviii – iStock photo

Page xix – iStock photo

Page 1 – iStock photo

Page 51 – iStock photo

Page 87 – iStock photo

Page 113 – iStock photo

Page 149 – iStock photo

Page 191 – iStock photo

Page 237 – iStock photo

Page 273 – iStock photo

Page 317 – iStock photo

Page 355 – iStock photo

Page 387 – iStock photo

Page 441 – iStock photo

Page 485 – iStock photo

Page 531 – iStock photo

Page 561 – Shutterstock photo

Solutions to Selected Review Exercises

Chapter 1

1. The set of natural numbers between -5 and 4 inclusive is $\{1, 2, 3, 4\}$, since the set of natural numbers is $\{1, 2, 3, \ldots\}$.

4. T. $\sqrt{7}$ is irrational and thus real.

6. F. -14 is a negative integer and therefore an integer.

19. $2.25\% = \dfrac{2.25}{100} = \dfrac{225}{10,000} = \dfrac{9}{400} = 0.0225$

23. T. $2(3) + 4 = 10$ 25. F. $3(1) - 4(2) = -5$

34. $2 - 3(-3) = 2 + 9 = 11$

37. $a + (b + c) = (a + b) + c$ associative (addition)
$= c + (a + b)$ commutative (addition)

39. $3(ab) = (3a)b$ associative (multiplication)
$= b(3a)$ commutative (multiplication)

41. $\dfrac{4 + a}{2} = \dfrac{4}{2} + \dfrac{a}{2} = 2 + \dfrac{a}{2}$

42. $-2(a - 3) = -2a + (-2)(-3) = -2a + 6$

43. $2(ab) = 2(ba) = (2b)a$

45. $\dfrac{|2 - 2(3)| + |-2 - 3|}{|(-2)3|} = \dfrac{|-4| + |-5|}{|-6|} = 9/6 = 3/2$

47. $\overline{AB} = |2 - (-3)| = |2 + 3| = |5| = 5$

49. $x \geq -1$

Chapter 2

5. $2(x - 1) = 4x - 3$
$2x - 2 = 4x - 4$
$-2 + 3 = 4x - 2x$
$1 = 2x$
$x = \dfrac{1}{2}$

7. Let $f = $ annual profit of the foreign division. Then the annual profit of the domestic division was $2f + 4$

Since the total annual profit was \$19 million,

$$f + 2f + 4 = 19$$
$$3f = 15$$
$$f = 5$$

The foreign profit was \$5 million; the domestic profit is $2f + 4 = 2(5) + 4 = 14$ million dollars.

9. Let x = exposure time for the fourth test print. Then

$$\frac{5 + 12 + 15 + x}{4} = 13$$

$$5 + 12 + 15 + x = 4(13) = 52$$

$$32 + x = 52$$

$$x = 20 \text{ seconds}$$

11. $$r = 2s + 4tu$$

$$r - 2s = 4tu$$

$$\frac{r - 2s}{4t} = u$$

17. $$2x + 3 \qquad\qquad > 5$$

$$2x > 5 - 3$$

$$2x > 2$$

$$x > 1$$

19. $$2(x + 2) < 3(x - 1)$$

$$2x + 4 < 3x - 3$$

$$4 + 3 < 3x - 2x$$

$$7 < x \quad \text{or} \quad x > 7$$

21. $$3 < 2x < 6$$

$$3/2 < x < 3$$

25. $$3x - 2 > -5$$

$$3x > -5 + 2$$

$$3x > -3$$

$$x > -1$$

29. $$-1 < 2x + 1 < 4$$

$$-1 - 1 < 2x < 4 - 1$$

$$-2 < 2x < 3$$

$$-1 < x < 3/2$$

33. Let x = number of orders placed.

$$120 + 1.5x > 180$$

$$1.5x > 180 - 120$$

$$1.5x > 60$$

$$x > 40$$

More than 40 orders must be placed.

37. $$\left|-y + 3\right| = 2$$

$$-y + 3 = 2 \qquad \text{or} \qquad -(-y + 3) = 2$$

$$-y = 2 - 3 \qquad\qquad\qquad y - 3 = 2$$

$$-y = -1 \qquad\qquad\qquad\quad y = 2 + 3$$

$$y = 1 \qquad\qquad\qquad\qquad y = 5$$

Check: $\left|-1 + 3\right|^{\overset{?}{}} = 2 \qquad \left|-5 + 3\right| \overset{?}{=} 2$

$$\left|2\right| \overset{\checkmark}{=} 2 \qquad\qquad \left|-2\right| \overset{\checkmark}{=} 2$$

39. $$\left|3r + 3\right| = 0$$

$$3r + 3 = 0$$

$$3r = -3$$

$$r = -3/3 = -1$$

Check: $\left|3(-1) + 3\right| \overset{?}{=} \left|-3 + 3\right| = \left|0\right| \overset{\checkmark}{=} 0$

43. $$\left|2x + 3\right| \qquad\qquad \leq 2$$

$$-2 \leq 2x + 3 \leq 2$$

$$-5 \leq 2x \leq -1$$

$$-5/2 \leq x \leq -1/2$$

Thus, $-5/2 \leq x \leq -1/2$

45. $$\left|2x + 1\right| = 2$$

$$2x + 1 = 2 \qquad \text{or} \qquad -(2x + 1) = 2$$

$$2x = 2 - 1 \qquad\qquad\qquad -2x - 1 = 2$$

$$2x = 1 \qquad\qquad\qquad\qquad -2x = 2 + 1$$

$$x = 1/2 \qquad\qquad\qquad\qquad -2x = 3$$

$$x = -3/2$$

Thus, $x = 1/2$ or $x = -3/2$

50. $$\frac{\left|4x - 2\right|}{3} \geq 4$$

$$\frac{4x - 2}{3} \geq 4 \qquad \text{or} \qquad \frac{4x - 2}{3} \leq -4$$

$$4x - 2 \geq 12 \qquad\qquad\qquad 4x - 2 \leq -12$$

$$4x \geq 12 + 2 \qquad\qquad\qquad 4x - 2 \leq -12 + 2$$

$$4x \geq 14 \qquad\qquad\qquad\qquad 4x \leq -10$$

$$x \geq 14/4 = 7/2 \qquad\qquad\qquad x \leq -5/2$$

$$x \geq 7/2$$

Thus, $x \leq -5/2$ or $x \geq 7/2$

Chapter 3

4. Let t = number of 20-cent stamps. We can arrange the given information as follows;

		× Denomination =	Value
20-cent	t	20	$20t$
40-cent	$t + 3$	40	$40(t + 3)$
1-dollar	$t - 3$	100	$100(t + 2)$
Total			560

Since

$$\text{total value} = \begin{pmatrix}\text{value of} \\ \text{20–cent} \\ \text{stamps}\end{pmatrix} + \begin{pmatrix}\text{value of} \\ \text{40–cent} \\ \text{stamps}\end{pmatrix} + \begin{pmatrix}\text{value of} \\ \text{1–dollar} \\ \text{stamps}\end{pmatrix}\text{''}$$

we have

$$560 = 20t + 40(t + 3) + 100(t - 2)$$
$$560 = 20t + 40t + 120 + 100t - 200$$
$$560 = 160t - 80$$
$$640 = 160t$$
$$t = 4$$

Thus,

$$t = \text{number of 20-cent stamps} = 4$$
$$t + 3 = \text{number of 40-cent stamps} = 7$$
$$t - 2 = \text{number of 1-dollar stamps} = 2$$

6. Let c = amount in classical music inventory

then

$12,000 - c$ = amount in popular music inventory

Displaying the information we have

	Amount	× Profit =	Rate of Return
Classical music	c	0.15	$0.15c$
Popular music	$12,000 - c$	0.20	$0.20(12,000 - c)$

Then

$$0.15c = 0.20(12,000 - c) - 1000$$
$$0.15c = 2400 - 0.20c - 1000$$
$$0.35c = 1400$$
$$c = \$4000 = \text{amount in classical music inventory}$$
$$12,000 - 4000 = \$8000 = \text{amount in popular music inventory}$$

9. Let x = average speed of slower aircraft

then

$$2x = \text{average speed of faster aircraft}$$

	Rate	×	Time	=	Distance
Slower aircraft	x		5		$5x$
Faster aircraft	$2x$		5		$10x$

Since after 5 hours the planes are 1500 miles apart,

$$5x + 10x = 1500$$
$$15x = 1500$$
$$x = 100 = \text{average speed of slower aircraft}$$
$$2x = 200 = \text{average speed of faster aircraft}$$

12. Let x = average speed of first aircraft

then

$$x + 100 = \text{average speed of second aircraft}$$

	Rate	×	Time	=	Distance
First aircraft	x		3.5		$3.5x$
Second aircraft	$x + 100$		3.5		$(3.5x + 100)$

After 3.5 hours the total distance covered is 3150 miles, so

$$3.5x + 3.5(x + 100) = 3150$$
$$3.5x + 3.5 + 350 = 3150$$
$$7x = 2800$$
$$x = 400 = \text{average speed of first aircraft}$$
$$x + 100 = 500 = \text{average speed of second aircraft}$$

16. Let x = number of pounds of Colombian coffee

Since the mixture is to consist of 25 pounds, we must have $25 - x$ pounds of Jamaican coffee.

Type of Coffee	Number of pounds	×	Price per pound	=	Value in cents
Colombian	x		400		$400x$
Jamaican	$25 - x$		500		$500(25 - x)$
Mixture	25		480		12,000

Since the value of the mixture is the sum of the two components, we have

$$12,000 = 400x + 500(25 - x)$$
$$12,000 = 400x + 12,500 - 500x$$
$$100x = 500$$
$$x = 5 = \text{ number of pounds of}$$
$$\text{Colombian coffee to be used}$$
$$25 - x = 20 = \text{ number of pounds of}$$
$$\text{Colombian coffee to be used}$$

Chapter 4

3. No, since x appears to the power of $-\frac{1}{2}$, which is not a nonnegative integer.

4. Yes, since all the exponents are nonnegative integers.

9. The degrees of the terms are 7, 3, and 0, so the degree of the polynomial is 7.

10. The degrees of the terms are 2, 4, and 5, so the degree of the polynomial is 5.

15. $-3(1)^3(-2) + (1)(-2)^2 - 2(1)(-2) + 3 = 17$

17. $(2x^3 - 3x + 1) + (3x^3 + 2x^2 - 3)$
$= (2 + 3)x^3 + (0 + 2)x^2 + (-3 + 0)x + (1 - 3)$
$= 5x^3 + 2x^2 - 3x - 2$

18. $(3a^2b^3 - 2a^2b + ab - a) - (-2a^3b^3 + ab^2 - 2ab + b)$
$= (0 + 2)a^3b^3 + (3 - 0)a^2b^3 + (-2 - 0)a^2b + (0 - 1)ab^2 + (1 + 2)ab + (-1 - 0)a + (0 - 1)b$
$= 2a^3b^3 + 3a^2b^3 - 2a^2b - ab^2 + 3ab - a - b$

22. $x(2x - 1)^2 = x(2x - 1)(2x - 1)$
$= x(4x^2 - 4x + 1)$
$= 4x^3 - 4x^2 + x$

26. $(a^2 + 2a + 3)(a^2 - a - 1)$
$= a^2(a^2 - a - 1) + 2a(a^2 - a - 1) + 3(a^2 - a - 1)$
$= a^4 - a^3 - a^2 + 2a^3 - 2a^2 - 2a + 3a^2 - 3a - 3$
$= a^4 + a^3 - 5a - 3$

28. $(b + 1)^2(2b - 1)^2$
$= (b + 1)(b + 1)(2b - 1)(2b - 1)$
$= (b^2 + 2b + 1)(4b^2 - 4b + 1)$
$= b^2(4b^2 - 4b + 1) + 2b(4b^2 - 4b + 1) + 1(4b^2 - 4b + 1)$
$= 4b^4 - 4b^3 + b^2 + 8b^3 - 8b^2 + 2b + 4b^2 - 4b + 1$
$= 4b^4 + 4b^3 - 3b^2 - 2b + 1$

31. $x^2(2x - 3)^2 = x^2(2x - 3)(2x - 3)$
$= x^2(4x^2 - 12x + 9)$

The x^3 term comes from $x^2(-12x)$, so the coefficient of x^3 is -12.

38. $16x^2 - y^2 = (4x)^2 - y^2$ (the difference of two squares)
$= (4x + y)(4x - y)$

39. $18x^2 - 24x + 6 = 6(3x^2 - 4x + 1)$
$= 6(3x + a)(x + b)$

so

$$ab = 1 \quad \text{and} \quad a + 3b = -4$$

The only integer factors satisfying $ab = 1$ are $a = 1$, $b = 1$ and $a = -1$, $b = -1$. We quickly see that $a = 1$, $b = 1$ does not satisfy $a + 3b = -4$ but that $a = -1$, $b = -1$ is a satisfactory choice. Thus,

$$18x^2 - 24x + 6 = 6(3x - 1)(x - 1)$$

40. $2rs + s - 2r - 1 = 2rs - 2r + s - 1$
$= (2r)(s - 1) + (s - 1)$
$= (2r + 1)(s - 1)$

44. $3a^2 + 2ab - 2b - 3a = 3a^2 - 3a + 2ab - 2b$
$$= 3a(a - 1) + 2b(a - 1)$$
$$= (3a + 2b)(a - 1)$$

46. $a^4 - 2a^2 + 1 = (a^2)^2 - 2a^2 + 1$
$$= (a^2 - 1)^2$$

50. $8x^3 + 125y^3$
$$= (2x)^3 + (5y)^3$$
$$= (2x + 5y)(4x^2 - 10xy + 25y^2) \quad \text{Sum of cubes}$$

52. $8x^3 - 125y^3$
$$= (2x)^3 - (5y)^3$$
$$= (2x - 5y)(4x^2 + 10xy + 25y^2) \quad \text{Difference of cubes}$$

56.
$$
\begin{array}{r}
4y \quad - 20 \\
y + 5\overline{\smash{\big)}\,4y^2 - 25} \\
\underline{4y^2 + 20y} \\
- 20y - 25 \\
\underline{- 20y - 100} \\
75
\end{array}
$$

$$\frac{4y^2 - 25}{y + 5} = 4y - 20 + \frac{75}{y + 5}$$

60.
$$
\begin{array}{r}
a \quad - 3 \\
a^2 + 2\overline{\smash{\big)}\,a^3 - 3a^2 - 2a + 6} \\
\underline{a^3 \qquad + 2a} \\
- 3a^3 - 4a + 6 \\
\underline{- 3a^2 \qquad - 6} \\
- 4a + 12
\end{array}
$$

$$\frac{a^3 - 3a^2 - 2a + 6}{a^2 + 2} = a - 3 + \frac{12 - 4a}{a^2 + 2}$$

Chapter 5

1. $\dfrac{5x + 10}{5} = \dfrac{5(x + 2)}{5} = x + 2$

3. $\dfrac{x^2 - 2x - 8}{x + 2} = \dfrac{(x + 2)(x - 4)}{x + 2} = x - 4$

7. $\dfrac{4x}{x + 1} \div \dfrac{2x^2}{x - 1} = \dfrac{4x}{x + 1} \cdot \dfrac{x - 1}{2x^2} = \dfrac{2(x - 1)}{x(x + 1)} = \dfrac{2x - 2}{x^2 + x}$

13. First we write the fractions
$$\frac{3y}{y^2 - 4} \qquad \frac{2}{y + 2} \qquad \frac{4y^2}{y^2 - 2y}$$

with factored denominators:
$$\frac{3y}{(y - 2)(y + 2)} \qquad \frac{2}{y + 2} \qquad \frac{4y^2}{y(y - 2)}$$

Then we fill in the following table to discover the factors of the LCD:

Factor	Highest power	Final factor
$y - 2$	1	$y - 2$
$y + 2$	1	$y + 2$
y	1	y

Thus, the LCD is $y(y - 2)(y + 2) = y(y^2 - 4) = y^3 - 4y$.

15. $\dfrac{2 - x^2}{x} + \dfrac{4 + 2x^2}{3x}$

The LCD is $3x$; thus, we have

$$\frac{3(2 - x^2)}{3x} + \frac{4 + 2x^2}{3x} = \frac{6 - 3x^2 + 4 + 2x^2}{3x} = \frac{10 - x^2}{3x}$$

18. $\dfrac{2y}{(2x + 3)(x - 1)} - \dfrac{y - 1}{2x + 3}$

The LCD is $(2x + 3)(x - 1)$. Thus, we have

$$\frac{2y}{(2x + 3)(x - 1)} - \frac{(y - 1)(x - 1)}{(2x + 3)(x - 1)}$$

$$= \frac{2y - (y - 1)(x - 1)}{(2x + 3)(x - 1)}$$

$$= \frac{2y - (yx - y - x + 1)}{(2x + 3)(x - 1)}$$

$$= \frac{2y - yx + y + x - 1}{(2x + 3)(x - 1)}$$

$$= \frac{3y - yx + x - 1}{(2x + 3)(x - 1)}$$

21. $\dfrac{2-\dfrac{1}{x}}{1+\dfrac{5}{x}}$

Multiply numerator and denominator by the LCD, x. Thus, we have

$$\frac{\left(2-\dfrac{1}{x}\right)x}{\left(1+\dfrac{5}{x}\right)x} = \frac{2x-1}{x+5}$$

23. $\dfrac{x-2}{2-\dfrac{1}{x+1}}$

Combining as one fraction in the denominator, we have

$$\frac{x-2}{\dfrac{2(x+2)-1}{x+2}} = \frac{x-2}{\dfrac{2x+4-1}{x+2}} = \frac{x-2}{\dfrac{2x+3}{x+2}}$$

$$= (x-2)\cdot\frac{x+2}{2x+3} = \frac{x^2-4}{2x+3}$$

31. $\dfrac{2x+1}{2x-1} = -\dfrac{2}{3}$

Multiplying both sides by $3(2x-1)$ to clear fractions, we obtain

$$3(2x+1) = -2(2x-1)$$
$$6x+3 = -4x+2$$
$$6x+4x = 2-3$$
$$10x = -1$$
$$x = -1/10$$

35. Let x = the number. Then $1/x$ is its reciprocal.

$$\frac{1}{2}+3\left(\frac{1}{x}\right) = 2$$

$$\frac{1}{2}+\frac{3}{x} = 2$$

$$2x\left(\frac{1}{2}+\frac{3}{x}\right) = 2x(2) \qquad \text{Multiply both sides by } 2x.$$

$$\frac{2x}{2}+\frac{6x}{x} = 4x$$

$$x+6 = 4x$$

$$6 = 3x$$

$$x = 2$$

37.

	Time alone	Rate	× Time =	Work done
Senior photographer	5	1/5	3	3/5
Junior photographer	x	1/x	3	3/x

Since

$$\left(\begin{array}{c}\text{work done by}\\\text{senior photographer}\end{array}\right) + \left(\begin{array}{c}\text{work done by}\\\text{junior photographer}\end{array}\right)$$

$$= 1 \text{ whole job}$$

we have

$$\frac{3}{5}+\frac{3}{x} = 1$$

$$5x\left(\frac{3}{5}+\frac{3}{x}\right) = 1$$

$$5x\left(\frac{3}{5}\right)+5x\left(\frac{3}{x}\right) = 5x$$

$$3x+15 = 5x$$

$$15 = 2x$$

$$x = \frac{15}{2} = 7.5 \text{ hours}$$

Thus, the junior photographer would take 7.5 hours to complete the job alone.

40. Let s = speed of the canoe in sill water.

	Rate	× Time	= Distance
upstream	s − 4	$\dfrac{30}{s-4}$	30
downstream	s + 4	$\dfrac{50}{s+4}$	50

$$\frac{30}{s-4} = \frac{50}{s+4}$$

Multiply both sides of the equation by the LCD. $(s-4)(s+4)$:

$$30(s+4) = 50(s-4)$$
$$30s+120 = 50s-200$$
$$20s = 320$$
$$s = 16$$

Thus, the speed of the canoe in still water is 16 km per hour.

45. $\dfrac{2}{2r+3} = \dfrac{1}{2}$

After clearing fractions by multiplying both sides by $2(2r+3)$, we have

$$2(2) = 1(2r+3)$$
$$4 = 2r+3$$
$$1 = 2r$$
$$r = \dfrac{1}{2}$$

46. $\dfrac{3}{r-2} = \dfrac{2}{r+3}$

Multiply both sides by $(r-2)(r+3)$:

$$3(r+3) = 2(r-2)$$
$$3r+9 = 2r-4$$
$$3r-2r = -4-9$$
$$r = -13$$

49. Let $x =$ cost of a 240-square-foot carpet. Since cost is proportioned to square footage,

$$\dfrac{600}{180} = \dfrac{x}{240}$$
$$600(240) = x(180)$$
$$144{,}000 = 180x$$
$$x = 800$$

Thus, the carpet costs $800.

Chapter 6

1. $B = (2-4, -3-1) = (-2, -4)$

3. II, since x is negative and y is positive

4. a and d, since

$$2(2)^2 - 5(3) = 8 - 15 = -7$$
$$2(-2)^2 - 5(3) = 8 - 15 = -7$$

14. $g(t) = \dfrac{3}{t^2+t-12} = \dfrac{3}{(t+4)(t-3)}$

Since the denominator cannot be zero, we must exclude the values $t = -4$ and $t = 3$ from the domain of g.

15. Not a function by the vertical line test

18. (a) $g(-5) = \dfrac{-5-3}{-5+1} = \dfrac{-8}{-4} = 2$

(b) $g(0) = \dfrac{0-3}{0+1} = -3$

(c) $g(3) = \dfrac{3-3}{3+1} = 0$

19. (a) When $t = 2$ seconds, $s = 16(2)^2 = 64$ feet
   When $t = 4$ seconds, $s = 16(4)^2 = 256$ feet

(b) With $s = 144$, solve

$$144 = 16t^2$$
$$t^2 = \dfrac{144}{16} = 9$$
$$t = 3 \quad (\text{reject } t = -3)$$

It takes 3 seconds to fall 144 feet.

29. (a) $C = \begin{cases} 0.15n, & 0 < n \le 5 \\ 0.075 + 0.10(n-5), & 5 < n \le 20 \end{cases}$

(c) $C = 0.75 + 0.10(16-5) = 0.75 + 1.10 = 1.85$

It costs $1.85.

37.

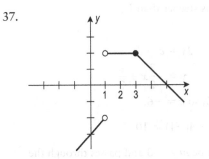

42. (a) $M = k/n^3$

(b) $\dfrac{1}{12} = \dfrac{k}{8}$, so $k = 2/3$

Hence,

$$M = \frac{2}{3n^3}$$

(c) When $n = 4$, $M = \dfrac{2}{3 \cdot 4^3} = \dfrac{1}{96}$;

when $n = 5$, $M = \dfrac{2}{3 \cdot 5^3} = \dfrac{2}{375}$.

n	2	3	4	5
M	1/2	2/81	1/96	2/375

45. $S = ktu^2$

Substituting $S = 18$, $t = 4$, and $u = 9$, we have

$$18 = k \cdot 4 \cdot 9^2$$

Then $k = 18/324 = 1/18$. When $t = 6$ and $u = 3$,

$$S = \frac{1}{18}tu^2$$

$$= \frac{1}{18}(6)(3)^2$$

$$= \frac{1}{18} \cdot 6 \cdot 9 = 3$$

51. Let

$a = $ the amount (in dollars) spent on advertising

$L = $ the length (in pages) of the manual

$R = $ revenue

$K = $ constant of proportionality

Then

$$R = k \cdot \frac{A}{L}$$

Substituting the given values, we have

$$1,000,000 = k \cdot \frac{50,000}{100}$$

$$k = \frac{1,000,000(100)}{50,000} = 2000$$

Thus,

$$R = 2000\frac{A}{L}$$

When $L = 120$ and $A = 75,000$,

$$R = 2000\left(\frac{75,000}{120}\right)$$

$$= 1,250,000$$

The firm would have received \$1,250,000.

Chapter 7

1. $P_1(-2, 3)$, $P_2(2, 5)$

$$m = \frac{y_2 - y_1}{x_2 - x_1} = \frac{5 - 3}{2 - (-2)} = \frac{2}{4} = \frac{1}{2}$$

4. falling, since $m < 0$

9. false, since L_1 is steeper than L_2

13. Solving for y:

$$2y = c - 3x$$

$$y = -\frac{3}{2}x + \frac{c}{2}$$

Then $c/2 = -3$, so $c = -6$.

17. yes, since $3(2) - 4(-1) = 10$

21. The line has slope $m = -3$ and passes through the point $(4, 0)$. Thus,

$$y - 0 = -3(x - 4)$$

$$y = -3(x - 4)$$

23. Since $m = 4$ and $b = -2$, $y = 4x - 2$.

25. Solving for y, we have

$$2x = 3y - 4$$

$$y = \frac{2}{3}x + \frac{4}{3}$$

Then $m = 2/3$, $b = 4/3$.

29. (a) $y = -3$ (b) $x = 2$

33. The slope of L is

$$m_1 = \frac{5 - 2}{-1 - 4} = -\frac{3}{5}$$

The slope of L' is

$$m_2 = \frac{3 - 2}{2 - 1} = 1$$

Since the slopes are unequal, the lines are not parallel.

35. Solving $3x - 2y = 4$ for y, we obtain

$$y = \frac{3}{2}x - 2$$

so $m = 3/2$. Thus, the equation of the line parallel to the given line is

$$y = \frac{3}{2}x + 5$$

37. Solving $5x - 2y = 4$ for y, we obtain

$$y = \frac{5}{2}x - 2$$

so $m = 5/2$. The slope of any line perpendicular to the given line is then $-2/5$. Since the line passes through $(4, 1)$,

$$y - 1 = -\frac{2}{5}(x - 4)$$

39. The slope of the line $2x - 3y = 4$ is $m_1 = 2/3$, and the slope of the line $2y + 3x = 6$ is $m_2 = -3/2$. Since $m_1 m_2 = -1$, the lines are perpendicular.

Chapter 8

3. $\left(-\dfrac{a}{b}\right)^5 = \left(\dfrac{-a}{b}\right)^5 = \dfrac{(-a)^5}{b^5} = \dfrac{(-1)^5 a^5}{b^5} = \dfrac{-a^5}{b^5}$

8. $\dfrac{(3a^3 b^2)^3}{(-2a^4 b^3)^4} = \dfrac{3^3 a^9 b^6}{(-2)^4 a^{16} b^{12}} = \dfrac{27 a^9 b^6}{16 a^{16} b^{12}} = \dfrac{27}{16 a^7 b^6}$

12. $a^{-4} a^4 a^2 = a^{-4 + 4 + 2} = a^2$

15. $\left(\dfrac{2xy^{-2}}{3x^{-2} y^{-3}}\right)^4 = \dfrac{2^4 x^4 y^{-8}}{3^4 x^{-8} y^{-12}} = \dfrac{81}{16 x^{12} y^4}$

17. $32^{2/5} = (2^5)^{2/5} = 2^2 = 4$

20. $\dfrac{81^{1/4}}{81^{5/4}} = \dfrac{1}{81^{5/4 - 1/4}} = \dfrac{1}{81^{4/4}} = \dfrac{1}{81}$

23. $\left(\dfrac{x^{2/3}}{x^{4/3}}\right)^{1/4} = \dfrac{x^{1/6}}{x^{1/3}} = x^{1/6 - 1/3} = x^{-1/6} = \dfrac{1}{x^{1/6}}$

25. $\sqrt{60} = \sqrt{4 \cdot 15} = 2\sqrt{15}$

29. $\dfrac{6a^7}{\sqrt{3b}} = \dfrac{6a^7}{\sqrt{3b}} \cdot \dfrac{\sqrt{3b}}{\sqrt{3b}} = \dfrac{6a^7 \sqrt{3b}}{3b} = \dfrac{2a^7 \sqrt{3b}}{b}$

33. $\sqrt[3]{3xy^2} + \sqrt[3]{5xy^2} = \sqrt[3]{3}\sqrt[3]{xy^2} + \sqrt[3]{5}\sqrt[3]{xy^2}$
$$= \sqrt[3]{xy^2}(\sqrt[3]{3} + \sqrt[3]{5})$$

36. $\dfrac{\sqrt{3x} - 1}{\sqrt{3x} + 1} = \dfrac{(\sqrt{3x} - 1)(\sqrt{3x} - 1)}{(\sqrt{3x} + 1)(\sqrt{3x} - 1)} = \dfrac{(\sqrt{3x} - 1)^2}{3x - 1}$

37. $\dfrac{2}{\sqrt{x - y}} = \dfrac{2}{\sqrt{x - y}} \cdot \dfrac{\sqrt{x - y}}{\sqrt{x - y}} = \dfrac{2\sqrt{x - y}}{x - y}$

40. $-i^{29} = -(i^{28} \cdot i) = -i = 0 - i$

41. $\sqrt{-20} = \sqrt{-5(2)^2} = 2\sqrt{5}i = 0 + 2\sqrt{5}i$

46. $(4 - 3i)^2 = 16 - 24i + 9i^2 = 16 - 24i - 9 = 7 - 24i$

47. $\dfrac{1}{\sqrt{3} + 2i} = \dfrac{1}{\sqrt{3} + 2i} \cdot \dfrac{\sqrt{3} - 2i}{\sqrt{3} - 2i} = \dfrac{\sqrt{3} - 2i}{3 - 4i^2}$
$$= \dfrac{\sqrt{3} - 2i}{7} = \dfrac{\sqrt{3}}{7} - \dfrac{2}{7}i$$

Chapter 9

3. $(x - 2)^2 = 9$

$x - 2 = \pm 3$

$x = 2 \pm 3$

$x = 5 \quad x = -1$

6. $2y^2 - 3y - 2 = 0$

$(2y + 1)(y - 2) \qquad = 0$

$y = -\dfrac{1}{2} \quad y = 2$

9. $\qquad x^2 - 5x = 3$

$x^2 - 5x + \left(\dfrac{5}{2}\right)^2 = 3 + \left(\dfrac{5}{2}\right)^2$

$\left(x - \dfrac{5}{2}\right)^2 = 3 + \dfrac{25}{4} = \dfrac{37}{4}$

$x - \dfrac{5}{2} = \pm \dfrac{\sqrt{37}}{2}$

$x = \dfrac{5}{2} \pm \dfrac{\sqrt{37}}{2}$

$x = \dfrac{5 + \sqrt{37}}{2} \quad x = \dfrac{5 - \sqrt{37}}{2}$

15. $a = 2, b = -2, c = 1$

$x = \dfrac{-b \pm \sqrt{b^2 - 4ac}}{2a}$

$= \dfrac{1 \pm \sqrt{1 - 8}}{4}$

$= \dfrac{1 \pm \sqrt{-7}}{4}$

$= \dfrac{1}{4} \pm \dfrac{\sqrt{7}}{4} i$

19. $9r^2 - 6r + 1 = 0$

$b^2 - 4ac = 36 - 4(9)(1)$

$= 36 - 36$

$= 0$ Since the discriminant is zero, there is a double real root.

29. $x + \sqrt{x + 10} = 10$

$\sqrt{x + 10} = 10 - x$

$x + 10 = (10 - x)^2$

$x + 10 = 100 - 20x + x^2$

$x^2 - 21x + 90 = 0$

$(x - 6)(x - 15) \qquad = 0$

$x = 6 \quad x = 15$

Test both answers:

$6 + \sqrt{6 + 10} \overset{?}{=} 10 \qquad 15 + \sqrt{15 + 10} \overset{?}{=} 10$

$6 + 4 \overset{\checkmark}{=} 10 \qquad\qquad 15 + 5 \overset{\checkmark}{\neq} 10$

31. $2x^4 + x^2 - 6 = 0$

Substitute $y = x^2$:

$2y^2 + y - 6 = 0$

$(2y - 3)(y + 2) \qquad = 0$

$y = -2 \quad y = \dfrac{3}{2}$

Then

$x^2 = -2 \quad \text{or} \quad x^2 = \dfrac{3}{2}$

$x = \pm i\sqrt{2}, x = \pm\sqrt{\dfrac{3}{2}} = \pm\dfrac{\sqrt{6}}{2}$

34. $\dfrac{x - 3}{x - 5} \geq 0$

The critical values occur where

$x - 3 = 0$

$x - 5 = 0$

So critical values are at

$x = 3, 5$

(Note: At $x = 5$ we have division by zero.)

Chapter 10

1.

$$\underline{1}|\ 2\quad 0\quad\ \ 6\quad -4$$
$$\qquad\ \ 2\quad\ \ 2\quad\ \ 8$$
$$\overline{\quad 2\quad\ \ 2\quad\ \ 8\quad\ \ 4}$$

$$\underbrace{\qquad\qquad}_{Q(x)}\quad\ \ \ |\quad R$$

$$Q(x) = 2x^2 + 2x + 8;\ R = 4$$

3.

$$\underline{-1}|\ 7\quad -3\quad\ \ 0\quad\ \ 2$$
$$\qquad\quad -7\quad\ 10\quad -10$$
$$\overline{\quad 7\ -10\quad 10\quad -8}$$

$$P(-1) = -8$$

$$\underline{2}|\ 7\ -3\quad\ \ 0\quad\ \ 2$$
$$\qquad\quad\ \ 14\quad 22\quad 44$$
$$\overline{\quad 7\quad\ 11\quad 22\quad 46}$$

$$P(2) = 46$$

5.

$$\underline{-2}|\ 2\quad\ \ 4\quad\ \ 3\quad\ \ 5\quad -2$$
$$\qquad\quad -4\quad\ \ 0\quad -6\quad\ \ 2$$
$$\overline{\quad 2\quad\ \ 0\quad\ \ 3\quad -1\quad\ \ 0}$$

Since $P(-2) = 0$, $x + 2$ is a factor.

8. $\dfrac{2 + i}{0 - 5i}\left(\dfrac{0 + 5i}{0 + 5i}\right) = \dfrac{10i + 5i^2}{-25i^2} = \dfrac{-5 + 10i}{25} = -\dfrac{1}{5} + \dfrac{2}{5}i$

14. With $\sqrt{-3} = \sqrt{3}i$, form the product:

$$(x - 3)(x - \sqrt{3}i)(x + \sqrt{3}i) = (x - 3)(x^2 + 3)$$
$$= x^3 - 3x^2 + 3x - 9$$

16. The number $1/2$ is a zero of the linear factor $(2x - 1)$, and -1 is a zero of the linear factor $(x + 1)$. Form the product:

$$(2x - 1)^2(x + 1)^2 = 4x^4 + 4x^3 - 3x^2 - 2x + 1$$

19. Divide by $x + 2$ to find the depressed equation:

$$\underline{-2}|\ 2\quad -1\quad -13\quad -6$$
$$\qquad\quad\ -4\quad\ \ 10\quad\ \ 6$$
$$\overline{\quad 2\quad -5\quad -3\quad\ \ 0}$$

$$\underbrace{\qquad\qquad\qquad}_{\substack{\text{depressed}\\\text{equation}}}$$

Solving $2x^2 - 5x - 3 = 0$, we have

$$(2x + 1)(x - 3) = 0$$
$$x = -\dfrac{1}{2}\quad x = 3$$

23. The polynomial

$$P(x) = x^5 - x^4 + 3x^3 - 4x^2 + x - 5$$

has 5 variations in sign and therefore has a maximum of 5 positive real zeros.

The polynomial

$$P(-x) = -x^5 - x^4 - 3x^3 - 4x^2 - x - 5$$

has no variations in sign, and therefore there are no negative real zeros.

25. The polynomial

$$P(x) = 3x^4 - 2x^2 + 1$$

has 2 variations in sign, so there can be at most 2 positive real roots. $P(-x) = P(x)$, so there can be at most 2 negative real roots.

28. The only possible rational roots are ± 1. Using condensed synthetic division, we find

$$\begin{array}{r|ccccc} & 1 & 3 & 2 & 1 & -1 \\ \hline 1 & 1 & 4 & 6 & 7 & \boxed{6} \\ -1 & 1 & 2 & 0 & 1 & \boxed{-2} \end{array}$$

Since neither remainder is zero, there are no rational roots.

29. Since the coefficients are all integers, the Rational Zero Theorem restricts the possible rational roots to

$$\pm 1,\quad \pm\dfrac{1}{2},\quad \pm\dfrac{1}{3},\quad \pm\dfrac{1}{6},\quad \pm 2,\quad \pm\dfrac{2}{3},$$

$$\pm 5,\quad \pm\dfrac{5}{2},\quad \pm\dfrac{5}{3},\quad \pm\dfrac{5}{6},\quad \pm 10,\quad \pm\dfrac{10}{3}$$

Testing by synthetic division,

$$\underline{-1}|\ 6\quad\ \ 15\quad -1\quad -10$$
$$\qquad\quad\ \ -6\quad\ -9\quad\ \ 10$$
$$\overline{\quad 6\quad\ \ 9\quad -10\quad\ \ 0}$$

we show that -1 is a root. The remaining roots are those of the depressed equation

$$6x^2 + 9x - 10 = 0$$

and are found by the quadratic formula

$$x = \dfrac{-9 \pm \sqrt{81 + 240}}{12} = \dfrac{-9 \pm \sqrt{321}}{12}$$

Chapter 11

2. $(f \cdot g)(x) = (x + 1)(x^2 - 1)$
$= x^3 + x^2 - x - 1$
$(f \cdot g)(-1) = (-1)^3 + (-1)^2 - (-1) - 1$
$= 0$

5. $(g \circ f)(x) = g(x + 1) = (x + 1)^2 - 1$
$= x^2 + 2x$

6. $g(x) = x^2 - 1$
$g(2) = 2^2 - 1 = 3$
$(f \circ g)(2) = f(3) = 3 + 1 = 4$

7. $(f \circ g)(x) = f(x^2) = \sqrt{x^2} - 2 = |x| - 2$

9. $(f \circ g)(-2) = |-2| - 2 = 0$

11. $(f \circ g)(x) = f\left(\dfrac{x}{2} - 2\right) = 2\left(\dfrac{x}{2} - 2\right) + 4 = x$

$(g \circ f)(x) = g(2x + 4) = \dfrac{2x + 4}{2} - 2 = x$

14. $2^{2x} = 8^{x-1} = (2^3)^{x-1}$ Write in terms of same base
$2^{2x} = 2^{3x-3}$ $(a^m)^n = a^{mn}$
$2x = 3x - 1$ If $a^u = a^v$, then $u = v$
$x = 3$ Solve for x

16. $S = P(1 + i)^n$ Compound interest formula

$i = \dfrac{r}{k} = \dfrac{0.12}{2} = 0.06$ Interest rate i per conversion period

$n = 4 \times 2 = 8$ Number of conversion periods

$S = 8000(1 + 0.6)^8$ Substitute for P, i, and n
$= 8000(1.5938)$ Use a calculator
$= \$12{,}750.40$

22. $\log_5 \dfrac{1}{125} = x - 1$

$5^{x-1} = \dfrac{1}{125}$ Equivalent exponential form

$5^{x-1} = 5^{-3}$ Write in terms of same base

$x - 1 = -3$ If $a^u = a^v$, then $u = v$

$x = -2$ Solve for x

24. $\log_3(x + 1) = \log_3 27$ If $\log_a u = \log_a v$, then $u = v$
$x + 1 = 27$
$x = 26$ Solve for x

25. $\log_3 3^5 = 5$ Since $\log_a a^x = x$
or
$\log_3 3^5 = x$ Introduce unknown x
$3^x = 3^5$ Equivalent exponential form
$x = 5$ If $a^u = a^v$, then $u = v$

28. $e^{\ln 3} = 3$ Since $a^{\log_a x} = x$
or
$e^{\ln 3} = 3$ Introduce unknown x form
$\ln x = \ln 3$ Equivalent logarithmic form
$x = 3$ If $\log_a u = \log_a v$, then $u = v$

30. $\log_a \dfrac{\sqrt{x - 1}}{2x} = \log_a \dfrac{(x - 1)^{1/2}}{2x}$ Exponent form of radical

$= \log_a(x - 1)^{1/2} - \log_a 2x$ Property 2
$= \log_a(x - 1)^{1/2} - [\log_a 2 + \log_a x]$ Property 1
$= \dfrac{1}{2}\log_a(x - 1) - \log_a 2 - \log_a x$ Property 3

34. $\ln 10 = 2.3026$, $\ln 5 = 1.6094$

$\log 5 = \dfrac{\ln 5}{\ln 10} = \dfrac{1.6094}{2.3026} = 0.6989$

36. $\log_5 75 = \dfrac{\ln 75}{\ln 5} = 2.6826$

Note: Values for $\ln 75$ and $\ln 5$ were obtained by using a calculator.

38. $\log 14 = \log(2 \cdot 7)$
$= \log 2 + \log 7$ Property 1
$= 0.30 + 0.85 = 1.15$ Substitute given data

41. $\log 0.7 = \log \dfrac{7}{10}$
$= \log 7 - \log 10$ Property 2
$= 0.85 - 1$ $\log_a a = 1$
$= -0.15$

42. $\dfrac{1}{3}\log_a x - \dfrac{1}{2}\log_a y = \log_a x^{1/3} - \log_a y^{1/2}$ Property 3

$= \log_a \dfrac{x^{1/3}}{y^{1/2}}$ Property 2

$= \log_a \dfrac{\sqrt[3]{x}}{\sqrt{y}}$ Radical form

43. $\frac{4}{3}[\log x + \log (x - 1)]$

$\qquad = \frac{4}{3} \log (x)(x - 1)$ Property 1

$\qquad = \log (x^2 - x)^{4/3}$ Property 3

46. $\log_b x = \dfrac{\log_a x}{\log_a b}$ Change of base formula

$\qquad\qquad\qquad\qquad x = 32, b = 8, a = 10$

$\quad \log_8 32 = \dfrac{\log 32}{\log 8}$ Substitute given data.

$\quad \log_8 32 = \dfrac{1.5}{0.9} = \dfrac{5}{3}$

$\quad$ Checking: $8^{5/3} = 32$ Write in equivalent

$\qquad\qquad\quad 32 = 32$ exponent form.

48. $\qquad 2^{3x - 1} = 14$

$\quad (3x - 1) \log 2 \qquad\qquad = \log 14$ Take log of both sides.

$\qquad\qquad x = \dfrac{1}{3} + \dfrac{\log 14}{3 \log 2}$ Solve for x.

49. $2 \log x - \log 5 \qquad\qquad = 3$

$\quad \log x^2 - \log 5 = 3$ Property 3

$\qquad \log \dfrac{x^2}{5} = 3$ Property 2

$\qquad\quad \dfrac{x^2}{5} = 10^3 = 1000$ Equivalent exponent form

$\qquad\quad x = \sqrt{5000}$ Solve for x.

Chapter 12

1. $d = \sqrt{(x_2 - x_1)^2 + (y_2 - y_1)^2}$

$\quad d = \sqrt{[2 - (-4)]^2 + [-1 - (-6)]^2}$

$\quad d = \sqrt{(2 + 4)^2 + (-1 + 6)^2}$

$\quad d = \sqrt{6^2 + 5^2} = \sqrt{36 + 25} = \sqrt{61}$

2. $d = \sqrt{(x_2 - x_1)^2 + (y_2 - y_1)^2}$

$\quad d = \sqrt{(3 - 3)^2 + (-2 - 4)^2}$

$\quad d = \sqrt{0^2 + (-6)^2}$

$\quad d = \sqrt{36} = 6$

4. $x = \dfrac{x_1 + x_2}{2} = \dfrac{-5 + 3}{2} = -1$

$\quad y = \dfrac{y_1 + y_2}{2} = \dfrac{4 - 6}{2} = -1$

9. By the distance formula,

$\quad \overline{AB} = \sqrt{170} \quad \overline{AC} = \sqrt{136} \quad \overline{BC} = \sqrt{34}$

Since $\overline{AB}^2 = \overline{AC}^2 + \overline{BC}^2$, triangle ABC satisfies the Pythagorean theorem and is a right triangle.

11.

y-axis test	x-axis test
Replace x with $-x$:	Replace y with $-y$:
$y^2 = 1 - (-x)^3$	$(-y)^2 = 1 - x^3$
$y^2 = 1 + x^3$	$y^2 = 1 - x^3$
no	yes

origin test

Replace both:

$(-y)^2 = 1 - (-x)^3$

$y^2 = 1 + x^3$

no

15. $x - h = x - 2 \qquad y - k = y + 3 \qquad r^2 = 9$

$\qquad\quad h = 2 \qquad\qquad k = -3 \qquad\quad r = \sqrt{3}$

$\quad$ center: $(2, -3); r = \sqrt{3}$

17. $\qquad x^2 + 4x + y^2 - 6y = -10$

$\quad (x^2 + 4x + 4) + (y^2 - 6y + 9) = -10 + 4 + 9$

$\qquad\quad (x + 2)^2 + (y - 3)^2 = 3$

$\quad$ center: $(-2, 3); r = \sqrt{3}$

19. $x^2 + y^2 - 6y + 3 = 0$

$\quad x^2 + y^2 - 6y = -3$

$\quad x^2 + (y^2 - 6y + 9) = -3 + 9$

$\quad\quad x^2 + (y - 3)^2 = 6$

$\quad$ center: $(0, 3); r = \sqrt{6}$

24. $\qquad y^2 + 4y = -x - 2$

$\quad y^2 + 4y + 4 = -x - 2 + 4$

$\quad (y + 2)^2 = -x + 2 = -(x - 2)$

$\quad$ Since $(y - k)^2 = 4p(x - h)$,

$\qquad$ vertex: $(h, k) = (2, -2)$

$\qquad$ axis: $y + 2 = 0 \quad$ or $\quad y = -2$

$\qquad$ direction: opens left, since $p < 0$

25. $2x^2 - 12x = y - 16$

$2(x^2 - 6x + 9) = y - 16 + 18$

$2(x - 3)^2 = y + 2$

$(x - 3)^2 = \dfrac{1}{2}(y + 2)$

Since $(x - h)^2 = 4p(y - k)$,

vertex: $(3, -2)$

axis: $x - 3 = 0$ or $x = 3$

direction: opens up, since $p > 0$

29. Dividing by 36, we have

$$\frac{x^2}{4} - \frac{y^2}{9} = 1$$

Setting $y = 0$, we have

$$x^2 = 4 \quad \text{or} \quad x = \pm 2$$

Setting $x = 0$, we see that there are no y-intercepts.

33. Dividing by 9, we have

$$\frac{x^2}{3} + \frac{y^2}{\frac{9}{4}} = 1$$

With $x = 0$, $y = \pm 3/2$.

With $y = 0$, $x = \pm\sqrt{3}$.

39. $2x^2 + 12x + y^2 - 2y = -17$

Completing the square, we have

$2(x^2 + 6x + 9) + (y^2 - 2y + 1) = -17 + 18 + 1$

$2(x + 3)^2 + (y - 1)^2 = 2$

Since the right-hand side is positive, $A \neq C$, and $AC > 0$, the graph is an ellipse.

Chapter 13

3. Substituting $x = 6y + 11$, we have

$$2(6y + 11) + 5y = 5$$

$$17y = -17$$

$$y = -1$$

$$x = 6y + 11 = 6(-1) + 11 = 5$$

Solution: $x = 5$, $y = -1$

6. Substituting $x = 5 - 3y$, we have

$$(5 - 3y)^2 + y^2 = 52$$

$$25 - 30y + 9y^2 + y^2 = 25$$

$$10y^2 - 30y = 0$$

$$10y(y - 3) = 0$$

$$y = 0 \quad \text{or} \quad y = 3$$

$$x = 5 - 3y = 5 \qquad x = 5 - 3y = -4$$

9. To eliminate x, multiply the first equation by -2 and the second equation by 1. Then add the two equations:

$$-2x - 8y = -34$$
$$\underline{2x - 3y = -21}$$
$$-11y = -55$$
$$y = 5$$
$$x + 4(5) = 17$$
$$x = -3$$

Solution: $x = -3$, $y = 5$

14. Rewriting the equations and adding, we have

$$x^2 + y^2 - 9 = 0$$
$$\underline{-x^2 + y - 3 = 0}$$
$$y^2 + y - 12 = 0$$
$$(y - 3)(y + 4) = 0$$
$$y = 0 \quad \text{or} \quad y = -4$$
$$x^2 = y - 3 = 0 \qquad x^2 = y - 3 = -7$$
$$x = 0 \qquad\qquad \text{no real solutions}$$

The circle and parabola are tangent at $(0, 3)$.

15. Let $x =$ the tens digit and $y =$ the units digit, so that

$x + y = 10$ The sum of the digits

Then

$10x + y =$ The number

$10x + y + x = 50$ The number plus its tens digit is 50

or

$11x + y = 50$

Solving the system of equations, we have

$$x = 4$$
$$y = 10 - x$$
$$y = 10 - 4 = 6$$

The number is 46.

17. x = cost per lb of hamburger

y = cost per lb of steak

Then

$$5x + 4y = 22.00$$
$$3x + 7y = 28.15$$

Solving, we find

$$x = \$1.80 \qquad y = \$3.25$$

18. x = speed of jogger

w = speed of wind

Then

$$(x + w)20 = 4 \quad \text{so} \quad 20x + 20w = 4$$
$$(x - w)30 = 4 \quad \text{so} \quad 30x - 30w = 4$$

Multiply the first equation by 3 and the second equation by 2 and then add:

$$60x + 60w = 12$$
$$60x - 60w = \ \ 8$$
$$\overline{}$$
$$120x = 20$$
$$x = \frac{1}{6}$$

$$20\left(\frac{1}{6}\right) + 20w = 4$$

$$w = \frac{1}{30}$$

speed of jogger: $\frac{1}{6}$ mi/min

speed of wind: $\frac{1}{30}$ mi/min

20.
$$C = 3300 + 5x$$
$$R = 8x$$
$$C = R$$

so

$$3300 + 5x = 8x$$
$$3300 = 3x$$
$$x = 1100$$
$$R = 8(1100) = 8800$$

21. Interchange equations 1 and 3:

$$-x + 4y + 2z = \ \ 15$$
$$2x + 5y - 2z = -9$$
$$-3x - \ y + \ \ z = \ \ 12$$

Add 2 times equation 1 to equation 2; add -3 times equation 1 to equation 3:

$$-x + 4y + 2z = \ \ 15$$
$$13y + 2z = \ \ 21$$
$$-13y - 5z = -33$$

Add equation 2 to equation 3:

$$-x + 4y + \ \ 2z = \ \ 15$$
$$13y + \ \ 2z = \ \ 21$$
$$-3z = -12$$

Using back-substitution:

$$-3z = -12 \quad \text{or} \quad z = 4$$
$$13y + 2(4) = 21 \quad \text{or} \quad y = 1$$
$$-x + 4(1) + 2(4) = 15 \quad \text{or} \quad x = -3$$

$$x = -3 \qquad y = 1 \qquad z = 4$$

35. The figure shows the set of feasible solutions and the coordinates of the vertices.

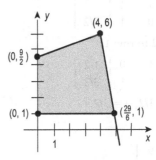

Evaluating the objective function at these points gives us the following information:

x	y	$z = 5y - x$
0	1	5
0	$\frac{9}{2}$	$\frac{45}{2}$
4	6	26
$\frac{29}{6}$	1	$\frac{1}{6}$

The maximum value, $z = 26$, occurs at $x = 4$, $y = 6$.

Chapter 14

12. From the third row, $x_3 = -3$. Then, from row 2,

$$x_2 + 3x_3 = -8$$
$$x_2 + 3(-3) = -8$$
$$x_2 = 1$$

From row 1,

$$x_1 - 2x_2 + 2x_3 = -9$$
$$x_1 - 2(1) + 2(-3) = -9$$
$$x_1 = -1 \qquad x_2 = 1 \qquad x_3 = -3$$

13. In matrix form,

$$\left[\begin{array}{cc|c} 1 & 1 & 2 \\ 2 & -4 & -5 \end{array}\right]$$

Add -2 times row 1 to row 2:

$$\left[\begin{array}{cc|c} 1 & 1 & 2 \\ 0 & -6 & -9 \end{array}\right]$$

Multiply row 2 by $-1/6$:

$$\left[\begin{array}{cc|c} 1 & 1 & 2 \\ 0 & 1 & 3/2 \end{array}\right]$$

Add -1 times row 2 to row 1:

$$\left[\begin{array}{cc|c} 1 & 0 & 1/2 \\ 0 & 1 & 3/2 \end{array}\right]$$

The solution is $x = 1/2$, $y = 3/2$.

19. In matrix form,

$$\left[\begin{array}{ccc|c} 1 & -2 & 3 & -9 \\ 2 & -1 & 4 & -9 \\ 3 & -2 & 1 & 1 \end{array}\right]$$

$$\left[\begin{array}{ccc|c} 1 & -2 & 3 & -9 \\ 0 & 3 & -2 & 9 \\ 0 & 4 & -8 & 28 \end{array}\right]$$

Replaced row 2 by the sum of itself and -2 times row 1.
Replaced row 3 by the sum of itself and -3 times row 1.

$$\left[\begin{array}{ccc|c} 1 & -2 & 3 & -9 \\ 0 & 4 & -8 & 28 \\ 0 & 3 & -2 & 9 \end{array}\right]$$

Interchanged rows 2 and 3.

$$\left[\begin{array}{ccc|c} 1 & -2 & 3 & -9 \\ 0 & 1 & -2 & 7 \\ 0 & 3 & -2 & 9 \end{array}\right]$$

Multiplied row 2 by 1/4.

$$\left[\begin{array}{ccc|c} 1 & -2 & 3 & -9 \\ 0 & 1 & -2 & 7 \\ 0 & 0 & 4 & -12 \end{array}\right]$$

Replaced row 3 by the sum of itself and -3 times row 2.

$$\left[\begin{array}{ccc|c} 1 & -2 & 3 & -9 \\ 0 & 1 & -2 & 7 \\ 0 & 0 & 1 & -3 \end{array}\right]$$

Multiplied row 3 by 1/4.

$$\left[\begin{array}{ccc|c} 1 & -2 & 0 & 0 \\ 0 & 1 & 0 & 1 \\ 0 & 0 & 1 & -3 \end{array}\right]$$

Replaced row 2 by the sum of itself and 2 times row 3. Replaced row 1 by the sum of itself and -3 times row 3.

$$\left[\begin{array}{ccc|c} 1 & 0 & 0 & 2 \\ 0 & 1 & 0 & 1 \\ 0 & 0 & 1 & -3 \end{array}\right]$$

Replaced row 1 by the sum of itself and 2 times row 2.

$$x = 2 \qquad y = 1 \qquad z = -3$$

29.

$$D = \begin{vmatrix} 2 & -1 \\ -2 & 3 \end{vmatrix} = 6 - 2 = 4$$

$$x = \frac{\begin{vmatrix} -3 & -1 \\ 11 & 3 \end{vmatrix}}{4} = \frac{2}{4} = \frac{1}{2}$$

$$y = \frac{\begin{vmatrix} 2 & -3 \\ -2 & 11 \end{vmatrix}}{4} = \frac{16}{4} = 4$$

Chapter 15

2.
$$a_n = \frac{n^3 - 1}{n + 1}$$

$$a_1 = \frac{1^3 - 1}{1 + 1} = \frac{0}{2} = 0$$

$$a_2 = \frac{2^3 - 1}{2 + 1} = \frac{8 - 1}{3} = \frac{7}{3}$$

$$a_3 = \frac{3^3 - 1}{3 + 1} = \frac{27 - 1}{4} = \frac{26}{4} = \frac{13}{2}$$

$$a_{10} = \frac{10^3 - 1}{10 + 1} = \frac{1000 - 1}{10 + 1} = \frac{999}{11}$$

3.
$$a_n = a_1 + (n - 1)d$$
$$a_{21} = -2 + (21 - 1)(2) = 38$$

5. Use the given information to determine d:

$$n = 16 \qquad a_{16} = 9 \qquad a_1 = 4$$
$$a_n = a_1 + (n - 1)d$$
$$9 = 4 + 15d$$
$$d = 1/3$$

Then find a_{13}:
$$a_{13} = a_1 + (n - 1)d$$
$$= 4 + 12\left(\frac{1}{3}\right) = 8$$

7.
$$S_n = \frac{n}{2}[2a_1 + (n - 1)d]$$

$$= \frac{25}{2}\left[-\frac{2}{3} + 24\left(\frac{1}{3}\right)\right] = \frac{275}{3}$$

9.
$$r = \frac{a_2}{a_1} = \frac{-6}{2} = -3$$

11.
$$a_2 = a_1 r = 5\left(\frac{1}{5}\right) = 1$$

$$a_3 = a_2 r = 1\left(\frac{1}{5}\right) = \frac{1}{5}$$

$$a_4 = a_3 r = \left(\frac{1}{5}\right)\left(\frac{1}{5}\right) = \frac{1}{25}$$

13.
$$r = \frac{a_2}{a_1} = \frac{6}{-4} = -\frac{3}{2}$$
$$a_n = a_1 r^{n-1}$$
$$a_6 = (-4)\left(-\frac{3}{2}\right)^5 = \frac{243}{8}$$

15. The sequence is

$$3, a_2, a_3, 1/72$$

With $a_1 = 3$, $a_4 = 1/72$, and $n = 4$,
$$a_n = a_1 r^{n-1}$$
$$a_4 = a_1 r^3$$
$$r^3 = \frac{1}{216}$$
$$r = \frac{1}{6}$$

Then

$$a_2 = a_1 r = 3\left(\frac{1}{6}\right) = \frac{1}{2}$$

$$a_3 = a_2 r = \left(\frac{1}{2}\right)\left(\frac{1}{6}\right) = \frac{1}{12}$$

16.
$$r = \frac{a_2}{a_1} = \frac{1}{2}$$

$$S_n = \frac{a_1(1 - r^n)}{1 - r}$$

$$S_n = \frac{\frac{1}{3}\left[1 - \left(\frac{1}{2}\right)^6\right]}{1 - \frac{1}{2}} = \frac{21}{32}$$

19.
$$r = \frac{a_2}{a_1} = -\frac{2}{3}$$

$$S = \frac{a_1}{1 - r} = \frac{3}{1 - \left(-\frac{2}{3}\right)} = \frac{9}{5}$$

21. By the binomial formula,
$$\left(\frac{x}{2} - 2\right)^4 = \left(\frac{x}{2}\right)^4 + \frac{4}{1}\left(\frac{x}{2}\right)^3(-2)$$
$$+ \frac{4 \cdot 3}{1 \cdot 2}\left(\frac{x}{2}\right)^2(-2)^2$$
$$+ \frac{4 \cdot 3 \cdot 2}{1 \cdot 2 \cdot 3}\left(\frac{x}{2}\right)(-2)^3 + (-2)^4$$
$$= \frac{x^4}{16} - x^3 + 6x^2 - 16x + 16$$

24. $\dfrac{13!}{11!2!} = \dfrac{13 \cdot 12 \cdot 11!}{11!2!} = \dfrac{13 \cdot 12}{2} = 78$

25. $\dfrac{(n - 1)!(n + 1)!}{n!n!} = \dfrac{(n - 1)!(n + 1)n!}{n!n(n - 1)!} = \dfrac{n + 1}{n}$

26. $\dbinom{6}{4} = \dfrac{6!}{4!2!} = \dfrac{6 \cdot 5}{2} = 15$

30. The six letters can be arranged in

$$P(6, 6) = 6! = 720$$

ways. However, the existence of two of the letter o will make half the arrangements indistinguishable. The answer is therefore

$$\dfrac{P(6, 6)}{P(2, 2)} = \dfrac{6!}{2!} = 360$$

31. $C(10, 6) = \dfrac{10!}{4!6!} = 210$

33. There are 8 successful outcomes:

1, 6	2, 5	3, 4
6, 1	5, 2	4, 3
5, 6	6, 5	

There are $6 \times 6 = 36$ outcomes. So

$$\text{probability} = \dfrac{8}{36} = \dfrac{2}{9}$$

34. We can select 2 white pens in $C(4, 2)$ ways. We can select 2 pens in $C(7, 2)$ ways. Therefore,

$$\text{probability} = \dfrac{C(4, 2)}{C(7, 2)} = \dfrac{2}{7}$$

Index

LANGENSCHEIDT'S
UNIVERSAL DICTIONARY

ENGLISH-ITALIAN
ITALIAN-ENGLISH

LANGENSCHEIDT
BERLIN · MUNICH · VIENNA
ZURICH · NEW YORK

Contents

Indice

© 1982 Langenscheidt KG, Berlin and Munich
Printed in Germany

Abbreviations

Abbreviazioni

The tilde (~, when the initial letter changes: ⌐) stands for the catchword at the beginning of the entry or the part of it preceding the vertical bar (|).

Examples:

abdicat|e; ~ion = abdication.

china; ⌐ = China.

Easter; ⌐n = eastern.

La tilde (~, quando l'iniziale cambia: ⌐) sostituisce la voce guida intera, oppure la parte che precede la riga verticale (|).

Esempi:

abdicat|e; ~ion = abdication.

china; ⌐ = China.

Easter; ⌐n = eastern.

---

a, adj adjective, *aggettivo.*

abbr abbreviation, *abbreviazione*

adv adverb, *avverbio*

aer aeronautics, *aeronautica*

agr agriculture, *agricoltura*

Am American English, *inglese americano*

anat anatomy, *anatomia*

aut automobilism, *automobilismo*

biol biology, *biologia*

bot botany, *botanica*

Brit British English, *inglese britannico*

cf confer, *confronta*

chem chemistry, *chimica*

com, comm commercial, *commerciale*

conj conjunction, *congiunzione*

eccl ecclesiastic, *ecclesiastico*

elec electricity, *elettricità*

etc et cetera, and so on, *eccetera*

f feminine, *femminile*

fam familiar, *familiare*

fig figurative, *figurato*

for forensic, law, *forense*

gast gastronomy, *gastronomia*

geog geography, *geografia*

gram grammar, *grammatica*

interj interjection, *interiezione*

irr irregular, *irregolare*

m masculine, *maschile*

mat mathematics, *matematica*

mech mechanics, *meccanica*

med medical, *medicina*

mil military, *militare*

mus music, *musica*
naut nautical, *nautico*
o.s. oneself, *sè (stesso)*
paint painting, *pittura*
phot photography, *fotografia*
pl plural, *plurale*
poet poetic, *poetico*
pol politics, *politico*
pp past participle, *participio passato*
prp preposition, *preposizione*
pron pers personal pronoun, *pronome personale*
pron poss possessive pronoun, *pronome possessivo*
qc, q.c something, *qualcosa*
qu, q.u someone, *qualcuno*

rail railway, *ferrovia*
s substantive, *sostantivo*
Scot Scottish *scozzese*
sg singular, *singolare*
s.o. someone, *qualcuno*
s.th. something, *qualcosa*
surg surgery, *chirurgia*
tel telephone, *telefono*
thea theatre, *teatro*
v/d defective verb, *verbo difettivo*
v/i intransitive verb, *verbo intransitivo*
v/r reflexive verb, *verbo riflessivo*
v/t transitive verb, *verbo transitivo*

Pronuncia delle parole inglesi

Guide to pronunciation of English words

Vocali e dittonghi

[ɑː]	*a* molto lunga, più che in *mare*: *far* [fɑː], *father* ['fɑːðə]
[ʌ]	*a* molto breve, più che in *paradiso*: *mother* ['mʌðə], *butter* ['bʌtə]
[æ]	*e* molto aperta e lunga, più che in *testa*: *man* [mæn], *fat* [fæt]
[ɛə]	dittongo composto di una *e* molto aperta e lunga e [ə]: *care* [kɛə], *there* [ðɛə]
[ai]	dittongo composto di [ɑː] e [i]: *time* [taim], *my* [mai]
[au]	dittongo composto di [ɑː] e [u]: *cloud* [klaud], *how* [hau]
[e]	*e* aperta e breve, più che in *bello*: *get* [get], *said* [sed]
[ei]	dittongo composto di una *e* lunga, seguita da un leggero suono di *i*: *name* [neim], *day* [dei]
[ə]	suono atono simile alla *e* nell'articolo francese *le*: *about* [ə'baut], *silent* ['sailənt]
[əː]	forma più prolungata del suono anteriore: *her* [həː], *bird* [bəːd]
[i]	suono molto breve tralla *i* di *fitto* e la *e* di *fetta*: *stick* [stik], *city* ['siti]
[iː]	*i* molto lunga, più che in *vino*: *need* [niːd], *tea* [tiː]
[iə]	dittongo composto di [i] e [ə]: *here* [hiə], *fear* [fiə]
[ɔ]	suono molto aperto tralla *o* di *lotta* e la *a* di *latte*: *not* [nɔt], *wash* [wɔʃ]
[ɔː]	*o* aperta e lunga, più che in *noto*: *law* [lɔː], *ball* [bɔːl] *poor* [puə], *sure* [ʃuə]

[ɔi]	dittongo composto di [ɔ] e [i]:
	point [pɔint], *boy* [bɔi]
[ou]	dittongo composto di una *o* lunga, seguita da un leggero suono di *u*:
	boat [bout], *bone* [boun]
[u]	suono molto breve tra la *u* di *tutto* e la *o* di *rotto*:
	book [buk], *put* [put]
[u:]	*u* lunga, più che in *fiume*:
	few [fju:], *fruit* [fru:t]
[uə]	dittongo composto di [u] e [ə]:

Consonanti

Le consonanti si pronunciano nella maggior parte dei casi quasi come in italiano. Le doppie si pronunciano come se fossero semplici.

[b]	come la *b* in *burro*:
	bag [bæg], *cab* [kæb]
[d]	come la *d* in *dare*:
	dear [diə], *ladder* ['lædə]
[f]	come la *f* in *forte*:
	fall [fɔ:l], *laugh* [la:f], *coffee* ['kɔfi]
[g]	come la *g* in *gatto*:
	give [giv], *stagger* ['stægə]
[h]	suono aspirato simile a quello della *c* di *casa* dei fiorentini
	whole [houl], *ahead* [ə'hed]
[j]	come la *i* in *ieri*:
	yes [jes], *use* [ju:s], *few* [fju:]
[k]	come la *c* in *casa*:
	come [kʌm], *back* [bæk]
[l]	come la *l* in *lungo*:
	land [lænd], *call* [kɔ:l]
[m]	come la *m* in *madre*:
	mean [mi:n], *summer* ['sʌmə]
[n]	come la *n* in *no*:
	night [nait], *can* [kæn]
[p]	come la *p* in *pane*:
	pot [pɔt], *top* [tɔp]

[r]	una *r* gutturale che si pronuncia soltanto quando precede una vocale:
	right [rait], *carol* ['kærəl]
[s]	*s* aspra come in *sono*:
	cycle ['saikl], *sun* [sʌn], *listen* ['lisn]
[t]	come la *t* in *torre*:
	take [teik], *letter* ['letə]
[v]	come la *v* in *valore*:
	vain [vein], *cover* ['kʌvə], *of* [ɔv]
[w]	come la *u* in *uomo*:
	wait [weit], *quaint* [kweint]
[z]	*s* dolce come in *rosa*:
	rose [rouz], *disease* [di'zi:z]
[ŋ]	come la *n* in *banca*:
	bring [briŋ], *singer* ['siŋə]
[ʃ]	come *sce* in *scena*:
	she [ʃi:], *machine* [mə'ʃi:n]
[tʃ]	come *ce* in *cento*:
	chair [tʃeə], *rich* [ritʃ]
[dʒ]	come *ge* in *gente*:
	join [dʒɔin], *range* [reindʒ]
[ʒ]	suono sonoro corrispondente di [ʃ] che non esiste in italiano:
	leisure ['leʒə], *usual* ['ju:ʒuəl]
[θ]	non esiste in italiano:
	think [θiŋk], *oath* [ouθ]
[ð]	non esiste in italiano:
	the [ðə], *lather* ['lɑ:ðə]
'	il segno dell'accento viene sempre collocato prima della sillaba accentata, es. *ability* [ə'biliti]

Trascrizione fonetica dei suffissi

Ecco la trascrizione fonetica dei suffissi che per economia di spazio tralasceremo di indicare nelle singole voci del dizionario:

-ability [-əbiliti]
-able [-əbl]
-age [-idʒ]
-al [-(ə)l]
-ally [-(ə)li]
-an [-(ə)n]
-ance [-(ə)ns]
-ancy [-ənsi]
-ant [-ənt]
-ar [-ə]
-ary [-(ə)ri]
-ation [eiʃ(ə)n]
-cious [-ʃəs]
-cy [-si]
-dom [-dəm]
-ed [-d; -t; -id]
-edness [-dnis; -tnis; -idnis]
-ee [-i:]
-en [-n]
-ence [-(ə)ns]
-ent [-(ə)nt]
-er [-ə]
-ery [-əri]
-ess [-is]
-fication [-fikeiʃ(ə)n]
-ial [-(ə)l]
-ian [-(jə)n]
-ible [-əbl]
-ic(s) [-ik(s)]
-ical [-ik(ə)l]

-ily [-ili]
-iness [-inis]
-ing [-in]
-ish [-iʃ]
-ism [-iz(ə)m]
-ist [-ist]
-istic [-istik]
-ite [-ait]
-ity [-iti]
-ive [-iv]
-ization [-aizeiʃ(ə)n]
-ize [-aiz]
-izing [-aizin]
-less [-lis]
-ly [-li]
-ment(s) [-mənt(s)]
-ness [-nis]
-oid [-ɔid]
-oidic [-ɔidik]
-or [-ə]
-ous [-əs]
-ry [-ri]
-ship [-ʃip]
-(s)sion [-ʃ(ə)n]
-sive [-siv]
-ties [-tiz]
-tion [-ʃ(ə)n]
-tious [-ʃəs]
-trous [-trəs]
-try [-tri]
-y [-i]